THE FIRST AND SECOND EPISTLES TO THE CORINTHIANS.

THE FIRST AND SECOND EPISTLES

TO THE

CORINTHIANS,

WITH NOTES CRITICAL AND PRACTICAL.

BY THE REV. M. F. SADLER,

RECTOR OF HONITON; PREBENDARY OF WELLS; AUTHOR OF "CHURCH DOCTRINE BIBLE
TRUTH," "CHURCH TEACHER'S MANUAL," "NOTES CRITICAL AND PRACTICAL
ON ST. MATTHEW, ST. MARK, ST. LUKE, ST. JOHN,
THE EPISTLE TO THE ROMANS," ETC.

WIPF & STOCK · Eugene, Oregon

Wipf and Stock Publishers
199 W 8th Ave, Suite 3
Eugene, OR 97401

The First and Second Epistle to the Corinthians
With Notes Critical and Practical
By Sadler, M. F.
ISBN 13: 978-1-62564-970-6
Publication date 6/20/2014
Previously published by G. Bell & Sons, 1889

INTRODUCTION TO THE FIRST EPISTLE TO THE CORINTHIANS.

I. TIME AND PLACE OF WRITING.

WE learn from 1 Cor. xvi., 8, "But I will tarry at Ephesus until Pentecost," that this Epistle was written from Ephesus, and shortly before Pentecost. Many have supposed, and with some reason, that on account of the allusion to the old leaven in v. 7, it was written at the time of the Passover, when the searching for leaven in Jewish houses would be fresh in his mind. Such an abrupt allusion to a purely Jewish custom seems to require some such explanation. Most expositors agree that it was written in 57, but Alford places it in 56, and Usher in the margin of our Bibles in 59.

II. OCCASION OF WRITING.

Two reasons seem to have united in causing St. Paul to write it. (1) Accounts had been brought to him of serious declensions in the Corinthian Church. They were distracted by parties, some calling themselves by the name of Paul, others of Apollos, others of Peter or Cephas, others of Christ. Some refused to acknowledge his Apostleship; some who desired mere human eloquence and a commanding presence, spoke disparagingly of their father in Christ; a fearful crime of such a character that it was not even named by the profligate Gentiles in whose midst they lived, was committed by one of their number, and apparently no notice had been taken of it, and the offender was suffered to continue in Church fellowship. And so far from entertaining proper brotherly feelings to one another as members of the same body, they dragged each other before the heathen tribunals.

(2) At the same time that he heard these reports, a letter was brought to him containing certain questions, respecting the solution of which they desired to have his opinion; such as whether a state of marriage or celibacy was preferable ?—what restrictions were to be put on the partaking of things offered to idols ?—for what reason did he refuse to receive that maintenance from them which other Apostles claimed as their right ? Then he had heard that they observed with some degree of faithfulness the traditions (probably respecting the conduct of their religious assemblies) which he had delivered to them, except, apparently, on two points, concerning their neglect of which he has to blame them severely—one, the veiling of women in their Church assemblies, the other, their disorderly conduct at the Agape, which apparently for schismatical or sensual purposes (xi. 20, 22) they had not kept distinct from the celebration of the Blessed Sacrament. They had also, it appears, sent him some questions respecting the relative value of their spiritual gifts, or perhaps he had heard that they abused one spiritual gift, that of tongues, through vanity or love of display. And he had also heard that there were some among them who had so declined from the faith which he first taught them as to deny the Resurrection of the Body, and, by consequence, the Resurrection of the Lord Himself.

To meet these evils, and to solve these questions, St. Paul was inspired by the Spirit of God to write this letter.

III. THE SPECIAL TEACHING OF THIS EPISTLE.

We have now to consider what is the Christian truth which St. Paul brings forward to meet these evils.

The dominant truth of this Epistle is, that Christ is the Head of a mystical Body, the Church, and that this Church is so the Body of Christ, that each member of the Church is a member of Christ, spiritually and sacramentally united to Him in one Divine organism. We will briefly review the Epistle in regard to this.

The whole Church is a body of men sanctified *in* Christ Jesus (i. 2). Grace is diffused throughout it, but "in" Christ Jesus. This, as it appears in the opening verses, is not so plain in our translation as it ought to be : for instance, "the grace given to you by Christ Jesus" (i. 4) ought to be "the grace given to you in Christ

INTRODUCTION.   vii

Jesus;" "enriched by Him" should be "enriched in Him."
Then he has to mention their divisions, and he significantly asks,
"Is Christ divided?" Then the Corinthians are of God in Christ
Jesus (i. 30). Then, as Christ is the one true temple of God (John
ii. 19, 20, 21), so are they the temple of God, and they must take
heed how they destroy or defile such a temple (iii. 17). They are
St. Paul's spiritual children, but "in" Christ (iv. 15). They must
purge themselves from the old leaven, because they have not
ten thousand paschal lambs, but One Paschal Lamb, of Whom
all partake (v. 7, 8). They must keep their bodies pure, not merely
because by impurity they contravene high ideas of morality, but
because they defile bodies which are members of Christ (vi. 15).
All members of the Church are one bread and one body, because
they are all partakers of One Inward Part in the great Sacrament
of Christian unity (x. 16, 17). Men are not to partake of things
presented on the altars or tables of demons, because, if so, they cannot partake savingly of the Lord's Body (x. 21). Because the head
of every man is Christ, women are not to pray or prophesy unveiled
in the Christian assemblies (xi. 3-16). In judging respecting
spiritual gifts the first principle to be taken into account is that
"by one Spirit we are all baptized into one body" (xii.13), that all the
members are endowed by the Spirit with spiritual gifts and faculties,
but all in subordination to the unity of the One Body. We are all
the body of Christ and members in particular or severally (xii. 27).
The offices of the mystical body, just as the members of the natural
body, are manifold, but the Spirit is the same, only manifesting
Himself differently in each. And lastly, this unity of the body of
Christ is not confined to this world, but has its issues in the spiritual
and eternal world: for we shall rise again, not *by*, or *in* ourselves,
but in Christ; He is the Second Adam, and as by receiving not the
soul only, or the spirit, but the flesh of the first Adam we all die, so
in Christ, the Second Adam, Who rose from the dead in a life-giving Body so capable of transfusion that it is, though a Body,
called a life-giving Spirit, we shall all be made alive (xv. 21-23).

All these remarkable things are said to the whole body of the
baptized without any limitation or reservation. It is assumed that
each baptized Corinthian maintaining a profession of the faith of
Christ, as distinguished from the denial of the same faith by Jews
or heathen (xii. 1-4), is a member of the body of Christ. If any
Corinthian has fallen into sin he is assumed to sin, not only against

his conscience, not only against his superior light, not only against his profession, but against the Body of Christ. Now this is actually said to be true of such a sin as fornication. "Know ye not that your bodies are the members of Christ? Shall I, then, take the members of Christ and make them the members of an harlot? God forbid." I must refer the reader to my note on this place (page 92), and also my notes on Romans vi. 1-12, on pages 114-124.

An attempt is made to get rid of the application of all this to the whole body of the baptised in our own day by calling the baptism of the early converts "believers'" Baptism, as distinguished from Infant Baptism, but all our Lord's words respecting the children of parents in outward covenant with God (who would naturally bring them up in the profession of the covenant) are such that we are compelled to believe that He would look upon them as just as capable of receiving grace from God suited to their years as those who could profess their faith. They come into union with the Second Adam for purposes of salvation, in the same state of unconsciousness as they came into union with the first by their conception and birth.

This truth of union with Christ through faith and Sacraments is the great leading doctrine of St. Paul; it pervades his Epistles to the Romans, Ephesians, and Colossians, as it does this Epistle, and I may say that of all Churches it is most explicitly declared by the Church of England in her formularies. It pervades our Baptismal Services, but, strange to say, is not alluded to in the Baptismal Service of the Romish Church. It is referred to in the Catechism as the first truth in which the Christian child has to be grounded. It is very distinctly recognized in the Eucharistic service (though totally ignored in the Canon of the Mass). It has a place in the Solemnization of Matrimony ("keep themselves undefiled members of Christ's Body") and in the Visitation of the Sick ("continue this sick member in the unity of the Church.")

IV. CHRONOLOGICAL TABLE.

It may be well to give a short table of the leading events in St. Paul's life, which took place between his first arrival at Corinth and his final departure.

INTRODUCTION.   ix

A.D.

51 or 52.   St. Paul's second Missionary journey, at the termination of which, after passing through Macedonia and Athens,

53 or 54.   He arrives at Corinth, Acts xviii. 1.

Continues at Corinth a year and a half.

Here he finds Aquila and Priscilla; lodges with them, xviii. 3.

Joined by Silas and Timotheus. Writes his Epistles to the Thessalonians.

Left the synagogue and preached at house of Justus, verse 7.

Converts Crispus; had a vision from Christ to encourage him, 9, 10.

Gallio refuses to hear the accusation of the Jews, 16.

After this tarries a good while with them, but how long is not mentioned, xviii. 18.

Sailed into Syria and came to Ephesus, 18, 19.

Continued there but a short time; sailed from Ephesus, 21.

Landed at Cæsarea, went up to Jerusalem, saluted the Church, and then went down to Antioch, 22.

54 or 55.   Starts on his third Miss. journey from Antioch, 23.

Passes through Galatia and Phrygia, 23.

Apollos appears on the scene, is fully instructed in the truths of the Gospel by Aquila and Priscilla, and departs for Corinth, xviii. 24-28.

54 or 55 to 57. Paul arrives at Ephesus, where he stays two years, xix. 10.

Purposes to go to Jerusalem through Macedonia and Achaia (Corinth).

Sends before him to Macedonia Timotheus and Erastus, xix. 22.

But himself stays in Asia for a season, *i.e.*, till Pentecost, 1 Cor. xvi. 9.

Writes First Epistle to the Corinthians. (During his stay at Ephesus he seems to have paid a short visit to Corinth, see notes on 2 Cor. i. 1, and on 2 Cor. xii. 14; xiii. 1.)

Departs from Ephesus to Macedonia, xx. 1.

x   INTRODUCTION.

 A.D. Sends Titus to the Church at Corinth to ascertain
 57.   its true state.
    Passes through Troas in much anxiety about this.
    Meets Titus in Macedonia, and is reassured by him
     respecting their state, 2 Cor. vii. 5, 6, 7.
    Sends his Second Epistle by the hands of Titus.
57 (late in year). Arrives at Corinth, and spends three months there,
    Acts xx. 2.
    Takes a circuit through Macedonia to avoid the
     "lying in wait" of the Jews, xx. 3.
    Passes through Philippi, Troas, Miletus, and
     thence by Tyre to Cæsarea and Jerusalem,
     Acts xx. xxi. 1-17.

V. AUTHENTICITY.

The authorship of the First Epistle to the Corinthians has never been doubted.

It is referred to as written by St. Paul, by Clement of Rome, who was the contemporary of the Apostle, in the words, "Take up the Epistle of the blessed Apostle Paul. What did he write to you at the time when the Gospel first began to be preached? Truly under the inspiration of the Spirit, he wrote to you concerning himself, and Cephas, and Apollos because even then parties (preferences) had been formed among you." (Ch. xlvii.)

Polycarp, "But who of us are ignorant of the judgment of the Lord? Do we not know that the Saints shall judge the world? (1 Cor. vi. 2), as Paul teaches?" (ch. xi.). Irenæus, "He proceeds to say, and such indeed were ye, but ye are washed, but ye are sanctified in the name of the Lord Jesus, and by the spirit of our God . . . and we have the precept, 'If any man that is called a brother be a fornicator,'" &c. Adv. Hær. iv. 27.

Clement of Alexandria quotes the Epistle above one hundred and fifty times. I give one place, "Writing in this wise, 'Brethren I could not speak unto you as unto spiritual, but as to carnal, to babes in Christ. I have fed you with milk not with meat,'" &c. Miscellanies, book v., ch. 4.

Tertullian quotes this Epistle an enormous number of times. One will suffice: "You have the Apostle enjoining people to marry in the Lord." "De Coronâ," ch. 13.

It would be impossible to forge such a document, for every line is stamped with the marked individuality of its author.

INTRODUCTION TO THE SECOND EPISTLE TO THE CORINTHIANS.

ST. PAUL wrote the Second Epistle to the Corinthians to prepare the Church for his coming to them at the end of his third journey. He did not desire—indeed, he dreaded to come to them as a severe reprover and stern judge; he would rather visit them as a loving spiritual father in Christ.

The circumstances under which it was written were these. He had received whilst in Ephesus very unfavourable reports of their factions and divisions—of their toleration of the incestuous person, of their going to law before the heathen tribunals, and other matters; and so he wrote to them his First Epistle, full of severe and well merited rebuke. This was not actually the first letter he had written (1 Cor. v. 9), but the first of the two which have been preserved. He despatched this Epistle so that it should arrive before the coming of Timothy, whom he sent, as he tells us, to bring to remembrance his ways in Christ—what he taught in every Church (1 Cor. iv. 17).

Timothy appears to have arrived in Corinth, and left before the arrival of this Epistle, or, if otherwise, the report of their reception of it was very unfavourable. Upon this he sent Titus, one whom he supposed would represent better the sterner aspect of his own character, to bring a report to him of their spiritual state: he himself setting out to come to them by way of Macedonia, Titus being ordered to meet him at Troas (2 Cor. ii. 12, 13). Finding that Titus had not arrived there, he was much discouraged, and instead of remaining some time at Troas, crossed over to Macedonia, and met him at one of the cities there, and sent Titus, and with him, perhaps, Luke, to Corinth with the present Epistle (2 Cor. viii. 17-24). The report which Titus had brought had reassured him of the loyalty of the great body of the Church, but had by no means set him at rest: for he learnt that his principal opponents, the Judaizing faction, were as malignant and as active as ever.

The contents of this second letter are very chequered. He thanks God for much, he praises them as far as he can; he gladly seizes the opportunity of speaking to them lovingly and hopefully respecting the collection for the saints at Jerusalem, but he must deal faithfully with them, for he had become painfully aware that their true hold on Christ, and their profession of the true Gospel of Christ depended much on his personal influence over them, and so on their allegiance and obedience to him as their only true Apostle. To this end he is forced to assert himself—his Apostolical power, his Apostolical labours, and his Apostolical visions and revelations. In writing all this he is, one might almost say, morbidly sensitive as to how they would receive this self-assertion, and the handle which his adversaries would make of it against him; but this matters not, his one object in writing in the way he did is given at the very end of the letter: "I write these things being absent, lest, being present, I should use sharpness, according to the powers which the Lord hath given me to edification and not to destruction" (xiii. 10).

Such is this second canonical letter to the Church of Corinth. What was its effect we know not. St. Paul stayed but a short time with them, and then went to Jerusalem by Macedonia. No doubt he intended to return to them—perhaps again and again: for they were "in his heart," but his long imprisonments—first at Cæsarea, then at Rome—would doubtless change all his plains. Clement of Rome writes to them as if, after St. Paul's departure, they continued free from the evils for which he rebuked them. Thus, in chap. ii., "Moreover ye were all distinguished by humility, and were in no respect puffed up by pride . . . thus a profound and abundant peace was given to you all, and ye had an insatiable desire for doing good . . . every kind of faction and schism was abominable in your sight. Ye mourned over the transgressions of your neighbours, their deficiencies ye deemed your own." And the seditions and deficiencies against which Clement wrote had arisen, he seems to imply, shortly before the writing of his own letter.

This Second Epistle is distinguished above others—even above those written by this Apostle—for its extraordinary personality. He

INTRODUCTION.

seems to let the Corinthians—and, through them, the world—into every secret of his soul. The transparency of the revelation of himself is to me something unequalled in all sacred literature. Let us run over a few examples of it in some of the first few chapters.

"God who comforteth us in all our tribulation that we may be able to comfort them which are in any trouble by the comfort wherewith we ourselves are comforted of God" (i. 4).

"Our consolation aboundeth by Christ" (i. 5).

"We had the sentence of death in ourselves that we should not trust in ourselves, but in God" (i. 9).

"Our rejoicing is this—the testimony of our conscience" (i. 12).

"We are your rejoicing—ye are our's" (i. 14).

"I call God for a record for my soul, that to spare you, I came not," &c. (i. 23).

"I determined I would not come again to you in heaviness" (ii. 1).

"Out of much affliction and anguish of heart I wrote unto you with many tears" (ii. 4).

"I had no rest in my spirit, because I found not Titus my brother" (ii. 13).

"We are the savour of life unto life—of death unto death" (ii. 16).

"Such trust have we through Christ to Godward" (iii. 4).

"As we have received mercy we faint not . . . by manifestation of the truth commending ourselves to every man's conscience" (iv. 1, 2).

"We have this treasure in earthen vessels" (iv. 7).

"Death worketh in us, but life in you . . . We also believe, and therefore speak" (iv. 12, 13).

"Our light affliction, which is but for a moment, worketh for us," &c. (iv. 17).

"In this we groan, earnestly desiring," &c. (v. 2).

"We walk by faith, not by sight" (v. 7).

"We give you occasion to glory on our behalf" (v. 12).

"Whether we be beside ourselves it is to God, or whether we be sober, it is for your cause" (v. 13).

"In all things approving ourselves as the ministers of God, in much patience," &c. (vi. 4).

"As deceivers, and yet true; as unknown, and yet well known" (vi. 8, 9).

INTRODUCTION.

"Our mouth is opened unto you, our heart is enlarged. Ye are not straitened in us," &c. (vi. 11, 12).

Now the question arises, how is it that a letter so almost purely personal, forms by God's providence a book, and by no means the smallest book, of the Canon of Scripture? We answer, because of these very personalities with which it abounds. It shows us how God, who has endowed us with personal qualities, with hearts, affections, sympathies, sensitiveness, yearnings after a requital of our love, does not intend these sensibilities to be hidden under a dignified reserve, but to be brought to bear on that which answers to them in our fellows. If there is a motto to be chosen for this letter—a human motto, touching the inmost spirit of its teaching—it should be "heart to heart."

It teaches us that such a type of Churchmanship as was exhibited in former times, and in some specimens reaching down to this time, the dignified ecclesiastic, wrapping himself up in his mantle of chilling reserve,[1] doing all he can to avoid the possibility of being called upon to give an opinion, always on the look-out to snub, to put down, to bow out—that such an one is in heart and soul utterly alien from *the* type set forth by the Spirit of God in the New Testament.

But there is another remarkable lesson to be learnt from this Epistle. How one and the same man, in the same letter, to the same persons, can at times, with the utmost sincerity, abase himself almost beneath the feet of his children, and yet at the same time threaten them, if they do not obey him, with the severest spiritual punishments, and these, too, in combination with temporal punishments, for no word of "fulmination" has ever gone beyond "to deliver such an one to Satan for the destruction of the flesh, that the spirit may be saved in the day of the Lord Jesus."

Consider the abasement. "Ourselves your servants for Jesus'

---

[1] A poor Welsh clergyman, well nigh broken hearted with discouragement, imagined that his bishop was the man to whom he might properly unburthen his griefs, so he speeds to the palace of one of the first—if not the first scholar in the kingdom—and begins his pitiful story; but is speedily cut short with the question, "My dear Sir, is there not in your village a shop or office with a blank pane or two of wood, and a slit in the pane with the words 'letter box' over it? Could you not have sent what you wish to tell me through that and—" Well, we need not finish. But would not a Bishop's time be thus unduly taken up? Would he not lose more than half an hour? Yes, but in that half hour he would at least learn patience, forbearance, and how this may lead to God's teaching him charity and sympathy, and so furthering his salvation.

INTRODUCTION.

sake." "We have this treasure in earthen vessels" (we are like Gideon's pitchers and lamps). "Death worketh in us, but life in you." "All things are for your sakes." "Whether we be beside ourselves it is to God, or whether we be sober it is for your sakes." "Receive us, we have wronged no man." "Ye are in our hearts to live and to die with you." "We were comforted in your comfort."

But consider the assertions of Church power: "I will come to you shortly, if the Lord will, and will know, not the speech of them which are puffed up but the power." "Shall I come to you with a rod?" (1 Cor. iv. 19, 20). "I beseech you that I may not be bold when I am present with that confidence wherewith I think to be bold against some." "Being ready to revenge all disobedience when your obedience is fulfilled." "Being absent now, I write to them which heretofore have sinned, and to all other, that if I come again I will not spare."

Now this abasement and this assertion is only natural. It is the outcome of his distrust and of his faith—his distrust of himself, as being nothing and less than nothing, apart from Christ: and his faith in Christ, as the Head of the Church, as the Ordainer of Sacraments, as the Institutor of severe, yet merciful discipline, as the Strength of His Ministers, accompanying their word, whether of binding or loosing, with His own power.

Altogether it is a study is this Epistle—a study in the school of Christ—a study of weak human nature, abiding as human nature, but to the uttermost sanctified, ennobled, informed, inhabited by the Spirit of God.

After all this it seems impertinent almost to speak of the genuineness of this Epistle, and its place in the Canon from the first.

It seems to be quoted at least three times in the Epistle of Polycarp, thus: (chap. iv. 14) "He who raised Him from the dead will raise up us also," ch. ii. "also (viii. 31) providing for that which is becoming in the sight of God and men," (ch. vi.) also (v. 10) "we must all appear before the judgment seat of Christ" (ch. vi.).

Also several times in Ignatius, thus: "For the things which are seen are temporal, but the things which are not seen are eternal." (Epistle of Ignatius to Romans iii.)

Irenæus quotes it many times (in an index now before me about twenty-five times), thus: "For as the Apostle does say in the second (Epistle) to the Corinthians: 'For we are unto God a sweet savour of Christ; in them which are saved and in them which perish.'" (Adv. Hær. iv. xxviii. 3.)

Clement of Alexandria quotes the Epistle above forty times, thus: "Only let us preserve free will and love: troubled on every side, yet not distressed; perplexed, but not in despair; persecuted, but not forsaken; cast down, but not destroyed." (Miscellanies, iv. 21.)

Tertullian above seventy times, thus: "But further, in recounting his own sufferings to the Corinthians, he certainly decided that sufferings must be borne. 'In labours,' he says, 'more abundant, in prisons very frequent, in deaths oft;' 'Of the Jews five times received I forty stripes save one.'" (Scorpiace, ch. 13.)

For MSS. and Versions, see the Introduction to the Romans, p. 18.

A COMMENTARY.

THE FIRST EPISTLE TO THE CORINTHIANS.

CHAP. I.

PAUL, [a] called *to be* an apostle of Jesus Christ [b] through the will of God, and [c] Sosthenes *our* brother,

[a] Rom. i. 1.
[b] 2 Cor. i. 1.
Eph. i. 1.
Col. i. 1.
[c] Acts xviii. 17.

1. "Paul, called to be an apostle of Jesus Christ through the will of God." "Called to be an apostle," literally "a called apostle." No doubt emphasis is to be laid on "called." He was not a self-appointed Apostle, as some were, but in writing to the Corinthians he thought it good to assert that he was an Apostle by special calling, as some among them had thrown doubts on this (ix. 1-6).

"By the will of God." All things take place by God's will: but in an extraordinary way God showed His will in the selection of St. Paul to the Apostolic office. With respect to the eleven, Christ had recognized them as the peculiar gift of His Father to Himself, "Thine they were, and thou gavest them me" (John xvii. 6); and so it was with St. Paul. This election or selection on the part of God the Father is asserted very markedly by him in Gal. i. 15: "It pleased God, who separated me from my mother's womb, and called me by his grace." In 1 Tim. i. 1 his Apostolate is "by the commandment of God our Saviour." In the economy of Redemption Christ does nothing apart from His Father: He does not even of Himself—of His separate Will—select His own special representatives.

"And Sosthenes our brother." Rather the brother, the well-

2 Unto the church of God which is at Corinth, ᵈ to them that ᵉ are sanctified in Christ Jesus, ᶠ called *to*

ᵈ Jude 1.
ᵉ John xvii. 19.
Acts xv. 9.
ᶠ Rom. i. 7.
2 Tim. i. 9.

known brother. He is supposed by some to have been the Sosthenes of Acts xviii. 17, who was beaten by the mob before the judgment-seat of Gallio; but this is doubtful. He could not well have been an obscure private person, if he was thus associated with St. Paul as a joint sender of the Epistle, but must have been someone well known to the Corinthian Church as a companion and fellow-helper of the Apostle. A more interesting question is, Why did St. Paul thus associate him with himself? Was he a prophet or evangelist? but even if this were the case, still it does not answer the question, for, from beginning to end, the Epistle bears the impress of one mind and one will. We should say without fear of contradiction that Sosthenes, or anyone else, did not add one idea to it, or compose of himself one line; and yet jointly with the great Apostle he is supposed to send the letter. The explanation seems to be that St. Paul had certain brethren of eminence amongst his disciples, whom he associated with himself and invested as far as possible with his own authority, that in his absence or on his removal they should take his place as rulers or presidents of local churches. And this, as I have shown elsewhere,[1] was the real foundation of the local Episcopate. He was certainly not the mere amanuensis, whose position appears, from Rom. xvi. 22, to have been very subordinate.

2. "Unto the church of God which is at Corinth, to them that are sanctified," &c. The Church of God is the mystical Body of Christ which exists in its entirety in all parts of the world, and is the Church in each particular place. It consists of those who are sanctified in Christ Jesus, that is, those who have been taken out of the first Adam, and grafted in Baptism into Him, the Second Adam. It is quite clear that by "sanctified" here the Apostle cannot mean effectually sanctified in heart and life, for many of the members of this Corinthian Church were not so purified, but needed internal holiness, and by being in Christ's Church were in the sphere, so to speak, of attaining complete sanctification

---

[1] "Church Doctrine Bible Truth," chap. vii.

be saints, with all that in every place ^g call upon the name of Jesus Christ ^h our Lord, ⁱ both their's and our's:

^g Acts ix. 14, 21. & xxii. 16.
2 Tim. ii. 22.
^h ch. viii. 6.
ⁱ Rom. iii. 22. & x. 12.

if they would but seek it. Their sanctification, then, consisted in their dedication to God—their membership in the one mystical Body, their possession of the means of grace. The Word of God and all its promises belonged to them—in the sense recognized by the Saviour when He speaks of those being "gods to whom the Word of God came" (John x. 35). But with all this some of them were unholy, some wilful sinners, especially led away by sins of the flesh, as was natural in a city so given to wickedness as was Corinth. Some had fallen from the faith so far as to say that there was no resurrection, and these all, throughout the Epistle, are warned by the Apostle to repent and separate themselves from sin because of their first sanctification, when they were first brought under the Covenant of Christ. The Apostle never ignores this first sanctification or dedication, but considers it always in force. To cite one instance out of many: "Know ye not," he writes, "that ye are the temple of God, and that the Spirit of God dwelleth in you? If any man defile [or destroy] the temple of God, him will God destroy; for the temple of God is holy, which temple ye are" (iii. 16, 17).

"Called to be saints." Called to belong to a holy calling, and to make good that calling by constant acts of self-dedication.

"With all that in every place call upon the name of Jesus Christ our Lord." It has been supposed that this "in every place" is to be taken literally, as referring to the whole world, but must it not be rather interpreted by the phrase in the parallel passage in 2 Cor. i. 1: "All the saints which are in all Achaia." The Epistle has now become, in the widest sense, a Catholic Epistle, being part of the Scriptures of the Catholic Church; but it is very improbable that it would be understood in this sense by those to whom it was addressed—indeed, so very general a designation would perhaps have hindered their prompt circulation of it through the neighbouring cities and villages.

"Call upon the name of our Lord Jesus Christ." Here Christians are described as those who worship Christ. The reader will remember Pliny's description of them as those who sung hymns to

3 ᵏGrace *be* unto you, and peace, from God our Father, and *from* the Lord Jesus Christ.

ᵏ Rom. i. 7.
2 Cor. i. 2.
Eph. i. 2.
1 Pet. i. 2.

4 ¹I thank my God always on your behalf, for the grace of God which is given you by Jesus Christ;

ˡ Rom. i. 8.

5 That in every thing ye are enriched by him, ᵐ in all utterance, and *in* all knowledge;

ᵐ ch. xii. 8.
2 Cor. viii. 7.

Christ as to God. This is a very direct proof of the Godhead of the Lord. To call upon the name of the Lord is an Old Testament phrase, denoting the worship of the one true God, thus Gen. iv. 26, Ps. cxvi. 17, Joel ii. 32; so that if Christ is thus invoked, it must be because He is with the Father and the Holy Ghost, the one true God.

"Both theirs and ours." Here we have the common Lordship of Jesus over the whole, and every particular Christian's interest and property in Him.

3. "Grace be unto you, and peace, from God our Father, and from the Lord Jesus Christ." Godet writes: "Grace is the Divine good-will, bending compassionately toward the sinner to pardon him; toward the reconciled child to bless him. Peace is the profound tranquillity with which faith in this Divine love fills the believer's heart." But this is much short of the truth. Grace is the Holy Spirit of God, given by God, and making the Christian partaker of all life from Christ. Peace is not only inward tranquillity in the heart, but outward tranquillity amongst the members of the Lord's mystical body. If there be not this peace—if there be enmity and divisions—all internal feelings of peace are delusive. That St. Paul meant to include this peace of the Church is evident from all that follows.

4, 5. "I thank my God always on your behalf, for the grace .... all knowledge." Why should he thank God always on the behalf of these Christians, that they had received gifts such as utterance and knowledge, which we consider mental rather than moral? Evidently for this reason, that such gifts were open manifestations to the world, both heathen and Christian, that the only true God, the Author of all good gifts, whether of mind or body, was among them and working in them, through that new system of Divine agency which on Pentecost had appeared amongst

CHAP. I.]   YE COME BEHIND IN NO GIFT.   5

6 Even as ⁿ the testimony of Christ was confirmed in you:

7 So that ye come behind in no gift; ᵒ waiting for the † coming of our Lord Jesus Christ:

ⁿ ch. ii. 1.
2 Tim. i. 8.
Rev. i. 2.
ᵒ Phil. iii. 20.
Titus ii. 13.
2 Pet. iii. 12.
† Gr. *revelation*, Col. iii. 4.

---

men. When were these Divine Gifts conferred upon them? Not on their conversion, for we never read of these gifts (except in one very special case, Acts x. 44-47) being conferred on conversion, nor at their Baptism (compare Acts viii. 16), but on the laying on of the Apostles' hands (Acts viii. 18, xix. 6; Rom. i. 11).

"In all utterance." [λόγῳ.] "In all word." It may have a more subjective meaning, "the word of truth within us;" but is usually translated as having the same meaning as in our Authorized, "In every form of utterance" (Ellicott), "In all discourse, and all knowledge, so that no kind of Christian aptitude of speech, or of Christian intelligence, is wanting among you." (Meyer.)

6. "Even as the testimony of Christ was confirmed in you." The testimony of Christ was the testimony of Paul and those with him to the Person and Redemptive work of Christ. Its confirmation was the supernatural gifts of knowledge, utterance, miracles, tongues, prophecy, &c., which were communicated by the hands of him who preached, thereby confirming the truth of what he preached, that it was from above, from the God of all power and wisdom.

7. "So that ye come behind in no gift." This does not mean that ye come behind in no gift of spiritual and sanctifying grace, *i.e.*, in responding to it: but it rather refers to the Church as a whole. No Church excelled them in the variety of their spiritual gifts.

"Waiting for the coming of our Lord Jesus Christ." An unnecessary difficulty has been made of this by not remembering that the universal hope of all Christians was fixed by the Apostles and early teachers on the Second Advent, rather than on the day of each Christian's death. If the expectations of the future life entertained by any body of Christians had now to be described, some cold and worldly persons would say that they looked forward to a future state, others that they had bright hopes of eternity, others that they one and all expected to go to heaven at death; whereas

8 ᵖ Who shall also confirm you unto the end, ᑫ*that ye may be* blameless in the day of our Lord Jesus Christ:

p 1 Thess. iii. 13.
q Col. i. 22.
1 Thess. v. 23.

---

in the first or Apostolic age death was ignored, and the one hope of all Christians who had any hope at all was the Second Advent. Whatever belief we express out of Church, *in* the Church we are certainly one with the Apostolic Christians in confessing our hopes in the Second Coming. "He shall come again with glory to judge both the quick and the dead." "At whose coming, all men shall rise again in their bodies, and shall give account for their own works." "We believe that thou shalt come to be our judge; we therefore pray thee help thy servants whom thou hast redeemed with thy precious blood: make them to be numbered with thy saints in glory everlasting."

8. "Who shall also confirm you unto the end, that ye may be blameless in the day," &c. "Who shall confirm you." No doubt it is Christ Who shall confirm or stablish them. Some suppose that it is God Who will thus confirm, but the Name of the Lord Jesus is the one last mentioned.

"To the end," *i.e.*, to His coming to judgment. It does not mean to the day of your death, but to the end of the dispensation, which is always connected with the Second Advent.

"You .... that ye may be blameless." Here he speaks not to individuals so much as to the Church or Body of Christ. Individuals may fall from it as they will be added to it; but the Church is the same, and will be presented at last to Himself as "a glorious Church, not having spot or wrinkle, or any such thing, but holy and without blemish" (Ephes. v. 27). This the Predestinarian may pronounce to be cold comfort; but the Apostle assumes that those to whom he writes will do their best by faith and prayer to continue in a body to which such grace has been assigned. He can give no comfort apart from continuance in faith and prayer. It is God's will, if we are to be guided by the writings of the New Testament, that salvation should belong to a fellowship. In it is acceptance, in it is pardon, in it is grace, in it is growth, in it is the Divine Food and Sustenance. Owing to the declensions, the divisions, the superstitions in the Church, we may have difficulty in realizing this, but in the pages of the New Testament it is so. It is the will

9 ʳ God *is* faithful, by whom ye were called unto ˢ the fellowship of his Son Jesus Christ our Lord.

10 Now I beseech you, brethren, by the name of our Lord Jesus Christ, ᵗ that ye all speak the

ʳ Isa. xlix. 7. ch. x. 13.
1 Thess. v. 24.
2 Thess. iii. 3.
Heb. x. 23.
ˢ John xv. 4. & xvii. 21.
1 John i. 3. & iv. 13.
ᵗ Rom. xii. 16. & xv. 5. 2 Cor. xiii. 11. Phil. ii. 2. & iii. 16. 1 Pet. iii. 8.

---

of God that individuals should to a great extent sink their individuality in the mystical fellowship. It is not to be constantly "I," "I," "Christ died for me," "I am saved." But it is, "He died for us," "We are saved," "We are in Him," "Our Father." We are to look to ourselves (2 John 8), but never, if possible, to assert ourselves. Constant self-assertion is a wretched sign.

9. "God is faithful, by whom ye were called unto the fellowship," &c. Notice here, too, how the calling is not to a heaven above the sky, but to a fellowship here on earth. If God has called you to the fellowship of His Son, He will assuredly show faithfulness in keeping His promises made to that Holy Fellowship. As long as you are in it you shall partake of its life, enjoy its spiritual gifts, partake, if you will, of its spiritual Food, and be animated by its hope.

10. "Now I beseech you, brethren, by the name of our Lord Jesus Christ .... same judgment." Observe the extreme seriousness and earnestness of the Apostle, "I beseech you by the name which is above every name, the name of the Saviour, the Son of God incarnate." It is quite clear, if he so beseeches them, that the matter respecting which he beseeches them cannot be of small importance, and indeed it is not. It is no other than this, that in them should be fulfilled the prayer of the Son of God, that all that believe in Him through the word of the Apostles should be one, even as the Father is in Him and He in the Father; and that this unity should not be merely a unity of spirit, but of outward expression—of word, that ye all speak the same thing on religion, on your common faith, on your common hope, on your duties. Now I do not think that this means that they should use the same words, but that the words which they used, though such words might express the same truth in different lights, or express different sides of the same doctrine, should mean or should have reference to one and the same

same thing, and *that* there be no †divisions among you; but *that* ye be perfectly joined together in the same mind and in the same judgment.

† Gr. *schisms*, ch. xi. 18.

---

thing. Dean Stanley translates it, "call yourselves by one common name;" but this cannot be, because, if so, the Apostle would have designated the common name. "Call yourselves Christians only. Let no one call you anything else than brethren." "Ye are called to be saints, call yourselves saints only." Their sin of calling themselves by the name of men could not have existed except as the expression of some difference of opinion respecting the truth, or respecting what is truth, on the part of those who ranged themselves under the names of particular leaders.

"And that there be no divisions among you." No schisms, in the sense of parties or factions. Attention is called by Stanley and others to the fact that what the Apostle reprobates are parties or factions within the Church, and not so much sects or bodies of men who had separated from the Church, thereby assuming that the one is not so evil or detrimental to Christianity as the other; but this is absurd. Just as factions in a particular national church prevent it acting together as one man, and so weaken it; so sects or schisms external to the catholic body weaken it, and are very rarely found on the side of that body in the assertion of the great truths of the faith.

"But that ye be perfectly joined together in the same mind and in the same judgment." Stanley notices that the noun of the verb, "that ye be perfectly joined together in the same mind," καταρτιστήρ, was the acknowledged phrase in classical Greek for a reconciler of factions, and Godet remarks that the verb generally implies the rectification of a disordered state of things, such as the re-establishment of social order after a revolution, or the repairing of an instrument (Mark i. 19, fishing-nets); but the signification here is probably rather that of making perfect. The Apostle does not exhort that the σχίσματα should be repaired, but that there should be none; and this could only be by unanimity as perfect as possible. "Mind" seems to mean, according to Godet, the Christian way of thinking in general—the same mind, full harmony of view in regard to Christian truth: and "judgment," or opinion, γνώμη, perfect agreement in the way of solving particular ques-

11 For it hath been declared unto me of you, my brethren, by them *which are of the house* of Chloe, that there are contentions among you.

---

tions. Men say that this is impossible, but how can that be impossible for which the Lord prayed, and which the Holy Spirit by the mouth of the Apostle commanded? If men of opposite parties or schools of thought would meet together, and not part till they had probed to the very root the reason of their differences—if they would never use ambiguous phrases, never charge their opponents with holding what they cannot really mean, never impute unworthy motives, never dogmatically pronounce that if a man holds what they think wrong he may be lawfully and charitably assumed to hold all the possible inferences from it—if men would also remember that upon a large number of Scripture doctrines there are in Scripture statements and counter-statements—if men would but act thus, the divisions in our own Church would be reduced to a minimum.

There seems, however, to have been less excuse for the existence of party divisions in the Church of Corinth, seeing that some among them had gifts of wisdom, others of knowledge, others of prophecy, others of discerning of spirits—all the gifts of one and the same Spirit.

11. "For it hath been declared unto me of you, my brethren . . . . contentions among you." It is doubtful, and indeed immaterial, whether this Christian lady was of Corinth or of Ephesus. It is to be noticed that the Apostle gave the name of his informant. In this case, no doubt, he acted with the consent of those who had brought the information. But if in similar cases it was the rule always to give the name of those who brought information respecting character and conduct, much slander would be prevented, as well as much suspicion. A says to B, "I tell you in confidence that people are saying such things of you." B asks for the name of one of those who had said the obnoxious things. A says he is not at liberty to give it, and the matter ends for the time with B entertaining evil surmisings against twenty persons, instead of, perhaps, having an amicable explanation with one.

12. "Now, this I say, that every one of you saith, I am of Paul; and I," &c. We are not to suppose that these were parties analo-

^u ch. iii. 4.   12 Now this I say, ^u that every one of you saith,

gous to our parties or schools of thought. It is probable that the divisions were personal, and arose naturally; but however they arose, they were typical of all party divisions and schisms, and in their effects very evil. An immense amount of learning and ingenuity has been expended in defining these marks of distinction, especially by German critics.

With respect to the first two, we have no ground whatever for supposing that there was the least difference between the theological or practical teaching of Paul and Apollos. If there had been, we may be sure that a man of the courage and zeal for truth of St. Paul would have asserted the difference: for in such a case, seeing that St. Paul was so especial an instrument of the Spirit, Apollos would have taught false doctrine. Is not the party feeling among the Corinthians amply accounted for by the difference between their gifts? Apollos was an eloquent man, Paul was not; Paul took no account of the way in which he presented the truths he was commissioned to teach; he presented them earnestly, fervently, at times, perhaps, passionately, whereas Apollos captivated by his eloquence, his admirable choice of words and phrases and rounding of sentences.

And in a mixed Church, which that of Corinth undoubtedly was, there would be many who would look to the expression of the truth more than to the truth itself. Those of Paul, then, would be those who owed themselves to him (Philemon 19), and would not hear of—perhaps fiercely resented—any comparison of him with other teachers. Those of Apollos would be constantly asserting—often as against Paul—his more eloquent setting forth of the same truth. Thus there would be a constant bringing-up of personalities and odious comparisons which would be the occasion of constant breaches of charity and goodwill, and misunderstandings, and scandals.[1]

---

[1] With respect to the opinions of Apollos, there is not the smallest ground for supposing that he was attached to the Alexandrian school of philosophy as represented in the writings of Philo. He was converted to the truth of Christ by the preaching of John, was baptized by him, and afterwards instructed in the faith more perfectly by Aquila and Priscilla. Not a syllable which he either spoke or wrote has come down to us. Some suppose, though without any reason, that he is alluded to somewhat disparagingly by St. Paul when he speaks of such things as "not with wisdom of words" or "I came not unto

I am of Paul; and I of ˣApollos; and I of ʸCephas; and I of Christ.

ˣ Acts xviii. 24. & xix. 1. ch. xvi. 12.
ʸ John i. 42.

With respect to those who said, "I am of Cephas," a corresponding party seems always to have existed in every Church where there was any Jewish element. The Jews never seem to have taken cordially to the doctrine of the equality of the Gentiles with themselves in the body of Christ. They would submit to it, rather than receive it. Such persons would never recognize with absolute cordiality the Apostolate of St. Paul. They would always be, at least, hinting the superiority of Cephas, in that he had seen and lived with the Lord, in that he had had the keys committed to him; such persons would always be trying, perhaps covertly, to bring the Gentiles under the yoke—if not in matters of importance, at least in minor matters, purifications, meats, drinks, &c. And they would appeal to the example of St. Peter, who was absent, for if he had been present, he would certainly have energetically repudiated such a use of his name. For, if we are to judge from his Epistles, there were not the smallest doctrinal or practical differences betwixt himself and St. Paul. They both held prominently the same doctrines of grace, and expressed them in very nearly the same way.

"And I of Christ." With respect to this party or faction, commentators are beyond measure divided. Godet has ten closely-printed pages upon it, and refers to the opinions of above five-and-twenty commentators. It may suffice to notice two.

(1.) Those who asserted their superior spirituality, or their unique holding of Christ and Christ alone. Doubtless they prided themselves on their spirituality and inward light, and looked down with contempt on those who professed to follow the opinion of any teacher. Perhaps they ignored the Apostolic teaching altogether, and proclaimed the doctrine of direct communion with God, without the aid of ministry or ordinances, like modern Quakers or Plymouth Brethren; and these, as well as the others, the Apostle rebuked.

---

you with excellency of speech or of wisdom;" others that he was the author of the Epistle to the Hebrews, as if an Alexandrian Jew, dwelling in Asia Minor or Greece, without any Apostolical authority on the one hand, or connection with Palestine on the other, would write such an Epistle for the use of Palestinian Jews.

13 ᶻIs Christ divided? was Paul crucified for you? or were ye baptized in the name of Paul?

ᶻ 2 Cor. xi. 4.
Eph. iv. 5.

---

13. "Is Christ divided?" Some translate this as an assertion, "Christ is divided." The Revisers give this translation in margin; but see below.

(2.) Others, however, as Godet, regard them as ultra Judaizers—not allowing to the Gentiles the liberty asserted for them in the Council at Jerusalem, but appealing to the example of Christ, Who was born under the law, was circumcised, was a constant attendant in the Temple, and Who said respecting the law that not one jot or tittle of it should pass away. Such would assert that not only St. Paul but the older Apostles had declined from the example and teaching of Christ, and would proudly and scornfully proclaim that they, and they alone, were "of Christ," and would bind upon the Gentiles everywhere every tittle of the law which Christ Himself observed. I incline to this latter view of the Christ-party, for it seems to me that the Apostles nowhere recognize that such a purely nineteenth century perversion of Christianity as Plymouth Brethrenism existed among their converts.

13. "Is Christ divided? was Paul crucified for you? or were ye baptized?" &c. Some understand, "Is Christ divided?" not as a question, but as an indignant assertion, "Christ is divided," answering to what we so often hear, "the seamless coat of Christ is rent." Bishop Ellicott, however, gives strong reasons for considering it to be an indignant question, and asserts that it is so translated by all the versions, all the Greek expositors, and the majority of the best modern commentators. It may be paraphrased, "If the name of Christ implies one Atonement, one Mediation, one Mystical Body, do not ye by your divisions do what in you lies to tear Him to pieces? Ye act as if ye would appropriate to yourselves Him Who is God's gift to all. Can this be without deadly sin?"

"Was Paul crucified for you?" This implies that by His Bloodshedding Christ purchased the whole Church with His Blood, that all should be the servants of Himself, their One Master.

"Or were ye baptized in the name of Paul?" Baptism into the name of Christ implied grafting into His Body, and Burial, and Resurrection with Him. "By calling yourselves by the

14 I thank God that I baptized none of you, but ª Crispus
and ᵇ Gaius;

15 Lest any should say that I had baptized in
mine own name.

ª Acts xviii. 8.
ᵇ Rom. xvi. 23.

---

15. "I had baptized in mine own name." So D., E., F., G., L., P., most Cursives (d, q, r), Syriac; but ℵ, A., B., C., some Cursives (e, f), Vulg., Copt. read, "ye were baptized."

names of men ye act as if they could be on your behalf what Christ is."

It has been noticed that if Christ had died only as an example, and not as a reconciling Sacrifice, there would have been no such great incongruity in men calling themselves by the name of Cephas or Paul, for they were both men who set examples of surpassing goodness.

14, 15. "I thank God that I baptized none of you, but Crispus and Gaius; . . . . baptized in mine own name." Crispus was the ruler of the Synagogue, respecting whom it is said that "he believed on the Lord with all his house" (Acts xviii. 8); and Gaius, or Caius, was the person at whose house St. Paul lodged.

It appears to have been the rule with the Apostles not to administer the Sacrament of Baptism themselves. Thus St. Peter, even in the case of Cornelius and his household, did not baptize them with his own hands, but commanded them to be baptized in the name of the Lord (Acts x. 48). And so the twelve men at Ephesus, who had been disciples of the Baptist, were probably baptized, not by the Apostle, but by some inferior minister (Acts xix. 5).

Paul assigns as the reason for his not personally administering the Sacrament his wish to make it impossible that any should say that he baptized in his own name, and the Apostles also may have declined in their own persons to administer it, that men might not be tempted to think that the Baptism of an Apostle was accompanied with greater grace than that of an ordinary minister; whereas, no matter who was the baptizer, it was always a Death and Resurrection with the Lord.

16. "And I baptized also the household of Stephanas," &c. The Apostle here suddenly remembered that there was one other whom, with his household, he had himself baptized. Stephanas who, with

16 And I baptized also the household of ᶜ Stephanas:
besides, I know not whether I baptized any other.
17 For Christ sent me not to baptize, but to

ᶜ ch. xvi. 15, 17.

---

his family, are called in chapter xvi. the first-fruits of Achaia,
was one of their foremost ministers, being commissioned by St.
Paul to rule as well as teach. His presence with St. Paul at the
time he wrote this letter would have recalled the well-nigh forgotten
fact to his memory.

17. "For Christ sent me not to baptize, but to preach the
Gospel." How is it that the commission of St. Paul and of the
original Apostles was different? They were sent to preach and
baptize (Matth. xxviii.): "Go, ye, and disciple all nations, baptizing them." He, on the contrary, seems to assert here that he was
sent to preach only. Now the full answer is to ask the question,
What Gospel did he preach? If we are to believe his letters, he
preached a Gospel, one chief article of which was that, in order to
partake of the Redemption of Christ, we are to submit to be baptized into His Death, and in order to partake of His Life, we are,
by the same act, to be baptized into His Resurrection. St. Paul
preached a Christ Who laid it upon His followers that by one most
holy rite they were to be brought into His mystical Body; and by
another they were to partake of His Flesh and Blood as their
Spiritual Food and Sustenance. It is certain that if St. Peter had
had to face the same error which St. Paul had, he would have expressed himself in the same way. Like St. Paul, he would have
first preached a Christ into whose Body all believers, if they would
be saved, must be baptized; and, like St. Paul, he would (as we
know he did) order that they should be baptized by the hands of
others. As Meyer well expresses it: "In the assured consciousness
that the design of his Apostolic mission was teaching, Paul recognized that baptizing, as an external office, and one that required no
special gift, should as a rule be left to others." None could preach
with the plenitude of inspiration which St. Paul had; but the
baptism by the hands of any minister whatsoever would equally
admit the catechumen into the same kingdom of grace.

It is miserable to think that this passage should have been used
to perpetuate the misunderstandings in the Church of England
respecting the Sacrament of Baptism, and that by one, at least, of

THE CROSS OF NONE EFFECT.

preach the gospel: ^d not with wisdom of ‖ words, lest the cross of Christ should be made of none effect.

^d ch. ii. 1, 4, 13. 2 Pet. i. 16.
‖ Or, *speech*.

her own bishops. It has been used to set Baptism against preaching, and to discourage the use of constant reference in our teaching to the grace we have therein received, as a grace for which we must hold ourselves to be answerable. It would be well if persons offending thus were to remember the words of Bishop Butler: "As it is one of the peculiar weaknesses of human nature where, upon a comparison of two things, one is found to be of greater importance than the other, to consider this other as of scarce any importance at all: it is highly necessary that we remind ourselves how great presumption it is to make light of any institution of Divine appointment; that our obligations to obey all God's commands whatever are absolute and indispensable; and that commands merely positive, admitted to be from Him, lay us under a moral obligation to obey them—an obligation moral in the strictest and most moral sense."

"Not with wisdom of words, lest the cross of Christ should be made of none effect." The word Gospel at once brings to his mind the perversions of the Gospel, which in all probability had already begun, for about five years after this he has to put the Colossian Christians on their guard against them. (Coloss. ii. 18.) He cannot, we repeat again, allude to the preaching of Apollos, for this man is described by St. Luke as "mighty in the Scriptures," and so far from "making the cross of Christ of none effect," he helped them much "that had believed through grace" (Acts xviii. 24-28). The Apostle, as he goes on to say in the next verse, would consider the Gospel a message of life or death, and would abhor with his whole soul any preaching of it which would divert men's minds from the message itself to the setting of it. It was from his point of view exceedingly simple—the Son of God incarnate, crucified, risen, ascended, and returning to judge. All words and ideas derived from Greek or Oriental philosophy merely obscured it, and blunted the sharpness by which it would penetrate the heart (Heb. iv. 12). Quesnel has an admirable remark: "It is to the humility of the preaching of the cross that God has annexed the grace of the conversion of sinners, and His power to save His elect. It is a deplorable abuse of preaching to have more regard to the taste

18 For the preaching of the cross is to ᵉ them that perish ᶠ foolishness; but unto us ᵍ which are saved it is the ʰ power of God.

* 2 Cor. ii. 15.
ᶠ Acts xvii. 18. ch. ii. 14.
ᵍ ch. xv. 2.
ʰ Rom. i. 16. ver. 24.

18. "The preaching of the cross;" lit. "the word of the cross." So Revisers, Vulg. verbum.

and judgment of a small number of worldly persons, who will never profit by it, than to the spiritual advantage of those whom God desires to save."

18. "For the preaching of the cross is to them that perish foolishness; but," &c. No words could express the scorn with which an educated Greek would regard the message that a poor despised Galilean had reconciled the world to God by His Death, and that the only way of being delivered from all evils of body and soul, temporal and eternal, was by believing that this crucified Man was not held by death, but was raised from the dead that He might be the present power of life to all, and the future Judge of all men. This, of course, would be utter folly and nonsense to him as long as he was in the way of destruction—as long as he was perishing by refusing to believe the abundant evidence presented to him that the Supreme Ruler of the visible and invisible worlds had interfered to save men from ruin.

"But unto us which are saved." "Unto us who are being saved." The same participle as in Acts ii. 47, where see note.

The power of the preaching of the cross is twofold. It is the power of God to draw to God all who hear it, because it exhibits as nothing else does the love of God, and love attracts, and the love of God, as displayed in the gift of His Son to die for us, attracts us to God, according to the words of St. John, "We love him because he first loved us;" and, again, the Lord says, "I, if I be lifted up from the earth, will draw all men unto me."

But, again, it is the power of God, because the Death of the Lord was never preached by the Lord apart from His Resurrection, and by His Resurrection He makes over to us the power of His New Life; and so the Apostle desires to know the power of his Lord's Resurrection (Phil. iii. 10).

19. "For it is written, I will destroy the wisdom of the wise," &c. This place, which St. Paul cites, is from Isaiah xxix. 14, but follows the Septuagint rather than the Hebrew. The Hebrew runs,

CHAP. I.] WHERE IS THE WISE ? 17

19 For it is written, ¹I will destroy the wisdom of the wise, and will bring to nothing the understanding of the prudent.

20 ᵏ Where *is* the wise? where *is* the scribe?

i Job v. 12, 13.
Isa. xxix. 14.
Jer. viii. 9.

k Isa. xxxiii. 18.

" The wisdom of their wise men shall perish, and the understanding of their prudent men shall be hid." The Septuagint reads, " I will destroy the wisdom of the wise, and will hide the understanding of the prudent."

But the place in Isaiah has primary reference to the deliverance of the Israelites from the Assyrian invasion; how is it applicable to redemption from sin? In this way. The Jews placed their hopes of deliverance in the politicians who had counselled alliance with Egypt. No worldly policy could seem wiser; but it was, or if the Lord had not Himself intervened it would have been, for their destruction. " The strength of Pharaoh shall be your shame, and the trust in the shadow of Egypt your confusion," &c. " And when they were on the point of complete national ruin, the Lord intervened and saved them. And God now proceeds on the same principle in saving the world. He snatches it from perdition by an act of His own love; and without deigning in the least to conjoin with Him human wisdom, which, on the contrary, He sweeps away as folly." (Godet.)

20. " Where is the wise? where is the scribe? where is the disputer of this world?" &c. "Where is the wise?" *i.e.*, where is mere human philosophy? What power could it afford against sin, what assurance of immortality and judgment, what proof of the efficacy of repentance, what atonement, and reconciliation to God?

" Where is the scribe? " The Jewish teacher or rabbi can only be here referred to. What had he to bring forward? Only glosses and false interpretations, which made void the law of God, and so prevented that law from leading men to Christ.

" Where is the disputer of this world?" Most probably the Apostle had in his mind the Greek sophists. Indeed, having mentioned Jewish human wisdom in the scribes, he cannot but here allude to the sophists, who, for purposes of gain, made the same bad use of philosophy as the cavilling and disputing Rabbis did of the Old Testament.

where *is* the disputer of this world? ¹hath not God made foolish the wisdom of this world?

21 ᵐFor after that in the wisdom of God the world by wisdom knew not God, it pleased God by the foolishness of preaching to save them that believe.

¹ Job xii. 17, 20, 24. Isa. xliv. 25. Rom. i. 22.
ᵐ Rom. i. 20, 21, 28. See Matt. xi. 25. Luke x. 21.

20. "Of this world;" rather, "of the world." So ℵ, A., B., C., D.; but E., F., G., L., most Cursives, Syriac, Copt., Arm., d, e, f, g, r, Vulg., read as in Text. Rec.

21. "After that." "Seeing that," Revisers.

"Preaching." Not so much "preaching" as the matter preached.

The form of the verse seems to be a reminiscence of Isaiah xxxiii. 18, "Where is the scribe? where is the receiver? where is he that counted the towers?" but only the form. And St. Paul so alters the latter clause, as to make it embrace all the departments of human speculation and wisdom whose spirit was opposed to the teaching of the Cross.

"Of this world?" refers to all three. St. Paul does not ask, "Where is the wise?" for he was in this very Epistle teaching the Church the highest wisdom; but this was a wisdom not having its origin in this world, but from above; and that there might be scribes not of this world, the Lord Himself asserts, when in Matth. xiii. 52, He speaks of "every scribe instructed unto the kingdom of heaven."

"Hath not God made foolish the wisdom of this world?" He hath made it foolish by showing that in the things of most importance to man, such as his deliverance from moral evil, and his eternal hopes, it had nothing to say which could be relied on.

And He made it foolish by the presence amongst us of the highest wisdom which it is possible for a creature to possess, a wisdom which unites us to God, and makes us partakers of His holiness.

21. "For after that in the wisdom of God the world by wisdom knew," &c. "In the wisdom of God." Two meanings have been given to this clause. Some have held that in the unsearchable wisdom of God He did not allow the world to know Him by wisdom, *i.e.*, by philosophy, or by the evidence of His own works of creation. He reserved the true knowledge of Himself to be given through revelation—particularly the revelation of Himself in His

CHAP. I.] THE JEWES REQUIRE A SIGN. 19

22 For the ⁿ Jews require a sign, and the Greeks seek after wisdom:

ⁿ Matt. xii. 38. & xvi. 1.
Mark viii. 11.
Luke xi. 16.
John iv. 48.

22. "A sign." So L., most Cursives, &c.; but ℵ, A., B., C., D., E., F., G., P., 46, 52, 63, 80, d, e, f, q, r, Vulg., Syr., Copt., Æth. read, "signs."

Son. Others, recoiling from the too predestinarian significance of this, consider the wisdom of God to be that displayed in the works of creation, and understand it as meaning that notwithstanding that the wisdom of God was so gloriously displayed in His works, the world, by its wisdom, which sought not to apprehend the Divine Wisdom, knew not God, *i.e.*, practically.

"It pleased God by the foolishness of preaching to save them that believe." It pleased God no more to approach them with what they deemed wisdom, but through what in their natural unregenerate state they would deem folly—the preaching of a crucified Jew as being through His Death the Deliverer from sin and death.

Preaching (κήρυγμα) signifies rather the contents of the message than the form of its delivery.

22. "For the Jews require a sign [or signs], and the Greeks seek after wisdom." This was the constant practice of the unbelieving Jews in our Lord's time. After He had traversed their land, healing in an instant all manner of sickness and all manner of disease—after He had fed the five thousand and the four thousand—they asked of Him "a sign from heaven." His miracles, they objected, were all done in the lower sphere of this earth; if He could do one which manifestly had its origin in heaven, as they falsely supposed the manna had, then they would believe. But they would not have believed. For He exhibited a power which could only have proceeded from the Supreme Lord of life and death when He raised Lazarus from the dead; and the power of the Supreme God alone could have raised Him from the dead; and yet these most perverse men still asked for signs. Even in Corinth, where so many exercised miraculous gifts, bestowed upon them by the hands of Paul, they asked for yet more signs.

"And the Greeks seek after wisdom." That is, instead of the Gospel, the account of the Son of God Incarnate, born of a virgin, dwelling in obscurity, speaking words of power to reach the heart and rectify the conscience, crucified, risen, ascended, and

WE PREACH CHRIST CRUCIFIED. [I. Cor.

o Isa. viii. 14.
Matt. xi. 6. &
xiii. 57. Luke
ii. 34. John
vi. 60, 66.
Rom. ix. 32.
Gal. v. 11.
1 Pet. ii. 8.

p ver. 18.
ch. ii. 14.

23 But we preach Christ crucified, ᵒ unto the Jews a stumblingblock, and unto the Greeks ᵖ foolishness;

24 But unto them which are called, both Jews

---

23. "Unto the Greeks." So most Cursives; but ℵ, A., B., C., D., E., F., G., L., P., several Cursives (5, 10, 17, 23**, 31, 37, 46, 71, 73, 80, 93), d, e, f, q, r, Vulg., Cop., Arm., Æth., &c., " unto the Gentiles."

speaking to the world through men of no commanding intellectual power, they required a Plato or an Aristotle, who should present to them an intellectual view of things. "The Greek ideal is quite different (from the Jewish): it is a masterpiece of wisdom: the Divine intellectualized in a system, eloquently giving account of the nature of the Gods, the origin, cause, or end of the universe." (Godet.)

23. "But we preach Christ crucified, unto the Jews a stumblingblock," &c. That is, we preach Christ in the lowest depth to which for our sakes He descended. "Taking the form of a slave, and being found in fashion as a man, he humbled himself and became obedient unto death, even the death of the cross." The Apostle did not for a moment conceal or put in the background the extreme humiliation to which the Lord of Glory descended. On the contrary, he put it in the foremost place of all, well aware that it would be a stumblingblock to his own countrymen, and the occasion of unbounded scorn and ridicule to the proud, self-sufficient, intellect-worshipping Greeks; but aware also that it would not fail in bringing about God's purpose—it would prosper in the thing whereunto God sent it, for he goes on—

24. "But unto them which are called, both Jews and Greeks, Christ the power of God." Those "which are called," *i.e.*, effectually called—those to whose innermost souls the call of God reaches, and in whom it abides [" My words abide in you "], and must we not say those who are described by the Lord in His parable of the Sower? "They which in an honest and good heart having heard the word, keep it, and bring forth fruit with patience" (Luke viii. 15).

"Christ the power of God." This is meant for the Jews who require signs—that is, exhibitions of the power of God. Christ Crucified is the power of God to attract sinners who feel the burden

CHAP. I.] CHRIST THE POWER OF GOD. 21

and Greeks, Christ ^q the power of God, and ^r the wisdom of
God.

25 Because the foolishness of God is wiser than
men; and the weakness of God is stronger than
men.

^q Rom. i. 4, 16. ver. 18.
^r Col. ii. 3.

of sin, and Christ Crucified is the power of God to atone for sin
and remit it. Christ Crucified is the greatest power in the moral
and spiritual world, for He is the power of the Love of God, and
through His Resurrection, which can never be dissociated from
His Death, He is the power of Life to a dead world. St. Paul
desires to "know Him and the power of His Resurrection, and
the fellowship of His sufferings—being made conformable to His
Death." (Phil. iii. 10.) The power of His Resurrection was exhibited
in His Apostles, when they did greater works than even He did—
greater works both in conversion and sanctification, and in the distribution of miraculous gifts, such as the gifts of tongues and prophecy: but all this was but the putting forth of His own power,
as when St. Peter said to Æneas, "Jesus Christ maketh thee
whole."

"And the wisdom of God." This was especially for those who
sought after wisdom. In Christ Crucified problems the most difficult and yet the most important for the interests of man are solved.
The reconciliation of the justice and mercy of God—the light in
which God regards humility as opposed to pride—self-surrender as
opposed to self-assertion, self-denial as opposed to self-love, the
efficacy of repentance, the power of faith, the surpassing grace of
patience, the virtue of the forgiveness of enemies and persecutors,
the strength of weakness, the indomitable courage of true reliance
on God. This is all exhibited on the human side of the Crucifixion.
On its Divine side is the love of God to sinners, the intense interest
which God takes in the warfare between good and evil, the bound-
less compassion of the Eternal Father even to His enemies.

25. "Because the foolishness of God is wiser than men; and the
weakness," &c. The foolishness and weakness of God means that
which is foolish and weak in the eyes of the worldly wise. Now
the preaching of the Cross with the view of saving men from the
guilt and power of moral evil, folly though it be in the eyes of the
world, is the highest wisdom and power. "The Apostle means
wiser than men with all their wisdom, stronger than men with all

26 For ye see your calling, brethren, how that ᵃnot many wise men after the flesh, not many mighty, not many noble, *are called*:

27 But ᵗGod hath chosen the foolish things of the world to confound the wise; and God hath chosen the weak things of the world to confound the things which are mighty;

ᵃ John vii. 48.

ᵗ Matt. xi. 25.
James ii. 5.
See Ps. viii. 2.

---

their strength. When God has the appearance of acting irrationally or weakly, that is the time when He triumphs most certainly over human wisdom and power."

26. "For ye see your calling, brethren, how that not many wise men after the flesh." "Your calling," not your calling in life, *i.e.*, your station—but your calling in the Gospel, the effectual calling by which the Gospel reaches and converts the heart.

"That not many wise men after the flesh," *i.e.*, not many of the Sophists, the rhetoricians, the teachers of philosophy: not many mighty, *i.e.*, not many magistrates or rulers of men, or captains, proprætors, &c.: not many noble, that is, not many of noble families.

Some of the Fathers, however, apply the word to the callers as well as to the called. Thus Ambrose on Luke vi.: "He chose the Twelve. Observe His Divine wisdom. He chose not the wise, nor rich, nor noble, but fishermen and publicans, lest He might appear to have drawn the world to Himself by wisdom, or to have redeemed it by wealth, or to have allured men by the influence of power or rank; and in order that the power of Divine truth, not the dreams of disputation might prevail." Chrysostom applies it to both callers and called: "Behold your calling, saith he: that not only teachers of an untrained sort, but disciples also of the like class, were objects of His choice."

27. "But God hath chosen the foolish things of the world to confound the wise," &c. This was apparent at the very beginning of the Church, when the High Priests and Sanhedrim perceived that the Apostles were "unlearned and ignorant men." But was it so afterwards? Was not St. Paul one who had profited in the Jews' religion, and was he not "exceedingly zealous of the traditions of his fathers"? Yes: but in preaching the Gospel, Paul, as

28 And base things of the world, and things which are despised, hath God chosen, *yea*, and ᵘ things ʳ which are not, ˣ to bring to nought things that are:

ᵘ Rom. iv. 17.
ˣ ch. ii. 6.

28. "Yea, and things." "Yea, and" omitted by ℵ, A., C., D., F., G.; retained by B., E., L., P., most Cursives, Vulg., Syr., Copt., Arm., &c.

far as was possible, laid aside all this, and devoted himself to the simple proclamation of the Crucified, and Salvation through Him.

"And God hath chosen the weak things of the world to confound," &c. Nothing was weaker in the eyes of men than the Gospel as an instrument for converting the world, and destroying heathenism and false philosophy; for we must remember that the Gospel was the message of Salvation through the Crucifixion and Resurrection of the Lord. It was not even the moral teaching of the Lord, expressed in well-chosen words and well-rounded sentences, so as to commend itself to the fastidious Greeks. It was "Christ Crucified" which came with power and light. He was "crucified through weakness," and that weakness confounded the might of Satan.

28. "And base things of the world, and things which are despised," &c.—*i.e.*, low-born Jews, despised by their own flesh and blood, not worthy of the smallest notice.

"Yea, and things which are not." This is the climax—"nothings" and "nobodies"—to bring to nought things that are. But was this the fact? Were the great powers and existences of the world brought to nought? Yes, it was soon felt by all heathendom that there was a new power in the world, and the more it was ignored the better; and about a century and a half afterwards a great Christian writer thus speaks of the Church, taking root downwards, and bearing fruit upwards: "Men cry out that the State is beset; that the Christians are in their fields, in their forts, in their islands. They mourn as for a loss, that every sex, age, condition, and now even rank is going over to this sect." (Tertullian, Apol. i. ch. i.) And Eusebius, speaking of the times of Commodus, writes: "So that now many of those eminent at Rome for their wealth and kindred, with their whole house and family yielded to their salvation." ("Eccles. Hist." v. ch. 21.) All this—that God had chosen the foolish, the weak, the base, the despised, the nothings, to confound the wise, the mighty, the great self-asserting, self-worshipping world—St. Paul, of course, said in faith. He saw but the

29 ʸ That no flesh should glory in his presence.

ʸ Rom. iii. 27.
Eph. ii. 9.

30 But of him are ye in Christ Jesus, who of

---

beginnings; but those beginnings were such that he knew that the stone was being "cut out without hands," which would become the great mountain, and fill the whole earth (Dan. ii. 45).

29. "That no flesh should glory in his presence." This "no flesh" is an Hebraism for no human being, and, of course, it equally applies to every intelligent creature, as flesh and spirit equally derive their existence from Him. But that which makes them unable to assert themselves before Him is that at times He makes their weakness to confound their strength. The weakness of the Lord Jesus in His utter desolation on the cross overcame the might of all evil. Then was He stronger than the strong man. Then He took from him all his armour, and divided the spoils.

30. "But of him are ye in Christ Jesus, who of God is made unto us wisdom," &c. This "but" signifies that though there is no boasting in self, or human wisdom, or power, there are those who have whereof to glory, not in themselves, but in what God has done and given.

"Of him"—that is, of God the Father—"of whom are all things, and we in him."

If things that were not have now become something, it is due to God alone. And very great things—the greatest things which the creature can receive—are "of him;" but we receive them not singly, not as separate, independent units, but in Christ Jesus, in union with Him.

"Who of God is made unto us wisdom, and righteousness," &c. This passage would be clearer if the order was adhered to, and the force of the particles observed. The Revisers translate: "Who was made unto us wisdom from God, as also righteousness, and sanctification, and redemption." It is as if the Apostle, having mentioned wisdom, suddenly remembered that wisdom was not all—there was righteousness too, and sanctification combined with it, and also redemption.

Christ of God, or from God, or on the part of God, is made unto us wisdom. He is the Word of God, the Wisdom of the Book of Proverbs, Whom "the Lord possessed in the beginning of His way," and Whose "delights were with the sons of men." But in a more excellent way He became wisdom from God to us, when He became

God is made unto us ᶻ wisdom, and ᵃ righteousness, and ᵇ sanctification, and ᶜ redemption:

ᶻ ver. 24.
ᵃ Jer. xxiii. 5, 6. Rom. iv. 25. 2 Cor. v. 21. Phil. iii. 9.
ᵇ John xvii. 19.
ᶜ Eph. i. 7.

---

incarnate, when He taught the people with authority—above all, when He exhibited the union of God's attributes of justice and mercy on the cross; and when He sent down the Spirit, and made men members of His body, that the wisdom of the Head should be infused into them.

But not only did He become to us wisdom, He became righteousness also. "God sent His own Son in the likeness of sinful flesh, that the righteousness of the law might be fulfilled in us." "He is the end of the law for righteousness" (Rom. viii. 4; x. 4).

And not only righteousness, but along with it sanctification. This does not mean merely purity of heart and life, but the dedication to God of all our faculties, so that we should be priests to God, offering up to Him spiritual sacrifices acceptable to Him through Jesus Christ.

The sanctification of the Old Testament especially signifies dedication—separation from all profane uses to the service of God alone. Thus the whole people were sanctified or dedicated to be a kingdom of priests—an holy nation. The altar, the tabernacle, its vessels, the priests were all sanctified—*i.e.*, set apart from profane to holy uses.

The Christian Sanctification is in Christ. He gave Himself for His Church, that He might sanctify and cleanse her with the washing of water by the word: "We are washed, we are sanctified, we are justified in the Name of the Lord Jesus, and by the Spirit of our God" (vi. 11).

"And redemption." There can be little doubt but that St. Paul means by this redemption the redemption of the body, to which he alludes in Rom. viii. 23: "Waiting for the adoption—to wit, the redemption of our body." The all-reconciling redemptive work upon the Cross, which is the foundation of all else, preceded, of course, our righteousness and sanctification in Him. And here redemption is mentioned last, whereas, if we are to confine the word to our Lord's purchase of us by His Blood upon the Cross, it would have come first. It signifies the final redemption at the day of Resurrection: thus, "Until the redemption of the purchased posses-

31 That, according as it is written, ^d He that glorieth, let him glory in the Lord.

^d Jer. ix. 23, 24. 2 Cor. x. 17.

---

sion," and "The Holy Spirit, whereby ye are sealed unto the day of redemption" (Ephes. i. 14; iv. 30).

Thus Bishop Ellicott: "Redemption, not merely from past sins and present sufferings, but also with a more inclusive reference to the final and complete redemption from sin, Satan, and death eternal." And Godet: "The Apostle seems to have in mind the principal phases of Christ's being—*wisdom*, by His life and teaching; *righteousness*, by His Death and Resurrection; *sanctification*, by His elevation to glory; *redemption*, by His future return."

31. "That, according as it is written, He that glorieth, let him glory in the Lord." The place where this is written is no doubt Jeremiah ix. 23, 24: "Thus saith the Lord, Let not the wise man glory in his wisdom, neither let the mighty man glory in his strength, let not the rich man glory in his riches. But let him that glorieth glory in this, that he understandeth and knoweth me, that I am the Lord which exercise loving-kindness, judgment, and righteousness, in the earth: for in these things I delight, saith the Lord."

How is it that the Apostle regards boasting as so evil? He constantly speaks against it; and, in doing this, he goes much deeper than Jeremiah, for the prophet will not have men boast in their wisdom, their might, their riches, whereas the Apostle will not have men boast of their virtue, their righteousness, their keeping of the law. Evidently for this reason, that all boasting arises from two very evil things in the heart—pride and self-dependence. Men boast because they constantly contemplate themselves; men boast because they have no feeling of dependence; they never ask the question, "What hast thou that thou didst not receive? now if thou didst receive it, why dost thou glory, as if thou hadst not received it?" (iv. 7.)

In this condemnation of boasting the Apostle is only carrying on the teaching of his Master, for Christ's first words were, "Blessed are the poor in spirit, for theirs is the kingdom of heaven;" His second, "Blessed are they that mourn, for they shall be comforted;" His third, "Blessed are the meek, for they shall inherit the earth."

CHAP. II.

AND I, brethren, when I came to you, ^a came not with excellency of speech or of wisdom, declaring unto you ^b the testimony of God.

2 For I determined not to know any thing among you, ^c save Jesus Christ, and him crucified.

a ch. i. 17.
ver. 4, 13.
2 Cor. x. 10.
& xi. 6.
b ch. i. 6.
c Gal. vi. 14.
Phil. iii. 8.

---

1. "The testimony of God." So B., D., E., F., G., L., P., most Cursives, d, e, f, g, Vulg., Sah., Æth., Arm.; but ℵ, A., C., Syr., Copt., read, "the mystery of God."

1. "And I, brethren, when I came to you, came not with excellency of speech," &c. As was the Gospel, so was its delivery. He did not wrap up that which was extremely simple in highflown words and phrases, which would have destroyed the power of its simplicity.

"Declaring unto you the testimony [or mystery] of God." The authorities for the two words are very evenly balanced, but the meaning and force are the same in either case, for the testimony of God—that which He testified by the Resurrection, viz., the true Sonship of the Only Begotten, and His Atoning Death—was mystery and must ever be : and the mystery of God was not wrapped up in a philosophy, but was a testimony, a testimony to the gift of His Son for the salvation of the world.

2. "For I determined not to know any thing among you, save Jesus Christ," &c. This does not mean that he determined to preach only the Crucifixion, because from all the first part of 1 Cor. xv. we gather that the principal fact of his Gospel, on which he laid most stress, was the Lord's Resurrection : but it means that in all his preaching of Jesus Incarnate, Dying and Rising again, he never kept back, but put in the foreground Jesus as Crucified. He never allowed any human motives or prudential considerations to make him keep back the offence of the Cross. Whatever temptations he might have to speak with reserve of the shame and indignity which the Lord suffered, he never yielded to

^d Acts xviii. 1, 6, 12.
^e 2 Cor. iv. 7. & x. 1, 10. & xi. 30. & xii. 5, 9. Gal. iv. 13.
^f ver. 1. ch. i. 17. 2 Pet. i. 16.
‖ Or, *persuasible*.
^g Rom. xv. 19. 1 Thess. i. 5.

3 And ^d I was with you ^e in weakness, and in fear, and in much trembling.

4 And my speech and my preaching ^f *was* not with ‖ enticing words of man's wisdom, ^g but in demonstration of the Spirit and of power:

---

4. "Of man's wisdom." So A., C., L., P., most Cursives; but ℵ, B., D., E., F., G., d, e, f, q, r, Vulg. (Cod. Amiat.), Syr., Sah., Arm., Æth., omit "man's."

them for a moment, but held up the Cross as the power of God for remission of sin and attraction of hearts to God.

3. "And I was with you in weakness, and in fear, and in much trembling." No doubt this took place because of those personal infirmities to which he so often alludes: thus in 2 Cor. x. 10 he makes his adversaries say of him (and no doubt they did say it) "that his bodily presence was weak, and his speech contemptible." And also in xi. 30: "If I must needs glory, I will glory of the things which concern mine infirmities." Again, "I will not glory but in mine infirmities." He seems to have had a painful consciousness of these infirmities, whatever they were, and dreaded exceedingly lest they should hinder the reception of the truths which he preached. Perhaps this dread also, for some wise reason, was permitted to have especial hold on him when he commenced his ministry in Corinth, for the Lord Himself appeared to him in a vision, supporting him with the words, "Be not afraid, but speak, and hold not thy peace, for I am with thee" (Acts xviii. 9). Someone has remarked that a peculiar undefined dread hanging over a preacher is very frequently the prelude to a particular blessing attending his ministry.

4. "And my speech and my preaching was not with enticing words," &c. The Corinthians seem especially to have expected these honied, enticing words from those who would move them, and so "Corinthian words" was a popular expression for exquisite phrases. (Stanley.)

"My speech" (λόγος), the form and words of speech; "my preaching," the thing preached, the substance of what he proclaimed.

"In demonstration of the Spirit and of power." "In demonstra-

CHAP. II.] NOT IN THE WISDOM OF MEN. 29

5 That your faith should not † stand in the wisdom of men, but ʰ in the power of God.

† Gr. *be.*
ʰ 2 Cor. iv. 7.
& vi. 7.

---

tion" means in clear proof, recognizable by all, that the Spirit of God accompanied his preaching.

Commentators are divided as to what this "demonstration of the Spirit" is. Some say that we must exclude from our view the miraculous gifts of the Spirit, and confine it to the internal working of the Spirit of God upon the soul, according to the words of the Lord, "He shall glorify me, for he shall receive of mine, and shall show it unto you." And no doubt conversion, especially that of one brought up in heathenism, is as manifest a work of the Holy Ghost as any miracle of bodily healing. Godet, a commentator who generally takes a believing view of Scripture, and so cannot be credited with a rationalistic dislike of miracles, goes so far as to write, "Chrysostom, and in our day Beet, apply these expressions to the outward miracles which St. Paul sometimes (?) wrought by the power of the Holy Spirit (2 Cor. xii. 12; Rom. xv. 19). Such an interpretation, allowable in the infancy of exegesis, should now no longer be possible." But did not the Spirit of God actually accompany the preaching of St. Paul with outward mighty signs and wonders? The Apostle, in the two places cited by Godet, expressly declares that He did. Take 2 Cor. xii. 12: "Truly the signs of an Apostle were wrought among you in signs, and wonders, and mighty deeds." These signs and wonders were wrought in Corinth before their eyes. They were the means, not perhaps by which they believed, but by which their attention was directed to the preaching of an obscure foreign Jew, as St. Paul was. Freely allowing that the miracle of miracles was the resurrection of a dead soul to the life of Christ, still this was a miracle in the compass of the heart only, and could, for a time at least, be known only to a few, whilst the outward miracles brought directly to the notice of thousands the working among them of the unseen Ruler of the universe. Considering the very great stress which the Apostle laid upon his miracles as the signs of his Apostleship, it is impossible to doubt but that he had them principally in his mind when he wrote this passage.

5. "That your faith should not stand in the wisdom of men, but in the power of God." That your faith should not stand in the

ⁱ ch. xiv. 20. Eph. iv. 13. Phil. iii. 15. Heb. v. 14.
^k ch. i. 20. & iii. 19. ver. 1, 13. 2 Cor. i. 12. James iii. 15.
^l ch. i. 28.

6 Howbeit we speak wisdom among them ⁱ that are perfect: yet not ^k the wisdom of this world, nor of the princes of this world, ^l that come to nought:

---

exhibition of the Gospel as a philosophical system expressed in the terms of human science and logic, but in the power of God, in the power of God within you, making you new creatures in Christ, with new views of God, and His Son, and His Spirit, and the eternal world, and confirming the truth and reality of this mighty change of all within you by signs and wonders which were in reality the effects of the Resurrection of Christ, and which took place in this visible state of things, so that you might be assured that your internal change was not a mental delusion, but a true work of Almighty God.

6. "Howbeit we speak wisdom among them that are perfect." The Apostle here corrects a misapprehension which might arise from what he had been saying. He had been speaking of God saving men "by the foolishness of preaching," of "the foolishness of God being wiser than men," of "God having chosen the foolish things of the world to confound the wise," of "not having come to them with excellency of speech and of wisdom." And from all this, they might think that there was no true wisdom, no deep philosophy, in the Cross: but here he assures them that if they thought so they would be wrong indeed, for amongst those fit to receive such instruction, whom he calls the perfect, *i.e.*, the full-grown, as opposed to the babes, they spoke wisdom, but not of this world, nor, he adds, of the princes of this world, that come to nought.

Why does he mention the princes of this world? Because the rulers of this world, *i.e.*, the heads of the Jewish Church and State, were directly instrumental in the crucifixion of the Lord, and he had just been speaking of knowing nothing among them save Jesus Christ and Him crucified. The mention of the Crucified brings to his mind the earthly wisdom to which the Cross was opposed, and this in its turn makes him revert to the fact that the Lord's crucifiers—Chief Priests, Scribes, and Pharisees—were, so far as his own nation were concerned, the possessors of the world's wisdom.

IN A MYSTERY.

7 But we speak the wisdom of God in a mystery, *even* the

"That come to nought." This probably means that they were doomed to disappear, and be destroyed in the swift approaching destruction of their city and temple.

7. "But we speak the wisdom of God in a mystery, even the hidden wisdom." "The wisdom of God in a mystery." What is this wisdom of God, and how is it in mystery (ἐν μυστηρίῳ)?

The wisdom of God is the knowledge of the greatest and highest matters which can be presented to the human intellect, such as the human and the Divine in the Person of Jesus of Nazareth, as set forth in the Epistles to the Colossians and Hebrews; the calling of the Gentiles and the casting away of the Jews, in that to the Romans; the Headship of Christ in the Epistle to the Ephesians, as well as the Revelation of the Anomos in the Thessalonians. These are the leading mysteries or leading parts of the one great mystery of Christ which we learn from the Epistles.

But how is this spoken in a mystery, or in mystery? There seems to be but one answer. This wisdom differs from human wisdom in that it is unsearchable by the human intellect. Men, in other respects apparently believers, tell us, or as good as tell us, that there is now no mystery in the usual sense of the word in the New Testament—that a mystery is a thing which was once hidden in God's foreknowledge, but being now revealed becomes a mystery no longer, but is brought into the domain of the human intellect. But let us take the Incarnation of our blessed Lord; this was prophesied of in Isaiah, and so was in the Divine foreknowledge. It was in due time made known to men; to the Virgin, in the words of the angel (Luke i. 35); to the Church, in the words of St. Paul, in Coloss. i., Phil. ii., also in Hebrews i., and in the first chapters of St. John's Gospel and Epistle. But when thus revealed, was it robbed of its mysteriousness, and brought down to our comprehension? No, it was made tenfold more mysterious, for then the human intellect first became thoroughly aware of the unfathomable depth with which it was brought face to face—the perfect union of the Divine and human in the Crucified.[1]

---

[1] Godet writes thus respecting the absence of a mystery properly so called in the New Testament. "The word mystery has taken, in theological language, a meaning which it has not in the New Testament, to wit, a truth which human reason cannot fathom. In Paul's writings it simply signifies a truth or a fact which the human understanding

hidden *wisdom*, ᵐ which God ordained before the world unto our glory:

8 ⁿ Which none of the princes of this world knew: for ᵒ had they known *it*, they would not have crucified the Lord of glory.

ᵐ Rom. xvi. 25, 26. Eph. iii. 5, 9. Col. i. 26. 2 Tim. i. 9.
ⁿ Matt. xi. 25. John vii. 48. Acts xiii. 27. 2 Cor. iii. 14.
ᵒ Luke xxiii. 34. Acts iii. 17. See John xvi. 3.

"The hidden wisdom," that is, hidden in the Divine foreknowledge which God ordained before the world, *i.e.*, before the ages—from all eternity.

"Unto our glory." This is an astonishing assertion: it seems at first sight to say that the one object of the revelation of these mysteries was for the glory of certain human beings. Now we know that these mysteries were revealed for the salvation of all men, and not only for the glory of the Apostles (Ephes. iii.). But one of the objects of this revelation assuredly was the glory of the Apostles and of those who believed in Christ through their word: and it is an astonishing honour put upon human beings that they should be able to apprehend in any degree the Trinity in Unity, and the wisdom and love of God in the Incarnation, Death, and Resurrection of Jesus Christ the Son of God. (See my notes on Rom. viii. 30.)

8. "Which none of the princes of this world knew: for had . . . . the Lord of glory." Such a title could not have been

cannot of itself discover, but which it apprehends as soon as God gives the revelation of it. Thus Jesus says, Luke viii. 10, ' It is given to you to know the mysteries of the kingdom ;' and Paul applies the word mystery to things which we can perfectly comprehend ; for example, Rom. xvi. 25." But is this true ? When the Lord says, ' To you it is given to know the mysteries of the kingdom,' what does He proceed to make known ? Why, the absolutely unsearchable mystery of the difference between souls which causes some to accept the truth and others to reject it. Some of these souls are compared to the roadside, some to stony ground, some to good ground, but how came it to pass that souls should have these inherent differences ? The great body of the Jews did not realize that there were such differences. The Apostles were told it as a fact, and accepted it because He told them, but in their case the mystery was only removed one step back. The state of particular souls so different, and yet all loved by the Creator, is as much a mystery as ever. Then in Rom. xvi. 25, the mystery which was hid is now made manifest, but surely the mystery of God, giving divine knowledge to one small nation only, and letting all the rest walk in blindness and ignorance, is as great a mystery as can well be presented to man. When St. Paul says, ' Behold I show you a mystery,' he proceeds to assert the reality of the spiritual body ; for the mystery in the words "we shall be changed " is a mystery ' which human reason cannot fathom.' The reason why some good men thus repudiate mystery in the New Testament is transparent—they desire to be rid of the Eucharistic mystery.

CHAP. II.]   EYE HATH NOT SEEN.   33

9 But as it is written, P Eye hath not seen, nor ear heard,
neither have entered into the heart of man, the   P Is. lxiv. 4.
things which God hath prepared for them that love him.

---

accorded to the Lord by a sincere Israelite like St. Paul, unless he
believed in the Lord's Godhead. "Who is the King of glory?"
asks the Psalmist: "The Lord of Hosts, He is the King of Glory."

9. "But as it is written," &c. I have considered in a foot-
note [1] (the substance of which comes from Neale) the difficulty
attached to this quotation—as to the exact place from which it was
taken. The Apostle quotes the passage according to his version
of it as expressing the three great means of acquiring natural knowledge, sight, hearing, and reflection or imagination ; and none of
them have enabled men to attain to the knowledge of the things
which the wisdom of God in a mystery—the hidden wisdom—has
given the knowledge of to the regenerate. The description,
as it most frequently is, may be applied to the joys of the unseen
and eternal world, of which the Lord will put the faithful into
possession at His coming: but the Apostle quotes the passage as
referring to what God gives us to know and realize, not hereafter,
but here.

---

[1] The Greek is ἀλλὰ καθὼς γέγραπται· ἃ ὀφθαλμὸς οὐκ εἶδε, καὶ οὖς οὐκ ἤκουσε, καὶ ἐπὶ καρδίαν ἀνθρώπου οὐκ ἀνέβη, ἃ ἡτοίμασεν ὁ Θεὸς τοῖς ἀγαπῶσιν αὐτόν. Now, on comparing this with the Septuagint version of Isaiah lxiv. 4 (ἀπὸ τοῦ αἰῶνος οὐκ ἠκούσαμεν, οὐδὲ οἱ ὀφθαλμοὶ ἡμῶν εἶδον Θεὸν πλὴν σοῦ, καὶ τὰ ἔργα σου, ἃ ποιήσεις τοῖς ὑπομένουσιν ἔλεον), which St. Paul is supposed to have quoted, it will be found that there is not one word the same in the two clauses, and yet this present passage is plainly meant to be a textual quotation : further, the relative ἃ, with which it opens, has no antecedent. It is remarkable that these difficulties are solved by a reference to the Liturgies of SS. James and Mark, in which occur prayers containing words exactly identical, *mutatis mutandis*, with the present verse, and giving also the antecedent (δωρήματα in St. James, and ἀγαθὰ in St. Mark) which St. Paul omits. It must therefore be concluded, either that St. Paul may have intended to quote Isaiah, and fell into the form of words as generally used in the Church, or else that he meant to quote directly from the Liturgies ; and that we are to infer that the Liturgies were so generally accepted that he does not hesitate to quote from them as from the Scriptures themselves. Neale adopts the latter view, and I agree with him ; and it is remarkable, too, that Clement of Rome (Ep. ii. 11) uses exactly the same form of words as SS. Paul, James, and Mark, only he puts the *ear* before the *eye* (" which ear hath not heard nor eye seen "), a variation to be readily expected, when he is quoting from a Liturgy probably learnt by heart in the first instance.

If the reader wishes to pursue the matter further, he must refer to Neale's " Essays on Liturgiology," p. 414, sq.

D

10 But ᑫ God hath revealed *them* unto us by his Spirit: for the Spirit searcheth all things, yea, the deep things of God.

ᑫ Matt. xiii. 11. & xvi. 17.
John xiv. 26. & xvi. 13.
1 John ii. 27.

---

10. "But God." So ℵ, A., C., D., E., F., G., L., P., most Cursives, d, e, f, g, Vulg., Syriac, Arm., Æth.; but B., with eight Cursives, Sah., Copt., read, "for God."

10. "But God hath revealed them unto us by his Spirit," &c. The Spirit here, of course, can be no other than the Third Person in the Godhead—the Holy Spirit. Rationalistic commentators either deny this, or pass it over as if the organ of communication on God's part was the spirit in man. But this is impossible, for the Christian Revelation did not rise up spontaneously, as it were, in the breasts of a number of good men, but spread from a local centre, and was propagated by preaching, which was witnessed to by marvellous works, which clearly proved that the Revelation was from the Lord of the whole universe, spiritual and natural.

This was in accordance with the word of prophecy, as Joel ii. 28, and, above all, with the word of Christ: "The Comforter .... shall teach you all things." "He will guide you into all truth" (John xiv. 26; xvi. 13).

"For the Spirit searcheth all things, yea, the deep things of God." The reader will notice a remarkable antithesis between this passage and Romans viii. 27. There we read, "He that searcheth the hearts knoweth what is the mind of the Spirit." Here, on the contrary, the Spirit searcheth the deep things of God. Chrysostom remarks well upon this: "The word to search is here indicative, not of ignorance, but of accurate knowledge; at least if we may judge from the fact that this is the same mode of speaking which he hath used even of God, saying, 'He that searcheth the hearts knoweth what is the mind of the Spirit.'"

"Searcheth all things." He searches in the sense of knowing accurately all the works of God, especially His work in the creation and continued existence of spiritual beings, such as angels and men: but above all, He knows accurately the deepest things of Him from Whom He proceeds—His being and attributes, the generation of that Eternal Word or Son from Whom also He proceeds, the Incarnation, the Atonement, and Intercession, as things in the Godhead between the Father and the Son, than which we can imagine nothing deeper or higher.

CHAP. II.] WE HAVE RECEIVED. 35

11 For what man knoweth the things of a man, ʳ save the spirit of man which is in him? ˢ even so the things of God knoweth no man, but the Spirit of God.

ʳ Prov. xx. 27. & xxvii. 19.
Jer. xvii. 9.
ˢ Rom. xi. 33, 34.

12 Now we have received, not the spirit of the

---

11. "For what man knoweth the things of a man, save . . . . Spirit of God." The human subject has that within him, viz., his highest part, his self-consciousness, which he can, as it were, at times project out of himself, so that it can look into him as from without, and examine into the whole state of his interior, his animal soul, and his mind, understanding, and will; and so the Spirit of God, proceeding from God, yet in God searcheth (or accurately knoweth) all that is in God.

I need hardly remark that nothing can go beyond this in proving the true and eternal Godhead of the Holy Spirit. "It is clear that the Spirit which searcheth the deep things of God, cannot be a creature or less than God" (Athanasius ad Serapion, i. sect. 22), quoted in Wordsworth, who also quotes a passage from Waterland, in which occurs: "He is in God, and knows the mind of God as perfectly as a man knows his own mind, and that in respect of all things, yea the deep things of God."[1]

12. "Now we have received, not the spirit of the world, but the spirit which is of God; that we might know," &c. "Now we have received." This "we" is emphatic, and may refer either to St. Paul and his brother Apostles, or to St. Paul and his fellow-teachers, most probably the latter, because the Corinthian Chris-

---

[1] Principal Edwards has an admirable note. He asks, "Does 'Spirit of God' here mean more than the self-consciousness of God? is not the force of the Apostle's argument in the analogy between the self-consciousness of man, knowing what is in man, and the self-consciousness of God, as it knows what is in God? Yes, say Osiander, Meyer, Kling after Baur ('New Test. Theol.,' p. 207). But it would be palpably absurd to say that God reveals anything to man through His own self-consciousness, unless the self-consciousness of God is identical with the Holy Spirit. This, again, would involve that the procession of the Spirit is prior in idea to God's self-consciousness—whereas His self-consciousness as Deus must be prior, in order of ideas, to His self-consciousness as fons deitatis. We must not, therefore, press the analogy. If we admit that the Holy Spirit knows the things of God, it is not necessary to the validity of the Apostle's reasoning that He should know them as man knows the things of man, by self-consciousness. Both are knowledge through introspection, and this is enough. . . . . If the Spirit is neither the human spirit, nor the Divine self-consciousness, a more decisive declaration of His Personality cannot be."

world, but ᵗthe spirit which is of God; that we might know the things that are freely given to us of God.

ᵗ Rom. viii. 15.

13 ᵘ Which things also we speak, not in the words which man's wisdom teacheth, but which the Holy Ghost teacheth; comparing spiritual things with spiritual.

ᵘ 2 Pet. i. 16.
See ch. i. 17.
ver. 4.

---

13. "Which the Holy Ghost teacheth." So E., L., P., and most Cursives; but ℵ, A., B., C., D., F., G., seven Cursives, d, e, f, g, r, Vulg., Syriac, &c., omit "Holy."

tians were brought more into contact with them than with the Apostles of the Circumcision.

"Not the spirit of the world." "This has been taken to mean Satan, the god of this world, or the principle of evil which binds together the kingdom of darkness, and makes it not a chaos, but a cosmos, an organization contrived to subvert the kingdom of Christ" (Edwards). But is it likely that the Apostle would feel it necessary to disclaim having received his inspiration from such a source? I think we must rather look to some spirit or spiritual influence which was not so absolutely opposed to the Spirit of God, but that it might be supposed to be the fountain of some Divine knowledge, and this we might take to be what Dean Stanley interprets it as being, "the spirit of mere human wisdom." This would be the highest form which the spirit of the world could take, but that was not the spirit which St. Paul and his fellows had received, for they had received

"The spirit which is of God; that we might know the things," &c. Might not "freely given to us of God" be translated "given by grace," not by knowledge or human endeavour, but by grace? For the whole system of the Gospel, or the Church, or Christianity, or by whatever name it is called, is a system of grace freely given on God's part, and received without human science or education or merit by us. The things thus given to us freely are, first of all, Christ Himself to the world; then Christ to each member of the Church, His mind, His will, His righteousness, His truth, His very human nature through His Body and Blood.

13. "Which things also we speak, not in the words which man's wisdom teacheth," &c. Not only are the things freely given to us—the things of grace, themselves taught by the Holy Spirit, but the same Spirit has taught us words wherein to give them fitting expression.

"Comparing spiritual things with spiritual." Great difficulties

THE NATURAL MAN.

14 ˣ But the natural man receiveth not the things of the Spirit of God : ʸ for they are foolishness unto

x Matt. xvi. 23.
y ch. i. 18, 23.

have been supposed to attach to this verse: first, from some uncertainty attaching to the meaning of the word comparing (συγκρίνοντες), of which Bishop Ellicott gives three renderings—combining, comparing, explaining: and secondly, from uncertainty as to whether the last word translated "spiritual" is masculine or neuter, and so whether it means explaining spiritual things by spiritual things, or explaining spiritual things to spiritual men; the last seems to agree best with the next verse.

But various passages in the Epistle itself seem to direct us to the true meaning, which is "explaining spiritual things by spiritual," which in point of fact amounts to the same as that indicated in our Authorized, comparing spiritual things with spiritual, for we compare in order to explain. I think St. Paul means we bring down spiritual things, as far as we are able, to the level of human apprehension, by the teaching of that which is most spiritual in the Old Testament—the teaching of the types. All through his Epistles St. Paul illustrates the New Testament truths by the significance of Old Testament types. Thus Christ our Passover in ch. v. 7, 8, and Christ our manna and spiritual drink in ch. x. 3, 4 ; and Isaac and Ishmael, and Hagar and Sarah as typical of the two Jerusalems in Gal. iv.

14. "But the natural man receiveth not the things of the Spirit of God," &c. The natural man is the psychical man, ψυχικὸς, the man under no higher influence than his animal soul, though that soul may have its intellectual or rational, as well as its sensual side. The spiritual man is the man in whom the spirit, his noblest part, does not lie buried under the weight of the animal, or merely mental or intellectual, but is alive to God, and takes in the things of God. We must remember that St. Paul, as we learn from 1 Thessal. v. 23, considers man to be of a tripartite nature :—1. The body ; 2. The soul, which is intermediate between the body and the spirit, and has its animal side which looks to the body, and its intellectual or even moral side, which looks to the spirit; and 3. The spirit, the πνεῦμα, which is that in him which looks to God, and is that part which the Spirit regenerates, and into which He infuses the knowledge of God, and of spiritual and eternal things.

So that, according to St. Paul, a philosopher may reason deeply

him: *neither can he know *them,* because they are spiritually discerned.

* Rom. viii. 5, 6, 7. Jude 19.

---

respecting intellectual and even ethical truths, and yet be ψυχικὸς, natural, since all may minister to his pride; as the Apostle says in Colos. ii. 18, he may be " vainly puffed up with his fleshly mind," and so with all his intellect he may be no nearer to God; but when, through the power of the Spirit of God, the true functions of his highest part, his spirit, are revived or regenerated, then he begins to apprehend God and the things of the Spirit of God.

Now the question arises, is the psychical or natural man here the unconverted individual person, and the spiritual man (he that is spiritual) of the next verse, the spiritual or enlightened person? I think not, and for this reason, the terms natural or psychical, and spiritual man, are used in the sense of the old man and the new man of Ephes. iv. 22, 24. The man, natural or spiritual, signifies the Adam, or, as we say, the spiritual principle which is in each man. None are perfectly spiritual, as we learn from Rom. vii., and many whom from their conduct or opinions we should pronounce only natural, show some spiritual perceptions. Again, we cannot infallibly pronounce respecting the good and virtuous heathen (Rom. ii. 14, 15), that they have no pneuma, and whether that pneuma may not be in some degree acted upon for good by "the law written on their hearts" by "the Light which lighteth every man that cometh into the world." Again I trust I shall be forgiven in what I say, but I firmly believe that when an Evangelical commentator asserts that there is no such thing as a mystery in the ordinary sense of the word in the New Testament, he makes that assertion at the inspiration of the natural or psychical man remaining within him, and not of the spiritual. For the first action of Christ through the Spirit on the human spirit is to humble it, and so put it in possession of the three first blessings wherewith He blesses His people.

What, then, the Apostle means is that the natural man—the psychical principle within each of us—does not apprehend the mysteries of the Kingdom of God. He has not the organ by which they are apprehended, or if he has such an organ, *i.e.*, the pneuma, it is in a dormant state: the Incarnation, the Atoning Death, the life-imparting Resurrection, the perpetual Intercession, the truths of the Mystical Body, the resurrection of the spiritual body, the true

JUDGED OF NO MAN.

15 ᵃ But he that is spiritual ‖ judgeth all things, yet he himself is ‖ judged of no man.

ᵃ Prov. xxviii. 5. 1 Thess. v. 21. 1 John iv. 1.
‖ Or, *discerneth*.
‖ Or, *discerned*.

discerning of the Sacramental Body, are foolishness unto him. He may acquiesce in them, or not deny them, because they may be a part of the Creed or body of divine truth of the Church to which he belongs, but he does not *see* them. He cannot know them, because they are spiritually discerned—till the Spirit takes of the things of Christ, and shows them to him, he cannot realize their amazing significance.

15. "But he that is spiritual judgeth all things, yet he himself is judged of no man." Judgeth ought perhaps to be rendered "discerneth." Judging in our language implies that we are superior, or for the moment take a superior position, to the things which we judge. The word is the same as that in the last verse, "they are spiritually discerned."

"He that is spiritual judgeth (or discerneth) all things." The spiritual man discerneth all things, even the deep things of God. His enlightened and strengthened spirit cannot altogether apprehend them, or compass them. They are to him as some vast object in some deep unfathomable abyss. He discerns that it is there. He discerns that side which is presented to him, but he cannot compass it or take the measure of it.

"All things." In this must be included human and worldly things. The spiritual man estimates at their right value the things of time and sense, the characters of men so far as one can do who cannot read the hearts, the relations of men to God, to Christ, and to one another. When any worldly scheme or political change is proposed, he instantly regards it in its relations to the Kingdom of God.

"Yet he himself is judged of no man." This means, of course, that the spiritual man—the new Adam within him—is judged by no unspiritual man. "The spiritual man has a new faculty by which he judges all, but cannot be judged by any who have it not. He understands the language in which other men speak, but they understand not the language in which he speaks." This, of course, applies not to the individual spiritual person, who partakes of the mixed character which there is in the best, but to the spiritual man or Adam in each. If the spiritual or enlightened person commits sin, or falls from grace, or acts contrary to what even the

16 ᵇ For who hath known the mind of the Lord, that he †may instruct him? ᶜ But we have the mind of Christ.

ᵇ Job xv. 8.
Is. xl. 13.
Jer. xxiii. 18.
Rom. xi. 34.
† Gr. *shall.*
ᶜ John xv. 15.

16. "Of Christ." So ℵ, A., C., E., L., P., most Cursives, d, e, Vulg., Syriac, Copt., Arm.; but B., D., F., G., f, g, r, read "of the Lord."

world acknowledges to be the highest principles of Christianity, then the worldly, unspiritual man rightly judges and condemns him.

Principal Edwards writes upon this:—"The judgment of the spiritual man is at once the widest and the highest. All things are subject to it, from it there is no appeal. It is unhesitating, authoritative, absolute, final." Now, however this may be true of the spiritual man—that is, the new Adam in each—it is not true of any particular spiritual person, for this reason, that those who from their language we should account the most highly spiritual people, constantly differ from one another. Again, it is exceedingly seldom that a spiritual man takes in the whole circle of spiritual knowledge. He has constantly a habit of discerning some truths, and shutting his spiritual eye to others. The will, in fact, constantly makes itself felt in the domain of the spirit. So that we have always need to adopt for ourselves the words of the Apostle, " I pray God that my whole spirit, and soul, and body be preserved blameless unto the coming of our Lord Jesus Christ" (1 Thess. v. 23).

16. "For who hath known the mind of the Lord, that he may instruct him?" &c. This is a remarkable assertion of the Divine sphere of knowledge into which the spiritual man has been uplifted. Who can instruct God? and God through the Spirit has made known to us His mind, and we through the Spirit dwelling in us have the mind of Christ or of the Lord, meaning Christ; so that so far as the things of God are concerned, who can judge us? who can even instruct us? who can impart to us truth which we have not in and through Christ?

The "we," however, is emphatic and must be applied only to St. Paul, and those who, like him (as the Apostles), have plenary divine knowledge of all things which the Church needs to know. Godet observes well, " In the ἡμεῖς, *we*, there is a well-marked contrast to the ὑμεῖς, *you*, of iii. 1-3. It is obvious how profoundly, in virtue of the revelation he has received, the Apostle distinguishes himself from the Church."

"We have the mind of Christ," *i.e.*, upon all things which it is necessary for the Church to be instructed in.

CHAP. III.

AND I, brethren, could not speak unto you as unto [a] spiritual, but as unto [b] carnal, *even as* unto [c] babes in Christ.

2 I have fed you with [d] milk, and not with

[a] ch. ii. 15.
[b] ch. ii. 14.
[c] Heb. v. 13.
[d] Heb. v. 12, 13. 1 Pet. ii. 2.

---

1. "As unto carnal." ℵ, A., B., C., D., 17, 67**, 71, read, σαρκίνοις, fleshy; E., F., G., L., P., and most Cursives read, σαρκίκοις, fleshly, *i.e.* sensual.

1. "And I, brethren, could not speak unto you as unto spiritual, but as unto carnal, even as unto babes in Christ." This means that though he did not speak unto them as unto those wholly unregenerate, for such could not be even babes in Christ—if they were babes in Christ they must have been brought into Him—but he spoke to them as those in whom the spiritual man was as yet scarcely at all developed; and so they were carnal, that is, the lower nature yet predominated in them.

"Carnal." The word is, according to the amended texts, founded on what are supposed to be the best manuscripts, σαρκίνοις, and is translated fleshy, whilst the word in the Rec. Text is σαρκίκοις, translated fleshly. In the former the idea of nature (flesh) is supposed to predominate—in the latter, character. St. Paul, however, evidently means to assert that there was something wrong in them which hindered their spiritual growth from infancy to manhood in Christ, and so he was only able to speak to them as to infants in grace, and not as to grown men.

2. "I have fed you with milk, and not with meat: for hitherto ye were," &c. What is this "milk" and what the "meat"? The question is more difficult than many suppose. Milk, according to Godet, "denotes the preaching of Christ crucified, with its simplest contents, and its most immediate consequences, expiation, justification by faith, the sanctification of the justified believer by the Holy Spirit," but surely the dullest Corinthian Christian must have asked, How could the Crucifixion of an unknown Jew make expiation for all sin? how could belief in such an One justify? It is quite clear that St. Paul must have preached to them how it was

meat: ᵉfor hitherto ye were not able *to bear it*, neither yet now are ye able.

ᵉ John xvi. 12.

---

that the Blood of Christ, as distinguished from that of any other man, could expiate, and what warrant he had for saying so. Now when we look to the latter part of this Epistle we find what it was which the Apostle preached to them *first of all*. "I delivered unto you *first of all*, that which I also received, that Christ died for our sins, that he was buried, and that he rose again the third day," &c. This was the milk with which beyond all doubt he began to feed them. It was his Gospel, and he could scarcely declare this without some reference to the relations of Christ to the unseen and unknown God—that He was His true, proper, and only Son. And all this was proved and enforced by miracles, and not only by miracles performed by the Apostle, but even by some among themselves. This, then, was the milk—the doctrine of Christ Incarnate, crucified, risen, ascended, and coming again to judge, if, that is, St. Paul preached the same Gospel doctrine to the Corinthians as he wrote to the Christians at Rome. But what would be the meat? Are we to look for any indication of what it is in this Epistle, or are we to suppose that because the Corinthians were yet carnal, we must look for it in Epistles addressed to more spiritual churches? We should have supposed that the great truth of Christians being one body in Christ, or of the resurrection of Christians in a spiritual body, would be meat for those full-grown in Christ: but both of these are treated more fully in this letter to "babes" than in any other Epistle. Again, the Eucharistic Mystery is more fully set forth in this Epistle than in any other; indeed, it is the only one in which specific mention is made of it.

It may be that the higher aspects of Election as set forth in Ephes. i.-iii., may be this strong meat, for unquestionably the view of election in Ephes. i. is higher than the view in the Epistle to the Romans even; or that the relations of Christ to God on the one side and the Church on the other, as set forth in Coloss. i.-iii., are higher doctrines, that is, require more spiritual power to assimilate them, than what are found in this Epistle.

It seems that as St. Paul advances in the writing of this Epistle, he finds himself compelled to set forth what only the more spiritual could apprehend and retain, just as pastors now must preach higher

YE ARE YET CARNAL.

3 For ye are yet carnal: for ⁱ whereas *there is* among you envying and strife, and ‖ divisions, are ye not carnal, and walk † as men?

<small>ᶠ ch. i. 11. & xi. 18. Gal. v. 20, 21. James iii. 16.
‖ Or, *factions*.
† Gr. *according to man?*</small>

---

truths to mixed congregations than they would if they could make some selection or separation amongst those who listen to them.

" Ye were not able to bear it, neither yet now are ye able." The latter clause seems to imply that they were, notwithstanding their declensions, somewhat advancing; and so he can now venture, as it were, to teach them what at his first sojourn among them he could not.

3. "For ye are yet carnal: for whereas there is among you envying and strife," &c. No passage of Scripture that I know of, brings out so sharply the difference between the Apostolic teaching in the primitive Church, and the state of Christian opinion amongst us as this. The Apostle regards envying, strife, and divisions as carnality, whereas this is the last thing to which such sins as envyings and strifes would now be attributed. Such things as drunkenness and fornication, and self-indulgence in food are now held to be carnal, and, as far as I know, only these; whereas it is not at all uncommon to hear religious strifes and divisions and factions vindicated. They are vindicated as assertions of the right of private judgment as inseparable from true freedom, and so on. There are sects whose one reason for their existence seems to be their profession of superior spirituality—they themselves being the sole judges of it. Now the Apostle treats religious strifes and party divisions as " of the flesh." They seem to us to be " of the Spirit," because so frequently have they to do with spiritual religion; but the Apostle denounces them as " of the flesh." How can this be? It is because the $\psi v \chi \dot{\eta}$, the soul, the carnal principle, having its intellectual side or part, intrudes into the domain of the spirit; or, it may be, that the spirit itself falls from its high estate, and suffers itself to be led by the flesh, by that which is lower, by self, by vain-glory, by desire of eminence, by the yet imperfectly subdued will. As Godet well says, " Such a state can only arise from self-complacency, either on the part of the leaders, or their adherents; and that is *the flesh*."

" Walk as men." According to the way of the world, according to man, for the world strives to bring about many of its ends,

4 For while one saith, ᵍ I am of Paul; and another, I am of Apollos; are ye not carnal?

ᵍ ch. i. 12.

5 Who then is Paul, and who *is* Apollos, but ʰ ministers by whom ye believed, ⁱ even as the Lord gave to every man?

ʰ ch. iv. 1.
2 Cor. iii. 3.
ⁱ Rom. xii. 3.
6. 1 Pet. iv. 11.

---

4. "Are ye not carnal?" So L., P., most Cursives, Syriac; but ℵ, A., B., C., D., E., F., G., 17, 67**, 71, d, e, f, g, r, Vulg., Copt., Æth., read, "are ye not men."

5. "Who then is Paul, and who is Apollos, but ministers," &c. So L., P., most Cursives, Syriac; but ℵ, A., B., C., D., E., F., G., 67, 71**, 177, d, e, f, g, r, Vulg., Copt., Arm., read, "Who then is Apollos, and who is Paul? (They are) ministers by whom," &c.

notably its political ones, by the use of party spirit and party organizations.

4. "For while one saith, I am of Paul; and another, I am of Apollos: are ye not carnal?" As it is not to be supposed that there was any difference between the views of Paul and Apollos respecting Divine truth, it is very probable that this ranging of themselves under these two leaders arose from mere personal considerations, such as the weight of St. Paul's teaching, and the eloquence of that of Apollos. "The carnal man neglects the truth, and is filled with the empty sound of words, which strikes his sense; this is no other than to despise and let go a treasure, and to hold fast the earthen vessel which contained it" (Quesnel).

"Are ye not carnal?" The oldest authorities have "Are ye not men?" *i.e.*, mere men, acting only on the principles, and following the example, of unregenerate men?

5. "Who then is Paul, or who is Apollos, but ministers by whom ye believed?" Apollos and Paul are ministers of Christ. They speak not in their own name, nor do they preach their own word, nor baptize into their own bodies. They are the mere instruments in the hands of One Who assigns to each minister his work, and accompanies that assignment with the exact success which He sees fit.

6. "I have planted, Apollos watered; but God gave the increase." St. Paul first preached the Gospel in Corinth, and so founded the Church. Apollos having been instructed in the way of God more perfectly by Aquila and Priscilla, went to Achaia (Corinth), and "helped them much which had believed through grace."

CHAP. III.] I PLANTED, APOLLOS WATERED. 45

6 ᵏ I have planted, ¹ Apollos watered; ᵐ but God gave the increase.

7 So then ⁿ neither is he that planteth any thing, neither he that watereth; but God that giveth the increase.

8 Now he that planteth and he that watereth

k Acts xviii. 4, 8, 11. ch. iv. 15. & ix. 1. & xv. 1. 2 Cor. x. 14, 15.
l Acts xviii. 24, 27. & xix. 1.
m ch. i. 30. & xv. 10. 2 Cor. iii. 5.
n 2 Cor. xii. 11, Gal. vi. 3.

"God gave the increase." It was only through the Spirit of God acting according to His Sovereign Will that souls were either converted, and then baptized into the Church, or grew up "in the unity of the faith, and of the knowledge of the Son of God into perfect men" (Ephes. iv. 13).

Wordsworth has a note drawing attention to the force of the Greek tenses here—"planted" and "watered" are in the aorist, denoting transitory acts; but God "was giving the increase" (in the imperfect), not by one act, but by a continuous bestowal of grace.

7. "So then neither is he that planteth any thing, neither he that watereth," &c. Neither of these ministers are anything of themselves, so that men should attach themselves specially to them, or call themselves by their names. They are neither called by themselves, nor did they come of their own mere will, neither do they preach their own message, nor, if they are faithful, do they add anything to it or take away anything from it; neither is any success which accompanies their labours to be put down to their account, as all is of God.

8. "Now he that planteth and he that watereth are one: and every man," &c. That is, they are one thing, one instrument, as if one human instrument had two or more parts, each having its own function, and yet so perfectly fitted together that all is but one in the hands of him who handled it.

The unity of action is not in themselves, of course, but in the mind of God.

But notwithstanding this unity in the hand and mind of God in using the instrument, it is not for a moment to be regarded as a mere lifeless machine. Each part has its distinct individuality, and, by consequence, its separate distinct responsibility; and this will be revealed at the last day, when

"Every man shall receive his own reward according to his own

º Ps. lxii. 12.
Rom. ii. 6.
ch. iv. 5. Gal.
vi. 4, 5. Rev.
ii. 23. & xxii.
12.

are one : º and every man shall receive his own reward according to his own labour.

---

labour." This is a tremendous statement of the Holy Spirit, particularly when we take into account that labour ($κόπος$) means not only working, but the toil, and trouble, and anxiety, the pains (as we say), and diligence, and industry, which should accompany work which is worth anything. As Quesnel says: "God does not crown the success, but the labour." Wesley has a noble note, which I will give in full : " Not only according to his success : but he who labours much, though with small success, shall have a great reward. Has not all this reasoning the same force still? Ministers are still barely instruments in God's hand, and depend as entirely as ever on His blessing to give the increase to their labours. Without this they are nothing, with it their part is so small, that they hardly deserve to be mentioned. May their hearts and hands be more united. And retaining a due sense of the honour God doth them, in employing them, may they faithfully labour, not as for themselves, but for the great Proprietor of all, till the day comes when He will reward them in full proportion to their fidelity and diligence."

Two or three remarks more on this verse.

First, the principle involved in it requires that the reward will be according to the self-denial exercised by the worker in his work. What is very hard work to some is easy to others ; what is to the taste of some is distasteful to others. What some commence and continue with fear and trembling, others rush into without a particle of misgiving, for the one regards more than the other the demands of the Master and the awfulness of the account.

Again, it is plain that work in the Church or Christian society must be in accordance with the declared intention of God respecting the Church, that it is to be a visible unity—one body as well as one spirit. Many labour much for the conversion of souls after their idea of conversion, who altogether disregard the prayer of Christ (John xvii. 21), and the injunctions of the Apostles respecting all being one.

Lastly, this passage shows how exceedingly wrong those are who presume to say that believers are above judgment. The persons who are here supposed to labour must be believers, but if they re-

LABOURERS WITH GOD.

9 For ᵖ we are labourers together with God: ye are God's ‖ husbandry, *ye are* ᵍ God's building.

10 ʳ According to the grace of God which is given unto me, as a wise masterbuilder, I have laid

ᵖ Acts xv. 4.
2 Cor. vi. 1.
‖ Or, *tillage*.
ᵍ Eph. ii. 20.
Col. ii. 7.
Heb. iii. 3, 4.
1 Pet. ii. 5.
ʳ Rom. i. 5.
& xii. 3.

---

10. "I have laid" (τέθεικα). So D., E., L., P., most Cursives; but ℵ, A., B., C., 17, 37*, 39, read, "I laid" (ἔθηκα).

ceive their own reward according to their own labours, it must be because both their work and themselves will have passed through a very scrutinizing judgment indeed.

"Stir up, we beseech thee, O Lord, the wills of thy faithful people, that they plenteously bringing forth the fruit of good works, may of thee be plenteously rewarded."

9. "For we are labourers together with God: ye are God's husbandry, ye are God's building." The word "God" is emphasized very strongly by being put at the beginning of each of the three clauses, "God's fellow-labourers are we; God's husbandry, God's building are ye."

What an astonishing honour put upon men that they should be fellow-labourers with God! and yet in all natural labour in the fields there is an analogous working together of God and man. Man must labour in the field in ploughing, sowing, and reaping; and yet God must work along with all in making the seed to germinate and the plant to blossom and bear fruit, and the grain to ripen.

"God's husbandry," "God's building." Here allusion is made not to the field or the actual building, but to the operations of husbandry and of building. God is at work upon you (and we under Him) as the plants in His field or vineyard, and the stones which are being builded together for His habitation through the Spirit.

10. "According to the grace of God which is given unto me," &c. "The grace of God," *i.e.*, the ministerial grace (compare Rom. xii. 3).

"As a wise masterbuilder." By applying to himself the term "wise," he does not arrogate to himself special wisdom, but simply asserts that he did what every competent builder would do, he laid the foundation, the one only secure foundation which it was given

s Rom. xv. 20. ver. 6. ch. iv. 15. Rev. xxi. 14.	ˢ the foundation, and another buildeth thereon. But ᵗ let every man take heed how he buildeth thereupon.
t 1 Pet. iv. 11.	
u Is. xxviii. 16. Matt. xvi. 18. 2 Cor. xi. 4. Gal. i. 7.	11 For other foundation can no man lay than ᵘ that is laid, ˣ which is Jesus Christ.
x Eph. ii. 20.	

---

to him by God to lay, and upon which alone those who came after him could build, if, that is, they built the Christian Church at all.

"And another buildeth thereon." This does not mean that St. Paul had ceased to build, for the whole of this Epistle is for the edification, that is, the building up, of the Church of Corinth. But having laid the foundation of this Church, he went and laid the foundation of other churches, and left others to do the work of building upon the foundation which he had laid.

"But let every man take heed how he buildeth thereupon." It is very often assumed that all that we have to do is to look to the foundation; that if the Foundation—Christ Jesus—be right, then the superstructure must also be right; but if we are to believe the Apostle, this is a very serious mistake, as we shall see in examining the next verses. Preachers on the One Foundation, Jesus Christ, may preach that which will not save souls in the day of the Lord.

11. "For other foundation can no man lay than that is laid, which is Jesus Christ." "Than that is laid," *i.e.*, by God Himself. This Foundation was decreed from eternity; its first enunciation is from the lips of Christ Himself to St. Peter, "Whom say ye that I am?" "Thou art the Christ, the son of the living God." "On this rock I will build my Church, and the gates of hell shall not prevail against it."

"Can no man lay." Christ is the historical Christ, and the Church is historically derived from Him, and rests solely on Him as its foundation, so that no matter how wrongly any man builds, he cannot build on any other foundation. If he does, what he erects is not the Church, the house or temple of God, but a building planned out of himself, a creation of his own imagination. What an unspeakable cause of thankfulness it is that God has so ordered the founding of Christianity, so planted it as the foremost fact in the history of the world, that no other foundation is possible—I

12 Now if any man build upon this foundation gold, silver, precious stones, wood, hay, stubble;

---

was going to say, conceivable. If the foundation is laid then the plan is laid, and we have to build according to the plan.

"Than that is laid." Rather, beside that laid by God. "When St. Paul preached Christ crucified and risen to the Corinthians, he used for them the one foundation on which alone their Church or any other Church could safely rest" (Ellicott).

12. "Now if any man build upon this foundation gold, silver, precious stones, wood," &c. Three different interpretations have been given to these materials.

(1.) They have been supposed to be doctrines; but as Godet rightly asks, is not this to forget that the edifice to be built is not a book of dogmatics, but the Church itself, composed of living personalities?

(2.) Then they have been supposed to be persons, but neither does this meet the point, for how would any builder knowingly build up such worthless persons as those which are indicated by hay and stubble into the fabric of the Church?

(3.) They are supposed to be good or worthless works produced by preaching in those joined to the Church—but evidently the building is a building of persons, not of things such as good works, and that persons are alone meant, is clear from the application of the contents of verse 16, "Know ye not that ye are the temple of God," &c. No passage of Scripture which I have yet come across has more variety of interpretations of every part of it, and so I hope I may be forgiven if I put forth a view of it differing from most.

What is the building? Evidently some part of the Church of Christ. The foundation being laid, parts of the edifice are given to various builders.

What is the act of building? Evidently preaching and teaching. It must include both: by preaching, additional stones are laid in the foundation; by teaching, they are worked into shape, chiselled, and laid securely in their places.

But what are the stones? Are they materials lying about from which the particular builder can choose what he pleases? This does not seem likely, for at first sight it would seem that no one having at his disposal gold and silver, and costly stones, such as marble, jasper, or agate, would reject them and build with such materials as wood and hay. And again, supposing that the various materials, gold, silver, costly stones, on the one hand, and wood, hay, stubble, on the other, were not yet built into the fabric, but were lying about, or otherwise at hand ready to be used by the builders, they must represent unconverted Gentiles of various moral characters. Now is it supposable that the various builders would have power to select these and put them into their places as they pleased?

Now I asked, Is it at all likely that one having gold and precious stones ready to his hand wherewith to build, would deliberately choose to build with wood and hay? and I answered in the negative; but this depends on the disposition of the builder and the sort of erection he desires to put up. Gold, silver, and precious stones are very expensive, and very intractable materials wherewith to work. If the stones are costly they are stones of exceeding hardness, and a temple, or part of one, erected of such materials would require years to be perfected, whereas a hovel or shanty of wood, with the interstices filled up with hay, and a roof of reeds, could be run up in a few days.

Now these considerations will, I think, at least point us to the true interpretation. Let us take the preaching of Christ crucified. What was the Apostolic preaching of Christ crucified? It was not only the preaching of Christ bearing our sins upon the cross, but also of Christ delivering us from sin so that we should live to God. It is all comprehended in the words, "He himself bare our sins in his own body on the tree, that we being dead to sins, should live unto righteousness" (1 Pet. ii. 24). Again, St. Paul writes, "They that are Christ's have crucified the flesh with the affections and lusts" (Gal. v. 24). What is this but the being made conformable to His death of Phil. iii. 10?

There are, then, no less than three ways of preaching Christ crucified. There is the preaching of Christ crucified merely as a sin-bearer. There is the preaching of Christ in His Crucifixion setting us an example, but virtually leaving out the atoning value of His Death, and there is the primitive Apostolic preaching—the preaching of Christ as SS. Peter and Paul preached Him, Sin-Bearer and Sanctifier at once, the Sin-Bearer never apart from the Sanctifier, the Sanctifier never apart from the Sin-Bearer.

Now these three sorts of preaching would attract different characters. The first would attract those who look for mere pardon without any deep concern about being crucified with Him in their

CHAP. III.] EVERY MAN'S WORK. 51

13 ʸ Every man's work shall be made manifest: ʸ ch. iv. 5.

flesh with its lusts. The second would attract those whose idea of Christianity was some small improvement in natural virtue, and who knew not, nor did they much desire to know, the love of God in the gift of Christ; the third would attract those for whom genuine Christianity was intended, those who desired to possess peace with God, and to be filled with the righteousness of God.

When, then, St. Paul said, "Let every man take heed how he buildeth thereupon," he seems to me to mean, Let every man take heed how he preaches Christ crucified, for he may so preach Him as to attract the wood and hay rather than the gold and silver—the light-hearted, the inconstant, the frivolous, rather than the earnest, the serious, and the devout.[1]

Now to this it may be replied, Does not the preaching, that is the building, change the materials—change the wood into precious stone? I answer that St. Paul here puts this out of sight, for the time. He speaks of it elsewhere abundantly, but not here. I take it that this figure, or, as we may call it, parable of St. Paul, resembles in this respect that of his Master, Who, in His parable of the Sower makes the seed fall into four sorts of ground without changing the ground, but really being changed by it; for instance, the casting in of the seed does not remove the rock, but the seed itself withers; the casting in of the seed does not make the fertile and good ground, but the seed is effectually fertilized by it.

13. "Every man's work shall be made manifest: for the day shall declare it," &c. The real quality of every man's work in the Church of Christ shall be manifested; not now, but hereafter, at *the day*—*i.e.*, the day of the Lord's Second Coming to Judgment. The value of each man's work cannot be manifested till that

---

[1] Godet, of all the commentators I have consulted, seems to me to come nearest to the true meaning—" Either the pastor, by his preaching, his conversation, his example, the daily acts of his ministry, succeeds in developing among his flock a healthy religious life, drawn from communion with Christ, abounding in the fruits of sanctification and love; and it is this strong and normal life which St. Paul describes under the figure of precious materials, or the pastor by his pathetic discourses, his ingenious explanations, succeeds indeed in attracting a great concourse of hearers, in producing enthusiastic admiration and lively emotions; but all this stir is only external and superficial; with it all there is no real consecration to the Saviour. This faith without energy, this love without the spirit of sacrifice, this hope without joy or elasticity, this Christianity saturated with egoism and vanity; such are the wood, hay, stubble."

52 THE FIRE SHALL TRY. [I. Cor.

for the day ᶻ shall declare it, because ᵃ it † shall be revealed by fire; and the fire shall try every man's work of what sort it is.

ᶻ 1 Pet. i. 7. & iv. 12.
ᵃ Luke ii. 35.
† Gr. *is revealed.*

---

13. "And the fire shall try." So ℵ, D., E., L., most Cursives, d, e, f, Vulg., Sah., Copt., Arm.; but A., B., C., P., some Cursives (eight), and Syriac, read, "the fire itself shall try."

day, for the real state of the souls which he has added to the Church or built up in the fabric of the Church, cannot be known till that day. This St. Paul sets forth in the next chapter, "Judge nothing before the time, until the Lord come, who both will bring to light the hidden things of darkness, and will make manifest the counsels of the hearts." It is clear that till the light of Christ's presence, at His appearing, reveals the real value of each man's work, we cannot speak certainly concerning it; and, indeed, we are expressly forbidden to judge it. ("Judge nothing before the time.")

"The day shall declare it, because it shall be revealed by [or in] fire." The day shall be revealed in fire, because it is the day of the Lord's coming, and the appearances of God in the present state of things are always accompanied with the brightness and searching power of fire. Thus the Lord descended on Mount Sinai in fire. The theophany of Psalm xviii. 13 is in fire, and that of Psalm l. is "Our God shall come, and shall not keep silence, a fire shall devour before him." Also in Isaiah xxx. 30, "With the flame of a devouring fire;" and in Malachi iv. 1, "The day cometh, that shall burn as an oven."

And the fire itself shall try every man's work of what sort it is.

The day will be revealed in material fire; but can this fire try spiritual work? At first sight, we should say not: the fire that can try spiritual work—the quality of souls, the value of their works, and their sincerity before God—must be itself spiritual. It must be the all-sifting and unerring judgment of Him Whose eyes are like a flame of fire. But we must not pronounce too dogmatically upon this, for we are profoundly ignorant of the relations which God may choose to bring about betwixt Matter and Spirit. Within the compass of our bodies what is material is constantly acting upon what is spiritual, and *vice versâ*. Pain occasioned by what is material has often a spiritual effect. So we may not judge too hastily of what the fire proceeding from God may do or may

14 If any man's work abide which he hath built thereupon, ᵇ he shall receive a reward. ᵇ ch. iv. 5.

15 If any man's work shall be burned, he shall suffer loss: but he himself shall be saved; ᶜ yet so as by fire. ᶜ Jude xxiii.

---

not do. What is material and what is spiritual in form are here apparently knowingly and deliberately mixed together, and in our haste we must not separate them.

14. "If any man's work abide which he hath built thereupon," &c. If any man's work abide, it shows that he has taken pains to ascertain and constantly to set forth the true doctrine of Christ; that he has applied the Word faithfully " for doctrine, for reproof, for correction, for instruction in righteousness; " that he has " reproved, rebuked, exhorted with all long-suffering and doctrine;" that he has "taken heed to himself and to the doctrine, and has continued in them, and so has saved himself and those who (effectually) heard him."

"He shall receive a reward"—that is, the special reward due to a faithful teacher and preacher, over and above the reward to those who have made their own calling and election sure (see Dan. xii. 3), "They that be wise shall shine as the brightness of the firmament, and they that turn many to righteousness as the stars for ever and ever."

15. "If any man's work shall be burned, he shall suffer loss," &c. That is, the loss of his expected wages or reward. He is not so much punished as mulcted; though it must be a severe punishment at that day, and in the presence of his Saviour and Judge, to see his work consumed. This implies that he could have done better. He had not taken heed how he builded on Christ. But he is not finally cast away: he is saved.

"Yet so as by fire." The figure seems to imply that he was employed in building when the conflagration came, and it consumed as in a moment the part of the building upon which he was employed, and he was only able to rush through the flames which were enwrapping all the building, and so escape.

What will be the precise reality of all this it is impossible to declare. It seems to me a matter of some uncertainty whether, if the part of the building of wood, hay, and stubble be souls, that

^d ch. vi. 19.
2 Cor. vi. 16.
Eph. ii. 21, 22.
Heb. iii. 6. 1
Pet. ii. 5.

16 ^d Know ye not that ye are the temple of God, and *that* the Spirit of God dwelleth in you?

---

their everlasting destruction in hell is here foretold. In ways unknown to us, the work which is burned, whether it be souls, or their character, or their works, may be proved worthless, and yet they may not be for ever with Satan and his angels.

The fire seems not to torment for ever, but to sweep rubbish away. This passage, almost every well-informed reader is aware, has been cited by Romanist divines as proving the doctrine of Purgatory; but this is impossible, for the fire of Purgatory is supposed to be a purging or cleansing fire which persons in their disembodied state have to undergo before the Day of Judgment, and the action of this fire, which, in all other places, is supposed to herald or accompany the appearance of God, does not take place till the Day of Judgment, and reveals that day; and the action of this fire is not purgatorial, but destructive.

16. "Know ye not that ye are the temple of God, and that," &c. "Know ye not." The Apostle appeals to their knowledge of this as if it were a first truth. And yet it is a truth almost unknown amongst us in these latter days, certainly till of late years. What Church in a place, what congregation would now attempt to realize that unitedly, and in the case of each separate member (vi. 19), they are the temple of God, because the Spirit of God dwelleth in them? In the eyes of the Apostle it is an undoubted and withal a fundamental truth.

"Temple of God." The word here is not *hieron*, signifying the whole sacred edifice, but *naos*, signifying the most sacred part—answering to the Holy of Holies of the Jewish temple, in which God was supposed more especially to dwell.

The article is wanting before "temple;" so we should not translate it, "the temple of God," as if the Corinthian Church was itself the Catholic Church; neither should we translate it, "a temple of God," as if it was separately and apart from the rest of the Church, *a* temple. The rendering which best preserves the sense is, God's temple.

How is it that the Corinthian Church was God's temple? Because of the indwelling of the Spirit. The fact which made the Temple of Jerusalem so holy was the dwelling of God therein; and

THE TEMPLE OF GOD IS HOLY.

17 If any man ‖ defile the temple of God, him shall God destroy; for the temple of God is holy, which *temple* ye are.

‖ Or, *destroy.*

18 ᵉ Let no man deceive himself. If any man among you seemeth to be wise in this world, let him become a fool, that he may be wise.

ᵉ Prov. iii. 7.
Is. v. 21.

---

the fact that made the Corinthian Church so holy was the indwelling of the Holy Spirit. God dwelt in it by the Spirit; and this clearly sets forth the true Godhead of the Spirit.

17. "If any man defile the temple of God, him shall God destroy." The translation of the Authorized is unfortunate, for the word rendered "defile" in the first clause, and "destroy" in the second, is the same. The Revisers render it, "If any man destroy the temple of God, him shall God destroy." By defiling or destroying, the Apostle evidently alludes to those who introduce or foment factions in the Church, or those who do not take heed how they build on the one foundation, and so undermine the connection of the whole with Christ, or sap the holiness of individual members.

The temple of God is holy, not in the sense of each member being absolutely holy in thought, word, and deed, but in the sense in which a temple is holy, because dedicated to God by being set apart from all profane uses. This holiness is sinned against by factions and divisions as well as by false doctrine, and the toleration of impurity of life.

The question, of course, arises, How can a body of men be holy, and so called the holy temple of God, which has within it a greater or less number of unholy members? To which we answer, Just as a temple may be holy, though some of its rafters be unsound, and some of its stones decaying. What is decaying has to be taken out and replaced with what is sound, and this is the work of each Church, and is effected through wholesome discipline, and God only knows what we lose by the abeyance of this discipline, as we acknowledge when, in our Commination Service, we confess its abeyance and desire its restoration.

18. "Let no man deceive himself. If any man among you," &c. This verse shows us that those who were destroying the Church were those who were introducing into it worldly maxims, and mixing up the Gospel of Christ crucified with some system of

19 For ᶠthe wisdom of this world is foolishness with God. For it is written, ᵍHe taketh the wise in their own craftiness.

ᶠ ch. i. 20. & ii. 6.
ᵍ Job v. 13.

---

this world's philosophy. The leaders of parties in that age would be those who would despise the humble and humbling doctrines of the Cross, and would be themselves unhumbled, and desirous of being looked up to by their fellows. Now the Apostle warns such that if they would desire to be wise in this world, *i.e.*, in this their state of probation, with the true wisdom, they must submit to the yoke of Christ. "Evangelical wisdom consists in renouncing the false knowledge of the wisdom of this world, in believing what this world judges to be impossible, in adoring what seems to this world contemptible, and in loving that which seems contrary to one's happiness, viz., humiliation and suffering." (Quesnel.)

19. "For the wisdom of this world is foolishness with God." This is literally true. If there be a Being, such as God is, Who sees all things as they really are, and knows all things perfectly, He sees the imperfection of all human wisdom. All mere human speculations, whether philosophical, or moral, or scientific, are to Him as the science or philosophy of a thousand years ago is to us. If there be any truth in them it is from Him, whether from His word or from the law written originally on the heart, but all that man has added to this (what the Apostle calls "of this world") partakes of his own ignorance and imperfection.

The leaders of parties in such a city as Corinth would, as I said, be, in all probability, those who added to the truth of Scripture human speculations such as those alluded to in Coloss. ii. 17-20. And in this our age, with what scorn must God regard those who lay themselves out, who bend all their energies, to deprive Him of the glory of His own creation, who teach that mere evolution without will, or design, or reason, has brought into being and orders all things: so that that which requires high intellect to apprehend it, is the product of mere unreasoning forces acting blindly, and utterly unconscious of what they are bringing about.

The quotation is from Job v. 13. The translation which St. Paul adopts is nearer to the original than that of the Septuagint, which he usually takes.

God sees the injury to themselves, into which their own craftiness

Chap. III.] LET NO MAN GLORY IN MEN. 57

20 And again, ʰ The Lord knoweth the thoughts of the wise, that they are vain.

21 Therefore ⁱ let no man glory in men. For ᵏ all things are your's;

ʰ Ps. xciv. 11.
ⁱ ch. i. 12. & iv. 6. ver. 4, 5, 6.
ᵏ 2 Cor. iv. 5, 15.

---

will lead them, and to show them their weakness and folly, permits them to be taken or snared by it.

20. "And again, The Lord knoweth the thoughts of the wise," &c. This is from Ps. xciv. 11, only the Apostle changes "the thoughts of man" into "the thoughts of the wise," and the Psalmist proceeds to speak of the blessedness of those who submit themselves entirely to the teaching of God: "Blessed is the man whom thou chastenest O Lord, and teachest him in thy law."

21, 22. "Therefore let no man glory in men. For all things are your's; whether Paul, or Apollos," &c. Why should you glory in men, and call yourselves after their names? For you do not belong to them, but they belong to you. And they belong to all of you. Paul, Apollos, Cephas, belong not to a section of the Church, but to the whole Church. Nay, they belong in their teaching, their ministrations, their gifts, their example, to every member of the Church alike.[1]

---

[1] A strange inference is drawn from this place by Principal Edwards (p. 91). "The world's wisdom, says St. Paul, is conquered by the Church. No man, therefore, can be sovereign over conscience." Now one of the worst things for Christianity is that so many men are sovereign over their own consciences. Many and many a man domineers over his own conscience. He treats it as a captive, he does not allow it to speak. When it asserts itself he silences it: and so his conscience is subdued to his will. And then the Principal proceeds:—"We may add, as a legitimate corollary, that the Apostle's argument is fatal to the theory that the Church consists, in so far as it has authority in controversies of faith, not of 'a congregation of faithful men,' or 'all who profess and call themselves Christians,' but only of a select number of the teachers." Now St. Paul says that, amongst other teachers, he belonged to the Corinthians; does he mean by this that the congregation of faithful men with which he had now especially to do, *i.e.* the Corinthians, had power to sit in judgment on his Epistles, and to put it to the vote whether they should be read in the Church as a message from the Holy Ghost, or not? The Apostle himself seems to allow no such power to the Church when he writes, "If any man think himself to be a prophet or spiritual, let him acknowledge that the things I write unto you are the commandments of the Lord" (xiv. 37). If "*all* who profess and call themselves Christians" are the ultimate judges, how are the decisions of such a multitude to be ascertained, and in such a case the office of teachers, a work of the Spirit, be it remembered, goes for nothing; and men who, in all probability, cannot find the places in their Bibles veto the decisions of those who have been prayerfully studying the Scriptures all their lives.

22 Whether Paul, or Apollos, or Cephas, or the world, or life, or death, or things present, or things to come; all are your's;

21, 22. "All things are your's; whether Paul, or Apollos," &c. First he makes mention of those whose names they claimed —these were the common possession of all, being ministers, not of a section of the Church, but of the Church; then he speaks of the world—all things in the world, if received as from God, and sanctified by His Word and Spirit, belong to the Christian, or it may mean that God makes all things, even the things of the world, work together for good to them that love God.

22. "Or life, or death." In his measure every true Christian can say "To me to live is Christ, to die is gain." "Whether we live we live unto the Lord, or whether we die we die unto the Lord; whether, therefore, we live or die, we are the Lord's" (Phil. i. 21; Rom. xiv. 8).

"Or things present." If God gives you happiness it will make you thankful: if He gives you unhappiness or disappointment it will drive you closer to God, the God of all comfort. The changes of the world will make you the more rely upon Him Who is unchangeable, the opposition of the world will make you realize the more that "greater is he that is in you than he that is in the world" (1 John iv. 4).

"Or things to come." The glories of the eternal world are yours, because you are sure of them, or at least it is in your power to be sure of them.

"All are your's."

23. "And ye are Christ's; and Christ is God's." "Whatever is created, and whatever happens in the world, it is all disposed and ordered by the providence of God, and made subservient to the forming of the Church, and to the salvation of the elect: as the whole Church and all the elect are designed only to form a body for Jesus Christ, and to compose One Single Christ (xii. 12), consisting of the Head and of the members: and as Jesus Christ made perfect and complete in all His members, is designed only to be an eternal priest to God and a Victim worthy of Him, and to offer up the Grand Sacrifice of eternity (and humanity) to Him in heaven . . . . The Church belongs to Christ, but the ministers to the Church." (Quesnel.)

23 And ¹ ye are Christ's; and Christ *is* God's.   ¹ Rom. xiv. 8. ch. xi. 3. 2 Cor. x. 7. Gal. iii. 29.

"Christ is God's." Not merely as man, as when He says, "I ascend unto my Father, and your Father, and to my God, and your God," but as being in the Godhead, as the Son Who is "of God" and is "in God." The Father being the Father of the Son, possesses that Son; the Son, though His equal in the Divine Nature, tenders to Him all loving obedience. "I came down from heaven, not to do mine own will, but the will of him that sent me." "If ye keep my commandments ye shall abide in my love, even as I have kept my Father's commandments, and abide in his love."

CHAP. IV.

LET a man so account of us, as of ª the ministers of Christ, ᵇ and stewards of the mysteries of God.   ª Mat. xxiv. 45. ch. iii. 5. & ix. 17. 2 Cor. vi. 4. Col. i. 25. ᵇ Luke xii. 42. Tit. i. 7. 1 Pet. iv. 10.

1. "Let a man so account of us, as of the ministers of Christ," &c. The first clause may be translated so as to join it more immediately with the preceding. "So then [from what we have said] let a man account of us, as the ministers of Christ." But the Authorized seems the more natural rendering.

"Stewards of the mysteries of God." In these descriptions the emphasis is to be laid on Christ in the first clause, and God in the second. They are not to be accounted ministers and stewards of men, but of Christ and of God.

These two offices are at the root the same. God has committed all the dispensations and mysteries of grace into the keeping of His Son, and so, by the fact of their being ministers of Christ, they are dispensers of the mysteries of God.

Stewards signifies dispensers. Whether these mysteries are the

2 Moreover it is required in stewards, that a man be found faithful.

2. "Moreover" (ὃ δὲ λοιπόν). So E., L., most Cursives; but א, A., B., C., D., F., G., P., 17, 31, 39, 67**, 71, d, e, f, g, Vulg., Syr., Copt., Arm., read, "here moreover" (ὧδε λοιπόν).

mysterious truths of the Gospel, or the Sacraments, or Absolution, they have wisely, yet generously, to dispense them. They have not to throw pearls before swine, but yet they have to see that the wants of Christian souls are supplied.

It is often said that the ministers of God are not priests. But if they are in any real sense dispensers of Sacraments, they are more than priests—more, that is, in the sense which the rationalism of this unbelieving age repudiates. Never respecting the body of any sacrifice which Aaron was commissioned to offer did God say, "This is my Body," "Give it to my people," nor respecting any blood of any victim did He say, "Drink ye all of it, for this is my Blood."

Priests are but ministers and dispensers. But what do they minister, and what do they dispense? If they dispense the mystery of the Incarnation either by word of mouth, or through Sacraments, they dispense infinitely more than Aaron was ever commissioned to do. And if they do this on the behalf of Christ, then by the very necessity of their office and function, they, by God's appointment, stand between Christ and His people. God, if He had so willed it, might have dispensed with all stewardship. He might have preached the Gospel to His people Himself with His own voice, as He gave them the law on Sinai; or He might have Himself with His own hand given to them the pledges of His love and grace. So that when we despise and deny the priesthood of the Christian ministry, we must take heed what we do, for we may despise and speak against that which all stewardship involves, viz., the dispensing of some, at least, of God's gifts through our fellow-sinners, whom God has commissioned so to do.

2. "Moreover it is required in stewards, that a man be found faithful." Instead of "moreover" the oldest uncials require us to read "Here moreover," here, that is, in this state of things.

"It is required" [or "ye require"] "in stewards, that a man be found faithful." The office of steward is not that of an owner, or landlord, but of an agent; and so the property of which he is the steward, not being his own, he has to give account of. None of

I KNOW NOTHING BY MYSELF.

3 But with me it is a very small thing that I should be judged of you, or of man's †judgment: yea, I judge not mine own self.

† Gr. *day*. ch. iii. 13.

4 For I know nothing by myself; ᶜ yet am I not hereby justified: but he that judgeth me is the Lord.

ᶜ Job ix. 2. Ps. cxxx. 3. & cxliii. 2. Prov. xxi. 2. Rom. iii. 20. & iv. 2.

the things which we have to dispense are ours—they are all God's and Christ's.

3. "But with me it is a very small thing that I should be judged of you, or of man's judgment," &c. We see here the true import of the verses of the last chapter, "All things are yours, whether Paul or Apollos," &c. All ministers of God belong to the Church, so that they should labour not for themselves, but for the Church —so that all their energies should be devoted to the advancement and edification of the Church; but they are not under the Church, that is, the private members of a particular Church, that they should be judged by the majority. St. Paul speaks, if it may be lawful to say so, with something like contempt of such a notion.

"Or of man's judgment." Literally " of man's day," contrasting, by implication, the day of man's judgment with the day of the Lord's.

"Yea, I judge not mine own self," *i.e.*, in the sense of condemning or acquitting myself after due examination, as if my judgment even of myself was final. What a contrast is this avowal of the Apostle's of his inability to judge himself, with the cool, self-confident way in which such numbers express themselves, as if they were quite sure what judgment Christ will pronounce upon them —in fact they go so far as to deny that He will judge them at all —being believers, being elect, God's dear ones, they are above judgment. They will stand by and see Apostles judged, but they will not be judged. Terrible mistake, as they will find!

4. "For I know nothing by [or against] myself; yet am I not," &c. Here we have an obsolete use of "by" as meaning against. Mr. Blunt gives two instances, one in a letter of Cranmer's respecting Anne Boleyn: "I am exceedingly sorry that such faults can be proved by the Queen as I heard of their relation." (Jenkyns' "Cranmer," i. 165.) And in Hollingshead's "Chronicle" Throckmorton says, "I then knew no more by Wyatt than by any other man."

5 ᵈ Therefore judge nothing before the time, until the Lord come, ᵉ who both will bring to light the

ᵈ Matt. vii. 1.
Rom. ii. 1, 16.
& xiv. 4, 10, 13.
Rev. xx. 12.
ᵉ ch. iii. 13.

The clause means that the Apostle, after strict examination of his conscience, mind, and motives, can find no unfaithfulness in the matter of his stewardship as entrusted with the mysteries of God.

"Yet am I not hereby justified." In the sense of acquitted, declared free from blame—not, of course, justified in the Christian or Pauline sense, which is through belief in the Resurrection of the Lord and the implantation of His nature, and the gift of His life to be ours.

"But he that judgeth me is the Lord." Here the Apostle declares that God, the Judge of *all*—all universally—now judges, and will judge him, Apostle though he is. An attempt is made to get rid of this by translating, "He that judgeth," by "He who maketh the only valid examination" (Godet), but what does the judge make the valid examination for, except for purposes of judgment? We need not for a moment give to this examination and this judgment the sense of examining with a view to find materials for condemnation. Quite the contrary—the rewards of the righteous are all supposed to be the result of judgment. It must have been so, if St. Paul wrote, "Every man shall receive his own reward according to his own labour," and if he represented his crown of righteousness, as given him by the "Lord, the righteous Judge" (2 Tim. iv. 8).

5. "Therefore judge nothing before the time, until the Lord come," &c. We must not take this as precluding all judgment, for a Christian must now judge what is contrary to the declared will of God to be sinful, and the Apostle himself, we shall soon find, severely blamed the Corinthian Church for not, after due investigation, putting away from among them a wicked person; but the judgment which he reprobates is that whereby they judged some leaders to be followed as worthy of all confidence, and others not.

"Until the Lord come." Does this mean that at the Second Coming they will exercise judgment? It may so mean, because the Apostle says, "We shall judge angels," but I think it is rather to be restricted to the pronouncing of judgment upon the hidden things of darkness, and will make manifest the counsels of the hearts: and ᶠthen shall every man have praise of God.   f Rom. ii. 29. 2 Cor. v. 10.

6 And these things, brethren, ᵍ I have in a figure transferred to myself and *to* Apollos for   g ch. i. 12. & iii. 4.

---

5. "Every man;" rather, "each man."

gifts and conduct of leaders and teachers, which was such a snare to them.

"Who both will bring to light the hidden things of darkness, and will," &c. The hidden things of darkness do not necessarily mean secret sins or insincerities, but include the good thoughts and intents and deeds which have been thought in the recesses of the heart, and done so secretly that none know them; but according to the Lord's assurance, these will then be rewarded openly.

"And then shall every man have praise of God." This is not the usual view which men take of the judgment of Christ. Many speak of it as if it was only to be associated with condemnation and hell, whereas here it is joined with praise and reward. The fact, as revealed in Scripture, is, that the judgment is as much for the righteous (or, if you please, for believers), that all men may see that they do not receive their crown out of mere favour, but that (under grace) they have won it. "How much good and how much evil lie concealed under the *darkness* of this present world, and in the secret recesses of the heart of man! how many blind judgments; how many unjust censures; how many ill-placed commendations, and how many false reputations! Let us wait with faith and patience for the light of the world to come." (Quesnel.)

6. "And these things, brethren, I have in a figure transferred to myself," &c. He means by this, I have not named all the party leaders, who are troubling you, but have represented myself only and Apollos (we who in all things teach the same and act together) as if we were the offenders and were causing the divisions. This I did when I wrote "Who then is Paul, or who is Apollos, but ministers by whom ye believed," &c. If he had mentioned Cephas, or those who unduly exalted him, it would have been represented that he had a sinister motive in so doing. But when he put himself and his co-

your sakes; ʰ that ye might learn in us not to think *of men* above that which is written, that no one of you ⁱ be puffed up for one against another.

7 For who † maketh thee to differ *from another?* and ᵏ what hast thou that thou didst not receive? now if thou didst receive *it*, why dost thou glory, as if thou hadst not received *it?*

ʰ Rom. xii. 3.
ⁱ ch. iii. 21. & v. 2, 6.
† Gr. *distinguisheth thee.*
ᵏ John iii. 27.
James i. 17.
1 Pet. iv. 10.

---

6. "To think." Omitted by ℵ, A., B., D., E., F., G., 46, d, e, f, g, Vulg.; but retained by L., P., most Cursives, Syriac, Copt., Arm.

Revisers translate, "that in us ye might learn not to go beyond the things," &c.

worker, Apollos, forward as exemplifying the evils of party followings, he, as far as he could, disarmed his traducers.

"That ye might learn in us not to think of men above that which," &c. Some MSS. omit "think;" but the omission or retention scarcely affects the sense. "That ye might learn in us," that is, in the example of us—by considering myself and Apollos as cases in point—"not to think of men above that which is written." What is written, and where is it written? No doubt the Apostle here alludes to the general tenor of the Scriptures, which set forth all ministers of God as mere servants, ministering only what God has commissioned them to minister, speaking only His Message.

"That no one of you be puffed up for one against another." The Apostle here speaks as if he considered pride as the root of all party divisions, such, that is, as those which he blamed in the Church of Corinth, and so it is. In exalting another man, one takes credit to himself for the admiration which he feels; one glories in being able to appreciate a superiority which others fail to know. The pride of the head of the party thus becomes the pride of the whole.

7. "For who maketh thee to differ from another? and what hast thou," &c. Thou canst not boast as if thou madest thyself, and enduedst thyself with excellences either of nature or of grace. Who maketh thee to differ? God only. "Let us suppose," says Chrysostom, "that thou art really worthy of praise, and that thou hast indeed the precious gift, and that the judgment of men is not corrupt: yet not even in this case were it right to be high-minded: for thou hast nothing of thyself, but from God didst receive it."

YE ARE FULL, YE ARE RICH.

8 Now ye are full, [1] now ye are rich, ye have reigned as kings without us: and I would to God ye did reign, that we also might reign with you.

[1] Rev. iii. 17.

Again: "For not to thee belong these excellences, but to the grace of God. Whether you name faith, it came of His calling; or whether it be the forgiveness of sins which you speak of, or the gifts of grace, or the word of teaching, or the miracles; thou didst receive all from thence. Now what hast thou, tell me, which thou hast not received, but hast rather achieved of thine own self? Thou hast nothing to say. Well, thou hast received, and does that make thee high-minded? Nay, but it ought to make thee shrink back into thyself."

8. "Now ye are full, now ye are rich, ye have reigned as kings without us." "Now ye are full," *i.e.*, filled to repletion with all the good things of the kingdom of grace. "Now ye are rich," in all spiritual gifts.

"Ye have reigned as kings without us." The kingdom of God in which ye will reign with Christ is already come to you, though it has by no means come to us. I would to God, I wish with all my heart (for in the original there is no invocation of the Divine name) ye did reign.

"That we also might reign with you." This is, as it were, the climax of absurdity to which he shuts them up—that they, the children, the disciples, the converts, should reign and their fathers in God, their instructors, those through whose faith and labour they believed, should not reign, but be well nigh overwhelmed with distress and worldly dishonour and disparagement.

This is irony, severe, cutting sarcasm, but it was good for them, and they richly deserved it. "It was therefore in mockery that he said to them, 'So quickly have ye come to the end,' which thing was impossible in the time; for all the more perfect things wait long in futurity: but to be 'full' with a little betokens a feeble soul; and from a little to imagine one's self 'rich,' a sick and miserable one. For piety is an unsatiable thing; and it argues a childish mind to imagine from just the beginnings, that you have obtained the whole: and for men who are not even yet in the prelude of a matter to be high-minded as if they had laid hold on the end." (Chrysostom.)

| Or, *us the last apostles as.*
m Ps. xliv. 22.
Rom. viii. 36.
ch. xv. 30, 31.
2 Cor. iv. 11. & vi. 9.
n Hebr. x. 33.
† Gr. *theatre.*
o ch. ii. 3.
p Acts xvii. 18. & xxvi. 24.
ch. i. 18, &c. & ii. 14. & iii. 18. See 2 Kings ix. 11.
q 2 Cor. xiii. 9.

9 For I think that God hath set forth ‖ us the apostles last, ᵐ as it were appointed to death: for ⁿ we are made a † spectacle unto the world, and to angels, and to men.

10 ᵒ We *are* ᵖ fools for Christ's sake, but ye *are* wise in Christ; ᵠ we *are* weak, but ye *are* strong; ye *are* honourable, but we *are* despised.

---

9. "And to angels and to men." Revisers, in margin, "both to angels and to men."

9. "For I think that God hath set forth us the apostles last, as it were," &c. Here St. Paul illustrates the lordly ideas of the Corinthians, and the worldly degradation of their fathers and teachers in Christ by the games or shows in the amphitheatre. He imagines that they were in conspicuous places amongst the spectators, whilst the Apostles were not merely amongst the gladiators or more honourable combatants, but were amongst the most degraded criminals, who were reserved to the last to be torn in pieces and devoured by wild beasts. Thus Tertullian translates this place, "God hath selected us, the Apostles [as] hindmost; like men appointed to fight with wild beasts, since we have been made a spectacle to this world, both to angels and to men." (Tertullian on "Modesty," chap. xiv.)

"To the world, and to angels and to men." The world, κόσμος, is here used in the sense of the universe, all things visible and invisible. "The vast range of an amphitheatre, under the open sky, well representing the magnificent vision of all created beings from men up to angels, gazing on the dreadful death-struggle; and then the contrast of the selfish Corinthians sitting by unconcerned and unmoved at the awful spectacle." (Stanley.)

10. "We are fools for Christ's sake, but ye are wise in Christ; we are weak," &c. The Apostle and his fellows determined to abide by "the foolishness of preaching," presenting the Gospel of Christ in all its simplicity, and not daring to make it a handle whereby to display their human wisdom.

"We are weak, but ye are strong." They assumed all the airs of those who claimed to be strong, to be perfect in Christ; whereas the Apostle was among them "in weakness, and in fear, and in

11 ʳEven unto this present hour we both hunger, and thirst, and ˢare naked, and ᵗare buffeted, and have no certain dwellingplace:

12 ᵘAnd labour, working with our own hands:

ʳ 2 Cor. iv. 8.
& xi. 23-27.
Phil. iv. 12.
ˢ Job xxii. 6.
Rom. viii. 35.
ᵗ Acts xxiii. 2.
ᵘ Acts xviii. 3.
& xx. 34.
1 Thess. ii. 9.
2 Thess. iii. 8.
1 Tim. iv. 10.

much trembling." The Apostle thought not of himself, but of his Master, and that Master's message, and this instead of exalting him, humbled him, as he says in 2 Cor. xii. 10: "I take pleasure in infirmities, in reproaches, in necessities, in persecutions, in distresses for Christ's sake: for when I am weak, then am I strong."

"Ye are honourable, but we are despised." Ye, on account of your assumption of worldly wisdom, and your pretence of knowledge and power—it may be by your vainglorious display of your spiritual gifts—are honoured by the heathen around you; we, who make no such pretensions, who dare not use for purposes of self-exaltation what God has given to us—we are despised.

11. "Even unto this present hour we both hunger, and thirst, ... no certain dwelling place." No place in Scripture exhibits more fully the power of the Cross than these two or three verses. The world was subdued to God by men whose lives were lives of want, and distress, and contumely.

"We hunger, and thirst, and are naked." Not that we continue hungry and thirsty, and shiver with cold because of the scantiness of our clothing; but God makes us constantly to feel these privations, that He may show to all how entirely we depend upon Him, and that He may subdue the world by those who have so little of the goods of the world.

"And are buffeted." We are constantly struck by insolent men, who would not dare to inflict upon us such outrages unless they knew that the protection of the law would be withheld from us.

"And have no certain dwellingplace." As yet there were no monasteries, no clergy-houses, no parsonages, in which those who preached the Gospel might be sure of finding a shelter at least, and a place in which to lay their weary limbs.

12. "And labour, working with our own hands." This appears from Acts xviii. 3: "Because he was of the same craft, he abode with them and wrought; for by their occupation they were tent-

^x Matt. v. 44.
Luke vi. 28. &
xxiii. 34. Acts
vii. 60. Rom.
xii. 14, 20. 1
Pet. ii. 23. &
iii. 9.
^y Lam. iii. 45.

^z 1 Thess. ii. 11.

^x being reviled, we bless; being persecuted, we suffer it:

13 Being defamed, we intreat: ^y we are made as the filth of the world, *and are* the offscouring of all things unto this day.

14 I write not these things to shame you, but ^z as my beloved sons I warn *you*.

---

makers." And, again, he asks (ix. 6), "I only and Barnabas, have not we power to forbear working?"

"Being reviled, we bless; being persecuted, we suffer it." They obeyed to the letter the words of the Lord, "Bless them that curse you." When ill-treated, they prosecuted not those who wronged them, but bore it all patiently.

13. "Being defamed, we intreat." It is doubtful whether this means, "We entreat God for them." It is explained by Godet: "They oppose to calumnies kindly intreating; they beseech men not to be so wicked, to return to better feelings, to be converted to Christ."

"We are made as the filth of the world, the offscouring of all things," &c. The words filth and offscouring signify the sweeping out of a room, rubbish (*quisquiliæ*). They are also supposed to refer to a piacular victim (or scapegoat) thrown into the sea to appease the anger of the gods; the off-scouring was the word addressed to those thus thrown into the sea, περίψημα ἡμῶν γενοῦ, "Be thou our sin-bearer;" but Godet and others think the allusion improbable. The words may contain a reference to Lamentations iii. 45, "Thou hast made us as the off-scouring and refuse in the midst of the people."

14. "I write not these things to shame you, but as my beloved sons I warn you." He now drops the tone of cutting irony, hoping that what he has written will have had the effect of showing their folly. "I write not these severe things for the mere purpose of putting you to shame, and leaving you in your shame, but I do all as a father. Take my words as not words of scorn and contempt, but of fatherly love."

15. "For though ye have ten thousand instructors in Christ," &c. By ten thousand teachers (pedagogues or tutors) he seems to

I HAVE BEGOTTEN YOU.

15 For though ye have ten thousand instructers in Christ, yet *have ye* not many fathers: for ª in Christ Jesus I have begotten you through the gospel.

16 Wherefore I beseech you, ᵇ be ye followers of me.

17 For this cause have I sent unto you ᶜ Timo-

ª Acts xviii. 11.
Rom. xv. 20.
ch. iii. 6. Gal.
iv. 19. Philem.
x. James i. 18.
ᵇ ch. xi. 1.
Phil. iii. 17. 1
Thess. i. 6. 2
Thess. iii. 9.
ᶜ Acts xix. 22.
ch. xvi. 10.
Phil. ii. 19.
1 Thess. iii. 2.

---

allude to the vast multiplication of teachers, or rather of those who considered themselves qualified to teach. This is the danger of all times of spiritual, as distinguished from moral activity. It is recognized by the Apostle in a later Epistle as a common danger of all Churches: "The time will come when they will not endure sound doctrine; but after their own lusts shall they heap to themselves teachers, having itching ears;" and by St. James: "My brethren, be not many masters, knowing that we shall receive the greater condemnation." (2 Tim. iv. 3; James iii. 1.)

"In Christ Jesus I have begotten you through the Gospel." The father is the instrument of engendering life: and as there can be but one natural father, so there could be but one spiritual father of the Corinthians, viz., the Apostle, who by his preaching moved them to "turn from idols to the living and true God," and to seek entrance by baptism into His Son's Church. (John iii. 5; Acts ii. 38; Rom. vi. 1-6.)

16. "Wherefore I beseech you, be ye followers of me"—since you are my children, and it is natural for children to follow their fathers. What a conscience void of offence the blessed Apostle must have had to give such a direction to his spiritual children.

17. "For this cause have I sent unto you Timotheus," &c. "For this cause." That is that they might, in all respects, be followers: of him.

"Have I sent unto you Timotheus." In Acts xix. 21, 22, we read "Paul purposed in the spirit when he had passed through Macedonia and Achaia to go to Jerusalem, saying, After I have been there I must also see Rome. So he sent into Macedonia two of them that ministered unto him, Timotheus and Erastus; but he himself stayed in Asia for a season."

No doubt this is the visit of Timothy alluded to. In the Acts it is only said that he sent Timothy to Macedonia, but inasmuch as

theus, ^d who is my beloved son, and faithful in the Lord, who shall bring you ^e into remembrance of my ways which be in Christ, as I ^f teach every where ^g in every church.

18 ^h Now some are puffed up, as though I would not come to you.

^d 1 Tim. i. 2. 2 Tim. i. 2.
^e ch. xi. 2.
^f ch. vii. 17.
^g ch. xiv. 33.
^h ch. v. 2.

Erastus, supposed to be a Corinthian and to hold high office in the city, was sent along with Timothy, no doubt they would go together to Corinth. In order that they might receive Timothy as became one who had been sent by the Apostle to supply his place for a time, he sent this letter, no doubt by sea, so that it should be read before Timothy arrived.[1]

"Who is my beloved son." He had called them sons, and so it was fitting that one who was begotten in Christ by his preaching, as they were, should be sent to represent him.

"Who shall bring you into remembrance . . . . every where in every church." Not instruct you, so much as remind you. Timothy had been St. Paul's companion on his first visit to Corinth, and was his constant fellow-helper in evangelizing everywhere, so no one would be more fitted to remind them of how he taught and what he taught.

"My ways which be in Christ." My ways which are in Christ is a phrase which at first seems not applicable to what the Apostle taught, but see Acts xviii. 26, "They expounded unto him the way of God more perfectly." The truth and walking in the truth should be inseparable.

"As I teach every where in every church." This is said to assure them that in laying upon them the necessity of unanimity and humbleness of mind, he did not inculcate what he did not universally teach and practise himself every where. His public teaching and private life were the same every where.

18. "Now some are puffed up, as though I would not come to you." As if some said, "We are of Cephas, we are of Christ. He dare not face us, he will only write severe letters; so he sends Timothy to bear the brunt of the conflict."

---

[1] Several undesigned coincidences are brought out by Paley in the "Horæ Paulinæ" on this passage.

CHAP. IV.] I WILL COME TO YOU SHORTLY. 71

19 ¹But I will come to you shortly, ᵏ if the Lord will, and will know, not the speech of them which are puffed up, but the power.

20 For ¹ the kingdom of God *is* not in word, but in power.

i Acts xix. 21.
ch. xvi. 5.
2 Cor. i. 15, 23.
k Acts xviii. 21.
Rom. xv. 32.
Heb. vi. 3.
James iv. 15.
l ch. ii. 4.
1 Thess. i. 5.

19. "But I will come to you shortly, if the Lord will," &c. He somewhat delayed his coming that they might repent and come to a better mind. He visits Macedonia first, and his reason is to be found written in 2 Cor. i. 23, "Moreover I call God for a record upon my soul, that to spare you I came not as yet unto Corinth."

"And will know, not the speech of them which are puffed up, but the power."

20. "For the kingdom of God is not in word, but in power." What is this power by which the Apostle, when he comes, will try the false apostles, the deceitful workers who oppose themselves to him?

Commentators are disagreed upon this. Godet and Edwards say that it is the spiritual power of converting souls; so Godet, "The power; by which he designates the effectual virtue of the Divine Spirit which brings back souls to themselves, makes them contrite, leads them to Christ, and begets them to a new life." Bishop Ellicott writes, "What power? Certainly not their power in reference to any miraculous manifestations (Chrysostom), and scarcely their power in its moral and ethical aspect (Osiander), or in spreading the Gospel (Meyer), but as verse 20 seems to suggest their power in its spiritual character." Yes, but if this power be neither manifested in miracles or in conversion, or in "moral and ethical aspects," how was it manifested, for manifested it must be? Dean Stanley actually takes no notice of the passage. Dean Alford, however, is wiser, "he (the Apostle) leaves it general and indefinite." There can be no doubt, I think, that he alludes to some miraculous manifestation, perhaps in the way of present judgment (see chap. v. 5, and 1 Tim. i. 20). It is exceedingly improbable that the Apostle would enter into some sort of contest with these men as to who should convert the greatest number of souls. Let the reader remember that the Apostle constantly refers to his exercise of miraculous powers as manifestations of his commission. (Rom. xv. 19; 2 Cor. xii. 12; Gal. iii. 5; also Acts xv. 12.)

21 What will ye? ^m shall I come unto you with a rod, or in love, and *in* the spirit of meekness?

^m 2 Cor. x. 2. & xiii. 10.

---

21. "What will ye? shall I come unto you with a rod," &c. Shall I come to you as a stern master, or as a father in Christ, with all affection and gentleness?

It is impossible that St. Paul could have written this if he had recognized in the congregation or church any inherent authority apart from the Apostolic ministry. According to every line of his writings bearing on the subject, all authority was from above, not from beneath; not from the Church ruling by the majority, but from Christ, first through the Apostles, then through their subordinates.

This verse is often considered as beginning a new paragraph or chapter, that, namely, which gives directions respecting the discipline to be exercised on the offending member.

CHAP. V.

IT is reported commonly *that there is* fornication among you, and such fornication as is not so much as ^a named among the Gentiles, ^b that one should have his ^c father's wife.

^a Ephes. v. 3.
^b Lev. xviii. 8. Deut. xxii. 30. & xxvii. 20.
^c 2 Cor. vii. 12.

---

1. "Not so much as named." So L., P., most Cursives, Syriac; but "named" omitted by ℵ, A., B., C., D., E., F., G., a few Cursives, d, e, f, g, Vulg., Copt.

1. "It is commonly reported that there is fornication among you," &c. "Commonly," rather "absolutely, actually." "Fornication is beyond all doubt reported (as being) among you." The fact is so notorious that the Apostle does not name his informants as he did in respect of the divisions or factions: "It has been declared unto me of you, my brethren, by them which are of the house of Chloe" (i. 11).

"And such fornication as is not so much as named among the Gentiles." The abhorrence in which such an act of incest was

2 ᵈ And ye are puffed up, and have not rather ᵉ mourned, that he that hath done this deed might be taken away from among you.   ᵈ ch. iv. 18.
ᵉ 2 Cor. vii. 7, 10.

3 ᶠ For I verily, as absent in body, but present   ᶠ Col. ii. 5.

---

3. "As absent." So E., F., G., L., most Cursives, d, e, f, g; but "as" omitted by ℵ, A., B., C., D., P., 17, 37, 39, 67, 80, 116, Vulg., Syriac, Copt., Æth., &c.

held by the Romans is apparent from the words of Cicero respecting a similar case, in his defence of Cluentius: "O incredible crime of a woman, and such as has never been heard of in this world, in any other than her solitary case." From the fact that such a marriage was forbidden both by the Roman and the Jewish law, it is probable that such an union had not been sanctioned by any legal form of marriage. The man only seems to have been a professing Christian, since no word is said of the woman's excommunication or restoration.

It has also been doubted whether the husband was alive. If 2 Cor. vii. 12 ("Not for his cause that hath done the wrong, nor for his cause that suffered wrong"), refer, as seems certain, to this case of adultery, then the son had seduced his father's second wife and was living with her in incest.

2. "And ye are puffed up," &c. That is, ye are self-satisfied and self-complacent, and behave yourselves as if ye were kings in spiritual matters, instead of hiding your heads for very shame at your connivance, even for a moment, at such extreme wickedness.

"And have not rather mourned, that he hath done," &c. Have not humbled yourselves by a public Church act of penitence, and no doubt of fasting, and at such a solemn assembly separated such an one from your fellowship.

Godet, however, supposes that the words "might be taken away," are not suitable to an act which the Corinthians might have done themselves, but are rather more in keeping with some act of God in striking the guilty one; but it is very improbable that the Apostle should blame them for not invoking so extreme a penalty from the Almighty. It was sufficient cause of blame that they had connived at the act by taking no public notice of it.

3. "For I verily, [as] absent in body, but present in spirit, have judged already," &c. "For I verily," the personal pronoun being expressed, shows the decision to be not of the Church, but of the

in spirit, have ‖ judged already, as though I were present, concerning him that hath so done this deed,

‖ Or, *determined*.

4 In the name of our Lord Jesus Christ, when ye are gathered together, and my spirit, [g] with the power of our Lord Jesus Christ,

[g] Matt. xvi. 19. & xviii. 18. John xx. 23. 2 Cor. ii. 10. & xiii. 3, 10.

Apostle, as overruling the action (or want of action) of the Church.

"Present in spirit." No doubt the case of Elisha and Gehazi is strictly one in point, "Went not mine heart with thee, when the man turned again from his chariot to meet thee?" (2 Kings v. 26). St. Paul was informed by the Spirit of God of all the circumstances, and instructed by Him in the way in which he was to act.

"Have judged already, as though I were present, concerning him." This is a remarkable assertion of plenary Apostolic power. There is a story told of some prince who was absent from his capital on some expedition, and hearing that his counsellors were about to meet and call in question some action of his, sent his sword and ordered that it should lie on the table before them during the debate; and though the Apostle sent no such visible sign of his authority, after reading this letter they would know that he who had wrought with such power, both of miracle and conversion, among them, was spiritually and effectually present, and weak though he was in personal appearance and speech, was able to exercise sharp discipline on the whole body, unless they submitted to the voice of God speaking through his mouth.

4. "In the name of our Lord Jesus Christ, when ye are gathered together," &c. "In the name of our Lord Jesus Christ." All was to be done in the Lord's Name, and by invoking the Lord's power to carry into effect the sentence both so far as it was outward or miraculous (for the destruction of the flesh) and spiritual or ecclesiastical, for the separation of the offender from the community of the faithful not only before men, but before God.

"When ye are gathered together." What does this mean? Does it mean that they were to call together a special assembly, or that it was to take place at the next ordinary assembly, just as in our Church at any ordinary Sunday after the Nicene creed "briefs, citations, and excommunications (are to be) read"? I think the

CHAP. V.] TO DELIVER UNTO SATAN. 75

5 ʰ To deliver such an one unto ⁱ Satan for the

ʰ Job ii. 6.
Ps. cix. 6. 1
Tim. i. 20.
ⁱ Acts xxvi. 18.

latter, because then the whole body of the faithful were most likely to be present.

But another question of far more importance is, Does the Apostle by the words, "When ye are gathered together" mean that he waits for their assent to his ruling in this matter? Impossible. The whole tone, not only of the passage which is now before us, but of the whole Epistle up to this point, is that he would have them look upon him as the Apostle, *i.e.*, the special messenger of Christ standing towards them through his special inspiration in the place of Christ towards them.

Godet puts it admirably. "There is not the faintest hint of making the pronouncing of the sentence dependent on the vote of the assembly which is to be held at Corinth, as if the Apostle's decision could be annulled by the contrary opinion of a majority. For his part everything is decided, and with his Apostolic competency he has judged to deliver over the offender; there will be joined to him, in the assembly which he convokes to take part in this terrible act, whoever wishes or dares."

"And my spirit." As if his spirit was present, and presided over their deliberations, which in fact was the case. The presence of his spirit was not by an act of sympathy or accord with what they were doing, but by a supernatural act, which if there was any place for supernatural acts in the life of the Apostle, seems to have been called for by the gravity of the occasion.

"With the power of our Lord Jesus Christ." What follows in the next verse seems to imply that this was to be something over and above an ordinary excommunication; and so the Apostle, by these words, pledges that Christ's power will follow upon their taking action, so that except there be almost immediate repentance on the part of the offender the sentence will be carried out in its utmost severity.

5. "To deliver such an one unto Satan for the destruction of the flesh," &c. What does this sentence import? Not mere excommunication, though it is, doubtless, included. It was a delegation to the Corinthian Church of a special power, reserved to the Apostles themselves, of inflicting corporeal death, or disease, as a punishment for sin. Of this we have notable instances in the case of

destruction of the flesh, that the spirit may be saved in the day of the Lord Jesus.

Ananias and Sapphira, and Elymas, and another hinted at in 1 Tim. i. 20: "Hymenæus and Alexander, whom I have delivered unto Satan, that they may learn not to blaspheme" (Alford). "This was the highest degree of punishment in the Christian Church. And we may observe, the passing this sentence was the act of the Apostles, not of the Corinthians" (Wesley).

"For the destruction of the flesh." Whatever disease, or bodily pain, or weakness, or "thorn in the flesh" was inflicted it would very speedily have terminated in death, had it not been averted by a timely repentance.

"That the spirit may be saved in the day of the Lord Jesus." There can, I think, be no doubt that the Apostle assumed that the guilty person would be cut off by death, but that this death would not be followed by eternal death, for the punishment of temporal death would be remedial, and either bring about a repentance, though a very late one, before he was taken away, or else his temporal death would be taken in mitigation of his punishment in the unseen world. Now we must fairly face this difficulty. If what was inflicted brought about repentance, which in this case it did, then the deadly blow was averted, and in this case there was no destruction of the flesh, and the offender survived, and the salvation of his spirit took place in the ordinary way, by an after life of penitence and faith: but if the blow took effect, then, in the view of the Apostle, it would be a sufficient punishment—sufficient, so far, that his spirit should be saved—perhaps saved as by fire, yet still saved. No doubt what the Apostle expected was the latter. His words, "that the spirit," &c., seem capable of no other meaning. Now suppose that the man had been cut off more or less suddenly. What should we have said? Why, that so great a criminal must have been, at the moment of his death, consigned to everlasting destruction; but it would not have been so at all: the temporal death, in the intention of the Apostle, was to avert eternal death.

Now this ought to show us how presumptuous we are in pronouncing upon the state of the departed. Respecting anyone taken off suddenly and in the flower of his days, we are utterly incompetent to

CHAP. V.] DISCIPLINE. 77

pronounce whether he has been taken off in judgment or in mercy. One may suddenly be cut off without apparently time for repentance, and the life of another may be prolonged, and he may die calmly and peacefully (may go off like a lamb, as the poor say), and yet all his life may have been that of one of the covetous, whom God abhorreth.

This place has received nothing like the attention which its importance demands, in our attempts, if such they may be called, to settle the eschatology of the New Testament. It takes its place by the side of the words of the Lord when (in Matth. xii. 32) He speaks of a sin which shall not be forgiven, "neither in this world, nor in the world to come," implying distinctly that sins may be forgiven in the future world.

Before leaving this most important passage we must make two further remarks.

And first respecting the incredible laxity of the Corinthian Church in taking no notice of so enormous a crime in one of their members. One would be tempted to think that the Church, as such, could have had no specific directions given to it respecting the exercise of discipline. To all appearance, unless the Apostle had so sharply intervened, no action would ever have been taken, for unless that action was taken at once, at the first, their feelings of shame would have been more and more blunted as time passed on, and in a comparatively short time the expulsion would have been, humanly speaking, impossible. The man must have been a powerful man, either from his wealth, or worldly status, or perhaps from his having taken the lead as the head of one of their principal factions.

Another matter is, How does all this bear upon us of the Church of England? It teaches us, I think, that there ought to be in every congregation or parish, a Church court, not of the clergy only, but of the communicants, and of the fittest among them, on account of age, intelligence, and spirituality—not a Church council to deliberate upon vestments, or changes in the service, or such things, which would only represent the factiousness of the parish or congregation; but a court to which no one would belong except under a deep sense of Christian obligation, knowing the odium to which he might be exposed, if he conscientiously did his duty.

But we are also taught by the example of St. Paul and the Corinthian Church respectively that there should be an external

6 ᵏ Your glorying *is* not good. Know ye not that ¹a little leaven leaveneth the whole lump?

7 Purge out therefore the old leaven, that ye

ᵏ ver. 2. ch. iii. 21. & iv. 19. James iv. 16.
ˡ ch. xv. 33. Gal. v. 9. 2 Tim. ii. 17.

---

7. "Purge out therefore." So C., L., P., most Cursives; but א, A., B., D., E., F., G., thirty Cursives, d, e, f, g, Vulg., Syriac, Copt., Goth., omit "therefore."

power, such as the bishop, to order the investigation of cases of open sin, where the parochial Church court failed in its duty, which, as the human nature of the Corinthians and of Englishmen is the same, it probably frequently would.

6. "Your glorying is not good." How hollow is your boasting of spiritual gifts or Divine knowledge, whilst you complacently tolerate such extreme wickedness!

"Know ye not that a little leaven leaveneth the whole lump?" The contagion of such unreproved licentiousness and open impurity must spread and contaminate more or less the whole Church.

7. "Purge out therefore the old leaven, that ye may be a new lump." "Purge out the old leaven—that is, this evil one. Not that he speaketh concerning this one only: rather he glanceth at others with him. For the old leaven is not fornication only, but also sin of every kind. And he saith not *purge*, but *purge out*. 'Cleanse with accuracy, so that there be not so much as a remnant, nor a shadow of that sort.' In saying, then, 'purge out,' he signifies that there was still iniquity among them. But in saying, 'that ye may be a new lump, as ye are unleavened,' he affirms and declares that not over very many was the wickedness prevailing. But though he saith, *as ye are unleavened*, he means it not as a fact that all were clean, but as to what sort of people ye ought to be." (Chrysostom.)

In using this figure of leaven, and of purging it out, some have supposed that the Apostle alludes to the Jewish Passover then near, and the scrupulous searching of each house, that there may be no crumb of leavened bread in any corner of it, which it is assumed that the Corinthians who observed the Passover would not omit. But St. Paul is not likely to urge such purely Jewish considerations on a Gentile Church. Christ is our Passover—the Passover of the world, in a heavenly and spiritual way; and Paul being the great Apostle of this truth, would not be likely to recognize any such remnants

CHAP. V.] CHRIST OUR PASSOVER. 79

may be a new lump, as ye are unleavened. For even ^m Christ our ⁿ passover ‖ is sacrificed for us:

8 Therefore ^o let us keep ‖ the feast, ^p not with

m Isai. liii. 7. John i. 29. ch. xv. 3. 1 Pet. i. 19. Rev. v. 6, 12.
n John xix. 14.
‖ Or, *is slain.*
o Exod. xii. 15, & xiii. 6.
‖ Or, *holiday.*
p Deut. xvi. 3.

---

7. "Sacrificed for us." So L., P., most Cursives, Syriac, Goth.; but ℵ, A., B., C., D., E., F., G., 17, 46, omit "for us."

of Judaism in an almost purely Gentile body. He would, no doubt, have in his mind the ancient law of the Passover, "Ye shall eat nothing leavened; in all your habitations shall ye eat unleavened bread" (Exod. xii. 20); but nothing further. Reference to such Jewish customs would not suit his purpose, which was to raise the Paschal view of Christ's Sacrifice above all mere Judaical forms, and make it Catholic.

"For even Christ our passover is sacrificed for us." Christ is our Passover, because, as the destroying angel, when he saw the blood of the Lamb over the door, passed over that house, and did not destroy the first-born of the family, so the wrath of God passes over the soul which has sought refuge from the guilt of sin in the Blood of the Son of God.

"Is sacrificed"—that is, He is slain as an all-atoning Sacrifice.

If Christ, then, be sacrificed, what follows? The Apostle tells us,

8. "Let us keep the feast." In order to realize this, we must remember that every Jewish sacrifice (except one, the burnt-offering) was partaken of, either by the priests or the sacrificers. In the case of the Passover, the whole was eaten as a Feast by the people.

If, then, the offering of Christ be a true Sacrifice, there must be means ordained whereby it is to be partaken of; and so there are. Christians have by Christ's own ordinance a means by which they may perpetually partake of Him as their Paschal Lamb; and this feast is to be partaken of after examination of their hearts and consciences. "Let a man examine himself, and so let him eat of that bread, and drink of that cup" (xi.).

Calvin has a remarkable exposition: "Now in the solemnity of this sacred feast we must abstain from *leaven*, as God commanded the fathers to abstain." But from what leaven? As the outward

old leaven, neither ^q with the leaven of malice and wickedness; but with the unleavened *bread* of sincerity and truth.

<small>q Matt. xvi. 6, 12. Mark viii. 15. Luke xii. 1.</small>

9 I wrote unto you in an epistle ^r not to company with fornicators:

<small>r See ver. 2, 7. 2 Cor. vi. 14. Ephes. v. 11. 2 Thess. iii. 14.</small>

---

9. "In an epistle." Properly, "in the epistle." Some epistle well known to you.

Passover was to them a figure of the true Passover, so its appendages were figures of the reality which we this day possess. If, therefore, we would wish to feed on Christ's Flesh and Blood, let us bring to this feast sincerity and truth. Let these be our loaves of unleavened bread. Away with all malice and wickedness, for it is unlawful to mix up leaven with this Passover. Again, Edwards: "But while the reference is to the Christian's life, the Apostle alludes especially to the Lord's Supper."

"Not with the old leaven," *i.e.*, by indulging the sinful desires of the first Adam, or old man.

"Nor with the leaven of malice and wickedness." If malice here is to be understood in the sense usually attached to it, then St. Paul probably alludes to the envy and ill-feeling which occasioned the factions or parties, and which was increased by such divisions.

"And wickedness" would probably mean the fornication for which he had to reprove them (2 Corinth. xii. 21).

"Sincerity and truth." Sincerity, according to Godet, means "transparency, and so the purity of a heart perfectly sincere before God." Truth can only mean truthfulness, straightforwardness, integrity of purpose. "Sincerity and truth seem to be put here for the whole of true inward religion" (Wesley).

9. "I wrote unto you in an [the] epistle not to company with fornicators." Many suppose that the epistle alluded to here is the first epistle to the Church; but there has as yet been no definite precept respecting the exclusion of such sinners from their company. It is alleged in favour of this view that if there had been such an epistle we should have heard more about it; but very probably it was a very short letter which he wrote to them, upon hearing of their laxity in associating with impure persons. Since St. Paul first visited Corinth in 54, and this first Epistle was written four or five years after at the least, it is probable that many

10 ⁵Yet not altogether with the fornicators ᵗ of this world, or with the covetous, or extortioners, or with idolaters; for then must ye needs go ᵘ out of the world.

ˢ ch. x. 27.
ᵗ ch. i. 20.
ᵘ John xvii. 15.
1 John v. 19.

11 But now I have written unto you not to keep company,

---

communications by letter had passed between the Apostle and the Church of Corinth, which was in many respects the most important which he had planted. In all probability, considering the anxiety which he had respecting the welfare of every Church which he had planted, and his constant communications with them through his subordinates (Timothy, Titus, Trophimus, &c.), we have not a twentieth part of the letters which he wrote to them now remaining. Such a passage as 2 Corinth. x. 10—"His letters, say they, are weighty and powerful"—implies that he gave much instruction by letter to the Churches.

If it be asked how it is that these letters have not been preserved, it may be answered that they would have so added to the bulk of the sacred volume that it would have rendered it the property of a few, not of all, as it now is.

10. "Yet not altogether with the fornicators of this world, or with the covetous," &c. But I did not mean by what I wrote that you should have no intercourse in the matter of business, or the necessary concerns of life, with the heathen around you, amongst whom this practice is not accounted to be sin—"nor with the covetous, nor with extortioners," for these sins also are tolerated, and those who are such are not excluded from society as criminals—"nor with idolaters," for if the heathen have any openly professed religion, it takes some form of idolatry.

"For then must ye needs go out of the world." It was not the intention of God that the Church should exist altogether aloof from the world. On the contrary, whilst living in the world, and taking part in all its lawful business—in the court, in the camp, in the forum, in the markets—it was to bear testimony against its sin by the example of men living in it, and yet uncontaminated by it.

11. "But now I have written unto you not to keep company, if any man," &c. There is some doubt about the way in which we are to understand this. Either we must take the "now" as it is usually understood: "but now (in this present letter) I write

G

[x] if any man that is called a brother be a fornicator, or covetous, or an idolater, or a railer, or a drunkard, or an extortioner; with such an one [y] no not to eat.

[x] Matt. xviii. 17. Rom. xvi. 17. 2 Thess. iii. 6, 14. 2 John 10.
[y] Gal. ii. 12.

(Epistolary Aorist) unto you not to keep company," &c.; but if the "I wrote" refers to what he had written in the former letter, then we must understand it as meaning, " but really I wrote," or "but, as it is, I wrote." They seem to have taken generally what he only meant to apply to those making a Christian profession. "Really I wrote to lay upon you not to eat with any professing Christian who is a fornicator, or covetous, or an idolater, or a reviler, or a drunkard, or an extortioner." Notice how, whilst limiting the prohibition to those calling themselves Christians, he extends its application to those practising many evil things besides fornication—to covetous, idolaters, extortioners, &c. It has been asked, how could any idolaters be reckoned amongst professing Christians? But is it not very probable that in such a mixed society of heathen and Christian, many professing believers should take part in idolatrous shows or feasts? In chap. viii. 10 he supposes the case, as if it were not by any means unknown, of Christians sitting at meat in an idol's temple; and many, in order not absolutely to break with their idolatrous relations and friends, might go even further, and affect some semblance of worship. I have heard of Christian Englishmen in India attending feasts in honour of Vishnu.[1]

A question also has arisen whether by the words "with such an one no not to eat," the Apostle alludes to the partaking of the Agapæ, or even of the Eucharist, with such sinners. His injunction seems to me to refer to private life, and it would seem most incongruous to exclude sinners from the Eucharist, and yet eat with them in private. This would be undoing privately what they had attempted to do publicly by Church censures. Eschewing the com-

---

[1] Dean Stanley and others understand this idolatry, not of worshipping false gods, but of sensuality and impurity: such sensuality and impurity being called idolatry because it was characteristic of the worship of such deities, as Aphrodite; but, in the first place, is it at all likely that the Apostle would veil fornication and lasciviousness under another name? Why should he? And, again, if Christians were under temptation to compromise themselves by taking part in idolatrous worship, surely it was the duty of the Apostle to denounce it.

CHAP. V.] PUT AWAY THAT WICKED PERSON.

12 For what have I to do to judge *them also that are without? do not ye judge ᵃ them that are within?

13 But them that are without God judgeth. Therefore ᵇ put away from among yourselves that wicked person.

ᶻ Mark iv. 11. Col. iv. 5. 1 Thess. iv. 12. 1 Tim. iii. 7.
ᵃ ch. vi. 1, 2, 3, 4.
ᵇ Deut. xiii. 5, & xvii. 7. & xxi. 21. & xxii. 21, 22, 24.

12. "Them also." So D. (Greek), E. (Greek), L., most Cursives, Arm., Goth.; but ℵ, A., B., C., F., G., P., 17, 31, 39, 46, 67, 73, d, e, f, g, Vulg., Copt., Syriac, Æth., omit "also."

13. "God judgeth," or "shall judge."

"Therefore put away." "Therefore" omitted by ℵ, A., B., C., D., F., G., P., fifteen Cursives, d, e, f, g, Vulg., Copt., Arm.

pany of fornicators, covetous persons, and drunkards, would form a necessary part of "purging out the old leaven" which he had just been pressing upon them.

12. "For what have I to do to judge them that are without?" As if he said, "Ye need not have misunderstood my meaning, for I have nothing to do in the way of judgment with those without, those external to the Church; but ye yourselves, by Church censures or excommunication, judge your fellow-members of the Church, and so ye might have known that I referred solely to them."

13. "But them that are without God judgeth." Either judgeth in the present, inasmuch as He now passes a judgment upon all, and in some cases exercises a present judgment, for He is "the Judge of all the earth"—or "shall judge," *i.e.*, at the last day.

"Therefore put away from among yourselves that wicked person." These words are taken verbatim from Deut. xxiv. 7: "If a man be found stealing any of his brethren of the children of Israel, and maketh merchandise of him or selleth him, then that thief shall die; and thou shalt put evil away from among you."

The "therefore" is perhaps not genuine. If it is not, it seems to read as if the Apostle dismissed the subject somewhat abruptly: "I have written enough. Put away at once the cause of offence."

CHAP. VI.

DARE any of you, having a matter against another, go to law before the unjust, and not before the saints?

^a Ps. xlix. 14.
Dan. vii. 22.
Matt. xix. 28.
Luke xxii. 30.
Rev. ii. 26. &
iii. 21. & xx. 4.

2 Do ye not know that ^a the saints shall judge the world? and if the world shall be judged by you, are ye unworthy to judge the smallest matters?

---

1. "Dare any of you, having a matter against another, go to law," &c. Bengel, who is quoted by most expositors, notices that the Apostle uses here a very lofty expression, as if going to law in heathen courts against one of the brethren is treason against the Church, the Body of Christ. ("Grandi verbo notatur læsa majestas Christianorum.")

If any Christians dared such a thing they came short in this matter of the faith and piety of the Jews, amongst whom it was a law that all disputes should be referred to the arbitration of approved men of their own faith and nation. This seems to have been recognized by Gallio, when he said to them, "If it be a question of words and names, and of your law, look ye to it, for I will be no judge of such matters"¹ (Acts xviii. 15).

"Go to law before the unjust, and not before the saints." The unjust, most probably because, being unbelievers, they were not justified. It can scarcely allude to any essential injustice in their modes of judicial proceedings, and this is confirmed by the heathen as ἄδικοι, and the saints as ἅγιοι, being opposed: the saints here can only mean those dedicated to God, the members of the Church of Christ, and so the unjust are those heathens whom God has at present not seen fit to make partakers of His righteousness.

2. "Do ye not know that the saints shall judge the world?" There seems here a clear reference to Daniel vii. 22: "Until the Ancient of days came, and judgment was given to the saints of the

---

¹ The Rabbinical prohibitions against going to law before Gentiles may be seen in Wetstein, *e.g.* "Statutum est ad quod omnes Israelitæ obligantur, eum qui litem cum alio habet non debere eam tractare coram Gentilibus" (Tauchuma, xcii. 2).

CHAP. VI.]   WE SHALL JUDGE ANGELS.   85

3 Know ye not that we shall ^b judge angels? how much more things that pertain to this life?   ^b 2 Pet. ii. 4. Jude 6.

---

most High; and the time came that the saints possessed the kingdom." This place should not be explained away as if the saints should judge the world in the sense of condemning it by the manifestation of their superior righteousness, nor that they should judge the world by the Imperial throne belonging, in the course of events, to a Christian Emperor as Constantine. It must refer to the saints being called by Christ, to be in some sort His assessors at the last day. Against this it is urged that Christ alone will judge, for He Himself said, "the Father judgeth no man, but hath committed all judgment unto the Son:" but it is not meant, when we plead for the literal meaning of this verse, that the judgment by the saints will be in the least degree apart from Christ, but simply under Him, by an act of His grace, and a sort of extension of His judgment.

As Godet remarks, "The idea of a real judicial act is demanded by the context." The Apostle speaks throughout of the judgment administered in this world by judges and courts of law, and his argument is that they who will actually take part in the judgment of the world are certainly competent to settle between themselves comparatively trivial matters of dispute which may arise among themselves.

3. "Know ye not that we shall judge angels? how much more things that," &c. Fallen angels must here be meant. It is scarcely conceivable that we shall pass sentence upon, or otherwise judge those who have, as ministering spirits, assisted us as heirs of salvation. Twice (2 Pet. ii. 4; Jude 6) we are told that evil angels have not yet been consigned to their final doom, and we may be called upon under Christ to judge them.

This also is one of those numerous places of Scripture which is taken little or no account of in our popular Eschatology. The circumstances under which we shall exercise this judgment are not told us, nor can we well imagine them; but the fact is revealed as one of the wonders of the Great Day. If men in the Name of Christ could cast out these evil spirits—if our conflict is not with flesh and blood, but with these principalities and powers—if they are (the very chief of them) even now bruised under our feet, it is no marvel if the Lord chooses to make those who were once their victims through sin, the instruments of His triumph over them.

4 ᶜIf then ye have judgments of things pertaining to this life, set them to judge who are least esteemed in the church.

ᶜ ch. v. 12.

5 I speak to your shame. Is it so, that there is not a wise man among you? no, not one that shall be able to judge between his brethren?

6 But brother goeth to law with brother, and that before the unbelievers.

7 Now therefore there is utterly a fault among you, because ye go to law one with another. ᵈ Why do ye not rather take wrong? why do ye not rather *suffer yourselves to* be defrauded?

ᵈ Prov. xx. 22.
Matt. v. 39, 40.
Luke vi. 29.
Rom. xii. 17, 19. 1 Thess. v. 15.

---

7. "A fault among you." So many Cursives; but ℵ, A., B., C., D., E., L., P., most Cursives, &c., read, " to you " ($ὑμῶν$), omitting $ἐν$.

4. "If then ye have judgments of things pertaining to this life, set," &c. Many understand this as an interrogative, "do ye set them to judge," &c.; others as if it was imperative, but spoken ironically. Taken in connection with the next verse it makes good sense either way.

5. "I speak to your shame. Is it so, that there is not a wise man," &c. They boasted of their knowledge and spiritual gifts, and yet acted as if there was not a prudent and intelligent person among them whom they could constitute arbiter in these secular matters.

6. "But brother goeth to law with brother, and that before the unbelievers." Here those who were in verse 1 called unjust are here called unbelievers. Quesnel remarks, " The good things of this world divide those who are most closely united to one another. The good things of heaven will reunite those who are most opposite and divided."

7. " Now therefore there is utterly a fault among you, because ye go to law one with another," &c. Translated by the Revisers, " Nay, already it is altogether a defect in you, that ye have lawsuits one with another."

The mere fact of your having these lawsuits is a loss of Christian grace to you. They manifest a loss of mutual forbearance and charity amongst those who by God's grace are one in Christ, and

YE DO WRONG AND DEFRAUD.

8 Nay, ye do wrong, and defraud, ᵉ and that *your* brethren.

ᵉ 1 Thess. iv. 6.

9 Know ye not that the unrighteous shall not inherit the

---

they cannot be tolerated amongst you without a loss of vitality to the whole Christian body (xii. 26). The word translated loss, $ἥττημα$, signifies deficiency, or coming short.

Why do ye not rather take wrong? Why do ye not rather suffer yourselves to be defrauded? This is in the spirit of the Lord's words: "I say unto you, that ye resist not evil, but whosoever shall smite thee on thy right cheek, turn to him the other also," &c. (Matth. v. 39.)

8. "Nay, ye do wrong, and defraud, and that your brethren." Notice how the Apostle here speaks to the whole Church, as if all were implicated. It might be rejoined by the Church that only a few had gone to law, just as only one had committed incest; but the Apostle looked upon the whole Church as one organic unity. It was one in grace, because all having been baptized into the unity of the same body, and partaking of one Bread, were one Body (x. 17); and so if sin in any member was not at once and energetically repudiated, the whole body was held responsible by the Apostle.

9. "Know ye not that the unrighteous shall not inherit the kingdom of God?" He speaks of it as a first principle which every Christian should know, that the kingdom of God being a kingdom of righteousness (Rom. xiv. 17), cannot have unrighteousness within it. In this imperfect state of its development the evil will be ever mingled with the good, but it will not be so when the perfect kingdom shall appear at the Second Coming—then the words of Christ will be fulfilled, "Then shall the Son of Man send forth his angels, and they shall gather out of his kingdom all things that offend, and them which do iniquity, and shall cast them into a furnace of fire." He begins with mentioning the unrighteous, which properly signifies those who act unjustly towards their neighbour, and then he naturally extends the meaning of the word, so as to cover every form of wickedness.

"Be not deceived." As if the Gospel gave you license to live in sin, instead of being intended to deliver you from its power.

"Neither fornicators, nor idolaters, nor adulterers." How is it that idolatry comes immediately after fornication? Evidently

kingdom of God? Be not deceived: ᶠ neither fornicators, nor idolaters, nor adulterers, nor effeminate, nor abusers of themselves with mankind.

10 Nor thieves, nor covetous, nor drunkards, nor revilers, nor extortioners, shall inherit the kingdom of God.

ᶠ ch. xv. 50.
Gal. v. 21.
Ephes. v. 5.
Tim. i. 9. Hebr.
xii. 14. & xiii. 4. Rev. xxii. 15.

---

because the idolatry of Corinth was so inextricably joined with filthiness and lewdness.

"Fornication, adultery." Notice how he distinguishes between the two. Though both will exclude from the inheritance, the latter is in many respects the worst crime, because through it the family is broken up, and a third person is irretrievably injured.

"Nor effeminate." μαλακοί are not the dainty or luxurious, those so enervated as to become like the weaker sex, but persons guilty of unnameable crimes. It would scarcely mean merely effeminate, if put as it is here, between adulterers and ἀρσενοκοῖται.[1]

Assuming that it means effeminate in the ordinary sense, Wesley has an admirable note:—"*Nor the effeminate.* Who live in an easy, indolent way, taking up no cross, enduring no hardship. But how is it that these good-natured, harmless people are ranked with idolaters and Sodomites? We may learn hence—that we are never secure from the greatest sins, till we guard against those which are thought the least, nor, indeed, till we think no sin is little, since every one is a step towards hell."

10. "Nor thieves, nor covetous, nor drunkards," &c. These two verses mention by name almost all the common sins of our natural state which men have to renounce before they can be admitted into the Church of Christ here, and which if persisted in will exclude from the kingdom of blessedness hereafter. The list, of course, is not exhaustive. Many more are enumerated amongst the works of the flesh in Gal. v.

11. "And such were some of you." God may have granted forgiveness and restoration to some who had in times past committed

---

[1] It is used in its darker sense by heathen writers, such as Dion. Halicarn. Ant., vii. p. 418, and Diogenes Laert., vii. c. 5, sec. 4. The Romans also used the term malacus in the same sense. In some later Lexicons this meaning is ignored. See also a remarkable description of such in Josephus, "Wars of the Jews," iv. ch. ix. sec. 10.

CHAP. VI.] YE ARE WASHED. 89

11 And such were ᵍ some of you: ʰ but ye are washed, but ye are sanctified, but ye are justified in the name of the Lord Jesus, and by the Spirit of our God.

ᵍ ch. xii. 2.
Ephes. ii. 2. &
iv. 22. & v. 8.
Col. iii. 7. Tit.
iii. 3.
ʰ ch. i. 30.
Hebr. x. 22.

the greatest of these abominations—such is the freedom of His Grace.

"But ye are washed, but ye are sanctified, but ye are justified." The neglect of giving the right force to the Aorist has well-nigh deprived this verse of its point and significance. It is " ye were washed (or washed yourselves), ye were sanctified (or consecrated to God), ye were justified (or were made partakers of the Life of Christ), in the name," &c. All these things took place at a definite moment in past time when ye were converted, and baptized in the Name of Christ, and by the Spirit were engrafted into the One Body (ch. xii. 13).

"Ye were washed." Therefore ye ought not to befoul yourselves again, as some of you are doing. Ye were sanctified or dedicated to God in your Baptism, and so ye became the temple of God; but some of you, I am afraid, have need to be told (as I have told you, iii. 17), that, "if any man defile the temple of God him will God destroy." Ye were justified or united to Christ as the Vine or Olive-tree of grace, but "you must continue in his goodness, otherwise you also shall be cut off" (Rom. xi. 22).

"Ye were sanctified" cannot possibly mean the sanctification of modern Evangelical language, otherwise it would not come between the washing of Christian Baptism and the Justification. It must be the dedication by which those who believed were in the act of Baptism set apart for ever to the service of God.[1]

"In the name of the Lord Jesus, and by the Spirit of our God." Grafting into Christ in Baptism, sanctifying grace and our Justifi-

---

[1] Many divines and pious writers are greatly exercised by the fact that St. Paul here does not give the proper Evangelical sequence—Justification first, then (perhaps) Baptism, then Sanctification; but the Apostle constantly names these things in what many good men now account to be the wrong order. In fact, it seems not the exception but the rule with him to invert the order. I have given a number of instances in full in "Church Doctrine Bible Truth," chap. xi. p. 375; I now merely give the references—1 Cor. vi. 11; 2 Thess. ii. 13; 1 Tim. i. 5; 1 Tim. iv. 12; 1 Tim. vi. 11; 2 Tim. ii. 22; Tit. ii. 2; Heb. x. 16, 17.

12 ¹All things are lawful unto me, but all things are not ‖ expedient: all things are lawful for me, but I will not be brought under the power of any.

13 ᵏ Meats for the belly, and the belly for meats: but God shall destroy both it and them. Now the body *is* not for fornication, but ¹for the Lord; ᵐ and the Lord for the body.

ⁱ ch. x. 23.
‖ Or, *profitable.*
ᵏ Matt. xv. 17.
Rom. xiv. 17.
Col. ii. 22, 23.
¹ ver. 15, 19, 20. 1 Thess. iv. 3, 7.
ᵐ Eph. v. 23.

---

cation by Christ's Risen Life, are all in the Name of Christ, and through the operation of the Spirit of God.

12. "All things are lawful unto me, but all things are not expedient." There is some difficulty in making out the connection between this verse and what immediately precedes, for in verses 9 and 10 he had been denouncing things which could not by any possibility be lawful, because some were unnatural and degrading, and some struck at the root of human society itself.

I think the connection is something of this sort. He had been speaking of things absolutely unlawful, and then it rises up in his mind that the use of lawful things may become unlawful if they are used wrongly, as, for instance, meats if eaten so as to give needless offence to others (Rom. xiv. 21). In such a case the use of such things would be unrighteous, and so go far to exclude the person thus needlessly and wantonly giving offence from the Kingdom of God.

And then in another way things lawful may become the occasion of sin, if they are used immoderately. The creatures are to be our servants and not our masters. But we may so use them, that we may be brought under their power. It is lawful to drink wine, but men may so drink as to become slaves of it. And so the Apostle means that all things are lawful, but that he will only use them in subordination to his spiritual progress.

13. "Meats for the belly, and the belly for meats: but God shall destroy," &c. Perhaps this is a proverbial saying, and was used by the Corinthians to excuse the gratification of gluttonous appetites, and St. Paul meets it by the fact that the sustentation of the body by meats is only for this life—for the risen spiritual bodies of the saints will not be sustained by food as their present gross bodies are; and if the nutritive functions of the body will be done away with at the Resurrection, so also will the generative,

14 And ⁿ God hath both raised up the Lord, and will also raise up us ᵒ by his own power.

15 Know ye not that ᵖ your bodies are the

ⁿ Rom. vi. 5, 8. & viii. 11.
2 Cor. iv. 14.
ᵒ Eph. i. 19, 20.
ᵖ Rom. xii. 5.
ch. xii. 27.
Ephes. iv. 12, 15, 16. & v. 30.

---

as the Lord said, " In the resurrection they neither marry nor are given in marriage, but are as the angels of God in heaven " (Matt. xxii. 30).

Just then as the body is not made for gratification of one sort, so much less is it made for sinful, soul-destroying gratification of another sort, to which the Corinthians were so grievously tempted.

For the body is "for the Lord," to be, when renewed and spiritualized, the instrument for carrying out His holy and heavenly purposes throughout eternity; and the Lord "for the body," *i.e.*, for the whole redeemed and renewed man, that He should be in him as his eternal life.

12. " And God hath both raised up the Lord, and will also raise up us by his own power." This is the reason why the body is for the Lord, and the Lord for the body. Our Lord's glorified body and the glorified bodies of His Saints are in the same sphere of being, as it were. God hath first raised up the Lord to be the type and model of the resurrection of His Saints, and to be the power of eternal life within them, and to rule the new state of things by them; and He will raise us up by His own power—by no power of nature, but by His own power—to be conformed to the Lord in body as well as in spirit, to be under Him as the Head, and to be directed by Him and do His bidding in the future and eternal world.

15. " Know ye not that your bodies are the members of Christ ? shall I then," &c. You are not only joined to Christ in soul and spirit, but also in body; for your body is part of your personality. The personality is not of the higher part only, but of the lower. Now God by uniting us to Christ in one body, has made our bodies members of Christ, so that we should be holy in body as well as in spirit, and we can only be thus holy by keeping our bodies in subjection, and not putting any member to a sinful use. And there is another figure also used to exemplify the same holy union. Christ is the bridegroom and the husband of His Church, and so each sepa-

members of Christ? shall I then take the members of Christ, and make *them* the members of an harlot? God forbid.

---

rate member of the Church being in the one bride or body of Christ, is so one with Him, that his body though composed of many members, is a member of Christ's body, and each member must be deemed consecrated to Him.

Before I go further I must say a word respecting the extreme importance of believing in this union, and accepting it in the very broad way in which it is delivered here by the Apostle, as applicable to every baptized Corinthian. St. Paul cannot possibly limit the application of it to only these Corinthians, who were, over and above their Baptism, converted and sanctified in the sense held by modern evangelical men; for, if so, he would undo his own purpose. His purpose was to bring about the holiness and purity of the whole Church, and as all the baptized were accounted members of the Church, and all the members of the Church accounted to be baptized, it was of the utmost importance that every baptized Corinthian should, on the assumption of his having been made a member of Christ in Baptism, keep himself from all sin, but especially from that sin which, in the eyes of the Apostle, was the most destructive to the soul and damaging to the whole Church, the sin connected with the sexual relations.

And if sins are the same then as now, and their destructive effects the same then as now, then the truth should be plainly declared, that we have all been made in our Baptism members of Christ, so that each baptized person (whether he has experienced such a change as is commonly called conversion since his Baptism matters nothing) should hold himself so a member of Christ, that all his members are consecrated to the service of God.

No minister of Christ, no teacher of classes of young men and young women, no catechist, can be accounted faithful to his Divine Master unless he teaches the holiness of the bodies of Christians owing to their Baptism into the Body or Church of Christ.

And, as a necessary corollary, all true conversion ought to be on St. Paul's principles—a conversion to the acknowledgment of, and the beginning to live in accordance with, the fact of their having been made members of Christ.

" Shall I then take the members of Christ, and make them the

16 What? know ye not that he which is joined to an harlot is one body? for ⁹two, saith he, shall be one flesh.

17 ʳBut he that is joined unto the Lord is one spirit.

q Gen. ii. 24.
Matt. xix. 5.
Ephes. v. 31.
r John xvii. 21, 22, 23.
Ephes. iv. 4.
& v. 30.

---

members," &c. I cannot express the lesson of this verse better than in the words of the Evangelical commentator, Thomas Scott: "Our bodies should be considered as 'for the Lord,' and be devoted to His service, that they may at length share His Resurrection, and be made like to His glorious Body. How degrading, then, how base, how ungrateful, how sacrilegious, to make the members of Christ the members of a harlot! Or to defile the temple of the Holy Spirit, and to alienate the Lord's peculiar property to the vile purposes of fornication." And again, a little before, "He did not form the body to be employed in fornication, and the promiscuous intercourse of the sexes, which counteract, and, if universal, would entirely defeat the design of the Creator in making them male and female, namely, the increase of the human species, the proper training up of children, and all the comforts and advantages of relative and domestic life, as springing from honourable marriage."

16. "What? know ye not that he which is joined to an harlot is one body? for two, saith he, shall be one flesh." The Apostle seems to anticipate an objection which he supposed someone might make, that he was speaking too strongly in saying that a man by sinning thus might make his members (which were the members of Christ) the members of an harlot; but he defends himself by reminding them of the words in which the mystery of the marriage union is set forth at its original institution, Genesis ii.: "The man shall be joined unto his wife, and they shall be one flesh." If then man and wife are one in a lawful holy union, the man and the harlot are one in an unholy deadly union. It is only in God that the union of the sexes is holy.

17. "But he that is joined unto the Lord is one spirit." "There is one Body and one Spirit, even as ye are called in one hope of your calling," Ephes. iv. 4. The Spirit proceeding from Christ, the Holy Spirit, so renews Christians that their spirits are one in Christ. They love and hate the same things, as our Apostle elsewhere says,

18 ⁵ Flee fornication. Every sin that a man doeth is without the body; but he that committeth fornication sinneth ᵗ against his own body.

ˢ Rom. vi. 12, 13. Hebr. xiii. 4.
ᵗ Rom. i. 24. 1 Thess. iv. 4.

"We have the mind of Christ," ii. 16. Here, of course, the Apostle uses it as an additional argument against sins such as he here reprobates. "By faith a man is one spirit with Christ, and shall he make himself one flesh with an harlot?" (Wesley.)

18. "Flee fornication." It has been well said that we must contend against other vices, but we must flee from fornication. Joseph, in this respect, is our example. If we would truly flee from fornication, we must not allow our minds to dwell even for a moment upon thoughts of it, we must not look upon forbidden objects; indeed, we must ever have in mind the words of the Lord, "He that looketh upon a woman to lust after her hath committed adultery with her already in his heart." And when we hear any filthy conversation we must reprove it, and even, if needful, stop our ears, and always leave the company where such talk is tolerated.

"Every sin that a man doeth is without the body; but he that committeth," &c. This is a passage of extraordinary difficulty; scarcely any two commentators are agreed upon its meaning.

And the subject is such that I cannot mention the greater part of them. It may be well, however, to notice what is certain in the passage, and what is difficult.

It is quite certain that the Apostle means to assert that fornication is peculiarly deadly and malignant—that its malignity consists in this, that it is a sin against, a dishonouring of, our bodies.

And the difficulty is in the saying that "every other sin which a man doeth is without the body." Now the Apostle had expressly mentioned drunkenness as a sin which will deprive those who commit it of the kingdom of God, so that he must have had it in his mind. But how can drunkenness be "without the body" as compared with fornication? It is a sinful or inordinate desire of the body, which finds its gratification solely, apparently, in a bodily gratification.

The only explanation I can hazard is, that in some mysterious way the sin of fornication touches the mystery of man's coming into being (Ephes. v. 30-33), which consists in man and wife being one flesh, and undoes that mystery—a mystery which only apper-

19 What? ᵘ know ye not that your body is the temple of the Holy Ghost *which is* in you, which ye have of God, ˣ and ye are not your own?

ᵘ ch. iii. 16.
2 Cor. vi. 16.
ˣ Rom. xiv. 7, 8.

---

tains to man, and so more than any other sin reduces man to the level of the brutes. Whether we acknowledge marriage to be a Sacrament or not, there is a sort of Sacramental mystery about it. It was ordained for the bringing into the world of a holy seed (see particularly Malachi ii. 14-15), and fornication undoes this, and so undoes the purpose of God more than any sin, and so more than any other destroys the dignity of man.

Perhaps upon the whole Alford's explanation seems the most reasonable. "The assertion . . . . is strictly true. Drunkenness and gluttony, *e.g.*, are sins done in and by the body, and are sins by abuse of the body—but they are still ἐκτὸς τοῦ σώματος—introduced from without—sinful not in their act, but in their effect, which effect it is each man's duty to foresee and avoid. But fornication is the alienating that body which is the Lord's, and making it a harlot's body—it is a sin against a man's own body in its highest possible state. . . . When man and wife are one in the Lord, united by His ordinance, no such alienation of the body takes place, and consequently no sin." Bishop Wordsworth also gives a very similar explanation, if not indeed the same, in other words.

19. "What? know ye not that your body is the temple of the Holy Ghost which is in you." Here is another consideration to make them keep their bodies holy. Not only are their bodies, and so their members the members of Christ: but these same bodies are the temple of the Spirit. He says "your body," *i.e.*, the body of each one, is the temple of the Spirit. It is designed for the worship of the Spirit. He dwells in it as His shrine, His Naos.

"Which ye have of God." Which comes to you and is given to you from God—from the Father and the Son. They then who dishonour their bodies by fornication, defile not only the members of the Son, but the shrine or dwelling-place of the Spirit. Mark how this truth, thus insisted upon by the Apostle, condemns utterly every approach to Antinomianism. Men say, "I do not sin in my soul or spirit, I sin in my flesh only, which is yet corrupt, and so what I do is no sin." Not so; your members are the members of

| y Acts xx. 28. |
| ch. vii. 23. |
| Gal. iii. 13. |
| Hebr. ix. 12. |
| 1 Pet. i. 18, 19. |
| 2 Pet. ii. 1. |
| Rev. v. 9. |

20 For *y* ye are bought with a price: therefore glorify God in your body, and in your spirit, which are God's.

---

20. "And in your spirit, which are God's." Omitted by ℵ, A., B., C., D., E., F., G., 17, 46, 67**, 71, 109, d, e, f, g, Vulg., Copt., Bas., Arm., Æth.; but retained by K., L., P., 37, most Cursives, and Syriac.

Christ—your body is the temple of the Spirit, and every sin which you commit in your body is a sin against Christ Whose members your members are, and against the Spirit Who dwells in your bodies.

"Ye are not your own."

20. "For ye are bought with a price: therefore glorify God in," &c. If your members are the members of Christ, if your body is the temple of the Holy Spirit, if you have surrendered yourselves to God, then indeed ye are not your own, and in addition to all this ye are bought, a ransom has been paid for you—the precious Blood of Christ; ye are "the Church of God which He hath redeemed with His own Blood."

"Therefore glorify God in your body." This is the conclusion of all. You are to glorify God in your body. You are to keep your body pure from sin as His temple. You are to give Him the worship of your bodies. There must be lowly adoration of body as well as soul.

The words "in your spirits," as the reader will see by turning to the critical note, are wanting in so many of the oldest MSS. and Versions that they must be held to be doubtful. They give, it is true, a more effective finish to the argument, but at the expense of its point and pertinency, for the Apostle is writing upon the sins of the body, and declaring the holiness of the body, and would have men reverence a body which will be raised again in the likeness of the glorious Body of Christ.

CHAP. VII.

NOW concerning the things whereof ye wrote unto me: ^a *It is* good for a man not to touch a woman.   ^a ver. 8, 26.

---

1. "Now concerning the things whereof ye wrote unto me : It is good for a man," &c. A considerable amount of words has been expended upon the question as to what party wrote to him asking him about marriage and celibacy. It is supposed that the Petrine party advocated marriage because St. Peter was married, and the Pauline advocated celibacy because St. Paul as evidently desired that, consistently with maintaining chastity, all Christians should be as free as he himself was from all bonds which would hinder them from serving the Lord without distraction.

I do not think we have any need to entertain the question whether it came from one of the "parties" or not. In a young community, such as was the Church of Corinth at this time, with terrible temptations to fall in with the prevailing licentiousness on the one side, and with the beginnings of asceticism on the other, some such question as this was sure to be asked of the inspired teacher.

"It is good for a man not to touch a woman," *i.e.*, it is good for a man to remain unmarried: for if he be married, he comes under the law expressed in verses 3 and 4.

A contrast has been drawn between these words of St. Paul, and those of God in Genesis ii., "It is not good that the man should be alone;" but such a comparison is absurd. It was not good that the man should be alone when he had no creature to converse with, and when the whole world required to be peopled; but it might be good for a man to be alone, *i.e.*, unmarried, when the world was crowded with people, and when those whose lot it was to evangelize it were daily exposed to imprisonment and death in carrying out their Master's orders.

"Good" is to be taken in its usual sense, not meaning that it is most honourable on the one side, nor merely expedient on the other, but that the state of celibacy in a man is absolutely be-

H

2 Nevertheless, *to avoid* fornication, let every man have his own wife, and let every woman have her own husband.

^b Exod. xxi. 10. 1 Pet. iii. 7.

3 ^b Let the husband render unto the wife due benevolence: and likewise also the wife unto the husband.

4 The wife hath not power of her own body, but the husband: and likewise also the husband hath not power of his own body, but the wife.

c Joel ii. 16. Zech. vii. 3. See Exod. xix. 15. 1 Sam. xxi. 4, 5.

5 ^c Defraud ye not one the other, except *it be* with consent for a time, that ye may give your-

---

3. "Due benevolence," &c. So K., L., most Cursives, Syriac; but א, A., B., C., D., E., F., G., P., Q., 6, 17, 46, 67**, 71, 177, d, e, f, g, Vulg., Cop., Basm., Arm., Æth., read, "the debt."

---

coming and worthy, and nothing in it contrary to the moral ideal. (Godet.)

2. "Nevertheless, to avoid fornication, let every man have his own wife," &c. Let "every man," *i.e.*, every man who feels that it is better for him to marry, or, with the temptations of such a city on every side, feels that it is dangerous for him to continue unmarried. (See verses 7, 8, 9.)

3. "Let the husband render unto the wife due benevolence," &c. The original word, no doubt (see Critical Note), is "the debt," the marriage due. Wesley has a pertinent remark: "Let not married persons fancy that there is any perfection in living with each other as if they were not married."

4. "The wife hath not power of her own body, but the husband, and likewise," &c. Chrysostom writes: "When therefore thou seest a harlot tempting thee, say, 'My body is not mine, but my wife's.' The same, also, let the woman say to those who would undermine her chastity, 'My body is not mine, but my husband's.'"

5. "Defraud ye not one the other, except it be with consent for a time." The word defraud, as Bengel notices, has reference to the debt or debitum. If any one is deprived of his due—of what is owing to him—he is defrauded. "Except it be with consent for a time, that ye may give yourselves to [fasting and] prayer." Fasting

CHAP. VII.] I SPEAK BY PERMISSION. 99

selves to fasting and prayer; and come together again, that ᵈ Satan tempt you not for your incontinency.

6 But I speak this by permission, ᵉ *and* not of commandment.

7 For ᶠ I would that all men were ᵍ even as I myself. But ʰ every man hath his proper gift of God, one after this manner, and another after that.

ᵈ 1 Thess. iii. 5.
ᵉ ver. xii. 25. 2 Cor. viii. 8. & xi. 17.
ᶠ Acts xxvi. 29.
ᵍ ch. ix. 5.
ʰ Matt. xix. 12. ch. xii. 11.

---

5. "Fasting and." Omitted by ℵ, A., B., C., D., E., F., G., P., ten Cursives, d, e, f, g, Vulg., Copt., Basm., Arm., Æth.; retained by K., L., most Cursives, Syriac, &c.

seems to have been suggested to early scribes from Acts xiii. 2, and xiv. 23, but the manuscript authority is decisively against it.

"And come together again." Notice how in all this the Apostle allows no ascetic consideration to come in. The permission is not to contravene the intention of marriage.

"That Satan tempt you not for your incontinency." That is, on account of your incontinency. One of the chief purposes of marriage being that you should be safe from this particular temptation.

6. "But I speak this by permission, and not of commandment." "By permission," that is, by way of allowance or indulgence. What does the Apostle allude to by the "this"? I speak *this*. Some, as Edwards and Bishop Ellicott, take it as referring to all that has gone before respecting the conjugal relations; others, as Alford, limit it to verse 5: "The recommendations all depended upon the possibility of their being tempted by incontinence; he gives it not, then, as a command in all cases, but as an allowance for those to whom he was writing, whom he knew and assumes to be thus tempted."

7. "For I would that all men were even as I myself." "I would that all believers who are now unmarried should remain eunuchs for the kingdom of heaven's sake (Matth. xix. 12). St. Paul having tasted the sweetness of this liberty, wished others to enjoy it as well as himself; but everyone hath his own proper gift from God. According to our Lord's declaration, all men cannot receive this saying, save they, the happy few, to whom it is given" (Matth. xix. 11). (Wesley.)

"Even as I am." This has been taken, as by Godet, to signify that St. Paul was not then married, and never was. For he asks,

8 I say therefore to the unmarried and widows, ⁱIt is good for them if they abide even as I.

9 But ᵏ if they cannot contain, let them marry: for it is better to marry than to burn.

ⁱ ver. 1, 26.
ᵏ 1 Tim. v. 14.

"How could he have expressed the desire that all men were widowers?" But if St. Paul had been married, he would, when God was pleased to deprive him of his wife, have become celibate, and able to "serve the Lord without distraction," as single and unencumbered, and that is all that is meant. It is most probable that St. Paul never was married, but his words here are no proof of it.

"But every man hath his proper gift of God, one after this manner," &c. This means that God hath given to one aptitude for life in celibacy, to another aptitude for married life. Dean Stanley says that gift ($\chi\acute{\alpha}\rho\iota\sigma\mu\alpha$) signifies here moral and natural gifts, but elsewhere preternatural gifts; but no doubt all gifts by which men are distinguished from their fellows are special gifts of God, and being gifts and not wages, are of grace or particular favour, though God may have hidden from us the mode in which He gives them.

8. "I say therefore to the unmarried and widows," &c. Some suppose that "the unmarried" here means widowers, but no reason whatsoever can be alleged for the restriction. A more probable supposition respecting the mention of widows is that, by becoming widows, they became more especially the servants of the Church. "We may with some confidence infer that in the Apostle's advice to widows not to contract a second marriage, we have a reference to those widows, for whose support the Church had already made provision (Acts vi. 1), and who afterwards acquired a more official position as deaconesses, or in a later age as members of the viduate ($\chi\acute{\eta}\rho\iota\kappa o\nu$). The present passage marks an intermediate stage in the growth of that office." (Edwards.)

"It is good for them if they abide even as I." That is, in a state in which there are none dependent upon them, to whose interests they are bound to look, so that in this state of celibacy they may "serve the Lord without distraction."

9. "But if they cannot contain, let them marry: for it is better to marry," &c. That is, if they have not continency, if they have not power over themselves, let them marry.

"It is better to marry than to burn," that is, to be consumed inwardly with evil desires.

CHAP. VII.] LET HIM NOT PUT HER AWAY. 101

10 And unto the married I command, ¹ *yet* not I, but the Lord, ᵐ Let not the wife depart from *her* husband:

11 But and if she depart, let her remain unmarried, or be reconciled to *her* husband: and let not the husband put away *his* wife.

12 But to the rest speak I, ⁿ not the Lord: If any brother hath a wife that believeth not, and she be pleased to dwell with him, let him not put her away.

13 And the woman which hath an husband that believeth not, and if he be pleased to dwell with her, let her not leave him.

¹ See ver. 12, 25, 40.
ᵐ Mal. ii. 14, 16. Matt. v. 32. & xix. 6, 9. Mark x. 11, 12. Luke xvi. 18.
ⁿ ver. 6.

---

10. "And unto the married I command, yet not I, but the Lord." He now takes up questions of separtion and divorce.

The words, "yet not I, but the Lord," refer to the commands of the Lord in the Gospels respecting divorce (Matth. v. 32; xix. 9; Mark x. 11; Luke xvi. 18). It is remarkable, however, that the Apostle should make prominent mention of the wife as being the one who desired to depart. And this, I think, refers to mixed marriages. If a Christian woman was married to a heathen man, she would very probably desire to leave a house where heathen idolatries and pollutions took place, which she had no power to prohibit or even to withdraw herself from, whereas the Christian man would be the ruler in his own house.

11. "But and if she depart, let her remain unmarried, or be reconciled," &c. The marriage contracted when both parties were in an heathen state, was the same, so far as its binding obligations on each party was concerned, as if contracted when they were Christians. It brought both under the law of Christ, that if the husband put away his wife he committed adultery against her, and if the wife put away her husband, she committed adultery (Mark x. 11, 12).

12, 13. "But to the rest speak I, not the Lord . . . . let her not leave him." I believe that in verses 10 and 11 he has an eye to mixed marriages (though not, perhaps, wholly), because, as I said, it was natural for the believing wife not to wish to live in an heathen household; now he considers the case of mixed marriages, where both parties had a desire to dwell together, but one or both had scruples respecting the continuance of intercourse with an

14 For the unbelieving husband is sanctified by the wife,

---

heathen. He declares that, so far as he knows (for he has had no special revelation respecting it), there is no ground for such scruples, and he gives a remarkable reason.

14. "For the unbelieving husband is sanctified by the wife, and the unbelieving," &c. This sanctification is not, of course, to be taken in the sense of being internally and spiritually holy, but relatively holy in so far as this, that their matrimony is holy matrimony; their intercourse is not sinful, and if they have children, the holiness of one parent saves the children from being considered or treated as heathen children; they are entitled to Baptism just as if both the parents were baptized Christians. We mistake altogether St. Paul's religious position, so to speak, if we conceive him to be a precursor of Luther or Calvin, much less of Zwingle or Knox. If ever man did, he believed in the Holy Catholic Church. He believed that the outward visible Church of Christ took the place of the Jewish body, and much more. Though its members might be very deficient in heart-sanctification or self-dedication, they were still in a real sense holy, and they were to believe this and act upon the belief, in order that they might attain to a higher sanctification. They were to hold not only their souls but their very bodies to be holy, because those bodies were the members of Christ. This Church is sanctified not merely by the preaching of the Word, but by the washing of water by the Word (Ephes. v. 26). The Church is one, not only because it is one in Christian opinion, or one in knowledge, or one in the possession of the Scriptures, but because it partakes of one Eucharistic Bread (1 Cor. x. 16, 17). Even what Christians eat is "sanctified by the word of God and prayer" (1 Tim. iv. 5). Angels are in their assemblies (xi. 10; Heb. xii. 22). Even whilst on earth they belong to the heavenly Jerusalem, they are in communion not only with one another, but with the general assembly and Church of the first-born, and with the spirits of just men made perfect (Heb. xii. 23). Such is St. Paul's idea of the Church, even of such a branch of it so imperfect as the Corinthian part of it; and we must carry with us all this in the reading of every verse of his Epistles. If we commit the folly of measuring him by Luther or Calvin, or the Puritans, or even by our best English Reformers, we mistake him and his teaching.

and the unbelieving wife is sanctified by the husband: else ° were your children unclean; but now are they holy. ° Mal. ii. 15.

14. "By the husband." ℵ, A., B., C., D., E., F., G., P., 17, 19, 46, d, e, f, g, Copt., Basm., read, "by the brother;" K., L., most Cursives, Vulg., Syriac, Arm., Æth., Goth., read, "husband."

Now let us apply these ideas of the Apostle of a great mixed body, being holy because of its profession and dedication, to the elucidation of the question: Has the Apostle the Baptism of Infants in his mind when he writes, "Else were your children unclean, but now are they holy"?

It has been said that the passage is against the practice of Infant Baptism in the Apostle's time, for he would have hardly founded an argument on the derivation of the children's holiness from their Christian parent or parents, if there had been a distinct act by which the children had themselves been admitted into the Christian Society. (Stanley.) Now to this it may be answered, that the Apostle knows of no holiness (among heathens, at least), apart from the Christian Church, and he asserts very distinctly, that that holiness comes not on the first act of belief, but through Baptism. (Ephes. v. 26; 1 Corinth. xii. 13; Titus iii. 5.) But those who thus lay down that this place is against the practice, assert equally strongly that the passage asserts the principle on which Infant Baptism is founded; thus (from the same commentator), "The children of Christian parents may therefore be considered as among the people of God, and from this would follow the natural consequence, that the whole family would participate in the same rites as belonged properly, and in the highest sense, only to those members, or that member of it who was strictly a believer."

But here we are asked to assume, that there was no practice of Infant Baptism, and yet that the words of St. Paul contain the whole principle of it. Surely he was a man who would understand the principles which underlay what he wrote, and would carry them out. If we bear in mind our Lord's treatment of infants, and what He said about them, as in some spiritual respects superior to adults —if we bear in mind the analogy of circumcision, and such a prophecy as that cited by St. Peter in Acts ii. 39—if we bear in mind that the Baptism not only of individuals, but of whole households, is expressly mentioned, and that children are addressed in

15 But if the unbelieving depart, let him depart. A

---

the Epistles to the Ephesians and Colossians, as members of the Christian Church just as much as their baptized elders (Ephes. vi. 1, Colos. iii. 20), then we see that the assertion by St. Paul that certain children of a Christian parent or parents were holy, postulates their Baptism. Of course, if we believe that St. Paul's views of the Church and its ordinances were those of Zwingle, then this assertion of his does not assume Baptism; but if his views respecting the Church and its ordinances were those which the Catholic Church has ever held, then it does.

This place, if taken simply and barely by itself, without reference to anything which St. Paul had written or our Lord had said, does not assume the practice of Infant Baptism; but if it be taken in connection with what St. Paul writes elsewhere respecting the holiness of the whole body of the Church and the sanctity of the several members of their bodies, and all this depending upon or assuming Baptism, then it does.

15. "But if the unbelieving depart, let him depart. A brother or a sister is not," &c. This means, apparently, If the unbelieving depart, you are under no obligation to attempt to live with him against his will, or to compel the unbeliever to live with you. You are not under such bondage in such cases. But the question further arises (and it is doubtful to me whether it is contemplated by the Apostle), do the words, "not under bondage," mean that they are at liberty—if finally deserted—to contract another marriage? Commentators of decided Catholic opinions have pronounced that they may. Thus Bishop Wordsworth: "Although a Christian may not put away his wife, being an unbeliever, yet, if the wife desert her husband, he may contract a second marriage." And Estius: "ut sensus sit. Christianum et Christianam cum infidelibus matrimonio copulatos, in hujusmodi rebus seu casibus, cujusmodi videlicet sermo proxime præcedens comprehendit, non esse subjectos servitute; ut vel inupti manere, vel cum conjugibus remanere, eisve digressis reconciliari debeant." Also Cornelius à Lapide: "Nota Apostolum permittere hoc casu non tantum thori devortium sed etiam matrimonii: ita ut possit conjux fidelis aliud matrimonium inire."

Chrysostom (here, at least), does not contemplate the Apostle referring to the Christian party who is deserted being permitted to marry again. "But what is the meaning of let the unbelieving

CHAP. VII.] GOD HATH CALLED TO PEACE. 105

brother or a sister is not under bondage in such *cases:* but God hath called us ᵖ † to peace.

16 For what knowest thou, O wife, whether thou shalt ᵍ save *thy* husband? or † how knowest thou, O man, whether thou shalt save *thy* wife?

17 But as God hath distributed to every man,

p Rom. xii. 18.
& xiv. 19.
ch. xiv. 33.
Heb. xii. 14.
† Gr. *in peace.*
q 1 Pet. iii. 1.
† Gr. *what.*

---

15. "Called us." So B., D., E., F., G., L., most Cursives, Ital, Vulg., Syriac, &c.; but ℵ, C., K., read, "you."

depart? For instance, if he bid thee sacrifice and take part in his ungodliness on account of thy marriage, or part company, it were better the marriage were annulled, and no breach made in godliness. If day by day he buffet thee, and keep up combats on this account, it is better to separate. For this is what he glances at, saying, 'But God hath called us unto peace.'"

"God hath called us to peace," or, "in peace." This must be taken in conjunction with "let him depart," *i.e.*, rather than by his presence and idolatrous practices be the constant occasion of wrangling and division. Or it may mean, if taken in connection with the usual meaning assigned to the next verse, Do what you can, consistent with your duty to God, to maintain peace, even when the husband or wife is unbelieving.

16. "For what knowest thou, O wife, whether thou shalt save thy husband?" There is a remarkable difference among commentators respecting the meaning of this verse; some asserting that it means, Do all you can to preserve union, in order that you may convert your unbelieving yoke-fellow, as St. Peter says, "If any obey not the word, they also may without the word be won by the conversation of the wives" (1 Pet. iii. 1). Others, on the contrary, interpret it as meaning, Let the unbeliever depart: hazard not for an uncertainty the peace in which you ought to be living as Christians, for what assurance have you that you will convert your unbelieving partners? it is most unlikely. So Alford. I need hardly say that the former way of taking the passage sounds the more Christian.

17. "But as God hath distributed to every man, as the Lord hath called," &c. The connection of the verse with what precedes is difficult and uncertain. Something of this sort seems to be the meaning. I have (in verse 15) asserted your liberty, that you are not in bondage, and so may change your state as regards your

as the Lord hath called every one, so let him walk. And ^r so ordain I in all churches.

18 Is any man called being circumcised? let him not become uncircumcised. Is any called in uncircumcision? ^s let him not be circumcised.

19 ^t Circumcision is nothing, and uncircumcision is nothing, but ^u the keeping of the commandments of God.

<small>r ch. iv. 17.
2 Cor. xi. 28.

s Acts xv. 1, 5, 19, 24, 28.
Gal. v. 2.
t Gal. v. 6. & vi. 15.
u John xv. 14.
1 John ii. 3.
& iii. 24.</small>

---

heathen partner; but this is to be held with this reservation—that God does not intend His religion to alter the social state of those whom He calls. For instance, the military life had connected with it much that seemed contrary to the Gospel, and yet it was quite possible that Christian soldiers might continue loyal servants both of God and of Cæsar. And so, if a person was called being married, he or she was not to seek occasion to change that condition, rather the contrary.

"And so ordain I in all churches." I do not merely recommend this as a Christian brother, but I ordain it as an Apostle, and would have men observe the rule which I lay down, that Christian liberty is not to make men loose to social bonds or relations. And now he gives two instances in point.

18. "Is any man called being circumcised? let him not become," &c. Let him not become so as to appear uncircumcised. Josephus alludes to this as undergone by apostate Jews, who desired to live as Gentiles: this happened in the time of Antiochus. (Ant. xii. v. sec. 1. See also 1 Mac. i. 11.)

18. "Is any called in uncircumcision? let him not be circumcised." That is, under the influence of Judaizing teachers. Let him not put himself under a law from the bondage of which Christ by His own obedience to the law has delivered him.

19. "Circumcision is nothing, and uncircumcision is nothing," &c. This, of course, is said with reference to the new standing of Christians in Christ. Before the coming of Christ it could not have been said without contravening the express words of God in Gen. xvii. 14: "The uncircumcised man child whose flesh of his foreskin is not circumcised, that soul shall be cut off from his people; he hath broken my covenant." But now that Christ was revealed and preached, "neither circumcision availeth anything, nor uncir-

CHAP. VII.]   USE IT RATHER.   107

20 Let every man abide in the same calling wherein he was called.

21 Art thou called *being* a servant? care not for it: but if thou mayest be made free, use *it* rather.

---

cumcision, but a new creature," and "in Christ Jesus neither circumcision availeth anything, nor uncircumcision, but faith which worketh by love" (Gal. v. 6, vi. 15).

20. "Let every man abide in the same calling wherein he was called." We are told that "calling" here cannot mean what we now designate "calling," *i.e.*, profession or manner of life. Grammatically it may not, but it is exceedingly difficult to explain it, especially to an English reader, except as referring to the calling in life. The calling, *i.e.*, the Divine calling, was to be a Christian, but the Apostle cannot possibly mean to say God's calling has called you to be a Christian, continue a Christian, do not apostatize. On the contrary he gives two illustrations of what this "calling" is, calling in circumcision, or calling in liberty—that is as a free man, in opposition to a slave, or *vice versâ*.

21. "Art thou called, being a servant [rather, slave]? care not." "Be not over anxious to become a freedman. God will temper thy servitude, and will make it, if thou committest thy way to Him, the means of thy greater spiritual freedom, and thy progress in the Divine life."

"But if thou mayest be made free, use it rather." This seems to mean, "If thou hast the opportunity of becoming free, seize the opportunity." But a singular diversity of opinion has prevailed upon the meaning of the place, most of the ancients and some moderns interpreting it as meaning, "If thou canst be made free, still abide in thy former state—continue in slavery, rather than not abide in the calling in which thou hast been called."

But verse 23 seems to render impossible such a meaning of the Apostle's words here.

Augustine (cited in Wordsworth) says that a man is to abide in his calling, if it be not hurtful to faith or morals; but slavery among the heathen involved many requirements contrary to both.

Respecting the two interpretations, "Take advantage of the offer of freedom," or "Remain in slavery though the offer is made," Dean Stanley remarks, "It is one of the most evenly balanced questions in the interpretation of the New Testament." The con-

22 For he that is called in the Lord, *being* a servant, is ˣthe Lord's † freeman : likewise also he that is called, *being* free, is ʸ Christ's servant.

23 ᶻ Ye are bought with a price; be not ye the servants of men.

ˣ John viii. 36.
Rom. vi. 18, 22. Philem. 16.
† Gr. *made free*.
ʸ ch. ix. 21.
Gal. v. 13.
Eph. vi. 6.
1 Pet. ii. 16.
ᶻ ch. vi. 20.
1 Pet. i. 18, 19.
See Lev. xxv. 42.

---

23. "Ye are bought." "Ye were bought."

duct of St. Paul himself in asserting his political freedom as a Roman citizen, seems to assure us that he valued it very greatly; and, if so, he would hardly say, "Even though thou canst be emancipated continue in slavery," but rather, "If thou art able, be as free as I am."

22. "For he that is called in the Lord, being a servant, is the Lord's freeman." He has been made free by Christ from the worst of all bondages, that of sin. He is free to serve God in his body, as well as in his spirit, which are God's. He is free whilst serving his earthly master to earn the highest possible reward—even an eternal one; for the Apostle teaches that if slaves do their duty to their earthly masters as to Christ they will receive the reward of the inheritance, for they serve the Lord Christ (Coloss. iii. 24).

"Likewise also he that is called, being free, is Christ's servant." The yoke of sin is broken from his neck, but he comes under the yoke of Christ. St. Paul was freeborn, and yet he delights to call himself the slave of Christ. In body, soul, and spirit he held that he belonged to Him Who had purchased him with His Blood.

23. "Ye are bought with a price; be not ye the servants of men." There seems to be an analogy between the emption of the Christian, in that a price has been paid for him, and the emption of the slave, in that he also has been bought, which decides the meaning of this verse: "Ye have been bought with a price, even with the precious Blood of Christ, that you should be His slaves. Now you can serve Him in continuing in submission to your earthly masters, for He will account that which you do for them as done to Him (Ephes. vi. 7, 8; Coloss. iii. 22), but you can serve Him best in a state of freedom. If free you can no more be compelled to take part in idolatrous worship or live in a house where all sorts of licentiousness prevails. Your time will be your own,

CHAP. VII.]   THEREIN ABIDE WITH GOD.   109

24 Brethren, [a] let every man, wherein he is called, therein abide with God.

[a] ver. 20.

that you can in a greater degree employ it in the active service of Christ." Such an interpretation is in accordance with what I cannot but think is, on Christian grounds, the natural interpretation of verse 21, "If thou mayest be made free, use it rather."

Many, however, take a different view. Bengel takes it as meaning, "If you are free do not sell yourself to be a slave." Principal Edwards, after Chrysostom, takes it as signifying, "Though you may be slaves in external condition, be not slaves in spirit;" but the whole context—indeed, the whole chapter, is occupied with external conditions, not with inward spiritual states.

24. "Brethren, let every man, wherein he is called, therein abide with God." This is a re-assertion of verse 20. What is the significance of the repetition? Evidently this: That Christianity, or the Church of Christ, should not have the ill name of being an institution disorganizing human society, but rather binding it together. Whatever we may think of enforced servitude, it was not only tolerated by God amongst His ancient people, but laws (sometimes severe ones) were laid down for its regulation. It could not be then, at that time, wrong in heathendom. No worse accusation could be brought against Christianity than that it unloosed what were then held to be the first principles of society. It would in time unloose them. Its first principles would first mitigate slavery, and afterwards abolish it. But this, of necessity, must be a matter of time, and postulated the conversion of the Empire to the nominal profession of Christianity, before it could be brought about.

This verse is to be taken, not as if it forbade the Christian changing his state of servitude for that of freedom if he could lawfully do so; but that he was to be in no haste about it. He was to remember that he could most effectually serve God whilst he was serving his earthly master, and that he was not to bring a scandal upon the Church by making men think that the spirit of the Church was one of insubordination.[1]

25. "Now concerning virgins I have no commandment of the Lord: yet," &c. He now comes to the case of young unmarried

---

[1] "The principle has been of incalculable importance in the development of the Church. It is by means of it that Christianity has been able to become a moral power at once sufficiently firm and sufficiently elastic to adapt itself to all human situations, personal

25 Now concerning virgins ᵇI have no commandment of the Lord: yet I give my judgment, as one ᶜthat hath obtained mercy of the Lord ᵈto be faithful.

26 I suppose therefore that this is good for the present ‖ distress, *I say,* ᵉthat *it is* good for a man so to be.

ᵇ ver. 6, 10, 40. 2 Cor. viii. 8, 10.
ᶜ 1 Tim. i. 16.
ᵈ ch. iv. 2. 1 Tim. i. 12.
‖ Or, *necessity*.
ᵉ ver. 1, 8.

---

women living in their fathers' houses: and who, it is to be remembered, were, as regards marriage, altogether under the control of the father: but he does not specifically consider their case till further on, in verse 36. His words till that verse apply to the unmarried in general, whether males or females.

"I have no commandment of the Lord." This has been taken to mean, "There is no specific commandment of Christ which I can cite as a general rule," as there was in verse 10; but need we restrict the allusion to the words of Christ as found in the Gospels, or in the current tradition? May not Christ, amongst the abundant revelations given to this Apostle, have given particular directions upon some things, as upon the Lord's Supper (xi. 23), and left him to his own enlightened judgment upon others? And so he goes on to say:—

"Yet I give my judgment, as one that hath obtained mercy of the Lord to be faithful." "To be faithful." The mercy of the Lord extends to this, that I should give a faithful, *i.e.,* trustworthy judgment upon things which are not matters of life and death, but which still have to do with Christian and Church life. As he has to say what he is about to say on his own authority, he puts that authority on the humblest and most unassuming ground: "he has obtained mercy to be faithful."

26. "I suppose therefore that this is good for the present distress." "The present distress." This has been taken as referring to the "distress of nations and perplexity," prophesied of by the Lord in Matthew xxiv., as immediately preceding His Second Coming, which the Apostles thought to be very near at hand; but may it not also refer to the persecutions of the Church which had begun before the writing of this Epistle, and which are always

---

domestic, national, and social. Thereby it is that, without revolution, it has worked the greatest revolutions, accepting everything to transform everything, submitting to everything to rise above everything, renewing the world from top to bottom, while condemning all violent subversion."—GODET.

CHAP. VII.] TROUBLE IN THE FLESH. 111

27 Art thou bound unto a wife? seek not to be loosed. Art thou loosed from a wife? seek not a wife.

28 But and if thou marry, thou hast not sinned; and if a virgin marry, she hath not sinned. Nevertheless such shall have trouble in the flesh: but I spare you.

29 But ᶠ this I say, brethren, the time *is* short:

ᶠ Rom. xiii. 11. 1 Pet. iv. 7. 2 Pet. iii. 8, 9.

assumed to be ready at any moment to burst upon it? Thus in Acts xiv. 22 we read of the Apostle long before the writing of this Epistle, "Confirming the souls of the disciples, and exhorting them to continue in the faith, and that we must through much tribulation enter into the kingdom of God."

They who have no wives or children are more independent of the world: they have not given hostages to it, as the saying is.

27. "Art thou bound unto a wife? seek not to be loosed," *i.e.*, by living separately, for the Apostle, in obedience to his Lord's command, could allow no divorce.

"Art thou loosed from a wife?" *i.e.*, "art thou free from the marriage tie?" Not, of course, in any other sense.

28. "But and if thou marry, thou hast not sinned; and if a virgin marry," &c. God instituted marriage, and therefore anyone who enters into the state commits no sin by so doing. But though perfectly lawful it may not be expedient, especially during times of persecution, such as I foresee are coming. "Such as marry shall have trouble in the flesh," *i.e.*, in their human relationship. Their partners and their children must in the ordinary course of things share in the troubles and distresses which they themselves suffer from the enmity of the world.

"But I spare you." The significance of this advice is also much disputed. Dean Stanley mentions two meanings: 1. "I refrain from dilating on these evils, to save you from the pain of hearing them; or, 2, I give you this advice to save you from these afflictions." Meyer agrees with the latter. "But I, for my part, deal tenderly with you, in advising you rather to remain unwedded; for by this advice, if you follow it, I spare you from such trouble."

29. "But this I say, brethren, the time is short: it remaineth," &c. The time is short. The word translated short (συνεσταλμένος) occurs only once elsewhere in the New Testament—in Acts v. 6,

it remaineth, that both they that have wives be as though they had none;

---

with reference to the wrapping up of the body of Ananias, or, perhaps, the making straight of his limbs. In accordance with this it is used here in the sense of being contracted, and so shortened.

Most expositors take the word "that" (ἵνα) as indicating the design of God; the time is short (or shortened) that henceforth "both they that have wives," &c.

It may be asked, Was the Apostle in the words "the time is short," referring to the nearness of the Lord's Second Coming, which all through the Apostolic age was thought to be impending? If so, his mind was in accordance with the mind of Christ, Who even in His own lifetime on earth, before He rose again and ascended, laid it on His followers that they should look for His Second Coming rather than for the day of their own deaths. They were always to live in the constant expectation of an event which might take place at any moment. In looking for this Coming then even in their own lifetime they were not mistaken. They were always in the very attitude of mind in which the Lord desired them to be—men who were waiting for their Lord, that the moment He knocked they might run and open to Him, for it might be at even, or at the midnight, or at the cock-crowing, or in the morning. And what He said to them, He said to all, "Watch." They were to regard the world then as if it had no certain lease of time, as it were, given to it. So far as it knows, or so far as God has revealed, the present state of things might have come, or now may come, to a sudden termination at any moment.

Now the Christian who is alive to this—*i.e.*, who has the mind of Christ and His Apostle—will always be loose to a world which has so uncertain a tenure of existence as this world has.

With respect to the marriage tie, the closest of all human bonds, he should ever remember that it is human, and the day will suddenly burst upon us, in which they who attain the resurrection from the dead will neither marry nor be given in marriage, but will be as the angels of God in heaven. Scarcely anything can be added to the words of Wesley on the detachment from the world set forth in these verses: "The time of our abode here is short. It plainly follows that even those who have wives be as serious, zealous, active, dead to the world, as devoted to God, as holy in all

CHAP. VII.] WITHOUT CAREFULNESS. 113

30 And they that weep, as though they wept not; and they that rejoice, as though they rejoiced not; and they that buy, as though they possessed not;

31 And they that use this world, as not ᵍabusing *it*: for ʰ the fashion of this world passeth away.

32 But I would have you without carefulness. ⁱHe that is unmarried careth for the things †that belong to the Lord, how he may please the Lord:

g ch. ix. 18.
h Ps. xxxix. 6. Jam. i. 10. & iv. 14. 1 Pet. i. 24. & iv. 7. 1 John ii. 17.
i 1 Tim. v. 5.
+ Gr. *of the Lord*, as ver. 34.

---

manner of conversation as if they had none. By so easy a transition does the Apostle slide from eveiything else to the one thing needful; and forgetting whatever is temporal, is swallowed up in eternity."

30, 31. " And they that weep, as though they wept not "—though sorrowful, yet alway rejoicing. "And they that rejoice, as though they rejoiced not." Tempering their joy with godly fear. " They that buy, as though they possessed not." Knowing themselves to be only stewards, not proprietors. "And they that use this world, as not abusing it." Not seeking happiness in it, but in God : using everything therein only in such a manner and degree as most tends to the knowledge and love of God. " For the whole scheme and fashion of this world . . . this marrying, weeping, rejoicing, and all the rest not only will pass, but now passeth away—is this moment flying off like a shadow." ¹

" They that use this world, as not abusing it." Revisers translate in margin, " as not using it to the full."

32, 33. " But I would have you without carefulness . . . please his wife." The Apostle having finished this short digression upon looseness to the world, because of its instability, as having no certainty of continuance, returns now to the subject of verse 28: " I would have you to be unencumbered with earthly cares; so that

---

1 St. Paul may possibly have had a reminiscence of a passage of the Second Book of Esdras in his mind (xvi. 40-44): " In those evils be even as pilgrims on the earth. He that sitteth let him be as he that fleeth away, and he that buyeth as one that will lose; he that occupieth merchandise as he that hath no profit by it, and he that buildeth as he that shall not dwell therein ; he that soweth as if he should not reap, so also he that planteth as he that shall not gather the grapes. They that marry as they that shall get no children, and they that marry not as the widowers."

I

33 But he that is married careth for the things that are of the world, how he may please *his* wife.

34 There is difference *also* between a wife and a virgin. The unmarried woman [k] careth for the things of the Lord, that she may be holy both in body and in spirit: but she that is married careth for the things of the world, how she may please *her* husband.

[k] Luke x. 40, &c.

33, 34. " How he may please his wife." Vulg. joins to this the first words of next verse : " quomodo placeat uxori et divisus est."

The readings are very uncertain. I can only refer the reader to the notes in Tischendorf and Tregelles, if he desire to compare them, which, however, make no difference to the sense. The Revisers give two in their margin.

your thoughts may not be distracted by them, but may be more continuously employed upon the things of God."

The Apostle assumes here a very high standard of devotion to Christ amongst the early Christian. It is not so now. Very frequently an unmarried man is one of the most selfish of men, spending most, if not all, his income upon himself, pleasing himself, giving nothing to others in comparison to what he might give: whereas the married man has to spend all on others—on their food, clothing, education; and so, even though he may be comparatively without religion, his selfishness at least is corrected in some measure. He is forced, if he has any decent human feeling (putting out of the question religious feeling), to think more about others than about himself, and this is very much to his moral advantage.

34 (and latter part of 33). " There is a difference also between a wife and a virgin. The unmarried woman," &c. The difference of punctuation, and the various readings of this passage make its meaning somewhat uncertain. The Revised version (1881) in its text is pretty nearly the same as the Authorized: " He that is married is careful for the things of the world, how he may please his wife. And there is a difference also between the wife and the virgin. She that is unmarried is careful for the things of the Lord." But in the margin the words, "there is a difference also," are rendered, " and is divided," and are taken with the latter part of the thirty-third verse: "He that is married is careful for the things of the world, how he may please his wife, and [so] is divided,"

CHAP. VII.]   WITHOUT DISTRACTION.   115

35 And this I speak for your own profit; not that I may cast a snare upon you, but for that which is comely, and that ye may attend upon the Lord without distraction.

36 But if any man think that he behaveth himself un-

---

i.e., he is divided between the world and the Lord. And there follows, "So also the wife and the virgin: she that is unmarried is careful," &c.

But there is also another difference of reading affecting the sense. The Codex Alexandrinus, and the Vulgate, put the full stop after "is divided," and read, "And the unmarried woman and the unmarried virgin (καὶ ἡ γυνὴ ἡ ἄγαμος καὶ ἡ παρθένος ἡ ἄγαμος) is careful for the things of the Lord, that she may be," &c.

But whichever way we settle the punctuation and readings, the Apostle's teaching is the same as prevails throughout the rest of this part of this chapter, that the unmarried state, both of the male and the female, has the advantage of being less in danger of being influenced by "present things."

35. "And this I speak for your own profit"—not to assert my authority in any way, or to force you to do as I am doing.

"Not that I may cast a snare upon you," *i.e.*, throw a net or noose over you. The metaphor is taken from hunting. Bishop Ellicott explains it as pointing, not to any snare of conscience which the Apostle might thus be laying for them, but simply to the coercive character which the command might carry with it, but which the Apostle here disavows.

"But for that which is comely" (or seemly). Meyer aptly explains this as such a manifestation of the inner life in all outward embodiment, as corresponds with consecration to the Lord.

"And that ye may attend upon the Lord without distraction." Commentators agree in supposing that St. Paul must have had in his mind Martha and her distraction (περιεσπᾶτο, Luke x. 40; ἀπερισπάστως, here).

Again let me remind the reader that though St. Paul was evidently on the side of celibacy, he had before him a state of society which was pervaded through and through with the desire of serving Christ, and not, as at present, a society permeated with the love of self.

36. "But if any man think that he behaveth himself uncomely

comely toward his virgin, if she pass the flower of *her* age, and need so require, let him do what he will, he sinneth not: let them marry.

37 Nevertheless he that standeth stedfast in his heart, having no necessity, but hath power over his own will, and

---

toward his virgin, if she pass," &c. To realize this verse we must remember that in Corinth, which was a colonia, the Roman law prevailed, that a man had absolute power over his family, particularly his unmarried daughters. It was not so much a matter of their choosing to be married, as if they had free will in the matter, but of his *giving* them in marriage.

And the Apostle seems to assume that there would be no difficulty about this—that there would be persons as ready to take his unmarried daughter as he would be to give her. A man then living in this state of things would deliberate *for* his daughter, whether she should serve the Lord by continuing unmarried, or whether he should give her in marriage. If such an one takes into consideration that his daughter is now of a marriageable age—in fact, that she may be passing that time, and that he is treating her in an unseemly way by not giving her in marriage, and need so require (*i.e.*, as Alford suggests, there may be danger to her living in chastity), "Let him do what he will." Since marriage is an holy estate, and ordained by God, he sinneth not; let them—*i.e.*, the maid and her lover—marry.

37. "Nevertheless he that standeth stedfast in his heart, having no necessity." I confess that the meaning of the Apostle in this verse is exceedingly difficult, because he here seems to pass from the idea of keeping his virgin, *i.e.*, his unmarried daughter, to the keeping of his own state of chastity, or rather celibacy. It seems to me as if through lapse of time or want of complete knowledge of the state of heathenism on the one side, or the Church on the other, we have lost some element necessary to the understanding of this verse.

I will give, however, a paraphrase of the verse on each of these two interpretations.

1. That the Apostle speaks of the father choosing for his virgin daughter, or ward. "He that stands firm of character, and therefore is not swayed by apprehension of this kind, having no necessity,

Chap. VII.] HE WILL KEEP HIS VIRGIN. 117

hath so decreed in his heart that he will keep his virgin, doeth well.

---

37. "Doeth well." So D., E., F., G., K., L., P., most Cursives, Itala, Vulg., Syriac, &c.; but ℵ, A., B., 6, 17, 46, 67**, Copt., Busm., read, "will do."

---

i.e., having no compulsion from his daughter's character or temptations, but hath power over his own will, *i.e.*, having the power of doing what he likes without regard to external circumstances (such as public opinion, which might severely blame him for keeping his daughter unmarried), and hath so decreed or determined in his heart that he will keep his virgin, *i.e.*, from the marriage state, or will keep her at home, doeth well."

2. That the Apostle speaks to a man himself with regard to his own celibacy. "If a man has no necessity; if, for example, he has incurred no obligations to marry by engaging himself to a particular woman, or if that engagement may be honourably dissolved, then it is expedient for him not to marry. But in that case he must also be sure that he has sufficient self-restraint to keep the virgin of himself (τὴν ἑαυτοῦ παρθένον), so that his abstinence from a lawful union may not lead him into unlawful excesses."

This last is from Mr. Blunt's annotations. It seems to me very much in accordance with the wording of this verse, but not in such accordance with what goes before, or comes after.[1]

38. "So then he that giveth her in marriage doeth well; but he that giveth," &c. In this verse the Apostle seems somewhat to

---

[1] The reader may thank me for giving the following from Godet: "This long sentence, loaded with incidental propositions, fully represents all the turnings which the father's original wish will have to take in order to reach at length a definite conclusion. This whole domestic drama has for its point of departure a firm conviction already formed in the father's mind, that celibacy is preferable to marriage for his child (ἕστηκεν ἑδραῖος); he has become and remains firm . . . . the father has become and remains firm, because there is nothing to hamper his liberty, neither the fear of opinion, nor the character and indomitable will of the virgin, nor too ardent a wish on the part of the mother. . . . . After measuring himself with all the difficulties of the situation, and finding none of them insurmountable, the father remains master of his own deliberate will, and may thus . . . . at length take the final resolution henceforth to refuse every offer for his daughter. These long circumlocutions do not at all suppose in him an arbitrary will which takes account of nothing but itself. On the contrary, they imply the fact that, before taking the final decision, everything has been heard, examined, weighed. . . . . The verb "to keep" does not signify to maintain his daughter as a virgin, but to keep her for the end to which she is consecrated—the service of Christ."

38 ¹ So then he that giveth *her* in marriage doeth well; but he that giveth *her* not in marriage doeth better.

39 ᵐ The wife is bound by the law as long as her husband liveth; but if her husband be dead, she is at liberty to be married to whom she will; ⁿ only in the Lord.

¹ Heb. xiii. 4.
ᵐ Rom. vii. 2.
ⁿ 2 Cor. vi. 14.

---

38. "Doeth"—"will do."
39. "By the law." Omitted by ℵ, A., B., D., Eᵃ, 17, 67, Vulg. (Cod. Am.), Basm., Arm., Æth., retained by E., F., G., L., P., most Cursives, and Syriac.

qualify what he had written in verse 36. There he had written somewhat disparagingly of marriage, "let him do what he will he sinneth not, let them marry:" here he writes, "he that giveth her in marriage doeth well," *i.e.*, he acts as a father, as a rule, acts in giving his daughter in marriage, and so fulfils the original institution of God.

"He that giveth her not in marriage doeth better." That is, he looks to the trials and temptations of life in the light of the "present distress;" he would have her "serve the Lord without distraction." In the then circumstances the one course of conduct is more Christian than the other.

39. "The wife is bound by the law as long as her husband liveth; but if her husband," &c. The Apostle here most probably answers very shortly a question which had been put to him respecting the second marriage of widows. Both Jews and heathens looked with somewhat of disapproval upon the second marriage of widows. The Jewish priest was to take a wife in her virginity, "a widow, or a divorced woman, or profane, or an harlot, these shall he not take." (Levit. xxi. 13, 14.) Again, the good example of the Jewish heroine Judith is mentioned to her credit, and the case of Anna the prophetess, who had continued a widow during a very long life, is recorded to her honour. Godet writes, that the heathen spoke contemptuously of the mulier multarum nuptiarum, and that they went the length of inscribing this title of honour on the tombstone of a woman, "univira." Here, however, the Apostle speaks with no disparagement of the second marriage of a widow. She is at liberty to be married to whom she will, but

"Only in the Lord," *i.e.*, only to one in the Lord, to a Christian, a member, like herself, of the Church of Christ.

40 But she is happier if she so abide, °after my judgment: and P I think also that I have the Spirit of God.

o ver. 25.
p 1 Thes. iv. 8.

40. "But she is happier if she so abide, after my judgment." After my judgment, *i.e.*, he had no specific command from Christ either in His discourses preserved in tradition, or in the Evangelists. So he is left by the Lord to act on his own enlightened judgment.

"And I think also that I have the Spirit of the Lord." This "I think" does not mean that he is uncertain, but he is quite assured that his private judgment is not alone, but is informed by the Spirit of God.

CHAP. VIII.

NOW ª as touching things offered unto idols, we know that we all have ᵇ know-

ª Acts xv. 20, 29. ch. x. 19.
ᵇ Rom. xiv. 14, 22.

1. " Now as touching things offered unto idols, we know that we all have knowledge." Here St. Paul proceeds to answer another question put to him by the Corinthians, one respecting the lawfulness of partaking in things offered unto idols. In this day we can scarcely realize how closely this question would affect the whole social life of the early Christians. For not only was the worship of the Gentiles sacrificial, but this worship was not confined to the temple precincts, but extended itself to their social gatherings, and even domestic meals. When an animal was offered in sacrifice to an idol, or to a false god represented by the idol, only a small part, such as the legs wrapped up in fat, or the intestines, were consumed by fire on the altar. The remainder was partaken of by the sacrificer and his friends, or those who were invited to the sacrificial feast, which took place either in the temple or in the adjoining grove, and to these sacrifices Christians might and would often be called (verse 10): or the remainder of the flesh, after what was burnt in honour of the idol, was claimed as their perquisite by the priests, and would be sold by them in the

ledge. ^cKnowledge puffeth up, but charity edifieth.

_{c Rom. xiv. 3, 10.}

---

shambles, and labelled as sacrificial, and the heathen would partake of it as meat of peculiar sanctity. The eating of these meats sacrificed to idols had been forbidden at the council held at Jerusalem, but this being the decree of a purely local Church would soon be considered in a measure obsolete by distant Churches, such as that at Corinth. Anyhow it seems from the question sent by the Corinthians to St. Paul not to have settled the matter, and they certainly wrote for the Apostle's direction as if they considered it an open question.

From the wording of the first verses it seems as if it had been put to the Apostle by those who took the side of liberty in this matter. They had framed the question in terms which implied that they thought there could be little doubt about the answer. They had boasted somewhat of their knowledge respecting the absolute nothingness of the objects of heathen worship, and St. Paul, perhaps somewhat ironically, took them at their word. "We know that we all have knowledge," if as Christians we know anything. If the Revelation of God in the Church has made us to know any single thing, it is the vanity and folly of idolatrous worship. But we have not compassed this knowledge of ourselves. God has given it to us, and like all other gifts of God it may be used improperly to our loss, or legitimately to our eternal gain. It is used to our loss if we dwell complacently upon the difference which it has made between us and the heathen. It then becomes the source of pride and self-complacency. It puffs us up with self-conceit. It is used to our eternal gain if it makes us regard those who worship false gods with loving pity, and strive to do nothing which may put a stumblingblock in their way, so that they should think that we regard their idolatry with indifference. And this our knowledge leads us into sin against our weaker brethren, if seeing us partaking of meat offered to idols they are emboldened to do the same, and eat with offence, *i.e.*, with sin, because they have a secret persuasion that there is something in an idol, as the representative or embodiment of a real evil existence.

"Knowledge puffeth up, but charity edifieth." This is a maxim of universal truth. Mere knowledge, even of divine things, unsanctified by the Spirit of God, inflates its possessor—makes him

CHAP. VIII.] THE SAME IS KNOWN OF HIM. 121

2 And ^d if any man think that he knoweth any thing, he knoweth nothing yet as he ought to know.

3 But if any man love God, ^e the same is known of him.

4 As concerning therefore the eating of those things that are offered in sacrifice unto idols, we

^d ch. xiii. 8, 9, 12. Gal. vi. 3. 1 Tim. vi. 4.
^e Exod. xxxiii. 12, 17. Nah. i. 7. Matt. vii. 23. Gal. iv. 9. 2 Tim. ii. 19.

---

constantly compare himself with others to his own advantage, whereas love or charity builds him up. Mere knowledge isolates him, and gives him the vices of isolation; whereas love builds him up as one stone in the great spiritual building of many stones. He is not by himself. He rests upon others. He is surmounted by others. He is encircled by others. He is cemented to those near him and so to all in the building. Love does away with the inherent selfishness of our possession of knowledge in that such possession leads a man to contemplate himself, whereas love leads him to contemplate others with the view of benefiting them.

2. "And if any man think that he knoweth any thing, he knoweth nothing," &c. Here the Apostle is lead to notice another defect of knowledge, which, if duly realized, would hinder us from being inflated by it. All knowledge is imperfect. The more real our knowledge is of any thing, the more we feel that we know it only in part. And this should make us humble. The idea entertained in us that we know anything really, so as to have mastered it, is a sign of our own ignorance. Now this applies to our knowledge of God, the true God, as compared with the variety of false gods. We can only know Him by love. No description of Him, no definition of Him can make us know as those do who love Him. They who love Him are known of Him, because they have intercourse with Him, and this mutual intercourse enables them to know Him personally (if we may so say), and there is no knowledge that can come near to this. But this knowledge comes by love—not by definition, not by mere contemplation of His attributes, but by loving, trustful prayer.

4. "As concerning therefore the eating of those things that," &c. In verses 2 and 3 he had been somewhat digressing. They had asserted their knowledge (γνῶσις), and he turns aside for a moment to tell them that this question required another element

know that ᶠan idol *is* nothing in the world, ᵍand that *there is* none other God but one.

5 For though there be that are ʰcalled gods,

ᶠ Is. xli. 24. ch. x. 19.
ᵍ Deu. iv. 39. & vi. 4. Isai. xliv. 8. Mark xii. 29. ver. 6. Eph. iv. 6. 1 Tim. ii. 5.
ʰ John x. 34.

---

for its solution, even love. Now he returns. "As concerning what you wrote to me about, we know that an idol is nothing in the world." He seems to mean by this that the Deity represented by the statue or idol had no existence except in the imagination of the worshippers. Ellicott translates it, "there is no idol in the world," *i.e.*, nothing corresponding to the representation. The Revisers render it, "no idol is anything in the world."

But how is this to be reconciled with 1 Cor. x. 20, where it is said in a quotation from Deut. xxxii. 17 ("They sacrificed to devils (demons) and not to God)," that those who sacrifice to false gods do not sacrifice to nonentities, but to demons having a real existence? The reconciliation seems easy. The Greek and Roman deities, Zeus, Aphrodite, &c., were not merely the creatures of poetical imagination, but the inspirations of evil spirits. No personifying of the powers of nature seems to me at all adequate to produce mythologies so elaborate, so beautiful, and yet so intensely wicked. The heathen then sacrificed to evil spirits, to images of the imagination, which were the creations of the enemy and his angels; and so the worship was rightly accounted to be demon-worship. Evil spirits may have made use of natural phenomena to give some colour or consistence of truth to the evil creations with which they peopled sky, earth, and ocean, but that is all. All that is personal in the conceptions of these gods seems to me not natural, but demoniacal. As Bishop Wordsworth well says, "Worship offered to any but the one true God, is accounted by God to be offered to devils which do exist, although it be offered by man to idols (*e.g.*, Jupiter, Venus, Bacchus), which do not exist."

"And that there is none other God but one." There is no being in the whole universe, seen or unseen, who can act as God in creating, preserving, restoring, saving, illuminating, sanctifying, except the one God.

5. "For though there be that are called gods, whether in heaven," &c. The Apostle's meaning in this verse is somewhat

CHAP. VIII.]   ONE GOD, THE FATHER.   123

whether in heaven or in earth, (as there be gods many, and lords many,)

6 But [1] to us *there is but* one God, the Father, [k] of whom *are* all things, and we ∥ in him; and

[1] Mal. ii. 10. Eph. iv. 6.
[k] Acts xvii. 28. Rom. xi. 36.
∥ Or, *for him*.

difficult to catch. He seems to mean something of this kind: " I have said that an idol is nothing, and though there may be evil representations of things in heaven and earth which are called gods, they possess nothing of Divine power; and though in the Old Testament continual reference is made to 'gods' and 'lords,' meaning by these either the principalities and powers in heavenly places, or the rulers of the darkness of this world."

"But to us," &c. The term "gods" is constantly applied to beings in the unseen world; thus, "Ye shall be as gods, knowing good and evil" (Gen. iii. 5); to human magistrates, perhaps, "Thou shalt not revile the gods" (Exod. xxii. 28). Again, when the true God is constantly called "the God of gods," it seems to mean much more than that He is the God of things which are non-existent. Again, the witch says to Saul, "I saw gods ascending out of the earth." Anyhow, the Apostle seems to imply that there may be beings which from the supernatural power with which God has gifted them may be in some appropriate sense called gods and lords.

6. "But to us there is but one God, the Father, of Whom are all things, and," &c. The Father is the Person of the Trinity in Whom is essentially the Godhead. The Son is God, because He is the Son. The Son is "of," *i.e.*, from the Father alone. He is God of, or out of, God; Light out of Light; Very God out of Very God. The Apostle is here asserting Monotheism in opposition to Polytheism; and so he asserts that the oneness resides in the Father. The Father is here emphatically styled one God, but without design to exclude the Son from being God also, as the Son is emphatically styled "one Lord;" but without design to exclude the Father from being Lord also.[1]

---

[1] The following extract from Bishop Pearson is valuable: "This priority (of the Father) doth properly and naturally result from the Divine Paternity; so that the Son must necessarily be second unto the Father, from whom He receiveth His origination, and the Holy Ghost unto the Son. Neither can we be thought to want a sufficient foundation for this priority of the first Person of the Trinity, if we look upon the nume-

124 ONE LORD JESUS CHRIST. [I. Cor.

^l John xiii. 13.
Acts ii. 36.
ch. xii. 3.
Eph. iv. 5.
Phil. ii. 11.
^m John i. 3.
Col. i. 16.
Heb. i. 2.
ⁿ ch. x. 28, 29.
^o Rom. xiv. 14, 23.

^l one Lord Jesus Christ, ^m by whom *are* all things, and we by him.

7 Howbeit *there is* not in every man that knowledge: for some ⁿ with conscience of the idol unto this hour eat *it* as a thing offered unto an idol; and their conscience being weak is ^o defiled.

---

7. "With conscience," συνειδήσει. So D., E., F., G., L., most Cursives, Vulg., Syriac; but א, A., B., P., 17, 46, 67, 80, 109, Copt., Basm., read, συνηθείᾳ, "by familiarity." See below.

"Of whom are all things, and we in him." In Him should rather be "unto Him" (εἰς αὐτόν)—as all things proceed from Him, inasmuch as He is the fountain of all existence, so they all tend to Him, at least all regenerate natures do; for the Apostle says, "*we* to him," to His glory, to union with Him.

"And one Lord Jesus Christ, by whom (or through whom) are all things, and we by him (or through him)." By Him we came into existence. Thus John i. 3: "All things were made by him, and without him was not anything made that was made;" and by, or through, Him we approach to the Father of Spirits: "Through him we have access by one Spirit unto the Father" (Ephes. ii. 18).

7. "Howbeit there is not in every man that knowledge." Even in a church of men converted by the Holy Spirit from the worship of idols there are some who have not got over their former feeling that the idol represents a real existence, and so

"Some with conscience of the idol unto this hour, eat it as a thing offered," &c. There is a remarkable difference of reading here. Many MSS. instead of συνειδήσει read συνηθείᾳ, "familiar intercourse," "familiarity through use," "habituation." This reading

---

rous testimonies of the ancient doctors of the Church, who have not stuck to call the Father the origin, the cause, the author, the root, the fountain, and the Head of the Son, or the Whole Divinity.

"For by these titles it appeareth clearly, first, that they made a considerable difference between the Person of the Father, *of whom are all things*, and the Person of the Son, *by whom are all things*. Secondly, that the difference consisteth properly in this—that as the branch is from the root, and river from the fountain, and by their origination from them receive that being which they have; whereas the root receiveth nothing from the branch, or fountain from the river; so the Son is from the Father, receiving His subsistence by generation from Him; the Father is not from the Son, as being what He is from none" (Pearson, on Creed, "I believe in God the Father," 38).

MEAT COMMENDETH US NOT.

8 But [p]meat commendeth us not to God: for neither, if we eat, ||are we the better; neither, if we eat not, ||are we the worse.

9 But [q]take heed lest by any means this ||liberty of your's become [r]a stumblingblock to them that are weak.

10 For if any man see thee which hast know-

[p] Rom. xiv. 17.
|| Or, *have we the more.*
|| Or, *have we the less.*
[q] Gal. v. 13.
|| Or, *power.*
[r] Rom. xiv. 13, 20.

---

8. The two last clauses reversed in some MSS.: "neither, if we eat not, are we the worse; nor, if we eat," &c. So Revisers.

is adopted by the Revisers, "Some being used until now to the idol," or as Ellicott, "by their being accustomed until now to the idol." This latter reading, whether correct or not, expresses the true idea. They have so long and habitually worshipped the idol as a reality, or representing a reality, that they cannot shake this off. They have given up as sinful the worship of the false God, but believe in his existence, and so if they eat of what is offered to it, they secretly think that they are polluted. They are emboldened to do so, and doing it without firm faith they sin (Rom. xiv. 23).

8. "For meat commendeth us not to God, for neither if we eat are we the better," &c. Here he teaches, as he does in Rom. xiv., the absolute indifference of eating or abstaining of itself. If we eat freely what is offered to idols, we are not on that account acceptable to God, and if we eat not, we are not the worse before Him.

9. "But take heed lest by any means this liberty of yours become a stumbling-block," &c. "But though this eating or abstaining from eating, may be a matter of indifference to you individually, it may be a serious hindrance to your weaker brother, and if knowing this, you so make use of your liberty as to cause him to commit sin, you will yourself become guilty before God." And he gives an instance in point.

10. "For if any man see thee which hast knowledge sit at meat," &c. Here the Apostle supposes an extreme case, one which we cannot but think must have been rare, but we learn from such a thing being supposable, the laxity into which some of the Corinthians had fallen. Perhaps it is cited because, if a nominal Christian was seen thus eating in the temple precincts, there could be no doubt, respecting the meat he was eating, that it must have

ledge sit at meat in the idol's temple, shall not ˢ the conscience of him which is weak be †emboldened to eat those things which are offered to idols;

11 And ᵗ through thy knowledge shall the weak brother perish, for whom Christ died?

12 But ᵘ when ye sin so against the brethren, and wound their weak conscience, ye sin against Christ.

ˢ ch. x. 28, 32.
† Gr. *edified*.
ᵗ Rom. xiv. 15, 20.
ᵘ Matt. xxv. 40, 45.

---

11. "And through thy knowledge," &c. The Revisers render this verse, "For through thy knowledge he that is weak perisheth, the brother for whom Christ died."

been meat which had been offered to the idol; whereas in other cases there could not have been such certainty. The man who did this might not think that he was guilty of idolatry—he might do it, as we say, out of bravado, but both the heathen and the weak brethren must have looked upon the act as in some sense done in honour of the idol.

"Shall not the conscience of him that is weak be emboldened," &c. The word for "emboldened" is built up, or edified—instead of being built up in the temple of God, he is built up in the temple of idolatry.

11. "And through thy knowledge shall the weak brother perish, for whom Christ died?" The verse is not a question, as in our Authorized, but rather an assertion. Rendered literally and according to the reading most widely accepted, the verse runs, "For the weak one perishes through thy knowledge [through its abuse—through thy want of love] even the brother for whom Christ died."

This verse refutes the Calvinistic error, that all those for whom Christ died will be saved, for (according to such a doctrine) He died for the elect only, who will all be saved. On the contrary, the Apostle assumes that because of his eating sinfully and against his conscience, the man on whose behalf Christ shed His Blood, is falling again into perdition. And this because of the inconsiderate and uncharitable conduct of the man who has knowledge.

12. "But when ye sin so against the brethren, and wound their weak conscience, ye sin against Christ." Wonderful the identification of Christ with His people. When He converted Saul He

13 Wherefore ˣif meat make my brother to   ˣ Rom. xiv. 21.
                                            2 Cor. xi. 29.

---

identified Himself with the persecuted saints, "Saul, Saul, why persecutest thou Me?" and now through the mouth of His Apostle He identifies Himself with the weak. "When ye make the weak to sin through your want of consideration and sympathy, ye sin against their and your Head. Ye sin against Christ."

13. "Wherefore, if meat make my brother to offend, I will eat no flesh while," &c. Now, since some weak brethren were made to offend by seeing others eat of things sacrificed to idols, does this mean that St. Paul at the time he wrote this verse was abstaining, and would hereafter abstain, from animal food? We cannot believe such a thing. The assertion is hyperbolical, and yet must not be dismissed as meaning nothing. It means that if St. Paul certainly knew that some weak brother was so influenced by his example, that as long as St. Paul abstained he would abstain, and so keep a clear conscience and not otherwise, then St. Paul would touch meat no more till his death.

But it seems to me quite clear that this recommendation of abstinence from animal food depends on times and places. At that time, and in such a city as Corinth, the greater part of the animal sold in the shambles or set before guests at feasts, was that which had been offered to idols, and so the weak brother would constantly be in danger of sinning; but in a city where there were few or no such social conditions as those at Corinth, the Apostle would, we are sure, have given no such recommendation; for to do so would be to tell his converts that they must, of set purpose, reject a gift of God. This verse has been used to recommend, or rather to enforce, total abstinence from wine, because so many abuse such a gift of God. Now, if any Christian determines to abstain from wine or such like liquors, which, taken in excess, are intoxicating, for the sake of his weaker brethren, he does a good thing; but, as he values his soul, he must take heed of two things, first, not to pronounce a most certain gift of God an evil thing in itself, for wine is as distinctly a gift of God as animal food is, and so to be received temperately with thanksgiving; and, secondly, he must take heed not to use or countenance the abusive and violent language which abstainers as a rule hurl against those who do not abstain; for if, instead of reprobating such language, he

offend, I will eat no flesh while the world standeth, lest I make my brother to offend.

---

encourages it by his presence and silence, he will assuredly offend God and provoke Him to withdraw His grace from one who, though he might begin with good intentions, goes on to act so presumptuously.

CHAP. IX.

^a Acts ix. 15. & xiii. 2. & xxvi. 17. 2 Cor. xii. 12. Gal. ii. 7, 8. 1 Tim. ii. 7. 2 Tim. i. 11.
^b Acts ix. 3, 17. & xviii. 9. & xxii. 14, 18. & xxiii. 11. ch. xv. 8.
^c ch. iii. 6. & iv. 15.

AM [a] I not an apostle? am I not free? [b] have I not seen Jesus Christ our Lord? [c] are not ye my work in the Lord?

---

1. "Am I not an Apostle? am I not free?" So D., E., F., G., K., L., most Cursives, d, e, f, g, &c.; but ℵ, A., B., P., some eight or nine Cursives, Vulg., Syr., Copt., Arm., Æth., &c., invert, "Am I not free? am I not an apostle?"

1. "Am I not an apostle? am I not free? have I not seen," &c. It is very difficult to make out the connection between this and what has immediately preceded. Many commentators make the assertion of freedom the connecting link, as if he had said, I am asking you to give up your freedom, or to exercise it not arbitrarily, but looking to the spiritual condition of your weaker brethren. I do the same. I am free, as the other Apostles are, to forbear manual labour for my own support, but I choose rather to labour, so that I may not be chargeable to you, but may minister the word of God to you without payment. In accordance with this, some of the best MSS., as the reader will see by the critical note, put the words, "Am I not free?" before "Am I not an Apostle?"

I cannot help thinking, however, that the Apostle here alludes to something in the letter of the Corinthians which reflected upon him as being not a true Apostle. He did not put forward the claims which the other Apostles did, for support for themselves and their wives; and this was attributed to his consciousness that he had no right to

THE SEAL OF MINE APOSTLESHIP.

2 If I be not an apostle unto others, yet doubtless I am to you: for ^d the seal of mine apostleship are ye in the Lord.

^d 2 Cor. iii. 2. & xii. 12.

3 Mine answer to them that do examine me is this,

4 ^e Have we not power to eat and to drink?

5 Have we not power to lead about a sister,

^e ver. 14. 1 Thes. ii. 6. 2 Thes. iii. 9.

---

4. "Power." Properly, "authority."

make such claims, not being an Apostle with the same authority which Cephas and others had. This seems alluded to in the words, "Mine answer to them that do examine me is this."

"Am I not an Apostle . . . . have not I seen Jesus Christ our Lord?" His opponents urged against his Apostolate the fact that whereas all the first elected Apostles had been companions of the Lord during nearly all His ministry, it was not so with St. Paul. In answer to this, he asks, Have I not seen the Lord? Did not the sight of the Lord as He appeared to me on the way to Damascus, and His subsequent appearances and revelations, fully make up for the companionship with Him in the days of His Flesh with which the rest of the Apostles were favoured?

"Are not ye my work in the Lord?"

2. "If I be not an apostle unto others, yet doubtless I am to you," &c. The fact that through his preaching they had been turned from darkness to light, ought to be a sufficient witness to them that he was truly sent by Christ as His Apostle. As seals attest the genuineness of a document, so their conversion attested the genuineness of his Apostolical commission.

3. "Mine answer to them that do examine me is this." This, apparently, refers to what had gone before. This is my answer to them that question my Apostleship—your own existence as a Church of Christ. But Chrysostom and others take it as referring to what comes after.

4. "Have we not power to eat," &c. Have we not power to demand maintenance of those to whom we preach the Gospel?

5. "Have we not power to lead about a sister, a wife, as well as other," &c. He had proved his Apostleship: now he proceeds to claim the full rights of an Apostle, in the maintenance of himself and of those whom he might bring with him.

K

a ‖ wife, as well as other apostles, and as ᶠthe brethren of the Lord, and ᵍCephas?

‖ Or, *woman*.
ᶠ Matt. xiii. 55. Mark vi. 3. Luke vi. 15. Gal. i. 19.
ᵍ Matt. viii. 14.

"A sister, a wife." It is by no means certain that the women (see margin) which other Apostles led about, were their wives. Theodoret interprets it of women like those who followed the Lord and His disciples, and ministered unto them (Luke viii. 2, 3, xxiii. 55). Still the reference to Cephas, of whom it is certain that he was a married man, seems to make it probable that some other Apostles took their wives with them.¹ The example of Cephas is, of course, sufficient for all controversial purposes.

"And as the brethren of the Lord." Assuming these to have been James, and Joses, and Judas, and Simon, the only "brethren of the Lord" mentioned in the New Testament, I have shown, in an excursus at the end of my volume of Notes on St. Mark, that they could not have been the Lord's uterine brothers, for they are all said to be the children of another Mary, the one who stood by the Lord when He was crucified.

"And Cephas?" The single intimation in Scripture, except this, that he was a married man, is in the account of the Evangelist that the Lord healed his mother-in-law (Mark i. 30).

6. "Or I only and Barnabas, have not we power to forbear working?" It is difficult to say why he should mention Barnabas.

---

¹ Bishop Wordsworth, who almost invariably takes the anti-Romanist line, has the following note :—"Though it is true that St. Paul does not say that they all *used* their power, yet his argument would have little force, if, for the most part, this power was not used as well as possessed by them. . . . In distinguishing himself and Barnabas as working with their own hands for their livelihood, he leads us to suppose that the other Apostles not only had the power *not* to work, but that they used the power which they had. So here: but we never hear of the Apostles travelling through the world with wives and children. If it had been so, St. Paul could hardly have said to ordinary Christians, that it was better for them to remain unmarried on account of the present necessity (vii. 26). And it was never supposed by Christian antiquity that all the Apostles were married. Tertullian ('De Monogam.' c. 8) says, 'Petrum solum invenio maritum inter Apostolos,' which is also St. Jerome's opinion ('Adv. Jovinian,' 1). And although other accounts vary from this (see in 'Euseb.' iii. 30), yet the ancient writers, who had this passage of Scripture before their eyes, never imagined St. Paul to suggest here that the Apostles generally were married, and carried their wives with them in their missionary tours. . . . Tertullian says that St. Paul does not say, 'Uxores ab apostolis circumductas, sed simpliciter mulieres.' Eusebius, in the place referred to, cites Clement of Alexandria as saying that some of the Apostles were married, but only mentions two, Peter and Philip."

DOTH GOD TAKE CARE FOR OXEN? 131

6 Or I only and Barnabas, ʰ have not we power to forbear working?

7 Who ⁱ goeth a warfare any time at his own charges? who ᵏ planteth a vineyard, and eateth not of the fruit thereof? or who ˡ feedeth a flock, and eateth not of the milk of the flock?

8 Say I these things as a man? or saith not the law the same also?

9 For it is written in the law of Moses, ᵐ Thou shalt not muzzle the mouth of the ox that treadeth out the corn. Doth God take care for oxen?

ʰ 2 Thess. iii. 8, 9.
ⁱ 2 Cor. x. 4. 1 Tim. i. 18. & vi. 12. 2 Tim. ii. 3. & iv. 7.
ᵏ Deut. xx. 6. Prov. xxvii. 18. ch. iii. 6, 7, 8.
ˡ John xxi. 15. 1 Pet. v. 2.
ᵐ Deut. xxv. 4. 1 Tim. v. 18.

---

9. "Doth God take care for oxen?" Revisers, "Is it for the oxen [alone] that God careth when he commanded this?"

The most probable explanation is that Barnabas, being associated with St. Paul in a missionary journey in which they were probably supported by the church at Antioch, and "took nothing of the Gentiles," continued in the same course of abstinence, and this was known to Paul, and here alluded to by him.

7. "Who goeth a warfare any time at his own charges? who planteth a vineyard," &c. St. Paul now draws the confirmation of his argument from the analogy of common life. The soldier receives wages or maintenance for his service in the field; the planter of the vineyard lives by the profit he gets from it; the tender of cattle or flocks lives on the milk by being nourished by it, or by its sale. Edwards notices that all these three vocations are types of the Christian ministry. The Apostle or Missionary first goes as the soldier of Christ to wage war on the world, then he plants the Church, and then he tends it as being the flock of Christ.

8. "Say I these things as a man? or saith not the law the same also?" Am I now relying on human reasoning or the analogy of common life? or have I not Scripture on my side?

9, 10. "For it is written in the law of Moses, Thou shalt not muzzle .... care for oxen? .... partaker of his hope." This citation from the law which St. Paul so energetically declares to have passed away as a means of justification, is of very great importance. The law is and must ever abide as the rule of life; and

10 Or saith he *it* altogether for our sakes? For our sakes, no doubt, *this* is written: that [n] he that ploweth should plow in hope; and that he that thresheth in hope should be partaker of his hope.

[n] 2 Tim. ii. 6.

---

10. "He that thresheth in hope should be partaker of his hope." ℵ, A., B., C., D., Syr., Sah., Copt., Arm., read, "he that thresheth (should thresh) in hope of partaking."

not only is it the rule of life even for Christians (*i.e.* of course when interpreted by the words of the Lord), but it contains principles of New Testament Church order. Here the inspired Apostle declares that when God gave, through Moses, this precept of humanity respecting oxen, He looked not only to the treatment of animals with kindness, not only to the maintenance of the ministers of the Old Testament, such as prophets; but that He had particularly in His foreknowledge and forethought the ministers of the Gospel. And, indeed, it must be so, if God has in mind when He utters His word all the right applications of that word. Amongst these there will be some far more important, and of more general application than others, and God must have respect to these.

God then, in dictating this precept, had in view the maintenance of the ministers of the Gospel. No plowing, or no threshing, can be so much as named in comparison with theirs.

The Revisers translate the latter part of verse 10, "Because he that ploweth ought to plow in hope, and he that thresheth to thresh in hope of partaking." Chrysostom, however, must have read the Greek somewhat differently: "Observe his wisdom in that from the seed he transferred the matter to the threshing-floor; herein also again manifesting the many toils of the teachers, that they in their own persons both plow and tread the floor. And of the ploughing, because there was nothing to reap but labour only, he used the word 'hope,' but of treading the floor he presently allows the fruit, saying, 'he that thresheth is a partaker of his hope.'"

Quesnel treats the verse entirely spiritually: "Those who belong to the field of the Church ought to imitate those labourers who work because they hope, and hope because they work. . . . . There must be no idleness, no sloth in an Evangelical labourer, nor any impatience at the delay either of the fruit or of the wages."

11. "If we have sown unto you spiritual things, is it a great

11 °If we have sown unto you spiritual things, *is it* a great thing if we shall reap your carnal things?   ° Rom. xv. 27. Gal. vi. 6.

12 If others be partakers of *this* power over you, *are* not we rather? ᵖ Nevertheless we have not used this power; but suffer all things, ᑫ lest we should hinder the gospel of Christ.   ᵖ Acts xx. 33. ver. xv. 18. 2 Cor. xi. 7, 9. & xii. 13. 1 Thess. ii. 6. ᑫ 2 Cor. xi. 12.

13 ʳ Do ye not know that they which minister about holy things ‖ live *of the things* of the temple? and they which wait at the altar are partakers with the altar?   ʳ Lev. vi. 16, 26. & vii. 6, &c. Numb. v. 9, 10. & xviii. 8-20. Deut. x. 9. & xviii. 1. ‖ Or, *feed*.

———

thing," &c. " If we have sown unto you spiritual things." By the preaching of the word, compared by our Lord to sowing, (Matth. xiii.), the Apostle and his fellows had made the Corinthians partakers of eternal good things—was it not then reasonable that they should partake of their infinitely inferior temporal good things, these temporalities being a mere pittance for their maintenance?

12. " If others be partakers of this power over you, are not we rather?" &c. Who are these others? They can scarcely be Apostles. We have no intimation of Peter or John, or any other Apostle having visited them. Most probably he alludes to some of the leaders of parties who made this claim in order that they might assume the greater authority.

" Nevertheless we have not used this power; but suffer all things." We have not insisted upon our just rights, but rather suffer all manner of privation, lest we should give our adversaries the opportunity of saying that we preach the Gospel for what we get by it, and so cause some to reject our teaching.

13. " Do ye not know that they which minister about holy things," &c. This does not mean the priests only, but all the servants of the temple. In preparing the sacrifices many besides the priests were employed; they had to kill the sacrifice, to flay it, to wash the inwards, &c., to prepare the fire, to carry the carcase up the steps to the top of the altar. All these had their maintenance from the " things of the temple."

" And they which wait at the altar are partakers with the altar." Here he alludes more particularly to the priests who had their part in all sacrifices except the burnt-offering (Levit. v. 13, &c.).

> ⁸ Matt. x. 10.
> Luke x. 7.
> ᵗ Gal. vi. 6.
> 1 Tim. v. 17.
> ᵘ ver. 12.
> Acts xviii. 3.
> & xx. 34.
> ch. iv. 12. 1
> Thess. ii. 9.
> 2 Thess. iii. 8.

14 Even so ˢ hath the Lord ordained ᵗ that they which preach the gospel should live of the gospel.

15 But ᵘI have used none of these things: neither have I written these things, that it should

---

14. "Even so hath the Lord ordained that they which preach the gospel should live of the gospel." The only words in which the Lord seems to ordain a maintenance for His ministers are those in Matth. x. 10, and Luke x. 7: "The labourer is worthy of his hire."

An absurd deduction has been drawn from this place as implying that ministers of the Gospel are not priests, and offer nothing that can properly be called a sacrifice, for if so they would derive their maintenance from it: but this is obviously to ignore the difference between the Jewish sacrifice and the Christian Eucharistic Oblation. The Jewish Sacrifice ordinarily supplied an abundant meal to the priests and the worshippers; the Eucharist, putting out of sight the love feast, was never to be eaten to satisfy the appetite.

The Christian ministers, then, never could be said to live of the Altar in the sense in which the Jewish priests did. They lived by the offerings of those who heard and received the Gospel, of which Gospel we shall soon see that the truth or doctrine of the Eucharist was an essential part.

This is a passage which Church people in many parishes should lay to heart. There are many so-called livings in the Church of England which do not supply anything like a decent maintenance to the Parish Priest. Those who worship at the Churches of such parishes should see to it that such a state of things is presently set at rights. They should not wait till matters are righted, which perhaps they never will be, by those in authority. They should consider that they themselves are contravening the Lord's ordinance as long as such a state of things exists, which they themselves, by a little exertion and self-denial, might obviate.

15. "But I have used none of these things: neither have I written these things," &c. I have never claimed any maintenance: on the contrary, I have with my hands worked so as to be independent of it, and what I am now writing respecting my claim to it is not to prepare the way for my receiving it from you.

be so done unto me: for ˣ *it were* better for me to die, than that any man should make my glorying void.   ˣ 2 Cor. xi. 10.

16 For though I preach the gospel, I have nothing to glory of: for ʸ necessity is laid upon me;   ʸ Rom. i. 14. yea, woe is unto me, if I preach not the gospel!

17 For if I do this thing willingly, ᶻI have a reward: but if against my will, ᵃ a dispensation *of the gospel* is committed unto me.

ᶻ ch. iii. 8, 14.
ᵃ ch. iv. 1.
Gal. ii. 7.
Phil. i. 17.
Col. i. 25.

"For it were better for me to die, than that any man should make my glorying void." The "glorying" was that he preached the Gospel without receiving his lawful remuneration. Now how was it that he insisted on this remuneration on behalf of others on no less a ground than that it was an ordinance of Christ, and refused to receive the same himself, and with such vehemence, that he said he would rather die than receive it? It seems a very strong hyperbolism, and so it is understood by Dean Stanley, who compares it with Rom. ix. 3, but it may not have been hyperbolical at all: for he himself only realized the difficulties of his position. He saw, perhaps, that it would be the destruction of his whole work, and fatal to the cause he had nearest to his heart, if in this matter he made himself to be as others.

16. "For though I preach the gospel, I have nothing to glory of . . . preach not the gospel!" I cannot boast of that to which I am compelled. If I was to decline preaching the Gospel after such manifestations of its truth, which I have personally experienced, I should be far more guilty and far more deserving of perdition than any of the sinners to whom I preach it.

17. "For if I do this willingly, I have a reward: but if against my will, a dispensation," &c. I have a reward, of course—the eternal reward of the faithful servants of God: but if I preach the Gospel unwillingly, even though I receive no reward, I am still compelled to preach it. I am entrusted with a stewardship, and no matter what happens to me, must give account of that stewardship. In this latter case, as Wordsworth remarks, "in that case I reduce myself to the condition of a domestic servant in an household, who does his duty merely because he is hired and obliged to do so."

18 What is my reward then? *Verily* that, ᵇwhen I preach the gospel, I may make the gospel of Christ without charge, that I ᶜabuse not my power in the gospel.

19 For though I be ᵈfree from all *men*, yet have ᵉI made myself servant unto all, ᶠthat I might gain the more.

20 And ᵍunto the Jews I became as a Jew, that I might gain the Jews; to them that are under the law, as under the law, that I might gain them that are under the law;

ᵇ ch. x. 33.
2 Cor. iv. 5.
& xi. 7.
ᶜ ch. vii. 31.

ᵈ ver. 1.
ᵉ Gal. v. 13.
ᶠ Matt. xviii. 15. 1 Pet. iii. 1.

ᵍ Acts xvi. 3. & xviii. 18. & xxi. 23, &c.

---

20. "As under the law." ℵ, A., B., C., D., E., F., G., P., many Cursives, Itala., Vulg., Sah., &c., add, "not being myself under the law;" but K., most Cursives, Syr., Copt., Æth., as in Rec. Text.

18. "What is my reward then? Verily that, when I preach the gospel," &c. "Reward" here should rather be translated hire or wages. The answer is, "to have no wages"—to preach the Gospel so absolutely freely, that I do not receive from those to whom I preach the maintenance I have a right to, so that I use not (or use not to the full) my power in the Gospel.

19. "For though I be free from all men, yet have I made myself servant," &c. Free from all men, *i.e.*, none have any claim upon me, because they maintain me: yet have I made myself servant of all. The way in which he did this we find in the next verses. It was the duty of a slave to obey his master's will in all things, and St. Paul made himself the slave of Jews, Legalists, Gentiles, weak brethren—of all who required his Apostolical sympathy.

20. "And unto the Jews I became as a Jew, that I might gain the Jews." He now proceeds to show how he made himself the servant of all. To the Jews he became as a Jew. He did this when he circumcised Timothy. It is expressly said in Acts xvi. 3: "He took and circumcised him because of the Jews which dwell in those quarters:" perhaps, also, he became as a Jew when he consented to "purify himself and be at charges with the four men which had a vow" (Acts xxi. 23, 24). He was also zealous for their honour, and could wish himself accursed for their sakes.

CHAP. IX.] TO THE WEAK BECAME I AS WEAK. 137

21 ʰ To ⁱ them that are without law, as without law, (ᵏ being not without law to God, but under the law to Christ,) that I might gain them that are without law.

ʰ Gal. iii. 2.
ⁱ Rom. ii. 12, 14.
ᵏ ch. vii. 22.

22 ˡ To the weak became I as weak, that I might gain the weak: ᵐ I am made all things to all *men*, ⁿ that I might by all means save some.

ˡ Rom. xv. 1. 2 Cor. xi. 29.
ᵐ ch. x. 33.
ⁿ

---

22. "Became I as weak." So C., D. Gr., E. Gr., F., G., K., L., P., all Cursives, f, g, Syriac, Sah., Copt., Arm., Æth.; but ℵ, A., B., d, e, Vulg., omit "as."

"To them that are under the law, as under the law . . . that I might gain," &c. Does he mean by "them that are under the law" the Jews only? I think rather he alludes to the religious proselytes. The principal Uncials add after "them that are under the law" the words "not being myself under the law." If these words are genuine, then St. Paul must mean, "not being myself justified by the law," *i.e.*, under the law for purposes of justification; or it may mean, "dead to the law by the body of Christ," as in Romans vii. 4, 5, 6, where see notes, and Gal. ii. 19.

21. "To them that are without law, as without law," &c. This he was when he forbade their being circumcised—when he ate with them, and reproved a brother Apostle because through fear of the Judaizers he declined to eat with them (Gal. ii. 11, 12). Again, he quoted their writers, and in all respects treated them, and would have them treated, as as much as the people of God as his own countrymen.

But here he inserts parenthetically lest he should be misunderstood as being an Antinomian—

"Being not without law to God, but under the law to Christ." Chrysostom well explains it: "So far from being without law, I am not simply under the law, but I have that law which is much more exalted than the older one, viz., that of the Spirit and grace." Alford translates ἔννομος as "a subject of the law of Christ."

He then condescended to the ways, and ideas, and scruples of all, that he might gain them—gain them to Christ.

22. "To the weak became I as weak, that I might gain the weak," &c. Meyer supposes that these weak ones were Christians weak as yet in discernment and moral power, and says that the term "gain" (κορδήσω) is not inconsistent with this view, for such

23 And this I do for the gospel's sake, that I might be partaker thereof with *you*.

---

23. "And this I do." So K., L., most Cursives, Syr., Goth.; but ℵ, A., B., C., D., E., F., G., P., 17, 37, 46, 67**, 73, 80, It., Vulg., Sah., Copt., Arm., Æth., read, "All things I do," &c.

believers would, by an inconsiderate conduct towards them, be made to stumble (viii. 11; Rom. xiv. 15); so also Bishop Ellicott.

"I am made all things unto all men, that I might by all means save some." "I have been made all things"—I have condescended to their infirmities, their prejudices, their errors, their mistakes—not, of course, that they should continue in these things, but that by bearing with them at first I might gradually strengthen their weaknesses, remove their prejudices, and rectify their mistakes.

This conduct of the Apostle teaches us what we should do in our present divided state. We should bear and forbear. We should not obtrude differences, we should make all possible allowances for differences of education, natural temperament, and worldly condition. We should do our best to discern what those whom we desire to win to the truth of God and the unity of the Church, really hold; we should recognize their truth before we denounce their error. We should make all allowances, knowing that we ourselves shall one day require all allowances to be made for us.

"That I might by all means save some." Why does not the Apostle say "all" rather than "some"? It has been said because of his humility, but may it not be because he had ever before his eyes that deep mystery of the differences between souls which we have in the Lord's parable of the sower? He became the servant of all that he might save some. So in Acts xxviii., "Some believed the words which were spoken, and some believed not."

23. "And this [or perhaps, all things] I do for the Gospel's sake, that I might," &c. "This is a short summing up: 'I labour then and make myself the servant of all for the Gospel's sake, that Gospel by which my Lord is glorified, and sinners brought into eternal union with Him, and that I may partake with you of what I preach to you.' Note the humility of the expression; he who laboured more than all others, has yet in view no higher reward for himself than just the salvation common to all believers." (Meyer). He is ambitious of nothing beyond this. When he

CHAP. IX.] SO RUN, THAT YE MAY OBTAIN.

24 Know ye not that they which run in a race run all, but one receiveth the prize? °So run, that ye may obtain.

° Gal. ii. 2.
& v. 7. Phil.
ii. 16. & iii. 14.
2 Tim. iv. 7.
Hebr. xii. 1.

speaks of the Lord in that day giving him his crown, he adds "not to me only, but to all who love His appearing" (2 Tim. iv. 8).

24. "Know ye not that they which run in a race run all, but one," &c. The Apostle in these verses draws an illustration from the earthly contests in the Isthmian games with which they were so familiar, to set forth the heavenly contest for the crown of righteousness. This seems to come in very abruptly, as during the verses just before he had spoken not so much of self-discipline as of adapting himself to various classes of persons—Jews, proselytes, Greeks, and weak ones. But the connection is probably in the last verse: "This I do for the Gospel's sake that I might be partaker thereof with you." This "being at last partaker of the heavenly good things of the Gospel," reminds him that very much more is required if they are to attain to this, than what he had been speaking of. They must take example of those whom they had often seen contending; how, knowing that of a multitude of competitors one only would receive the prize, they ran with all their might—each exerted himself to the uttermost, though the chance, so to speak, of each one was very uncertain.

Now the Apostle, though covertly, alludes to the difference between the earthly and the heavenly race in the words, "run all, but one receiveth the prize." In the earthly race, if a man did not win he might as well have not run at all. He suffered the disgrace of being defeated, whereas in the contest for God's eternal reward it is not so. "In this our blessed course He Who crowns is willing to crown not the first only but the last, not those only who have from the first ever run steadfastly, untiringly, but those who, sluggish at first, have at last been quickened and run. Yet must all run in a certain way. '*So* run that ye may obtain.'" (Pusey).

What this "so running" is we learn from another Epistle. We are to run laying aside every weight, and the sin which doth so easily beset us, and we are to run with *patience* the race that is set before us, and we are to run looking unto Jesus, the author and finisher of our faith (Hebrews xii. 1, 2).

p Eph. vi. 12. 1 Tim. vi. 12. 2 Tim. ii. 5. & iv. 7.	25 And every man that ᵖ striveth for the mastery is temperate in all things. Now they *do it* to
q 2 Tim. iv. 8. James i. 12. 1 Pet. i. 4. & v. 4. Rev. ii. 10. & iii. 11.	obtain a corruptible crown; but we ᑫ an incorruptible.

25. "And every man that striveth for the mastery is temperate in all things." "Striveth for the mastery," *i.e.*, striveth in the games; the words "for the mastery" are too general.

"Is temperate in all things," exercises self-control and self-discipline. The discipline lasted for ten months preparatory to the contest, and was at this time so severe as to be confined to the professional athletes. It chiefly consisted in diet, and is thus described by Epictetus (Ench. c. 29, § 2). "Thou must be orderly, living on spare food; abstain from confections, make a point of exercising at the appointed time, in heat and in cold, nor drink cold water, nor wine at hazard; in a word, give thyself up to thy training master as to a physician, and then enter on the contest." (Dean Stanley.)

We are also told that none were permitted to contend who had not satisfied the authorities that they had faithfully observed this discipline.

"Now they do it to obtain a corruptible crown, but we an incorruptible." The Apostle here alludes to the perishable nature of the crown, or, as we should rather call it, garland. It was not even of gold or silver, but of parsley or ivy leaves; in the case of the Isthmian games, of pine sprigs. In a very short time it faded away, and though great honours might be heaped upon him who had won it, as that he should re-enter his native town through a breach in the walls; that his victory should be celebrated by some poet whose verses have long since perished; that in all future games he should occupy one of the foremost seats among the spectators; yet all was soon forgotten, whereas the Christian's victory will be written in the book of God and of the Lamb, and will be remembered throughout eternity.

It is well to remember that the crown with which the triumphant Christian will be crowned, is a crown or garland of victory, not a kingly crown. The kingly crown, *i.e.*, the diadem, may be hereditary, or may be the reward of rebellion or treason, whereas the crown won by the contenders in the race had no value, except

26 I therefore so run, ʳ not as uncertainly; so fight I, not as one that beateth the air: ʳ 2 Tim. ii. 5.

---

as a thing fairly won in a lawful contest. The victor's crown is the *stephanos*, the monarch's the *diadēma*. The Christian, if he is to wear the victor's crown, must have gained the victory, but only One Brow wears of right the diadēma (Rev. xix. 12). If this had been always remembered, much cant and unreality would have been avoided.

It undoes all the glory and virtue of his reward if his crown, his stephanos, is given to him of mere favour.

26. "I therefore so run, not as uncertainly; so fight I, not as one," &c. "There was no want of clearness in course or direction; he ran with no uncertain or unsteady step, he knew whither and in whose presence he was running the great race of eternal life." (Ellicott.) Meyer renders it, "Not without a clear, conscious assurance and certainty of running so as to reach the goal." And this seems better, because it brings out that, in the case of the Christian, there must be good hope, if there is to be good progress.

"So fight I, not as one that beateth the air." Here there is a remarkable change from the metaphor of a racer to that of a pugilist; but who, in this latter case, is the opponent against whom he deals his blows? No other than himself, *i.e.*, his carnal self, his flesh, the nature of the old Adam within him. Conscious of his sincerity in the contest—conscious that every blow he aims is directed with his whole will and energy, he says, "So fight I, not as one that beateth the air."

In this fight with their flesh, their evil nature, many fight at random. They make but a show of fighting; they do not sincerely wish that their blows shall punish that which is a part of themselves, because they are afraid of the pain of such well-directed blows. Not so with St. Paul, not so with the sincere Christian. He heartily desires to give no quarter to his sinful flesh, his old Adam. He is ashamed of it and hates it, and desires its death, and so, casting away all secret tenderness, he aims his blows with all his skill, with all his might, and with his whole will.

27. "But I keep under my body, and bring it into subjection: lest that I," &c. "I keep under my body." This word "keep under" [ὑπωπιάζω] is in the original a very remarkable expression. It signifies "I give one a blow under the eye, so as to beat his face

27 ˢBut I keep under my body, and ᵗbring *it*

ˢ Rom. viii. 13. Col. iii. 5.
ᵗ Rom. vi. 18, 19.

black and blue." It expresses very graphically the determination, the fierceness, so to speak, with which the Apostle meets his adversary, *i.e.*, his own fleshly nature.

"And bring it into subjection," *i.e.*, lead it captive as a slave. Dr. Pusey, in a Sermon on Fasting ("Parochial Sermons," vol. i., series x.) has a remarkable passage on the necessity of Christians endeavouring to subdue their flesh by outward bodily means, as well as by spiritual:—"Rather it must be feared, that it is one of the subtlest devices of the enemy to persuade us that we may become spiritual through means merely spiritual; that we can cherish better the things of the Spirit by neglecting those of the flesh; that we can have the victory over the flesh without fighting against it; that being in the body we can transfer the conflict wholly to the soul; that we can cultivate spiritual feelings, desires, longings, love, without discipline of the body, which would obstruct them and weigh them down. This self-deceit is not a snare of these times only. It has been practised on system before, as now, only then by heretics, who thinking the spirit alone worthy of God, the body, which He also created, all evil, thought it no evil to do all evil with it. It is so not unfrequently now with those who make spiritual feelings the test of holiness. It will ever be that they who think themselves more spiritual than the Church, or seek these easier, shorter roads, will find their spirituality to be sickly and carnal, puffed up by some false spirit, rather than borne aloft by the indwelling Spirit of God."

"Lest that, by any means, when I have preached to others, I myself should," &c. "Having preached to others." This word preaching, rather heralding ($\kappa\eta\rho\nu\xi\alpha\varsigma$) is generally supposed to bear a covert allusion to the herald of the games, who proclaimed the laws of the contest or the names of the victors. But why need it mean more than preaching as John the Baptist came preaching? It is fearful to think of one who has proclaimed salvation to others not attaining to it himself. "Who is there," asks Quesnel, "whom St. Paul's fear on this account will not terrify? What presumption and delicacy can resist the force of such an example of humiliation and mortification in so great an Apostle? Can any one pretend, after this, to be saved without penitential exercises? Whoever

CHAP. X.] ALL OUR FATHERS. 143

into subjection: lest that by any means, when I have preached
to others, I myself should be ᵘa castaway.   ᵘ Jer. vi. 30.
2 Cor. xiii.
5, 6.

excuses himself from them and spares his body under pretence of
the labour of preaching, never learned this in the school of the
Apostle."

"A castaway," ἀδόκιμος, the word elsewhere translated "re-
probate," but it really means unapproved, or rejected (as the
Revisers render it). We need not give it the harshest meaning
possible, as that it means enduring the torments of hell for ever.
No doubt all unfaithfulness leads to a final and an irrevocable fall
from God. But I do not think St. Paul has this in his mind (as
he has in Thess. i., 8, 9). The thought to him would be unbearable, that he in any way came short of the approval of his Lord
and Master.

CHAP. X.

MOREOVER, brethren, I would not that ye should
be ignorant, how that all our fathers were under

1. "Moreover" (δὲ). So K., L., most Cursives, Syriac; but ℵ, A., B., C., D., E., F.,
G., P., a few Cursives, It., Vulg., Sah., Copt., read, "for" (γὰρ).

1. "Moreover, brethren, I would not that ye should be ignorant,
how that all," &c. The Apostle had just been writing of the
necessity that even he was under that he should keep his body
under subjection, lest he should be unapproved at the last by the
Judge, and now he goes on to apply this to the members of the
Church of Corinth, all of them, and he does this by reminding them
of an immense body of men, 600,000 in numbers, who all set out
on their way to their rest under the most favourable conditions
possible, and yet all but two failed to attain to that rest.

"I would not that ye should be ignorant." By this he does not
mean their being ignorant of the bare facts of the narrative, for
they were the most striking in the Old Testament, but of their

^a Exod. xiii. 21. & xl. 34. Numb. ix. 18. & xiv. 14. Deut. i. 33. Neh. ix. 12, 19. Ps. lxxviii. 14. & cv. 39.
^b Ex. xiv. 22. Numb. xxxiii. 8. Josh. iv. 23. Ps. lxxviii. 13.

^a the cloud, and all passed through ^b the sea;

---

typical meaning—their spiritual significance—their practical application.

This practical application he finds in the analogy between the deliverance of the Israelites from Pharaoh and his hosts, and their sustentation in the wilderness by the Manna on the one side, and the two Sacraments of the Church, Baptism and the Holy Communion on the other. The great point of comparison is that all the Israelites were brought into a state of comparative freedom by their passage through the Red Sea, and were all sustained in the wilderness by the manna, and all the members of the Corinthian Church had received Baptism into the Body of Christ, and all received the heavenly Food of the Body and Blood of Christ to sustain the new Life of grace which they were assumed to have received in Baptism.

The deliverance of all the Israelites in the Red Sea, and their sustentation by the manna must have been typical of some benefit or blessing which all the members of the Corinthian Church had received in the one Sacrament, or were receiving in the other; or the comparison drawn by the Apostle would have failed.

But just as the Baptismal deliverance of the Israelites at the commencement of their career, and their daily eating of the heavenly bread were, in a measure, thrown away upon them because of their disobedience, so that they did not finally possess the inheritance for which God baptized them in the sea, and fed them in the wilderness, so it might be with the members of the Corinthian Church: it was quite possible that through their disobedience they might fail to attain to the better inheritance which God designed for each and all of them, when by His Providence He had caused them to be baptized into His Son's Church and then fed them with His Son's Body and Blood.

We will now more carefully examine this remarkable passage. First, the Apostle calls the Israelites "our fathers." This does not point to any large proportion of a Jewish element in the Corinthian Church, but simply to this, that the Israelites might be well accounted the progenitors of the Christian Church in the favour of God. By the term "our fathers" the Apostle would claim for the Gentile Corinthians that they had a right to all the

ALL BAPTIZED UNTO MOSES.

2 And were all baptized unto Moses in the cloud and in the sea;

2. "Were all baptized." Aorist passive (ἐβαπτίσθησαν). So ℵ, A., C., D., E., F., G.; but aorist middle (ἐβαπτίσαντο) in B., K., L., P., most Cursives. Ellicott remarks that "in later Greek the difference between the aorist middle and the aorist passive is, in cases such as the present, practically scarcely appreciable."

Old Testament promises, many of which, as those in the present case, were enshrined in types.

"Were under the cloud and all passed through the sea." The cloud betokened the immediate presence of the angel of the covenant, or it may be, of God. Thus Exod. xiv. 19: "The angel of God, which went before the camp of Israel, removed and went behind them, and the pillar of the cloud went from before their face and stood behind them;" and immediately after this the passage of the Red Sea took place, so that the water of the cloud was over them, and the sea on each side of them. Thus were they baptized, not only with water, but with the symbol of the presence of God. It was the Almighty Power in the cloud which gave them deliverance through and by the water.

The cloud and the sea may be taken to adumbrate the water and the Spirit which are joined in our Baptism.

2. "And were all baptized unto Moses in the cloud and in the sea." "Baptized unto Moses." Baptized into him, as their leader, or perhaps into his dispensation, Moses being the Mediator of the people—standing between them and God, and offering prevailing intercession on their behalf (Exod. xxxii. 30, 31 ; Deut. v. 5 ; Gal. iii. 19).

Of course Moses was not the head of any mystical body as Christ was, neither had he died and risen again for the people, so that they could not be baptized into his body, or be buried and raised again in him as this Apostle assures us that all Christians are buried and raised again with Christ in Holy Baptism (Rom. vi. 1-6).

Some grammarians endeavour to show that the tense being the aorist middle, there was something voluntary on their part in submitting to this Baptism, but is it conceivable that these ignorant and stiff-necked Israelites imagined that they were voluntarily submitting to the religious yoke of Moses? They were simply escaping, as fast as they could, from the pursuing Egyptians.

c Exod. xvi.
15, 35. Neh.
ix. 15, 20.
Ps. lxxviii. 24.
d Exod. xvii.
6. Num. xx.
11. Ps. lxxviii.
15.

3 And did all eat the same ^c spiritual meat;
4 And did all drink the same ^d spiritual drink:

3, 4. "And did all eat the same spiritual meat; and did all drink," &c. There can, as far as I can see, be but one meaning attached to this word "spiritual," and that is, having a spiritual significance—in fact, "typical."

The manna was in no other sense spiritual meat. Our Lord draws attention to this unspeakable difference between the manna and the living Bread, even His Flesh, when He says, "Moses gave you not that bread from heaven, but my Father giveth you the true bread from heaven:" and again, "Your fathers did eat manna in the wilderness, and are dead. This is the living bread which cometh down from heaven, that a man may eat thereof and not die." (John vi. 32, 49.)

The manna, perhaps, might be called in another sense spiritual, because of the spiritual lesson it taught, that the God Who gave these people their daily bread by a daily miracle, was the only God to be worshipped and relied upon; but this lesson they utterly failed to learn.

4. "And did all drink the same spiritual drink: for they drank," &c. There is very considerable difference of opinion amongst theological writers and expositors as to what this spiritual rock means, or to what is the allusion. Some think that the Apostle refers to a Rabbinical tradition that the Rock itself (probably a boulder from the neighbouring Horeb), followed them in all their wanderings, and furnished them with a supply of water. Others have conjectured that a stream flowing from the rock followed them, but this latter would necessitate much more miraculous action on God's part.

Now before we proceed further we must distinctly remember that, unless the Israelites always encamped close to the rock, or within such reach of it that their women and servants were always able to go to it for water, God must have continued His miraculous action to bring the water to them, or they would have perished with thirst. The account in Exod. xvii. 5, 6, speaks about Moses smiting the rock, but says nothing about the continuance of the stream. In fact, for anything we learn from that passage, the supply might

for they drank of that spiritual Rock that ‖ followed them: and that Rock was Christ.

‖ Or, *went with them.*
Deut. ix. 21.
Ps. cv. 41.

have been only for a day or two. The older traditions, then, are, that either the rock, or a part of it, accompanied the Israelites, and furnished them with a perpetual supply of water, or that a stream from the rock followed the camp of Israel in all its wanderings through this waterless region. Many moderns, however, deny that there is any reference to the Rabbinical tradition, and would have us adhere as literally as possible to the words "That rock was Christ." After carefully reading what Meyer has written, I can come to no other conclusion than that he believes that the rock was either a manifestation of Christ Himself personally, or such a manifestation of Him as was identical with Himself. I give in a note the passage at full length.[1] Bishop Ellicott gives substantially this explanation: "The rock out of which it (the water) came, whether at Rephidim or Kadesh, if the occurrences are really different, or elsewhere, was no earthly rock, but a spiritual rock, a manifestation on each occasion of the spiritual and wonder-working presence of Christ, who as the λόγος ἄσαρκος thus vouchsafed to accompany and help His people."

Now we must remember that God has not revealed to us the way in which He supplied the Israelites with water all the time between the first striking of the rock in Rephidim (Exod. xvii. 6), and the last occasion, when Moses, contrary to God's command, struck the rock a second time (Numb. xx. 11). He has not, that is, revealed it to us in the Mosaic narrative, but we are told by the Apostle that the water was a miraculous creation. It was the same water, and from the same rock, wherever they were. The analogy of the manna compels us to believe that just as the Israelites were sustained by a daily re-

---

[1] "The thoughts to which Paul here gives expression are the following:—(1.) To guard and help the Israelites in their journey through the wilderness, Christ accompanied them, namely, in His pre-existent Divine Nature, and consequently as the Son of God (= the Logos of John), who afterwards appeared as man (comp. "Wisdom," x. 15). (2.) The *rock* from which the water that they drank flowed was not an ordinary natural rock, but a πέτρα πνευματική: not the mere appearance or phantasm of a rock, but an actual one, although of supernatural and heavenly origin, inasmuch as it was the *real self-revelation* and manifestation of the Son of God Who invisibly accompanied the host on its march; it was, in other words, the very Christ from heaven, as being His own substantial and efficient presentation of Himself to men."

5 But with many of them God was not well pleased: for they ᵉ were overthrown in the wilderness.

ᵉ Numb. xiv. 29, 32, 35. & xxvi. 64, 65. Ps. cvi. 26. Hebr. iii. 17. Jude 5.

peated miracle with the same bread, so, by an equally continuous exercise of God's power, they were refreshed with the same water from the same rock. Whether that spiritual rock was a type of Christ, or Christ Himself, matters not to the Apostle's argument, which is that it was the *same* water from the *same* rock, of which all the people drank. This it was which he brought to bear upon the Corinthian Christians. It was evidently God's design in bringing *all* the people by a Baptism through the Red Sea, and by feeding *all* of them in all their wanderings with supernaturally produced bread and supernaturally produced water, to bring them to the inheritance which He had promised to their fathers, and it was as evidently God's design in having caused all the Corinthian Christians to be baptized into Christ's body, and in having caused them all to be fed and refreshed with the Body and Blood of Christ, to bring all these Corinthian Christians, without exception, into the possession of a heavenly inheritance.

Now let the reader mark this. The typical Baptism of the Israelites, and their eating of the spiritual food, must have been a reality in every case; for it realized to each Israelite the present favour of God, and was the assurance to each one that God designed him to possess some part of Canaan ; and so it must have been with the Sacraments which the Corinthian Christians received—Baptism must have been to each one of them, and the Eucharistic elements must have been to each one of them, a reality—to use the words of our article, "They must have been certain sure witnesses, and effectual signs of grace and God's good will towards them, by which He worked invisibly in them."

We can now proceed with the argument of the Apostle.

5. "With many of them God was not well pleased: for they were overthrown," &c. This Red Sea Baptism, and this daily eating of spiritual food, was a real sign of the good will of God, but it was not an absolute sign, *i.e.*, a sign independent of their conduct, for they were overthrown in the wilderness. One act of disobedience after another cut them off from the favour of God, till at last, of the 600,000 men who came out of Egypt, only

6 Now these things were †our examples, to the intent we should not lust after evil things, as ᶠthey also lusted.

7. ᵍNeither be ye idolaters, as *were* some of them; as it is written, ʰThe people sat down to eat and drink, and rose up to play.

8 ⁱNeither let us commit fornication, as some

† Gr. *our figures.*
f Num. xi. 4, 33, 34. Ps. cvi. 14.
g ver. 14.
h Exod. xxxii. 6.
i ch. vi. 18. Rev. ii. 14.

---

two, Caleb and Joshua, attained to the inheritance which God designed for all.

6. " Now these things were our examples, to the intent that we," &c. These things were our examples—in the Greek, our types: but not as Alford says, in the usual acceptation of the word type with us; "these things" are the things which happened to the Israelites— their passage of the Red Sea, their manna, the rock from which the water flowed, and their behaviour under all this—all these things were examples, or as we say, cautions for us, that we, having infinitely greater spiritual privileges, should not fail to realize ours as they failed to realize theirs.

" To the intent that we should not lust after evil things, as they also lusted." It was the intention of God, in causing these things to be recorded in the Old Testament history, to put us on our guard, lest we fall from the grace of our Sacraments by sin—especially by the sins by which they were destroyed. The Apostle mentions "lust" because most, if not all the sins, through which the Israelites were destroyed, were some form of evil desire. Their evil lust and its punishment is especially mentioned in Numb. xi. 4. "The children of Israel also wept again, and said, Who shall give us flesh to eat?"

7. "Neither be ye idolaters, as were some of them; as it is written," &c. "Neither be ye idolaters," *i.e.*, by taking part in the idolatrous feasts, and eating publicly of the things offered to idols. The account of the Israelitish idolatry is especially connected with the feasting on the offerings (Exod. xxxii. 6).

" And rose up to play," *i.e.*, to dance. Then there was an opening for the idolatry being connected with acts of lewdness.

8. " Neither let us commit fornication, as some of them committed," &c. Here reference is made to the people committing whoredom with the daughters of Moab (Numbers xxv.) This was not common, but idolatrous fornication, *i.e.*, the Israelites would

^k Numb. xxv. 1, 9. Ps. cvi. 29.
^l Ex. xvii. 2, 7. Num. xxi. 5. Deu. vi. 16. Ps. lxxviii. 18, 56. & xcv. 9. & cvi. 14.
^m Num. xxi. 6.

of them committed, and ^k fell in one day three and twenty thousand.

9 Neither let us tempt Christ, as ^l some of them also tempted, and ^m were destroyed of serpents.

---

9. "Neither let us tempt Christ." So D., E., F., G., K., L., most Cursives, Ital., Vulg., Syriac; but אֵ, B., C., P., some Cursives, Arm., and Æth., read, "the Lord," and A. reads "God."

not have fallen into it unless they had obeyed the invitation of the Moabites to partake of the sacrifices of their gods. Owing to the immense number of prostitutes who took part in the worship carried on in the temple of Venus at Corinth, this must have been a very dangerous temptation to the members of the Corinthian Church, and necessitated their absolute separation from the heathen in everything approaching to participation in their idolatrous rites.

"Fell in one day three and twenty thousand." The account in Numbers xxv. 9 makes it four and twenty thousand. "St. Paul speaks of the mortality of one day only, Moses of the whole." (Wordsworth: but see my notes on Acts vii. 16.)

9. "Neither let us tempt Christ, as some of them also tempted." "To try the Lord" means generally, "to let it come to the point whether He will shew Himself to be God"—in fact, it means to try His patience. The Israelites are continually said to have tempted God when they provoked Him to cut them off. (Thus Exod. xvii. 7; Numb. xiv. 22, Deut. vi. 16). It is important to observe here that the sin against the Jehovah of the Old Testament becomes a sin against Christ, or a tempting of the Lord in the New: for if we read "the Lord," it can only mean here the Lord Christ. Christ has now all rule over the Church put into His hands. It is He Who in righteousness severely exercises discipline, as well as directs, and guides, and comforts, and saves.

"And were destroyed of serpents." The punishment of Israel by the fiery serpents when they were healed by looking to the brazen serpent. (Numbers. xxi. 5-9).

10. "Neither murmur ye, as some of them also murmured." This command that they were not to murmur has been taken (and

CHAP. X.] NEITHER MURMUR YE. 151

10 Neither murmur ye, as ⁿ some of them also
murmured, and ° were destroyed of ᵖ the destroyer.

11 Now all these things happened unto them
for ‖ ensamples: and ᑫ they are written for our

ⁿ Ex. xvi. 2.
& xvii. 2.
Numb. xiv. 2,
29. & xvi. 41.
° Num. xiv.
37. & xvi. 49.
ᵖ Ex. xii. 23.
2 Sa. xxiv. 16.
1 Chron. xxi.
15.
‖ Or, *types.*
ᑫ Rom. xv. 4.
ch. ix. 10.

11. "Happened unto them for ensamples" (types). So D., E., F., G., L., most Cursives, Sah., Copt.; but ℵ, A., B., C., K., P., read typically (τυπικῶς).

by commentators from whom I should have scarcely expected such an interpretation) as meaning that the Corinthians were not to murmur against St. Paul and Apollos, and other inspired teachers, but I cannot conceive St. Paul threatening them with God's vengeance if they murmured against him as they did against Moses. He usually receives the discontent of his converts far more meekly, and in the spirit of all Christian love exhorts them to a better mind. Why should we restrict it to murmuring against himself, seeing that murmuring against the dispensation of God's providence is the sure indication of a rebellious and discontented spirit? The murmuring referred to is probably that of Numbers. xiv. 27-29.

"Were destroyed of the destroyer," *i.e.*, of the destroying angel. Their destruction came not of any natural cause. They seemed to be mown down by a pestilence, but it was by the hand of an angel. In Exod. xii. 23, the destroyer is the angel who smote the firstborn, and in 2 Sam. xxiv. 16, he is the angel of the Lord, who was commanded by God to stay his hand.

11. "Now all these things happened unto them for ensamples," &c. The best MSS., instead of τύποι read τυπικῶς, by way of figure. Were then the events historically true? Certainly, but God, without in any way interfering with the action of free responsible agents, so overruled them that, when recorded in His word, they furnish examples to us that we should avoid the sins which destroyed them. Meyer explains it as meaning—These facts (*i.e.*, those which are referred to in verses 6-10) happened to them in a typical fashion, in such a way that as they fell out, a typical character, a predictive reference impressed itself upon them (*i.e.*, on the facts). Wordsworth says that they happened to them (the Israelites) typically, so that they, *i.e.*, the rebellious Israelites, might

r ch. vii. 29. Phil. iv. 5. Heb. x. 25, 37. 1 John ii. 18.	admonition, ^r upon whom the ends of the world are come.
s Rom. xi. 20.	12 Wherefore ^s let him that thinketh he standeth take heed lest he fall.

---

see Christ in them by the eye of faith; but is it at all likely that God intended to impart to these besotted Israelites high evangelical ideas, when they seem to have been utterly unable to grasp the first truths respecting God and goodness?

"They are written for our admonition, upon whom the ends of the world are come." Illustrative of this are the words of St. Peter respecting the prophecies of the prophets, "Unto whom it was revealed that not unto themselves, but unto us, they did minister the things which are now reported unto you by them that have preached the Gospel unto you," &c., (1 Pet. i.) And as they through their falls or their steadfastness ministered to our instruction, so our use or abuse of Gospel privileges will furnish instruction hereafter to the angelic world. (Ephes. iii. and my Excursus on Election in Notes on the Epistle to the Romans).

12. "Wherefore let him that thinketh he standeth take heed," &c. Estius and others suppose that, though St. Paul's words in this verse contain a general axiom, yet that he had especially in his mind those who thought they stood or were strong in the matter of partaking of things offered to idols; such men thought they stood in their knowledge, (ch. viii. 1, 2, 10), but such self-confidence might be the prelude to a grievous fall.

The axiom, then, is of the most general application. All self-confidence is very dangerous. St. Peter found it so after he had said so boastingly, "If I should die with thee, I will not deny thee in any wise" (Mark xiv. 31). There is nothing that we can rely upon absolutely. The use of sacraments, the possession of the Bible—nay, even an extensive knowledge of it, a supposed spiritual hold on Christ, lively feelings, zeal for the truth, or some particular truth—by none of these we stand sure if we think we stand. Our one confidence is constantly to commit our souls to God's safe keeping. "Into thy hands I commend my spirit, for thou hast redeemed me, O Lord, thou God of truth." With such passages as this in the Scripture, it is very wonderful that men who profess to be guided by Scripture should make confident belief in

GOD IS FAITHFUL.

13 There hath no temptation taken you but such as is ‖ common to man: but ᵗ God *is* faithful, ᵘ who will not suffer you to be tempted above that ye are able; but will with the temptation also ˣ make a way to escape, that ye may be able to bear *it*.

‖ Or, *moderate*.
ᵗ ch. i. 9.
ᵘ Ps. cxxv. 3. 2 Pet. ii. 9.
ˣ Jer. xxix. 11.

---

our own final acceptance the one test of our state in the sight of God. They write as if God had made it impossible for men to deceive themselves, whereas God warns them at every turn against self-deception. By the mouth of this very Apostle He even tells those who stand by faith that they are not to be high-minded, but fear (Rom. xi. 20).

13. "There hath no temptation taken you but such as is common to man." Literally human, and because all men partake of the same human nature, all men are liable to the same temptations. As one form of evil predominates in one man, and another in another, so some may be more easily led away by some temptations than others, but no man is absolutely alone in the form of the temptations that assail him. He may think so—he may think no one is so strangely tempted as he is; and yet those who probe souls with a view to their guidance will tell him that numbers are in the main tempted just as he is.

As, then, the children of God in times past have (some of them at least) resisted the very temptations by which you are assailed, so God will so order matters now that there shall always be a way of escape. If the temptation seems irresistible, your faithful God will either carry you through by His grace, or will open out to you a means of escape, by flight. Only for this you must look out. You must not secretly desire to be overcome, and so yield, but you must without a moment's parley avail yourselves of the way of escape, and flee.

"That ye may be able to bear it." A man equally bears the temptation, *i.e.*, does not succumb to it, when he either resists in God's strength, or promptly avails himself of God's open door of escape. Quesnel wisely concludes with the words: "The most violent temptations are only an occasion of triumph to those who are in the hand of God; but the lightest are a snare, and an abyss of destruction to those who are in their own hands."

14 Wherefore, my dearly beloved, ʸ flee from idolatry.

15 I speak as to ᶻ wise men; judge ye what I say.

16 ᵃ The cup of blessing which we bless, is it

ʸ ver. 7. 2 Cor. vi. 17. 1 John v. 21.
ᶻ ch. viii. 1.
ᵃ Matt. xxvi. 26, 27, 28.

---

14. "Wherefore, my dearly beloved, flee from idolatry." "Flee from idolatry." Do not dally with it—do not expose yourselves to temptations from this quarter by accepting invitations to idolatrous feasts, under the idea that you are strong enough to resist, but keep resolutely out of the way of all such allurements.

15. "I speak as to wise men; judge ye what I say." Wise men here means sensible men—men who have intelligence sufficient to understand the significance of their own ordinances. This is to be connected with what follows: "Judge ye whether what I say is not in accordance with the Eucharistic Mystery, of which ye all are partakers."

16. "The cup of blessing which we bless, is it not the communion," &c. In the next six verses the Apostle resumes the consideration of the danger of eating things offered to idols, from the fact that participation in the Eucharist made Christians partakers of the Body of Christ, and so because of such partaking they were one body in Christ: and it was the most utterly incongruous, and, indeed, wicked thing, after they had thus entered into the most intimate fellowship with Christ, to partake of heathen sacrifices, and so enter into fellowship with the demons to whom these sacrifices were offered.

Now in order to realize the Apostle's meaning we must remember that in the next two verses he is not teaching certain Eucharistic doctrine for the first time to the Corinthians, which they are supposed to be ignorant of, but he is teaching an inference from the well known and (amongst Christians) universally acknowledged doctrine of the Eucharist which in the verses before he had said they knew, or at least might know when he said, I speak as to sensible men—judge ye of the truth of what I say.

The truth which he sets forth respecting the Eucharist is its unifying nature. We must go back to verses 3 and 4. The Israelites did all eat the same spiritual meat. They did all drink the same spiritual drink, after all partaking of the same Baptism under the same cloud and in the same sea. So far, then, as it was possible

THE COMMUNION OF THE BLOOD.

not the communion of the blood of Christ? ᵇThe

ᵇ Acts ii. 42, 46. ch. xi. 23, 24.

for men to be one before the Incarnation they were *one*—one Church, in the highest sense that men could be one Church before Pentecost. They had fellowship at once with God, and with one another. And in addition to this, they all had fellowship with God because they partook of the sacrifices offered on the one altar. The altar made all their sacrifices one—one bread of God (Levit. xxi. 6 ; Numb. xxviii. 2).

Now this daily receiving from God of miraculously produced meat and drink, and this constant communion in His altar, made their sin in polluting themselves with idolatry the more inexcusable. And it is to be remembered that the worship of the idol was always a sacrificial worship. It was not a worship of words, but a worship always associated with altars, victims, priests, and feasting. So that their sin was very great when, after partaking of the food from God's holy Altar, they partook of the idolatrous sacrificial offerings of false gods. And the Apostle now proceeds to show that the sin of the Corinthian Christians, if they did the like, was far greater, because the one sacrificial act of worship of the Church made them participate in an unity and fellowship to which that of the Israelites was as nothing.

"The cup of blessing," he says, "which we bless, is it not the common participation of all of us in the Blood of Christ, *i.e.*, in the Life of Christ (the life is in the blood) ? "

What is the "blessing" here ? Some say, as Dean Stanley, that it is in allusion to the fourth and most sacred cup of the Paschal feast, which was so called from the words pronounced over it, "Blessed be thou, O Lord our God, the king of the world, who has created the fruit of the vine " (Lightfoot *ad loc.*) ; but it is beyond measure unlikely that St. Paul should bring in the terms of a bygone ordinance, and a strictly Jewish one, to designate the Catholic sacrament which the Corinthians enjoyed. Others have said that it is so called because of the blessings in which it made the devout communicants partake ; but can there be a doubt but that it refers to the action of Christ in blessing the contents of a cup, which blessing He commanded to be ever hereafter imitated or followed by the ministers of His Church, when he said, "Do this in remembrance of me"? In every Eucharist, from the time of

bread which we break, is it not the communion of the body
of Christ?

Christ to the present, this blessing, or giving thanks over, or consecrating the contents of a cup, has been one of the two features
of the Eucharist.

"Which we bless." By a very large number of modern expositors
and commentators, we are told that the "we" involved in εὐλογοῦμεν
refers not to the Apostle and his co-ministers, but to the Apostle or
minister associated with the congregation of laymen, of whom he
is but one—that, in fact, he is but the minister or mouthpiece, not
so much of Christ as of the congregation. Now this view seems to
me to be totally incompatible with the original institution. The
Lord, when He instituted the Eucharist, did not invite the Apostles
to bless and break, but He Himself alone did it. He afterwards
sent His Apostles to act in His place, not as the representatives of
the people, but as His representatives, when He said, "As my
Father sent me, so send I you." It is quite true that the congregation said "Amen" at the end of the Consecration prayer,
which signifies their solemn approval of the act, but we are never
told that they themselves said that prayer, nor has any vestige of
any approach to such a mode of blessing or consecration come
down to us. Surely if at any time we are to account ministers to
be "ministers of Christ and stewards of the mysteries of God," it is
in the celebration of the Eucharist.

"Is it not the communion of the Blood of Christ?" What is
the idea in the communion here? It is a co-partaking of something which makes those who partake of it one. It implies much
more than our word "fellowship" does. Take the most common use of the word, "The communion of the Holy Ghost." The
communion of the Holy Ghost is the actual indwelling of the Holy
Ghost, the third Person of the Trinity, in a vast number of human
beings, making them one in God inasmuch as the Holy Ghost is
the Spirit of God, and one with one another in faith, hope, and
love.

The communion of the Holy Ghost implies of necessity the possession of the Holy Ghost Himself, not of a figure of the Spirit—
not of the mere teaching of the Holy Spirit as of one external to the
person taught—not of the leading of the Spirit as of one going
before men, but still apart from them; but of the actual co-par-

17 For ^cwe *being* many are one bread, *and* one body: for we are all partakers of that one bread. c Rom. xii. 5. ch. xii. 27.

---

taking of the Spirit by His dwelling in them. "He dwelleth with you, and shall be in you." Now what immediately succeeds this verse teaches us that the κοινωνία of the Spirit is analogous to the κοινωνία of the Body and Blood of Christ. The Body and Blood of Christ is actually in certain persons to bring about a κοινωνία, or there would be no κοινωνία of the Body of Christ, or in one Body the Church.

"The bread which we break, is it not the communion of our body of Christ?" Why does the Apostle, having spoken of the cup being the cup "which we bless," go on to speak of "the bread which we break"? Does the breaking of the bread in all respects answer to the blessing of the cup, seeing that the bread itself is blessed (λαβὼν τὸν ἄρτον, καὶ εὐλογήσας ἔκλασε, St. Matth. xxvi. 26)? No; but the bread is broken first to set forth the breaking of the Lord's Body; secondly, the partaking of that Body, for to be one Divine Food to all it must be broken that each one may have a part. By being broken it continues the same bread, but all partake of it.

17. "For we being many are one bread, and one body: for we are all partakers," &c. There is some difference of opinion respecting the translation of this. The exact translation in the order of the Greek words is, "Because one bread, one body are we, the many (*i.e.*, the many who partake), for we all of the one bread partake." The Revisers in their text give pretty nearly the same meaning as our Authorized, but in their margin they give what appears to me to be the true translation, carrying with it the true sense: "Seeing that there is one bread, we, who are many, are one body, for we all partake of the one bread."

What is the "one bread"? Evidently the Inward Part or Thing Signified of the Sacrament (I write, of course, for members of the Church of England), for the outward part of or sign is not one. On the contrary, it may not be made of the same materials. In countries where there is no wheaten bread, it may be barley, oaten, rye, as well as wheaten. And even if it is of wheaten flour it is not one. It is of different seeds, sown in different fields, reaped by different hands, ground in different mills; and in some parts of the Church it is leavened, and in others it is unleavened. But

18 Behold ^d Israel ^e after the flesh: ^f are not they which eat of the sacrifices partakers of the altar?

19 What say I then? ^g that the idol is any thing, or that which is offered in sacrifice to idols is any thing?

^d Rom. iv. 12. Gal. vi. 16.
^e Rom. iv. 1. & ix. 3, 5. 2 Cor. xi. 18.
^f Lev. iii. 3. & vii. 15.
^g ch. viii. 4.

---

the Spiritual food is one because of the presence of the Inward Part.

No matter what the figure, form, or taste, of the outward sign, the Inward Part—the Most Holy Thing, whose Presence is signified and therefore assured to the Communicants—is the True Bread, the Living Bread—" The bread which cometh down from heaven that we may eat thereof and not die," the bread of which Christ said, "He that eateth my flesh, and drinketh my blood, dwelleth in me, and I in him" (John vi. 50, 56).

This bread being the means of continued union with Christ, continues us in the Unity of His Body. God "does assure us thereby of His favour and goodness towards us; and that we are very members incorporate in the mystical Body of His Son, which is the Blessed Company of all faithful people."

Such is the Unity of the Church. It is made by St. Paul to depend upon the Sacrament having everywhere and in every place the same Inward Part which the faithful everywhere partake of under the veil of bread.

18. "Behold Israel after the flesh," &c. He now proceeds to another point. Those of the fleshly Israel who partook of the sacrifices were partakers of the altar. Now this altar was no other than "the table of the Lord" (Ezek. xli. 22, Malachi i. 7, 12). They who partook of the things offered upon it, partook of food from His table, and so were in communion with the Lord.

19. "What say I then? that the idol is any thing, or that which," &c. This appears to me to be a tacit reference to viii. 4. There he had said, "We know that an idol is nothing in the world," but if an idol be nothing, then the things offered to idols are nothing. They are meaningless, and so harmless. And so we may offer them or partake of them without sin. "No, by no means," he proceeds to say, "I am quite aware of the non-existence of heathen Deities, but notwithstanding this—

THEY SACRIFICE TO DEVILS.

20 But *I say*, that the things which the Gentiles [h] sacrifice, they sacrifice to devils, and not to God: and I would not that ye should have fellowship with devils.

[h] Lev. xvii. 7.
Deu. xxxii. 17.
Ps. cvi. 37.
Rev. ix. 20.

21 [i] Ye cannot drink the cup of the Lord, and

[i] 2 Cor. vi. 15, 16.

---

20. "I say, that the things which the Gentiles sacrifice, they sacrifice to devils (demons)," &c. This means the deities of the heathen mythologies. Jupiter, Venus, Minerva, have no existence out of our imaginations, but they are not the mere creations of poets. The whole system of idolatry is demoniacal and Satanic: and so they who worship at these heathen altars by sacrifice, put themselves more and more into fellowship with fallen spirits, as Godet well puts it: "Behind all that mythological phantasmagoria there lie concealed malignant powers, which, without being Divinities, are nevertheless very real and very active, and which have succeeded in fascinating the human imagination, and in turning aside the religious sentiment of the heathen nations to beings of the fancy; hence the idolatrous worships addressed to those diabolical powers and not to God. . . . . The words of the Apostle do not imply the idea that every false God worshipped by the heathen corresponds to a particular demon; they signify merely that heathen religions emanate from these malignant spirits, and that consequently the man who takes part in such worship puts himself under their influence."

"I would not that ye should have fellowship with devils." The words "have fellowship" is "be in communion." This clearly implies that in idolatrous sacrificial worship there was a real communion with evil spirits; God in His mercy might interpose and prevent the full effects of such intercourse, but it actually took place.

21. "Ye cannot drink the cup of the Lord, and the cup of devils: ye cannot," &c. "Ye cannot" may be taken in one of two ways; either "ye cannot with any consistency—indeed, without the greatest sin—drink the cup of the Lord," &c.; or "ye cannot be in communion with the Lord, which ye are by drinking His cup, and with devils by drinking their cup, for the Lord will deeply resent such profanation, and instead of communicating Himself to you

the cup of devils: ye cannot be partakers of the Lord's table, and of the table of devils.

22 Do we ˡ provoke the Lord to jealousy? ᵐ are we stronger than he?

ᵏ Deut. xxxii. 38.
ˡ Deut. xxxii. 21.
ᵐ Ezek. xxii. 14.

---

21. "Devils," demons.

for purposes of salvation, ye will eat and drink your own condemnation, not discerning His Blood and Body."

This verse is of great importance, as it decides the question, "Is the Lord's table an altar?" Unquestionably it is; for St. Paul here makes it analogous to, and parallel with, the "tables" of devils, which were unquestionably altars. This question is even now bebated amongst ourselves with great heat and vehemence. Now this seems to me to arise out of what I cannot help characterizing as a most stupid misunderstanding. They who refuse the name of altar to the piece of church furniture on which the consecrated elements rest, do so on the ground that the altar is a thing *on* which the animal offered in sacrifice was slain. Thus we have a popular hymn, beginning

> "Not all the blood of beasts
> On Jewish altars slain,"

but no beast was ever slain on the altar, Jewish or heathen. It was slain by or near the altar. Its blood was poured forth or sprinkled (Levit. i. 5), round about the altar, and the altar itself, instead of being an instrument of slaughter, was a means of communion between God and the worshippers. For the animal that was offered was wholly, or in part, laid on the altar to be consumed, and the part which was not consumed by fire was partaken of by the worshippers in token that they were in communion or amity, or reconciliation with God. And so the name of "The table of the Lord" was given to the Jewish altar. (Ezek. xli. 22; Mal. i. 7.)

So the Lord's table in our churches is, in the strictest sense, an altar, for from it we partake of the Body of the Adorable Victim by means of the consecrated elements. Christ our Passover has been slain, or immolated for us, and there at our altars we keep the feast (v. 7, 8).

22. "Do we provoke the Lord to jealousy? are we stronger than he?" Idolatry is represented as not simply kindling the anger of

CHAP. X.] LET NO MAN SEEK HIS OWN. 161

23 ⁿ All things are lawful for me, but all things are not expedient: all things are lawful for me, but all things edify not.   n ch. vi. 12.

24 ᵒ Let no man seek his own, but every man another's *wealth*.

o Rom. xv. 1, 2. ver. 33. ch. xiii. 5. Phil. ii. 4, 21.

25 ᵖ Whatsoever is sold in the shambles, *that* eat, asking no question for conscience sake: p 1 Tim. iv. 4.

---

23. " All things are lawful for me." "For me" (μοι) omitted by ℵ, A., B., C., D., E., F., G., P., 46*, 67**, 118, 179, d, e, f, g (Vulg. Cod. Amiat.), Sah., Copt., Goth.; but retained in H., K., L., most Cursives, Syriac, Arm.

the Lord, but provoking His jealousy. "Thou shalt not bow down to them nor worship them, for I the Lord thy God am a jealous God." And this takes place even when the God worshipped has no real existence. "They have moved me to jealousy with that which is not God." (Deut. xxxii. 21.)

23. "All things are lawful (for me), but all things are not expedient," &c. He now proceeds to conclude this matter of Christian liberty in its bearing upon the eating of things offered to idols by a few general rules. He refers to, or repeats what he had said in ch. vi. 12. "All things," *i.e.*, external things, "are lawful." I may partake without defilement of any meats, any drink, nor am I polluted by any company: but still I may commit grievous sin by so eating or drinking, as to give offence to my weaker brother, and cause him to fall from God.

"All things are lawful, but all things edify not," *i.e.*, do not build up the soul or the Church. Chrysostom has a very good comment. "Seest thou his great wisdom? Because it was likely that they might say, 'I am perfect, and master of myself, and it does me no harm to partake of what is set before me.' 'Even so,' saith he, 'perfect thou art, and master of thyself; do not, however, look to this, but whether the result involve not injury—nay, subversion.'"

24. "Let no man seek his own, but every man another's wealth." So in Rom. xv. 1: "We that are strong ought to bear the infirmities of the weak, and not to please ourselves," &c.; and xiii. 5: "Charity seeketh not her own." Wealth, of course, is to be taken as meaning well-being; and, first of all, spiritual well-being.

25. "Whatsoever is sold in the shambles, that eat, asking no question," &c. Not inquiring, that is, whether it has been offered

26 For ^q the earth *is* the Lord's and the fulness thereof.

27 If any of them that believe not bid you *to a feast*, and ye be disposed to go; ^r whatsoever is set before you, eat, asking no question for conscience sake.

28 But if any man say unto you, This is offered in sacrifice unto idols, eat not ^s for his sake that

q Ex. xix. 5. Deu. x. 14. Ps. xxiv. 1. & l. 12. ver. 28.
r Luke x. 7.
s ch. viii. 10, 12.

---

28. "This is offered in sacrifice to idols." So C., D., E., F., G., K., L., P , all Cursives, Goth., Vulg., Cop., Arm.; but ℵ, A., B., H., Sah., read simply, "offered in sacrifice," ἱερόθυτον, instead of εἰδωλόθυτον.

to an idol or not. "He doth not even suffer them to *question*, *i.e.*, to search and enquire whether it be an idol sacrifice, or no such thing: but simply to eat everything which comes from the market, not even acquainting oneself with so much as this, what it is that is set before us. So that he that eateth, if in ignorance, may be rid of anxiety." (Chrysostom.)

26. "For the earth is the Lord's, and the fulness thereof." Therefore all food as His creation is good; and He hath removed the restrictions which were imposed in the Old Dispensation on certain meats, permitting all to be eaten indifferently. "Meats, which God hath created to be received with thanksgiving of them which believe and know the truth" (1 Tim. iv. 3).

27. "If any of them that believe not bid you to a feast, and ye be disposed," &c. The invitation might be to a relative or to a friend: and St. Paul had laid down considerable liberty in the matter of intercourse with such in v. 9, 10. If they went they enjoyed the same liberty in partaking of what was set before them, as they did when they bought in the shambles.

28. "But if any man say unto thee, This is offered in sacrifice unto idols," &c. If the man who said this to him were an heathen, then by eating he seemed to regard the idol as a real Divinity, with whom he desired to be in communion, and so the heathen man is confirmed in his idolatry; whereas if the Christian abstained he would see that the Christian abhorred anything approaching to honouring an idol. If, however, the neighbour sitting by him, were a weak Christian, he would be emboldened to act contrary to his conscience, as is laid down in ch. viii. 10, 11; and so having formally received such information the true Christian is bound to abstain.

CHAP. X.] FOR CONSCIENCE SAKE. 163

shewed it, and for conscience sake; for ᵗthe earth *is* the
Lord's, and the fulness thereof:

29 Conscience, I say, not thine own, but of the
other: for ᵘ why is my liberty judged of another
man's conscience?

30 For if I by ‖ grace be a partaker, why am I
evil spoken of for that ˣ for which I give thanks?

ᵗ Deu. x. 14.
Ps. xxiv. 1.
ver. 26.
ᵘ Ro. xiv. 16.

‖ Or, *thanksgiving.*
ˣ Rom. xiv. 6.
1 Tim. iv. 3, 4.

---

28. " For the earth is the Lord's, and the fulness thereof." Omitted by ℵ, A., B., C., D., E., G., H*., P., twelve Cursives, Ital., Vulg., Syr., Sah., Copt., Arm.; but retained in H* *., K., L., and most Cursives.

"For the earth is the Lord's," &c. The principal MSS. omit this clause, and most critics regard it as a mistake of the copyist, who probably was deceived by the word "conscience" (συνείδησιν) a little above, and carelessly copied the sentence which followed it.

29. "Conscience, I say, not thine own, but of the other." His last words had been (eat not) "for conscience sake;" but lest he should seem by the mention of conscience to be undoing what he had laid down respecting Christian liberty, he explains: "Conscience, not thine own, but of the other." "Thine own conscience is free, it ought not to be tormented by any scruples; yet it is well for thee to abstain, for if thou indulgest, thy liberty is judged and condemned by another man's conscience." There have been most contrary interpretations given of this verse. I think Chrysostom's by far the best: "And what he means is this. God hath made me free, and above all reach of injury, but the Gentile knoweth not how to judge of this high morality of mine, nor to see into the liberality of my Master, but will condemn and say to himself, Christianity is a fable; they abstain from the idols, they shun demons, and yet cleave to the things offered to them. Great is their gluttony. And what then? it may be said. What harm is it to us if he judge us unfairly? But how much better to give him no room to judge at all."

30. "For if I by grace be a partaker, why am I evil spoken of," &c. The argument seems to be something of this sort: I by the grace of God, in freeing me from the bondage of the law, and making all things lawful to me, am able to partake of these meats without defiling my own conscience; but there is a further consideration: by partaking I may wound the consciences of others, and cause my

164   DO ALL TO THE GLORY OF GOD.   [I. COR.

<small>y Col. iii. 17.
1 Pet. iv. 11.
z Rom. xiv. 13.
ch. viii. 13.
2 Cor. vi. 3.
† Gr. *Greeks*.
a Acts xx. 28.
ch. xi. 22.
1 Tim. iii. 5.
b Rom. xv. 2.
ch. ix. 19, 22.
c ver. 24.</small>

31 ʸ Whether therefore ye eat, or drink, or whatsoever ye do, do all to the glory of God.

32 ᶻ Give none offence, neither to the Jews, nor to the † Gentiles, nor to ᵃ the church of God:

33 Even as ᵇ I please all *men* in all *things*, ᶜ no

---

liberty in partaking to be spoken against as verging upon idolatry or giving countenance to it. Why should this be? "What! that for which a believer gives thanks, the other converts into a ground of defamation against him. What sort of religion is that? the heathen would say who were witnesses of both actions." (Godet.)

31. "Whether therefore ye eat or drink, or whatsoever ye do, do all to the glory of God." Here St. Paul gives the only safe rule to carry them through these entanglements and difficulties, and doubtful cases of conscience, unharmed—consciously and of set purpose do all, even the meanest daily actions, to the glory of God. Constantly dedicate yourselves afresh to Him, constantly commit your daily life to Him. The Apostle gives a parallel rule in Coloss. iii. 17: "Whatsoever ye do in word or deed, do all in the name of the Lord Jesus, giving thanks unto God and the Father by him." You will then experience the truth of the promise, "The name of the Lord is a strong tower, the righteous runneth into it and is safe." (Prov. xviii. 10.)

32. "Give none offence, neither to the Jews, nor to the Gentiles, nor to the," &c. All these three classes would be offended in different ways by the same thing: by your unduly using your liberty in the matter of partaking of meats offered to idols, the Jews would be offended because they would think you were conformed to, or at least made light of, idolatrous worship; the Gentiles, seeing you do that which implied a partaking of their sacrifices, would think that you considered idolatry no serious matter, and would say among themselves, Why should I renounce idolatry, seeing that these Christians make no scruple of partaking of what they know is consecrated to idols? and the Church of God, in the persons of the weak brethren, would be emboldened to eat against their consciences, and so sin against God.

33. "Even as I please all men in all things, not seeking mine own profit," &c. This is a repetition in terser language of what he

seeking mine own profit, but the *profit* of many, that they may be saved.

had said in ch. ix. 19, "For though I be free from all men .... I am made all things to all men that I might by all means save some." "Many" ought to be translated "the many," the greater number, in fact, all. In asking the Corinthians to make these sacrifices, he only asks them to do what he himself did: he had first shown them by his own example how they ought to do the will of God, and then he concludes all this matter of partaking in the idolothuta with the words:—

CHAP. XI.

BE [a] ye followers of me, even as I also *am* of Christ.

2 Now I praise you, brethren, [b] that ye re-

[a] ch. iv. 16.
Eph. v. 1.
Phil. iii. 17.
1 Thess. i. 6.
2 Thess. iii. 9.
[b] ch. iv. 17.

1. "Be ye followers of me as I also am of Christ." This ought to have been put at the end of chap. x. It is the same as what he had inculcated in Rom. xv. 2, "Let every one of us please his neighbour for his good to edification. For even Christ pleased not himself," &c. One writes, "We do not find in St. Paul's Epistles the notice of Christ's earthly life being a pattern or ideal, after which men ought to fashion their lives. His mind is absorbed in the greatness of the self denial manifested by the Son of God in taking upon Him the form of a Servant, and humbling Himself by His obedience unto the death of the Cross." (Edwards.) Not wholly true this, for St. Paul in the next Epistle beseeches these very Corinthians " by the meekness and gentleness of Christ." He could not have done this unless he had instructed his converts in the lessons of the daily life of Christ.

2. "Now I praise you, brethren, that ye remember me in all things," &c. The Apostle now enters upon a subject connected with reverence in worship, and that due subordination and order

member me in all things, and ^c keep the ‖ ordinances, as I delivered *them* to you.

^c ch. vii. 17.
‖ Or, *traditions*, 2 Thess. ii. 15. & iii. 6.

---

which should be manifested throughout the conduct of all the members of such an institution as the Church, which is not to be regarded as a heap of stones, however precious, thrown together accidentally, but not united, each one being separate from its neighbour stones; but on the contrary, the whole is intimately connected with the order of the universe, each member being united to Christ as his Head, and Christ being under the Father as the First Person in the Godhead.

He has to blame them for tolerating that which contradicts the principle of this order or subordination ; but, before blaming them, as a wise teacher he praises them.

"I praise you that ye remember me in all things, and keep the ordinances," &c. No doubt this means that they followed the regulations which he had laid down respecting a large number of what we should deem secondary matters. The ordinances or traditions or paradoseis are the laws and rules respecting public worship and private conduct which he delivered to them to observe. He did not preach the Gospel to them, and then say, I have done my part, now you are at liberty to follow your own fancy, and to make what ecclesiastical regulations you think will suit you best. Nothing of the sort. We find that he uses such expressions as "as I teach everywhere in every church," "so ordain I in all churches," "stand fast and hold the tradition which ye have been taught, whether by word or our epistle" (1 Cor. iv. 17; vii. 17; 2 Thess. ii. 15).

It may be asked why have these ordinances or traditions not been preserved and come down to us? To which we answer, we do not know whether these traditions, many of them, at least, have not come down to us. In all human probability they form part of that body of Church observance which we find everywhere recognized in the very early fathers, and prevailing in all parts of the Catholic Church.[1] Anyhow, the ship of the Church from the first

---

[1] Such, for instance, as the reverent use of the Cross ; the remarkable features common to all the typical Liturgies; Infant Baptism; the early rather than the late celebration of the Eucharist.

THE HEAD OF CHRIST IS GOD.

3 But I would have you know, that ᵈ the head of every man is Christ; and ᵉ the head of the woman *is* the man; and ᶠ the head of Christ *is* God.

ᵈ Eph. v. 23.
ᵉ Gen. iii. 16.
1 Tim. ii. 11, 12. 1 Pet. iii. 1, 5, 6.
ᶠ John xiv. 28. ch. iii. 23. & xv. 27, 28. Phil. ii. 7, 8, 9.

has gone in one direction, in the Catholic direction, in the direction of Catholic dogmas and marked ritual observance, and it is impossible to conceive how it could have done so if these "traditions" of St. Paul, and doubtless of his brother Apostles, had been conceived in a Puritan rather than in a Catholic spirit. The direction in which the Church was to sail must have been given from the first.

The Apostle now proceeds to consider the propriety of women having their heads covered when in worship, and to this he devotes sixteen verses of the comparatively little space at his disposal. The modern religious sentiment prevalent amongst us would consider such a thing totally unworthy of the Apostle's notice, much less that so much precious space should be devoted to it, and still less that it should involve great principles of Divine order.

On the contrary the Apostle fully considers it, writes upon it earnestly—instead of compressing it, he enlarges upon it, and repeats himself in his discussion of it, and bases it upon the primacy of God Himself.

3. "But I would have you know that the head of every man is Christ," &c. Are we to consider this "every man" as every man born into the world, or every man baptized into the Church? It is quite true that Christ being the Second Adam is the Head of the race, but here I think, having only the conduct of members of the Church in his mind, he means every man born again into the Church.

"And the head of the woman is the man." She was created for him to be an helpmeet for him, and to be in subjection to him, as it is written, "Thy desire shall be to thy husband, and he shall rule over thee."

"And the head of Christ is God." The Son of God, Jesus Christ, deriving His Divine Nature from the Father, is subordinate to Him in the Godhead, and this the Son of God constantly asserts, as when He says, "I came down from heaven, not to do mine own will, but the will of him that sent me" (John vi. 38).

In these cases of subordination which he has cited, there is also

4 Every man praying or ^g prophesying, having *his* head covered, dishonoureth his head.

5 But ^h every woman that prayeth or prophe-

g ch. xii. 10, 28. & xiv. 1, &c.
h Acts xxi. 9.

---

unity. Man and wife are one flesh. Christ is One with us as the Head of His mystical body. Christ and the Father are One.

4. "Every man praying or prophesying, having his head covered, dishonoureth his head." This was in a Grecian city, and was a Gentile practice, adopted into Christian worship. It was contrary to the Jewish ritual of prayer, which required that every Jew, in prayer, should wear a sort of veil called the tallith. This symbolized that in the Jewish state of things he was not able to behold God with open face, but must come to Him with head covered in token of shame for sin, not wholly but only typically cleansed.[1] The Romans also prayed to the gods with covered head; but the Greeks always with head uncovered, and this, though heathen and national, was adopted at once into the Church on account of its accordance with the idea of freedom and boldness in our access to God.

"Dishonoureth his head." In the first place he dishonours his own head by keeping upon it a badge of servitude, and by this means dishonours Christ his Head, "in whom we have boldness and access with confidence." (Ephes. iii. 12.) The uncovered head betokens the dignity as well as freedom of the standing in Christ.[2]

A question has been raised whether the *men* of the Christian assembly covered their heads. Most probably not, but the Apostle desires to give the divine principle underlying the conduct of the man and the woman respectively.

5. "But every woman that prayeth or prophesieth with her head uncovered." In what way does she dishonour her head? She

---

[1] Most probably there is an allusion to this in the Liturgy of St. James, where, in the prayer introducing the Lord's Prayer, we have, "Grant, O Lord, that we may boldly and without blame, with a pure heart and contrite mind, without shame and confusion, and with sanctified lips presume to call upon Thee our God and heavenly Father, and say, Our Father," &c.

[2] Mr. Blunt gives a remarkable case in point in a passage in St. Cyprian, who writes thus to some confessors who had refused to sacrifice, "Your heads remained free from the impious and wicked veil with which the captive heads of those who sacrificed were then veiled." (Cyprian on the lapsed, ii.)

CHAP. XI.] ALL ONE AS IF SHE WERE SHAVEN. 169

sieth with *her* head uncovered dishonoureth her head: for that is even all one as if she were [i] shaven.   [i] Deut. xxi. 12.

---

may dishonour it by undue assumption of equality with the man. Anyone who exalts himself through pride or arrogant assumption really dishonours himself. His exaltation is sure, in the providence of God, to be ignominiously humbled. It is the glory of the creature to abide in the position in creation which God has assigned to him. It is consequently the glory of the woman to abide in due subjection, and that is signified in public worship by the woman being veiled in that worship, and the man being uncovered. If she prays or prophecies in the Christian assembly with her head uncovered, it is as if she acted immodestly—without the shamefacedness and sobriety (the $αἰδώς$ and $σωφροσύνη$) which the Apostle would have women adorned with (1 Tim. ii. 9).

Taking "head" here to have reference to the man ("the head of the woman is the man"), she dishonours her head by assuming equality with him by keeping her head uncovered.

And now the Apostle hints at another reason which he thus expresses:

"For that is even all one as if she were shaven." The woman having long hair is, in the Apostle's view of things, a sign of subjection, and of her subordinate position with reference to man. If then she be uncovered in Church, it is as much a dishonour to her as if she were shaven. Her long hair is an honour to her head: but if she is unveiled in Church, the whole significance of the fact that God has given to her long hair is undone. She might as well be shaven.

But how are we to reconcile " that prayeth or prophesieth," with the very strict injunction of the Apostle in xiv. 35, "It is a shame for women to speak in the Church"? Very easily, I think. He means, "It is a shame for a woman to speak by herself, to take the lead in a Church where men as well as women are assembled, by publicly praying or prophesying." Prophesying here does not mean preaching, but joining in hymns and psalms, and spiritual songs. We must adopt some explanation like this if we are to have any respect for the very categorical command of the Apostle (xiv. 34), "let your women keep silence in the churches, for it is not permitted unto them to speak, but they are commanded to be under obedience."

6 For if the woman be not covered, let her also be shorn: but if it be ᵏa shame for a woman to be shorn or shaven, let her be covered.

ᵏ Num. v. 18. Deut. xxii. 5.

7 For a man indeed ought not to cover *his* head, forasmuch as ˡ he is the image and glory of God: but the woman is the glory of the man.

ˡ Gen. i. 26, 27. & v. 1. & ix. 6.

8 For ᵐ the man is not of the woman; but the woman of the man.

ᵐ Gen. ii. 21, 22.

9 ⁿ Neither was the man created for the woman; but the woman for the man.

ⁿ Gen. ii. 18, 21, 23.

One of these passages must give way to the other, and if we take, as we may very well do, praying and prophesying as joining in prayers and prophesyings, we do no violence to the consistency of Scripture. Observe also that the Apostle speaks with some degree of contempt of the woman who would desire to pray uncovered.

6. "For if the woman be not covered, let her also be shorn: but if it be a shame for a woman," &c.

7. "For a man indeed ought not to cover his head, forasmuch as he is the image," &c. He is what no other creature of God in this world is, the image and glory of God, and therefore in his approach to God, and when taking part in the worship of God, he ought not to wear any sign of inferiority or subjection.

"But the woman is the glory of the man."

8, 9. "For the man is not of the woman, but the woman of the man. Neither was the man," &c. In what respect the woman is the glory of the man is to be found in the next two verses. The woman's glory is not an independent glory as if she were a separate creation. She was made out of man, and so the glory which she has is from him. And besides this, the man was not created for the woman, but the woman for the man, and so her glory looks, as it were, to him. It is part of the glory of man that such a being as woman should be created out of him, out of his flesh and bones, and for him, to be not independent of him, much less have any authority over him, but to be his helper.[1]

---

[1] There have been various shades of meaning given to these verses by different writers. Edwards writes, "The man's glory as distinguished from God's consists in subjection. The final glory of the Son of God Himself, in so far as He is Man, will be His subjection

POWER ON HER HEAD.

10 For this cause ought the woman ° to have || power on *her* head ᵖ because of the angels.

° Gen. xxiv. 65.
|| That is, *a covering, in sign that she is under the power of her husband.*
ᵖ Eccles. v. 6.

---

10. "For this cause ought the woman to have power on her head." There can be not the smallest doubt but that the Apostle by " power on her head," means " the sign of power on her head," and the whole context requires that the sign should not be one of her own power, but of that of the man as exercised over her. Meyer puts it tersely when he writes " to have a power upon her head, *i.e.*, the sign of a power (to wit, as the context shows, of her husband's power, under which she stands) by which power the Apostle means a covering for the head."

Very many reasons why the Apostle should call a covering of the head " power " or authority are to be found in the commentators. A passage in Diodorus Siculus is appealed to in which βασιλεία signifies a symbol of one's own power, that is, a diadema. Another takes it to signify a token of honour of the married woman over the single. Others take it to mean a sign of authority to speak in public. The reader will find a number of such explanations in Meyer's commentary, to which I refer him.

"Because of the angels." Chrysostom and Theodoret seem to see not the smallest difficulty in this; the former simply and shortly explains it, " For although thou despise thine husband, saith he, yet reverence the angels,—reverence them, that is, as present in the assemblies of the faithful, pleased with every sign of reverence and devotion, and displeased at signs of pride, and undue

---

to God (xv. 28). It follows that the woman manifests man's glory by manifesting in her subjection to him his subjection to God." Godet writes: " It is an honour, the highest of all undoubtedly, for one being to become the object of another's love and devotion; and the more the being who loves, and is self devoted, is exalted in talent and beauty, the more is this honour increased. Can there therefore be a greater glory to man than to possess as a loving and devoted helpmeet a being so admirably endowed as woman? All the perfection that belongs to her is homage rendered to the man for whom and from whom she was made, especially where she consecrates herself freely to him in the devotion of love." Meyer says, " St. Paul has in his eye the relation of marriage, in which rule is conferred on the man alone. The woman accordingly has, in harmony with the whole connection of the passage, to appear simply as δόξα ἀνδρός, inasmuch, namely, as her whole wedded dignity, the high position of being spouse to the man, proceeds from the man, and is held in obedience to him, so that the woman does not carry an independent glory of her own, an ἰδία δόξα, but the majesty of the man reflects itself in her, passing over to her immediately, and, as it were, by derivation."

q Gal. iii. 28.   **11** Nevertheless ^qneither is the man without

assumption of superiority." Now the moderns have, as a rule, found the utmost difficulty in this place. They have some of them explained it as meaning presiding elders or bishops, as in Rev. ii. 8, "the angels of the churches." Others have taken it to refer to bad angels who might be tempted by the beauty of the women, as in Gen. vi. 2.

Now it seems to me a matter of considerable interest to ascertain, seeing that the Apostle gave this reason for the head of the woman being reverently veiled in Church, why such a commentator as Chrysostom sees not the smallest difficulty about it, and why so many modern commentators endeavour to explain it away.

The Apostle assigns such a reason because the angelic world was to him an intense reality. He speaks of the Apostle's suffering as "a spectacle to the world, and to *angels*, and to men" (iv. 9). One article of the mystery of Godliness in his eyes was that Christ was "seen of angels" (1 Tim. iii. 16). He charges Timothy "before God and the elect angels" (1 Tim. v. 21). The law was ordained by angels in the hand of a mediator. (Gal. iii, 19.) He asks, "Know ye not that we shall judge angels?" (vi. 3). Now such a man would realize the presence of angels everywhere, and especially in the assemblies of the saints. When, then, he thus speaks of the becomingness of women being veiled in Church, he naturally figures to himself the presence of angelic beings, as well as of men, and such have holy feelings similar to ours. A commentator like Chrysostom, believing intensely in the supernatural world, would take such a reason as a matter of course, and commentators, now semi-rationalists, and having, to say the least, no realization of the spiritual universe, would give, as they do, any explanation rather than the literal one.

Well, if angels are in our assemblies, can they see us worship without themselves worshipping? And how should we demean ourselves in the presence of such fellow-worshippers? Would it not add to our seriousness, that amongst us there are those who "always behold the face of our Father in heaven"? (Matth. xviii. 10). And might not such a thought reprove the sin of those who are "almost in all evil in the midst of the congregation and assembly"? (Prov. v. 14).

11, 12. "Nevertheless, neither is the man without the woman

the woman, neither the woman without the man, in the Lord.

12 For as the woman *is* of the man, even so *is* the man also by the woman; ʳ but all things of God.   ʳ Rom. xi. 6.

13 Judge in yourselves: is it comely that a woman pray unto God uncovered?

14 Doth not even nature itself teach you, that, if a man have long hair, it is a shame unto him?

15 But if a woman have long hair, it is a glory to her: for *her* hair is given her for a ‖ covering.   ‖ Or, *veil*.

. . . . all things of God." Here the Apostle guards what he has said from being misunderstood. In asserting the supremacy of the man, and how such supremacy is to be notified, even in public worship, he must not be taken to mean that the man is independent of the woman. The man and the woman are not isolated, but one in Christ. They are counterparts of one another. The Church is not a Church of males, in whose flesh alone could be the sign of God's covenant, but of females also, who along with men are members of Him in Whom is "neither male nor female." And the mode of the continuance of the human family is also a witness to this: for though the first woman was taken out of the man, yet, ever since, each man comes into the world by being born of a woman.

" But all things of God "—by the institution of marriage, by the blessing of fruitfulness acting, not by man's will, but by God's providence, in the case of every one born into the world. The man and wife are dependent upon one another, but both are in Him in Whom alone their marriage is an holy estate.

13-15. "Judge in yourselves: is it comely? . . . . her hair is given her for a covering." This seems to be a repetition, with some difference of expression, of the argument in verses 4, 5, 6. If a woman prays to God uncovered she goes contrary to the principle of subordination which the Creator had in view in giving her long hair. She, for the time, affects equality with the man, and so does what is not comely or becoming ($\pi\rho\acute{\epsilon}\pi o\nu$). They themselves, of their own common sense, might judge respecting this, if they simply asked what is natural: now nature makes us have a feeling

16 But *if any man seem to be contentious, we have no such custom, †neither the churches of God.

17 Now in this that I declare *unto you* I praise *you* not, that ye come together not for the better, but for the worse.

* 1 Tim. vi. 4.
† ch. vii. 17. & xiv. 33.

---

of shame when we see a man wearing long tresses. We call him effeminate, and so, also, if we saw a woman with closely cropped hair, we should say that it was unseemly—masculine—in fact, unnatural in her.[1]

16. "Now if any man seem to be contentious, we have no such custom," &c. This has been understood as signifying, If any man seem to be contentious, we have no such custom of contentiousness; but must it not rather refer to what he had been discussing in these sixteen verses—We have no such custom of permitting the women to remain unveiled in the Christian assemblies?

"Neither have the churches of God," *i.e*, anywhere, in any place. The custom that the women should be clad as those that are in subjection, is universal—the contrary is unknown.

17. "Now in this that I declare unto you I praise you not, that ye come together," &c. At the beginning of the last paragraph, on the matter of the subjection of women, he had begun with the words "I praise you;" now a graver matter by far rises before him, no other than the profanation of the Holy Eucharist, and he prefaces it with "I praise you not that ye come together, not for the better, but for the worse."

This reads us a lesson. How anxious we are that there should be large congregations: and yet how many in any congregation may be much the worse for coming, even to what is rightly accounted the house of God. If professedly Christian people come to see and be seen—if they come to criticize, to idle away in vain thoughts

---

[1] At the time the Apostle wrote, the long hair in a man was regarded as a mark either of effeminacy or savage manners. Among the later Romans, especially after the year B.C. 300, the long locks by which their ancestors were distinguished were laid aside, and the derivation of cæsaries, the hair of the male sex, from cædo, to cut, although etymologically false, is historically true. And Juvenal speaks of the gathering-up of the thick tresses into a golden head-dress, as the last climax of effeminacy and profligacy: "Reticulumque comis auratum ingentibus implet," Sat. ii. 96. In the East men usually shave the whole head, leaving only one long lock. (Stanley.)

CHAP. XI.] THERE MUST BE HERESIES. 175

18 For first of all, when ye come together in the church, ᵘ I hear that there be ‖ divisions among you; and I partly believe it.

19 For ˣ there must be also ‖ heresies among you, ʸ that they which are approved may be made manifest among you.

ᵘ ch. i. 10, 11, 12. & iii. 3.
‖ Or, *schisms*.
ˣ Matt. xviii. 7. Luke xvii. 1. Acts xx. 30. 1 Tim. iv. 1. 2 Pet. ii. 1, 2.
‖ Or, *sects*.
ʸ Luke ii. 35. 1 John ii. 19. See Deut. xiii. 3.

18. "In the church." ℵ, A., B., C., D., E., F., G., K., L., P., and thirty Cursives omit article.

---

the most precious time which God gives them here on earth, if they come to have their ears tickled, or their self-importance asserted by the place they claim, do they not come together for the worse rather than for the better?

18. "For first of all, when ye come together in the church, I hear that there be divisions among you," &c. These divisions cannot well be exactly the same as those he had animadverted on in chap. i. They seem to have been divisions or heresies, which were manifested in the church or room where they assembled for prayer and Eucharist. Perhaps the separate parties into which they were divided at the love feasts (verse 21) may have been connected with them, the members of the various parties or factions eating together, and excluding the rest from their company.

19. "For there must be also heresies among you, that they which are approved," &c. Why *must* there be heresies or divisions? Because of the sinfulness of our nature—because of the Old Adam which is present even in the regenerate.

"That they which are approved may be made manifest among you." Divisions and heresies are the fruits of our evil nature, and when men reject God's supernatural cleansing and sanctifying work in the scheme of redemption, He not only permits our corrupt nature to take its course and produce these evil fruits, but He makes use of them to bring good out of them. They are a part of that plan by which, before the final judgment, He allows evil to manifest its true malignity. Divisions and heresies in the Church already manifest those who are approved and those who are not. They suck into their vortices the self-asserting, the self-opiniated, the quarrelsome, the meddlesome, and as a rule

20 When ye come together therefore into one place, ‖ *this* is not to eat the Lord's supper.

‖ Or, *ye cannot eat.*

---

they fail to influence the poor in spirit, the meek, the humble-minded.[1]

20. "When ye come together, therefore, into one place, this is not to eat," &c. The place of meeting for celebration of the Eucharist, prayer, and instruction. This, I think, does not mean a place where the whole Church assembled—very probably they would be too numerous all to meet in one room—but the various upper rooms or courts where particular groups or congregations assembled.

"This is not to eat the Lord's Supper." "When ye meet together to celebrate the Lord's Supper, that which ye do is not to eat the Lord's Supper, but something very different." (Estius.) Another sense is, "Ye so conduct yourselves that it is not a right thing for you to eat the Lord's Supper after ye have feasted so profanely."

Very considerable differences are found in commentators and divines as to what this Lord's Supper (Cæna Dominica, κυριακὸν δεῖπνον) is. Some, as Augustine, understand it as the Blessed Sacrament of the Body and Blood of Christ. So also Theodoret, "He calls the Lord's Sacrament the Lord's Supper." (Æcumenius, Lombard, Thomas Aquinas, and others.) But many others, and with reason, suppose that the Apostle means the Agapæ, or love feasts, which were held in commemoration not of the first Eucharist, but of the Paschal feast which preceded it. The reader will find this question very learnedly and lucidly discussed in Estius. He argues that the disorders which actually took place, and are described in verses 21 and 22, could not have taken place at the celebration of the Eucharist, which was only bread and a mingled cup, but were very likely to have taken place at such a meal as the Agape, in which each brought his own provision, which was intended to be shared by all.

---

[1] I am not here speaking of the larger divisions of Christendom in general, or of the sects of this country. Some of the latter have arisen from laxity, abeyance of discipline, want of distinctive teaching, and failure of the parochial system among ourselves. A vast amount of our Dissent is now hereditary. But what I mean is, that if there be factions and heresies in any Christian community, it will be found that those who are drawn into these factions are the unhumbled, and those who are not so drawn are the humble, and so, in the Lord's view, the better Christians.

DESPISE YE THE CHURCH OF GOD.

21 For in eating every one taketh before *other* his own supper: and one is hungry, and ᶻanother is drunken.   ᶻ 2 Pet. ii. 13. Jude 12.

22 What? have ye not houses to eat and to drink in? or despise ye ᵃthe church of God, and   ᵃ ch. x. 32.

---

21. "For in eating every one taketh before other his own supper: and one is hungry," &c. They brought their provisions with them—the rich would bring much, the poor man would come very scantily provided. Those who came first began to eat at once without waiting till all had come; and so in this Agape, this feast of love, they did not set forth that regard for one another which was the characteristic of any purely secular entertainment.

"One is hungry, and another is drunken." One is hungry, *i.e.*, the poor man who came perhaps with nothing, expecting that as it was a feast of charity he would share the bounty of his richer brethren.

"Another is drunken." He has brought more wine than is necessary for his own private use, and consequently, not having shared it with his brethren, has himself taken too much, and is, of course, utterly unfit to take part in any further worship.

22. "What? have ye not houses to eat and to drink in? or despise ye the Church of God?" The Church of God, that is, the place where the living Church assembled. This is the first intimation in the New Testament of holiness attaching to places, because of the very sacred actions which were performed therein. Though we have no reason to believe that the places of Christian assembly in Corinth were more than rooms somewhat larger than the ordinary rooms of a house, yet in these the Mystical Body assembled, and in these the Sacramental Body was offered and distributed, and this made the Apostle ask indignantly, "Despise ye the Church of God?" Here he cannot mean the mere assembly; he most certainly associates with it its place of meeting, for he had immediately before mentioned houses as opposed to the Church of God.

"And shame them that have not?" "Them that have not" cannot well be those without dwellings, but must rather signify

178   I PRAISE YOU NOT.   [I. Cor.

^b shame ‖ them that have not? What shall I say to you?
shall I praise you in this? I praise *you* not.
23 For ^c I have received of the Lord that which

^b James ii. 6.
‖ Or, *them that are poor?*
^c ch. xv. 3. Gal. i. 1, 11, 12.

---

those who were not able, owing to their poverty, to bring any provisions, and were abashed at seeing others feasting when they had nothing.

"What shall I say?" What shall I say to your display of selfishness, even at the feast of charity—to your greediness—to your irreverence?

"Shall I praise you in this? I praise you not." As if he said, I praised you that ye remembered me in all things, and kept the ordinances or traditions, but I must make one great and terrible exception. I cannot praise you respecting your conduct at these feasts of charity.

23. "For I have received of the Lord that which also I delivered unto you." And now the Apostle, apparently very abruptly, delivers to them the account which he had received from the Lord Himself respecting the original Institution of the Eucharist.

The first question which has to be answered is this,—Why did the Apostle introduce this account here, for he had been speaking of disorders at the Agape, not at the Eucharist? There can, I think, be but one answer—the Corinthians had mixed up the Agape with the Eucharist. I will not say that they had confounded the two, but they had done what was sure to lead to confusion between the two. They had habitually observed the Agape a little before the Eucharist. They had no real sense of the profound significance, as well as awfulness, of the Holy Communion of the Lord's Body and Blood. And so they seem to have put it into a subordinate position, in comparison with the Agape. This was very natural, for the Blessed Sacrament, though given in earthly elements, was in the very highest sphere of the supernatural and spiritual. Nothing in it ministered to the appetite. Its joy was wholly "in the Lord," whereas the Agape might, and frequently was so perverted, as to minister to self-indulgence, even to gluttony and drunkenness. Now the only way to remedy this was to separate between the two. It seems almost certain that the Agape was not an institution of Christ, at least in nothing like the

CHAP. XI.] THE LORD JESUS TOOK BREAD. 179

also I delivered unto you, ^d That the Lord Jesus the *same* night in which he was betrayed took bread : ^d Matt. xxvi. 26. Mark xiv. 22. Luke xxii. 19.

sense in which the Eucharist was.[1] And so, if tolerated on account of the good feeling and hospitality to which, if religiously observed, it might minister, it must be kept in its subordinate place, and the dominant position of the Eucharist asserted. This the Apostle proceeds to do in a very marked fashion. I, that is, "I myself," as distinguished from the other Apostles, have received of the Lord, *i.e.*, by special revelation.[2] If he had received it, as some suppose, by tradition, from the other Apostles, he would most certainly have said, "*We* received it," whereas by the almost abnormal use of the personal pronoun, ἐγώ, he emphasizes the fact that he had received it himself personally, whether by vision or more direct communication, we are not told.

"That which also I delivered unto you." This place is also much to be remarked. When he first instituted the celebration of the Eucharist among them, he gave them the account of the Institution as he had received it from the Lord, but they had to a great extent failed to realize its significance, and it was only because of the disorders which had attended the Agape that he repeated this in writing. So that we owe the most circumstantial of the four accounts of the Institution of the Blessed Sacrament to the forgetfulness, not to say the profanity, of these Corinthians. This emphasizes the fact that in no one book of the New Testament have we the full account of any doctrine of the faith. Every epistle presupposes that those to whom it is addressed had been instructed in all the doctrines of the faith, so that the Scriptures of the New Testament come into the hands of those who are already by Apostolic traditions in possession of almost all truth, though much

---

[1] Lightfoot, quoted in Wordsworth, says: "It is not improbable that the Jewish Christians, looking back at their own Passover, on which the Holy Communion had been engrafted, regarded the Eucharist as an appendage to a domestic religious meal, such as the Passover was, in which households of about twelve partook together by families; and that hence arose those separate δεῖπνα which the Apostle condemns, in which it is likely that the Gentile Christians would not be disposed or admitted to partake before the Holy Communion."

[2] It has been objected that if so, the preposition παρά would have been used instead of ἀπό, as signifying direct transmission, but, as Godet remarks, this preposition is involved in παρέλαβον.

24 And when he had given thanks, he brake *it*, and said,

---

of it might be unrealized and much forgotten. They come into the hands of the Church, which had been fully instructed in the truth before a line of the New Testament was in writing.

"That the Lord Jesus the same night in which he was betrayed took bread." Why is the time of the Institution characterized as the night, or time in which He was betrayed? Because His betrayal was His being delivered up for our sakes. He had said very emphatically, "No man taketh my life from me, but I lay it down of myself; I have power to lay it down, and I have power to take it again" (John x. 18). And the time when He solemnly and sacerdotally surrendered it was when He said, "This is my body which is given for you." Then He parted with all power over His own life. Thus He was betrayed to be crucified, and in less than a day the sacrifice was consummated.[1]

"Took bread." There must have been something particularly solemn and reverential in this taking of bread, for it is particularly mentioned in each of the four accounts. With it was no doubt joined the lifting up of His eyes to heaven; and this is intimately combined with it in the most ancient Liturgies. Thus the Clementine, "For in the same night that He was betrayed, taking bread into His holy and immaculate hands, and looking up to Thee, His God and Father." So also the Liturgies of St. Mark and St. James.

24. "And when he had given thanks, he brake it." When He had given thanks ($εὐχαριστήσας$). In the Eucharistic passages of the New Testament, the word is apparently used interchangeably with " having blessed." On this occasion the blessing partook of a double character, so as to be both a benediction and thanksgiving; for St. Matthew and St. Mark represent our Lord as having blessed the bread ($εὐλογήσας$), and having given thanks ($εὐχαριστήσας$) over the cup; and St. Luke and St. Paul represent Him as having given thanks ($εὐχαριστήσας$) over the cup; and in x. 16, St. Paul speaks of the cup as the cup of blessing ($εὐλογία$).

---

[1] This is recognised in two of the most ancient Liturgies—that of St. Mark, "For our Lord himself, our God and Supreme King, in the same night wherein He delivered Himself for our sins," &c., and St. James, "In the same night that He was offered, or, rather, offered up Himself for the life and salvation of the world."

THIS IS MY BODY.

Take, eat: this is my body, which is broken for you: this

24. "Take, eat." Omitted in אּ, A., B., C., D., E., F., G., 3, 17, 23*, 31, 46*, 57, 67**, 70, 71, 73, 178, d, e, f, g, Vulg. (Cod. Amiat), Sah., Copt., Arm.; retained in K., L., P., most Cursives, Syriac, Goth., Æth. † ᴜ V.

24. "Which is broken for you." אּ*, A., B., C*., 17, 67, omit "broken," and read, "which is for you;" but E., F., G., K., L., P., most Cursives, d, e, g, Syriac, Goth., read, "broken."

"He brake it." The English Eucharistic office alone of all Liturgies seems to put the actual breaking of the bread into its becoming place, for it takes place in the consecration itself. The fraction in no other liturgy is so placed as to warrant this most Holy Sacrament being called "The Breaking of Bread." I owe this to Archdeacon Freeman.

"And said, Take, eat." These words are not in St. Luke's account, which so closely agrees with that of St. Paul, that it was evidently derived from him. From the little manuscript authority for them it may be that they have at an early period been inserted from the accounts in St. Matthew and St. Mark. There is not the smallest doubt, however, but that the Lord said them.

"This is my body, which is broken for you." As each volume of this exposition is intended to be, as far as possible, independent of the others, I shall not content myself with referring to my notes on the Synoptics. I shall now consider, as far as we in this present state of things may venture to do so, the import of these words. Are they devoid of mystery, or do they set forth a mystery?

A believing commentator, Godet, treats them as no revelation of a mystery whatsoever, when he writes: "The simplest explanation is this: Jesus takes the bread which is before Him, and, presenting it to His disciples, He gives it to them as the symbol of His Body which is about to be given up for them on the cross, and to become the means of their salvation; the verb *be* is taken in the same sense as that in which we say, as we look at a portrait, ' It is so and so.' " Nothing can be less mysterious than this. If we may dare to call anything which occurred in the life of our Blessed Lord —God and man—commonplace, it would be this.

Now it does not alter the non-mysteriousness, if I may coin a word, of this explanation, if we suppose that this symbol is ordained to be the means of conveyance of certain benefits of redemption to the worthy recipient as a seal to a document which conveys an estate, or a ring given in the investiture of any one with a dignity or an

| Or, *for a remembrance*.   do ‖ in remembrance of me.

---

24. " In remembrance of me." "*In meam commemorationem.*"

office. Such an use of the symbol does not add in the least degree to its mystery, only to its value.

From the first age to the present in all branches of the Catholic Church, the solemn rite of the consecration and participation of the Eucharist has been called "the mysteries;" and for this one and only reason, that in the reception of the consecrated elements the Body and Blood of the Lord are understood to be received also. To take the two earliest accounts which treat of the mystery, we read in Justin Martyr, who lived seventy or eighty years at the outside after the time of the writing of this Epistle: "Not as common bread or common drink do we receive these: but in like manner as Jesus Christ our Saviour, having been made flesh by the Word of God, had both flesh and blood for our salvation, so likewise have we been taught that the food which is blessed by the prayer of His Word, and from which our blood and flesh by transmutation are nourished, is the flesh and blood of that Jesus Who was made flesh." Now though there may be obscurities in this passage, one thing is certain, that it never could have been written by one who held the bread and wine after consecration to be merely symbols.

The second passage is from Irenæus (book iv., chap. xviii. 5). "But our opinion is in accordance with the Eucharist, and the Eucharist, in turn, establishes our opinion. For as the bread, which is produced from the earth, when it receives the invocation of God, is no longer common bread but the Eucharist, consisting of two realities, earthly and heavenly; so also our bodies, when they receive the Eucharist, are no longer corruptible, having the hope of the Resurrection to eternity."

Such are the earliest accounts of any length of the mystery of the Eucharist. A tenth part of the references to the mystery in all the subsequent writers of the Catholic Church would fill a library. We only have space to notice how the idea of the profoundest mystery attaching to this sacrament is stated in our formularies. First we claim the use of this very word "mystery"—"He hath instituted and ordained Holy Mysteries." We speak of ourselves as we who have received " these holy mysteries." We pray God that we may receive and do an unsearchably mysterious thing, that we may "so eat the flesh of His dear Son and drink His blood, that our sinful bodies may be made clean by His Body, our souls washed through His most precious Blood, and that we may ever more dwell in Him, and He in us;" thereby proclaiming our belief that the most extraordinary words in the whole compass of the Bible, those of John vi., refer to the Eucharistic eating and drinking.

In addition to this, in our catechism we reproduce, if not the words, at least the exact idea of Irenæus, when we ask, "What is the outward part or sign of the Lord's supper?" and put into the child's mouth the answer, "Bread and wine, which the Lord hath commanded to be received." And we follow this up with the question, "What is the Inward Part or Thing Signified?" and the answer, "The Body and Blood of Christ, which are verily and indeed taken and received by the faithful in the Lord's Supper."

We, then, of the Church of England, are pledged to look upon the union or identity of the Lord's Body and Blood with the outward part of the Sacrament, as a deep and unfathomable mystery, as a secret known only to God. We repudiate the gross and unscriptural way of Transubstantiation on the one side, and, if the words of our formularies are to be taken in their natural sense, we equally repudiate any meaning given to the Lord's sacramental words which would make it more proper for Him to have said, "This is not my Body—this is not really my Body; this is a figure, a symbol, a representation, a picture of my Body."

Now, inasmuch as figures and types are constantly employed in Scripture, why cannot we be content with looking upon this as one amongst many similar figures? We answer most emphatically, that there is no similar figure. There is no similar figure, for in this matter of the Holy Sacrament the Lord directs our attention to the lower part of His nature—His Body and Blood—rather than to Himself. In all other figures—"I am the Door," "I am the Shepherd"—the Lord directs attention to His spiritual nature, His action as a Divine Spirit. Here He directs attention to His lower and passive nature as that through which we are to receive the benefits of His Redemption.

Then in the next place we must believe that if our Lord intended to give the bread as a mere symbol He would have plainly said so, for if He had but once so explained it, it would have saved the Church from 1700 or 1800 years of most gross misconception concerning the meaning and import of the leading rite of His Religion. But is there any necessity why we should partake of His lower nature of Flesh and Blood, as well as of His higher? He must be the Judge of that, and He lays it down that there is when He says, "Except ye eat the flesh of the Son of man, and drink his blood, ye have no life in you."

May I be permitted to reproduce what I have written elsewhere upon this? "Every sincere believer in the supernatural, as revealed in the Scriptures, must allow that there may be reasons connected with our own nature of flesh and blood, and the sin and weakness, and death transmitted to us through flesh and blood, why we should receive the Lord's very Body and Blood. There is mystery enough about a Body which the eternal Son of God assumed, which was conceived and born totally out of the course of nature, which was the Body of the Second Adam, the New Head of the race; which ascended far above all heavens, and now sits at the right hand of God. There is mystery enough, I say, about such a Body to help us take His words in humble and submissive faith. What limit can we put to its capacities, seeing that in Him dwelleth all the fullness of the Godhead bodily?"

If Christ be our Second Adam it seems not so unlikely that we should supernaturally partake of His Flesh and Blood, seeing that by naturally having within us the flesh and blood of the old Adam we are in sin and death. So that three mysteries—the profound mystery inherent in our own nature of flesh and blood, in which mind and spirit are, as it were, incarnated, and sin in the whole—the still profounder mystery of the nature which is in store for us, the nature of the Resurrection body—the profoundest mystery of all, the union of the Divine and Human, the eternal Word and the human flesh, in the Person of our blessed Lord—all these things make for our taking the words of Christ not in the carnal or miraculous but in the sacramental way set forth in the oldest accounts and in our own formularies, a way by which we hold that the bread and wine remain in their natural substance, but that when we receive them we verily and indeed take and receive the Body and Blood of Christ, so that we may have eternal life, and be raised up by Him at the last day.

"Which is broken for you." The Lord's Body unquestionably was broken for us. This does not mean that any of His bones were broken. To fulfil a very direct prophecy it was ordered that they should not be; but when His Sacred Body was scourged and crowned with thorns, when His hands and feet and side were pierced, His Body, His Flesh, was indeed broken.

"This do in remembrance of me." This means "take bread, bless it, break it, and say over it what I say." The words which Christ said as he delivered the bread have been said over the bread ever since as a part of the institution.

"In remembrance of me." Rather for my commemoration—for my anamnesis.

The question now arises, What is this remembrance? Is it only a private act of remembrance which we make in our own souls, so that we use the blessed Sacrament as a reminder of what Christ has done for us just as we might read over the account of the Crucifixion in any one of the Gospels, or in the twenty-second Psalm, or in the fifty-third chapter of Isaiah? This is impossible, not only because the Church has never held it to be such a private reminder, but because the Sacrament itself, considered apart from its adjuncts, its prayers, praises, and thanksgiving, would remind no one of Christ; a sermon on the Death of Christ, or a Cross, much more a Crucifix, would be a more direct reminiscence of Him.

The word which the Lord uses is a remarkable one, ἀνάμνησις. It is, apart from its use in Luke xxii. 19, and in this place, only once used in the New Testament, and that is in Hebrews, x. 3, "in those sacrifices," *i.e.*, those offered on the great day of Atonement, "there is a remembrance again made of sins every year." This is undoubtedly a solemn sacrificial remembrance made before God and God alone, for it was expressly commanded that no one was to be in the tabernacle except the High Priest, when he made the atonement. (Levit. xvi. 17.)

What then is meant by "Do this in remembrance of me?" I cannot give the answer better than in the words of Jeremy Taylor in his "Holy Living."

"1. The celebration of the Holy Sacrament is the great mystery [mysteriousness] of the Christian religion, and succeeds to the most solemn rite of natural and Judaical religion, the law of sacrificing. For God spared mankind, and took the sacrifice of beasts, together with our solemn prayers, for an instrument of expiation. But these could not purify the soul from sin, but were typical of the Sacrifice of something that could. But nothing could do this, but either the offering of all that sinned, that every one should be the Anathema or devoted thing; or else by some one of the same capacity, who by some superadded excellency, might in his own personal sufferings have a value great enough to satisfy for all the whole kind (or race) of sinning persons. This the Son of God, Jesus Christ, God and Man, undertook and finished by a Sacrifice of Himself upon the altar of the Cross.

"2. This Sacrifice, because it was perfect, could be but One, and that once; but because the needs should last as long as the world itself, it was necessary that there should be a perpetual ministry established, whereby this one sufficient Sacrifice should be made eternally effectual to the several new arising needs of all the world who should desire it, or in any sense be capable of it.

"3. To this end Christ was made a 'Priest for ever;' He was initiated or consecrated on the Cross, and then began His Priesthood which was to last till His coming to judgment. It began on earth, but was to last and be officiated in Heaven, where He sits perpetually representing and exhibiting to the Father that great effective Sacrifice which He offered on the Cross, to eternal and never failing purposes.

"4. As Christ is pleased to represent to His Father that great Sacrifice as a means of atonement and expiation for all mankind, and with special purposes and intendment for all the elect, all that serve Him in holiness; so He hath appointed, that the same ministry shall be done upon earth too, in our manner, and according to our proportion; and therefore hath constituted and separated an order of men, who, by showing forth the Lord's Death by sacramental representations, may pray unto God after the same manner that our Lord and High Priest does: that is, offer to God and represent in the solemn prayer and sacrament, Christ, as already offered, so sending up a gracious instrument, whereby our prayers may, for His sake, and in the same manner of intercession, be offered up to God on our behalf, and for all them for whom we pray, to all those purposes for which Christ died." ("Holy Living," ch. iv. sec. x.[1])

---

[1] I have given in Appendix A. of my work entitled "The One Offering," some extracts from early Fathers and Ecclesiastical writers in which they confess the Sacrificial Nature of the Eucharist. I will now give a few short extracts. Thus, Clement of Rome—"Our sin will not be small if we eject from the Episcopate those who have blamelessly and holily offered the gifts" (Epistle to Corinthians, ch. xliv.) Ignatius, A.D. 100 or so—"Take ye heed then to have but one Eucharist, for there is one Flesh of our Lord Jesus Christ, and one Cup for the unity of His Blood, one Altar, as there is one Bishop, along

HE TOOK THE CUP.

25 After the same manner also *he took* the cup, when he

---

25. "After the same manner also he took the cup, when he had supped," &c. This was a mingled cup—not of wine only, but of wine and water. This mingling of the cup is mentioned in the first account of the Eucharist—to be found in the Fathers. That in Justin Martyr: "There is then brought to the president of the brethren bread and a cup of wine mixed with water; and he, taking it, gives praise and glory to the Father of the Universe, through the Name of the Son, and of the Holy Ghost, &c. And when the president has given thanks, and all the people have expressed their assent, those who are called by us deacons give to each of those present to partake of the bread and wine mixed with water, over which the thanksgiving was pronounced, and to those who are absent they carry away a portion."

The same is noticed in the Liturgy of St. Clement: "Likewise also having mingled the cup with wine and water and blessed it, he gave it to them, saying, 'Drink ye all of it,'" &c. And also in that of St. James: "Likewise after supper He took the cup, and mixed it with wine and water," &c.

"When he had supped." What is meant by this? It is supposed by many that there was an interval—perhaps a considerable one—between the consecration and distribution of the bread and

---

with the Presbytery and deacons," &c. Justin Martyr (A.D. 140)—"Accordingly God, anticipating all the Sacrifices which we offer through His Name, and which Jesus the Christ enjoined us to offer, *i. e.* in the Eucharist of the Bread and the Cup," &c. Again, Irenæus (A.D. 180)—"He took that created thing, bread, and gave thanks and said, This is my Body, and the cup likewise, which is part of the Creation to which we belong, He confessed to be His Blood, and taught the New Oblation of the New Covenant which the Church, receiving from the Apostles, offers to God throughout all the world," &c.

To these I may add a testimony from the lately exhumed "Didache of the Apostles," a very ancient monument of Jewish or Palestinian Christianity, which, I believe, represents that phase as it flourished before the end of the first century—"And on each Lord's Day of the Lord be ye gathered together, and break bread and give thanks, after confessing your transgressions, that our sacrifice may be pure. And let none that hath a difference with his fellow come together with you until they be reconciled, that our Sacrifice be not defiled. For this is that which is spoken by the Lord (Malachi i. 11). In every place and time offer me a pure sacrifice: For I am a great King, saith the Lord, and my name wonderful among the Gentiles."

The two previous passages (chap. ix. and x. page 129-131 of Dr. Taylor's edition), which are supposed to refer to the Eucharist, cannot possibly do so, as they have not the smallest reference to the Sacrifice of Christ. They are in all probability Jewish Thanksgivings used at the Agape in Palestine, which was not then separated from the Eucharist.

had supped, saying, This cup is the new testament in my

---

25. "Testament;" rather "covenant."

that of the cup. Thus Gresley in his "Harmony" makes an interval between the delivery of the bread and of the cup, during which the Lord spake the words contained in John xiv.; and that, as He was rising up to leave, He consecrated and delivered to them the cup. St. Matthew and St. Mark seem to know of no interval whatsoever between the delivery of the bread and of the cup; and we, at this distance of time, and not knowing exactly all the particulars of the Paschal Rite, cannot say with any certainty anything about it. The bread which the Lord took was probably the cake which was eaten last of all, and the cup which He took was some cup at the conclusion of the whole solemnity. I can only repeat here what I have said in my commentary on St. Luke xxii. 17: "There were four cups at least solemnly blessed and used at the Passover solemnity; and this (that of Luke xxii. 17—not, of course, that of Luke xxii. 20) was most likely the second. This has been called "the cup of the Old Testament or Covenant," being strictly a part of the Ancient Passover which was then for ever passing away. The next (or rather last cup), that of verse 20, being part of the New Rite—the Eucharistic Sacrament—into which a somewhat later part of the solemnity of breaking bread, and blessing and handing round a cup, was turned by the Lord."

Why, however, is this, "after he had supped" mentioned? Most commentators, and, I think, with reason, suppose that it was to distinguish the Eucharist from every other meal, no matter how sacred.

The two consecrations must of necessity be united, because, ever since the Apostles' time, they form part of one prayer.

"Saying, This cup is the new testament in my blood." This must be perfectly synonymous with "This is my blood of the new testament," and is of inconceivable value as showing us that, in receiving the Blood, we receive that for which the Blood was shed—that is, the New Covenant. The Blood of Christ was shed to

---

[1] Mr. Blunt supposes that the words, "when he had supped," apply to the whole action, and do not mean that the consecration of the bread and of the wine was broken by a considerable interval, as if one took place in the midst of the supper and the other only after its conclusion.

blood: this do ye, as oft as ye drink *it*, in remembrance of me.

26 For as often as ye eat this bread, and drink this cup,

---

bring about and inaugurate a New Covenant, which is described in Jeremiah xxxi. 33: "This shall be the covenant that I will make with the house of Israel; After those days, saith the Lord, I will put my law in their inward parts, and write it in their hearts, and will be their God, and they shall be my people. . . . . I will forgive their iniquity, and I will remember their sin no more." To apprehend that we receive this with the Blood of Christ, we must have faith—faith in the Lord as the Institutor of this Sacrament—faith in His being the same yesterday, to-day, and for ever—to make this Sacrament to us now what it was to St. Paul's converts then. And no matter what our faith be in other respects—our conversion, our illumination, our spiritual feelings—can we be said to be in this New Covenant, unless we receive the seal of It?

"This do ye, as oft as ye drink it, in remembrance of me"—that is, for My solemn Church anamnesis or memorial.

The repetition of this is to be noticed. The two elements of the Most Holy Sacrament are not to be divided. Both are to be taken as the solemn memorial of the Passion and Death of the Son of God. With what face, then, can any Church deny to the great body of her members the cup, seeing that in it the memorial is made, as well as in the bread; seeing, too, that it is the sign and seal of the New Covenant—rather, that the New Covenant is in it?

26. "For as often as ye eat this bread, and drink this cup, ye do shew," &c. It has been said that this "shew" is to be taken in the sense of proclaiming or preaching, for that is the usual sense of the word καταγγέλλω. But is this possible? For the Sacrament of the Lord's Body has never been a preaching ordinance. In primitive times it was celebrated with closed doors, and only before the faithful, not to the world, who much more than the faithful require the preaching of Christ to convert them. I think we shall see the meaning, if we consider well the question, What did a Jew in old time do when he offered a sacrifice? He set forth, shewed forth, proclaimed his belief that the God of Israel had ordained the sacrifice to be an atonement for him; and he did this not so much before his fellow Israelites as in the sight of God, for the sacrifice

| Or, *shew ye.*
e John xiv. 5.
& xxi. 22.
Acts i. xi.
ch. iv. 5. &
xv. 23. 1
Thess. iv. 16.
2 Thess. i. 10.
Jude 14. Rev.
i. 7.
f Num. ix. 10,
13. John vi.
51, 63, 64. &
xiii. 27. ch.
x. 21.

|| ye do shew the Lord's death ᵉ till he come.

27 ᶠ Wherefore whosoever shall eat this bread,

was not offered to men, but to God. It was an act of worship, and worship is not offered to be seen of men, but to propitiate God.

The best illustration of the Apostle's meaning is to be found in one of the earliest Liturgies—that of St. James—where the Priest, having consecrated the cup, says, "Do this in remembrance of me: for as oft as ye eat this bread, and drink this cup, ye do shew forth the Death of the Son of Man, and confess His Resurrection until His coming again."

And to this the people respond :

"O Lord, we shew forth thy Death, and confess thy Resurrection."

"Till he come." This shows in opposition to some modern sectaries, that the Holy Eucharist is intended to be a permanent ordinance, to be celebrated till the Second Coming. Just as the Jewish sacrifices, by anticipation, set forth the Lord's Death till His First Coming, so the Eucharist shows forth His Death till His Second.

27. "Wherefore whosoever shall eat this bread, and [or] drink this," &c. Almost all authorities read "or." "ἤ [or] has a peculiar significance here, because, as the context shows, St. Paul has been censuring the Corinthians for two several *sins*, opposed respectively to the *two* several elements of the Lord's Supper. The first sin is that of eating meats offered to idols, and of gluttony generally, and particularly at the meals before the Communion (v. 21), a sin especially opposed to communion in the Eucharistic Bread (see 1 Cor. x. 21). The second sin—that of Drinking the Cup of Devils, or false Deities (1 Cor. x. 2), and of intemperance in the meals before the Communion (v. 21)—a sin especially opposed to the Eucharistic Cup" (Wordsworth).

The Bread of the Lord—not the bread which the Lord eat, but the Bread of which the Lord said, "I am the true bread, the living bread."

"Unworthily." What is meant by this "unworthily"? It may mean in a state of sin, without repentance, without faith, without love, without self-examination, without prayer. Or it may mean

LET A MAN EXAMINE HIMSELF.

and drink *this* cup of the Lord, unworthily, shall be guilty of the body and blood of the Lord.

28 But g let a man examine himself, and so let him eat of *that* bread, and drink of *that* cup.

g 2 Cor. xiii. 5.
Gal. vi. 4.

27. "And drink this cup." Almost all MSS. and versions read, "or;" so ℵ, A., B., C., D., E., F., G., K., L., P., most Cursives, Versions, &c.

in an unbelieving manner, as if it was a common meal, common bread, common wine, a mere adjunct of the love feast. Now this latter was undoubtedly the sin of the Corinthians. They discerned not the Lord's Body, making no difference between consecrated elements and ordinary food. But it is quite clear that if men take the Blessed Sacrament whilst they are living in a state of wilful sin, and determining to continue in that state, they profane that which is given them to enable them to resist sin. It is given them for the strengthening and refreshing of their souls by the Body and Blood of Christ. They go clean contrary to the intent for which God gives them the Body and Blood of Christ, which is that "Christ may dwell in them and they in Him," and how can a man invite Christ into himself to dwell in him along with that sin from which Christ died to deliver him?

"Shall be guilty of the body and blood of the Lord." If the consecrated elements are symbols then he profanes these figures which God (no matter how we regard them) has ordained for a most holy use; but the whole reasoning of the Apostle in the following verses implies that they are far more than symbols—they are most blessed and yet tremendous realities; for in profanely using them it is in our power to eat and drink our own condemnation, not discerning the Lord's Body.

"Guilty of the body and blood," must mean, guilty of the Body and Blood itself, not of a mere representation of it.

28. "But let a man examine himself," &c. The examination in this context must refer to the nature of the guilt which is to be avoided. If the guilt is a profanation through receiving in impenitence, then we must examine ourselves as regards our hatred and fear of sin, so that we should receive the blessed Sacrament as a strengthening against sin, and of spiritual refreshment in our conflict with sin. But if it refers to a profanation through not considering and duly reverencing the Inward Part of the Sacrament

29 For he that eateth and drinketh unworthily, eateth and

29. "Unworthily." So ℵ, A., B., C., 17, Sah., omit "unworthily;" but D., E., F., G., K., L., P., almost all Cursives, Itala., Vulg., Syriac, Cop., Arm., Goth., retain.

then we must earnestly pray for faith in the words of Christ in which He instituted this Sacrament, and in the words of Christ in which He prepared His apostles to receive in it the greatest benefits of Redemption.

"And so let him eat of that bread, and drink of that cup." Observe that the Apostle never contemplates the possibility of anyone abstaining from partaking of the Eucharist. If anyone on examination finds himself unworthy, on account of sin persisted in, he must resolve against sin, and pray to God through Christ to give him instant deliverance.

29. "For he that eateth and drinketh unworthily .... not discerning the Lord's Body." The word unworthily is not in the four principal Uncials, but is in all other authorities. If omitted the verse will read "he that eateth and drinketh, eateth and drinketh condemnation to himself, if he discern not the Lord's Body," and the difference in meaning is scarcely perceptible. The latter rendering makes all unworthy eating—all eating to condemnation—to consist in failing to discern the Lord's Body. The Lord's Body is to be discerned not only as there, but as there so that it should be received for the highest purposes of salvation, "that we should dwell in him and he in us," that "we should have eternal life and be raised up at the last day." The eating of the Flesh of the Son of man is not the absolute end, but takes place that we may be one with Christ and Christ with us, which is, as far as the mind of man can comprehend, the absolute end. Of course it is not meant that all who fail to realize fully receive unworthily, for in so profoundly deep and holy a matter there must be many degrees of apprehension; but if we begin as the Church teaches us, devoutly and seriously to consider the DIGNITY of that Holy Sacrament, we shall be led on by God to worthier and still worthier degrees of realization.

"Damnation to himself." This rendering has been, so far as the eye of man can see, a very unfortunate one. It has impressed upon the minds of many, especially among the poor and uneducated, a deep-seated conviction that it is safer to stay away from Holy Communion than to communicate. Still there is this to

drinketh ‖ damnation to himself, not discerning the Lord's body.

‖ Or, *judgment*, Rom. xiii. 2.

29. "The Lord's Body." So D , E., F., G., K., L., P., most Cursives, Syr., Copt., Arm., Goth.; but ℵ, A., B., C., 17, 67**, Vulg. (Cod. Amiat.), Sah., omit "the Lord," and read "the Body."

be considered that as we have no primitive discipline worth speaking of, men should be brought to exercise discipline upon themselves.

The meaning of the word is judgment: this judgment may be temporal or eternal—in this world or in the world to come. In the case of these unworthy receivers amongst the Corinthians the judgment was temporal, as is clear from the next verse, but any persistence in a state of heart which incapacitates us from discerning the Lord's Body, or renders us unfit to receive it, must be a state very displeasing to God, and which sooner or later He will punish severely.

"Not discerning the Lord's body." This is explained as meaning either—

(1.) Not discriminating, not making a difference between Bread which the Lord called His Body and common bread, not realizing that the Sacrament has an Inward Part, or

(2.) Not forming a judgment on the Lord's Body, *i.e.*, as there for our salvation. The word discerning—discerning that it is there—seems to be best, and we may also notice the word "considering," which we have in our Eucharistic office. "Considering" cannot mean considering that the Lord has a body which is now in heaven, but considering—devoutly, humbly, prayerfully considering—that God gave His Son not only to die for us, but also to be our spiritual food and sustenance in that Holy Sacrament.[1]

---

[1] Some, as Dean Stanley, have said that the Body here means not the Sacramental Body of the Lord, but the Church which is called His Body; but how can this be said with the smallest degree of reason when the Body of Christ, as signifying the Church, has not been mentioned throughout the entire context? The Apostle begins with citing the Lord's words, "This is my Body;" surely He does not mean "this is My Church;" then He speaks of the Cup being His Blood or the New Covenant in His Blood. Then the Apostle proceeds to show the end of the purpose of this eating and drinking, "to show the Lord's Death till he come." Then he shows that unworthy eating and drinking makes men guilty of the Body and Blood of the Lord; and, lastly, a man is to examine himself before he eat of that Bread, and then, after all this allusion to Sacramental Bread, we are told that, in the 29th verse, the discerning of this Body is the discerning of the Church. A

30 For this cause many *are* weak and sickly among you, and many sleep.

ʰ Ps. xxxii. 5. 1 John i. 9.

31 For ʰ if we would judge ourselves, we should not be judged.

---

31. "For if we would," &c. So C., K., L., P., most Cursives, Syriac, Sah., Copt., Arm.; but ℵ, A., B., D., E., F., G., 17, 46, 109, g, Goth., Æth. [quod si d, e, f, Vulg.], read, "but if" (εἰ δὲ).

I shall consider the question, What do the wicked eat or receive, in an Excursus at the end of the book.

30. "For this cause many are weak and sickly among you, and many sleep." This can only refer to temporal weakness or sickness and death, not to spiritual; for the spiritual decay and death was in the state of heart which suffered them to treat the Sacrament as common food. In the first beginnings of the Church temporal punishments were inflicted by God on profane persons, as on Ananias and Sapphira. There seems to have been a strange and fatal mortality in the Corinthian Church, and St. Paul here speaking by inspiration of God, declares it to have been a visitation of God.

"Many"—not a few—a sufficient number to indicate the anger of God on the Church—the ἱκανοί being perhaps intended here to mark something less than the πολλοί, though still sufficiently numerous to arouse serious attention.

31. "For if we would judge ourselves, we should not be judged." If we judged ourselves, *i.e.*, if we would look into ourselves, if we would narrowly examine ourselves, and accuse ourselves before God of the evil we find within us and bewail it, and bring it before God to be forgiven, then we should not be judged, either now or hereafter, by the Lord.

"We should not be judged," refers to the judgments on the Corinthians: we should not have been judged as we have been. (So Wordsworth.)

Mark how St. Paul here identifies himself with those who suffered by using the first person plural "we."

---

more dishonest handling of Scripture cannot be conceived: and yet we shall see presently that if any rationalistic or Zuinglian view of the Sacrament is to be entertained, the Sacramental view of this verse must be got rid of.

CHAP. XI.]   TARRY ONE FOR ANOTHER.   195

32 But when we are judged, [1] we are chastened of the Lord, that we should not be condemned with the world.

[1] Ps. xciv. 12, 13. Heb. xii. 5-11.

33 Wherefore, my brethren, when ye come together to eat, tarry one for another.

---

32. "But when we are judged, we are chastened of the Lord," &c. The judgments inflicted by God on the Corinthians were not inflicted wholly in judgment, but in mercy as well. And they took place not merely to arouse and convert them to a better mind, but to be a real punishment, which God inflicted on them in this world, that He might not punish them with extreme severity in the world to come. The case seems to have been analogous to the punishment of death with which the Apostle threatened the incestuous Corinthian, whom he delivered unto Satan for the destruction of the flesh, that the spirit might be saved in the day of the Lord Jesus (v. 5); and in some degree analagous also to that inflicted on Hymenæus and Alexander, whom he delivered to Satan—not that he might have eternal dominion over them, but that they might be delivered from his eternal dominion by being taught not to blaspheme (1 Tim. i. 20).

"That we should not be condemned with the world." The world is under condemnation. Those who believe in Christ, and are united in His fellowship, are delivered from this condemnation, but they may fall back into it if they make not their calling and election sure.

33, 34. "Wherefore, my brethren, when ye come together to eat, tarry one for another." The Apostle having sufficiently asserted the uniqueness of the Eucharist and its awful nature, so that they who eat it profanely are guilty of the Body and Blood of the Lord, now resumes for a moment the consideration of the love feasts, and gives a short, but sufficient direction against the practice which was the occasion of the disorder. He had said (ver. 21), "In eating every one taketh before other his own supper, and one is hungry and another is drunken." The Apostle now tells them that they must make it what its name implies—a love feast—and tarry one for another, so that the rich may not have consumed all their provisions ere the poor arrive, and find there is nothing left, and entertain bitter feelings in consequence.

k ver. 21.
l ver. 22.
|| Or, *judgment*.
m ch. vii. 17.
Tit. i. 5.
n ch. iv. 19.

34 And if any man ᵏhunger, let him eat at ˡhome; that ye come not together unto || condemnation. And the rest ᵐwill I set in order when ⁿI come.

It is impossible to suppose that the words "tarry one for another" refer to the celebration of the Eucharist, for there must have been an appointed hour for such celebration, and it is ridiculous to imagine that St. Paul would have had the commencement of the Eucharistic celebration delayed to accommodate those who were unpunctual. And the words, "if any man hunger, let him eat at home," cannot of course possibly refer to the eating in the Eucharist.

"That ye come not together unto condemnation." The love feast, being held in the Christian assemblies, was a sacred meal, and its intention was that all ranks of Christians should be partakers of a common meal which was not, as the Eucharist, a sacrificial act of worship done to God, but partook more of the character of a secular feast. So it might be taken irreverently and without due regard to the place and the purpose, and so to condemnation.

"And the rest will I set in order when I come." No doubt he did set matters in order, but not a word respecting the manner of his doing so has come down to us. Judging from his remarks, we must believe that his setting in order would, amongst other things, take the form of separating the Eucharist from every other feast or meal, for the mixing up of the Eucharist and the Agape had led to the profanity. In the earliest notice of the celebration of the Eucharist in Justin Martyr, it appears as a rite or Sacrament absolutely unique, and the partaking of it *the* reason why Christians came together on the Lord's Day.

CHAP. XII.

NOW ^a concerning spiritual *gifts*, brethren, I would not have you ignorant.

2 Ye know ^b that ye were Gentiles, carried away unto these ^c dumb idols, even as ye were led.

a ch. xiv. 1, 37.
b ch. vi. 11. Ephes. ii. 11, 12. 1 Thess. i. 9. Tit. iii. 3. 1 Pet. iv. 3.
c Ps. cxv. 5.

---

2. "Ye know that ye were Gentiles." So F., G. (Greek), many Cursives, d, e, Syriac, Copt.; but ℵ, A., B., C., D., E., L., P., fifty Cursives, f, g, Vulg., Sah., Arm., Æth., read, "when ye were Gentiles ye were carried away."

1. "Now concerning spiritual gifts, brethren, I would not have you," &c. Comparing the wording of this with that of chap. vii. 1, and viii. 1 (the same form περὶ δὲ κ. τ. λ. occurring in all three places), we should gather that they had put a question to him respecting spiritual gifts, and, from the way in which he answers it, we should gather that they had asked him about the comparative greatness of some of these gifts. Some had boasted that the gifts which they possessed were greater than those which others had received. They had apparently despised those which were not outwardly striking, in comparison with such a gift as that of tongues, which from chap. xiv., it appears that some had used for vain-glorious display, and ranked above others, such as prophesying, which were far more edifying to the Church.

He takes the opportunity thus offered him of instructing them in the whole subject of the work of the Spirit in the Mystical Body. And first of all he tells them that that profession of faith in Christ, which they all had in common, and without which they could have received no other grace or gift of the Spirit, was "by the Spirit."

2. "Ye know that ye were Gentiles, carried away unto these dumb," &c. He contrasts their former with their present state. They had all of them a little before this been Gentiles, not only worshippers of false Gods, but borne away unto them as men are borne to execution. There is supposed to be a reference to the irresistible force with which some seem impelled. Thus Chrysostom, "In the idol temples, if any were at any time possessed by an unclean spirit, and began to divine, even as one dragged away,

d Mark ix. 39. 1 John iv. 2, 3.
‖ Or, *anathema.*
e Matt. xvi. 17. John xv. 26. 2 Cor. iii. 5.

3 Wherefore I give you to understand, ^dthat no man speaking by the Spirit of God calleth Jesus ‖ accursed : and ^e*that* no man can say that Jesus is the Lord, but by the Holy Ghost.

---

3. "Calleth Jesus accursed." "Calleth Jesus Lord;" so D., E., F., G., K., L., P., most Cursives, d, e, g, Sah.; but א, A., B., C., 6, 17, 46, 109, Cop., Arm., Æth., read, "Jesus is accursed." "Jesus is Lord."

so was he drawn by that spirit in chains, knowing nothing of the things which he utters."

3. "Wherefore I give you to understand, that no man speaking by the Spirit of God," &c. What can the Apostle mean by this? Who in the Christian assemblies would call Jesus accursed? And some commentators have referred to the followers of Cerinthus, who separated between the man Jesus and the Christ within Him, and held that the one was accursed because suffered to hang on the tree, whilst the Christ, or Word once dwelling within Him, had left Him and ascended to heaven.

But the most natural way of understanding it is by supposing that St. Paul does not in the least refer to utterances in Church, but to the Jews and heathen, particularly the former. God had promised (Haggai ii. 5) that His Spirit should remain among them, and yet the unconverted among them cursed the All Holy Name. This showed on the face of it that they had none of the Spirit of God, but, on the contrary, the confession of the Christians that Jesus was the Lord, could only have been brought about by the power of the Holy Ghost. Their conversion from heathenism to the faith of Christ was as great a miracle in the spiritual world, as any performed by the Name of Jesus in the outward and visible world, such as the healing of diseases, and the speaking with tongues. I think, however, we must take this statement in the broadest way possible. We must not narrow it by explaining it as " No man can truly say, can devoutly say, can savingly say—that Jesus is the Lord"; but no man can at all profess that Jesus is the Lord, but by the Spirit of God. I believe it means that what we call the outward profession of Christianity was certainly in that day a work of the Spirit, and may not the continuance of men in the outward profession of the faith in this day be a gift—a work of the Spirit? It surely is a good thing not to

CHAP. XII.]   DIVERSITIES OF GIFTS.   199

4 Now ᶠ there are diversities of gifts, but ᵍ the same Spirit.

5 ʰ And there are differences of ‖ administrations, but the same Lord.

6 And there are diversities of operations, but it is the same God ⁱ which worketh all in all.

ᶠ Rom. xii. 4, &c. Hebr. ii. 4. 1 Pet. iv. 10.
ᵍ Ephes. iv. 4.
ʰ Rom. xii. 6, 7, 8. Ephes. iv. 11.
‖ Or, *ministeries*.
ⁱ Ephes. i. 23.

---

deny that Jesus is the Son of God. Considering the vast numbers who hold Him to have been a mere man, it is something to hold the mere acknowledgment of His being the Son of God. It may lead, if well handled by the preacher or teacher, to the realization of all saving truth.

4. "Now there are diversities of gifts [*charismata*] but the same Spirit." No matter what the difference in the gifts themselves they are all gifts of the One Spirit; the gifts which have to do with the healing of the body, and those which have to do with the edification of the soul or spirit, proceed from the One Holy Spirit.

5. "And there are differences of administration, but the same Lord." Administrations, ministrations or ministries (" Or ministry, let us wait on our ministering," Rom. xii. 7) are here referred to the Lord Jesus, Who is the Head of all ministry in the Church, for under Him and by His appointment all ministries are exercised.

6. "And there are diversities of operations, but it is the same God," &c. Operations are the " effects, results and outward manifestations of the in-working power " (Ellicott), not simply synonymous with the gifts, or with the ministries or ministrations, but the practical and powerful effect of them. Thus the Holy Spirit gives a man a gift of grace, Christ employs that man as His minister in some department of His Church, but God makes the gift exercised by the minister powerful and effectual; as the Apostle says (iii. 7), " Neither is he that planteth anything, neither he that watereth, but God that giveth the increase." So that the action of the three Persons of the Ever-Blessed Trinity are inseparably combined in every work of the Church. The gift or ability by which a Christian does any work, is of the Spirit; the ministration or working is under the Lord as the Head of the Church; the effectual working for good is through the power of the Father: thus

> 7 ᵏ But the manifestation of the Spirit is given to every man to profit withal.
>
> 8 For to one is given by the Spirit ¹the word

ᵏ Rom. xii. 6, 7, 8. ch. xiv. 26. Ephes. iv. 7. 1 Pet. iv. 10, 11.
¹ ch. ii. 6, 7.

---

8. "By the Spirit;" lit. "through the Spirit" (διὰ).

even Christ said, "The Father that dwelleth in me, he doeth the works" (John xiv. 10).

7. "But the manifestation of the Spirit is given to every man to profit withal." The manifestation of the Spirit is not so much the manifestation that the man has the Spirit, but that the Spirit manifests certain things (wisdom, knowledge, &c.) through him.

"To every man." "To each one," Revisers. Without laying undue stress upon this "each" or "every" as referring to all absolutely, there is no doubt but that the Apostle meant that the gifts were very generally diffused. The gift implied in being able to confess the Lord Jesus, was, of course, common to all (Titus iii. 6), and teaches us that the Spirit was poured forth, not sparingly, but abundantly.

"To profit withal," *i.e.*, for the edification and strengthening of the whole Church, not for each man's particular glory or advantage.

8. "For to one is given by the Spirit the word of wisdom." There are nine gifts of the Spirit here enumerated, and expositors from the time of Tertullian to the present, have attempted (I am constrained to say with what appears to me very indifferent success) to classify them or group them together. Some have made three, some four, and another no less than five divisions among the nine; the last one makes prophecy, as teaching power, one, and discerning of spirits, as critical power, another. Then they have been said to have been arranged by the Apostle in the order of their importance, the "word of wisdom" being the most important, and the interpretation of tongues the least. But can this be so? for surely the word of knowledge is not above faith, taking faith to be here a more than ordinarily vivid realization of unseen things; and, then, can the working of miracles be put before prophecy, seeing that the Apostle says "desire . . . rather that ye may prophesy"? I scarcely think then that such a classification was in the Apostle's mind.

8. "For to one is given by the Spirit the word of wisdom; to another the word of knowledge," &c. The reader will notice that

CHAP. XII.] THE WORD OF KNOWLEDGE.

of wisdom; to another ᵐ the word of knowledge by the same Spirit;

ᵐ ch. i. 5. & xiii. 2. 2 Cor. viii. 7.

"Knowledge by the same Spirit;" "according to the same Spirit" (κατὰ).

the two gifts here mentioned are not wisdom and knowledge, but the outward expression of these gifts—the word of wisdom and the word of knowledge.

It is most discouraging to think that the expositors, nearly every one, take a different view of what wisdom and knowledge are respectively. Godet, for instance, in a single page repudiates the meanings given by Neander, Bengel, Hofmann, Heinrici and Edwards.

The Apostle evidently considers wisdom as the highest state of mind, when he says, "We speak wisdom among them that are perfect," (ii. 6), and St. James seems to include in it all good moral qualities when he writes, "The wisdom that is from above is first pure, then peaceable, gentle, and easy to be intreated, full of mercy and good fruits, without partiality, and without hypocrisy" (James iii. 17). But, above all, Christ is called "The wisdom of God." The wisdom then here must be the representation of His Mind, and the word of wisdom of His teaching.

Now, what is the characteristic of the Lord's teaching? It is pre-eminently moral. It appears to me that He never reveals any truth for a merely intellectual purpose—always for a practical one. He reveals the Mystery of His own Sonship, to show that the Father loves Him, and in giving Him shows His Love to all mankind. And because of this they should love Him and keep His commandments. Such then is the word of wisdom.

But what is the word of knowledge? St. Paul evidently, in this very Epistle, treats it as in a sphere below wisdom, when he says, "We know that we all have knowledge. Knowledge puffeth up, but charity edifieth" (viii. 1). Knowledge is our cognitive faculty, apprehending a multitude of truths, either made known to us in the Scripture, or given to us through the revelations made by God to those inspired by Him, and the word of knowledge is the right way of expressing these truths, putting them in their right order, and bringing them down, as far as they can be, to the level of the human intellect—in fact, teaching. Godet seems to illustrate the difference well: "We see in gnosis, a notion of effort, investigation, dis-

> n Matt. xvii. 19, 20. ch. xiii. 2. 2 Cor. iv. 13.
> o Mark xvi. 18. James v. 14.

9 ⁿ To another faith by the same Spirit; to another ^o the gifts of healing by the same Spirit;

---

9. "By the same Spirit;" lit. "in the same spirit." So Revisers. "Gifts of healing by the same Spirit;" "in the one Spirit."

covery (compare xiii. 2, where this term is connected with the idea of knowing all mysteries); and in sophia, on the contrary, the idea of a calm possession of truth already acquired, as well as of its practical application. Gnosis makes the teacher: wisdom the preacher and pastor."

9. "To another faith by the same Spirit." This can hardly be the rudimentary faith which is given at the very outset. It has been generally explained as the faith which enabled Christians in those days to perform miracles, as this Apostle says in a later chapter, xiii. 2, "And though I have all faith so that I could remove mountains;" and it is noticed that "the gifts of healing," and "the working of miracles" immediately follow it. But both these seem to me, by being mentioned as separate gifts, to require us to interpret this faith as a something apart from either of these, and I would take it to be a more than ordinary realization of the powers of the spiritual world, an almost overwhelming evidence of things not seen, a constant sight of Him Who is invisible.

If it be asked, how did this faith show itself apart from miraculous manifestation? I should answer by a life more than ordinarily above the world—by prayer which was certain of its answer, and which believed that it received what it asked for. I should say, then, that the outward sign of the faith was constant prayer. Godet speaks of it as the possession of salvation taking the character of assurance in God of heroic daring, resolutely attacking and surmounting all the obstacles which are opposed to God in a given situation, "Father, I know that thou hearest me always." The lives of men and women endued with this faith are the best sermons.

"To another the gifts of healing by the same Spirit." Not, of course, healing all who came in their way, but those whom by some secret impression of the Spirit they were impelled to heal. St. Paul was impelled to restore Eutychus to life, but was not permitted to heal Epaphroditus (Phil. ii. 25).

TO ANOTHER PROPHECY.

10 ᵖ To another the working of miracles; to another ᑫ prophecy; ʳ to another discerning of

p ver. 28, 29.
Mark xvi. 17.
Gal. iii. 5.
q Rom. xii. 6.
ch. xiii. 2. &
xiv. 1, &c.
r ch. xiv. 29.
1 John iv. 1.

10. "To another the working of miracles." What are these workings of miracles as distinguished from gifts of healing? Evidently exorcisms, or driving out of evil spirits, perhaps in some cases miraculously multiplying food. "To possess the power of working miracles and gifts of healing is not the same thing, for he that had a gift of healing used only to do cures; but he that possessed powers for working miracles used to punish also. For a miracle is not the healing only, but the punishing also, even as Paul inflicted blindness, as Peter slew": so Chrysostom. This power, however, seems to have been confined to the Apostles. There are no instances of others exercising it.

"To another prophecy." This is supposed to be something answering to our preaching, only of a character more directly inspired by the Spirit. Thus, it is said of Judas and Silas, that being prophets themselves, they exhorted the brethren with many words, and confirmed (strengthened) them (Acts xv. 32). Sometimes, however, the prophet, as in the case of Agabus, actually foretold future events. The characteristic of the prophet seems, however, to have been not to foretell the future, but to say, "Thus saith the Lord," and he foretold the future, because the revelation of God which he received generally took the form of threats of judgment to come on the wicked.

"To another discerning of spirits." This was not apparently a power to read the heart, but a power to pronounce upon certain prophetical utterances, whether they came from beneath or from above. The work of the Spirit in "prophecy" was permitted by God to be counterfeited. St. John writes: "Beloved, believe not every spirit, but try the spirits whether they are of God: because many false prophets are gone out into the world" (1 John iv. 1), and he gives a direction how they should try them, which seems to show that the false prophets promulgated Gnostical or Cerinthian errors. This discerning of spirits, however, mentioned here, implies a sort of judgment passed at once on the utterance of the prophet, independent of any lengthened application of some doctrinal test. As Bishop Ellicott says, "This gift was not dependent

spirits; to another * *divers* kinds of tongues; to another the interpretation of tongues;

* Acts ii. 4. & x. 46. ch. xiii. 1.

11 But all these worketh that one and the self-

---

on after reflection, but showed itself in an intuitive and instinctive perception."

"To another divers kinds of tongues; to another the interpretation of tongues." I have entered fully into the scope and meaning of this gift of tongues in an Excursus at the end of my volume of Notes on the Acts. Notwithstanding any seeming difficulties, I believe it to be what it is said to be in the proper Preface for Whitsunday, the "gift of divers languages," and I shall hope to make this clearer by a fuller examination of chap. xiv.

"To another the interpretation of tongues." This need not by any means be restricted to the interpretation of the utterances of those who had the gift of tongues. Supposing that any Christian from some distant land who knew Greek very imperfectly was desirous to address them, the office of the interpreter of tongues would come in. In all cases where one spoke in a tongue which he was unable to interpret, the interpreter had to be present to make known the meaning.

And now before we proceed we must consider the question, How came the Christians of Corinth, or of any other place to possess these gifts? Evidently by the laying on of the Apostles' hands. It was so in Ephesus (Acts xix. 6), and it was not likely to be otherwise in Corinth. St. Paul desired to be present with the Roman Christians, in order that he might impart unto them some spiritual gift. Why could not this have been done from a distance? Because God saw fit that the gift or gifts should be plainly seen to proceed from the Apostle, to establish their faith in that freeness of the Gospel which was the speciality of his mission.

Now we have this same rite of "laying on of hands." Ought we not to pray very earnestly that those who receive it may not only have given to them the ordinary gifts of the Spirit, but extraordinary ones suited to these times, such as the word of wisdom, of knowledge, of faith, and of prophesying, in the sense in which Judas and Silas possessed the gift?

11. "But all these worketh that one and the self-same Spirit, dividing," &c. No matter what the gifts, whether in the mind or

same Spirit, ^t dividing to every man severally ^u as he will.

12 For ^x as the body is one, and hath many members, and all the members of that one body, being many, are one body : ^y so also *is* Christ.

^t Rom. xii. 6.
ch. vii. 7. 2
Cor. x. 13.
Ephes. iv. 7.
^u John iii. 8.
Hebr. ii. 4.
^x Rom. xii. 4,
5. Ephes. iv.
4, 16.
^y ver. 27.
Gal. iii. 16.

---

12. "All the members of that one body." ℵ, A., B., C., F., G., K., L., P., 10, 17, 23, 31, 73, 115, 119, 122, 137, f, g, Vulg., Syriac, Cop., Arm., Æth., omit "one," and read, "of the body;" but D., E., most Cursives, d, e, Goth., insert "one."

spirit as wisdom and faith, whether on the body as gifts of healing, whether in the outer world as miracles, the One Spirit of God worked them all.

We have in this verse the plainest proofs possible both of the Godhead and the Personality of the Spirit—of His Godhead, in that He communicated to Christians such surprising gifts of supernatural insight and power; and of His distinct Personality—in that He divided the gifts to each one separately, according to His own free choice. He was not a mere afflatus from the Father and the Son, but in communicating each gift to a separate person, He was guided by His own all-wise Will.

12, 13. "For as the body is one, and hath many members, and all the members," &c. The connection between the last verse and this one is this. The formation of the Church and its inherence in Christ as the Body of which He is the Head, is the work of the Holy Spirit, Who, when He baptizes any one into Christ, assigns to Him a position in the mystical body as one of its members, and afterwards endows him with the grace by which he will be enabled to fulfil his function, as a member of that body.

Thus, it is in the Body of Christ, *i.e.*, His Church, as it is in the natural human body. The body is one, and yet this very oneness of the human body postulates a variety of members, and the multiplicity of members does not imply a multiplicity of separate organisms or bodies, but one organism only, and as it is with our human mortal bodies, so it is with Christ as the Head of His Body, the Church, with which He is one, so that instead of the Apostle saying the Body of Christ, he actually says "Christ," Christ and His Body in the Apostle's eyes forming, as it were, one Personality.

^z Rom. vi. 5.
^a Gal. iii. 28.
Ephes. ii. 13, 14, 16. Col. iii. 11.
† Gr. *Greeks*.
^b John vi. 63. & vii. 37, 38, 39.

13 For ^z by one Spirit are we all baptized into one body, ^a whether *we be* Jews or † Gentiles, whether *we be* bond or free; and ^b have been all made to drink into one Spirit.

---

13. "Into one Spirit." So E., K. (L.), most Cursives; but ℵ (A), B., C., D., F., G., P., 17, 47, 73, 80, 137, d, e, g, Vulg. (Amiat.), &c., omit "into" ("to drink of one Spirit.")

13. "For by one Spirit are we all baptized into one body, whether we," &c. This means that by the operation of the Spirit in Holy Baptism we are all baptized into, that is, are all made members of, the One Mystical Body. It may be well to consider for a moment the question, Does this refer to the visible Sacrament whereby we are made members of Christ, or does it refer to an invisible baptism by the Spirit, altogether distinct from the outward sacrament, and very seldom simultaneous with it? Now it may be sufficient to answer that the Holy Apostle knows nothing of such a baptism introducing us into an inner body or church apart from the outer. On the contrary, such an idea neutralizes the greater part of his teaching, which is, that all the professing members of the Church should consider themselves as having a real connection with Christ. There is but one Church from his point of view, an outward visible body endowed all of it with invisible graces and powers: so that each baptized person, instead of doubting that his baptism brought him into connection with Christ, should have no manner of doubt about it, but be assured that if he does not live as a member of Christ so much the worse for him, and that if he does realize his union with Christ so much the more power has he against sin and on the side of holiness.

"Whether we be Jews or Gentiles, whether we be bond or free." The original distinction between Jew and Gentile, and this distinction done away in Christ, was ever before the mind of the Apostle, and also at this time the distinction between bond and free was in his mind as appears from chap. vii. All distinctions of nationality and worldly conditions are done away with in Christ. "In him is neither Jew nor Greek, Barbarian, Scythian, bond nor free" (Coloss. iii).

"And have been all made to drink (into) one Spirit." There seems to be a reference to the cup of the Eucharist here. The

THE BODY NOT ONE MEMBER.

14 For the body is not one member, but many.

15 If the foot shall say, Because I am not the hand, I am not of the body; is it therefore not of the body?

---

types of Christians, the children of Israel in the wilderness, "all drank of the same spiritual drink," and St. Paul in applying this writes, "The cup of blessing which we bless, is it not the communion of the blood of Christ?" (x. 16.) Still it may be asked why does he not mention the bread, which is that part or sign which more especially has to do with unity? It may be answered that in x. 16, he mentions the cup first, and as Bishop Wordsworth notices, St. Ignatius, within fifty or sixty years after this, speaks of "one cup into the unity of His Blood." (Epistle to Philadelphians.)

Still we must be very careful not to suppose that the Inward Part of the Cup is the Holy Spirit. It is the Blood of Christ which is made effectual to us by the operation of the Spirit.

Godet explains this, "being made to drink," of the laying on of hands: "The new fact in the mind of the Apostle seems to me to be the communication of the gifts of the Holy Spirit which accompanied the laying on of hands after baptism (Acts viii. 17, xix. 6). By Baptism the believer is bathed in the Spirit as the source of new Life; by the act which follows the Spirit enters into him as the principle of certain particular gifts," &c. I cannot help thinking that the explanation given by Chrysostom is nearest the truth, "And give us all the same watering, for this is the meaning of 'we were all made to drink into One Spirit.'"

14-17. "For the body is not one member, but many." "If the foot shall say . . . If the ear . . . If the whole body were an eye," &c. The reader will remember the parable of the belly and members, as given in Livy, which I give in a note.[1] There is,

---

[1] "In that time in which the members of the human body were not in a state of unity, as they now are, but each member had its own separate judgment and tongue, all the rest became full of indignation because whatever was provided by their care, labour, and industry was spent upon the belly; while the belly, lying at ease in the midst of the body, did nothing but enjoy whatever ministered to its pleasure and delight. They conspired, therefore, among themselves that the hands should not carry food to the mouth, nor the mouth receive what was offered to it, nor the teeth grind it between them. Thus carrying out their revenge, whilst they were taming the belly into subjection by hunger, every particular member, and the whole body itself, began to waste away to nothing. Thus it came to be evident that the belly did not live so lazily as was supposed, and that

16 And if the ear shall say, Because I am not the eye, I am not of the body; is it therefore not of the body?

17 If the whole body *were* an eye, where *were* the hearing? If the whole *were* hearing, where *were* the smelling?

c ver. 28.
d Rom. xii. 3.
ch. iii. 5.
ver. 11.

18 But now hath ᶜGod set the members every one of them in the body, ᵈ as it hath pleased him.

---

however, a very considerable difference in the line taken by the Roman general Menenius Agrippa and the Apostle; for, whilst the heathen general advocates the necessity of one member, and that apparently the idlest, and all the other members are on the point of perishing because they refuse to contribute any longer to its nourishment, the Apostle shows the necessity to the whole body of all the members, even the most feeble.

16, 17. "If the ear shall say . . . . If the whole were hearing," &c. A ludicrous but very pertinent illustration is given by one of our most popular writers. He describes those who run after preachers simply to have their sense of hearing gratified as if they were all ear, the ear having become gigantic and out of all proportion with the rest of the body; and some are just as if they were all hands or all feet, always running about, always bustling, always meddling, having their fingers in every pie; and yet never taking in anything, never learning, never submitting, never retiring.

18. "But now hath God set the members every one of them in the body, as it hath," &c. In these verses the Apostle seems to contemplate a spirit of discontent in those who had not prominent offices or functions, as if, because they were not ministers or teachers, they were nothing. And so he reminds them of the power and wisdom of God in appointing its proper place and function to every particular member of the human body. If all the members had but one office there could be no human body. On the contrary, no member of the body can assert itself as having no need of the help of any one of the rest.

And not only so but the feeblest members and those which are

---

the other members of the body did not nourish it more than it nourished them; for that it rendered up to every part that which gives life and strength, digesting the food given to it, so that the life blood formed from that food might be distributed throughout the body" (Livy's Hist., ii. 32).

MANY MEMBERS, ONE BODY.

19 And if they were all one member, where *were* the body?

20 But now *are they* many members, yet but one body.

21 And the eye cannot say unto the hand, I have no need of thee: nor again the head to the feet, I have no need of you.

22 Nay, much more those members of the body, which seem to be more feeble, are necessary:

23 And those *members* of the body, which we think to be less honourable, upon these we ‖ bestow more ❙ Or, *put on.* abundant honour; and our uncomely *parts* have more abundant comeliness.

---

less honourable, and so are kept covered, are as necessary as any.

To apply this to the Body of Christ—those who live lives of silent prayer, and out of their deep poverty give alms secretly, and never obtrude themselves, but spend the little time at their own disposal in intercession, and have a word of Christian comfort or encouragement for all who need it; these are the members which we in our ignorance esteem so feeble, and the day will come when we shall know how the humble faith, the secret prayers and good deeds of these have been of untold value to the Church, have called down God's grace upon it, or turned away from it His just displeasure.

23. "And those members of the body, which we think to be less honourable, upon these," &c.,—by keeping them always clothed. Naturally, no member of the body can be dishonourable or uncomely, since God has made each and all to subserve the purposes for which the whole frame of members is put together; but owing to the fall, by a sort of second nature, we esteem some members less honourable than others. But as Dean Stanley says, "The covering of the body and uncovering of the face is probably one chief point of the comparison." Are there, however, any members of the Church of Christ which we think to be "less honourable" and "uncomely" as distinguished from the feeble members of the previous verse? Bernardino à Piconio says, "Hic verbis et similitudinibus docet Apostolus non modo minores, infirmos, senes,

24 For our comely *parts* have no need: but God hath tempered the body together, having given more abundant honour to that *part* which lacked:

|| Or, *division*. 25 That there should be no || schism in the body; but *that* the members should have the same care one for another.

26 And whether one member suffer, all the members suffer

---

pauperes, omnibus, ut videtur, donis et talentis destitutos ; sed etiam aliquâ notâ infames, verum pænitentes, contritos, humiles; hos, inquam, omnes contemni non debere ; sed foveri, conservari, ornari, quia sæpe Deo gratiores et ideo Ecclesiæ, suis precibus et meritis sunt maxime necessarii."

24, 25. "For our comely parts have no need: but God hath tempered the body together . . . . that there should be no schism in the body," &c. God hath so ordered the human body that in its healthy normal state there should be no division in it of part against part. It is only when it is diseased that one part unduly asserts itself, or is swollen, or takes more than its share of nourishment, and so robs the rest. Now God intends that there should be no disease in the mystical Body of Christ, but owing to the sin of man by asserting himself, and separating himself, and looking down on his fellow members, or by neglecting his proper functions, and ceasing from prayer, or falling from the faith, schisms are begun by which whole churches and congregations are inexpressibly weakened.

Again, schisms are occasioned by not giving due honour to the feebler, or the supposed less honourable members. They are unnoticed, uncared for, untended, and so they go astray, and wander out of the pale of the Church to find that with which the Church has neglected to provide them.

"That the members should have the same care one for another. And whether one member suffer, all the members suffer," &c. The Apostle passes here somewhat abruptly from the natural truth, that in the physical organization all the members are necessarily more or less dependent upon one another, to the spiritual truth, that in the great mystical Body each member ought to have a care to promote the interests of all the rest. In this Christ, the Head, sets the example, for when Saul persecuted the Church, the

YE ARE THE BODY OF CHRIST.

with it; or one member be honoured, all the members rejoice with it.

27 Now ^e ye are the body of Christ, and ^f members in particular.

^e Rom. xii. 5. Ephes. i. 23. & iv. 12. & v. 23, 30. Col. i. 24.
^f Ephes. v. 30.

Lord said to him, "Why persecutest thou Me? I am Jesus whom thou persecutest"—not why persecutest thou my disciples, my followers, but "why persecutest thou me? When the least member of my body is persecuted, I feel it, I resent it." As in the natural body a sting in one of the fingers is felt up the arm, and the whole body is affected and seems full of pain; so in the spiritual body, an envenomed dart of Satan, piercing the smallest limb, affects the whole body. It may not seem to us to do so, but the eye of the All-seeing Head sees that it does. When a minister or some important member of a local church falls, one sees what a scandal there is in the parish, which reaches the whole neighbourhood, and the Church is everywhere ashamed and depressed; but so it is with *every* member. The Church has need of the prayers, and the example, and the help of every member, and if it is deprived of such prayers and such example, it invariably suffers loss far beyond what the eye of man can see.

"Or one member be honoured, all the members rejoice with it." "Honoured," that is, by being made the instrument of doing some good, or setting forth its inward life by a holy outward conversation. All the members who have the life of God in them "rejoice with it." What examples do we find of self-denial and devotion in what is called humble life if we will but look out for them and observe them! In every parish in which I have ministered the Word of God I have found some souls—a very few, but some—holy, prayerful, self-denying, never speaking evil, always, if possible, speaking good of others, always ready to help, full of mercy, and of good fruits, in fact, as near perfection as can well be in this state of things. At the sight of these all seem to rejoice. Even those who have little of the Divine life seem to acknowledge the presence of such as a token for good from God.

27. "Now ye are the Body of Christ, and members in particular." Observe how he seems to be anxious to include all in the unity of this body. He might have spoken very differently: he might

28 And ᵍGod hath set some in the church, first ʰapostles, secondarily ⁱprophets, thirdly teachers, after that ᵏmiracles, then ˡgifts of

ᵍ Ephes. iv. 11.
ʰ Ephes. ii. 20. & iii. 5.
ⁱ Acts xiii. 1. Rom. xii. 6.
ᵏ ver. 10.
ˡ ver. 9.

have said, "See that ye become of the body of Christ. Ye are not all in the one body for ye are not all converted." But he says exactly the contrary. His words are, "Ye are the Body of Christ and members each one," and his inference is, "See that ye be sound members; see that ye be strong, healthy limbs; see that ye do your part; see that ye seek grace; see that ye keep your places, and envy none of your brethren; see that as members of Christ ye keep yourselves holy and undefiled."

28. "And God hath set some in the church." The Apostle here sets forth the Gifts of the Spirit, according to their importance.

First of all the gift of the Apostleship as the first in importance, because it comprehended all other gifts, and because it branched out more directly from Christ. It comprehended the witness to the Resurrection of Christ (Acts. i. 21, 22, x. 41 ; 1 Cor. ix. 1, xv. 8, 9), the possession of all other gifts, prophecy, miracles, tongues, and absolute rule over all churches planted by each particular Apostle. So naturally he mentions it as the first.

"Secondarily prophets"—those who spake by Inspiration. They not only foretold future events, as Agabus; but they exhorted and confirmed (Acts xv. 32). They seem to have been withdrawn from the Church when the Canon of the New Testament was completed, for in the Epistles of St. Paul and of the other Apostles, and in the Apocalypse, we have preserved to us the prophesyings of the Apostles themselves. We want no other truths than those contained in their writings, but we want the exposition and application of these to ourselves.

"Thirdly teachers." "Teaching" here is classed among the supernatural gifts of the Spirit, but as coming after prophesying.

Pastors and teachers are in Ephes. iv. 11, joined together, so that their functions were probably exercised more locally than the gifts of the Apostolate and prophecying. The office seems to have been the exposition and application of the Scriptures, rather than the delivery of messages from heaven. The care of the prophet was rightly to divide (or handle) the word of truth (2 Tim. ii. 15).

healings, ᵐ helps, ⁿ governments, ‖ diversities of tongues.

ᵐ Numb. xi. 17.
ⁿ Rom. xii. 8. 1 Tim. v. 17. Hebr. iii. 17, 24.
‖ Or, *kinds*, ver. 10.

"After that miracles." Most probably exorcism.

"Then gifts of healings"—to be exercised when God, as I said, directed them to minister this gift.

"Helps." This is by some supposed to comprehend the functions of the diaconate, but by others, as Cornelius à Lapide, as indicating a ministry for the assistance of the sick and infirm, not by miracle, but by ordinary works of mercy, as by our sisters of charity and nursing sisterhoods.

"Governments." In the ordinary acceptation of the word, this would imply rule over the whole Church, but it cannot mean this, as so important a function for the well-being of the Church, by whomsoever exercised, would not be placed so low down in the list. It must rather mean the superintendence and disposal of the temporal affairs of the Church, as Cornelius à Lapide suggests:— "Those who preside over the regulation of the temporal matters which the faithful offered to the Church. Such were the functions of the deacons who were deputed by the Apostles to preside over the distribution of alms to the widows.[1]

It is to be remembered that at this very early period there was no independent government exercised by the Church of Corinth, or any other Church. All government was kept in the hands of the Apostle himself, who was (we say it with all reverence) the dictator. He laid down rules and regulations upon all matters, even the head-dresses of the women in Church. He suffered no woman to speak in the Christian assembly. He ordered all matters touching the exercise of the spiritual gifts. He praised them that they kept the traditions *as he had himself delivered them* unto them. He bade them wait till he came for the final orders respecting the love-feasts and the celebration of the Eucharist, and he delivered a very gross offender to Satan for the destruction of the flesh, that the spirit might be saved in the day of the Lord

---

[1] Godet explains it in a similar way " as the various kinds of superintendence needed for the external good order of the assemblies, and the worship of the Church." Perhaps the office which most nearly represents it now is that of the Churchwarden.

29 *Are* all apostles? *are* all prophets? *are* all teachers? *are* all ‖ workers of miracles?

‖ Or, *powers.*

30 Have all the gifts of healing? do all speak with tongues? do all interpret?

31 But °covet earnestly the best gifts: and yet shew I unto you a more excellent way.

° ch. xiv. 1, 39.

Jesus:"[1] so that literally there was no room for any government, in the higher sense of the word, excepting his own.

"Diversities of tongues." This is put the last on the list, as being one which, except it were exercised for the special benefit of those for whose sake God gave it (xiv. 22; also Acts ii. 8-11), was the least edifying.

29, 30. "Are all Apostles .... do all interpret?" It has been asserted by many commentators who desire to represent everything in the early Church as unsettled and in a loose and fluid state, that offices and functions were not distinguished; but here the Apostle seems anxious to distinguish each one from another, and it seems to have been probable that those who had one function or gift of service, were not likely to have others.

31. "But covet earnestly the best gifts, and yet shew I unto you," &c. How could they show that they desired earnestly the more excellent gifts? Evidently by their more earnest prayer for such better gifts. St. Paul would not press upon them the desire, unless he knew that God, probably through the laying on of his hands, would meet their desire.

"A more excellent way." The more excellent way of Christian love, which he now proceeds to describe and enforce. It was through want of this that they had exercised their gifts wrongly and vain-gloriously, and so sinfully. It is only through love that the highest gifts can be exercised beneficially to the Church, and with safety to the person who has received them.

---

[1] 1 Cor. iv. 18, 19, 21; v. 3, 4, 5, 13; xi. 1, 2, 17, 18, 33, 34; xiv. 29, 33, 34, &c.

CHAP. XIII.

1. "Though I speak with the tongues of men and of angels, and have," &c. The remarkable chapter now before us stands by itself. It seems scarcely a part of this Epistle, for all the rest of this long letter is more or less controversial. With the exception of the short Epistle to the Galatians, it is more full of blame and reproach than all the rest put together; but here we seem to have the product of a direct Inspiration, raising the soul of the Apostle out of an atmosphere of war and tumult, and causing it to rest in a very heaven of love and peace.

And yet this paragraph on love arises directly out of the previous context. The Apostle had been enumerating the gifts of the Spirit —the word of wisdom, of knowledge, faith, prophecy; and now he pauses, and says in effect, These are not Christianity. They are necessary to Christianity, if it is to subdue the world, if it is to become, as the Lord intended it to be, a great power in the world; but they are not Christianity—altogether they are not Christianity, no more than the shell is the kernel. I will show you the most excellent way, for I will tell you what Christianity is. It is the mind of Christ, the heart of Christ, the spirit of Christ, the love of Christ, as exhibited in His life of love. It was for the reproduction of Himself in His members that the Son of God, Jesus Christ, became incarnate, and lived, and died, and rose again; and I will show you the form and fashion of this reproduction of Christ in us.

But it is a hard thing to describe. I cannot teach it you. The love of God cannot be taught; it must be shed abroad in your hearts by the Holy Ghost, which is given to you. No one can describe love—love must be felt if it is to be learnt. I can only tell you its importance, its eternal imperishable nature, and what it is incompatible with.

And now, first with respect to the word used throughout this chapter—though it is derived from a word in common use ($\dot{a}\gamma a\pi\acute{a}\omega$), it is not a classical word; it is a word peculiar to the language of the Church—to Christianity. With respect to its translation, though rendered here by the word "Charity," it is elsewhere ren-

THOUGH I speak with the tongues of men and of angels,

---

dered "love." Thus, in Rom. v. 5, the same word is rendered "love," where it is said "the love of God is shed abroad in our hearts." And in Rom. xiii. 10: "Love worketh no ill to his neighbour, therefore love is the fulfilling of the Law." Throughout the Epistle of St. John it is rendered "love"—"God is love" (ἀγάπη), i.e., God is charity.

Now some object to the use of the word charity as the translation of this agape, and they give as a reason that charity has declined in its significance, and has come to signify one branch of charity. Thus we have "sisters of charity"—those who nurse and otherwise attend to the poor; and we have "charity" sermons; and we speak of the "charities" of a place. But would it do to have only the word "love,"—for is not love misunderstood? Is it not dragged through the gutter of lust? Does it not signify unholy love, worldly love, family love, which often is the preference of ourselves, of what is like us, of what comes from us, and is compatible with injustice to those who are not ours? So that it seems to me well to have two words to express this agape; so that if men take the lower view of charity, we may tell them that there may be charity without love; and if men speak of love, as they often do, in terms which seem to imply lust, or private irreligious preference, we have to tell them that the love which God asks of us and works in us is religious, and that charity always implies religion.

And now we come, God helping, to the exposition.

1. "Though I speak with the tongues of men and of angels." This is his starting-point. They had put into undue prominence the gift of tongues, because it seems to have lent itself to their vanity and love of display; and in reproof of this, he says, "Though I speak with the tongues of men and of angels." Now what are the tongues of men? They must be intelligible tongues. They cannot be the expression of religious ecstasy, for, if so, they would not be called the tongues of men. These tongues of men can be nothing but the languages in which the various races of men express themselves.

"And of angels." Have, then, the angels various languages? We should think not, for the variety of languages is a punishment, which we have reason to believe will one day be done away (Zeph.

CHAP. XIII.]   SOUNDING BRASS.   217

and have not charity, I am become *as* sounding brass, or a tinkling cymbal.

2 And though I have *the gift of* ᵃprophecy, and understand all mysteries, and all knowledge;

ᵃ ch. xii. 8, 9, 10, 28. & xiv. 1, &c. See Matt. vii. 22.

---

iii. 9). But probably what the Apostle says is hyperbolical—"If I could express myself as clearly and as sweetly as the angels." Some have compared it with, "Though we or an angel from heaven preach any other Gospel" (Gal. i. 8).

With respect to the words of angels which are recorded in the Scriptures, nothing can be plainer, more direct, and, we may say, more unimpassioned. They seem to say with the utmost conceivable plainness what they have been commissioned to say, and nothing more. No words are less the words of ecstasy than theirs. The most sublime words in which they chant the praises of God in His unclouded Presence are the simplest conceivable, "Holy, holy, holy, Lord God Almighty, which was, and is, and is to come."

"And have not charity, I am become as sounding brass, or a tinkling cymbal." I am, that is, in the sight of God, as bad as the brass which, being struck, has given an unmeaning and discordant sound. The one meaning which God looks for in every human utterance is love—the love of Himself when we speak to Him; the love of our brethren when we speak to them. This is the true melody which God listens for.

"A tinkling"—rather a clanging cymbal, having no meaning, no variety, no expression in its sound.

2. "And though I have the gift of prophecy, and understand all mysteries," &c. Chrysostom takes the understanding of mysteries and knowledge as marking the high character of the prophesying. "And this gift again with an excellency. For as in the former case he mentioned not tongues, but the tongues of all mankind, and as he proceeded, those of angels, and then signified that the gift was nothing without charity, so also here he mentions, not prophecy alone, but the very highest prophecy, in that having said, 'Though I have prophecy,' he added, 'and understand all mysteries and all knowledge,' expressing this gift also with intensity." "'All mysteries,' all the mysteries, or the mysteries all of them" (Wordsworth). The mystery of Godliness (1 Tim. iii. 16); the mystery of the Gospel (Ephes. vi. 19); the mystery of the calling of the Jews

and though I have all faith, [b] so that I could remove mountains, and have not charity, I am nothing.

[b] Matt. xvii. 20. Mark xi. 23. Luke xvii. 6.

---

first (Ephes. iii. 3, 4, 9); the mystery of the resurrection of the body (xv. 51)—all these are instances.

"All knowledge"—everything natural or supernatural which God has given to men to know. Perhaps there is here a reference to the "word of knowledge" of xii. 8, wisdom not being mentioned here, because wisdom, though joined with knowledge, is in a sphere above it, and always implies a moral element which knowledge may not.

"And though I have all faith, so that I could remove mountains:" πᾶσαν τὴν πίστιν, all faith, *i.e.*, faith in its fullest form and nature, not every form of it (πᾶσαν πίστιν) but all the fulness of it (Ellicott). We are told that this faith is not saving faith, but wonder-working faith; but how can we make such distinctions? Wonder-working faith is here represented as the highest degree of faith which the Apostle knew of, and yet in the eyes of the Apostle he who possesses it without charity is not saved or justified—he is nothing. James and John had this faith, or they would not have asked Christ if they might not call down fire from heaven upon the Samaritans who would not receive Him, but they were sharply reproved by the Lord, and told that they knew not what manner of spirit they were of.

Wonder-working faith must be some outcome of ordinary faith, and apparently greater in intensity than it; and yet, if it be without love, it may be worthless. It is astonishing that men who write and speak sensibly can be blind to this fact, that no matter what test we insist upon to prove the existence of faith in the soul, it may exist in it without love. Expressions of faith, lively feelings and emotions, zeal for the truth, or some truth which is undoubtedly a truth of God; constant attendance at Evangelical preaching and the evident enjoyment of that preaching—and I do not use the word Evangelical here in any party or in any invidious sense—all these may exist, and yet love, as described in this chapter, may be wanting, utterly wanting. We are taught this in some shape or other in almost every page of Scripture, and we are taught it by the experience of daily life. St. Paul never could have written "In Christ Jesus neither circumcision availeth anything, nor uncircumcision, but faith which worketh by love," unless, as far as

CHAP. XIII.] IT PROFITETH ME NOTHING. 219

3 And ^cthough I bestow all my goods to feed *the poor*, and though I give my body to be burned, and ^{c Matt. vi. 1, 2.} have not charity, it profiteth me nothing.

3. "To be burned" (καυθήσομαι). So D., E., F., G., L., and many Cursives (C., K. read καυθήσωμαι), and d, e, f, g, m, Vulg., Syriac, Copt., Arm., Æth., Goth.; but ℵ, A., B., and Latin copies mentioned by Jerome, " that I may glory," καυχήσωμαι.

the eye of man can see, faith may exist without love. It is not true to say that unless faith works by love it is not true, or genuine. It is true and genuine so far as it goes, but it must go further into the domain of love or charity, or it is nothing in the sight of God.[1]

3. "And though I bestow all my goods to feed the poor," &c. The word "bestow .... to feed the poor" is one word (ψωμίζω), and signifies to put food or morsels of food into the mouth, as nurses feed children; literally, to give all one's property in small doles of food, or mouthfuls: "Who that has witnessed the almsgiving in a (Roman) Catholic monastery, or the court of a Spanish or Sicilian bishop's or archbishop's palace, where immense revenues are syringed away in farthings to herds of beggars, but must feel the force of the Apostle's half-satirical ψωμίσω?" (Stanley).

"And though I give my body to be burned." It is supposed by some that the Apostle had in his mind the three holy children who gave their bodies to be burned (Dan. iii. or 2 Mac. vii. 5). An account is given of a Hindoo who, in the time of Augustus, accompanied an embassy from India to Augustus, and caused himself to be burned alive at Athens. His tomb was to be seen in Athens with the inscription, "Zarmochegas, the Indian from Bargosa, according to the ancient custom of India, made himself immortal and lies

---

[1] Godet has a valuable note. "How are we to suppose speaking in tongues apart from faith, and faith divorced from charity, which is its fruit. Is not the Apostle's supposition merely a threat fitted to alarm his readers? Experience proves that a man, after opening his heart with faith to the joy of salvation, may very soon cease to walk in the way of sanctification, shrink from complete self-surrender, and, while making progress in mystical feeling, become more full of self and devoid of love than he ever was. Such is the issue of the religious sybaritism of which revivals furnish so many examples. Christianity, instead of acting as a principle of devotion, turns into poetry, sentimentality, and fine speaking. It may even happen that, after a real and serious conversion, love may be at first developed in the heart and life, but afterwards, in consequence of some practical unfaithfulness, and through a want of vigilance, leading to spiritual pride, charity may be gradually chilled. The gifts originally received remain in some measure, but the inner life has disappeared."

4 ^d Charity suffereth long, *and* is kind; charity

<small>d Prov. x. 12.
1 Pet. iv. 8.</small>

---

here." Considering the way in which, in the early ages of the Church, martyrdom was courted, and the reputation in which those who suffered it were held, it is too probable that many suffered through vainglory rather than the love of Christ.

For the reading, "Give my body that I may glory," see critical note above.

"It profiteth me nothing." "Without this love whatever I speak, whatever I have, whatever I know, whatever I do, whatever I suffer, it profiteth me nothing." (Wesley.)

4. "Charity suffereth long, and is kind," &c.—love that has the mind of God, Who is pre-eminently long suffering. As the Lord says of God His Father when He sets His long suffering forth as an example, "Pray for them which despitefully use you and persecute you, that ye may be the children of your Father which is in heaven, for he maketh his sun to rise on the evil and on the good, and sendeth rain on the just and on the unjust" (Matth. v. 44, 45). Quesnel's remarks on this are peculiarly valuable, because they take into full account the love and submission to God as well as the love of our neighbour. "Charity suffereth the delays of God, waits with patience for His proper season. . . . . She feels and suffers her own miseries, complains of them before God, and looks for deliverance from Him. She bears the imperfections of others without vexation, waits for their amendment without impatience, and begs it earnestly of God without being weary or growing cold."

"And is kind." "Quiet and peaceable in her own actions, good-natured, and far from giving trouble to anyone." (Quesnel.)

"For not at all with a view to light up the fire, to those who are inflamed with anger, do they deal more mannerly with them, but in order to appease and extinguish it; and not only by enduring nobly, but by soothing and comforting do they cure the soul and heal the wound of passion" (Chrysostom).

"Charity vaunteth not." The Divine Charity, the love which is a gift of the Spirit, regards everything as coming from God, and given by Him. If God has seen fit to give a gift to one and not to another, the other, who has charity, looks upon God as just in all His gifts, and is sure that anything which is withheld is withheld for a good purpose, and that those who have more from God have more to answer for. Such an one has a deep feeling that God has

envieth not; charity ‖ vaunteth not itself, is not puffed up,

5 Doth not behave itself unseemly, ᵉ seeketh not her own, is not easily provoked, thinketh no evil;

‖ Or, *is not rash.*
ᵉ ch. x. 24.
Phil. ii. 4.

---

given to each one what is best for glorifying Him and attaining to salvation: and yet this Divine contentedness does not prevent the charitable, loving soul from coveting, *i.e.* desiring earnestly, the best gifts, but beyond the desire for the best gifts, it desires still more earnestly the "more excellent way" which the Apostle here describes.

"Charity vaunteth not itself." Expositors differ much respecting the meaning of this word. The ancient commentators sometimes take it as meaning acting with precipitancy, which is inconsistent with true charity—we do not wish that men should act rashly or with precipitancy towards us, judging our motives without due care and thought, and we too should be careful to avoid the same wrong disposition. Thus Chrysostom: "It renders him who loves both considerate, and grave, and steady in his movements." Also Theodoret: "He that loveth cannot endure to do anything rash." Wesley has an excellent explanation: "Love acteth not rashly—does not harshly condemn anyone, never passes a severe sentence on a slight or sudden view of things."

Many, however, take it according to our translation, vaunteth not itself, displays not itself, does not show itself off.

"Is not puffed up." Here there seems a reference to chap. viii. 1. The best gifts—such as knowledge—puff up, if internally dwelt upon as possessed by ourselves rather than by others, and so minister to vainglory.

5. "Doth not behave itself unseemly." He, perhaps, alludes to the conduct of the women in abstaining from wearing in public worship the veil, the sign of subjection and modesty; perhaps, also, to the unseemly conduct at the love-feasts. Any want of respect in our outward conduct to the presence and feelings of those in whose company we are betrays a want of consideration of what is due to them, which they will probably resent; and this will be a sin in us and in them.

"Seeketh not her own." This seems the chief feature of all. The opposite of charity is selfishness. "Look not every man on

6 ᶠRejoiceth not in iniquity, but ᵍrejoiceth ‖ in the truth.

Ps. x. 3.
Rom. i. 32.
g 2 John iv.
‖ Or, *with the truth.*

---

his own things." "Let this mind be in you which was also in Christ Jesus." "Even Christ pleased not Himself."

This is the hardest precept of all. We have in some measure to love ourselves, or we should not be told to love our neighbour as ourselves; and yet if our aim is to seek our own interest, we have not this gift of the Spirit—we have not the mind of Christ.

"Is not easily provoked." Perhaps, as Godet suggests, there is a reference here to the dissensions and law suits; but the precept is of the most general character—"is not put into a passion." We have need of another word of the Apostle, where he says, "Be ye angry, and sin not" (Ephes. iv.). It is a bad sign if we are not moved at the sight of sin; but we should at the same moment be moved to prayer for the sinner, and pity for his fall. With respect, however, to private injuries and slights, how often are we disturbed in mind; perhaps (it may be for but a short time) boil with anger at what, perhaps, a year after, we shall wonder that we took any notice of. But here it should be remarked that some are of more quick and hasty tempers than others; and if such by prayer and divine grace subdue their tempers, so much the more are they pleasing to God, for He has said, "He that is slow to anger is better than the mighty, and he that ruleth his spirit than he that taketh a city" (Prov. xvi. 32).

"Thinketh no evil," *i.e.*, imputeth no evil: does not keep an account of the evil which it suffers from any one that some day it may pay him off in full, but rather strives to forget it, and blot it out of its books, as it hopes that God will blot out all its evil out of His books.

6. "Rejoiceth not in iniquity." The truly charitable man—the man in whose heart the love of God and of his neighbour is shed abroad by the Holy Ghost—does not secretly rejoice when he hears that his enemy or his theological or political opponent has fallen into sin. He rather prays for him, knowing that, unless he repents, a far more terrible punishment will overtake him than any which his bitterest enemy could desire. We should look very searchingly into ourselves respecting this matter. If thoughts of exultation or satisfaction arise in our breasts at hearing of the iniquity of those

7 ʰ Beareth all things, believeth all things,   ʰ Rom. xv. 1.
                                                Gal. vi. 2.
                                                2 Tim. ii. 24.

we dislike, we share the joy of Satan. We are glad at that which God hates and abhors. As Godet well puts it, "Charity feels no criminal joy on seeing the faults which may be committed by men of an opposite party." Chrysostom understands it in the sense that charity delights not in seeing what an enemy unjustly suffers. Wesley says, "Weeps at the sin or folly of even an enemy; takes no pleasure in hearing or repeating it; but desires it may be forgotten for ever."

"But rejoiceth in the truth." The expression is remarkable. It really is "rejoiceth with the truth"—congaudet autem veritate (Vulg.). Some suppose that love and truth are here personified as two sisters, who rejoice together when either of them triumphs, or is honoured. Or it may be supposed that Charity, being a sympathetic and social virtue, rejoices not alone, but shares its joy with the good everywhere. We have, however, to consider why iniquity is not here so much opposed to righteousness and goodness as to the truth. The idea seems the same as that in John iii. 20, 21, where "he that doeth evil" is opposed, not to him that doeth good, but to him that "doeth truth"—not so much believeth in the truth as doeth the truth (see my note on that place). It seems as if all iniquity, all unrighteousness, all injustice is pervaded by an element of falsehood. The truth not only thinks truly, but acts truly—*i.e.*, justly and fairly; and in this charity rejoices. "The truth" has also been explained as meaning the truth of the Gospel, which is the real antidote to all that can be called evil or unrighteousness; and, of course, he who is under the influence of the Spirit of God will rejoice in the triumph of the Gospel as the only real triumph of righteousness.

7. "Beareth all things." This "bearing" is taken by some in the sense of enduring; but as the verse ends with "endureth all things," it is probable that it means "covereth all things," in the sense of 1 Peter iv. 8, "charity shall cover the multitude of sins." The word στέγει, which St. Paul uses, has the sense of bearing up and resisting, as a roof keeps out rain and snow; but its ordinary meaning is that of covering over for the purpose of shelter. "Love covereth all things." Whatever evil the lover of mankind sees, hears, or knows of anyone, he mentions it to none; it never goes out of his lips, unless where absolute duty constrains to speak.

hopeth all things, endureth all things.

"Believeth all things." Believes, that is, all the good which it can of anyone. Some take it as meaning believing all that is said by anyone, so as not to suppose him guilty of falsehood; so Theodoret. Godet remarks well: "The term *believe* usually refers to God; here it denotes, apparently, confidence in man; but in reality this confidence has for its object the Divine in man, all that remains in him of God's image."

"Hopeth all things." It entertains hopes even of the very worst, because it knows the power of the grace of God, and His love to sinners, as Chrysostom says, "It doth not despair of any good thing in the beloved one, even though he be worthless: it continues to correct, to provide, to care for him." "It puts the most favourable construction upon everything, and is ever ready to believe whatever may tend to the advantage of anyone's character; and when it can no longer believe well, it hopes whatever may excuse or extenuate the fault which cannot be denied. Where it cannot even excuse, it hopes God will give at length repentance unto life." (Wesley).

"Endureth all things." Bearing much for the sake of others: bearing much ill-temper, ill-conduct, even ill-will from others; but the Apostle says, " endureth not *much*, but endureth *all things*. Now in this, as he is bound to do, he describes what is perfect; for if he did not—if he put in much about the impossibility of attaining this character—he would simply undo all, for people would rest contented in uncharitableness, and cease striving after an ideal which they were told was impossible.

But is this character attainable? It is not, and it is. If measured by the standard of absolute perfection, it is not: for we have not yet put on the Resurrection body. But yet it is. In a long ministry I have known some—not many—but some who very fairly come up to this standard. They suffer long, they are kind, they never vaunt themselves; are the reverse of being overbearing and consequential; they behave themselves well in all companies, even in the company of those who seem not to respect them; they certainly seek not their own, their chief aim is to benefit others; they are not easily provoked, in fact one marvels at the things which they endure without resentment; they betray not the slightest satisfaction at the faults of others, and so they never

CHAP. XIII.] CHARITY NEVER FAILETH. 225

8 Charity never faileth: but whether *there be* prophecies, they shall fail; whether *there be* tongues, they shall cease; whether *there be* knowledge, it shall vanish away.

---

encourage scandal-mongering and tale-bearing; they never expose the faults or weaknesses of others; they believe even where it seems unlikely; they hope the best, and they endure what most of their neighbours would not put up with for a moment. And all this evidently has its roots in their belief in Jesus Christ. And is it a marvel that there should be such? Why cannot the Holy Ghost make a good man? The marvel ought to be that, in the Church, with such sacraments, such promises, such prayers for the Spirit, characters of this sort do not abound.

8. "Charity never faileth: but whether there be prophecies, they shall fail," &c. "Never faileth," *i.e.*, it never comes to an end, because there is no longer any need of it; on the contrary, it is imperishable and eternal. This does not mean that love or charity in particular individuals does not grow cold, for our Lord says that it will (Matth. xxiv. 12), but it lasts through this present state as a preparation for a better, and in the better state it forms the joy of all holy souls. It is the character of God, and so must ever be that to which all elect spirits tend.

"Whether there be prophecies, they shall fail." The Apostle now illustrates the eternal nature of the grace of charity by exhibiting the temporal character of the greatest of the gifts on which the Corinthians had prided themselves.

"Whether there be prophecies, they shall fail." The gift of prophecy is intended for the benefit of those who are in an imperfect state. Whether it reveals the future, or the will of God respecting the present, or sets forth and explains hidden mysteries, it will have no place in a state where the blessed will know as by intuition the deep things of God.

"Whether there be tongues, they shall cease." Various languages and their interpretation will exist no longer, as the curse of Babel will have been removed, and in the words of the prophet, "God will have turned to the people a pure language, that they may all call upon the name of the Lord, to serve Him with one consent" (Zeph. iii. 9).

"Whether there be knowledge, it shall vanish away." "Vanish

Q

9 ¹ For we know in part, and we prophesy in part.

ⁱ ch. viii. 2.   10 But when that which is perfect is come, then that which is in part shall be done away.

---

away" is the same word as that translated "they shall fail," in the first clause of the verse. How can real knowledge be said to vanish away? Because it gives way to a knowledge so deep, so clear, so intuitive that the former is as nothing in comparison. This is the state which the prophet Jeremiah refers to when he prophecies, "They shall teach no more every man his neighbour, and every man his brother saying, Know the Lord: for they shall all know me," &c. (Jerem. xxxi. 34.)

This transformation of knowledge has taken place in our day in respect to several sciences, as, for instance, chemistry and electricity. The knowledge which the most advanced scientists of one hundred years ago had of these branches of knowledge is, when compared with what we have now, absolute ignorance. Rückert, as quoted by Godet, says, "It is not the true knowledge which shall cease; it is only the various fragments of knowledge, received here below (γνώσεις) which shall pass away to give place to perfect knowledge."

9, 10. "For we know in part, and we prophesy in part. . . . . in part shall be done away." This is the explanation of the fact why such things of the Spirit as prophecy and knowledge fail, or come to nothing, or are destroyed. They pass away to be superseded by a knowledge and a mode of communicating that knowledge far more perfect.

It has been made a matter of question what time the Apostle alludes to as the one in which these manifestations of the Spirit shall cease, and some have supposed that the present state of the Church, in which prophesy and tongues have ceased, is that to which he alludes, but this to me seems impossible. Surely this, our present state, is anything but perfect. It certainly is not perfect in love, for it has declined from the love of the first age. The perfect state is evidently that in which our bodies will be raised in the likeness of Christ's, and our faculties of receiving knowledge will not be clogged then as they are now by the conditions and limitations of our unrenewed frames, but the body will then answer to the spirit in its highest state.

11. "When I was a child, I spake as a child, I understood as a child," &c. The Apostle here illustrates what he has said respect-

WHEN I WAS A CHILD.

11 When I was a child, I spake as a child, I understood as a child, I ‖ thought as a child: but when I became a man, I put away childish things.

12 For ᵏ now we see through a glass, † darkly;

‖ Or, *reasoned.*

ᵏ 2 Cor. iii. 18. & v. 7. Phil. iii. 12.

† Gr. *in a riddle.*

ing that which is " perfect," superseding that which is " in part " by the comparison of childhood. The child knows nothing respecting any human thing thoroughly, and he speaks, understands, and thinks according to his very imperfect knowledge; and so it is in spiritual things. At present we speak of them, understand them, and think or reason about them very imperfectly; hereafter we shall look back upon our present state as comparative ignorance. This is not to be taken as if the knowledge of the child is false. He knows that he has parents, he knows them personally in a way that no stranger can know them, he knows when and how he pleases them, or displeases them, he knows that he owes all to them and depends upon them. And what in spiritual things is analogous to this knowledge is true—that no matter to what scale of existence we shall be permitted to advance, we shall never look upon this knowledge as false. All further development of utterance or intellect must be founded upon this, built upon this infantile knowledge as true, and every advance must be a further and more complete realization of what we knew when we first exercised our faculty of cognition. A further illustration may be taken from the comparison of the Old Dispensation with the New. Nothing in the Old Dispensation was false and yet it has passed away. Take the offering of sacrifices. It was not false worship; it was, when offered faithfully, acceptable to God, but it has utterly passed away, and is superseded by an infinitely higher showing forth of the All-atoning Death.

12. "For now we see through a glass, darkly; but then face to face," &c. The word translated glass (ἐσόπτρον) never signifies a window, but always a mirror; and it would be a mirror of highly polished brass or other metal, for making which the Corinthians were famous. We now see spiritual things as if we were looking at their reflexion in a mirror, and this was always more or less dim or blurred or imperfect. So Chrysostom: "Because the glass sets before us the things seen in some way or other," he adds, "darkly, to show very strongly that the present knowledge is most partial." We can only determine the meaning of "darkly,"

but then ¹face to face: now I know in part; but then shall I know even as also I am known.

¹ Matt. xviii. 10. 1 John iii. 2.

(or in an enigma) by the expression "face to face," to which it is opposed. The passage seems to be parallel to that in St. John where the Apostles say to the Lord, " Lo, now speakest thou plainly, and speakest no proverb" (or parable); and to what God says about Moses: "If there be a prophet among you, I the Lord will make myself known unto him in a vision, and will speak unto him in a dream. My servant Moses is not so . . . . With him will I speak mouth to mouth, even apparently, and not in dark speeches; and the similitude of the Lord shall he behold" (Numbers xii. 6-8). Being profoundly ignorant of the conditions under which God reveals Himself to us even now, and much more so of what will be accorded to us in the beatific vision, even an Apostle can only express himself in such terms as "darkly," as opposed to "face to face"— "knowing in part," as opposed to "knowing as I am known." We must reverently close our lips, or if we speak we must be content to say after the Psalmist: "As for me, I will behold thy face in righteousness: I shall be satisfied, when I awake, with thy likeness." (Ps. xvii. 15.)

But how can it be said that we shall know God even as we are known of Him? This does not mean that we shall know Him as perfectly as He knows us, for we shall always be finite and He infinite, and the finite cannot compass the infinite; but we shall know Him not through His works, not through His scriptures, or through His revelations, but as one intelligent being knows another. He knows us, not by our works, or by anything else which proceeds from us, such as our words, by which we show ourselves to our fellows, but as we are in ourselves, and we shall know Him by a similar knowledge clearly and distinctly, but not by an equal knowledge.

13. "And now abideth faith, hope, charity, these three, but," &c. I do not think that because the Apostle here pronounces charity or love to be greater than faith and hope that therefore he means that faith and hope only exist in this state of things, and faith will in the future state of blessedness be "lost in sight," and hope will be lost in fruition. Faith must always be exercised by the creature, for faith is dependence upon the supreme God, and the highest

13 And now abideth faith, hope, charity, these three; but the greatest of these *is* charity.

---

angels feel their entire dependence upon Him far more than any below them do, and every creature must hope that God will ever sustain him in holiness, and look forward to higher and higher degrees of nearness to God ; but love is the greatest because love is the character of God. God, Who knows all things, cannot believe as His creatures do, and God, Who inhabits eternity cannot hope as His creatures do, but God can love—God is love. It cannot be said that God is faith, nor can it be said that God is hope, but it is said that God is love.

CHAP. XIV.

FOLLOW after charity, and ᵃ desire spiritual *gifts*, ᵇ but rather that ye may prophesy.

ᵃ ch. xii. 31.
ᵇ Numb. xi. 25, 29.

1. "Follow after charity, and desire spiritual gifts, but rather that ye may prophesy." Literally, "pursue charity." Bishop Wordsworth supposes that there is here an allusion to the games. "Pursue her with the earnestness with which the runners strive after the prize. Make charity your aim and end (σκοπὸς) in the whole race of your spiritual life."

"And desire spiritual gifts, but rather that ye may prophesy." Spiritual gifts being all of them, if sensibly and devoutly used, of the greatest benefit to the Church, are to be desired, but the Apostle specifies prophecy as the most useful.

We now come to a comparison, drawn out at great length, between the usefulness of the gift of tongues and that of prophecy. There is no passage of the New Testament which gives us such an insight into the spiritual state of the earliest Church, at least as it existed in such a city as Corinth. It lets us into its extraordinarily abnormal, rather, perhaps, if one might say so, prenormal state. For here are actually gifts of the Holy Ghost used by converted Christians for vain-glorious purposes—used not for edification, but in a disorderly way, so that if a heathen man came in, and found the Church as a body exercising a particular one of these gifts, he would pronounce them to be mad. It appears that one at least of these gifts might be used senselessly, without regard to the purpose for which God had apparently given it, so much so that many learned men holding the highest rank amongst expositors write as if God had no intelligible purpose in bestowing it.

I have examined in Excursus III. in my volume of notes on the Acts, to which I must refer the reader, the two rival theories which have been held on this subject; the first of these, held by all ancient expositors, being that the gift of tongues was an ability to speak in human languages, which those who possessed it had never learnt; the second that it was the expression of ecstatic devotion, that it was unintelligible to the hearers, and, according to many, generally so to the speaker.

I shall now briefly recapitulate my reasons for believing that the gift of tongues was the gift of speaking in human languages not previously learnt by the utterer, and then, as I proceed with the exposition, draw attention to several places in this chapter which absolutely require that such should be the meaning, and are incompatible with any other explanation whatsoever.

1. Christ, in his parting charge, as given by St. Matthew, says, "Go ye and teach all nations;" and as given by St. Mark, says, "Go ye to all the world, and preach the Gospel to every creature." Apparently He seemed to command an impossibility, for the Galileans to whom He gave these charges were "unlearned and ignorant men," and being probably not young men, would find it very difficult to acquire the knowledge of any language so as to teach in it the mysteries of the faith.

2. On the day of Pentecost a great number of Jews residing in different countries were gathered together in Jerusalem, and these men were astonished beyond measure at hearing the Apostles, and perhaps others, who only knew Aramaic imperfectly, speak to them in their own tongues the wonderful works of God. It is clear from this that the Apostles did not speak to them in Greek, which was extensively used as a common mode of intercourse throughout the East, but in Parthian, in Median, in Persian, or in Mesopotamian; and this was the aspect of the miracle which impressed them. Quite independent of any actual instruction which they

received, the fact that men who but a short time before knew not a word of their particular language now addressed them in that language, convinced them that there was here a putting forth of the power of God, such as had never been recorded in their sacred history since the confusion of tongues. They constantly heard of miracles of healing, and with prophecy, true or false, they were familiar, but neither Moses nor any succeeding prophet had ever given to men such a power as was now given from heaven by Jesus of Nazareth. But let this be noticed, that the force of the miracle in convincing them of the truth of the Gospel wholly depended on their understanding the tongue. If it had been some tongue which no one of the assembled multitude could understand—much more, if it had been some ecstatic utterance—it would have been no sign whatsoever of the truth of the Gospel, or of the power and presence of the Holy Spirit.

Now this account of the Pentecostal gift of tongues must rule all other notices of it; so that whenever the gift of tongues is mentioned, it must mean such languages as were spoken at Pentecost,— intelligible tongues, tongues spoken by some race or other which some present, or some who might be present, could verify. And with this accords the remarkable fact, that all the places in which the gift of tongues is spoken of as exercised, are places to which men of different nationalities resorted : 1. In Jerusalem, where devout men from every nation under heaven were gathered together ; 2. In Cæsarea, more a Gentile than a Jewish city, and the port of Palestine, thronged by soldiers and sailors from all parts of the world ; 3. In Ephesus, the resort for commerce or pilgrimage of all Asia Minor ; 4. and in Corinth, the city with two ports, having merchants and sojourners from all the coasts of the Mediterranean and the Euxine.

We now come to the exposition of the chapter, which presents no difficulty if the reader bears in mind that the gift of tongues was used by the Corinthians in a wrong way. It was given that the foreigners outside the pale of the Church might be witnesses of a miracle by which they might understand that the power of the Creator of the human mind was put forth on behalf of Christianity ; so that the proper place for its use was where men of all nations flocked together for commerce or any other purpose. Instead of this, it was used in the Church where all spake the same tongue, and no one could verify it.

2 For he that ᶜspeaketh in an *unknown* tongue speaketh not unto men, but unto God: for no man †understandeth *him*; howbeit in the spirit he speaketh mysteries.

ᶜ Acts ii. 4. & x. 46.
† Gr. *heareth*, Acts xxii. 9.

3 But he that prophesieth speaketh unto men *to* edification, and exhortation, and comfort.

4 He that speaketh in an *unknown* tongue edifieth himself; but he that prophesieth edifieth the church.

---

2. "He that speaketh in an unknown tongue speaketh not unto men, but unto God: for no man understandeth him." This evidently implies that what he spoke was not unintelligible jargon, but perfectly intelligible if there were persons present who could understand it. Whatever was spoken was, so far as the action of the Holy Spirit was concerned, intended to be understood. Edwards writes: "It was a conspicuous feature of the gift, that the tongues were unintelligible. Could the Apostle say of any man that speaks in a foreign language, that he speaks not to men but to God?" Certainly, we answer, if any man prays to God in a language not known to the people about him, he speaks only to God. He may do such a thing perfectly blamelessly, but it is of no use to the people present, and so the Apostle discourages it if there be no interpretation or interpreter.

"Howbeit in the spirit he speaketh mysteries." Mysteries to be spoken of in a way consonant with reverence must be spoken of intelligently; and the man described by the Apostle must first understand the mysteries, and then put what he understands into intelligible language. This he did not do, and so he was useless to the Church, just as if a man were to insist on saying the Te Deum—in which the greatest mysteries of the faith are very plainly expressed—in the original Latin, the congregation not understanding a word of it.

3. "But he that prophesieth speaketh unto men to edification," &c. That is, because he utters his prophecies in a language which they know. Notice that in this account of prophecy there is no allusion to its function of making man acquainted with future events, but only to its power of confirming and edifying.

4. "He that speaketh in an unknown tongue edifieth himself." How can a man edify himself unless he speaks to himself what he

5 I would that ye all spake with tongues, but rather that ye prophesied; for greater *is* he that prophesieth than he

---

5. "For greater" (γὰρ). So D., E., F., G., K., L., almost all Cursives, d, e, f, g, Vulg., Syriac, Arm., Æth.; but ℵ, A., B., P., 39, Copt., read "but" (δὲ).

himself understands, and yet a writer, expounding this chapter, tells us that these tongues "were the expressions, not of thoughts, but of feelings, unintelligible always if uninterpreted to the listener, and sometimes to the utterer himself." [1]

5. "I would that ye all spake with tongues, but rather that ye prophesied." According to the modern interpretation, this must mean: "I would that ye all were in an ecstacy, and so expressed yourselves in the language of ecstacy." But what is ecstacy? There may be two sorts of ecstacy, a true and a false. The true would arise out of an overwhelming apprehension of the goodness of God as set forth in the mysteries of the faith, in the Incarnation especially, and the unspeakable love displayed in the Lord's giving Himself to Death for our sakes—amongst Catholics in the ineffable nearness of the Lord in the Eucharist, and amongst Calvinists in the sense of God's electing love. Now we have the lives, the writings, the experiences of very holy men who seemed to be at times raised above themselves in the contemplation of one or more of these truths, but in no case does their ecstacy express itself in unknown language. Take the following writers, whose glowing devotion reached as high a point as can well be conceived—Augustine, Bernard, Thomas à Kempis, St. Francis de Sales, Guion, Bishop Hall, Bishop Ken, the Wesleys, John Newton, not to mention those living so near to us as Keble or Faber. The characteristic of what has come down to us of the writings of these most devout persons is their exceeding clearness. If they ever express themselves obscurely, the obscurity arises out of their lack of power over their own language, not because they have made the smallest approach to expressing themselves in some unknown language of rapture.

To return, when the Apostle says, "I would that ye all spake with tongues," it is beyond measure unlikely that he means "I

---

[1] So also Bishop Ellicott, "The one who speaks in a tongue ministers to himself edification—not necessarily by any knowledge of the purport of what he says, but by the glow of soul associated with the exercise of the charisma."

that speaketh with tongues, except he interpret, that the church may receive edifying.

6 Now, brethren, if I come unto you speaking with tongues, what shall I profit you, except I shall speak to you either by [d] revelation, or by knowledge, or by prophesying, or by doctrine?

[d] ver. 26.

---

would that you were all in such an ecstatic state of rapture that your native tongue or any other known language was insufficient to express the fervour of your thoughts, but that you must be impelled to use tones and articulations which, for the most part, are beyond even your own comprehension." If the reader thinks this way of putting matters somewhat exaggerated, let him remember that the modern explanation of this gift is, that it is not a gift of itself, but the outcome of a religious state of mind, and that the Apostle must desire that they first possessed this extremely exalted fervour of mind, or else he would desire that they should exhibit the manifestation of that which they did not actually experience. "I would then that ye all spake with tongues" must mean "I would that ye all could make known the way of salvation to the various tribes resorting to your city, so that they might be astonished beyond measure, and be turned to the true worship of Him Who has such power over the human intellect and the human organ of speech."

"But rather that ye prophesied, for greater is he that prophesieth." Prophecy is greater than speaking with tongues, because prophecy is the inspiration of the Holy Spirit, making known to the innermost spirit the deepest mysteries of the faith, and enabling the person endowed with it to speak those mysteries to all about him in the vernacular tongue; whereas the gift of tongues is a more outward gift, acting in or through that function of the soul which is able to understand or express words, and is a very inferior function to that which enables it to apprehend God.

"Except he interpret, that the church may receive edifying." This implies that the tongue is not a mere ecstatic rhapsody, but has a meaning, which if it be interpreted to the Church may edify it just as much as if the man prophesied.

6. "Now, brethren, if I come unto you speaking with tongues, what shall I profit?" The Apostle now does as he had done in

CHAP. XIV.] THINGS WITHOUT LIFE. 235

7 And even things without life giving sound, whether pipe or harp, except they give a distinction in the sounds, ‖ how shall it be known what is piped or harped? ‖ Or, *tunes.*

8 For if the trumpet give an uncertain sound, who shall prepare himself to the battle?

iv. 6, he transfers the matter to himself—that if even he, Apostle though he was, came speaking with a tongue, they would receive no profit unless he interpreted the words of the tongue as conveying some revelation received from God, or some Divine knowledge, or some mystery or future event, or some doctrine according to godliness.[1]

7. "And even things without life giving sound, whether pipe or harp, except," &c. Even lifeless instruments, if they are to speak in the language of music, and affect the feelings or passions of those who hear them, must give a distinction in the sound, *i.e.*, "be subject to the laws of tone and rhythm, to the intervals of scale and measure;" and so unknown languages, volubly uttered, might be to those that heard them just as bewildering as musical sounds without intervals and proper articulation. "Even in those inarticulate sounds there is need of some distinctness: and if thou strike not or breathe not into the pipe according to art, thou hast done nothing. Now if from things without life we require so much distinctness, and harmony, and appropriateness, and into these inarticulate sounds we strive and contend to infuse so much meaning, much more in men endued with life and reason, and in spiritual gifts ought one to make significancy an object." (Chrysostom.)

8. "For if the trumpet give an uncertain sound, who shall," &c. "An uncertain sound," *i.e.*, a sound which cannot be understood, as it would be if one who knew no music was making a noise with it. The Apostle seems to look upon all utterances in the Church of God as preparations for the great battle in which all the soldiers

---

[1] There is much difference amongst expositors respecting the relations of these four. Dean Stanley says, "He gives these four gifts or utterances as exhausting all the modes of teaching. (1.) ἀποκάλυψις, unveiling of the unseen, as in "the Apocalypse;" (2.) γνῶσις, insight into Divine truth, as in the "wisdom" of xi. 6; (3.) προφητεία, message of exhortation, or "consolation," as in verse 3; (4.) διδαχὴ, regular teaching, like the continuous teaching of our Lord's discourses and parables, as in Acts ii. 42."

9 So likewise ye, except ye utter by the tongue words †easy to be understood, how shall it be known what is spoken? for ye shall speak into the air.

10 There are, it may be, so many kinds of voices in the world, and none of them *is* without signification.

† Gr. *significant.*

---

of Christ were to be engaged, and if for any reason these sounds were not understood, the enemy might attack them when they were off their guard.

9. "So likewise ye, except ye utter by the tongue words easy to be understood." This precept or direction is wholly incompatible with the "tongues" being the expression of rapturous devotion or ecstacy; for such expression would not be under the control of him who was in the state of ecstacy. In the accounts of the utterances of the Irvingites, which we are told are an "illustration" of these gifts of the Spirit, the afflatus came upon them usually with uncontrollable power. They must speak the words dictated by the Spirit (?). Like Jeremiah, "His word was in their heart, as a burning fire shut up in their bones, and they were weary with forbearing and could not stay" (Jer. xx. 9). Who was the Apostle that he should presume to regulate the times and occasions, the mode and manner of expression of an ecstatic rapture which, if it was not false or diabolical, must be the work of the Holy Spirit in the soul, and yet here he says, "Except ye utter by the tongue words easy to be understood, how shall it be known what is spoken? for ye shall speak unto the air." How could the inspired Corinthian control the expression of ecstatic rapture, which, as we are told, was very frequently unintelligible to the utterer himself?

When the Apostle here blames them for speaking what is not significant, and so speaking to the air, he evidently blames them for speaking in languages which were not understood by the Church, and so were out of place in it, but which, if they were true gifts of God, must have had some place or places for their lawful exercise, which would be the resorts of foreigners, or, as in the day of Pentecost, of devout Jews brought up in, and usually speaking the languages of, distant places.

10. "There are, it may be, so many kinds of voices in the world, and none of them is without signification." "Kinds of voices," here signify kinds of languages, each separate language being a

11 Therefore if I know not the meaning of the voice, I shall be unto him that speaketh a barbarian, and he that speaketh *shall be* a barbarian unto me.

12 Even so ye, forasmuch as ye are zealous †of spiritual *gifts*, seek that ye may excel to the edifying of the church.

† Gr. *of spirits.*

---

different one; "and none of them without signification," that is, there are no languages like the inarticulate cries of animals, or of birds, but every word in each language represents an idea or an external object.

11. "Therefore if I know not the meaning of the voice, I shall be unto him that speaketh," &c. Cornelius à Lapide quotes a verse of Ovid, complaining of his exile in Pontus: "Barbarus hic ego sum, quia non intelligor ulli." Now in these two verses the Apostle proceeds on the idea that the languages which the Corinthians uttered were, each of them, exact counterparts of some known language spoken somewhere on earth, which some nation or other understood, but which was not understood in the Greek congregation where the utterance took place. If there had been a language or languages devised and taught by the Holy Spirit for the purpose of expressing a devotion so exceedingly ecstatic and rapturous that no human tongue could express it, could he have cited the speaking in these foreign languages as in the least degree analogous? When the ecstatic afflatus or rapture comes upon such a person he must speak, and by all principle or rule of the exercise of linguistic powers he must speak in the hearing of others; for a gift of language could not be given for the purpose of private devotions.

12. "Even so ye, forasmuch as ye are zealous of spiritual gifts, seek," &c. "Spiritual gifts" ought rather to be translated "spirits." Some suppose that it signifies the influence of spirit upon spirit, others simply all manner of inspiration of the Spirit. Seeing they were zealous respecting spiritual things or influences, let them, above all, seek those which would edify their fellow Christians, for speaking in an unknown tongue would not, and so he proceeds to say,—

13. "Wherefore let him that speaketh in an unknown tongue pray that he may interpret." Two interpretations have been given of this; the first, which is that of the ancient expositors and many modern

13 Wherefore let him that speaketh in an *unknown* tongue pray that he may interpret.

14 For if I pray in an *unknown* tongue, my spirit prayeth, but my understanding is unfruitful.

15 What is it then? I will pray with the spirit, and I will

---

ones, "Let him pray that he may have the gift of interpreting what he has said in the tongue;" the second, "In giving himself up to the Spirit who leads him to pray in a tongue, let him do so with the intention, and with the settled aim beforehand to reproduce the contents of his prayer afterwards in intelligible language" (Godet). So that in the first case he simply prays for a separate spiritual gift, which "the interpretation of tongues" is; in the second he intends with settled aim, and apparently without special prayer, to do what of himself he certainly has no power to do. It may appear at first sight strange that a man should be able to speak in a tongue which he could not interpret without a special gift of Divine assistance, but a moment's consideration will show that it was not at all unlikely; for if the man used the knowledge of the unknown language for the purpose for which God had given it to him, to preach the Gospel to the strangers and foreigners who crowded the places of public resort in Corinth, he would have no need to interpret it. The hearers would exclaim, "We hear the works of God in our own tongues wherein we were born." Whereas if he spoke it in the Church, where they all spoke Greek only, he would have to translate words with which he was not himself familiar, and which a Superior Power had enabled him to speak at that time, and the result, unless he had the separate gift of interpretation, might be anything but edifying.

14. "For if I pray in an unknown tongue, my spirit prayeth, but," &c. If he uses the words of some tongue unknown to the congregation in prayer to God, he realizes in his own spirit what he says to God, but his understanding (or mind) is unfruitful. As Theodoret says: "The fruit of him who speaks is the advantage which the hearers derive." If, then, he speaks in an unknown language, and brings no interpretation to bear on his auditory, he has not the fruit which he ought to have from every spiritual exercise.

15. "What is it then? I will pray with the spirit, and I will pray," &c. The spirit is that part of the inner man by which it

CHAP. XIV.] I WILL SING WITH THE SPIRIT. 239

pray with the understanding also: ᵉI will sing with the spirit, and I will sing ᶠwith the understanding also.

ᵉ Eph. v. 19.
Col. iii. 16.
ᶠ Ps. xlvii. 7.

16 Else when thou shall bless with the spirit, how shall he that occupieth the room of the unlearned say Amen ᵍat thy giving of thanks, seeing he understandeth not what thou sayest?

ᵍ ch. xi. 24.

---

rises into the closest communion with God. The understanding is that comparatively lower part by which, through the medium of speech, a man makes his thoughts intelligible to his fellow-creatures.

St. Paul then says in effect, " I will pray in the spirit, but I will not allow myself to be so carried away, even though I have the gift of tongues, as to utter what is unintelligible ; and so, with what I sing, my whole spirit shall mount up in the psalm or hymn, but I will so sing it that all who hear shall understand. I will use no language that all do not understand, whether known or unknown, whether of men or angels ; for, if so, I minister to my own vanity, not to edification."

16. "Else when thou shalt bless with the Spirit, how shall he . . . say Amen at thy giving of thanks," &c. There can be little doubt but that "he that occupieth the place of the unlearned," means the private or non-official person—*i.e.*, the layman, and that the Amen is not a common Amen, but the one said by the whole congregation after the Consecration. It is alluded to at some length twice by so ancient a writer as Justin Martyr as follows : " After this, bread and a cup of wine mixed with water are brought to the president; and he taking them gives praise and glory to the Father of the Universe, through the Name of the Son and of the Holy Ghost, and offers thanksgiving at considerable length for our being counted worthy to receive these things at His Hands. And when he has concluded the prayers and thanksgivings, all the people express their assent by saying Amen " (Apol. i. 65).

There is a remark upon this place in Chrysostom's Commentary, which is still more confirmatory of the above. "And what he saith is this: If thou shalt bless in a barbarian tongue, not

17 For thou verily givest thanks well, but the other is not edified.

18 I thank my God, I speak with tongues more than ye all:

---

18. "With tongues." So B., K., L., P., most Cursives, Syriac, Copt., Æth.; but ℵ, A., D., E., F., G., 17, 31, d, e, f, g, Vulg., Arm., read "with a tongue."

knowing what thou sayest, nor able to interpret, the layman cannot respond the Amen. For not hearing the words, 'for ever and ever,' which are at the end, he saith not the Amen." Now when we turn to the most ancient of Liturgies, the Clementine, we find that this long prayer ends with "both now and ever, and world without end." And then there comes a special rubric or direction, "And let all the people say Amen." It is to be noted that the word is with the article in this verse—not Amen, but *the* Amen (τὸ ἀμήν).

It may be asked, would any one be so foolish as to give the Eucharistic Thanksgiving in an unknown tongue? St. Paul does not say that any one had actually done so, but by supposing the case he shows its absurdity. The layman would not only be unable to understand, but even to give his solemn assent to the principal feature in the worship.

17. "For thou verily givest thanks well, but the other is not edified." That is, with fervency and devotion, but the other cannot either understand or respond. The prayer or thanksgiving, it is clear, must have been in some articulate language, for it is inconceivable that any Eucharistic prayer could have been expressed in ecstatic devotion, probably above the comprehension of the offerer.

18. "I thank [my] God, I speak with tongues more than ye all." Literally (and adopting the reading *tongue*) "I thank God that I speak (or, am speaking) in a tongue more than ye all." If "tongue" here means languages, then St. Paul means "I speak in languages more than ye all," which really amounts to "I speak in more languages than ye all," and this was needful for him, for he was the world's missionary. If tongue, however, means ecstatic devotion, then it means, I pray to God, and praise Him in the highest raptures of ecstatic devotion, more than all of you, for I know your thoughts, and the state of your souls even when I am

CHAP. XIV.]   IN UNDERSTANDING BE MEN.   241

19 Yet in the church I had rather speak five words with my understanding, that *by my voice* I might teach others also, than ten thousand words in an *unknown* tongue.

20 Brethren, ʰ be not children in understanding: howbeit in malice ⁱ be ye children, but in understanding be † men.

21 ᵏ In the law it is ˡ written, With *men of*

ʰ Ps. cxxxi. 2. Matt. xi. 25. & xviii. 3. & xix. 14. Rom. xvi. 19. ch. iii. 1. Eph. iv. 14. Heb. v. 12, 13.
ⁱ Matt. xviii. 3. 1 Pet. ii. 2.
† Gr. *perfect*, or, *of a ripe age*, ch. ii. 6.
ᵏ John x. 34.
ˡ Isa. xxviii. 11, 12.

absent from you, and I know that I excel you all in the ecstatic rapture of my prayer, but I pray thus privately, for in all that I am now writing, I am showing you how unedifying the speaking with tongues in the Church usually is.¹

Let the reader judge for himself, would it be likely—is it credible that the Apostle would thus expose before others his preeminence in a very peculiar kind of devotion, which arose entirely out of the rapturous character of his love to God?

19. "Yet in the Church I had rather speak five words with my understanding." "With my understanding." "In a rational manner, so as not only to understand myself what I say, but to be understood by others."

20. "Brethren, be not children in understanding: howbeit in malice be ye children," &c. They were children in understanding if they used such a gift as the speaking in foreign languages, where there were none to interpret, or none to understand. If, however, it was an afflatus which came upon them from without to enable them to express the extreme rapture or ecstasy of their souls, then they could not restrain themselves, and the Apostolic reproof would scarcely apply to them.

"Howbeit in malice be ye children." Rather "Be ye infantile." Notice how pervaded the Apostle's mind is with the exalted place of charity above all other Christian dispositions.

"But in understanding be men"—"be as those of full age; be ripe; be perfect."

21. "In the law it is written, With men of other tongues, and other lips," &c. This quotation is exceedingly difficult to apply

---

¹ "After paying this homage to glossolation, the Apòstle consigns this gift to its place. This place is the domain of private edification, not of public worship" (Godet).

R

other tongues and other lips will I speak unto this people; and yet for all that will they not hear me, saith the Lord.

---

21. "And other lips" (ἑτέροις). So D., E., F., G,, K., L., P., most Cursives; but ℵ, A., B., 5, 6, 10, 17, 31, 39, 67**, 73, read, "with the lips of others" (ἑτέρων).

---

to the matter upon which the Apostle is writing—the abuse of the gift of tongues. So difficult is it that Edwards actually supposes that this gift of tongues, which the Apostle desired that all the Corinthian Christians should possess, was given by way of punishment on themselves. His words are: "The Apostle taunts the Corinthians as the prophet taunts Israel, with being children in understanding; and as the Lord threatens to speak to Israel in the, to them, unintelligible language of the Assyrians, so the childish vanity and ostentation of the Corinthians is visited with an outburst of ecstatic cries in the Church assemblies. The tongues are an example of analogical retribution, childishness receiving childish gifts." We read this with amazement, when we remember Acts xix. 6, "The Holy Ghost came upon them, and they spake with tongues and prophesied;" or 1 Cor. xii. 8-10, "For to one is given by the Spirit the word of wisdom—to another divers kinds of tongues—to another the interpretation of tongues;" (xiv. 5), "I would that ye all spake with tongues," and many other places. One is staggered at a Christian speaking thus of the gifts of the Spirit. St. Paul writes against the abuse of a gift which, if taken in its proper meaning, demonstrates more than any other the power of God on the side of the Gospel. He reminds his hearers that God had prophesied that some time in their future, "with other tongues, and with other lips he would speak to this people." This was fulfilled on the day of Pentecost, in Cæsarea, in Ephesus, and at Corinth. Now the Apostle's reasoning is, "This speaking with other tongues and other lips" was for the unbelieving Jews, that they might hear, but so perverse were they that they rejected the testimony of the extraordinary greatness of the gift, and stopped their ears. But this did not undo the fact that some of them heard and believed the Word. Much stress is to be laid on the words, "Yet for all that," as showing not only the greatness of the gift, but its fitness for converting unbelievers. It is clear that in the words "For all that they will not hear," there can be no covert allusion to the Corinthian

TONGUES ARE A SIGN.

22 Wherefore tongues are for a sign, not to them that believe, but to them that believe not: but prophesying *serveth* not for them that believe not, but for them which believe.

23 If therefore the whole church be come together into one place, and all speak with tongues, and there come in *those that are* unlearned, or unbelievers, ᵐ will ᵐ Acts ii. 13. they not say that ye are mad?

Christians, for on one hypothesis their belief extended to ecstasy in devotion, and on the other (the ancient one) the Spirit had been given to them to enable them to perform an astonishing miracle on the side of the truth.

22. "Wherefore tongues are for a sign, not to them that believe, but to them, &c." Tongues can only be a sign to those who understand them, and who also are sure that those who speak them have not learned them in the ordinary way. When these two conditions meet no miracle performed in favour of the Gospel could be greater, if so great: but if one came to them speaking in a tongue of ecstatic rhapsody, of which they would not understand one word, they would naturally say, as the Apostle tells us in the next verse, that the speaker was out of his senses. And even if the meaning of the words of ecstasy was given to them by an interpreter, it seems to me that it would be most unlikely to convert them. What would convert them would be the account of the Death and Resurrection of Jesus of Nazareth, powerfully evidenced by external miracles, and not the expression of feeling which prompted the ecstatic tongue, which I think would be, till they were converted, as unintelligible to them as the tongue itself.

"But prophesying serveth not for them that believe not, but for them which believe." Prophesying was for the edification, or building up of those in whose hearts the foundation was laid by repentance and faith. The prophet seems ordinarily not to have been the Evangelist sent to the heathen. His work was rather, as expressed in verse 3, the edification, exhortation, and comfort of Christians.

23. "If therefore the whole church be come together into one place, . . . ye are mad?" If an unlearned layman, or an unbeliever, enter into the Church when those who have the gift of tongues are exercising it, he would be utterly confounded at the apparent

24 But if all prophesy, and there come in one that believeth not, or *one* unlearned, he is convinced of all, he is judged of all:

---

jargon and confusion. This, of course, would be the case whatever we take the gift of tongues to be, whether the gift of ecstatic utterance or of foreign languages.

It is very important, however, to notice it, as some who hold the ecstatic language theory maintain that the tongue was given to the unconverted heathen in judgment—to convince them of a fast approaching retribution; but here St. Paul supposes a totally different effect—that instead of the heathen being led to fear judgment to come they would be led to believe in the insanity of the utterer of the tongue.[1]

24. "But if all prophesy, and there come in one that believeth not, or one unlearned, he is convinced of all," &c. The prophet (verse 3) is supposed to speak to men, "to edification, and exhortation and comfort;" and particularly it is assumed that he speaks in the vernacular language. When then the private person or unbeliever hears the exhortation to believe in Jesus, and receive from Him a new life, or when he hears words of comfort which assure him of the abundant consolation here for all the evils of life, and the good hope of eternal life hereafter, then under God's grace he is convinced of all—that is, everyone who prophesies brings some-

---

[1] Thus Edwards:—"The ecstatic cries in the Church assemblies were intended by God to be a sign to the unbelievers (the heathens of Corinth) that the day of the Lord was near." But this seems impossible, unless we suppose that the day of grace was absolutely closed to the people of Corinth. Godet takes it in a somewhat different sense. He likens it to our Lord speaking in parables. "It is a sign of His growing breach with the mass of the nation. So it is with tongues, glossolalia is neither a means of conversion, nor a sign of approaching judgment on unbelievers. It is a demonstration given to their own conscience of the state of unbelief which God sees them to have reached. Would a God of light manifest Himself in the midst of His own by unintelligible sounds? Here there is a sign of severance, which is gradually carried out." So far M. Godet. But he does not tell us plainly to whom this sign of unintelligible speech is addressed. It cannot be to the Corinthian Church assembly, for assuredly we are not to believe that they were in such a state of unbelief that Jesus Christ was gradually withdrawing himself from them. There is not one word of such a withdrawal in all the rest of these two Epistles. And it cannot be the heathen of Corinth; for how could they possibly guess that people speaking in unintelligible utterances was an assurance that a certain obscure prophecy and a certain mysterious conduct of our Lord to His fellow countrymen was a sign to them? How could they be expected to know the purport of Isaiah xxviii. 11, 12, or of the facts recorded in Matthew xiii.?

25 And thus are the secrets of his heart made manifest; and so falling down on *his* face he will worship God, and report ⁿ that God is in you of a truth. ⁿ Isa. xlv. 14. Zech. viii. 23.

26 How is it then, brethren? when ye come together, every one of you hath a psalm, ᵒ hath a ᵒ ver. 6. ch. xii. 8, 9, 10.

---

25. "And thus." These words omitted in א, A., B., D*., F., G., ten Cursives, d, e, f, g, Vulg., Syriac, Copt., Arm., Goth., Æth.; but retained by K., L., most Cursives, &c.

thing home to his conscience—he is judged of all, *i.e.*, everyone that so prophesies in words that he can understand shows him his real state.

25. "And thus are the secrets of his heart made manifest; and so," &c. The effect of all Divine teaching is, first of all, the revelation of a man's heart to himself—in fact, conviction of sin, of righteousness, and of judgment. This is the first thing, the foundation on which all the spiritual edifice is built, and without which it is uncertain and insecure. It is that also which manifests the presence of the Searcher of hearts, and so, being convinced that He is present in the Church, the man falls down and worships. A singular interpretation of this is given by Edwards. "The unbeliever falls on his face in shame that the hidden sins of his heart should have been brought to light." But is it to be supposed that a man's secret sins should be made known to the whole Church? Why may not the man fall on his face in adoration, as the seraphim employ four out of their six wings to show reverence at the presence of God (Isaiah vi. 2)? If Christ fell on His face (Matt. xxvi. 39) why should not we?

26. "How is it then, brethren? when ye come together, every one of you hath a psalm," &c. This sounds as if there were something of blame in it, but we need not so understand it. He had said that "the manifestation of the Spirit is given to every man to profit withal," and then he exemplifies it by recounting the gifts which various persons in their assembly were likely to possess.

The first of these is singular. "Everyone of you hath a psalm." Was this one of the one hundred and fifty, or was it a hymn like those poured forth by inspiration, such as the song of the Blessed Virgin, or of Zacharias, or of Simeon? Most likely one of the latter, composed by some individual Christian under the special teaching of the Spirit.

doctrine, hath a tongue, hath a revelation, hath an interpretation. ᵖ Let all things be done unto edifying.

ᵖ ch. xii. 7.
2 Cor. xii. 19.
Eph. iv. 12.

26. "Hath a tongue." These words put after "hath a revelation" in ℵ, A., B., D., E., F., G., 17, 73, 93, d, e, f, g, Vulg., Syr., Copt., Æth.; but L. and most Cursives have "hath a tongue" before "hath a revelation."

But how came such psalms or hymns to be lost? Very probably because, when so many had the power of composing them, they were little thought of, after their first utterance: and their places were supplied by others. But why have we not inspired hymns? Well, we do not know whether we have not. It is very probable that many of the hymns in our most popular hymn book, containing the productions of holy men in all ages, are as much inspired by God as were these psalms of the Corinthians. It is questionable whether the most of them would have had more genuine inspiration than "Glory be to Jesus," or "Rock of Ages," or "The Church's One Foundation," or "O Sacred Head surrounded," or, "Jesu, Lover of my Soul."

It is scarcely probable that they were altogether extemporaneous, though, like the Magnificat, many might have been. In Tertullian's time (about 190 or 200 A.D.) it appears that each one in turn might be called upon to sing.[1]

"Hath a doctrine." Probably what we now call an instruction.

"Hath a tongue." Probably this should come after the next,— "Hath a revelation;" the order being "hath a revelation, hath a tongue," &c. The revelation is, most probably, a prophetical announcement, coming more directly from the Spirit than the διδαχή, or instruction.

Such an abundance of gifts seems to put the earliest Church far above the present; but it is not so, for it is to be remembered that the Corinthian Church had but a small part of our New Testament —indeed, probably one Gospel, and the Epistle which St. Paul was

---

[1] This fact appears in a description of the love feast. "Men sit not down to meat before tasting in the first place of prayer to God. They eat as much as hungry men desire; they drink as much as is profitable for chaste men; they are so filled as men who remember that during the night also they must pray to God; they so discourse as those who know that God heareth. After that water for the hands and lights are brought, according as each is able, out of the Holy Scriptures, or of his own mind, he is called upon to sing publicly to God. Hence it is proved in what degree he hath drunken" (Tertullian, Apol., i. 39.)

CHAP. XIV.] IF THERE BE NO INTERPRETER. 247

27 If any man speak in an *unknown* tongue, *let it be* by two, or at the most *by* three, and *that* by course; and let one interpret.

28 But if there be no interpreter, let him keep silence in the church; and let him speak to himself and to God.

---

now writing. It is possible that they might have had the two short Epistles to the Thessalonians, but no more.

Whereas we, though we have no prophecy, no apocalypses, no tongues, have the teaching or prophesying of the Apostles in a permanent form in their Epistles which have come down to us, as well as such sources of Divine instruction as St. Luke's and St. John's Gospels.

"Let all things be done unto edifying." Not to self-exaltation, not to the display of gifts, but let there be but one aim, one purpose, the building up of the body of Christ in Christ.

27. "If any man speak in an unknown tongue, let it be by two, or at the most," &c. "Let it be by two, or at the most by three." Ellicott renders this, "To the number of two, or at the most three." Why does St. Paul permit the speaking of tongues at all in a Church assembly where all spoke one language? Blunt suggests, and with great probability of truth, that there might be present strangers from other countries, particularly sea-faring men, who had been moved to embrace the Gospel, and that those who had the gift had specially such in view, but inasmuch as the greater part used the Greek language, one who had the gift of the interpretation of tongues must always be present. It is not in the least degree likely that there were many in the Church, if any, who were in a state of ecstacy. Considering how the Apostle has to blame them for sinful divisions, for party spirit, for uncomely behaviour in the house of God, for the abuse of the Agape, for want of realization of the meaning and intent of the Eucharist, and for want of charity, it is extremely unlikely, I say, that there would be much, if any, true ecstatic rapture among them, which must perforce vent itself in sounds unintelligible to the assembled Church. There might be false ecstacy, unreal rapture, but this could hardly take the form of a gift of God's Holy Spirit.

28. "But if there be no interpreter, let him keep silence." But if, as some commentators hold, this gift of unintelligible utterance

29 Let the prophets speak two or three, and ᑫ let the other judge.

ᑫ ch. xii. 10.

---

29. "The other." Properly, "others."

was given as a sign of judgment (see Edwards, Godet, and Bishop Ellicott, on verse 21), why should the man thus endowed keep silence? By doing so he would withhold the needful warning—for, according to these expositors, the very unintelligibleness of the tongue was a sign of judgment to come.

"Let him speak to himself, and to God." This might be possible in a congregation in England. A man may speak to God in the Hebrew words of a Psalm, or in the Greek words of such a hymn as the Magnificat, or in the Latin words of the Te Deum, and be blameless; but he would appear to be guilty of great vanity and foolishness if he spoke all this aloud in the congregation.

29. "Let the prophets speak two or three, and let the other (others) judge." He now proceeds to regulate, or set limitations to the prophetic utterances—two or three only were to speak (apparently) at each meeting of the Church.

"And let the others (οἱ ἄλλοι) judge." But if prophecy was a gift of the Spirit, and if the prophets spoke by the Spirit, how could their utterances be judged? This seems to imply a very great gulf between the utterances of the great prophets, whose prophecies have been embodied in the Canon of Scripture, and those of these somewhat inferior prophets of the Church. Were there degrees of inspiration? but whatever degrees there were, prophecy in each one is reckoned by St. Paul as a gift of the Spirit. Perhaps the key is to be found in 1 John iv. 1, "Beloved, believe not every spirit, but try the spirits, whether they are of God . . . . Every Spirit that confesseth that Jesus Christ is come in the flesh is of God," &c. And so it was in the times of the Old Covenant. There was very great abundance of prophecy, but much of it was false, and the people of God had constantly to be guarded against false prophets.[1] (See particularly Ezek. xiii, and Jer. iv. 9, v. 13, 31, and many other places.)

Perhaps, however, the word "judge" may be taken in the sense

---

[1] The author of the "Didache" gives a very clear warning respecting the danger from false prophets: "not every one that speaks in the spirit is a prophet, but only if he have the manners of the Lord" (ch. xi.).

CHAP. XIV.] LET THE FIRST HOLD HIS PEACE. 249

30 If *any thing* be revealed to another that sitteth by, ʳ let the first hold his peace.

31 For ye may all prophesy one by one, that all may learn, and all may be comforted.

ʳ 1 Thess. v. 19, 20.

---

of "discerning." It seems strange that what we account to be utterances of the Spirit should need to be judged before being accepted by the Church: if so the Christian assembly must have sometimes taken the form of a debating society. Is it possible that the power of prophecy—*i.e.*, the eloquence—the ready choice of words and expressions was one thing, and the matter of the prophecy another? Commentators notice the extraordinary difference between this rule of St. Paul's, and that given by the unknown author of the Didache, who lays it down that it is the sin against the Holy Ghost to judge the prophetic utterance, "Ye shall not tempt, neither judge of any prophet, speaking in the Spirit; for every sin shall be forgiven, but this sin shall not be forgiven" (Chap. xi.).

Altogether the whole subject of prophecy, both as it appears in the Old Testament and in the New, is exceedingly mysterious—quite as much, if not more so, than that of the tongues.

30. "If any thing be revealed to another that sitteth by, let the first hold," &c. This that was revealed to the other being from the Spirit, was a sign that the first had prophesied sufficiently, and that it was now the turn of another. Thus Chrysostom: "Since what need was there further, that when the second was moved to prophecy, the first should speak? Ought they, then, both? Nay, this were profane, and would produce confusion. Ought the first? This, too, were out of place. For to this end, when the one was speaking, the Spirit moved the other, in order that he, too, might say somewhat."

31. "For ye may all prophesy one by one, that all may learn," &c. There seems not to have been a particle of jealousy in the Apostolic mind respecting prophecy interfering with Church rule or Church order. He seems to have had altogether the mind of Moses, "Would God that all the Lord's people were prophets, and that the Lord would put His Spirit upon them." (Numb. xi. 29.)

May I be permitted to repeat here what I have written on Acts ii. 17, 18? "The Apostle here declares that the gift of the Spirit shall

32 And ^s the spirits of the prophets are subject to the prophets.

33 For God is not *the author* of † confusion, but of peace, ^t as in all churches of the saints.

^s 1 John iv. 1.
Gr. *tumult*, or, *unquietness*.
^t ch. xi. 16.

---

33. Some connect the latter part of this verse with the rest, "as in all churches of the saints, let the women keep silence in the churches." So Tischendorf.

not be in any way confined to the educated and respectable of the world, but shall reach to servants and slaves. We of the Church of England should look to this. If "the Lord gives the word, great may be the company of the preachers," and He may not see fit to confine the great prophetical gift to those educated in universities or colleges. We shall in such cases have to fall in with His mind, and find suitable spheres for those who have undoubtedly gifts of the Spirit directly from Him, and we may rest assured that such gifts, if truly and indeed from Him, will not tend to the disintegration, but to the Unity of the One Mystical Body."

"That all may learn, and all may be comforted." This implies that each one gifted with the prophetic spirit has, or may have, his own individual message, and his own power of imparting comfort. Does this mean that each and every member of the Church may speak, or is it, as Godet appears to think, to be limited to those who have the prophetic gift? Very probably the Church then had powers of instantly recognizing a true prophetic utterance which have not been recorded.

32. "And the spirits of the prophets are subject to the prophets." This has been taken to mean that the prophetic utterances are subject to the judgment of the body or company of those similarly inspired, or it may mean that the prophetic impulse in each man is under the control of his own spirit. Thus Wordsworth: "They who professed to be moved by the Spirit might allege that they were not and could not be subject to any laws of order and discipline, and therefore the Apostle teaches that it is the very essence of genuine prophecy, as distinguished from that which is spurious, to be regulated according to the laws prescribed by God, for the good order and edification of His Church;" and with this agrees what follows.

33. "For God is not the author of confusion, but of peace, as in all churches of the saints." This is an universal axiom, that

CHAP. XIV.] LET WOMEN KEEP SILENCE. 251

34 "Let your women keep silence in the churches: for it is not permitted unto them to speak; but ^x*they are commanded* to be under obedience, as also saith the ^y law.

^u 1 Tim. ii. 11, 12.
^x ch. xi. 3.
Eph. v. 22.
Col. iii. 18.
Tit. ii. 5. 1 Pet. iii. 1.
^y Gen. iii. 16.

---

whatever in a church tends to dissension is not from God. Ought not then false doctrines, or superstitious worship, to be protested against? Yes; but in trembling subordination to the Unity of the Body. If men are not hasty, not ambitious of being leaders, and revolt at originating schism, God, we believe, will find out a way of removing error and establishing the truth.

If the latter words of this verse, "as in all churches of the saints," are to be connected with the first part, then the Apostle in them emphasizes the maxim that God is the author of peace everywhere. He is, as we address Him as being, "The author of peace and lover of concord, in knowledge of whom standeth our eternal life."

34. "Let your women keep silence in the churches, for it is not permitted," &c. This precept is so exceedingly plain and direct, that it must of necessity overrule all inferences in favour of women speaking in the church, drawn from chap. xi. 5, and also from Acts xxi. 9. Whatever form the praying or prophesying of women assumed it must not be such as would enable them to be for the time superior in the public assemblies to men, as the teacher of necessity places himself over the taught. They are to be in subjection, under obedience, and the first words in which God, after the fall, assigns to the sexes their relative positions is a testimony to this, "Thy desire shall be to thy husband, and he shall rule over thee." This verse of Genesis contains the principle which is contravened wherever a woman is allowed to preach publicly.[1] This rule is constantly infringed among the sects, but how any woman by profession belonging to the Church of England with this place in her Bible can desire to do such a thing seems inexplicable.

35. "And if they will learn any thing, let them ask their husbands," &c. The prohibition extends even to their asking

---

[1] An occasion took place lately on which I was present, when a Christian woman was allowed to speak in an assembly of clergy and representative laity, and the result was most distressing.

35 And if they will learn any thing, let them ask their husbands at home: for it is a shame for women to speak in the church.

36 What? came the word of God out from you? or came it unto you only?

37 ˣ If any man think himself to be a prophet, or spiritual, let him acknowledge that the things that I write unto you are the commandments of the Lord.

ˣ 2 Cor. x. 7.
1 John iv. 6.

---

35. "For women." So D., E., F., G., K., L., most Cursives, d, e, g, Syriac; but ℵ, A., B., some Cursives, Vulg., Copt., Basm., Arm., Æth., read, "a woman."

37. "Are the commandments." So E., K., L., most Cursives; ℵ, A., B., 17, Copt., Æth., read, "is the commandment;" but D., E., F. (Gr.), G., d, e, g, read merely, "are of the Lord."

questions. Their voices are not to be heard in the Christian assembly.

"For it is a shame for women (or a woman) to speak in the church." It is contrary to modesty and propriety, and in so far as it is a contravention of a great scripture principle it is sinful and wrong.

36. "What? came the word of God out from you? or came it unto you only?" They had acted in the matter of allowing women to preach and to worship with heads uncovered, and of assigning that particular value and position to the various works of the Spirit which their fancy dictated, and of measuring the Eucharist by the Agape—they had acted, in all these matters, as if they were the authors of their own Christianity—as if, because of their manifold spiritual gifts, the word of God had come forth from Corinth, instead of from Jerusalem. The Apostle reminds them that instead of such being the case the word of God was brought to them by himself, and those under him. They had received all from him— even the first gifts of the Spirit had come, as in all other churches, through the laying on of Apostolic hands.

37. "If any man think himself to be a prophet, or spiritual, let him acknowledge," &c. This is a most decisive dictum. It scatters to the winds any idea respecting the independence of local churches. If any Church had any right to assert such independence because of the manifold gift of the Spirit in its members, it was this Church of Corinth. They might rejoin to all that the Apostle had written

COVET TO PROPHESY.

38 But if any man be ignorant, let him be ignorant.

39 Wherefore, brethren, ^a covet to prophesy, and forbid not to speak with tongues.

^a ch. xii. 31. 1 Thess. v. 20.

---

to them in the way of blame or direction, "If you have the spirit so have we." And to this the Apostle replies, "If you have the spirit He will not say one thing in you and another in me." You with your divisions, and parties, and differences from all other churches, and pride and self-seeking, are not likely to have the Spirit in such measure that you are able to criticize what I deliver by inspiration of God. The evidence on your part of having the Spirit will be seen in your at once acknowledging that what I write is from the Lord through the Holy Ghost.

This passage may also be taken not only as an assertion of a higher inspiration, which it is, but as a vindication of his own action in all his dealings with them. He had not, as Godet says, directed the Church in ways of his own choice, but by the light which is assured to him as an Apostle, charged with founding and governing the Churches of the Gentiles.

38. "But if any man be ignorant, let him be ignorant." If any man is, or professes to be, ignorant that what I say is from direct inspiration, let him be ignorant—there is no help for him if he chooses to make naught of the proofs of my inspiration, such as that I have imparted to you the Gospel, and with it the gifts of the Spirit, and that I do more miracles, and speak with more tongues than you all. (See 2 Corinth. xii. 12.)

39. "Wherefore, brethren, covet to prophesy, and forbid not to speak with tongues." "Covet to prophesy." This is in accordance with what he had said at the beginning of the chapter, "Desire spiritual gifts, but rather that ye may prophesy."

"Forbid not to speak with tongues." This permission he had given in verse 27, but with this proviso, that there was to be an interpreter in the church. If there were no interpreter, and if he could not himself interpret, as might well be the case (see note on verse 5), then he must keep silence. It is to be remembered that the gift of speaking in a language not learnt by natural means was a most wonderful miracle of God's power over the human mind, and if used intelligently in the Church, and understood by the hearers through the interpreter, was a most manifest sign of the

40 ᵇ Let all things be done decently and in order.

ᵇ ver. 33.

40. "Let all things." So K., L., and almost all Cursives; but ℵ, A., B., D., E., F., G., P., fifteen Cursives, Ital., Vulg., Syr., Copt., Arm., read, "but let all things" (δὲ).

presence in the Church of the Spirit of Power. On this account it might be permitted in the Church, though the proper place for exercising it were places to which foreigners resorted. But I beg the reader to try and realize how impossible it was for the Apostle to say such a thing as "forbid not to speak with tongues," if these tongues (or this tongue) were the outward sign or effect of inward ecstatic or rapturous devotion. How could he say "forbid not the outward manifestations of the most extreme love for God or Christ, or the raptures of the first experience of forgiveness, or the exceedingly warm glow of soul at the consciousness of the Spirit within one, or of heaven brought close to one?"

40. "Let all things be done decently and in order." "Decently." Here he is supposed to hint at the conduct of the women, and the disorders in the Agape, and the celebration of the Eucharist. Such disorders were unseemly and indecorous. And they were not likely to be alone, for where the spirit of reverence for the Church of Christ was wanting, the spirit of laxity and disorder was sure to find entrance.

"And in order." Here he is supposed to refer to the want of order in the use of the gifts of the Spirit, which he reproves and corrects in verses 23-33.

But he enunciates an axiom which should be ever present in the conduct of all public worship—a precept which forbids all slovenliness—all haste—all want of that carefulness which we should observe in our approaches to One Whom we should regard with such profound reverence. It contains the spirit of such words as "Worship the Lord in the beauty of holiness;" "Serve the Lord with fear, and rejoice unto him with reverence." "I am a great King, saith the Lord of hosts, and my name is dreadful among the heathen" (Mal. i. 14).

As the matter contained in this chapter is of very great importance to our right conception of the Holy Spirit's working, it may be well to recapitulate the reasons for accepting the ancient view of this great work of God, and rejecting the modern one.

1. The account of the gift of tongues on the day of Pentecost,

being the first in order, and the most definite as regards the aim, exercise, and purpose of the gift, must rule all other notices.

2. Of this Pentecostal gift, a writer who believes in the ecstatic devotion theory (Edwards) says:—"If we had only the narrative in the Acts, no one would have supposed the gift of tongues meant anything else than the power of speaking in languages, colloquial knowledge of which had not, in the ordinary way, been acquired by the Apostles" (p. 319).

3. The same writer goes on to say:—"If, on the other hand, we possessed only the references to it in this Epistle, it is hard to believe anybody would have suspected that the gift of tongues meant this, though it would be difficult to say what it did mean!"

4. In order to assign some meaning to the account in our Epistle, the gift of tongues has been supposed to be some unknown language, a work of the Holy Spirit, devised by Him to enable certain of the Corinthians to express the ecstatic rapture of their love to God and joy in Jesus Christ, which could not be done adequately in the Greek language which they commonly used.

5. In such a case the gift of tongues was not a gift in itself, but the expression of a state of internal feeling respecting God and Christ and eternal things, which betokened the highest state of devotion possible. Then Godet describes it: "I can only regard the gift of tongues as the expression in a language spontaneously created by the Holy Spirit of the new views, and of the profound and lively emotions of the human soul set free *for the first time* from the feeling of condemnation, and enjoying the ineffable sweetness of the relation of Sonship to God." But let the reader remark that M. Godet's explanation postulates but one exercise of the gift in each person, and that is, at conversion, whereas the Apostle's account is, that the exercise of it constantly recurred and required to be restrained.[1]

6. I have examined in the preceding pages this chapter very

---

[1] In the extraordinary manifestations of religious feeling which took place in the north of Ireland somewhere about 1858 or 1859, the persons affected were thrown into a trance, and when they awoke out of it gave vent to their feelings in a prayer (it is said) of extraordinary fervour and beauty of language; but this was in the vernacular, nor was there any case of utterances unintelligible to the bystanders. As far as I can gather the utterance of this prayer occurred but once. From what I have heard, the effects of this Revival were in the long run most lamentable, as might be expected when we learn that the religious meetings were prolonged till after midnight.

carefully verse by verse, and have, I trust, shown that in no case were the tongues unintelligible. In every case they are supposed to be capable of interpretation. There is no association whatever of ecstasy, or of rapturous devotion, with their use. On the contrary, the language in which the Apostle speaks of them is quite incompatible with this modern explanation, that they are the expression of real genuine Christian ecstasy. And every mention of them throughout the whole account implies that they were a gift of speaking in foreign languages analogous to the great Pentecostal gift, only not intelligently or wisely used, but perverted to the purposes of religious display. And this is quite in accordance with the character of many members of the Corinthian Church— perhaps of a considerable number of them, as we learn from numerous places in the Epistle (i. 12 ; iii. 1, 3, 18, 21 ; iv. 7, 8, 9, 10 ; v. 2, 6 ; viii. 1, 2 ; xi. 21, 22).

7. Not only is the whole chapter inconsistent with the ecstatic devotion theory, but some places markedly so, as particularly verses 10, 11, 18, and 22 ; and to my notes on these verses I desire to refer the reader.

8. It has been said that the part of the world which was evangelized by the Apostles Peter, Paul, and John did not need any special gift of speaking foreign languages, because Greek or Latin was spoken more or less in all the coasts of the Mediterranean ; but this is a mistake. The merchants and seamen from the shores of the Black Sea and other distant parts who frequented the marts and docks of Corinth no doubt knew enough Greek to enable them to unlade and victual their vessels, and bargain about the prices of their goods ; but the vast bulk of them would be unable to understand at first the simplest sermon respecting the claims of Jesus of Nazareth to be the Christ—the Saviour of the world.

9. It has been said that we have no account of the Apostles or others using this gift for missionary purposes, but this is said in flat contradiction to the account in Acts ii., where persons of all nationalities heard them speak in their own tongues the wonderful works of God. What is this but a missionary use of the gift at its very beginning ! And what is still more to the purpose, we have no account of any Apostle or Apostolic man spending a considerable time in acquiring the language of those to whom he was commissioned to preach, which account we always find in the life of every modern missionary.

In concluding this summary I desire the reader to remember that what I am really contending for is the identity of the gift of tongues in Acts ii. and 1 Cor. xiv. On the ecstatic devotion theory they are wholly different.

Tertullian has been appealed to as the one Father who has taken the modern view, but I think wholly without reason. He refers to it thus in his book against Marcion (book v. chap. viii.): "Now compare the Spirit's specific graces, as they are described by the Apostle, and promised by the prophet Isaiah. 'To one is given,' says he, 'by the Spirit the word of wisdom.' This we see at once is what Isaiah declared to be the 'Spirit of wisdom.' 'To another the word of knowledge.' This will be the prophet's 'Spirit of understanding and counsel.' To another, 'faith by the same spirit.' This will be the Spirit of religion and the fear of the Lord. 'To another the gifts of healing, and to another the working of miracles.' This will be 'the Spirit of might.' 'To another prophecy, to another discerning of spirits, to another diverse kinds of tongues, to another the interpretation of tongues.' This will be the 'Spirit of knowledge '"—not, let the reader remark, the Spirit of rapture or of ecstasy, but the Spirit which most differs from it, 'the Spirit of knowledge.' I have noticed in my Excursus at the end of my volume on the Acts, two or three passages from very early Fathers bearing on the use of this gift. Irenæus, who lived within one hundred years after the writing of the Acts, says: "Luke relates that the Spirit descended on the disciples after the Ascension of the Lord, on the day of Pentecost, in order that all nations might enter into life; wherefore they united in all languages in praising God the Holy Spirit, bringing distant tribes into unity, and offering the first-fruits of all nations to God." (Irenæus iii. 17, cited in Wordsworth on Acts ii.) Also Irenæus speaks as if the gift yet remained in the Church: "In like manner we do also have many brethren in the Church who possess prophetic gifts, and who through the Spirit speak all kinds of languages, and bring to light for the general benefit the hidden things of men and declare the hidden mysteries of God" (v. 6). Also Origen on Rom. i., "I suppose that he was made a debtor to different nations, because, through the grace of the Holy Spirit, he had received the gift of speaking in the languages of all nations, as he also himself saith, 'I speak in tongues more than ye all.'" Of the "illustrations" of this great Pentecostal gift, which are cited by upholders of the modern view, I cannot find one which is in point till we come to the Irvingite manifestations. Some of the prophets of the Cevennes spoke sentences of Hebrew, or Greek, or Latin (which languages they are supposed never to have learned), but not in the language of ecstasy. Some manifestations also among the early Methodists are cited, but Wesley himself, in his notes on this chapter, makes not the slightest allusion to them.

The manifestations of the Irvingites I have treated of in an excursus at the end of my volume on the Acts. I would ask one question of those who cite these manifestations as illustrations of the Pentecostal gift. Do they mean to imply that both alike were gifts of the Spirit of God? Because if so, why do they not pay serious attention to the accounts of them, and search and see in a spirit of humble submission whether God has sent any message to us through these comparatively unknown persons in whom it seems He has revived a gift of the Spirit which has been in abeyance for eighteen hundred years?

If these Irvingite manifestations are real, let us treat them as such—as actual works of the Holy Spirit sent at first as a sign to those that believe not—*i.e.*, to us, so that we may accept the message, whatever it be, which they make known. If they are not real, let us cease to cite them as "illustrations" of the work of God at Pentecost, or we may commit a grievous sin against the Holy Spirit Himself.

CHAP. XV.

ON THE RESURRECTION OF THE BODY.

INTRODUCTORY.

We have in this chapter the Resurrection of the Dead set forth as it is nowhere else in Scripture, and we may make the same remark respecting this sublime enunciation of doctrine as we did respecting that of the truth of the Eucharist in Chapter XI. It is the especial prerogative of God to bring good out of evil, and as He made the profanation of the Eucharist by the Corinthians an occasion for bringing out the Institution of the Holy Communion, together with its doctrinal significance, more circumstantially than it is elsewhere revealed, so He has here made the unbelief of the Corinthians respecting the Resurrection of the Body the occasion for a vindication of the truth respecting that Resurrection which seems to exhaust the subject, and to leave nothing to be desired by the Christian soul to aid it in its adoring contemplation of this mystery of Godliness.

The circumstance which gave rise to his writing this chapter is to be found in verse 12, " Now if Christ be preached that he rose from the dead, how say some among you that there is no Resurrection of the dead?" The contents of this chapter are not so much a declaration of the truth of the Resurrection, *per se*, as of the necessary connection between Christ's Resurrection and ours. The Resurrection is not based upon any natural law, though a natural law is used as an illustration in verse 36; neither is it made to depend upon a mere arbitrary putting forth of Almighty power; but it is treated as a result, an outcome of the Resurrection of Christ. The whole chapter may be considered as an expansion of the Lord's words, " Because I live, ye shall live also."

To this end it commences with an account of the evidences of Christ's appearances in His risen Body which may with the utmost propriety be called a fifth Gospel. It contains more notices of appearances than any of the four, and it is to be remembered that it is the earliest written form of the Gospel of a Risen Christ.

This setting forth of the Resurrection as *the* Gospel is eminently Pauline. The enunciation of the Gospel at the commencement of the Epistle to the Romans is that He " was made of the seed of David according to the Flesh, and declared to be the Son of God with power by the Resurrection from the dead." Justification of life is intimately connected with belief in the Resurrection. (Rom. iv. 24, 25.) So also Salvation, " We shall be saved by His Life." (v. 10.) " If . . . . thou shalt believe in thine heart that God raised Him from the dead thou shalt be saved." (x. 9.) Again, " It is Christ that died, yea rather that is risen again." (viii. 34.) Again, " Remember that Jesus Christ was raised from the dead according to my Gospel." (2 Tim. ii. 8.) On this account, then, the Holy Spirit inspired the Apostle to commence this Revelation of this cardinal truth of Christianity with a declaration of his Gospel. This Gospel was the fact of Christ's Resurrection, and it was

MOREOVER, brethren, I declare unto you the gospel ᵃ which I preached unto you, which also ye have received, and ᵇ wherein ye stand;

ᵃ Gal. i. 11.
ᵇ Rom. v. 2.

---

declared, or re-declared by the Apostle, because the very outward fact witnessed to the resurrection of the dead.

Let us consider for a moment the significance of the Resurrection of the Lord. It is the Father's assurance of the truth of the Lord, of the truth of all that the Lord had said respecting His Sonship, His Atonement by His Death, His Life given to be our Life, His Second Coming and Judgment. (1) His Sonship—that He was the own, the very, the only Son of God. (2) That His Death had accomplished the purpose for which He submitted to Death—to be our ransom. (3) That by His renewed Life He could be the Bread of Life, the Living Bread, the assurance of immortality to the body, as He said, "He that eateth my Flesh and drinketh my Blood, hath eternal life, and I will raise him up at the last day." (4) His Second Coming,—"All that are in the graves shall hear the voice of the Son of Man, and shall come forth."

Now the Resurrection of Christ is the assurance of the truth of all this, but its very outward form and manner is, in an especial manner, the assurance of our Resurrection. The Resurrection of Christ bears upon the Resurrection of the Christian more directly and palpably than upon any other truth of the Gospel, and so the Apostle begins with it.

1. "Moreover, brethren, I declare unto you." "I declare unto you"—I make known unto you. The same word, γνωρίζω, is used in Gal. i. 11, where it is translated, "I certify you." Bishop Ellicott's explanation seems the best: he says, "It is accompanied with some tinge of reproach, marking that the Apostle was forced, as it were, *de novo*, to make known the tenour and import of the Gospel, since they seem not to realize it."

"The Gospel which I preached unto you." The Apostles were especially witnesses of the Resurrection. "With great power gave the Apostles witness of the Resurrection of the Lord Jesus." (Acts iv. 33.)

"Which also ye have received." The mere fact that they had renounced heathenism, and were professedly members of the

CHAP. XV.] BY WHICH YE ARE SAVED. 261

2 ^cBy which also ye are saved, if ye ‖ keep in memory †what I preached unto you, unless ^dye have believed in vain.

^c Rom. i. 16.
ch. i. 21.
‖ Or, *hold fast*.
† Gr. *by what speech*.
^d Gal. iii. 4.

Christian Church, was a proof that they had *received* this great truth, however they might have failed to realize its vast issues.

"And wherein ye stand." So in Rom. v. 2. "By whom also we have access by faith into this grace wherein we stand." Chrysostom asks, "How saith he that they who were so tossed with waves stand ? He feigns ignorance to profit them, desiring not to repel them, as if they had no hold of the truth, but to encourage them by the assumption that they had." Just as we in speaking to our congregations do not assume that they are unbelievers, but that they believe what they profess.

2. "By which also ye are saved." Salvation is always by the Apostle Paul intimately connected with the Lord's Resurrection. "If thou shalt confess with thy mouth the Lord Jesus, and shalt believe in thine heart that God hath raised him from the dead, thou shalt be saved" (Rom. x. 9). In these latter days belief is fixed by teachers and preachers on the Death of Christ, and often no allusion is made to His Resurrection. But in the first ages this could not be: for it was nothing then to tell a heathen man that a Jew had been crucified, and had died, but it was a great thing, and demanded the whole submission of his soul to God to tell him that God had raised up on the third day this crucified Jew, to assure men that He was His Son, and the Saviour of the world.

"If ye keep in memory what I preached unto you." The expression is peculiar—"if ye hold fast with what word I preached it to you (or, I evangelized you)." Godet explains: "By which also ye are put in possession of salvation, if ye hold it (the word) as I have taught it to you. The word λόγος here denotes the exact meaning Paul had given to the facts here related. Faith should grasp not only the fact, but also the Divine Thought realized in the fact."

The fact of the Resurrection even might be assented to apathetically, so there must be a realization in our inmost souls of the purpose of Divine love contained in the fact preached.

The "if" (IF ye hold fast) shows that he doubts whether some of them had a firm hold of the Gospel itself. This doubt in the Apostle's mind is not inconsistent with the words, "in which ye

3 For ^e I delivered unto you first of all that ^f which I also received, how that Christ died for our sins ^g according to the scriptures;

4 And that he was buried, and that he rose

<small>e ch. xi. 2, 23.
f Gal. i. 12.
g Ps. xxii. 15, &c. Isai. liii. 5, 6, &c. Dan. ix. 26. Zech. xiii. 7. Luke xxiv. 26, 46. Acts iii. 18. & xxvi. 23. 1 Pet. i. 11. & ii. 24.</small>

---

stand." He does not doubt their spiritual condition. Their lapse had not yet passed the limit of a lax hold of truth.

"Unless ye have believed in vain" (or believed). Unless your faith be dead, or unfruitful, or only nominal. It may, however, mean, as in verse 14, "Unless the Resurrection be not true, and so ye have no foundation for your faith."

3. "For I delivered unto you first of all that which I also received." He received it of those who first instructed him in the Christian faith. He does not mention from whom—probably not from Christ Himself, or he would have mentioned so important a fact as he does in chap. xi. 23; and probably, also, not from the Apostles themselves, as he seems not to have seen them till some time after his conversion, and it was the Lord's Will that he should be as independent of them as possible.

"How that Christ died for our sins according to the scriptures." If he preached the Resurrection of the Lord he must have preached His previous Death, and this Death was an all-atoning one—it was "for our sins." The proclamation of the Resurrection would have been of no value—it would have proclaimed an universal Resurrection to condemnation, except we had been reconciled to God through the Death of Him Who rose again.

"For our sins according to the scriptures." If the Death of the Messiah was according to the Scriptures, it must have been an atoning and reconciling death; for the place which above others sets forth the Death of the Messiah, sets it forth in such terms as "He was wounded for our transgressions; he was bruised for our iniquities . . . all we like sheep have gone astray, and the Lord hath laid on him the iniquity of us all."

4. "And that he was buried." Why is this particularly mentioned? No doubt because the circumstances of His Burial witness to the reality both of His Death and of His Resurrection. The request of Joseph of Arimathea led to Pilate's inquiring as to the

HE ROSE AGAIN THE THIRD DAY.

again the third day ᵇ according to the scriptures: ᵇ Ps. ii. 7.
& xvi. 10.
Isa. liii. 10.
Hos. vi. 2.
Luke xxiv. 26, 46. Acts ii. 25-31. & xiii. 33, 34, 35. & xxvi. 22, 23. 1 Pet. i. 11.

reality of the Lord's Death. His Burial, or rather the preparation for it, as recorded in the Gospels, and the laying of Him for a short time in the tomb, guarded by soldiers at the instigation of the chief priests, are all assurances of His absolute Death, and by consequence of the reality of His coming to life again in the same body in which He had suffered death.

"And that he rose again the third day according to the scriptures." The principal place of Scripture in which the Resurrection of Christ on the third day is foretold is Hosea vi. 2: "After two days he will revive us; on the third day he will raise us up, and we shall live in his sight." In the preceding verse we have the words of penitent Israel, "Come and let us return unto the Lord, for he hath torn, and he will heal us, he hath smitten and he will bind us up." The prophet here speaks by inspiration of Him in Whom His people, indeed all men, die and are buried and rise again. "What Christ our head did, He did, not for Himself, but for His redeemed, that the benefits of His Life, Death, Resurrection and Ascension might redound to all. He did it for them; they partook of what He did. In no other way could our participation in Christ be foretold.

It was not the prophet's object here, nor was it so direct a comfort to Israel, to speak of Christ's Resurrection in itself. He took a nearer way to their hearts. He told them, "all we who turn to the Lord, putting our whole trust in Him, and committing ourselves wholly to Him to be healed of our wounds, and to have our griefs bound up, shall receive Life from Him, shall be raised up by Him." They could not understand *then* how He would do this. The "*after two days*," and "*in the third day*," remained a mystery to be explained by the event. But the promise itself was not the less distinct, nor the less full of hope, nor did it less fulfil all cravings for life eternal and the sight of God, because they did not understand *how shall these things be?* Faith is unconcerned about the "how." Faith believes what God says, because He says it, and leaves Him to fulfil it, "how" He wills and knows. The words of the promise which faith had to believe were plain. The life of which the Prophet spoke, could only be life from death whether of

5 ¹And that he was seen of Cephas, then ᵏ of the twelve:

ⁱ Luke xxiv. 34.
^k Matt. xxviii. 17. Mark xvi. 14. Luke xxiv. 36. John xx. 19, 26. Acts x. 41.

---

the body or of the soul, or both. For God is said to *give* life only in contrast with such death. Whence the Jews, too, have ever looked, and do look, that this should be fulfilled in the Christ (Targum) though they know not that it has been fulfilled in Him. They too explain it (Targum), "He will quicken in the day of consolation, which shall come in the day of the quickening of the dead; He will raise us up and we shall live before Him."

In shadow the prophecy was never fulfilled to Israel at all. The ten tribes were never restored: they never, as a whole, received any favour from God, after He gave them up to captivity. And unto the two tribes (of whom, apart from the ten no mention is made here) what a mere shadow was the restoration from Babylon, that it should be spoken of as the gift of life or of resurrection, whereby we should live before Him. The strictest explanation is the truest. The *two days* and the *third day* have nothing in history to correspond with them, except that in which they were fulfilled when Christ 'rising on the third day from the grave, raised with him the whole human race.'" (Pusey on Hosea vi. 2.)

It is also to be noticed that on the third day Abraham in a figure received Isaac from the dead, and Jonah was cast up by the fish on the third day. (See Matth. xii. 40.)

5. "And that he was seen of Cephas," &c. It has been said that St. Paul must have received this from St. Peter himself, when he abode with him fifteen days in Jerusalem (Gal. i. 18), but it was well known among the disciples on the very day on which it occurred (Luke xxiv. 34). What took place at this interview we are not told. May I conjecture that the Lord then revealed to Simon how He had preached in the world of spirits, because in the Epistle of St. Peter alone have we any word of this action of His in the unseen state?

"Then of the twelve." This, no doubt, was the appearance chronicled in Luke xxiv. and John xxi. The "twelve" is the designation of the Apostolic band as distinguished from other disciples, though, of course, on this occasion neither Judas nor Thomas were present. (See particularly my notes on St. Luke xxiv. 36-43.)

HE WAS SEEN OF JAMES.

6 After that, he was seen of above five hundred brethren at once; of whom the greater part remain unto this present, but some are fallen asleep.

7 After that, he was seen of James; then [1] of all the apostles.

[1] Luke xxiv. 50. Acts i. 3, 4.

---

6. "After that, he was seen of above five hundred brethren at once," &c. This must have been in Galilee, for only there was it probable that five hundred believers could be gathered together in one place, the number in Jerusalem being only one hundred and twenty. I believe (as I said in my notes on St. Matthew, page 467), that this appearance was a manifestation to the body of believers as distinguished from the Apostles. Chrysostom notices that some in his day took ἐπάνω above, as meaning that He appeared to them above in the heavens, or raised above the earth, and this is very likely if He desired to be recognized by them all. Still it was not likely that there would be exactly five hundred, and so "above," as indicating number, is not unlikely.

"Of whom the greater part remain unto this present, but some," &c. The words "fallen asleep" would seem to point to the fact that in their case death had been abolished and was only a sleep of their bodies. (So 1 Thess. iv. 14, 15.)

7. "After that, he was seen of James," &c. Not the son of Zebedee, but the one who became the first Bishop of Jerusalem. In the Apocryphal Gospel according to the Hebrews, quoted by Jerome, the following account is given: "After His Resurrection the Lord went unto James, and appeared unto him. Now James had sworn that he would not eat bread from the hour in which he had drunk the cup of the Lord until he should see Him again, after that He had arisen from among them that sleep. . . . . Then the Lord said, Bring hither a table and some bread . . . . and He took the bread and blessed it, and brake it, and afterwards gave it to James the Just, and said unto him, 'Eat thy bread, my brother, for the Son of man hath risen from among them that sleep.'" (Hieron, de Viris Illustris, ii., quoted in Blunt.)

"Then of all the apostles." Most probably on the day of His Ascension.

8. "And last of all he was seen of me also, as of one born out of due time." The words "one born out of due time" most probably

8 ᵐAnd last of all he was seen of me also, as of ‖ one born out of due time.

9 For I am ⁿthe least of the apostles, that am not meet to be called an apostle, because ᵒI persecuted the church of God.

10 But ᵖby the grace of God I am what I am: and his grace which *was bestowed* upon me was not in vain; but ᵠI laboured more abundantly

m Acts ix. 4, 17. & xxii. 14, 18. ch. ix. 1.
Or, *an abortive.*
n Eph. iii. 8.
o Acts viii. 3. & ix. 1. Gal. i. 13. Phil. iii. 6. 1 Tim. i. 13.
p Eph. iii. 7, 8.
q 2 Cor. xi. 23. & xii. 11.

---

signifies an abortion, and the meaning may be that he was as unworthy to be called an apostle as an abortion is to be considered a man. Some seem to explain it as referring to the irregular, and, so to speak, unnatural mode of St. Paul's appointment to the Apostleship; for all the rest of the Apostles had been the companions of the Lord, and, compared with St. Paul, came into their office naturally, whereas St. Paul's election was sudden and violent. Stanley remarks, " The corresponding word (*abortiones*) in Latin was metaphorically applied as here, to such senators as were appointed irregularly." (Suet Oct. c. 35, 2.)

9. " For I am the least of the apostles, that am not meet to be called," &c. This fact that he had been a persecutor was constantly before his mind, as if he never forgave himself for it. Thus Gal. i. 13, 23; Phil. iii. 6; 1 Tim. i. 13, 15, 16.

10. " But by the grace of God I am what I am . . . . abundantly than they all," &c. He was a successful Apostle only through grace, *i.e.*, through the unmerited favour of God, and through the powerful working of Christ within him.

" More abundantly than they all." This is taken by some commentators to mean more abundantly than all the rest put together, but this would seem far more than the Apostle would wish to say of himself, for seeing that the twelve were dispersed all over the world, how could he know it? But it seems quite true for him to say it with reference to the better known Apostles, Peter, James, aud John, that in the way of journeyings by land and sea and shipwrecks, and the care of all the churches which devolved upon him as the Apostle of the Gentiles, he laboured more abundantly than them all. Such a series of hardships and struggles as we have

CHAP. XV.] SO WE PREACH. SO YE BELIEVED. 267

than they all: ʳ yet not I, but the grace of God which was
with me.

11 Therefore whether *it were* I or they, so we
preach, and so ye believed.

12 Now if Christ be preached that he rose from
the dead, how say some among you that there is
no resurrection of the dead?

ʳ Matt. x. 20.
Rom. xv. 18,
19. 2 Cor. iii.
5. Gal. ii. 8.
Eph. iii. 7.
Phil. ii. 13.

---

recorded in his second Epistle (xi. 21-30) seems not to have been undergone by any other Apostle or Apostolic man whatsoever.

"Yet not I but the grace of God which was with me." What is this grace? evidently the peculiar grace of the Apostleship, but along with this, of course, the grace of Sacraments and of insight into the Divine word, and so the grace which was common to each Christian as a member of the body of Christ. Notice how, even when he was forced to assert himself, he yet ascribed nothing to himself, but all to the grace of God.

"Therefore whether it were I or they, so we preach," &c. Whatever differences evil minded men had insinuated between his teaching and that of the other Apostles, on this matter of the Resurrection all preached exactly the same—"so we preached;" and all who called themselves Christians accepted this Gospel of the Resurrection in its literal sense—"so ye believed."

12. "Now if Christ be preached that he rose from the dead, how say," &c. Various reasons have been given for this denial on the part of the Corinthians of the Resurrection of the Body. Some say that it was through the influence of Sadduceeism amongst the Jews who generally constituted the nucleus of each Gentile church; but this is exceedingly unlikely. Sadducees would be the last persons to be converted to the Gospel. Indeed it is impossible to see how they could, whilst retaining any tincture of Sadduceeism, be converted to the faith of a Saviour Who, if He had not risen from the dead, would have by that very fact been proved to be an impostor. Others have referred to the mention of Hymenæus and Philetus, 2 Tim. ii. 17, who said that the Resurrection was passed already, and have inferred that some of the Corinthians had taught that the real resurrection took place at the conversion of the soul, and that no other was to be looked for. But must we not look to the prevalent Greek philosophy for the key to this unbelief? The view of Plato

13 But if there be no resurrection of the dead, ᵃthen is Christ not risen:

ᵃ 1 Thess. iv. 14.

14 And if Christ be not risen, then *is* our preaching vain, and your faith *is* also vain.

---

that matter (ὕλη) was essentially evil, and that the perfection of the soul consists in its deliverance by death from the innate pollution of the body, was almost universally held by the heathen,[1] and some of the Corinthians were not at their conversion thoroughly delivered from this misbelief. It was this opinion which was the root of Gnosticism, and extended even to the denial of the true human nature of Christ—some asserting the blasphemy that His Body was a mere phantom, and that His Spiritual or Divine Part alone ascended into heaven. This lingering Platonism, or rather perhaps incipient Gnosticism was quite sufficient to account for the denial of the Resurrection by some amongst the Corinthians.

Of course those who denied this Resurrection of the Body held firmly to the immortality of the soul, but this, in St. Paul's view, was no real Christianity.

13. "But if there be no resurrection of the dead," &c. If it be out of the power of God, or if it be contrary to some law which He has imposed upon Himself, to allow of a Resurrection at all, then Christ is not risen. The Resurrection of Christ is not an isolated fact, because He Himself is not an isolated person. He so took upon Him our nature that He is one with us in Life, Death, and Resurrection. If we, then, cannot rise again, neither can our Head have risen. The logic of the Apostle has been called in question, but it is the logic of one who had written, "as the body is one, and hath many members ... so also is Christ." (1 Cor. xii. 12.)

14. "And if Christ be not risen, then is our preaching vain, and your faith," &c. Our preaching is vain, because we have preached as the foundation of all belief and all hope that which has, on the unbelieving hypothesis, never taken place; and your faith is vain,

---

[1] Wordsworth quotes two passages from the Tragedian:—

ἀνδρὸς δ' ἐπειδὰν αἷμ' ἀνασπάσῃ κόνις·
ἅπαξ θανόντος οὐκέτ' ἔστ' ἀνάστασις.

Æschylus, Eumen., 655.

and

οὐκ ἔστι θνητῶν ὅστις ἐξανίσταται.

Eurip., Alcestis, 783.

CHAP. XV.] IF THE DEAD RISE NOT. 269

15 Yea, and we are found false witnesses of God; because ^t we have testified of God that he raised up Christ: whom he raised not up, if so be that the dead rise not. ^t Acts ii. 24, 32. & iv. 10, 33. & xiii. 30.

16 For if the dead rise not, then is not Christ raised:

17 And if Christ be not raised, your faith *is* vain; ^u ye are yet in your sins. ^u Rom. iv. 25.

---

because it rests not on human reasoning, nor on the proof of the immortality of the soul, but on the fact of the Lord's Resurrection.

15. "Yea, and we are found false witnesses of God; because we have," &c. Notice how the Apostle tacitly repudiates the idea that they could possibly have been deceived. They could not have been deceived. There could have been no room for deception in the circumstances of that appearance of the Lord which changed the tenour of his whole life. He could not have been deceived as to the light from heaven which blinded him—as to the momentary sight of the Lord in that light—as to the voice from heaven, which dispersed all doubt as to Whom he saw. His brother Apostles, Peter, John, James, could not have been deceived. They knew the Lord too well. If not deceived, they must have been deceivers. But for what did they deceive men? In order that they might suffer the loss of all earthly things? In order that they might live lives of ignominy, persecution, and distress?

16, 17. "For if the dead rise not, then is not Christ raised . . . ye are yet in your sins." These verses may seem to some a needless repetition of verses 13 and 14, but they are not. The point of the two former verses is, that if Christ be not risen, their faith is vain. The point of verses 16 and 17 is, If Christ be not risen they are yet in their sins. The argument is: If the dead rise not, then is Christ not risen, your faith is vain—now faith in a risen Christ is the means of your justification—Rom. iv. 5; if, then, He be not raised, ye are unjustified, ye cannot be in Him for purposes of life if He be dead. If He rose not again, then the ransom which He promised has not been paid, ye are unforgiven, ye are yet in your sins. If Baptism be for the remission of sins, it must be a Baptism into One Who has atoned for sin by His Death, and risen again to make us partakers of His justifying life, according to the Apostle's words in the Epistle to the Romans: "We were buried with Him

18 Then they also which are fallen asleep in Christ are perished.

---

by Baptism into His Death, that like as Christ was raised up from the dead by the glory of the Father, even so we also should walk in newness of life." (Rom. vi. 3, 4.)

But the Apostle, though he does not express it, evidently implies the impossibility of such a thing as that they were yet in their sins. They knew that they were not. They knew by the internal peace and the internal strength, that they had been delivered from sin. The promise had, in the case of some among them, been fulfilled, "Sin shall not have dominion over you." That could be no delusion, which had broken such a power.

18. "Then they also which are fallen asleep in Christ are perished." Godet suggests that this "perished" means that they would awake and find themselves in eternal punishment, but such a harsh supposition is its own refutation. What the Apostle means is that there is no immortality of the soul revealed apart from that of the body, or rather, apart from the Lord's Resurrection. Whatever philosophy may have to say about it, a mere immortality of the soul is not revealed. It does the utmost violence to the idea planted in us of an eternal Justice, to think that the best men have the same end as the worst.

In the hope of the Resurrection the martyrs of Christ had lived lives such as had never yet been seen on earth: can they perish as the brutes? No, because life and immortality are brought to light by the Gospel, and that Gospel is the Gospel of the Resurrection. In such ways the Apostle shows the absurdity to which men are driven if they reject the Resurrection.

19. "If in this life only we have hope in Christ, we are of all men most miserable." There is a difference of translation suggested, owing to the emphatic position of "only" at the end of the clause, "if we have only hoped in Christ in this life," &c., but then in the world to come we shall not *hope* in Christ, we shall enjoy the sight of Him in His Kingdom. Cornelius à Lapide thus paraphrazes. "The word 'hoping,' or 'men hoping,' signifies here, not the act of hope (for it is certain that this exists only in this life), but the object of hope, forsooth, the thing hoped for, as if he said, 'If in Christ we are hoping for only those good things which are in this life, we are of all men most miserable.'"

19 ˣ If in this life only we have hope in Christ, we are of all men most miserable. ˣ 2 Tim. iii. 12.

"What sayest thou, O Paul, How in this life only have we hope, if our bodies be not raised, the soul abiding and being immortal? Because, even if the soul abide, even if it be infinitely immortal, as indeed it is, without the flesh, it shall not receive those hidden good things, as neither truly shall it be punished . . . . If the body rise not again, the soul abides uncrowned, without that blessedness which is in heaven," &c. (Chrysostom.)

Now does this "most miserable" principally consist in present persecutions and distress, with hope of joy hereafter? Have not other men misery besides Christians? And if other men are miserable without Christian hope of a Resurrection, and Christians themselves have no hope of a Resurrection, is there not an equality? No: we are to take into account other things which Christ reveals, which very much intensify the evil plight of those who, if such a thing can be, have only hope in Him so far as this world is concerned. For Christ reveals to us God. He not only reveals God to us, but makes us acquainted with Him, so that we know Him, or suppose that we know Him, as our friend.

How unspeakably miserable, then, it would be, if through Christ we should have hoped that we had been made to know God, and conversed with Him, and received answers of peace from Him, and after we have been removed hence after a short time find that all this is a delusion. Such would, indeed, be a miserable end—the future all the darker because of its delusive brightness. We should, in such a case, be the greatest dupes among men to have had such intense hopes, and to be at last disappointed would be the lowest depth of misery.

This passage opens out to us the most irrefragable proof of the truth of Christianity. In the far-seeing wisdom of God, our religion was promulgated, and the Church founded by men who had no worldly motive whatsoever for preaching Christ. Supposing that, from the first, ministers of Christ had had before them anything like the same worldly prizes which they now have, would it not be said that they preached because it was their worldly interest to do so? But now this cannot be said. Men may choose present distress and toil and pain if there be some certainty of future recompense, but that men should live such lives as the Apostles lived,

20 But now ʸ is Christ risen from the dead, *and* become ᶻ the firstfruits of them that slept.

21 For ᵃ since by man *came* death, ᵇ by man *came* also the resurrection of the dead.

ʸ 1 Pet. i. 3.
ᶻ Acts xxvi. 23. ver. 23. Col. i. 18. Rev. i. 5.
ᵃ Rom. v. 12, 17.
ᵇ John xi. 25. Rom. vi. 23.

20. "And become." So K., L., most Cursives, Syr., Goth.; but omitted by ℵ, A., B., D., E., F., G., P., 6, 17, 67**, 71, 177, d, e, f, q, r, Vulg., Sah., Copt., Basm., Arm., Æth.

with the full knowledge that the hopes of the future, which they pretended to have, were a delusion, because they knew that Christ had not risen—this is far more contrary to nature than all the miracles in the Evangelists put together.

20. "But now is Christ risen from the dead, and become the firstfruits," &c. The Apostle, after showing the absurdity of a denial of the Lord's Resurrection, dismisses the thought with indignant scorn and impatience. "Now is Christ risen from the dead, the first fruits of them that slept." (The word "become," $ἐγένετο$, is probably, spurious, and it takes away from the spirit of the assertion that Christ is risen as the firstfruits.) The Resurrection of Christ is the earnest of the Resurrection of those who are in Him and then of all mankind.

The Lord ordained that at each harvest the children of Israel were to bring a sheaf of the first-fruits of their harvest unto the priest, "And he shall wave the sheaf before the Lord, to be accepted for them" (Levit. xxiii. 10-11). Christ, then, was typified by the sheaf of the firstfruits. His Body raised again was the pledge of the mighty harvest of redeemed bodies which shall rise like an exhalation at the last day.

21. "For since by man came death, by man came also the resurrection of the dead." Great is the mystery here. God saves men, and yet he saves them through themselves—through one of themselves. God saves us by no act of mere power. He sent His Son amongst us in the likeness of sinful flesh. This Son of His by coming amongst us became naturally, as it were, the Head of the race. How could God incarnate, if He be amongst us as one of ourselves, be other than our Head? And by His submission to the death which we derived from man He was enabled as man to restore us to life.

CHRIST THE FIRSTFRUITS.

22 For as in Adam all die, even so in Christ shall all be made alive.

23 But ^cevery man in his own order: Christ the firstfruits; afterward they that are Christ's at his coming.

^c ver. 20.
1 Thess. iv. 15, 16, 17.

22. "For as in Adam all die, even so in Christ shall all be made alive." A very grave and difficult question presents itself here. Is the "all" of the second clause to be taken as universally as the "all" of the first? In Adam all are by nature, and so die. In Christ only some are by grace, for the Lord says, "Ye will not come to me that ye may have life." There can be no doubt that all those who are abiding members of Christ's Mystical Body will rise with Him their Head; but how about those who are not members of the Mystical Body, or have been cut off from it by sin? (John xv. 6). Will these be made alive in Christ? Now we have the assurance of Christ Himself that all universally will rise again by His power and at His call. "All that are in the graves shall hear His voice, and shall come forth; they that have done good unto the resurrection of life, and they that have done evil unto the resurrection of damnation" (John v. 28, 29). But there must be a difference between the Resurrection of the righteous and of the wicked. If the good are raised because they abide in Christ the wicked cannot be so raised, for they have not Christ in them: but still Christ is the Head not only of the Church, but of the race. And they may rise in Him as the Head of the race. A parallel distinction seems to be recognized in 1 Tim. iv. 10: "The living God, who is the Saviour of all men, specially of those that believe." The greatest differences have existed about this amongst divines and theological writers. According to Edwards, Chrysostom, Theodoret, Ambrosiaster, Calvin, Meyer, De Wette, Olshausen, &c., the second "all" is as universal as the first; but Augustine, Estius, Grotius, Bengel, Rückert, Hofman, and Heinrice, consider that it only refers to believers.

23. "But every man in his own order." Theodoret and others make this to mean either in the order of the good, or of the wicked. Others consider the order to be differences of rank and happiness according to the degree of sanctification in each one. Others refer it to various resurrections as, first that of Christ, then that of those who have fallen asleep in Him before His coming, then that of those

24 Then *cometh* the end, when he shall have delivered up ^d the kingdom to God, even the Father;

^d Dan. vii. 14, 27.

---

24. "He shall have delivered up." So K., L., most Cursives, Ital., Vulg.; but ℵ, A., B., D., E., F., G., P., 31, 67, 80, read, "He shall deliver up."

who, like St. Paul, are in the Lord when He comes (1 Thess. iv. 15, 16, 17), then the general Resurrection of Rev. xx. 12. The latter seems to agree best with the remainder of the verse.

"Christ the firstfruits; afterwards they that are Christ's at his coming." "They that are Christ's at his coming." This seems to be the first Resurrection, the Resurrection from out of the dead of Philippians iii. 11, the ἐξανάστασις. It is also that of Rev. xx. 5, 6. "Blessed and holy is he that hath part in the first Resurrection: on such the second death hath no power, but they shall be priests of God and of Christ, and shall reign with him a thousand years."

24. "Then cometh the end, when he shall have delivered up (shall deliver up)." We cannot consider these verses without reverently bearing in mind the saying of the Lord to the Apostles: "It is not for you to know the times or the seasons, which the Father hath put in his own power" (Acts i. 7). The first question which arises on this verse has to do with the first word "*Then*." "Then cometh the end." The last verse ends with the parousia ("they that are Christ's at his coming) *then* cometh the end." What time and what events does this "then" cover? The end is evidently the delivering of all things to the Father. But the proper translation, according to the oldest authorities, is, "Then cometh the end, when he shall deliver up (not have delivered up) . . . when he shall have put down all rule," &c. So that there may be an interval (how long we know not) between the coming (parousia) and the end of all things, during which He shall put down all rule. Thus Bishop Ellicott: "Whether any, and, if any, what interval is to be supposed to exist between this coming (παρουσία) and the end (τὸ τέλος) of the following verse (24)—in fact, between the ἔπειτα and the εἶτα, the sober interpreter cannot presume even to attempt to indicate. This only may be said, that the language *seems* to imply a kind of interval; but that there is nothing in the particles or in the passage to warrant our conceiving it to be longer than would include the subjugation of every foe and every power of evil, and all that may

PUT DOWN ALL RULE.

when he shall have put down all rule and all authority and power.

be immediately associated with the mighty τέλος which is specified in the succeeding verse. . . . It must be carefully remembered that the Apostle is here dealing with a single subject, the Resurrection of the dead, and not with the connected details of eschatology. These must be gathered from other passages and other portions of Scripture."

The great difficulty in Christian eschatology is the exact position which all that is specified in Rev. xx. 4, is to hold in the sequence of the future which is to be unfolded.

"When he shall have delivered up [or deliver up] the kingdom to God, even the Father." There would be no difficulty about this place if we considered sufficiently that God the Father for a time seems to have given His "Monarchia" into the hands of the Son. Thus the Lord says: "All things are delivered unto me of my Father." "All power is given to me in heaven and in earth" (Matth. xi. 27; xxviii. 18) and He especially specifies the exercise of judgment, which we should have considered to be of necessity exercised solely by the Father, to be in future exercised by Himself, so that "the Father judgeth no man, but hath committed all judgment unto the Son" (John v. 22). This supreme power is committed unto Him not as God, for as the Eternal Word it was always His, but as the Son of Man; and it is for a dispensation of time—till, that is, He has subdued all things to Himself and to God. This rule is His Mediatorial Rule. The Deity now acts, and reigns, and judges as the son of Man till the time when the purpose of God in suffering this conflict between good and evil is fulfilled.

When He delivers up the kingdom to God His Father He will cease to rule visibly and palpably as man, but He never can cease to rule in the unity of the Godhead.

"All rule, and all authority, and power." There can be no doubt but that by these words "rule," "authority," and "power," the Apostle means evil spirits. Just as there is a hierarchy amongst the good angels, for the Apostle speaks of "principalities and powers in heavenly places" (Eph. iii. 10), so there is a similar gradation of power amongst the evil angels, for he says, "We wrestle not against flesh and blood, but against principalities, against powers, against the rulers of the darkness of this world" (Eph. vi. 12). How this evil hierarchy reigns in this world, and under what

25 For he must reign, ᵉ till he hath put all enemies under his feet.

26 ᶠ The last enemy *that* shall be destroyed *is* death.

ᵉ Ps. cx. 1.
Acts ii. 34, 35.
Eph. i. 22.
Heb. i. 13. &
x. 13.
ᶠ 2 Tim. i. 10.
Rev. xx. 14.

---

conditions or limits we know not; but many things in the course of events in past times and in the present seem to show that there is a supernatural maintenance of evil, a solidarity, as it were, of evil men holding evil principles, a fellowship of darkness, as well as of light.

25. "For he must reign, till he hath put all enemies under his feet." So then we gather from this that the reign of Christ is not a reign of peace, but of warfare. The rider on the white horse Who had the crown given to Him, rides forth conquering and to conquer (Rev. vi. 2). There is a time apparently of peace for one thousand years, but it is terminated by the last outbreak of evil (Rev. xx. 4, 10), which itself is terminated by the Consummation.

Does He then cease to reign when His enemies are all put under His feet? It can only be in a sense; for we have so many intimations that Christ shall reign for ever, that they cannot be disregarded. Thus Rev. xi. 15, "The kingdoms of this world are become the kingdoms of our Lord and of His Christ, and He shall reign for ever and ever." Thus Luke i. 33, "Of his kingdom there shall be no end." Thus it was said to God the Son by the Father, "Thy throne, O God, is for ever and ever" (Hebrews i. 8); also Dan. ii. 44, vii. 13, 14.

As I said, His Mediatorial Kingdom must pass away or be delivered up when its purpose is fulfilled, but His rule as a Person in the Godhead cannot pass away: for He said, "I and the Father are one," and He said, "I am Alpha and Omega, the beginning and the ending, which is, and which was, and which is to come, the Almighty" (John x. 30; Rev. i. 8).

26. "The last enemy that shall be destroyed is death." What is the meaning of this, for death is not an entity, an individual existence, as an angel is, and even the angel of death is not an enemy of God, but some holy spiritual being, who, at His command, executes His purpose of punishment? The destruction of death signifies the abolition of the curse, "Dust thou art, and unto dust shalt thou return." Thus in the account of the final restitution we

CHAP. XV.] ALL THINGS UNDER HIS FEET. 277

27 For he ^g hath put all things under his feet. But when he saith all things are put under *him, it is* manifest that he is excepted, which did put all things under him.

g Ps. viii. 6.
Matt. xxviii.
18. Heb. ii. 8.
1 Pet. iii. 22.

have, " There shall be no more curse: but the throne of God and of the Lamb shall be in it; and his servants shall serve him " (Rev. xxii. 3). The destruction of death then signifies the abolition of the curse—the reconciliation of all things to God (Coloss. i. 20).

How is it said, then, in Rev. xx. 14, that "death and hell were cast into the lake of fire "? It may mean that death shall exist only in Gehenna in the form of the Second Death; or it may mean that those who have resisted all the invitations of God's mercy, and when spiritual life was offered to them, have of their own free will continued in the death of sin, shall be under death for ever in the lake of fire.

Cornelius à Lapide says well: " The first enemy of Christ and of Christians is the devil, who was conquered by Christ on the cross; the second is sin, which through the grace of Christ is conquered by Christians in this life; the third is death, which, as the last of all, will be conquered at the Resurrection."

27. " For he hath put all things under his feet. But when he saith," &c. It seems strange to us that St. Paul should draw attention to the fact that when God the Father surrendered all things into the hands of the Son, and gave Him the monarchy of the universe for a time, He did not put *Himself* under His Son. Some seem to explain this as if it were put in to emphasize the universal dominion of Christ, that *all* things whatsoever are put under Him except God—the exception, as it were, proving the absolute universality of His rule. I cannot but think that there is some truth in the suggestion of Theodoret, who says, that this is written to meet any misconception which might arise from reminiscences of the heathen mythology, in which the supreme ruler attains his high estate by deposing him who ruled before him. The Father is not subjected because the whole universe is committed into the hands of the Son. On the contrary, the Father acts in all that the Son does for the subjugation of evil. It is the Father Who says to the Son, " Sit thou on my right hand till I make thine enemies thy footstool." The Son has all things committed to Him, and yet the Son says, " I can do nothing of myself." " Whatsoever things the

h Phil. iii. 21.
i ch. iii. 23. & xi. 3.

28 ʰ And when all things shall be subdued unto him, then ⁱ shall the Son also himself be subject

---

Father doeth, these doeth the Son likewise." (See John v. 19, 30; ix. 4; xii. 49; xiv. 10.)

28. "And when all things shall be subdued unto him, then shall," &c. Much difficulty has been made of this expression, "the Son also himself shall be subject unto him that put all things under him," as if it detracted from the Divine honour of the Son if He were perfectly subordinate to His Father. But this is a great mistake. The most exalted idea of Sonship is perfect equality in nature with Him that begat Him, and yet perfect subjection in love and will. If there be a true begetting, the Father must transmit to the Son all His nature and attributes, so that so far as Godhead and its perfections are concerned, the Son must be equal. This is recognized as fully as possible in the Lord's words in John v. 17, "My Father worketh hitherto, and I work." No mere human being could say such a thing as this, for it implies on the face of it (and still more when it is taken in connection with the context) that the two workings are the same. The Jews understood this as an assertion of that Sonship which implies equality of nature, and particularly of power, and so they took up stones to stone Him because He said also that God was His Father, rather His own Father (ἴδιον), making Himself equal with God. Our Lord, instead of denying His equality with the Father, reasserted it in connection with His subordination in the words, "The Son can do nothing of himself, but what he seeth the Father do; for what things soever he doeth, these also doeth the Son likewise," and this He extended even to the raising of men from the dead (John v. 21).

We trust we may, without presumption or irreverence, illustrate the matter as follows: A king who has an only son whom he associates with himself in all his counsels, finds an important province in rebellion. He says to his son, "I will give this province entirely into your hands, I will appear as little as possible on the scene, and you shall have, till you have thoroughly subdued it, the entire charge of the province." When after he has accomplished this, he comes back and puts the conquered province entirely into the hands of his father, does he lose any of his original human attributes which he has in common with his father, because he possesses the same nature? It is absurd to suppose so. The subjection or sub-

unto him that put all things under him, that God may be all in all.

---

ordination of the Son adds, if one may so say, to our view of his moral perfection, "I have kept my Father's commandments and abide in his love."

A strange view has been taken of the termination of the mediatorial dispensation by Dean Stanley, and after him by the Rev. T. Teignmouth Shore, and perhaps others, which is, that not only the mediatorial rule of Christ, but all rule whatsoever, will cease at the time of this consummation. Mr. Shore writes: "Not only all hostile rule, and authority, and power, but all intermediate rule of any sort, good and bad. The direct government by God of all creatures is to be at last attained. All the interventions of authority and power, which the fall of man rendered necessary, will be needless when the complete triumph of Christ comes in. Thus humanity, having for ages shared the condition of fallen Adam, will be finally restored to the state of unfallen Adam. Man will see God, and be ruled by God face to face."

But if this is to be, God will cease to have servants, for all the servants of God mediate in some degree between God and some part of His creation. God could do everything without intervention of any sort, but He has constituted the services of angels and men in order that they may do what He Himself could do, but has seen fit to employ others in doing. The idea of the abolition of all intermediate action on God's part seems to me to postulate a dead level of equality in all His spiritual or intelligent creation. It is hard to see how there can be degrees in created beings, unless the higher grades in some way superintend the lower. And again, this non-intervention idea seems by the author I have quoted to be a consequence of the Fall, but surely the hierarchy of heaven—the principalities and powers in heavenly places—was not first instituted at the time of the Fall.

"That God may be all in all." Many, many are the interpretations which have been given to this wonderful revelation. We can only say as Calvin said respecting another unspeakably deep mystery, "we can only feel after it rather than attempt to grasp it."

It may point to a fuller and more direct manifestation of the Father than has been accorded hitherto to the intelligent creation. Hitherto the Father has been known by the Son. It may be that

29 Else what shall they do which are baptized for the dead, if the dead rise not at all? why are they then baptized for the dead?

---

after the consummation He will show Himself more directly, or it may be that the explanation is to be found in the true meaning of such profound places as " My Father will love him, and we will come to him and make our abode with him" (John xiv. 23). One thing is certain, that the presence of the Father will not exclude that of the Son, and that of the Holy Ghost.

It is not said that the Father will be all in all, but that God will be all in all. God is, in the Unity of the Divine Nature the Father, the Son, and the Holy Ghost—and these will be all in all in the redeemed, and the Presence of none of these Persons can possibly be excluded from their state of final perfection.

The subordination of the Son is inherent in His being the Word. A word must be subordinate to him who speaks it. A conception must be subordinate to him who conceives, Sonship must be subordinate to Fatherhood. We have no faculties for realizing any submission or subjection on the part of the Son, beyond that expressed in His own words, John xii. 49: " I have not spoken of myself; but the Father which sent me, he gave me a commandment, what I should say, and what I should speak."

I confess to having a great difficulty in the explanation of this place, but the difficulty to me is simply this. In Ephes. iv. 6, this same Apostle writes of the Father: " One God and Father of all, who is above all, and through all, and in you all." What can the subjection of the Son add to this?

29. " Else what shall they do which are baptized for the dead," &c. A large number of explanations have been given of this passage. It will be quite sufficient to mention two.

Some have supposed that there is a reference to a superstitious practice, which seems to date from the earliest times, of baptizing a living person as a sort of proxy for one who had died without Baptism. The difficulty is that the Apostle should have drawn an argument from a practice of which, as we suppose, he could hardly have approved; and yet it is not impossible that this practice might have gained a footing in the Corinthian Church, and that the Apostle here alludes to it as an extreme case in point; as if he said, You are so anxious about the future of those who die by

30 And ᵏwhy stand we in jeopardy every hour?

31 I protest by ‖¹your rejoicing which I have in Christ Jesus our Lord, ᵐI die daily.

ᵏ 2 Cor. xi. 26.
Gal. v. 11.
‖ Some read, *our*.
¹ 1 Thess. ii. 19.
ᵐ Rom. viii. 36. ch. iv. 9. 2 Cor. iv. 10, 11. & xi. 23.

---

31. "By your rejoicing which I have." So D., E., F., G., L., most Cursives, d, e, f, g.; but ℵ, A., B., K., P., fifteen Cursives, Vulg., Goth., Syr., Sah., Copt., Basm., add, "brethren."

some accident unbaptized that you baptize others on their behalf by a rite which has no meaning, unless it is supposed to give them a part in a Death and a Resurrection following close after the Death.

Chrysostom, after alluding to this Baptism by proxy as that of heretics, explains the Apostle's words thus: "After the enunciation of those mystical and fearful words, and the awful rules of the doctrines which have come down from heaven, this also we add at the end when we are about to baptize, bidding them say, '*I believe in the Resurrection of the dead*,' and upon this faith we are baptized. I say, after we have confessed this, together with the rest, then at last are we let down into the fountain of those sacred streams. This, therefore, St. Paul recalling to their minds said, 'If there be no resurrection why art thou then baptized for the dead?' *i.e.*, the dead bodies. For, in fact, with a view to this art thou baptized, affirming a resurrection of thy dead body, that it no longer remains dead. And thou indeed in the words makest mention of a Resurrection of the dead; but the priest as in a kind of image signifies to thee by very deed the things which thou hast believed and confessed in the appointed words . . . . when thou hast done thine own part, then also doth God fully assure thee. How, and in what manner? By the water: for the being baptized, and immersed, and then emerging, is a symbol of the descent into hell, and the return thence."

30. "And why stand we in jeopardy every hour?" If the dead rise not, why do we expose ourselves to all manner of danger, even of our lives? All the persecutions and distresses which we endure are not because we preach a future state on the same grounds as some of your philosophers, but because we preach a crucified and risen Christ, and a resurrection of our bodies as the consequence of His.

31. "I protest by your rejoicing which I have in Christ Jesus

32 If ‖ after the manner of men ⁿI have fought with beasts at Ephesus, what advantageth it me, if the dead rise not? ᵒlet us eat and drink; for to morrow we die.

‖ Or, to speak *after the manner of men.*
n 2 Cor. i. 8.
o Eccles. ii. 24.
Isa. xxii. 13.
& lvi. 12.
Luke xii. 19.

---

our Lord, I die daily." This follows upon "Why stand we in jeopardy every hour?" Not only am I in jeopardy, but "I die daily:" I live a dying life (compare "In perils by mine own countrymen, in perils by the heathen, in perils in the city, in perils in the wilderness," 2 Cor. xi. 26). "I protest:" I swear that this is true by your rejoicing or boasting which I have in Christ Jesus. He strengthens what he says respecting his daily dying by an asseveration grounded on his boast of them as his work in Christ.

32. "If after the manner of men I have fought with beasts at Ephesus," &c. After the manner of men, *i.e.*, as Meyer says, "after the manner of ordinary men, *i.e.*, not in divine striving and hoping, but only on account of temporal reward and glory, whereby the unenlightened man is wont to be moved to undertake great risks."

"I have fought with beasts at Ephesus, what advantageth it me?" Some think that this should be taken literally—that he was cast to the wild beasts then, but was delivered by God's power as Daniel was: but the objection is that no mention is made in the Acts of the Apostles of such an event, which, if it had taken place literally would have been the most extraordinary deliverance which the Apostle had ever experienced. But it is a well known phrase used both in the Old Testament, and in classical writers, to signify conflicts with fierce and bloodthirsty men. Thus Ps. xxii. 12, 16, "Many bulls have compassed me . . . . dogs have compassed me." Again, lvii. 4, "My soul is among lions," &c. Pompey in Arrian B.C. 11, says, "With what wild beasts do we fight?" And Ignatius in his Epistle to the Romans speaks of persecution by evil men as fighting with beasts by land and sea, and of himself as being bound to ten leopards—meaning ten soldiers.

"If the dead rise not, let us eat and drink, for to-morrow we die." The first clause ought most probably to be taken with the second, not with what goes before. "Let us eat and drink," &c., is taken from Isaiah xxii. 12. "In that day did the Lord of Hosts call to weeping . . . . and behold joy and gladness, slaying oxen and killing sheep, eating flesh and drinking wine : let us eat and drink ; for

CHAP. XV.] AWAKE TO RIGHTEOUSNESS. 283

33 Be not deceived: [p]evil communications corrupt good manners.

34 [q]Awake to righteousness, and sin not; [r]for some have not the knowledge of God: [s]I speak *this* to your shame.

p ch. v. 6.
q Rom. xiii. 11.
Eph. v. 14.
r 1 Thess. iv. 5.
s ch. vi. 5.

---

to-morrow we shall die." If there be no resurrection why should not sensual and selfish men act on this principle? but if there be a resurrection, had not such rather lay to heart the words of the wise man? "Rejoice, O young man, in thy youth; and let thy heart cheer thee in the days of thy youth, and walk in the ways of thine heart, and in the sight of thine eyes; but know thou that for all these things God will bring thee into judgment." (Eccles. xi. 9.)

33. "Be not deceived: evil communications corrupt good manners." He seems to advert to unrestrained intercourse with the heathen, or with lapsed Christians (v. 11). Communication is an unfortunate translation. It does not, in our day, bring out the fact that what St. Paul would guard them against is evil discourses (colloquia). These, in the case of the Resurrection, would be what we now call sceptical, or free-thinking, or naturalistic, explaining away on some "vision" theory the Resurrection of the Lord, and reducing that of Christians to the immortality of the soul. The Apostle here quotes either a passage in the Thais of the heathen poet Menander, or a well-known proverb which Menander himself had quoted. Tertullian supposes the former, for he speaks of it as a verse sanctified by St. Paul's use of it. (Ad uxorem, i. 8.)

34. "Awake to righteousness, and sin not; for some have not the knowledge of God," &c. We gather from this that the denial of such a doctrine as the Resurrection was in Christians not a matter of opinion, but of unrighteousness. Righteousness embraces not only our duty to our neighbour, but our duty to God: and if God has revealed to us certain unspeakably great benefits which He intends to confer upon us, it is our duty to meet His loving offers with grateful acknowledgment. If we do not we are ungrateful, and so unrighteous.

"Awake to righteousness" would be more literally translated "awake righteously." Chrysostom renders it "with a view to what is profitable and useful." Observe how, by calling on them to awake, he implies that some may be sleeping the sleep of sin and death.

35 But some *man* will say, 'How are the dead raised up? and with what body do they come?

36 *Thou* fool, "that which thou sowest is not quickened, except it die:

^t Ezek. xxxvii. 3.
^u John xii. 24.

Thus in Ephes. v. 14, he says, 'Awake, thou that sleepest, and arise from the dead, and Christ shall give thee Light.'"

"For some have not the knowledge of God." How could men who denied the power and willingness of God to bring about a Resurrection have any true knowledge of God?

35. "But some man will say, how are the dead raised up? and with what body," &c. Here is a new departure. An objector, who knows, or affects to know, no higher laws or processes than those of the present course of nature, scornfully asks, "How are the dead raised up?" That is, with what power? By what means? What is the process? And with what body do they come? Are they raised up in the same sort of bodies as those in which they lived here, or, if not, what are the properties of the bodies in which they are raised?

36. "Thou fool, that which thou sowest is not quickened, except it die." Thou senseless one, thou man without mind, hast thou not observed the commonest process of nature, the process by which thou art thyself fed and sustained? "That which thou sowest is not quickened except it die." As long as it remains in thy bag or on thy barn floor, it is a dead thing—there is a germ of life in it, but that is to all appearance as if it did not exist. It can only start into life by being buried in the earth, and the whole body of the seed thus buried decays and dies, whilst the new plant springs out of it from a germ infinitesimally small. The real atom which contains the life is unsearchable. It cannot be seen or distinguished till it has attained some size by having acquired nourishment from the decayed seed: so that here is the greatest mystery of nature, patent on all sides of us, the beginning of a new life from a dead seed.[1] Now this, of course, is only an analogy, and an analogy is

---

[1] The analogy of the chrysalis, which develops into the butterfly, has been used for the same purpose as the Apostle uses that of the seed developing into the plant, but it is infinitely inferior, for the chrysalis is not a dead thing, but moves slightly if touched, and is more like a creature in a womb which developes organs secretly till it is fit to use them.

37 And that which thou sowest, thou sowest not that body that shall be, but bare grain, it may chance of wheat, or of some other *grain*:

38 But God giveth it a body as it hath pleased him, and to every seed his own body.

---

not a proof : for the proof of the Resurrection is historical. It is the Resurrection of One Who, during His life, displayed supernatural power and wisdom, and whose Resurrection was proclaimed by men who lost every worldly advantage, and exposed themselves to death daily, because they asserted its truth. This, in the Apostle's view, was *the* proof of the Resurrection, but when men asked, how are the dead raised up, as if it were an impossible thing, then the Apostle used the analogy of the seed and the plant. How the seed is actually developed from the plant is as great a mystery as the Resurrection—not, of course, as great a thing—but as great a mystery—as inexplicable—as unsearchable. And the atheist, or agnostic, who says that it is produced by a law of nature, only introduces a still greater mystery—the mystery of laws not imposed by any intelligent being, but acting no one knows how—blindly, unintelligently, though they require the highest intellect of the race to describe or measure their action.

37. "And that which thou sowest, thou sowest not that body that shall be," &c. When a man sows in a field, he does not sow the fully developed plant, but a seed as unlike it as possible, bare grain, having no outward promise of beauty or fertility.

38. "But God giveth it a body as it hath pleased him, and to every seed," &c. Not only is the development of any plant from a seed a thing of the deepest mystery, but still more mysterious is that uniform action of God, by which each seed developes not into any plant, but into *the* plant which God has appointed from the first: so that, as far as we can see, not only are there an infinite variety of seeds, but an infinite variety of lives, *i.e.*, principles of life. There is a particular character of life in the seed of the rose and a different one in the seed of the lily, and they never interchange. The seeds of the rose and of the lily may produce varieties, but naturalists tell us that they all have a tendency to revert to the original form. Now the Apostle introduces this consideration because he means not merely life out of the dead seed, but a particular

39 All flesh *is* not the same flesh: but *there is* one *kind
of* flesh of men, another flesh of beasts, another of fishes,
and another of birds.

40 *There are* also celestial bodies, and bodies terrestrial:
but the glory of the celestial *is* one, and the *glory* of the
terrestrial *is* another.

---

form of life from each different seed. Does he not also hint that the
difference of bodies at the day of the Resurrection will also be, not according to any mere order of nature, but as God has decreed, "He
that soweth to his flesh shall of the flesh reap corruption, but he
that soweth to the Spirit shall of the Spirit reap life everlasting"?

Or it may be that he, in this clause, begins the answer to him
who asks, " with what body do they come?" "From the endless
variety of organization in things seen, he argues the possibility of a
new organization, yet to be disclosed hereafter." (Stanley.)

39. "All flesh is not the same flesh: but there is one kind of
flesh," &c. St. Paul now mentions the extraordinary variety of
organized bodies composed of flesh and blood. None of these classes
of living creatures have the same flesh. When examined by the
microscope their flesh is, as regards its cellular tissue and fibres, all
different, and their blood, which nourishes the flesh, is different in
all. If God, then, from animal tissue can produce such a variety
of forms of life adapted to live some on earth, some in the water,
some in the air, why cannot there be an immense variety of forms
in the unseen world answering to the variety in this world?

40. "There are also celestial bodies, and bodies terrestrial, but,"
&c. These celestial bodies are, most probably, the bodies of the
angels, from which in a way unknown to us light proceeds. They
are also such visible, palpable frames as those in which Moses and
Elias appeared on the Mount of Transfiguration. The "bodies
celestial" of the angels appear to us as men, and frequently it is
said that men appeared when we know that they were angels, as in
Acts i. 10, and so in Luke xxiv. 4: "Two men stood by them in
shining garments," and Mark xvi. 5.

Some have supposed that these celesial bodies are the heavenly
bodies of the next verse, but the Apostle would scarcely enunciate
such a truism as that the glory of the sun and moon is one, and
that of human beings is another; whereas, although the bodies

41 *There is* one glory of the sun, and another glory of the moon, and another glory of the stars: for *one* star differeth from *another* star in glory.

42 ˣ So also *is* the resurrection of the dead. It is sown in corruption; it is raised in incorruption:

ˣ Dan. xii. 3. Matt. xiii. 43.

---

of the angels resemble those of men—so that angels are very frequently called men—yet the difference of the glory or brightness of the one and the other is so great that it clearly shows that God can invest the same form with very different degrees or glory.

41. "There is one glory of the sun, and another glory of the moon," &c. It is to be remembered that here the Apostle drops for a moment the idea of organized body, and speaks of degrees of glory.

The sun seems to be a fountain of perennial light in himself, the moon reflects his light, and the stars have each their particular degree of glory or brightness. The latest discoveries of modern science teach us that the stars do not differ in brightness merely because they differ in distances, some being almost infinitely more remote than others, but that some of their glory depends upon their composition, or the constitution of their photospheres.

Some have supposed that the Apostle notices this variety in the glory of the stars as illustrating the variety of glory in the risen bodies of the saints, but it may be only cited as another instance in the variety of God's works in all parts of the universe: the aim of the Apostle being not so much to illustrate the degrees of reward in brightness or in glory, as the power of God to produce an infinite variety of existences; so that the more we think of it the more absurd becomes the atheistical question: "How are the dead raised? with what body do they come?"

42. "So also is the resurrection of the dead. It is sown in corruption; it is raised in incorruption," &c. This "so" is not to be limited to the analogy contained in the last verse, or that before it. It rather goes back to verses 36-38 where the seed is sown to die, and is laid in the clods of the earth as in a grave, in order that it may spring up a plant wholly differing in form and beauty from the seed sown.

"It is sown in corruption." We must understand here the word "body." No matter what efforts are made to preserve it from

43 ⁷ It is sown in dishonour; it is raised in glory: it is sown in weakness; it is raised in power:

ʸ Phil. iii. 21.

44 It is sown a natural body; it is raised a spiritual

---

mouldering away, it is under the power of corruption, till the morning of the Resurrection. No folly can be greater than that of attempting to preserve the form when the life is gone. The sooner it is dissolved and returns to its original dust the better. To make a show of attempting to stay the work of dissolution is as if one doubted the power of God to raise it incorruptible and immortal, equal in glory and beauty to an angel of heaven.

43. "It is sown in dishonour; it is raised in glory." This dishonour can hardly refer to any dishonour put upon the Christian during life, for continuance in life cannot well be called sowing. The sowing takes place at the death, or the burial. "What," asks Chrysostom, "is more unsightly than a corpse in dissolution?" Who more beautiful than Sarah, who more honoured than the mother of the chosen race? Who more beloved of the father of the faithful, and yet he bowed down before the Hittites to give him a portion of a field and a cave in which he might bury Sarah out of his sight.

"It is raised in glory." The Lord speaks of those who attain to this glory as being equal to the angels, and as being the children of God, being the children of the Resurrection (Luke xx. 36), and as shining forth as the sun in the kingdom of their Father (Matth. xiii. 43). St. Paul speaks of our vile bodies as being fashioned like unto Christ's glorious body (Phil. iii. 21), and Daniel describes them as shining like the stars (xii. 3).

"It is sown in weakness, it is raised in power." The risen body will have the same sort of faculties in kind though not in degree as the Lord's risen Body has. It will move with incredible swiftness. It will pass through all obstacles as the Lord's Risen Body did. But in another respect also it will be raised in power, for—

44. "It is sown a natural body; it is raised a spiritual body." The natural (or psychical) body is, through the fall, weak compared to the spirit within it. All its physical power is derived from the immaterial essence which is incarnate within it. And not only morally but physically the spirit is willing, but the flesh is weak. Now the body will be so raised that it will fulfil at once

body. There is a natural body, and there is a spiritual body.

45 And so it is written, The first man Adam *was   * Gen. ii. 7.

---

44. "There is a natural body, and there is a spiritual body." So E., K., L., most Cursives, Syriac; but ℵ, A., B., C., D., F., G., some nine Cursives, d, e, f, g, Vulg., Copt., Arm., read, "If there is a natural body there is also a spiritual body."

---

all the desire of the Spirit. The present body is a clog—a hindrance to the Spirit; the future body will be its help-meet, as we read in the vision of Ezekiel, "whithersoever the Spirit was to go they went." This will be brought about by the most transcendent exercise of God's power; for no putting forth of God's power upon creatures can be conceived greater than that by which He makes the same body to have at one and the same time the properties of matter and of spirit. The Lord said to the Apostles, "Handle me and see, for a spirit hath not flesh and bones as ye see me have," and yet this body was a spiritual body, for it appeared and disappeared at will. It passed through the closed doors, and it ascended into heaven.

"There is a natural body, and there is a spiritual body." Here the Apostle again categorically asserts the fact. It is raised a spiritual body, because there is such a creation of God as a spiritual body.

Theologians, as Cornelius à Lapide, gather from these verses four endowments of the glorified body: Impassibility, or a state incapable of suffering, from the first antithesis of the Apostle, "It is sown in corruption, it is raised in incorruption;" Brightness, for the Apostle says, "It is sown in dishonour, it is raised in glory;" Agility, from the third antithesis, "It is sown in weakness, it is raised in power;" Subtlety, for "it is sown a natural, it is raised a spiritual body."

45. "And so it is written, The first man Adam was made a living soul," &c. The "so" refers to the preceding clause, "There is a natural body, and there is a spiritual body," and so in the account of man's creation in Genesis it is said, "man (Adam) was made a living soul."[1]

There is a very general misunderstanding among the readers of

---

[1] The quotation is not perfectly literal. The Hebrew does not comprehend the words the "first man;" it is simply, "and man was (or became) a living soul."

made a living soul; ᵃthe last Adam *was made* ᵇ a quickening spirit.

46 Howbeit that *was* not first which is spiritual,

ᵃ Rom. v. 14.
ᵇ John v. 21.
& vi. 33, 39, 40, 54, 57.
Phil. iii. 21.
Col. iii. 4.

the English Bible of the meaning of this verse (Gen. ii. 7). It is generally supposed to teach that man was made different to the other animals in that he had given to him a living soul—a soul alive with the Life of God—living in a state of moral and spiritual life; but it by no means appears to teach this, for the word soul (nephesh) means rather the animal life which man shares with all other creatures, and seems by no means interchangeable with spirit. St. Paul is here drawing out the distinction between the two heads of the race. The first was not spiritual as the second was. He was psychical only; his body was a natural or psychical body only, a "nephesh hayah," even before his fall. Of course man had, and even after the fall retains, a moral nature, but this the Apostle is at present taking no account of. He is marking the difference between the two Adams as regards their life-communicating natures with reference to the Resurrection. The first man was a living creature, not a spirit, but a soul; he communicated animal life to his descendants only in a natural or carnal way, as the other animals did, whereas the Second or Last Adam was constituted a life-giving Spirit. This refers not to the Mind or Spirit of Christ, but to His Body. The bread (staff of life) which He gives is His Flesh which He gives for the life of the world (John vi. 51). Whatever powers of communicating life He had before His Resurrection, at His Resurrection His Body became a spiritual body capable of communicating its peculiar life.

Wesley has a short and pithy but admirable note, which expresses the mystery in the fewest words: "The first Adam was made a living soul—God gave him such life as other animals enjoy, but the last Adam, Christ, is a quickening Spirit. As He hath Life in Himself so He quickeneth whom He will; giving a more refined life to their very bodies at the Resurrection."¹

46. "Howbeit that was not first which is spiritual, but that which," &c. This does not mean that the natural or psychical has

---

¹ That Christ was the Second Adam was a Rabbinical doctrine. "Adamus postremus est Messias." "Neve Shalom," ix. 9 (Schötgen).

CHAP. XV.]   OF THE EARTH, EARTHY.   291

but that which is natural; and afterward that which is spiritual.

47 ^c The first man *is* of the earth, ^d earthy: the second man *is* the Lord ^e from heaven.

48 As *is* the earthy, such *are* they also that

^c John iii. 31.
^d Gen. ii. 7. & iii. 19.
^e John iii. 13, 31.

---

47. "The Lord from heaven." So A., K., L., P., most Cursives, Syriac, Arm., Goth.; but א, B., C., D., E., F., G., 17, 67**, d, e, f, g, Vulg., Copt., Æth., omit " Lord."

---

any tendency to develope into the Spiritual, but that in the order of His gifts God first gives the natural in the first Adam, and then the Spiritual in the Second. There is no *natural* progress from nature to grace. After nature has been tried and found wanting, then comes in, or rather comes down, the highest form of grace in the Second Adam.

47. "The first man is of the earth, earthy: the second man," &c. This is exceedingly clearly brought out in the account of the original creation of man, " The Lord God formed the Adam, dust from the ground (or Adamah)," Gen. ii. 7. The Apostle does not, I think, say this by way of reproach, but simply asserts a fact. It teaches us, I think, that we should not make too much of the spirituality of the first Adam before the Fall. If he was so spiritually perfect as some would have him to have been, how was it that he yielded so quickly to the tempter?

"The second man is the Lord from heaven." The Lord constantly asserts this, as when He says, " The bread of God is he which cometh down from heaven, and giveth life unto the world " (John vi. 33). Again, " Ye are from beneath; I am from above: Ye are of this world; I am not of this world " (John viii. 23). But how can it be said that the second man is from heaven when He assumed our mortal nature in the womb of the Virgin? Evidently because the Personality of the Eternal Son made the very flesh which He took heavenly. That which was conceived of the Holy Ghost was heavenly—raised above the elements of earth, both by the conception by the Holy Ghost, and by His own in-dwelling.

48. " As is the earthy, such are they also that are earthy," &c. That is, such a nature as the first Adam had, we have, liable to sin and death, and all the wretchednesses of such a body—pain, disease, corruption.

are earthy: ᶠand as *is* the heavenly, such *are* they also that are heavenly.

49 And ᵍas we have borne the image of the earthy, ʰwe shall also bear the image of the heavenly.

50 Now this I say, brethren, that ⁱflesh and blood cannot inherit the kingdom of God; neither doth corruption inherit incorruption.

ᶠ Phil. iii. 20, 21.
ᵍ Gen. v. 3.
ʰ Rom. viii. 29. 2 Cor. iii. 18. & iv. 11. Phil. iii. 21. 1 John iii. 2.
ⁱ Matt. xvi. 17. John iii. 3, 5.

---

49. "We shall also bear." So B., 46, a few Cursives, Arm., Æth.; but ℵ, A., C., D., E., F., G., K., L., P., most Cursives, Ital., Vulg., Goth., Copt., read, "let us bear."

"And as is the heavenly, such are they also that are heavenly." "Who shall change our vile body, that it may be fashioned like unto his glorious body" (Phil. iii. 21), and again, "We know that when he shall appear, we shall be like him," &c. (1 John iii. 2).

49. "And as we have borne the image of the earthy, we shall also bear the image of the heavenly." "The image of the earthy," *i.e.*, of the first Adam, formed out of the dust, and through his fall liable to sin and death.

"We shall also bear the image of the heavenly," *i.e.*, we shall be raised up in bodies having the likeness, in their spiritual nature, of the glorified Body of Christ.

The greater part of manuscripts and versions read, "Let us bear," but though this is a prayer that it would be well for all of us to put up to God, it is scarcely likely to be the true reading, for throughout this chapter St. Paul has only in mind the Resurrection of life, and treats it as if no manner of doubt could be entertained that it would take place in all who had died in Christ.

50. "Now this I say, brethren, that flesh and blood cannot inherit," &c. "Flesh and blood," *i.e*, human nature, or the human subject in its unregenerate state. Thus our Lord says, "Flesh and blood hath not revealed it unto thee": "I conferred not with flesh and blood," Gal. i. 16, also Eph. vi. 12. It must be renewed by the power of God before it can be fit to take its place in the heavenly inheritance.

"Neither doth corruption inherit incorruption." This is a parallelism more fully explaining the first clause of the verse—"Flesh

CHAP. XV.] WE SHALL BE CHANGED. 293

51 Behold, I shew you a mystery; ᵏ We shall not all sleep, ˡ but we shall all be changed,

52 In a moment, in the twinkling of an eye, at the last trump: ᵐ for the trumpet shall sound, and the dead shall be raised incorruptible, and we shall be changed.

ᵏ 1 Thess. iv. 15, 16, 17.
ˡ Phil. iii. 21.
ᵐ Zech. ix. 14. Matt. xxiv. 31. John v. 25. 1 Thess. iv. 16.

---

and blood" answering to "corruption," the "kingdom of God" to "incorruption."

The question has been raised upon this verse, whether the renewed bodies of the saints will have blood as well as flesh. Our Lord, with respect to His own Body, mentions flesh and bones but not blood. The body or flesh is renewed by the blood, and if the spiritual body is so above the condition of our present bodies that it needs no food, it will not need the circulation of the blood which we now have; but it is better not to speculate upon the adjuncts of a body of the mode of existence of which we know nothing.

51. "Behold, I shew you a mystery." Behold, I show you what with our present faculties we cannot so much as approach to the understanding of. This term "mystery," as in most other cases, does not signify a matter once unrevealed, but now revealed, and which by being revealed is deprived of its character of mysteriousness; but it signifies something the apprehension of which is altogether beyond the reach of our present faculties of mind or spirit. The instantaneous change of the bodies of those who are alive when the Lord comes is evidently as great a mystery, in the sense of being incomprehensible, as any which the Lord has revealed. (See my note on ii. 7.)

"We shall not all sleep, but we shall all be changed."

52. "In a moment, in the twinkling of an eye, at the last trump: for the trumpet," &c. This is, no doubt, the "great sound of the trumpet" alluded to by the Lord in Matth. xxiv. 31: "He shall send his angels with a great sound of a trumpet," and by St. Paul, in 1 Thess. iv. 16, "The Lord shall descend from heaven with a shout, with the voice of the archangel, and with the trump of God."

It is called the last trump, because on other occasions God manifested His coming to judgment by the voice of the trumpet; thus on Sinai, as we read in Exod. xix. 16; but on this occasion the race

53 For this corruptible must put on incorruption, and
ⁿ this mortal *must* put on immortality.

ⁿ 2 Cor. v. 4.

54 So when this corruptible shall have put on incorruption, and this mortal shall have put on immortality, then shall be brought to pass the saying that is written, ᵒ Death is swallowed up in victory.

ᵒ Isa. xxv. 8.
Heb. ii. 14, 15.
Rev. xx. 14.

---

will be gathered together to receive judgment. It is the last trump in the same sense in which we speak of the last day.

"For the trumpet shall sound, and the dead shall be raised incorruptible, and we shall be changed."

53. "For this corruptible must put on incorruption," &c. Thus Chrysostom: "Then lest any, hearing that flesh and blood cannot inherit the kingdom of God, should suppose that our bodies do not rise again, he adds, 'This corruptible must put on incorruption, and this mortal immortality.' Now the body is corruptible, the body is mortal, so that the body indeed remains, for it is the body which is put on; but its mortality and corruption vanish away when immortality and incorruption come upon it."

"Must put on." If our present bodies are to become incorruptible and immortal they must indeed be changed, so that that decay which is inherent in all nature must be done away, and they will then become as incapable of dying as they are now incapable of living beyond their allotted time.

54. "So when this corruptible shall have put on incorruption," &c., ... Death is swallowed up in victory." These words are from Isaiah xxv. 8. The prophet is seemingly occupied with the thoughts of some temporal deliverance of the Jews; but, as it is in many other prophecies, the terms in which he expresses himself are in their grandeur and poetic power of inspiration infinitely beyond thanksgiving or praise for any earthly deliverance. They can be only interpreted with any propriety of the final deliverance of the race: for what otherwise can we make of, "He will destroy in this mountain the face of the covering cast over all people, and the veil that is spread over all nations; He will swallow up death in victory; and the Lord God will wipe away all tears from off all faces?" What else can a Christian call to mind when he reads this but Rev. xxi. 4?

CHAP. XV.] O DEATH, WHERE IS THY STING?

55 ᵖO death, where *is* thy sting? O ∥ grave, where *is* thy victory?

56 The sting of death *is* sin; and ᑫthe strength of sin *is* the law.

p Hos. xiii. 14.
∥ Or, *hell.*
q Rom. iv. 15.
& v. 13. & vii. 5, 13.

---

55. "Grave." ℵ, B., C., D., read, "death." Vulgate reads, " Ubi est, mors, victoria tua? ubi est, mors, stimulus tuus?" Syriac exactly as English.

The quotation is from the Hebrew, not from the Septuagint, the word "netzah," generally rendered "for ever," is translated "victory" in 1 Chron. xxix. 11, and rightly so, for it is one among such substantives as greatness, power, glory, and majesty.

55. " O death, where is thy sting? O grave, where is thy victory?" The same may be said of this prophetical passage as of the one just quoted. The terms used in it are infinitely beyond any temporal deliverance of the fleshly Ephraim. The words refuse to be tied down to a temporal deliverance—a little longer continuance in Canaan is not a redemption from the power of the grave, nor was Ephraim so delivered. Words of God cannot mean so little while they express so much. " Then, and then only, were they fulfilled in their literal meaning when God the Son took our flesh, that through death He might destroy him that had the power of death, that is the devil, and deliver them who, through fear of death, were all their life-time subject to bondage." (Pusey on Hosea xiii. 14.)

The words of the prophet are quoted by the Apostle mainly from the Septuagint, which reads, " Where is thy penalty (δίκη) O death? O Hades, where is thy sting?"

There are differences of reading, as the reader will see by the critical note, but the meaning under all is the same. Death is deprived of his real power to hurt. The grave, or Hades, or death, is deprived of victory: though he seems to subdue all, he does not do so, for through the grave and gate of Death we pass to our joyful resurrection. Looked at in the light of the Resurrection of Christ, he is the end of a transitory and miserable life, and the beginning of an eternal and glorious one.

56. " The sting of death is sin; and the strength of sin is the law." The thing which makes death terrible is the sense of sin, an accusing conscience, the conviction that if there is an eternal Justice presiding over the universe there must be a future retribu-

57 ʳBut thanks *be* to God, which giveth us ˢthe victory through our Lord Jesus Christ.

58 ᵗTherefore, my beloved brethren, be ye stedfast, unmoveable, always abounding in the

ʳ Rom. vii. 25.
ˢ 1 John v. 4, 5.
ᵗ 2 Pet. iii. 14.

---

tion, and in the case of many, a very terrible one. The word translated sting ($\kappa \acute{\epsilon} \nu \tau \rho o \nu$) is rendered "prick" in the sense of goad in Acts ix. 5 ; xxvi. 14, but in Revel. ix. 10 it is used of the venomous sting of a scorpion, which is evidently the allusion here, for the rendering "goad," as a sharp pointed stake to drive men, is inadmissible; whereas sting, in the sense of a sharp point conveying deadly venom, is very applicable to death.

"The strength of sin is the law." Here we have the first instance in St. Paul's writings of that antagonism between the law and grace which forms one of the main subjects, if not *the* main subject of his Epistle to the Romans. Strange, passing strange, that the law of God, holy, just, and good, the rule of life for all His children, should be the strength of sin. But even if St. Paul had not taught it, we should learn it by experience. That which is unholy within us rises in rebellion against the assertion of God's holiness. Such is our natural alienation from God that the rule of His holiness calls out the contradiction of our nature to Him. Sin is pleasant because it is forbidden. (See notes on Rom. vii. 7-25.)

57. "But thanks be to God, which giveth us the victory through our Lord Jesus Christ." The victory is our justification—our being put in possession of Christ as our wisdom, righteousness, sanctification, and redemption. We cannot stand in ourselves before God, but we can stand in Him. God accepts us as branches of the True Vine, as members of the Mystical Body. Being in Him, we are delivered from the curse of the law,—*i.e.*, from the strength of sin— we are delivered from the fear of death, whereunto we were once subject to bondage.

58. "Therefore, my beloved brethren, be ye stedfast, unmoveable, always," &c. "Therefore," *i.e.*, because of the certainty of the Resurrection of the Lord, and your Resurrection in Him. "Therefore," because through Jesus Christ, God has given you the victory over sin and death, and redeemed you from the curse of the law.

"Be ye stedfast." Stedfast in the faith of the Resurrection.

"Unmoveable" by any doubts insinuated into your minds by

CHAP. XV.] YOUR LABOUR NOT IN VAIN. 297

work of the Lord, forasmuch as ye know ^u that your labour
is not in vain in the Lord. ^u ch. iii. 8.

---

the great enemy, as to how the dead are raised up, and as to the
body in which they come.

"Always abounding in the work of the Lord." Always keeping
in subjection your own bodies—always doing what good you can to
the bodies and souls of your neighbours, always striving for the
faith of the Gospel, for the Unity and Sanctity of the Church,
always continuing in prayer and thanksgiving.

"Forasmuch as ye know that your labour is not in vain in the
Lord." Do all, having respect to the recompense of the reward.
The Resurrection assures us that every man shall receive his own
reward according to his own labour; but this must be in Christ.

"There is not one moment wherein we have no need that God
should subdue sin in us by the grace of Jesus Christ. Without
Him there is nothing in us but inability and unworthiness. Our
only refuge is to address ourselves, and to adhere to Him by a lively
faith and an humble prayer, to labour in Him by an abundant
charity, and to expect from Him, by a firm and unmovable hope,
the eternal recompence and reward." Such are the words in which
Quesnel concludes his comment on this chapter. We will join
with them the words of a kindred spirit. "Let us also endeavour,
by cultivating holiness in all its branches, to maintain this hope in
its full energy, longing for that glorious day when, in the utmost
extent of the expression, 'death shall be swallowed up for ever,'
and millions of voices, after the long silence of the grave, shall
burst out at once into that triumphant song, 'O Death, where is
thy sting? O Hades, where is thy victory?'" (Wesley.)

CHAP. XVI.

NOW concerning ᵃthe collection for the saints, as I have given order to the churches of Galatia, even so do ye.

2 ᵇUpon the first *day* of the week let every one of you lay by him in store, as *God* hath prospered him, that there be no gatherings when I come.

ᵃ Acts xi. 29.
& xxiv. 17.
Rom. xv. 26.
2 Cor. viii. 4.
& ix. 1, 12.
Gal. ii. 10.
ᵇ Acts xx. 7.
Rev. i. 10.

---

2. "As God hath prospered him," or, "What his means allow him to give." "Quod ei bene placuerit" (Vulg.).

1. "Now concerning the collection for the saints, as I have given order," &c. This direction comes in with marked appropriateness after the concluding exhortation of the last chapter, "Be ye always . . . . abounding in the work of the Lord." No work of the Lord occupies a higher place in the Scriptures than the assistance of the poor and needy. It seems probable, comparing the way in which he introduces the subject with that in which he begins upon "marriage" and "things offered to idols" (vii. 1, viii. 1), that they had asked him some question respecting the collection.

The saints were the poor Christians of Jerusalem, who shared, of course, in the constant famines and dearths which were occurring at this time (see my notes on Acts ii. 45, and xi. 28). I have there shown that this distress could not possibly have been owing to the community of goods which prevailed on and after Pentecost—for that distribution must have rather abated than increased the distress among the poor saints.

"As I have given order to the churches of Galatia, even so do ye." This order may have been by letter, or it may have been communicated personally, when he went over all the country of Galatia before he came to Ephesus (Acts xviii. 23).

2. "Upon the first day of the week let every one of you lay by him in store," &c. On each first day of the week—an Hebraism, the days of the week being reckoned from the Sabbath.

"Let every one lay by him in store." The words "lay by him" seem to imply that he was to put it aside on that day, and keep it

3 And when I come, ^c whomsoever ye shall approve by *your* letters, them will I send to bring your †liberality unto Jerusalem.

4 ^d And if it be meet that I go also, they shall go with me.

c 2 Cor. viii. 19.
† Gr. *gift*.
2 Cor. viii. 4, 6, 19.
d 2 Cor. viii. 4, 19.

---

4. "If it be meet that I go also." Some translate, "If it (the sum collected) be worthy that I go."

in his own house. But taken in connection with the fact that this was to be done on the day of their religious assembly, and so that there should be no trouble or time lost in collecting it when he came, it is rather to be inferred that on each Sunday it was to be deposited in the treasury of the church. Chrysostom, however, takes it in the first way.

"As God hath prospered him." This is to be ruled in its sense by the words "every one of you." It was not those who had been exceptionally prosperous who were to lay by, but all.

"That there be no gatherings when I come." That when I come your time may not be wasted in making collections, but employed in listening to my instructions. Chrysostom notices that by small weekly contributions the burden would be less felt, and also that if it was left to the time of his coming, some might not be able to give at one time as much as they would, had the collection been made weekly.

3. "And when I come, whomsoever ye shall approve by your letters," &c. Notice here the mixture of authority and loving confidence. It was their collection, but *he* sent it, and yet only by those whom *they* approved. The Corinthians themselves were to choose their agents, probably to prevent the possibility of misappropriation, as others had been chosen for a like purpose by the other churches (see 2 Cor. viii. 18-20; Stanley).

4. "And if it be meet that I go also, they shall go with me." "If it be meet that I go also." Meyer and others make this "meet" to have reference to the sum collected. If it turned out to be a paltry sum, then it would be beneath the dignity of his office to go with it. If it was a sum worthy of the occasion, he would himself accompany the messengers.

5. "Now I will come to you, when I shall pass through Macedonia," &c. The Apostle does not mean by this that he is now

5 Now I will come unto you, ^e when I shall pass through Macedonia: for I do pass through Macedonia.

^e Acts xix. 21. 2 Cor. i. 16.

6 And it may be that I will abide, yea, and winter with you, that ye may ^f bring me on my journey whithersoever I go.

^f Acts xv. 3. & xvii. 15. & xxi. 5. Rom. xv. 24. 2 Cor. i. 16.

7 For I will not see you now by the way; but I trust to tarry awhile with you, ^g if the Lord permit.

^g Acts xviii. 21. ch. iv. 19. James iv. 15.

8 But I will tarry at Ephesus until Pentecost.

9 For ^h a great door and effectual is opened unto me, and ⁱ *there are* many adversaries.

^h Acts xiv. 27. 2 Cor. ii. 12. Col. iv. 3. Rev. iii. 8.
ⁱ Acts xix. 9.

---

passing through Macedonia, but that he has determined to do so. This Epistle was written from Ephesus, not from Philippi, as is erroneously stated in the subscription at the end in our English Bibles.

6, 7. "And it may be that I will abide, yea, and winter with you," &c. He is not sure what places he will visit after he has stayed some time in Corinth; and, besides this, he did not come to Corinth as early as he intended, but waited to see what effect his letters had upon them, so that when he came he might not be compelled to exercise severe discipline.

He desired not to pay them a passing visit, but to stay some time with them.

8, 9. "But I will tarry at Ephesus until Pentecost. . . . . many adversaries." In writing from one Gentile Church to another he would scarcely have mentioned Pentecost as a sacred season, unless it had already begun to be observed among Christians. Why should it not? If any fact in the history of God's dealings with man deserved to be had in remembrance, it was—next, of course, to the Resurrection—the descent of the Holy Ghost.

"For a great door and effectual is opened unto me," &c. The account of this great and effectual opening for the Gospel, and the virulence of the adversaries, we learn in Acts xix. "All they which dwelt in Asia heard the word of the Lord." Special miracles were wrought by touching handkerchiefs or aprons which had themselves touched the body of the Apostle—fear fell on all the neighbourhood—"the Name of the Lord Jesus was magnified." But it

CHAP. XVI.] LET NO MAN DESPISE HIM. 301

10 Now ᵏ if Timotheus come, see that he may be with you, without fear: for ˡ he worketh the work of the Lord, as I also *do*.

11 ᵐ Let no man therefore despise him: but conduct him forth ⁿ in peace, that he may come unto me: for I look for him with the brethren.

ᵏ Acts xix. 22. ch. iv. 17.
ˡ Rom. xvi. 21. Phil. ii. 20, 22. 1 Thess. iii. 2.
ᵐ 1 Tim. iv. 12.
ⁿ Acts xv. 33.

---

was not likely that Satan would suffer this without opposition. There was no small stir which ended in the dangerous riot in the theatre, and St. Paul's hurried departure to Macedonia.

10. "Now if Timotheus come, see that he may be with you without fear," &c. In iv. 17 he had written, "For this cause have I sent unto you Timotheus, who is my beloved son, and faithful in the Lord, who shall bring you into remembrance of my ways which be in Christ, as I teach every where in every Church." Now Timothy was young, and very inferior to the Apostle, as it appears, not only in Church standing, but in determination and energy, so that it was very possible that he would be cowed by the virulence of that opposition which had made some of the leaders of the factions question the Apostolic authority of their father in Christ. This exhortation ("see that he be with you without fear") was very necessary. The words, "if Timotheus come," imply some doubt whether, through accidental circumstances, he would arrive before Paul.

"He worketh the work of the Lord, as I also do." This does not mean that he worked with the zeal and the spirit with which St. Paul did, and yet in many things took his own line; but that he worked in the same way, used the same outward form or ritual, and in all things acted as if he could not well improve upon the Apostle's model. It, in fact, means the same as "he shall remind you of my ways which are in Christ, as I teach every where in every Church " (1 Cor. iv. 17).

11. "Let no man therefore despise him: but conduct him forth in peace." That is, escort him, and provide him with everything needful for the journey. Great stress seems to have been laid on this "speeding of the parting guest" in the early Church: thus (3 John 6), "whom if thou bring forward on their journey after a godly sort, thou shalt do well."

"That he may come unto me: for I look for him with the

12 As touching *our* brother °Apollos, I greatly desired him to come unto you with the brethren: but his will was not at all to come at this time; but he will come when he shall have convenient time.

13 ᴾ Watch ye, ᑫstand fast in the faith, quit you like men, ʳ be strong.

14 ˢ Let all your things be done with charity.

° ch. i. 12. & iii. 5.

ᴾ Matt. xxiv. 42. & xxv. 13. 1 Thess. v. 6. 1 Pet. v. 8.
ᑫ ch. xv. 1. Phil. i. 27. & iv. 1. 1 Thess. iii. 8. 2 Thess. ii. 15.
ʳ Eph. vi. 10. Col. i. 11.
ˢ ch. xiv. 1.
1 Pet. iv. 8.

---

brethren." No doubt the Apostle meant that he would meet him somewhere in Macedonia.

"With the brethren"—that is, with Erastus, and Titus who bore the Second Epistle, and others.

12. "As touching our brother Apollos, I greatly desired him to come," &c. What was the reason why Apollos declined to accord to the wish of Paul? It could not have been any worldly reason; but in all probability he thought that his presence would increase or embitter the spirit of faction. Some amongst them had set him over against Paul as superior to him in eloquence, and he dreaded that he should be the occasion of increasing this schismatical feeling in the Church.

13, 14. "Watch ye, stand fast in the faith, quit you like men, be strong . . . . with charity." The comment of Chrysostom on this verse is remarkable for its terse eloquence. "Not in the wisdom which is without: for there it is not possible to stand, but to be borne along. Now in saying these things he seems indeed to advise; but he is reprimanding them as indolent. Wherefore he saith, *Watch*, as though they slept; *stand*, as though they were rocking to and fro: *quit you like men*, as though they were playing the coward, *Let all your things be done in charity*, as though they were in dissensions."

"But what means 'All things with charity?' 'Whether any one rebuke,' saith he, 'or rule, or be ruled, or learn or teach, let all be with charity;' since, the things which have been mentioned arose from neglect of it. For if this (charity) had not been neglected, they would not have been puffed up, they would not have said: 'I am of Paul, and I of Apollos.' If this had existed they would not have gone to law before heathens, or rather, they would not have gone to law at all. If this had existed, that notorious

THE FIRSTFRUITS OF ACHAIA.

15 I beseech you, brethren, (ye know ^t the house of Stephanas, that it is ^u the firstfruits of Achaia, and *that* they have addicted themselves to ^x the ministry of the saints,)

16 ^y That ye submit yourselves unto such, and to every one that helpeth with *us*, and ^z laboureth.

17 I am glad of the coming of Stephanas and Fortunatus and Achaicus: ^a for that which was lacking on your part they have supplied.

^t ch. i. 16.
^u Rom. xvi. 5.
^x 2 Cor. viii. 4. & ix. 1. Heb. vi. 10.
^y Heb. xiii. 17.
^z Heb. vi. 10.
^a 2 Cor. xi. 9. Phil. ii. 30. Philem. 13.

---

person would not have taken his father's wife; they would not have despised the weak brethren; there would have been no heresies among them; they would not have been vainglorious about their gifts. Therefore it is that he saith, 'Let all things be done with charity.'"

15. "I beseech you, brethren, (ye know the house of Stephanas, that it is the firstfruits,") &c. Stephanas himself was apparently with the Apostle at this time, and so the Apostle commends to them his house, *i.e.*, the near relatives who had assisted him in his holy work.

"They have addicted themselves to the ministry of the saints." Some, as Blunt, suppose that they were not ministers, but rather helped other Christians with their hospitality; but there is no reason why they should not have been endowed with powers of government (governments, xii. 28), inasmuch as he proceeds to say to the Corinthian Christians—

16. "That ye submit yourselves unto such, and to every one that helpeth with us, and laboureth." Dean Stanley supposes that the ministry of the saints is the contribution to the necessities of the saints in Judæa, which is called by this name in 2 Corinth. viii. 4, and ix. 1; but this would seem to require co-operation rather than submission. The call upon them to submit also to all his co-helpers and labourers, seems to imply a ministry acting with and under him.

17. "I am glad of the coming of Stephanas . . . . they have supplied." Of Fortunatus and Achaicus nothing is known. One Fortunatus is mentioned in Clement's Epistle to the Corinthians, "Send back to us in peace and with joy these our messengers to

18 ^b For they have refreshed my spirit and your's: therefore ^c acknowledge ye them that are such.

19 The churches of Asia salute you. Aquila and Priscilla salute you much in the Lord, ^d with the church that is in their house.

20 All the brethren greet you. ^e Greet ye one another with an holy kiss.

^b Col. iv. 8.
^c Phil. ii. 29. 1 Thess. v. 12.
^d Rom. xvi. 5, 15. Philem. 2.
^e Rom. xvi. 16.

---

19. "Priscilla." ℵ and D. read "Prisca."

you, Claudius, Ephebus, and Valerius, Bito, and Fortunatus," &c., but inasmuch as we cannot put the writing of this Epistle before the year A.D. 90, it is very improbable that they were the same persons.

"That which is lacking on your part they have supplied." Very probably this means that these men out of their own private means had supplied the Apostle with what the body of the Corinthian Church had been remiss in giving. (1 Cor. ix. 5-15.)

18. "For they have refreshed my spirit and yours: therefore acknowledge ye them," &c. They have refreshed my spirit by acts of kindness, and they refreshed yours by spiritual comfort. (Wordsworth). Or it may be that the Apostle has in view the sympathy that all Christian souls must have with one another—they have refreshed my spirit, and when you know what comfort they have given to me they will have refreshed yours also. We have the same idea in the next Epistle i. 6, "whether we be comforted it is for your consolation and salvation."

"Therefore acknowledge ye them that are such." Acknowledge them as leaders, as examples, as benefactors of the Church.

19. "The churches of Asia salute you." That is of Proconsular Asia. Seven of them receive messages from the Lord through St. John in the Apocalypse.

"Aquila and Priscilla salute you much in the Lord, with the church," &c. They were at Corinth when St. Paul first arrived there (Acts xviii. 2). Afterwards they came to Ephesus with Paul, and were instrumental in conveying a more accurate knowledge of the faith to Apollos.

20. "All the brethren greet you. Greet ye one another with an holy kiss." The salutation by a kiss was always common in the East. Thus the Lord says to His host, who had been deficient in kindly courtesy, "Thou gavest me no kiss" (Luke vii. 45).

CHAP. XVI.] ANATHEMA MARAN-ATHA. 305

21 ᶠ The salutation of *me* Paul with mine own hand.

22 If any man ᵍ love not the Lord Jesus Christ, ᵗ let him be Anathema ⁱ Maran-atha.

f Col. iv. 18.
2 Thess. iii. 17.
g Eph. vi. 24.
h Gal. i. 8, 9.
i Jude 14, 15.

22. "Love not the Lord Jesus Christ, let him be," &c. "Jesus Christ" omitted by ℵ, A., B., C., M., 17, 73, 74; K., P., thirty Cursives, Syr. (Schaaf), Æth., read, "our Lord" (ἡμῶν); but D., E., F., G., K., L., P., most Cursives, d, e, f, g, Vulg., Syriac, Copt., Goth., retain, "Jesus Christ."

If this had been carried out as the Apostle commanded it would have been a more serious matter than we now should suppose; for the leaders of factions and fomenters of division would have had to exchange the kiss of charity, and what hypocrisy would they have been guilty of if they had done this without laying aside their divisions!

The kiss of peace or charity was incorporated into the Eucharistic office, and was not discontinued in the Western Church until the thirteenth century. (See note on Rom. xvi. 16.)

21. "The salutation of me Paul with mine own hand." Hitherto he had written, as he usually did, by an amanuensis. Now he takes the pen into his own hand to give the loving salutation.

22. "If any man love not the Lord Jesus Christ, let him be Anathema Maran-atha." Fearful words from the lips of him who was one of the most loving and sympathising of men; but his spirit within him had been stirred, his heart was on fire, he looked on the spiritual state of these his children in Christ, and saw that the evils he had denounced amongst them sprang from one source. Their hearts had not been true to Christ. They who profess to love the Crucified Son of God must strive to please Him, or how can they love Him? We strive to please those whom we love. It is the one test of our love. And so, as Chrysostom says, "How could they love Christ who made their members the members of an harlot, those who put stumbling blocks in the way of their brethren, by the things offered in sacrifice to idols (viii. 12), those who occasioned schisms by naming themselves after men; those who refuse to believe in the Resurrection?"

Anathema signifies a thing accursed, and so devoted to destruction (thus Rom. ix. 3, Gal. i. 8), corresponding to "sacer" in the Latin, and "cherem" in the Hebrew. It is to be remembered that the Apostle here only anathematizes or devotes to destruction those

x

23 ᵏ The grace of our Lord Jesus Christ *be* with you.

ᵏ Rom. xvi. 20.

24 My love *be* with you all in Christ Jesus. Amen.

---

who, by their opposition to the will of Christ and resistance to His Spirit, had already anathematized or devoted themselves to destruction.

"Maran-atha." This signifies "The Lord cometh," Maran being the longer and more emphatic form of "Mar," or Lord. The word for our Lord throughout the Syriac is "Moryeh." The word is not necessarily connected with "Anathema," but was added to it to emphasize it. Let him who loves not the Lord Jesus be anathema, and the Lord cometh to confirm the judgment.

23. "The grace of our Lord Jesus Christ be with you." This is a solemn invocation of grace from the Lord as the fountain and treasury of Divine grace, and so Lord and God.

24. "My love be with you all in Christ Jesus." Thus, though he had had much occasion to rebuke, and even threaten, he sends his love to all, even to those who caused division, who called themselves by the names of men, who had abetted the fornicator, who had denied the Resurrection. They had none of them sinned so as to be out of the reach of the love of God, and so he sends to them his love. His love would be the love of one who had them ever in his heart, his prayers, his sympathy.

THE SECOND EPISTLE TO THE CORINTHIANS.

CHAP. I.

PAUL, ^a an apostle of Jesus Christ by the will of God, and Timothy *our* brother, unto the church of God which is at Corinth, ^b with all the saints which are in all Achaia :

2 ^c Grace *be* to you and peace from God our Father, and *from* the Lord Jesus Christ.

^a 1 Cor. i. 1.
Eph. i. 1.
Col. i. 1.
1 Tim. i. 1.
2 Tim. i. 1.
^b Phil. i. 1.
Col. i. 2.
^c Rom. i. 7.
1 Cor. i. 3.
Gal. i. 3. Phil.
i. 2. Col. i. 2.
1 Thess. i. 1.
2 Thess. i. 2.
Philem. 3.

---

1. "Paul, an Apostle of Jesus Christ by the will of God, and Timothy," &c. This second letter was written from some city of Macedonia, and Timothy had returned, and was now with the Apostle. The same may be said of St. Paul's association of Timothy with himself as I have said of that of Sosthenes (1 Cor. i. 1). In all probability not one line of the Epistle was written or dictated by Timothy. Every sentence was the overflow of the Apostle's own mind, but he thought good to associate his chief companions in labour with himself, in order that the Churches might as far as possible look upon them as identified with himself, and honour and obey them as his partners in the Lord.

"Unto the Church of God which is at Corinth, with all the saints which are in all Achaia." The parallel phrase in 1 Cor. i. is "with all that in every place call upon the name of Jesus Christ our Lord, both theirs and ours."

2. "Grace be unto you and peace from God our Father, and from the Lord Jesus Christ." The Lord Jesus Christ is, side by side with God, the fountain of blessing. "The river of the water of life, clear as crystal," proceeds out of the throne of God and of the Lamb (Rev. xxii. 1).

3 ^d Blessed *be* God, even the Father of our Lord Jesus Christ, the Father of mercies, and the God of all comfort;

^d Eph. i. 3.
1 Pet. i. 3.

4 Who comforteth us in all our tribulation, that we may be able to comfort them which are in any trouble, by the comfort wherewith we ourselves are comforted of God.

^e Acts ix. 4.
ch. iv. 10.
Col. i. 24.

5 For as ^e the sufferings of Christ abound in us, so our consolation also aboundeth by Christ.

---

3. "Blessed be God, even the Father of our Lord Jesus Christ, the Father," &c. Instead of the usual, "I thank my God," we have a doxology similar to that in Ephes. i. 3, 4: "The Father of our Lord Jesus Christ—the Father of mercies." He personifies, as it were, the mercies which come to us in and through Jesus Christ. This teaches us that God's mercies are not gifts apart from Himself, but come, if one may so say, from His very Essence. Similarly He is called the Father of Glory and the Father of lights.

4. "Who comforteth us in all our tribulation, that we may be able to comfort," &c. Wonderful truth! We should suppose that any comfort under any private trouble is for ourselves alone—that it cannot belong to others, and can only be enjoyed by ourselves; but here we are told that when God imparts comfort to any soul, it is that that soul may be enabled in its turn to impart the same comfort to its afflicted brother.

5. "For as the sufferings of Christ abound in us, so also our consolation (comfort)," &c. There is a remarkably analogous passage in Coloss. i. 24: "Who fill up that which is behind of the afflictions of Christ in my flesh for his body's sake, which is the Church." Compare also Phil. iii. 10: "That I may know him and . . . . the fellowship of his sufferings." It seems to mean that the sufferings of Christ are reproduced in the sufferings of the members of His mystical Body, in order that they may be comforted with no human consolation, but may partake of the consolation with which Christ was consoled. And this not for the private consolation of any particular sufferer, but, as he proceeds to say,—

6, 7. "And whether we be afflicted, it is for your consolation

6 And whether we be afflicted, *it is* for your consolation and salvation, which ‖ is effectual in the enduring of the same sufferings which we also suffer: or whether we be comforted, *it is* for your consolation and salvation.

f ch. iv. 15.
‖ Or, *is wrought.*

7 And our hope of you *is* stedfast, knowing, that ᵍ as ye are partakers of the sufferings, so *shall ye be* also of the consolation.

g Rom. viii. 17.
2 Tim. ii. 12.

8 For we would not, brethren, have you ignorant

---

6. There is some difference amongst manuscripts respecting the order of the words. The Revisers, following A., C., D., read, " Whether we be afflicted, it is for your comfort and salvation, or whether we be comforted, it is for your comfort, which worketh in the patient enduring—and our hope for you is steadfast."

and salvation .... so shall ye be also of the consolation." Many suggestions are given of the meaning of this verse. That given by Chrysostom seems in every way satisfactory: " Your salvation is not our work alone, but your own as well; for both we in preaching the word to you, endure affliction, and ye, in receiving it, endure the very same; we to impart to you that which we received, ye to receive what is imparted, and not let it go." The afflictions and consolations of ministers, especially, are often intended for the sake of the people as well as themselves, that by their own example, experience, counsels, and exhortations, they may promote the salvation and consolation of others also. For these blessings are commonly brought home to the hearts of men, and the word of God is rendered effectual for every saving purpose by means of trials and afflictions; and the minister who is a stranger to sufferings and divine consolations, can seldom duly sympathise with the mourners, counsel the tempted, encourage the dejected, or even bear with the infirmities of the weak.

7. " And our hope of you is steadfast, knowing, that as ye are partakers," &c. He could scarcely have written this in his first Epistle—so full of misgiving and upbraiding: but now having received from Titus the account of their repentance and altered state of mind towards him, he can say with confidence, " as ye are partakers of the sufferings, so shall ye be also of the consolation."

8. " For we would not, brethren, have you ignorant of our trouble, which came," &c. Two or three explanations have been given of this

of ^h our trouble which came to us in Asia, that we were pressed out of measure, above strength, insomuch that we despaired even of life:

9 But we had the ‖ sentence of death in ourselves, that we should ⁱ not trust in ourselves, but in God which raiseth the dead:

10 ^k Who delivered us from so great a death, and doth deliver: in whom we trust that he will yet deliver *us*:

h Acts xix. 23.
1 Cor. xv. 32.
& xvi. 9.

‖ Or, *answer*.
i Jer. xvii. 5, 7.

k 2 Pet. ii. 9.

---

10. "And doth deliver." So E., F., G., K., L., M., most Cursives, f; but A., D., d, e, Syriac, omit, and ℵ, B., C., P., 17, 47, 73, 93, 211, g, Vulg. (Amiat.), read, "shall deliver."

"trouble in Asia." The first, and by far the most probable, is that it was the dangerous riot described in its leading incidents in Acts xix. 23-41, in which the Apostle narrowly escaped being murdered. This seems most consonant with the words "our trouble *in Asia*." Others, as Dean Plumptre, consider it to have been a dangerous illness which had brought him to the gates of the grave; and others suppose, but I think with very little reason, that it was the disheartening news from Corinth respecting the state of his beloved Church there which well-nigh overwhelmed him.

9. "But we had the sentence of death in ourselves, that we should," &c. That is, we were as certain of death as one who had had the sentence of death pronounced upon him by a judge, and for whom, humanly speaking, there could be no escape or reprieve. So that there was no human hope; the only source of hope was to trust in that God Who not only rescueth from death, but restoreth the dead to life.

10. "Who delivered us from so great a death, and doth deliver: in whom," &c. He delivered us from so imminent a death. Nothing could exceed the fury of the silversmiths, and yet nothing could be more remarkable than the sudden cessation of the riot, and the escape of the Apostle (Acts xx. 1).

We cannot, however, help noticing the evangelical application of this verse. The Lord *hath* delivered us by His Death and Resurrection from death in its three terrible forms—death temporal, death spiritual, death eternal. "He doth deliver." He *doth* de-

CHAP. I.]   OUR REJOICING IS THIS.   311

11 Ye also ¹helping together by prayer for us, that ᵐ for the gift *bestowed* upon us by the means of many persons thanks may be given by many on our behalf. ¹ Rom. xv. 30. Phil. i. 19. Philem. 22. ᵐ ch. iv. 15.

12 For our rejoicing is this, the testimony of our conscience, that in simplicity and ⁿ godly sincerity, ᵒ not with fleshly wisdom, but by the grace ⁿ ch. ii. 17. & iv. 2. ᵒ 1 Cor. ii. 4, 13.

---

12. "In simplicity." So D., E., F., G., L., most Cursives, d, e, f, g, Vulg., Goth., Syriac; but ℵ, A., B., C., K., M., P., 17, 37, 67**, 73, Copt., Arm., read, "in holiness."

liver us now from the assaults of Satan and from the dominion of our evil passions, and He *will* deliver us from every evil work, and make us partakers of His heavenly kingdom.

11. "Ye also helping together by prayer for us, that for the gift bestowed upon us." St. Paul seems to have had an extraordinary sense of the value of intercessory prayer. In the Epistle to the Philippians he seems to make even his own salvation in a measure to depend upon it. "I know that this shall turn to my salvation through your prayer, and the supply of the Spirit of Jesus Christ" (Phil. i. 19).

"Bestowed upon us by the means of," &c. He seems to think it a great advantage to all that they should pray for him, and then that their prayers having been answered, they should give thanks to God. All intercourse with God such as this cannot but be most acceptable to God and beneficial to their souls.

"This he said, at once to stir them up to prayer for others, and to use them always to give thanks to God for whatever befalleth others, showing that He too also willeth this exceedingly . . . . and observe, I pray you, this also, that even if God doeth anything in mercy, yet prayer doth mightily contribute thereunto. For at the first he attributed his salvation to His mercies; for 'the God of all mercies' he says Himself delivered us; but here to their prayers also." (Chrysostom.)

12. "For our rejoicing is this, the testimony of our conscience," &c. The word translated "rejoicing" is usually rendered "boasting."

"The testimony of our conscience." This was a great matter with St. Paul. Before the Sanhedrim he affirmed, "I have lived in all good conscience before God unto this day." "Herein," he

of God, we have had our conversation in the world, and more abundantly to youward.

13 For we write none other things unto you, than what ye read or acknowledge; and I trust ye shall acknowledge even to the end;

14 As also ye have acknowledged us in part, p that we are your rejoicing, even as q ye also *are* our's in the day of the Lord Jesus.

p ch. v. 12.
q Phil. ii. 16. & iv. 1.
1 Thess. ii. 19, 20.

---

says again, "do I exercise myself to have always a conscience void of offence towards God and towards men."

"That in simplicity and godly sincerity, not with fleshly wisdom," &c. My conscience witnesses to me that I have done nothing underhand; in all my intercourse with you and with others I have been candid and sincere, not relying on worldy wisdom, but on the grace of God; and if I have acted thus openly with others, I have especially behaved myself thus in my intercourse with you.

This verse is the introduction to another paragraph of the Epistle. Titus had informed him that doubts had been thrown upon his sincerity in the matter of his coming. He had threatened to come (1 Cor. iv. 19, &c.), and had not yet come. All sorts of sinister motives had been imputed to him because he had not fulfilled his promise. These he now proceeds to rebut.

13. "For we write none other things unto you than what ye read or acknowledge," &c. What we write to you in our Epistle is plain, and there is no other meaning than that which is on the surface. The teaching or meaning is what ye read, or acknowledge to be true. It is the plain truth of God applied to your conduct, and I trust for your own sakes ye will always receive it as such.

14. "As also ye have acknowledged us in part, that we are your rejoicing," &c. He is careful to say "in part," inasmuch as some among them had questioned his Apostolical authority.

"Even as ye also are our's in the day of the Lord Jesus." He had taught them that the coming of the Lord was ever impending, and so, instead of saying, "ye are our rejoicing when we all die and go to heaven," he said, "ye are our rejoicing when, as I trust, I shall present you as a chaste virgin to Christ when He comes." (2 Cor. x. 2.)

CHAP. I.] DID I USE LIGHTNESS ? 313

15 And in this confidence ʳ I was minded to come unto you before, that ye might have ˢ a second ‖ benefit;

16 And to pass by you into Macedonia, and ᵗ to come again out of Macedonia unto you, and of you to be brought on my way toward Judæa.

17 When I therefore was thus minded, did I use lightness ? or the things that I purpose, do I purpose ᵘ according to the flesh, that with me there should be yea yea, and nay nay ?

ʳ 1 Cor. iv. 19.
ˢ Rom. i. 11.
‖ Or, *grace*.
ᵗ 1 Cor. xvi. 5, 6.

ᵘ ch. x. 2.

---

15. "A second benefit" (or "grace"). So ℵ, A., C., D., E., F., G., K., most Cursives, Ital., Vulg.; but B., L., P., and five Cursives read, "joy."

15, 16. "And in this confidence I was minded to come unto you before . . . . to be brought on my way toward Judæa." "I was minded to come to you before." Wordsworth notices that the word, "I was minded," does not signify a steady determined purpose, but rather a wish which was controlled and overruled by the will—a will which was conformed to the will of God, and willed what He willed. "That ye might have a second benefit"— that is, that he should visit and stay with them twice rather than once—the first time on his way from Ephesus to Macedonia, the second on his way back from Macedonia to Judæa.

"And of you to be brought on my way"—*i.e.*, with an escort in a way befitting the respect they should have to an Apostle of Christ, and to their spiritual Father, to whom under Christ they owed their souls.

17. "When I therefore was thus minded, did I use lightness? or the things," &c. "Did I use lightness?"—that is, levity or fickleness.

"Or the things that I purpose, do I purpose according to the flesh, [*i.e.*, in purposing a journey, am I guided by merely human considerations?] that with me there should be yea yea, and nay, nay"—*i.e.*, as Meyer explains it, that affirmation and denial may exist together; that I, according as the case stands, may assent to the fleshly impulse, and in turn renounce it—to-day yea, and to-morrow nay, or yea and nay, as it were in one breath. No, this cannot be. I am not such an one.

18 But *as* God *is* true, our ‖ word toward you was not yea and nay.

‖ Or, *preaching.*

19 For ˣ the Son of God, Jesus Christ, who was preached among you by us, *even* by me and Silvanus and Timotheus, was not yea and nay, ʸ but in him was yea.

ˣ Mark i. 1.
Luke i. 35.
Acts ix. 20.
ʸ Heb. xiii. 8.

---

18. "Was not." So K., L., most Cursives, Syriac, Æth.; but ℵ, A., B., C., D., F., G., P., 17, 23, 57, 70, d, e, f, g, Vulg., Goth., Copt., Arm., read, "is not."

18, 19. "But as God is true, our word toward you was not yea and nay. . . . . in him was yea." Let the reader notice that the impulse or determination which we should call "human" the Apostle calls "fleshly." This teaches us that unless in all things we defer to the teaching of the Spirit of God, our resolves are in the flesh, and so have the nature of sin. "Whatsoever ye do in word or deed, do all in the name of the Lord Jesus" (Col. iii. 17).

He now, by what some persons would call an extraordinarily illogical turn of the argument, leaps from his resolve in this particular matter of the change of the plan of his journey to his general teaching of the Gospel. It is a sort of appeal to their common sense. Would one whose whole life was bound up in the teaching of the most positive, plain, unchangeable truth possible, be fickle and uncertain in a matter closely connected with the proclamation of that truth? The infinite importance of the word which he preached would not only give him holiness, and joy, and comfort, but its exceeding strength, and immobility, and unchangeableness would, even if he were naturally fickle, impart to him of its own steadfastness and unchangeableness. "Our word towards you was not yea and nay." It was not one thing one day and another another. It was always the same, and that because of its Divine Unchangeable Subject. And so he proceeds:—

19. "For the Son of God, Jesus Christ, who was preached . . . . not yea and nay, but in him was yea." Nothing can be more remarkable, when one looks into it, than the affirmative nature of the Teaching, and Life, and Person of Jesus Christ. The law as set forth in the Decalogue was mainly prohibitive (nay)— "Thou shalt not, thou shalt not;" whereas the New Law as set forth in the Beatitudes is, "Blessed are the poor in spirit—they that mourn—the meek," &c. The whole life of Christ was positive

CHAP. I.]   IN HIM YEA, AND IN HIM AMEN.   315

20 ᶻ For all the promises of God in him *are* yea, and in him Amen, unto the glory of God by us.   ᶻ Rom. xv. 8, 9.

20. "And in him Amen." So E., K., L., most Cursives; but ℵ, A., B., C., F., G., Ovi., P., 10, 17, 31, 37, 38, 80, 137, f, g, Vulg,, Goth., Syr., Copt., Arm., read, "Therefore through him also is the Amen."

good, affirming the benevolence, the justice, the holiness, the compassion of the unseen Father. The Incarnation affirmed the reality of the Fatherhood, in that He had an only Son. The Death revealed the Infinite Love of the Father, and the submission of the Son to His Will. The Resurrection is beyond measure affirmative. It affirms Christ to be the Son of God—the perfect Sacrifice—the new Source of Life—the future Judge.

Dean Plumptre draws attention to the use of the Amen, the "so it is," or the "so be it," in the discourses of the Lord. When the Lord says, "Verily, I say unto you," it is "Amen, I say unto you." When the Lord, in St. John, says, "Verily, verily, I say unto you," it is "Amen, amen, I say unto you." And nothing is, outwardly at least, more characteristic of His teaching than this constantly recurring solemn affirmation.

20. "For all the promises of God in him are yea, and in him Amen." The word Amen is from the Hebrew root "aman," which signifies to establish, to make firm, to uphold. St. Paul refers to the confirmation of all the promises of God in Christ in his first sermon in Antioch in Pisidia (Acts xiii. 34), where he quotes the Prophet Isaiah as saying, "I will give you the sure mercies (or holy things) of David." The *sure* mercies[1] are the firm or established mercies of David—in fact, following literally the Hebrew, "the mercies of David, the amened ones."

So this verse means, "All the promises of God in Him are affirmed (said 'yea' to), and in him established." And so it is. All the ancient promises of forgiveness, of cleansing, of the law written in the heart, of the new heart and the right spirit, of the Resurrection, of the eternal glory of the righteous, are reaffirmed and established in Him.[2]

---

[1] Isaiah lv. 3. חַסְדֵי דָוִד הַנֶּאֱמָנִים.

[2] Some, as Wesley, and, if I understand him, Meyer, say that the promises are yea with respect to God's promising, Amen with respect to men believing; yea with respect to the Apostles, Amen with respect to their hearers; but the Apostle applies both terms to Christ.

21 Now he which stablisheth us with you in Christ, and [a] hath anointed us, *is* God;

22 Who [b] hath also sealed us, and [c] given the earnest of the Spirit in our hearts.

[a] 1 John ii. 20, 27.
[b] Eph. i. 13. & iv. 30. 2 Tim. ii. 19. Rev. ii. 17.
[c] ch. v. 5. Eph. i. 14.

"To the glory of God," Who has, notwithstanding the sins of His ancient people, glorified His truth and faithfulness in the Revelation of His Son.

"By us." Without our preaching and teaching the stability of God's promises in Christ would not have been proclaimed to the world.

21, 22. "Now he which stablisheth us with you in Christ, and hath anointed us, is God." The word "stablish" carries on the idea of the Amen in its Hebrew significance of strengthening. Note how he says not "us" alone, or "you" alone, but "us with you." St. Paul and his converts are partakers in all respects of the same saving grace.

"And hath anointed us [*i.e.* with His Holy Spirit] is God," *i.e.*, the Father. Here are the three persons of the Godhead working together in the matter of each one's salvation. We are established, not by earthly wisdom, not in an earthly system, but into Christ, and this by God the Father, Who hath anointed us and sealed us, and given to us the earnest of the Spirit.

"Anointed" refers to Christ the Anointed, and seems to point to baptism.

"Sealed" seems to refer to that which was called the seal of the Lord, or the "laying on of hands."

"And given the earnest of the Spirit in our hearts." The earnest —arrhabön [1]—is a small sum of money given as an earnest that the whole shall be given when the contract is completed. If the Holy Spirit is now working in the heart, sanctifying the inner man, raising the affections above the world to God and to Christ—then there is an earnest within us that all God's promises will be fulfilled in due time.

23. "Moreover I call God for a record upon my soul, that to

---

[1] This word is a remarkable one. It was originally Hebrew, and is found for the first time as early as Gen. xxxviii. 17, 18, 20. It got into Greek, and is used by Menander and other Greek writers. It appears in Latin as *arrha*, in French as *les arrhes*, and in popular Scotch even as *artes*. (Wordsworth and Plumptre.)

23 Moreover ^d I call God for a record upon my soul, ^e that to spare you I came not as yet unto Corinth.

24 Not for ^f that we have dominion over your faith, but are helpers of your joy: for ^g by faith ye stand.

d Rom. i. 9. ch. xi. 31. Gal. i. 20. Phil. i. 8.
e 1 Cor. iv. 21. ch. ii. 3. & xii. 20. & xiii. 2, 10.
f 1 Cor. iii. 5. 1 Pet. v. 3.
g Rom. xi. 20. 1 Cor. xv. 1.

spare you," &c. If he had come when he first heard of their sins and defections, he would have had to come with the rod of severe discipline, which might have alienated them still more from him their father in Christ. So he solemnly calls God to record, God Who alone knows the secrets of the hearts, that to spare them he delayed his journey till he had had a more favourable report of them from Titus.

24. "Not for that we have dominion over your faith, but are helpers of your joy." Why does he make this disclaimer? because he had used the word "to spare you," and so to prevent them from supposing that he desired to put himself in the place of God, Who alone has dominion over faith, he declares that he and his fellow-workers are helpers of their joy. He, apostle though he was, had required of them a belief in no new article of faith. What he set forth was the faith which they had heard from the beginning.

But we must beware how we take "not that we have dominion over your faith," as if he disclaimed any authority to require them to hold fast to the faith into which they had been baptized. On the contrary, when he heard that they had declined from but one article of the faith—the Resurrection of the dead—he wrote to them with the utmost seriousness and earnestness, reminding them of what he had delivered unto them first of all, that Christ rose from the dead, and that their present unbelief was a falling from that their first faith, and a virtual denial of the Resurrection of Christ Himself (1 Cor. xv. 13, 16).

"For by faith ye stand," *i.e.* by the faith, τῇ πίστει. He had written to them to remind them of the faith, or Gospel, which he had preached unto them, "wherein," he said, "ye stand," (1 Cor. xv. 1) and now he says again, " By the faith ye stand." By your realizing belief in the Incarnation, the Death, and the Resurrection of the Lord, and with it all that necessarily depends upon it and is involved in it, "ye stand."

CHAP. II.

BUT I determined this with myself, ^athat I would not come again to you in heaviness.

^a ch. i. 23. &
xii. 20, 21. &
xiii. 10.

2 For if I make you sorry, who is he then that maketh me glad, but the same which is made sorry by me?

---

1. "But I determined." So ℵ, A., C., D., E., F., G., K., L., O., P., most Cursives, d, e, f, g, Vulg., &c.; but B., 17, 37, Copt., read, "for" (γὰρ).

"I would not come again to you in heaviness." So some Cursives; but most authorities, ℵ, A., B., C., D., E., F., G., K., L., O., P., most Cursives, Ital., Vulg., read, "I would not again in heaviness come to you."

1. "But I determined this with myself, that I would not come again to you in heaviness." This verse depends for its meaning on the position of the word "again." If we read it according to the authorized, it signifies that he would not come again, *i.e.*, a second time in heaviness. This implies that he had come but once to them, *i.e.*, at his first visit, and that his second visit should be deferred till he could come with more satisfaction than at present. If however we put the word "again" (πάλιν) before "come," it seems to favour the idea that he had before this made a short visit to them, which, on account of their conduct, had been a bitter one; and that he would now try the effect of letters, such as the one which has been lost (1 Corinth. v. 9), and the first Epistle (*i.e.*, the canonical first Epistle). The effect of these (coupled with the visit of Titus) we shall see was that he could again visit them with some degree of joy.

2. "For if I make you sorry, who is he then that maketh me glad, but," &c. Some suppose that "he that maketh me glad," is general in its application, and signifies any one whom he had brought to repentance by his letters; others suppose that he alludes particularly to the incestuous person who above all others was made sorry ("ye ought rather to forgive him and comfort him lest such an one should be swallowed up," &c.), but in whose repentance the Apostle now the more rejoiced as a signal triumph of the grace of God. I think the latter the true meaning.

3 And I wrote this same unto you, lest, when I came, ᵇ I should have sorrow from them of whom I ought to rejoice; ᶜ having confidence in you all, that my joy is *the joy* of you all.

4 For out of much affliction and anguish of heart I wrote unto you with many tears; ᵈ not that ye should be grieved, but that ye might know the love which I have more abundantly unto you.

ᵇ ch. xii. 21.
ᶜ ch. vii. 16.
& viii. 22.
Gal. v. 10.

ᵈ ch. vii. 8, 9, 12.

3. "And I wrote this same unto you, lest, when I came, I should have," &c. "This same," *i.e.*, the severe words of the first Epistle (and perhaps of the lost Epistle), such, for instance, as "I could not speak unto you as unto spiritual, but as unto carnal"—"Ye are yet carnal"—"As my beloved sons I warn you"—"Some are puffed up,"—"Shall I come to you with the rod?"—"That one should have his father's wife," and "ye are puffed up"—"Your glorying is not good," &c. &c. He wrote this and much more to bring them to their senses, so that he should not be grieved with those over whom he ought to rejoice.

"Having confidence in you all, that my joy is the joy of you all." "I have confidence in the reality of the Christianity which ye possess, which will make my joy the joy of you all. I rejoice when I know that our Lord has brought back a wandering sheep in His arms unto His fold, and I am sure that because of your love of Christ, and of the souls for which He died, you will rejoice with the same joy."

4. "For out of much affliction and anguish of heart I wrote unto you," &c. "What more tenderly affectioned than this man's spirit is; for he showed himself to have been not less pained than they who had sinned, but even much more. For he said not out of affliction merely but out of *much*, nor with *tears*, but with *many* tears and anguish of heart, that is, I was suffocated, I was choked with despondency; and when I could no longer endure the cloud of despondency, I wrote unto you, not that ye should be grieved, but "that ye might know the love," saith he, "which I have more abundantly unto you." And yet what naturally followed was to say, "not that ye might be grieved, but that ye might be corrected, for with this purpose he wrote. This, however, he doth not say,

5 But ^e if any have caused grief, he hath not ^f grieved me, but in part: that I may not overcharge you all.

6 Sufficient to such a man *is* this ‖ punishment, which *was inflicted* ^g of many.

7 ^h So that contrariwise ye *ought* rather to forgive *him*, and comfort *him*, lest perhaps such a one should be swallowed up with overmuch sorrow.

<small>e 1 Cor. v. 1.
f Gal. iv. 12.
‖ Or, *censure*.
g 1 Cor. v. 4, 5. 1 Tim. v. 20.
h Gal. vi. 1.</small>

---

but more to sweeten his words, and win them to a greater love, he puts this for it, showing that he doth all from love." (Chrysostom.) Notice how little fear the Apostle had that they should take advantage of his expressions of love and turn haughtily or sulkily upon him, and proudly assert their right to do as they liked, as many sinners do to their pastors, when they have begun to fall away, resolving to carry it with a high hand. St. Paul was not afraid of this; he had confidence in the work of the Spirit within them, that they would show a better mind.

5. "But if any have caused grief, he hath not grieved me, but in part." Many explanations have been given of this verse. The one that commends itself to myself is something of this sort. The incestuous person had caused grief, but not to the Apostle only, but to all the right-minded persons in the Church, who shared with the Apostle in his grief at the scandal, and the Apostle says this that he might not lay too heavy a burden upon all of them, which he would have done if he had represented himself as the only person aggrieved. On the contrary, he desired to share the scandal with the whole body of the Church.

6. "Sufficient to such a man is this punishment which was inflicted of many." That is, the solemn excommunication, and perhaps some severe bodily disorder, threatening the destruction of the flesh, and the exclusion from the society of all who were like-minded with the Apostle.

"Of many." Of the many—of the Church gathered together.

7. "So that contrariwise ye ought rather to forgive him, and comfort him, lest," &c. Is it possible that one could be too sorrowful for having committed so enormous a sin? Yes, if his sorrow made him despair of forgiveness. He might seek to put an end to himself; he might become morose; his mind might be unhinged;

OBEDIENT IN ALL THINGS.

8 Wherefore I beseech you that ye would confirm *your* love toward him.

9 For to this end also did I write, that I might know the proof of you, whether ye be ¹obedient in all things. ¹ ch. vii. 15. & x. 6.

10 To whom ye forgive any thing, I *forgive* also: for if

---

9. "Whether ye be obedient." So ℵ, C., D., E., F., G., K., L., O., P., &c.; but A. B., read, "wherein" or "how."

he might become incapable of performing the proper duties of his station.

8. "Wherefore I beseech you that ye would confirm your love towards him." They might "confirm their love" either by acts of private love or friendship, or by the removal of the Church's censure, but this latter, I think, was probably removed by Titus as the representative of the Apostle whose act the excommunication really was. (1 Cor. v. 3, 4, 5.) After the excommunication had been removed some might say that it was well that he should yet feel the disgrace which he had brought upon them, but the Apostle judged that the punishment had been sufficient.

9. "For to this end also did I write, that I might know the proof of you," &c. There is some difference of opinion as to whether he means what he wrote to them in his first Epistle, or what he is now writing to them. Probably the former, but the matter to be particularly noticed is the way in which he demands their submission to him as an Apostle, *i.e.*, as the direct representative of Jesus Christ, one of those to whom the Lord said, "He that heareth you heareth me," Luke x. 16. This was one purpose of his writing, besides the measures he commanded to be taken to bring the incestuous person to repentance.

10. "To whom ye forgive any thing, I forgive also: for if I forgave any thing," &c. "To whom ye forgive any thing, I forgive also." This must refer, not to the removal of the excommunication, but to the forgiveness and comfort of verse 7, and it signifies, "I thoroughly am in accord with you in any kindness ye show him in order to reassure him;" and this follows upon the removal of the excommunication which he now reasserts, "If I forgave any thing to whom (or wherein) I forgave it, for your sakes forgave I it in the person of Christ."

I forgave any thing, to whom I forgave *it*, for your sakes
forgave I it ‖ in the person of Christ;

| Or, *in the sight*.

11 Lest Satan should get an advantage of us:
for we are not ignorant of his devices.

---

10. "To whom I forgave it." So K., L., 17, most Cursives; but ℵ, A., B., C., F., G., O., &c., read, "what I forgave" (ὃ κεχάρισμαι εἴ τι κεχάρισμαι).

The excommunication had been the action of the Apostle absent in the flesh, but present in the spirit. So 1 Cor. v. 3: "I verily, as absent in the body but present in spirit, have judged already . . . in the Name of our Lord Jesus Christ when ye are gathered together, and my spirit, with the power of our Lord Jesus Christ, to deliver such an one to Satan," &c. The removal of the sentence also was his doing. "If I forgave anything, to whom I forgave it, for your sakes forgave I it in the person of Christ." This implies that he had already pronounced his absolution. Both the binding and the loosing were in the Name of Christ: and were each an assertion of that authority which the Lord had given for discipline, in the words, "Whosesoever sins ye remit, they are remitted unto them," &c. It can hardly be said that, in the retention of the sin of the incestuous person he acted with the concurrence of the Corinthian Church, for, from what we can gather from the first Epistle, they would not have stirred a finger in the matter unless he had commanded them. He could not be present personally; and so they were to do it, not of themselves, but as if he was present in spirit.

It is remarkable that this is the only account of the exercise of retaining and remitting sins in the New Testament, and it is exercised by St. Paul—not by St. Peter or St. James, but by the Apostle who is constantly quoted as the vindicator of liberty; whereas in his writings alone do we find the whole Church system either asserted or carried out in its fulness.

11. "Lest Satan should get an advantage of us; for we are not ignorant," &c. Chrysostom has a good remark: "Satan destroys even under the show of piety. For not only by leading into fornication can he destroy, but even by the contrary, the unmeasured sorrow following on the repentance of it. . . . Wherefore also with reason did he call it getting advantage, when he even conquereth with our own weapons. . . . For to take by sin is his proper work: by repentance, however, is no more his: for *ours* not *his* is that weapon. When then even by this he is able to take,

NO REST IN MY SPIRIT.

12 Furthermore, ᵏ when I came to Troas to *preach* Christ's gospel, and ¹ a door was opened unto me of the Lord,

ᵏ Acts xvi. 8.
& xx. 6.
¹ 1 Cor. xvi. 9.

13 ᵐ I had no rest in my spirit, because I found not Titus my brother: but taking my leave of them, I went from thence into Macedonia.

ᵐ ch. vii. 5, 6.

14 Now thanks *be* unto God, which always causeth us

---

think how disgraceful is the defeat, how he will laugh to scorn, and make ravage on us as weak and pitiful, if at least he is to subdue us with our own weapons."

12, 13. " Furthermore, when I came to Troas to preach Christ's gospel . . . thence into Macedonia." The Apostle gives another proof of his overwhelming anxiety on behalf of the spiritual welfare of the Corinthian Church. He had sent Titus to Corinth to bring him a faithful account of what was going on there. Titus was to meet him at Troas on his (St. Paul's) way to Macedonia, but when he came to Troas and did not find Titus there, his anxiety was such that he left a place where a door was opened for him to preach the Gospel (*i.e.* where he had every prospect of preaching with great success), and went at once to Macedonia, with the view of meeting Titus. He did meet him, probably at Philippi, from which, or from some other city of Macedonia, he wrote this letter.

14. " Now thanks be unto God, which always causeth us to triumph," &c. The rendering, "causeth us to triumph," though it is certainly that which Chrysostom accepted, is considered by most moderns inadmissible. They say that θριαμβεύειν means, properly, to lead in triumph; but, as Alford remarks, there are always two kinds of persons led in triumph, the participators of the victory and the victims of the defeat.

But who are the victims of the defeat ? If Christ, the conqueror of all sin and evil, triumphs, then those who are conquered by Him, *i.e.* the Apostles, and notably St. Paul, and all who are by Him turned to God, are the victims led in procession.

I cannot, however, believe that this last is the meaning. It seems incongruous to render it "leads us in triumph," when it so obviously means here causes us to triumph.¹ For St. Paul had just been

---

¹ So Liddell and Scott and Grimm—the latter of whom speaks of it as being used hiphilitice, that is, after the Hebrew hiphil.

to triumph in Christ, and maketh manifest ⁿthe savour of his knowledge by us in every place.

n Cant. i. 3.

15 For we are unto God a sweet savour of Christ, °in them that are saved, and ᵖin them that perish:

o 1 Cor. i. 18.
p ch. iv. 3.

16 ᑫTo the one *we are* the savour of death

q Luke ii. 34.
John ix. 39.
1 Pet. ii. 7, 8.

---

16. "Of death unto death." So D., E., F., G., K., L., most Cursives, It., Vulg., Arm.; but א, A., B., C., some Cursives, &c., read, "from" (ἐκ θανάτου).

led, through the lapse of so many of the Corinthians, to expect a serious defeat in his warfare with the kingdom of Satan: and now, unexpectedly, he finds he has cause for triumph; and, looking back on his past life, he remembers so many instances of God thus bringing good out of evil, that he thanks God that it is *always* so.

"And maketh manifest the savour of his knowledge by us in every place." As in the Roman triumph, there was the swinging of censers and the diffusion of the sweet odour of the incense all around; so in the life of the Apostle, wherever he went there was the diffusion of the knowledge of Christ crucified and risen again through the preaching of the Gospel.

15, 16. "For we are unto God a sweet savour of Christ in them that are saved (being saved) and in them that perish. To the one we are the savour of .... life unto life." The best explanation of this seems to be that the incense of the Roman triumphal procession typifies either prolonged life, or swift approaching death to those who inhaled it. To those who shared in the conqueror's triumph, it was the sweet forecast of further wealth and honour from a grateful country; to the captives it was the sign of approaching death, when they should be hurried out of the glittering procession to be slain barbarously in cold blood, or be cast headlong into the lowest depths of the Mamertine prison. Now so it was with the Gospel: to those who accepted it willingly and gratefully it was like the incense to the conquerors, a pledge of a happier and more glorious future; but to those who rejected it, because they would not "have this Man to reign over them," it was the savour of death unto death, it bid them prepare to receive the doom in store for the enemies of God.

Terrible is this figure, that the same odour of sweetness should be the prelude of life or death, but it is a fact to each one of us, in our

CHAP. II.] THE SAVOUR OF DEATH AND LIFE.

unto death; and to the other the savour of life unto life. And ʳ who *is* sufficient for these things?   ʳ 1 Cor. xv. 10. ch. iii. 5, 6.

spiritual life now, and we must face it. On this one occasion only was the fume of incense the harbinger of life and death. And the Apostle fastens on it, and singles it out, and treats it as a parable of the outward world, which teaches us, in a remarkable way, a truth which we would fain shut our eyes to.

For the preaching of the Gospel never can be a matter of indifference—it never can leave a soul in the same state as that in which it finds it. It either softens it to eternal life, or hardens it to reject that life, and abide the more pertinaciously in death. This double effect of the Gospel is set forth in the words of holy Simeon, "This child is set for the fall and rising again of many in Israel" (Luke ii. 34), and in the words of the Lord Himself, "For judgment I am come into this world that they which see not might see, and that they which see might be made blind" (John ix. 39).

But what are we to understand by the words, "are unto God"? Is the perishing of the wicked a sweet savour unto God—that God Who has said by His prophet, "Have I any pleasure at all that the wicked should die, saith the Lord God, and not that he should return from his ways and live?" (Ezek. xviii. 23.)

No; what he means is this, that the preaching of the Gospel of His Son is always well pleasing to God, notwithstanding that it may turn to the greater condemnation of those who reject it. Though it may be that some who hear it will be the worse for doing so, we are yet to preach it, and leave the consequences to God.

Wordsworth has a suggestive note: "Indeed, it is a solemn truth that in the Christian scheme nothing that God has done is indifferent. Everything is a two-edged sword. All Christian privileges, all the means of Grace, Scriptures, Sermons, Sacraments, Sundays, Churches, Chapels, Liturgies, and all things that Christ's ministers do and teach in His Name are, according as they are used, either blessings or banes, either physic or poison, they are either for weal or woe, either an odour of life unto life eternal, or of death unto death eternal, to the souls of all to whom they come."

"And who is sufficient for these things?" What things? For being the instruments of Christ's triumph — for making manifest the savour of His knowledge in every place. The answer is given in chap. iii. 5, "Our sufficiency is of God."

| Or, *deal deceitfully with.*
ª ch. iv. 2. &
xi. 13. 2 Pet.
ii. 3.
ᵗ ch. i. 12. &
iv. 2.
|| Or, *of.*

17 For we are not as many, which || ªcorrupt the word of God: but as ᵗof sincerity, but as of God, in the sight of God speak we || in Christ.

17. "For we are not as many, which corrupt the word of God." "As many"—rather, as "the many" who corrupt the Word of God. The word *capelos* (κάπηλος) signifies a huckster, particularly a retailer of wine who adulterated it; and hence here, those who for gain or ambitious purposes mixed up men's devices with the Word of God, to suit the depraved taste of their hearers (2 Tim. iv. 3), are said to huckster it, or, as in the margin, deal deceitfully with it.

"Many" ought rather to be translated "the many;" and it seems that from the first the Church was in danger from the multitude of false teachers. Thus, in this very Epistle, notice is taken of those who taught that immorality was venial, that there was no danger in publicly partaking of things offered to idols, that St. Paul was not a true Apostle, and that the resurrection of the dead was doubtful.

"But as of sincerity." This may refer either to sincerity of mind in the delivery of the message, or to the message itself as being pure and unadulterated.

"As of God," knowing and acting upon the knowledge that all we speak is from God and in Christ.

CHAP. III.

ª ch. v. 12.
& x. 8, 12.
& xii. 11.
ᵇ Acts xviii. 27.

DO ª we begin again to commend ourselves? or need we, as some *others*, ᵇ epistles of

1. "Do we begin again to commend ourselves? or need we, as some others," &c. The Apostle in the next three chapters reasserts his Apostolical authority. He had written (1 Cor. ix. 2), "If I be not an apostle to others, yet doubtless I am to you, for the seal of my apostleship are ye in the Lord." He had heard probably from Titus that what he had written in his first letter had

commendation to you, or *letters* of commendation from you?

2 ^cYe are our epistle written in our hearts,   c 1 Cor. ix. 2. known and read of all men:

3 *Forasmuch as ye are* manifestly declared to be the epistle of Christ ^d ministered by us, written   d 1 Cor. iii. 5.

---

not restrained some from persisting in questioning his Apostleship. Apollos had come to them with commendatory letters (Acts xviii. 27), so probably had some of the Judaizing teachers; and he now proceeds to treat with somewhat of contempt the conduct of those who had disparaged him, because he had not brought such letters in his hands.

"Do we begin again to commend ourselves?" He was bound, not from personal considerations, but from his allegiance to Christ, Who had constituted him the Apostle and special teacher of the Gentiles, to assert his Apostolical authority; and this he could hardly do without putting prominently in the foreground his labours and his success: his labours—" he laboured more abundantly than they all, yet not he but the grace of God with him; " and his success—not only was he the sweet savour of Christ in every place, but the Church of Corinth was, under God, his creation. And so he needed no letters of commendation to them, as others did, and he was not so absurd as to ask letters of commendation [1] from those who were his spiritual children, and under his authority as their Apostle.

2, 3. "Ye are our epistle written in our hearts, known and read of all men. Forasmuch as ye are manifestly declared to be the epistle of Christ," &c. "Written in our hearts." He uses this metaphor of a written letter to signify two things—(1) Ye are our letter written in our hearts. The conversion of so many of them from the power of Satan to God was deeply written in his

---

[1] Perhaps these letters were less formal than those used in the Church of the succeeding age. According to Mr. Blunt they were given in three cases. First, the clergy and others received such letters of commendation from the bishops when they were travelling, so that they might claim the right of Christian fellowship among strangers. Secondly, they were given as certificates of communion. Thirdly, the clergy received such epistles under the name of letters dimissory, when they removed from one diocese to another, to show that they left in peace with their bishop.

not with ink, but with the Spirit of the living God; not ⁿin tables of stone, but ᶠin fleshy tables of the heart.

4 And such trust have we through Christ to God-ward:

ⁿ Exod. xxiv. 12. & xxxiv. 1.
ᶠ Ps. xl. 8.
Jer. xxxi. 33.
Ezek. xi. 19.
& xxxvi. 26.
Hebr. viii. 10.

---

3. "In fleshy tables of the heart." So F., K., most Cursives, It., Vulg., Goth., Syr., Cop., Arm.; but ℵ, A., B., C., D., E., G., L., P., about twenty-five Cursives, read, "in tables that are hearts of flesh." So Revisers.

own heart. Thus he said of the Philippian Christians that he was confident that He Who had begun a good work in them would continue it because "he had them in his heart." The Apostle looked upon the faithful and true Christian heart as especially the domain of God, and if God had written the Corinthian Christians in his heart, there was no need of anything further to commend them to him or him to them; but (2) the writing was not only in his heart, to be read by him—it was of such a character that it was known and read of all men. The conversion of such a number of persons in so wicked a city as Corinth from such a religion of idolatry and filthiness to one of such godliness and purity, was an Epistle which commended the Apostle and his work to all men. Let men of any understanding consider what they were and what they are; whom they then worshipped, and what they now worship; what were their hopes then, and what their hopes are now, and he would be bound to acknowledge that their Christianity was not a matter of paper and ink, but of that writing which the finger of God—that is, the Spirit—only can inscribe. It was like the writing of the finger of God upon the tables of stone which God gave to Moses, but with this amazing difference, that whereas God wrote the ten commandments on a hard substance, typifying the hardness of their hearts to whom the law was given, now He had written the law in hearts softened by Divine grace, according as Ezekiel had prophesied, "I will take the stony heart out of their flesh, and will give them an heart of flesh" (Ezek. xi. 19). And so the Apostle says, "written not in tables of stone, but in fleshy tables of the heart."

4, 5. "And such trust have we through Christ to God-ward.... our sufficiency is of God." "Such trust." That is, trust that He will make all Christians whom we convert to be living Epistles manifesting the power and truth of the Gospel which we preach—and

CHAP. III.] OUR SUFFICIENCY IS OF GOD. 329

5 ^g Not that we are sufficient of ourselves to think any thing as of ourselves; but ^h our sufficiency *is* of God;

6 Who also hath made us able ⁱ ministers of ^k the new testament; not ^l of the letter, but of the

g John xv. 5. ch. ii. 16.
h 1 Cor. xv. 10. Phil. ii. 13.
i 1 Cor. iii. 5. & xv. 10. ch. v. 18. Ephes iii. 7. Col. i. 25, 29. 1 Tim. i. 11, 12. 2 Tim. i. 11.
k Jer. xxxi. 31. Matt. xxvi. 28. Heb. viii. 6, 8.
l Rom. ii. 27, 29, & vii. 6.

this not as if we desired to arrogate to ourselves any credit, or as if we had any real power in the matter, but all our ability to enable souls to manifest the glory of God is entirely His Work.

6. "Who also hath made us able ministers of the new testament [or covenant]; not of the letter, but of the spirit: for the letter killeth," &c. "Who hath made us able ministers." Perhaps it would be better to translate it "Who hath fully qualified us to be ministers"—hath made us sufficient or fit. "Of the New Testament," rather of the New Covenant—the Covenant promised in Jeremiah xxxi. 31: "Behold the days come, saith the Lord, that I will make a new covenant . . . . not according to the covenant that I made with their fathers." This is the Covenant: "I will put my law in their inward parts, and write it in their hearts. . . . I will forgive their iniquity, and remember their sin no more." It was not like the Old Covenant, a mere command, but it was a promise. It was not so many letters which could be counted, but it was a promise of the Spirit writing the law in the heart; and the law was to be written not by the mere learning of some ten, or twenty, or a hundred precepts, but by the heart being expanded and purified, and warmed, and animated with the life of God breathed into it; so that the man thus changed in heart never could be content with obedience to the letter, but desired with all his soul obedience to the full spirit—in fact, conformity to the will of God.

"Not of the letter, but of the Spirit." Every revelation which is contained in a book, or is capable of being so contained, must have letters, and in the Old Covenant the leading matter is the letter (even ten commandments, and He added no more); but the book of the New Covenant is pervaded by a Spirit, the Spirit of Christ—the Life of Christ displayed in His Own Life and that of His servants, the Death of Christ as displaying the love of God, the Resurrection as verifying and applying it. Must we then

spirit: for ^m the letter killeth, ⁿ but the spirit ‖ giveth life.

7 But if ^o the ministration of death, ^p written *and* engraven in stones, was glorious, ^q so that the

<small>m Rom. iii. 20. & iv. 15. & vii. 9, 10, 11. Gal. iii. 10.
n John vi. 63. Rom. viii. 2.
‖ Or, *quickeneth.*
o Rom. vii. 10.
p Exod. xxxiv. 1, 28. Deut. x. 1, &c.
q Exod. xxxiv. 29, 30, 35.</small>

---

7. "Written and engraven in stones." Lit., "in letters and engraven on stones."

---

adhere to the letter of the New Testament?¹ Certainly, but on this principle, that God, in giving us His perfect revelation, has chosen the best words, and we cannot improve on them.

"For the letter killeth, but the Spirit giveth life." The letter killeth, because it brings the knowledge of sin, and convicts of sin (Rom. vii. 9), and unless it be followed by the promises of God, shuts men up in despair; but the Spirit, *i.e.*, the Holy Spirit, giveth life. He imparts to the soul the very life of Christ Himself, so that in us is fulfilled the word of Christ, "Because I live ye shall live also."²

7. "But if the ministration of death, written and engraven in stones was glorious," &c. How could the giving of the law be called the ministration of death? Because its leading feature was the threatening of death. If any one of the Israelites came near to the mount within the bounds, he was to be put to death (Exod. xix. 13). When the children of Israel were assembled between

---

<small>1 Of course, in what he says respecting the letter and the spirit the Apostle speaks broadly, as it were, for there is the very spirit and essence of the Gospel in Isaiah liii. and in Psalm xxii., and there are the highest conceivable expressions of piety and union of spirit with God in the Psalms; but still, the very Apostles who had constantly read that chapter and used those Psalms had, till Pentecost, no idea that the Messiah was to triumph over sin and the grave by the Cross.

2 Chrysostom takes a somewhat lower view of the words, "the letter killeth," as meaning the law punisheth; but his remarks are very grand. "The law, if it lay hold on a murderer, putteth him to death; the Gospel, if it lay hold on a murderer, enlighteneth and giveth him life. And why do I instance a murderer? The law laid hold on one that gathered sticks on a Sabbath Day, and it stoned him. This is the meaning of 'the letter killeth.' The Gospel takes hold on thousands of homicides and robbers, and baptizing, delivereth them from their former vices. This is the meaning of 'the Spirit giveth life.' The former maketh its captives dead from being alive, the latter rendereth the man it hath convicted alive from being dead: for 'come unto me all ye that labour and are heavy laden,' and he said not, I will punish you, but I will refresh you."</small>

children of Israel could not stedfastly behold the face of Moses for the glory of his countenance; which *glory* was to be done away:

8 How shall not ʳ the ministration of the spirit be rather glorious? ʳ Gal. iii. 5.

Gerizim and Ebal, the curses only seem to have been uttered aloud, and the people said Amen only to the curses.

And how could it be said to be glorious? Because the outward manifestations of the glory of God were infinitely greater in the eyes of men than the wonders that attended the giving of the Gospel—whether at the Incarnation and Nativity—at the Crucifixion or the Resurrection—or Ascension—or even at Pentecost. All these latter manifestations of power might be deemed private and partial. Even with respect to the ministry of the Messiah, so full of miracles and wisdom, it was described in the words, " He shall not strive nor cry, neither shall any man hear his voice in the streets " (Matth. xii. 19). Whereas the outward and visible glory of the appearance of God was such that the countenance of Moses, because he had been face to face with God, shone so that the children of Israel could not bear to look upon his face. The Person of the Lord was only on one occasion enveloped in light, and that in the sight of but three persons, and certainly no glory shone from the faces of those who were in constant communication with Him; whereas the face of Moses, after he had been in the presence of God, shone with unbearable brightness.

" Which glory was to be done away." The meaning of this is twofold. First the glory of the shining of Moses' face was transitory. It was for a time exceedingly bright, so that Moses had to hide his face under a veil, but this was only for a short time; it soon came to an end. And the glory of the dispensation also was exceeding great at the first, but only at the first. The glories of the Exodus—of the stricken rock—of the manna—of the mountain burning with fire—of the brightness of Moses' face, were never equalled in the latter days, and the restoration after the Babylonian captivity was in very deed tame and commonplace when compared with the glories of the Exodus.

8. " How shall not the ministration of the spirit be rather glorious?" The glory of the ministration of death was a glory of

9 For if the ministration of condemnation *be* glory, much more doth the ministration ᵇ of righteousness exceed in glory.

ᵇ Rom. i. 17.
& iii. 21.

10 For even that which was made glorious had no glory in this respect, by reason of the glory that excelleth.

11 For if that which is done away *was* glorious, much more that which remaineth *is* glorious.

---

sight. It was intended to influence the children of Israel from without, being addressed to their outward senses, whilst the glory of the ministration of the Spirit was within, from within, unseen for the most part by the eye of man, and yet its glory was infinitely greater, for it was the glory of spirit rather than of flesh. It was conformity to that which is the highest glory of God, even His moral glory, His loving and righteous character.

9. " For if the ministration of condemnation be glory, much more," &c. The ministration of righteousness was not without its outward visible glory. The sight of the angels and that of the multitude of the heavenly host, the star of the Magi, the descent of the Holy Ghost as a dove, the Transfiguration, were all forecasts of never-ending glory. The glory of the Crucifixion, the "Father, forgive them," the "This day shalt thou be with me in paradise," the "I thirst," the "It is finished," all in the eyes of faith far eclipse the glories of Sinai. The Resurrection was the most wondrous work of God, in that it was the investment of a human body with all the powers and attributes of a Divine spirit. The Ascension, though seen only by the Apostles, was the greatest visible triumph of righteousness over evil that the hosts of the angels had ever seen (Psalms xxiv., cx., John xvii. 5, and Coloss ii. 15), and all leading on to the final triumph of Righteousness at the Second Advent when the Son of Man shall come in His own glory, and that of His Father, and of the Holy Angels.

10, 11. " For even that which was made glorious . . . much more that which remaineth," &c. Not only does the glory of the dispensation of righteousness exceed that of the ministration of condemnation in that it is moral and spiritual as well as outward and physical, but the glory of the ministration of righteousness far exceeds the glory which preceded it, in this respect, that it is permanent. The righteous shine forth as the sun not for a time, but for

GREAT PLAINNESS OF SPEECH.

12 Seeing then that we have such hope, [t] we use great ‖ plainness of speech:

13 And not as Moses, [u] *which* put a vail over his face, that the children of Israel could not

[t] ch. vii. 4.
Ephes. vi. 19.
‖ Or, *boldness*.
[u] Exod. xxxiv. 33, 35.

---

ever and ever (Matt. xiii. 43; Dan. xii. 3). A glorious beginning makes a shameful ending more deplorable. Now the new dispensation began in humiliation, but that humiliation being the humiliation even unto death of the Eternal Son, makes His reward, which reward He shares with His people, infinitely more glorious.

12. " Seeing then that we have such hope, we use great plainness of speech." The word translated plainness is the same word which in Acts iv. 13, and in most other places where it occurs, is translated boldness. " Seeing, then, we have such hope of future transcendent glory, we speak very boldly, lest men lose, through our want of earnestness, their conviction of the deep reality of what we hold out to them; and not only do we speak boldly, but plainly, knowing that mere human eloquence detracts from the simplicity of our Gospel, and endangers its real reception by making men think of the casket in which the jewel is presented to their acceptance rather than of the jewel itself."

13. " And not as Moses, which put a vail over his face, that the children of Israel could not stedfastly look," &c. St. Paul, in this allusion to Moses as veiled, takes a very different view of it from what we have been accustomed to take through our Authorized English Version. We, *i.e.*, the great majority of the readers of the English Bible, have been accustomed to suppose that Moses put a veil upon his face to hide the glory which made first Aaron and the elders of the people, and then all the Israelites, afraid to approach him to receive from him the words of God. This seems the natural interpretation of the account as we read it in Exod. xxxiv. 29—35. But this does not accord with the lesson which the Apostle seems to draw from it, which is a mystical lesson. Moses, according to the Apostle's interpretation, put a veil on his face, not to hide the glory, but lest the children of Israel should see the diminution or ending of the glory. And if we compare the Hebrew with the English we shall find the reason for this, for verse 33 of Exod. xxxiv. should be translated " *when* Moses " (not till) but " *when* Moses had done

^x Rom. x. 4. stedfastly look to ^x the end of that which is abolished:

---

speaking with them," he put a veil on his face (and so LXX., and other versions). So that the true account of the transaction seems to be this. Moses came down from the Mount where he had been speaking face to face with God with his face resplendent with light. Aaron and the elders feared to approach him whilst his face thus shone, but he called unto them, and no doubt bid them fear nothing, and after this the whole congregation were emboldened to come near, and when Moses had done speaking to them, then he put the veil on his face, and the Apostle seems to say that he did this (whether consciously or not does not in the least affect the question) for a typical purpose,—that the Israelites should not see to the end, that is the evanescent nature or transitoriness of the glory of the law. Many difficult questions, however, arise from this. It could not be said of such a servant of God as Moses, that in order that he might not lose the prestige of having this light ever streaming from his face, he by means of the veil deliberately concealed from the children of Israel its evanescence. It was evanescent—are we to suppose that he tried to make them believe that it was a permanent glory? But again: on this hypothesis we are to suppose that, except for a few short intervals when he disappeared from the view of the congregation to speak with God, he was always veiled. He must have been, if the illusion, the typical illusion, was to be kept up. But have we the smallest reason to suppose that he was among the people of Israel as a " veiled prophet"? If so, the most extraordinary fact of his long life is unmentioned. The present passage, however, is plainly allegorical, and we may now turn to it as such.

In a note [1] I give the comment of Chrysostom, who translates

---

[1] "Putting them in mind of this history, he says, verse 13, 'And not as Moses, which put a vail over his face, so that the children of Israel could not stedfastly look to the end of that which was abolished.' Now what he says is of this nature. There is no need for us to cover ourselves as Moses did; for ye are able to look upon this glory which we are encircled with, although it is far greater and brighter than the other. Seest thou their advance? For he that in the former Epistle said, 'I have fed you with milk and not with meat,' says here, 'we use much plainness of speech,' and he produces Moses before them, carrying forward the discourse by means of comparison, and thus leading his hearers upwards.

"Verse 14. 'But their minds were blinded: for until this day,' &c. See what he establisheth by this. For what happened, then, once, in the case of Moses, the same

CHAP. III.] THEIR MINDS WERE BLINDED. 335

14 But ʸ their minds were blinded: for until this day remaineth the same vail untaken away in the reading of the old testament; which *vail* is done away in Christ.

15 But even unto this day, when Moses is read, the vail is upon their heart.

ʸ Is. vi. 10.
Matt. xiii. 11,
14. John xii.
40. Acts
xxviii. 26.
Rom. xi. 7, 8,
25. ch. iv. 4.

---

according to the Hebrew and Septuagint, and yet evidently considers that Moses veiled his face to conceal the glory itself, not to conceal the termination of it. The shining of Moses' face typified the real glory of the law, and the end of the law also. This glory and this end was Christ. Christ was the One to Whom the law and the prophets bare witness. He was also the end or the fulfilment of the law for righteousness unto all them that believe. But for certain wise reasons, till He came and manifested Himself, the law manifested Him very obscurely. There was a veil upon its glory and upon its intention, which veil, though it was typified by the veiling of Moses' face to hide its brightness from the Israelites, was in reality the antitypical, not on the face of Moses, but on the hearts of the children of Israel, and so St. Paul proceeds to say—

14, 15. "But their minds were blinded: for until this day remaineth the same vail," &c. Here the veil which in type covered the face of Moses now rests upon the hearts of the unconverted Jews in the reading of the Old Testament. This seems to confirm the view we have taken that Moses was directed by God to put on the veil, not to conceal the evanescence of the dispensation of the law, but to conceal its real glory, the sight of which the Israelites in their then state could not endure.

There seems something supernatural in the blindness of the Jews all through their history to the witness of the law to Christ. They must have looked beyond their carnal sacrifices to some spiritual

---

happeneth continually in the case of the law. What is said, therefore, is no accusation of the law, as neither is it of Moses, that he then veiled himself, but only of the senseless Jews. For the law hath its proper glory, but they were unable to see it. Why, therefore, are ye perplexed, he saith, if they are not able to see this glory of the Grace [of Christ] since they saw not that lesser one of Moses, nor were able to look steadfastly upon his countenance: and why are ye troubled that the Jews believe not Christ, seeing, at least, that they believe not even in the law. For they were ignorant of the Grace [of Christ] also, because they knew not even the Old Covenant, nor the glory which was in it. For the glory of the law is to turn men to Christ."

16 Nevertheless *when it shall turn to the Lord, ᵃ the vail shall be taken away.

17 Now ᵇ the Lord is that Spirit: and where the Spirit of the Lord *is*, there *is* liberty.

* Exod. xxxiv. 34. Rom. xi. 23, 25.
ᵃ Is. xxv. 7.
ᵇ ver. 6.
1 Cor. xv. 45.

17. "Is that Spirit." "Is the Spirit."

one. They must have looked in the recitation of their Psalms to some One greater than David. The grandeur and wisdom of Solomon and his failure must have led them to expect a greater than Solomon. The prophecies of Isaiah must have led them to the idea at least of a Messiah suffering as well as glorified. They did look for a Messiah, but it was not an honest looking. Their spiritual vision was obscured by a carnal veil; and Christians who are carnal, and take the Jewish or carnal view, have the veil over their hearts.

16. "Nevertheless when it shall turn to the Lord, the vail shall be taken away." The "it" probably alludes to the future national turning of all Israel to the Lord. Thus, in Rom. xi. 25, 26, 32: "Blindness in part is happened unto Israel . . . so shall all Israel be saved. God hath concluded all in unbelief that he may have mercy upon all."

Some suppose that in the words "when it shall turn to the Lord, the vail," &c., there is an allusion to the fact that Moses, when he turned into the tabernacle to speak unto the Lord, took the veil from off his face; but this seems doubtful.

17. "Now the Lord is that Spirit, and where the Spirit of the Lord is," &c. The introduction of the Spirit and His identification with the Lord is exceedingly abrupt, and we must look to where the mention of the Spirit last occurs to explain it. In verse 6 St. Paul says, "that God hath enabled the Apostles to be ministers of the New Covenant, not of the letter, but of the Spirit, for the letter killeth, but the Spirit giveth life;" and in the 8th verse, "How shall not the ministration of the Spirit be rather glorious?" Now what is the Spirit in these two places? It is not so much the ministration of the Third Person by Himself, but it is the Third Person ministering the Second, ministering His wisdom, and His Righteousness. Now Christ is the Spirit of both Testaments, in the Old more obscurely, but in the New more plainly. Comparing verses 16 and 17, we have "when it, (the Jews or the particular

18 But we all, with open face beholding [c] as in a glass [d] the glory of the Lord, [e] are changed into

[c] 1 Cor. xiii. 12.
[d] ch. iv. 4, 6. 1 Tim. i. 11.
[e] Rom. viii. 29. 1 Cor. xv. 49. Col. iii. 10.

18. Revisers translate this verse—"But we all, with unveiled face reflecting as a mirror [or, beholding as in a mirror] the glory of the Lord, are transformed into the same image from glory to glory, even as from the Lord the Spirit."

soul) shall turn" from the mere letter to the Spirit which underlies the letter, the veil shall be taken away; but the Spirit to which it turns is the Lord Himself. He is the fulfilment of all the types, the substance of all the shadows, the thing really hinted at in the obscure allusions: in fact the testimony of Jesus is the Spirit of prophecy. So that when the Jew begins to realize the law it is by his turning to its Spirit, that is, to the Lord Jesus, and this at once gives him freedom. The Son makes him free, and he is free indeed; free, not only from the bondage of ordinances, which, as St. Peter says, "neither we nor our fathers were able to bear," but from the dominion of sin.

With respect to the teaching of this verse it has been often taken to be a categorical assertion of the Godhead of the Third Person: but the context will scarcely allow of this, for such an assertion here would be too abrupt: neither can it be taken to be an assertion of the spiritual nature of the Lord Himself, *i.e.*, of His Godhead. It must mean, I think, that the Lord in His Redeeming and Sanctifying work is the Spirit of all God's dispensations to this fallen world.

18. "But we all, with open face beholding as in a glass the glory of the Lord." "We all:" in the account in Exodus Moses alone received the revelation; now we all draw nigh to God as effectually as Moses did. There is no veil on our hearts to prevent us from receiving the full glory of the revelation of God.

"With open face," that is, with unveiled face. As long as Moses veiled his face, no glory from God shone from it upon the Israelites, but we all reflect the glory of God. Our faces as mirrors receive light from Christ, and reflect it as mirrors do. This is the translation of the Revisers, "We all with unveiled face reflecting as a mirror."

"Beholding the glory of the Lord, are changed into the same image from glory to glory." The contemplation of the image of the Son of God acts upon our moral and spiritual nature as the presence

the same image from glory to glory, *even* as ‖ by the Spirit
of the Lord.

‖ Or, *of the Lord the Spirit*.

of God did upon the face of Moses. It causes us to shine forth with some of His glory. The humblest Christian who looks constantly to Christ as his Redeemer and Exemplar and Source of Spiritual life, reflects in his own life something of the glory of Christ; and if he faithfully continue to do this he reflects it more and more, and goes from strength to strength. Are there any other words with which we may describe this process, and so make it clearer, and bring it within the reach of all? Yes. Christians looking thus to Christ and reflecting Him, " add to their faith virtue, and to their virtue knowledge, and to their knowledge temperance, and to their temperance patience, and to their patience godliness, and to their godliness brotherly kindness, and to their brotherly kindness charity." (2 Pet. i. 5, 6, 7.)

"Even as by the Spirit of the Lord" [even as from the Lord the Spirit]. The words in the original may have either of these meanings. As St. Paul has not yet mentioned the action of the Third Person in the Godhead, and as it is peculiarly His province to transform or regenerate the Christian, we should judge it best to understand it of the Holy Ghost.

CHAP. IV.

ᵃ ch. iii. 6.
ᵇ 1 Cor. vii. 25. 1 Tim. i. 13.

THEREFORE, seeing we have ᵃ this ministry, ᵇ as we have received mercy, we faint not;

1. "Therefore, seeing we have this ministry, as we have received mercy, we faint not." This ministry of the Spirit, this ministry whose prerogative it is to receive of the glory of God, and reflect it upon you, that ye may be changed into the same image of Christ—this ministry we have received through the mercy of God, as he says elsewhere, "For this cause I obtained mercy, that in me first Jesus Christ might show forth all long-suffering." (1 Tim. i. 16.)

"We faint not." Because we have received it through mercy we

CHAP. IV.] NOT WALKING IN CRAFTINESS. 339

2 But have renounced the hidden things of † dishonesty, not walking in craftiness, ^c nor handling the word of God deceitfully; but ^d by manifestation of the truth ^e commending ourselves to every man's conscience in the sight of God.

3 But if our gospel be hid, ^f it is hid to them that are lost:

† Gr. *shame.*
Rom. l. 16. &
vi. 21.
c ch. ii. 17.
1 Thess. ii. 3, 5.
d ch. vi. 4, 7.
& vii. 14.
e ch. v. 11.
f 1 Cor. i. 18.
ch. ii. 15.
2 Thess. ii. 10.

3. " That are lost "—rather " that are being lost."

faint not. Alford translates it, "We do not behave ourselves in a cowardly manner." As Waite explains it, "He does not fail in the courage which both the mercy and the ministry demand of him."

2. "But have renounced the hidden things of dishonesty, not walking," &c. He has continually before him the corruption of the word of God through false teachers. Thus in this Epistle ii. 17: "We are not as the many who corrupt (or deal deceitfully with) the word of God." These were probably the Judaizing teachers who put forward those passages in the Old Testament which seemed to favour their views of the permanency of Judaism as it had come down to them, and carefully kept in the background prophecies which speak of the New Covenant superseding the old.

"But by manifestation of the truth commending ourselves to every man's conscience." The truth of God is adapted to man's fallen nature, to raise him out of its corruption, and give him power and grace to live as becomes a true child of God. The manifestation of such truth commends itself to the conscience of each man, revealing to him his sin, and showing him at the same time the true remedy.

3. "But if our Gospel be hid [veiled], it is hid [veiled] to them that are (being) lost." Here he recurs to the image of the veil. If our Gospel be hidden under a veil so that men cannot look upon its brightness, and be changed thereby, it is because they are perishing or being lost. It is a mistranslation to render it, "that are lost," as if the fiat had gone forth from God that they were no longer to be accounted in a state of grace, that repentance henceforth would be impossible to them and, if possible to them, unavailing. It means rather "to them that are being lost,"—who are not repenting and using faithfully the means of grace.

4. "In whom the god of this world hath blinded the minds of

THE GOD OF THIS WORLD. [II. Cor.

^g John xii. 31. & xiv. 30. & xvi. 11.
Ephes. vi. 12.
^h Isai. vi. 10. John xii. 40. ch. iii. 14.
ⁱ ch. iii. 8, 9, 11, 18. ver. 6.
^k John i. 18. & xii. 45. & xiv. 9. Phil. ii. 6. Col. i. 15. Hebr. i. 3.
^l 1 Cor. i. 13, 23. & x. 33.

4 In whom ^g the god of this world ^h hath blinded the minds of them which believe not, lest ⁱ the light of the glorious gospel of Christ, ^k who is the image of God, should shine unto them.

5 ^l For we preach not ourselves, but Christ

---

4. "World." "Age," "æon."
5. "Christ Jesus." א, A., C., D., E., &c., read, "Jesus Christ;" B., H., K., L., most Cursives, as in Rec. Text.

them which believe not," &c. The god of this world hath blinded their minds because they were of this world, and so virtually chose to be under him rather than under Christ. The god of this world means properly the god of this æon, or this age, and may signify the whole period or æon from the fall to that time, or even to this present time.

"The minds of them which believe not" may mean either the minds of the unconverted Jews, or of the heathen who refused the Gospel when it was preached to them, or of those nominal Christians who refused to be sanctified by the truths of the Gospel which they professed to believe.

"Lest the light of the glorious gospel of Christ, who is the image of God," &c. So that men may have the light of the Gospel shining all around and directed full upon them, and yet be blinded, and blind themselves to it. They are like men in a dark cave or chamber, who resolutely keep out the light, and when they have begun to do this they are assisted by one far more powerful than themselves in their evil work of keeping themselves in darkness.

"Who is the image of God." Why is this introduced? I think for this reason: The face of Moses was illuminated because he had been in the presence of God, and so Christ reflects perfectly the glory of God, because He is "the express image of His Person," and "he who hath seen Him hath seen the Father."

5. "For we preach not ourselves, but Christ Jesus the Lord; and ourselves your servants," &c. "We preach not ourselves." There must have been some amongst the false teachers who preached themselves as if what *they* preached had power of itself to build men up in Christ. In answer to them the Apostle said, "We preach Christ crucified;" and again, "the Son of God, Christ Jesus, who was

CHAP. IV.] OURSELVES YOUR SERVANTS. 341

Jesus the Lord; and ᵐ ourselves your servants for Jesus' sake.

6 For God, ⁿ who commanded the light to shine

m 1 Cor. ix. 19. ch. i. 24.
n Gen. i. 3.

---

preached among you by us" (2 Cor. i. 19). What is it to preach Christ? It is to preach His Person, God and Man; His work—Redeeming, Sanctifying; His Relation to His Church as its Head, His Character as all Holy, and the Standard to which we are to be conformed. If St. Paul's Epistles set forth the preaching of Christ, then there can be no true preaching of Him without the setting forth of His Sacraments as means whereby His grace becomes ours. Altogether, the preaching of Christ is the preaching of the whole Christian system as in Him, rendered efficacious by His presence, and subservient to His glory.

" And ourselves your servants for Jesus' sake." Not your lords, but still less your servants in the sense of being appointed and controlled by you. We minister to you His word in our preaching, and His grace in the Sacraments we give in His Name. Calvin has an admirable remark: "Here, however, all pastors of the Church are admonished as to their state and condition, for by whatever title of honour they may be distinguished they are nothing more than the servants of believers, and unquestionably they cannot serve Christ without serving His Church at the same time. An honourable servitude, it is true, this is, and superior to any principality, but still it is a *servitude*, so that Christ alone may be elevated to distinction—not encumbered by the shadow of a single rival. Hence it is the part of a good pastor not merely to keep aloof from all desire of domineering, but to regard it as the highest pitch of honour at which he aspires, that he may serve the people of God. It is the duty of the people, on the other hand, to esteem the servants of Christ first of all, on the ground of the dignity of their Master, and then, further, on account of the dignity and excellence of their office, that they may not despise those whom the Lord hath placed in so illustrious a station."

6. "For God, who commanded the light to shine out of darkness, hath shined in our hearts," &c. Why must we preach Christ Jesus the Lord? Because God, the Father of lights, the original Creator of the visible light, is He Who hath shined into our hearts, to cause to exist there a more divine and life-giving light. This better and ever-enduring light is "the light of the knowledge of the glory of

out of darkness, † hath ° shined in our hearts, to *give* ᵖ the light of the knowledge of the glory of God in the face of Jesus Christ.

7 But we have this treasure in ᑫ earthen vessels, ʳ that the excellency of the power may be of God, and not of us.

8 *We are* ˢ troubled on every side, yet not distressed; *we are* perplexed, but ‖ not in despair;

† Gr. is he who hath.
° 2 Pet. i. 19.
ᵖ ver. 4. 1 Pet. ii. 9.
ᑫ ch. v. 1.
ʳ 1 Cor. ii. 5. ch. xii. 9.
ˢ ch. vii. 5.
‖ Or, *not altogether without help*, or, *means*.

God in the face of Jesus Christ." Here there seems to be a contrast between the face of Moses emitting an external light upon the faces of the children of Israel, and the face of Jesus Christ, Who, being looked upon by the eye of faith, causes the light of the knowledge of the glory of God, not to shed light upon the face, but to arise as the Sun of Righteousness in the heart itself.

Chrysostom remarks a difference between the external and the spiritual creation of light. "Howbeit *then*, He said, Let it be, and it was: but *now* He said nothing, but Himself became light for us. For he (the Apostle) said not hath also now commanded, but hath Himself shined. Therefore neither do we see sensible objects by the shining of this light, but God Himself through Christ."

All through this verse there is also a clear reminiscence of his own conversion, inasmuch as he had seen the face of Jesus Christ, and the sight of this had changed the darkness of his own light into the light of God through Christ.

7. "But we have this treasure in earthen vessels, that the excellency of the power may be of God," &c. There seems to be here a reference to the lights carried in pitchers by the men of Gideon, which diffused their light after they were broken, and not so much to the cheapness and vileness of the clay of the earthen vessel; and with this agrees what comes after, in which the Apostle speaks of the uncertain character of the outward circumstances of the Apostles, who were always on the point of extinction, and yet never extinguished.

8, 9. "We are troubled on every side, yet not distressed; we are perplexed . . . . not destroyed." There are some alterations suggested in the translation which emphasize the contrasts. Thus the Revisers have, "We are pressed on every side, yet not straitened."

CHAP. IV.]   DEATH IN US : LIFE IN YOU.   343

9 Persecuted, but not forsaken; ^t cast down, but not destroyed;

10 ^u Always bearing about in the body the dying of the Lord Jesus, ^x that the life also of Jesus might be made manifest in our body.

11 For we which live ^y are alway delivered unto death for Jesus' sake, that the life also of Jesus might be made manifest in our mortal flesh.

12 So then ^z death worketh in us, but life in you.

^t Ps. xxxvii. 24.
^u 1 Cor. xv. 31. ch. i. 5, 9. Gal. vi. 17. Phil. iii. 10.
^x Rom. viii. 17. 2 Tim. ii. 11, 12. 1 Pet. iv. 13.
^y Ps. xliv. 22. Rom. viii. 36.
1 Cor. xv. 31, 49.
^z ch. xiii. 9.

The way in which our adversaries press upon us and environ us, seems in no way to take from the power of our words. We utter freely what we desire.

"Perplexed, yet not in despair." We know not sometimes whither we are to turn to be extricated from our difficulties, but we are quite sure, from past experience, that a door will be opened.

"Persecuted (or pursued), yet not forsaken"—when in the dungeon we sang at midnight hymns to God. Some translate it, "pursued, yet not abandoned."

"Cast down, but not destroyed." Cast down in soul, yet not destroyed. "Patience," as he says elsewhere, "worketh experience, and experience hope" (Rom. v. 4). "My grace is sufficient for thee, for my strength is made perfect in weakness" (xii. 9).

10. "Always bearing about in the body the dying of the Lord Jesus," &c. "And what is the dying of the Lord Jesus, which they bare about? Their daily deaths, by which also the Resurrection was shewed. 'For if any believe not,' says he, 'that Jesus died and rose again, beholding us every day die and rise again, let him believe henceforward in the Resurrection.' Seest thou how he has discovered yet another reason for the temptations?

"What, then, is this reason? That His life also might be manifested in our body. He says, 'by snatching us out of the perils.' So that this, which seems a mark of weakness and destitution, this [I say] proclaims His Resurrection. For His power had not so appeared in our suffering no unpleasantness, as it is now shown, in our suffering indeed, but without being overcome." (Chrysostom.)

12. "So then death worketh in us, but life in you." These forms of a living death, in which we exist, are your salvation. They work

13 We having ^a the same spirit of faith, according as it is written, ^b I believed, and therefore have I spoken; we also believe, and therefore speak;

14 Knowing that ^c he which raised up the Lord Jesus shall raise up us also by Jesus, and shall present *us* with you.

15 For ^d all things *are* for your sakes, that ^e the abundant grace might through the thanksgiving of many redound to the glory of God.

^a Rom. i. 12.
2 Pet. i. 1.
^b Ps. cxvi. 10.
^c Rom. viii. 11.
1 Cor. vi. 14.
^d 1 Cor. iii. 21.
ch. i. 6. Col.
i. 24. 2 Tim.
ii. 10.
^e ch. i. 11. &
viii. 19. & ix.
11, 12.

---

life in you, because God has ordained them to be the channels by which you live to God, according to the saying, "The Blood of the martyrs is the seed of the Church."

13. "We having the same spirit of faith, according as it is written, I believed, and therefore," &c. St. Paul quotes this as an axiom of universal truth, that what a man of any truthfulness believes, that he speaks, and this is particularly so in the matter of any revelations he may have received from God. Thus, "my heart was hot within me, and while I was thus musing, the fire kindled, and at the last I spake with my tongue." This is the characteristic of the spirit of faith, it forces the man to utter what he believes.

14. "Knowing that he which raised up the Lord Jesus," &c. Now the truth which burnt in the very bones of the Apostle, and made him as a man on fire, was the Resurrection of Jesus, and our resurrection in and with Him; and not only so, but the fact that God had raised up Jesus, not as a solitary man, but as the Head of a great redeemed race, as the Head of a great mystical body, in which were first the Apostles, and then their converts who endured to the end.

15. "For all things are for your sakes, that the abundant grace," &c. To enter fully into the meaning of the Apostle here we must have something of his mind respecting the importance of Eucharistia—of praise and thanksgiving. The lifting up of the spirits and souls of men to God in thanksgiving was in one sense the most important thing which they could do. It was the acknowledgement by all within them of God—His goodness, His love, and His power, put forth on their behalf. And so it was the purpose for which the abundant grace was given. What, humanly speaking, is the rain given for, but to call forth the fruits of the earth; and

16 For which cause we faint not; but though our outward man perish, yet ^f the inward *man* is renewed day by day.

^f Rom. vii. 22. Ephes. iii. 16. Col. iii. 10. 1 Pet. iii. 4.

what is the abundant grace given for, but that the many might be thankful, and show forth God's praise, not only with their lips, but in their lives. The greatest glory of God is the return which answers to His Grace, consisting first of all in the thankfulness and gratitude which cause the heart to overflow towards God as the Personal Giver of good. Thankfulness is acknowledgment to a person. It cannot be given to a thing. It must be accorded to a good and holy being.

The word that the Apostle uses for thanksgiving is "Eucharistia," from which the name of "Eucharist," as applied to the Blessed Sacrament, is derived. Now when he uses such words as "the thanksgiving" (eucharistia) of the many, does he think of the Eucharist? We answer, How can he exclude it from his thoughts? The Eucharist, or Holy Communion, was in his view a solemn commemoration of the Death of Christ, and a setting forth of His Death till He came again. The Apostle most certainly believed with all his heart and soul that all blessings came wholly through the Death of Christ, and would consider that the closer we associate all our graces and blessings with that Death the better; and assuredly, to say the least, the Apostle would hold that the Eucharist afforded to believing Christians the closest connection possible of these thanksgivings and prayers with the Body and Blood of the Lord.

16. "For which cause we faint not; but though our outward man perish," &c. "For this cause "—that is, because of the Resurrection of the Lord by the Father, and our interest in that Resurrection.

"Though our outward man perish," through such afflictions and distresses as he had recounted in verses 7, 8, 9, 10.

"Yet the inward man is renewed day by day." The distresses by which the outward man was on the point of perishing were so blessed by God that they were made means of union with the sufferings of Christ, and so, whilst there was outward decay, there was inward renewal.

17. "For our light affliction, which is but for a moment, worketh for us," &c. The Apostle had spoken of the affliction in such terms as "troubled" or "hemmed in on every side," "perplexed," "per-

17 For ^g our light affliction, which is but for a moment, worketh for us a far more exceeding *and* eternal weight of glory;

18 ^h While we look not at the things which are seen, but at the things which are not seen: for

^g Matt. v. 12. Rom. viii. 18. 1 Pet. i. 6. & v. 10.
^h Rom. viii. 24. ch. v. 7. Hebr. xi. 1.

---

17. "Our light affliction." "Our" omitted by B. and Syriac; retained by ℵ, D., E., F., G., K., L., P.

secuted," "cast down," "always bearing about in the body the dying of the Lord Jesus." Now he calls this affliction light in comparison with the weight of glory, which under God's grace it was the means of procuring for us.

"A far more exceeding and eternal weight of glory." "He sets side by side the things present with the things to come, the momentary with the eternal, the light with the weighty, the affliction with the glory. And neither is he content with this, but he addeth another expression doubling it, and saying in excess and unto excess (καθ' ὑπερβολὴν εἰς ὑπερβολὴν)." (Chrysostom.)

"Weight of glory." As if the contemplation of it was what one might call oppressive—the mind not able fully to sustain the continued thought of it. "O world to come in exchange for the present! O eternity for a moment! O everlasting rest for a transitory labour! O eternal communion in the holy, blessed, and eternal life of God, for the sacrifice of a criminal, miserable, and corruptible life here on earth! Whoever sets no value on this seed of a blessed eternity knows not what it comprehends." (Quesnel.)

18. "While we look not at the things which are seen, but at the things which," &c. We look not at (*non contemplantibus*), we regard not the things of the present life. For if they are good, their good is not lasting; and while it lasts, it is dangerous to our faith and hope. And if they are evil, their evil may be turned into good; and the evil itself, though entailing pain and distress, passes away.

"At the things which are not seen." "We endure as seeing Him Who is invisible. We look for a city which hath foundations. We esteem the reproach of Christ better than the treasures of Egypt, for we have respect unto the recompense of the reward."

"The things seen are temporal"—no matter what it is which the fleshly eye looks upon, whether good or evil, it will pass away.

"But the things which are not seen," but which the eye of faith

the things which are seen *are* temporal; but the things which are not seen *are* eternal.

---

sees, are eternal. The ever Blessed Trinity, the Holy Angels, the Incorruptible Body, the crown of righteousness—these the eye of flesh cannot see, and these are eternal.

"O God, the Protector of all that trust in Thee, without Whom nothing is strong, nothing is holy, increase and multiply upon us Thy mercy, that Thou being our Ruler and Guide, we may so pass through things temporal that we finally lose not the things eternal."

CHAP. V.

FOR we know that if ᵃour earthly house of *this* tabernacle were dissolved, we have a building

ᵃ Job iv. 19.
ch. iv. 7.
2 Pet. i. 13, 14.

1. "For we know that if our earthly house of this tabernacle were dissolved, we have," &c. "We know." Notice the Apostolic certainty. He writes as one who knew and believed that there was not only a resurrection body, but one prepared for him. On what grounds did he know this? On two grounds. First, on the ground of the Resurrection of the Lord; on that was based the truth of the doctrine. But he knew that he had a part in the sufferings here—for now in this life he could say, "Always bearing about in the body the dying of the Lord Jesus, that the life also of Jesus might be made manifest in our mortal body." If he suffered now with Jesus, he knew that the Lord would not in death and in eternity desert His fellow-sufferer.

"If our earthly house of this tabernacle were dissolved." He calls the present body a tabernacle or tent; but inasmuch as it has an inhabitant, which is the soul, it is a tabernacle and a house—a tabernacle, that is, a tent which may be at any time taken to pieces, and yet a house or dwelling, because it is a shelter for the soul for a period.

"Be dissolved"—*i.e.*, broken up as a tent is. He scarcely

of God, an house not made with hands, eternal in the heavens.

^b Rom. viii. 23.

2 For in this ^b we groan, earnestly desiring to be clothed upon with our house which is from heaven:

---

alludes to what we call the dissolution of the body in the earth, but to the taking down for removal of the goats'-hair tents with which he was so familiar.

"We have a building of God, an house not made with hands." Our present earthly frames are buildings of God; but compared with that body that shall be, they, though fearfully and wonderfully made, are as nothing. In the building of the future glorified and spiritual body God will put forth infinitely more power, for it will be a body with the functions and endowments of a spirit. Its very mode of existence exceeds all our present faculties of comprehension.

It will be "a house not made with hands," not made by human or even by angelic hands—but it will be of (ἐκ) God, proceeding directly from Him. In the term, however, "not made with hands," he alludes to the future body as the house or resting-place of the soul or spirit, for all our houses or resting-places are made with hands. Compare "He looked for a city which hath foundations, whose builder and maker is God" (Heb. xi. 10).

"Eternal in the heavens." This probably means that it is to be for ever incorruptible in the heaven of heavens; but some have suggested that it is being prepared by God now, to be fitted to the souls at the time of the Lord's appearance; but this seems contrary to the identity of the resurrection body with the suffering one. It seems contrary to St. Paul's words, "He shall change our vile body that it may be fashioned like unto his glorious body" (Phil. iii. 21).

2. "For in this we groan." The expression of this groaning we have in Rom. vii. 24, "O wretched man that I am, who shall deliver me from the body of this death?" And the external side of it in the last chapter, "We are troubled on every side," &c.; and in the next chap. (vi. 4), "In much patience, in afflictions, in necessities;" and in xi. 23-28.

"Earnestly desiring to be clothed upon with our house," &c.

3 If so be that ᶜbeing clothed we shall not be found naked.   ᶜ Rev. iii. 18. & xvi. 15.

4 For we that are in *this* tabernacle do groan, being burdened: not for that we would be unclothed, but ᵈclothed upon, that mortality might be swallowed up of life.   ᵈ 1 Cor. xv. 53, 54.

The expression of the same desire in different words is to be found in Rom. viii. 23: "We ourselves groan within ourselves, waiting for the adoption, to wit, the redemption of our bodies." The Apostle, however, has at the present his mind full of the idea of a tent or tabernacle, easily taken down, and so he uses words which rather imply a dwelling, "Our house is from heaven," *i.e.* from God, not from the earth, not a house of clay, but from being corruptible we shall put on incorruption.

3. "If so be that being clothed we shall not be found naked." There is considerable difference amongst expositors as to what is alluded to by the term "naked." Stanley supposes that the Apostle considers the state of a bodiless soul as one of nakedness, derived from the heathen ideas of spirits in Hades, and he instances the legend of a woman appearing to her husband after death, intreating him to burn dresses for her as a covering for her disembodied spirit; the root-conception of the Apostle being that the new glorified body will be a covering for the soul: but Wesley, Cornelius à Lapide, and others, understand "naked" in the sense of not being clothed with grace and good works; as the Lord casts out the servant who had a place at the feast, but had not on the wedding garment. The word naked is in Rev. iii. 17, 18, and xvi. 15, used to denote the absence of spiritual grace.

4. "For we that are in this tabernacle do groan, being burdened." Blunt quotes, as a most apposite illustration, the words of the book of Wisdom: "For the corruptible body presseth down the soul, and the earthly tabernacle weigheth down the mind that runneth upon many things" (Wisdom ix. 15).

"Not for that we would be unclothed, but clothed upon." This seems to mean that we desire not to be disembodied spirits in the intermediate state, but to be raised up in the likeness of the glorious Body of our Lord. What God promised, that His servant Paul desired. His desires were not that he should be a mere spirit, even though in

5 Now ᵉ he that hath wrought us for the selfsame thing is God, who also ᶠ hath given unto us the earnest of the Spirit.

6 Therefore *we are* always confident, knowing that, whilst we are at home in the body, we are absent from the Lord :

7 (For ᵍ we walk by faith, not by sight :)

ᵉ Isai. xxix. 23. Ephes. ii. 10.
ᶠ Rom. viii. 23. ch. i. 22. Ephes. i. 14. & iv. 30.
ᵍ Rom. viii. 24, 25. 1 Cor. xiii. 12. ch. iv. 18. Hebr. xi. 1.

---

heaven, but that his body should be like that of the Lord when He appeared.

5. "Now he that hath wrought us for the self same thing is God," &c. "He that hath wrought us"—He Who hath worked for us, and upon us, and in us for this self-same thing, viz., the redemption of our bodies. All the work of God in the world and in the Church, the Incarnation, Death, and Resurrection of the Eternal Son, all the work of God upon our own souls in our Conversion, Regeneration, Justification, Sanctification, Discipline, Comfort; all the grace of Sacraments, the Burial, and Resurrection with Christ in the one, the feeding on His Body and Blood in the other—all are for this selfsame thing, and a pledge of its certainty. He hath given to us the pledge of the Spirit. This pledge being the indwelling of a Person of the Trinity cannot but be a pledge of the highest blessing which God can bestow on His creature.

6. "Therefore we are always confident, knowing that, whilst we are at home," &c. Confident, or rather bold, of good courage; because of what God so far has wrought us to be, and because He hath also given to us the pledge or earnest of the Spirit that He will give us yet more glorious things. "Always thus being confident, or of good courage, knowing that whilst we are at home," &c. As long as we sojourn here we are strangers and pilgrims, absent from our true home, and from Him Who presides over it.

7. "For we walk by faith, not by sight." A reminiscence of what he had said in iv. 18, "Whilst we look not at the things which are seen, but at the things which are not seen." Sight here does not mean the faculty of seeing, but the things or appearances which are seen.

8. "We are confident, I say, and willing rather to be absent

PRESENT WITH THE LORD.

8 We are confident, *I say*, and ʰ willing rather to be absent from the body, and to be present with the Lord.

ʰ Phil. i. 23.

9 Wherefore we ‖ labour, that, whether present or absent, we may be accepted of him.

‖ Or, *endeavour*.

10 ⁱ For we must all appear before the judgment seat of Christ; ᵏ that every one may receive

ⁱ Matt. xxv. 31, 32. Rom. xiv. 10.
ᵏ Rom. ii. 6. Gal. vi. 7. Ephes. vi. 8. Col. iii. 24, 25. Rev. xxii. 12.

10. "Appear." Rather, "be made manifest."

from the body," &c. Does this mean that he desires to be in the unseen state when he will not yet be clothed upon with his house which is from heaven? Yes, because when he departs this life, his sufferings will be at an end, and he will be no longer liable to fall, and there will be imparted to him and those with him some visible Presence of the Lord which has not yet been vouchsafed to men. He will be in the state in which he was caught up out of the body into Paradise, and heard the unspeakable words (xii. 1-8).

9. "Wherefore we labour, that, whether present or absent, we may be accepted," &c. We labour, rather "we are ambitious," a stronger word than labour, implying not only the labours of the body, but the eagerness and earnest desire of the mind.

"That whether present or absent." Present, of course, means in the body, but must we infer that if absent, *i.e.* unclothed with our mortal frames, we must yet be ambitious to be acceptable to the Lord? Yes, the angels are ambitious, and do their best with all their powers to serve their king. The unseen state is not one of mere quietude or repose, but it is one in which beings who are formed for active service will be active and zealous in that service.

10. "For we must all appear before the judgment seat of Christ," &c. This word "appear" should rather be reckoned "be made manifest." All our thoughts, words, and works will then be plainly declared, so that it may be seen that God, in apportioning to us our eternal rewards, deals with us in absolute justice; so we have in 1 Cor. iv. 5: "Until the Lord come who both will bring to light the hidden things of darkness, and will make manifest the counsels of the hearts."

Observe that the Apostles will be judged as well as others. In the face of this how can men have the hardihood to say that the things *done* in *his* body, according to that he hath done, whether *it be* good or bad.

---

believers are in a sphere above judgment. Wesley has a very suggestive note: "*Must appear*—openly, without covering, where all things will be revealed, probably the sins even of the faithful, which were forgiven long before. For many of their good works (as their repentance, their revenge against sin) cannot otherwise appear."

"The things done in his body," literally, "through the body," the body being the instrument of the Spirit wherein the will dwells. If the flesh be subdued to the Spirit, then the works done are holy and righteous, but if the man lives after the flesh then the works of the flesh are manifest in him. (Gal. vi. 8.) He sows to the flesh and of the flesh reaps corruption.[1]

The question arises, how is such a truth to be reconciled with that other truth, that men are saved by grace through faith? Perfectly so; there need not be a moment's hesitation (I was almost going to write a moment's thought) about it if we remember that men are answerable for grace, and that some men receive God's grace, and continue in it and improve it, and that others fall from it. Every single thing in which men differ from one another is owing to God's particular providence and bounty (1 Cor. iv. 7.) The Lord lays this down as an universal truth, "Unto whomsoever much is given, of him shall be much required." (Luke xii. 48.) Supposing, then, that any two men have the same religious privileges, and one of them repents and turns to God, or is converted under them, and the other is not, the latter has to answer for the rejection, but the former is not raised into a state in which he is

---

[1] Dean Plumptre has an admirable note. "'*That every one may receive the things done in his body.*'—It would have seemed almost impossible, but for the perverse ingenuity of the system-mongers of Theology, to evade the force of this unqualified assertion of the working of the universal law of Retribution. No formula of justification by faith, or imputed righteousness, or pardon sealed in the blood of Christ, or priestly absolution, is permitted by St. Paul to mingle with his expectations of that great day as revealing the secrets of men's hearts, awarding to each man according to his works. 'Whatsoever a man soweth, that shall he also reap' (Gal. vi. 7), was to him an eternal unchanging law. The Revelation of all that had been secret, for good or evil; the perfectly equitable measurement of each element of good or evil; the apportionment to each of that which, according to this measurement, each one deserves for the good and evil which he has done, that is the sum and substance of St. Paul's eschatology here and in 1 Cor. iv. 5."

11 Knowing therefore ¹ the terror of the Lord, we persuade men; but ᵐ we are made manifest unto God; and I trust also are made manifest in your consciences.

¹ Job xxxi. 23. Hebr. x. 31. Jude 23.
ᵐ ch. iv. 2.

above accountability: quite the contrary. No mistake has been more terrible in its consequences to the Church of Christ than the idea that grace, no matter what form it takes—Converting, Regenerating, Sanctifying, Sacramental, Enlightening—raises men above the necessity of fearing God, above the necessity of making their calling and election sure, above the necessity of patiently continuing in well-doing, and of working out their salvation with fear and trembling. Is a man forgiven? He is forgiven for this purpose, that he should sin no more. Is a man enlightened? It is that he should walk in the light. Is a man baptized? It is that he should walk in newness of life. Does a man receive the Eucharist? It is that Christ may evermore dwell in that man, and he in Him. A man received into any degree of God's grace should see to it that he has written in his heart the axiom with which the next chapter begins, "We then, as workers together with him, beseech you also that ye receive not the grace of God in vain."

11. "Knowing therefore the terror of the Lord, we persuade men." This should rather be rendered "the fear of the Lord," and yet every faithful minister is bound to re-echo the words of his Master, "I say unto you my friends (not my enemies, but my friends) be not afraid of them which kill the body . . . . but rather fear Him who after he hath killed hath power to cast into hell." (Luke xii. 4.)

"But we are made manifest unto God; and I trust also are made manifest," &c. "We are made manifest unto God." God who knows the hearts, knows the sincerity of our life and ministry. This seems said with reference to the manifestation before the judgment-seat of Christ. 'Before our manifestation at that great day we trust to be manifest as sincere in the eyes of God, who trieth the hearts, and also to you in your consciences.' Notice his anxiety in the matter of his standing perfectly right in the sight of his fellow-men. He loved these Corinthians with more than a father's love, and it cut him to the heart to think that they had any doubts about his perfect honesty of dealing, and besides this he knew well that if they distrusted him who had come with such

WE COMMEND NOT OURSELVES. [II. Cor.

12 For ⁿ we commend not ourselves again unto you, but give you occasion ᵒ to glory on our behalf, that ye may have somewhat to *answer* them which glory † in appearance, and not in heart.

n ch. iii. 1.
o ch. i. 14.
† Gr. *in the face.*

13 For ᵖ whether we be beside ourselves, *it is* to God: or whether we be sober, *it is* for your cause.

p ch. xi. 1, 16, 17. & xii. 6, 11.

---

12. "For we commend not." "For" omitted by אֲ, B., C., D., F., G., 10, 39, 67, 139, d, e, f, g, Vulg., Goth., Syriac, Cop., Arm.; retained by E., K., L., most Cursives.

"On our behalf." So C., D., E., F., G., K., L., P., most Cursives; but א, B., 17, read, "your."

---

credentials from Christ, their hearts were not perfectly right with Him Who had sent him, so that it was a matter of anxiety with him, not only on his own, but on their account, that his ministry should in all respects be commended to their consciences.

12. "For we commend not ourselves again unto you, but give you occasion to glory on our behalf," &c. He here excuses himself for having seemed to commend himself. "We do not thus defend or commend ourselves simply on our own account, but in order that you may be able to speak boldly in answer to those who glory in appearance." See how he assumes that they—the body of them—are with him, and only want to know what answer to give, which will shut the mouths of these gainsayers.

What does he mean by "those which glory in appearance only"? Some suppose that he refers to those who judged of him by his personal defects (his bodily presence is weak and his speech contemptible); others, to the fact that he carried with him no letters of commendation; perhaps, however, he alluded to false assumption of spirituality on the part of his adversaries, to their display of eloquence rather than plain speaking, to their appearance of zeal (compare Gal. iv. 17, "They zealously affect you, but not well"), and other tricks to which false teachers resort.

13. "For whether we be beside ourselves, it is to God: or whether we be sober," &c. "We be beside ourselves." Some suppose that in this there is an allusion made to his preaching of such mysteries as the Resurrection, which made Festus exclaim, "Thou art beside thyself:" others quote the words, "I thank God I speak with more tongues than ye all," as implying that he constantly used these unknown tongues in the face of the congregation as the only speech

THE LOVE OF CHRIST.

14 For the love of Christ constraineth us; because we

fitted to express his internal ecstacy of feeling; but this would have been contrary to his own advice (1 Cor. xiv. 19), and would have been unworthy of him.

May we not explain it of the vehemence with which he asserted and defended the truths which he held? Cold, semi-believing, worldly men, hearing a man speak with uncontrollable emotion of such things as Christians being one body in Christ, their very members members of His body, of the extreme impropriety of women being unveiled in Church, of men who partake of the Eucharist unworthily as eating and drinking their own damnation, of there being a spiritual body as well as a natural—unsympathizing, half-believing men, I say, hearing him speak as if he was on fire about such things, would say of him as those like them said of his great Master, "He hath a devil, and is mad, why hear ye him?" (John x. 20).

"It is to God." It is in the cause of His truth. It is that men should be subdued to the faith of His Gospel. In His cause we cannot be lukewarm.

"Or whether we be sober, it is for your cause." This "sobriety," or soundness of mind, may have been alleged against him by his enemies, because of his worldly wisdom—he made himself, at times, all things to all men, that he might by all means save some (1 Cor. ix. 22). He would be thus sober minded, when, as he describes in the next chapter, he gave no offence in anything, that his ministry might not be blamed, but in all things approved himself as a minister of God.

But it may be simply the opposite of that vehemence and fervour, and perhaps, at times, undue gesticulation, which had made them call him mad. If he, at times, spoke very calmly and with logical argument rather than warmth, it was for their sakes. Sometimes the minister must show vehemence, sometimes mildness and placidity, according as befits the state of mind of those listening to him.

14. "For the love of Christ constraineth us; because we thus judge," &c. What is the love of Christ here? Is it Christ's love to us, or our love to Christ? Undoubtedly the former; for if ever Christ's love in us constrains us to do that which pleases Him, it is because we love Him because He first loved us.

| q Rom. v. 15. | thus judge, that q if one died for all, then were all dead: |

| r Rom. vi. 11, 12. & xiv. 7, 8. 1 Cor. 6, 19. Gal. ii. 20. 1 Thess. v. 10. 1 Pet. iv. 2. | 15 And *that* he died for all, r that they which live should not henceforth live unto themselves, but unto him which died for them and rose again. |

---

14. "Then were all dead." "Therefore all died," Revisers.

"Constraineth us." To what? "To labour that, whether present or absent, we may be accepted of him" (verse 9). To endeavour to persuade men—to be made manifest to the conscience of all true believers—to be at times as if beside ourselves in showing energy and zeal.

"Constrains us," hems us in, so that we cannot turn to the right hand or to the left, but must go straight forward in the Lord's battle.

"Judging thus." Having come to this judgment or determination "that if one died for all, then were all dead."

This has been rendered in two or three ways. "Then were all dead," *i.e.*, under sentence of death—under the dominion of death; or "then were all dead," *i.e.*, in trespasses and sins—or rather, perhaps, as by Revisers, "therefore all died." There can be no doubt that this last is more in accordance with the Greek and with the context; for the Apostle is speaking of Christ as dying in the place of all—as their atonement, as their sponsor, in their place. When He died, all died in Him; and when He rose again all rose in Him. Compare Rom. xiv. 9, "To this end Christ both died, and rose, and revived, that he might be Lord both of the dead and living."

15. "And that he died for all, that they which live should not henceforth live unto themselves," &c. His death was an atonement for the sins of the whole world; not for a certain number who accept that atonement, but for the whole world.

It was His purpose in dying for all mankind to save all. His atonement was sufficient for the sins of all, and His will in making the atonement was one with that of His Father, "Who will have all men to be saved, and to come unto the knowledge of the truth" (1 Tim. ii. 4). But in making man in His own image, God permitted him to have a will of his own, which must be, on

16 ˢWherefore henceforth know we no man after the flesh: yea, though we have known Christ after the flesh, ᵗyet now henceforth know we *him* no more.

ˢ Matt. xii. 50, John xv. 14.
Gal. v. 6.
Phil. iii. 7, 8.
Col. iii. 11.
ᵗ John vi. 63.

man's part, voluntarily conformed to the Divine Will, and because of this freedom of will, men are not all saved; that is, so far as we can see, they do not all repent and believe, and become holy, even though God desires them to be so. Apparently He cannot make them holy and good absolutely in spite of themselves; but He works upon them and bears with them and forbears to the utmost that the freedom of will, which He must respect, will allow. He must be served freely—it is contrary to His glory and to the order of the universe that He should be served by puppets; and if men are not to be puppets this freedom of will must be respected, even to their own extreme loss.

"Live not unto themselves, but unto him which died for them, and rose again." In requiring them, because He died for them, to live not to themselves, but to Him Who died for them and rose again, He requires them to imitate His conduct towards themselves. He lived not for Himself, but for them, He died for them, He pleased not Himself, but did all to please His Father in carrying out His designs of love for mankind. Henceforth He requires men, through the lips of such deniers of self as the Apostles, to live to Him Who died for them, and rose again for them. If He requires them to live to Him for His own sake He has a right to demand it, but He requires them to live to Him in order that they may attain to the greatest height of perfection of which a creature is capable.

It has been asked whether we can consider that He rose again for us in the same sense as He died. Yes surely; He died not only in our place as our surety, but for our benefit. He died as the Second Adam, that as all die in Him, so should all rise again in Him. There is, of course, a difference: He died to make atonement for all, He rose again to impart His Life to all if they will accept it.

Thus the love of Christ constrained the Apostle—may the same love constrain us.

16. "Wherefore henceforth know we no man after the flesh," &c. To know a man after the flesh has been explained as knowing him

358   THE NEW CREATION.   [II. COR.

u Rom. viii. 9.
& xvi. 7.
Gal. vi. 15.

|| Or, *let him be.*

17 Therefore if any man ᵘ *be* in Christ, || *he is*

---

17. "If any man *be* in Christ, *he is* a new creature." "Si qua in Christo nova creatura," Vulg.

as belonging to an earthly nation, or an earthly family, or as having a certain worldly station: but may it not rather allude to the great divisions of Jew and Gentile, into which God had divided mankind? This only, I think, will account for the Apostle putting in the words, "Yea, though we have known Christ after the flesh." We know in Christ neither Jew nor Gentile—all are one in Him: neither do we know Him as belonging to a particular race, for we know Him now only as the Second Man, the Head of the race, and of a Church redeemed out of all nations and tongues. St. Paul here, no doubt, alludes to those Judaizers who boasted of Christ as a Jew, and would have all men become Jews as He was when He lived upon earth. But the Apostle meets this with the truth that Christ is raised to a sphere in which He is infinitely above such distinctions of the flesh, for He is now the quickening Spirit of the race.

17. "Therefore if any man be in Christ, he is a new creature: old things," &c. Before considering the meaning of this most important verse it will be necessary to look to its proper translation. In our authorized, and by most modern expositors, it is divided into two sentences in a most arbitrary way, and a stop (comma), and words to which nothing answers in the original are inserted to complete each sentence. The words of the original, exactly in the order in which they stand, without addition or punctuation, are "So that if any in Christ new ktisis (order of things, dispensation, &c.) the ancient things (not old things) are passed away," &c.

The only words wanted to complete the English sense would be "there be "—" So that, if *there be* any new creation in Christ, ancient things are passed away." Now this is the rendering of the oldest translation, the Vulgate, and if thus construed as one sentence it is entirely in accordance with the context. For the Apostle had been speaking of Christ dying for all (verse 14) as the Second Adam, the New Man: and then he had been speaking of "knowing no one after the flesh," *i.e.*, no one had, owing to his birth, a greater claim on Christ than another; and even as regards Christ Himself He must henceforth be considered as belonging to the whole world, not to

CHAP. V.]   ALL THINGS ARE BECOME NEW.   359

ˣ a new creature: ʸ old things are passed away; behold, all things are become new.

ˣ Gal. v. 6. & vi. 15.
ʸ Is. xliii. 18, 19. & lxv. 17. Eph. ii. 15. Rev. xxi. 5.

---

17. "All things." So E., K., L., P., most Cursives, Goth., Arm.; but א, B., C., D., F., G., d, e, f, g, Vulg. (Cod. Amiat.), Cop., omit "all things." "They are become new."

any section of it. In Him there was neither Jew nor Greek, &c. And now, strictly following up this line of thought, he proceeds, "so if that there be any new Creation (*i.e.*, new order of things—new access to God) in Christ—the ancient things, the ancient mode of access, the ancient law of ordinance, the ancient ministry, the ancient standing in Abraham or Moses, are all passed away." "For behold," saith Chrysostom, "a new soul (for it was cleansed), and a new body, and new worship, and promises new, and covenant, and life, and table, and dress, and all things new absolutely. For instead of the Jerusalem below, we have received that mother city which is above; and instead of a material temple, have seen a spiritual temple; instead of tables of stone, fleshy ones; instead of Circumcision, Baptism; instead of the manna, the Lord's Body; instead of water from a rock, Blood from His Side; instead of Moses' rod, the Cross; instead of the promised land, the kingdom of heaven; instead of a thousand priests, one High Priest; instead of a Lamb without reason, a Spiritual Lamb; with these and such like things in His thoughts He said, All things are new."

I have no doubt that this is the true idea. He is not speaking so much of the new state of the soul as of its new surroundings as it were. It is in a new kingdom. It has new and better grace, altogether different from that of the Old Covenant. It has a new standing, and that in Christ. It has new nourishment, even His Body and Blood. There is a New Scripture, a new ministry of reconciliation, new powers of serving God through the New Birth, and a new hope.

But let the reader remember that though this is, I believe, the true meaning of the Greek words as they stand, yet the way of taking them as two sentences yields a perfectly true meaning. For if any man be in Christ, *i.e.*, savingly, and really, and permanently, such a man is a new creature. He has new hopes, new desires, new affections, he has a new conflict within, and new strength to aid him in maintaining it. And this is true, whether we

> x Rom. v. 10.
> Eph. ii. 16.
> Col. i. 20.
> 1 John ii. 2.
> & iv. 10.

18 And all things *are* of God, ᶻ who hath re-

look upon him as brought into Christ once for all in baptism, or as reinstated in Him by a true and hearty repentance, or a genuine conversion.

No matter how we look upon his entrance into Christ, if he be a branch of the vine, the Divine Husbandman will come round to see if there be fruit in him. If he bears fruit then he is in the condition which is usually supposed to be meant by the words "new creature." If any man be truly in Christ, he is a new creature, that is, a real Christian.

Calvin and others understand the first part of the verse as if it should be rendered "let him be a new creature." Calvin's paraphraze is, "If any one is desirous to hold some place in Christ, that is, in the Kingdom of Christ, let him be a new creature. By this expression he condemns every kind of excellence that is wont to be in much esteem among men, if renovation of heart be wanting. Learning, it is true, and eloquence, and other endowments, are valuable and worthy to be honoured, but when the fear of the Lord and an upright conscience are wanting, all the honour of them goes for nothing."

But it is clear that to the words of the original we have no more right to add "Let him be," than " he is."

"Old things are passed away; behold, all things are become new." The word for old, archaios, rather signifies ancient. The old thing which we have to put away, the old man, or Adam, is palaios. As long as the old Adam is yet allowed to exist in the Christian it cannot be said strictly that old things *are* passed away, though it can be said with the utmost strictness that the ancient things, the things of the ancient economy, have entirely passed away. The whole of this Epistle is written to those in Christ, and yet almost every line of it implies that much of the old man lingers in the greater part of them, and St. Paul writes to the Ephesians, who, as a Church, seem to have been in a higher spiritual state than the Corinthians, that even they should put off the old man, be renewed in the spirit of their minds, and put on the new. (Ephes. iv. 22.)

18. "And all things are of God, who hath reconciled us to himself," &c. All things, *i.e.*, all these new things, whether external

RECONCILIATION.

conciled us to himself by Jesus Christ, and hath given to us the ministry of reconciliation :

---

18. "Jesus Christ." ℵ, B., C., D., F., G., P., It., Vulg., Syr., Copt., omit "Jesus;" but E., K., L., and most Cursives, retain.

things, such as new means of grace, a new ministry, a new mystical body; or internal, as a new heart, a new spirit, a cleansed conscience, a renewed will, are of God as directly as the things of the old economy, but in a much more gracious and glorious way, being through the Incarnation and Mediation of Jesus Christ.

It has been made a question whether God has reconciled Himself to us, or whether we are reconciled to Him by His enabling us, once enemies, to love Him and willingly obey Him. But a little thought will show us that the two are at the root the same: for God must have looked with extreme displeasure at man's sin, and yet with extreme love on the race of men if He gave His Son to die for them. So that even when He was angry in one sense, He was reconciled in another; for if one man desires to do another, who is his enemy, the greatest conceivable benefit, he must be really and in heart reconciled to him, though he may require the man, for his own sake, to endure some discipline. And with respect to our being reconciled in heart and feeling towards God, the very atonement itself, unless it brings this about, will, as far as we can see, stop short of benefiting us in the way in which we most require benefit : for alienation of heart from God is the root-evil of all, and if this be removed we are on the side of God and are His true children.

"And hath given to us the ministry of reconciliation." It seems to be called the ministry of reconciliation, as distinguished from the word of reconciliation, because in its exercise the minister ministers to the sinner more than mere words. 1. He ministers the word, *i.e.*, the preached word of repentance and faith. Then (2) the Sacrament of Baptism by which sinners are grafted into the Mystical Body. Then (3) the Body and Blood of Christ to be the Spiritual Food and Sustenance of His people, and, lastly, Absolution, which is but a further ministering of the atoning power of the Blood of Christ.

19. "To wit, that God was in Christ, reconciling the world unto himself," &c. God the Son, Who shared with His Father all the attributes of the supreme God, had become incarnate in Jesus

19 To wit, that ᵃ God was in Christ, reconciling the world unto himself, not imputing their trespasses unto them; and hath † committed unto us the word of reconciliation.

ᵃ Rom. iii. 24, 25.
† Gr. *put in us.*

20 Now then we are ᵇ ambassadors for Christ, as ᶜ though God did beseech *you* by us: we pray *you* in Christ's stead, be ye reconciled to God.

ᵇ Job xxxiii. 23. Mal. ii. 7. ch. iii. 6. Eph. vi. 20.
ᶜ ch. vi. 1.

Christ, to make atonement for the sins of the world, and had been lifted up to draw all men to Himself: but if we take God as meaning the Father, then we have to remember the words of the Lord, "Believest thou not that I am in the Father and the Father in me," and "the Father that dwelleth in me, he doeth the works." (John xiv. 10.)

"Not imputing their trespasses unto them; and hath committed unto us," &c. If God had imputed their trespasses to the world of sinners, He would not have sent them the message of reconciliation. The very fact of His sending them such offers of mercy showed that whatever mind they had towards Him, His mind was pacified towards them.

"And hath committed unto us the word of reconciliation."

20. "Now then we are ambassadors for Christ, as though God did beseech you by us." If the ministers of Christ are His ambassadors, then by His appointment they stand between sinners and Himself just as much as priests do: in fact, more so. But the office of ambassador implies not a mere desire to represent Christ to sinners, but a commission so to do.

"Ambassadors for Christ, as though God did beseech you by us." Notice here the assertion of the Godhead of Christ. Ambassadors for Christ act for God as if Christ were God. When Christ beseeches by His ambassadors, it is God Who beseeches by the same persons.

"We pray you in Christ's stead, be ye reconciled to God." It seems strange that the Apostle should call upon those who had been converted and brought into the Body of Christ, to be reconciled to God, but if they had anything of the old Adam within them, they had that in them which was contrary to God, and which must be put away if they were to abide in Christ. In so far as they were carnal, litigious, divided into parties, indifferent to impurity and idolatry, irreverent in worship, and unbelieving about such an

CHAP. V.] SIN FOR US. 363

21 For ^d he hath made him *to be* sin for us, who knew no sin; that we might be made ^e the righteousness of God in him.

^d Is. liii. 6, 9, 12. Gal. iii. 13. 1 Pet. ii. 22, 24. 1 John iii. 5.
^e Rom. i. 17. & v. 19. & x. 3.

article of faith as the Resurrection, they had great need to put away from them such things as these, all which were irreconcilable with a state of true peace with God.

18. "For he hath made him to be sin for us, who knew no sin; that we might," &c. We have here the idea which pervades the Epistle to the Hebrews, that God made Christ, or that Christ made Himself, to be an atoning Sacrifice. It also runs through Isaiah liii., "The Lord hath laid on him the iniquity of us all." God could not possibly make Christ actual sin, but He could treat Him, or by His providence bring about that He should be treated, as a sinner. This took place at His Crucifixion. He was condemned by both Jewish and heathen judges. He was executed between two notorious sinners. The death which was inflicted upon Him was that inflicted only on the vilest criminals: so that so far as could be, short of His being made to commit sin, He was made sin. He was made sin in a sacrificial sense; not, I think, in a forensic so much as in a sacrificial sense. The animal, in the preparatory dispensation, was accepted for the offerer to make atonement for him (Levit. i. 4). Farther than this we cannot go. The redemptive work was a transaction between Two Persons in the Godhead, but it is represented to us in Scripture under the figure of One offering a Sacrifice, and the Other accepting it, and with this we must be content, and in humble faith we must throw ourselves into God's mind respecting both the expression and the realization, on our own part, of this great mystery.

"That we might be made the righteousness of God in him." The whole purpose of the redemptive work of Christ was that we should be reconciled to God, not by an outward or forensic or imputative reconciliation, but by an inward one; that is, by our souls being cleansed from all that keeps them apart from God, and by having the life of God put into us, that we should live lives of dedication to God. This is most fully set forth at the beginning of Romans viii. "God sent His own Son in the likeness of sinful flesh, and for sin (as a sin offering: περὶ ἁμαρτίας) condemned sin in the flesh, that the righteousness of the law might be fulfilled in us who walk not after the flesh, but after the Spirit."

CHAP. VI.

WE then, as ^aworkers together *with him,* ^bbeseech *you* also ^cthat ye receive not the grace of God in vain.

^a 1 Cor. iii. 9.
^b ch. v. 20.
^c Heb. xii. 15.
^d Is. xlix. 8.

2 (For he saith, ^dI have heard thee in a time accepted, and in the day of salvation have I suc-

---

1. "We then, as workers together with him, beseech you also that ye," &c. "As workers together with him." So 1 Cor. iii. 9: "We are labourers together with God."

"Beseech you also that ye receive not the grace of God in vain." What is this grace? It may stand for all grace, conversion, regeneration, sacraments; but I rather think that here, taking into account what precedes it and what follows it, we must consider it to be the grace of the Apostolic message of salvation, for he had said, "Now then, we are ambassadors for Christ, as though God did beseech you by us; we pray you," &c. And he illustrates this grace by the quotation from Isaiah, "I have heard thee in a time accepted—behold now is the accepted time."

It is the great underlying truth of all St. Paul's Epistles that those to whom he writes are already in a state of grace, and must see to it that they receive it not in vain—*i.e.,* that they receive it without conscious efforts to live to it, and to bring forth fruit answering to what they have received.

2. "For he saith, I have heard thee in a time accepted, and in the day," &c. The question which arises respecting these words is, Does St. Paul quote them as containing a general truth falling in with the purpose of his argument, or does he quote them having reference to their context? Now the whole passage from which they are taken is a very clear prophecy of Christ. Thus the verse before (Isaiah xlix. 7): "Thus saith the Lord, the Redeemer of Israel, and his Holy One, to him whom man despiseth, to him whom the nation abhorreth, to a servant of rulers, Kings shall see and arise, princes also shall worship, because of the Lord that is faithful, and the Holy One of Israel, and he shall choose thee. Thus saith

coured thee: behold, now *is* the accepted time; behold, now *is* the day of salvation.)

3 ᵉGiving no offence in any thing, that the ministry be not blamed: ᵉ Rom. xiv. 13; 1 Cor. ix. 12. & x. 32.

---

the Lord, In an acceptable time have I heard thee, and in a day of salvation have I helped thee: and I will preserve thee, and give thee for a covenant of the people . . . that thou mayest say to the prisoners, Go forth," &c. All this is in the highest degree Messianic; and if St. Paul remembered it, he must have had in his mind the Intercession of the Messiah, the one thing which made that day far beyond any which had preceded it, a day of salvation.

"Behold, now is the accepted time; behold, now is the day of salvation." Now—not always. Let us remember the words of the Lord :· "Strive to enter in at the strait gate: for many, I say unto you, will seek to enter in, and shall not be able. When once the master of the house is risen up," &c. (Luke xiii. 24).

These words are, of course, the words of the Apostle, applying the words of God in Isaiah, "I have heard thee in an acceptable time." It is as if God said to the Messiah, "I have heard Thee in an acceptable time, when I brought Thee up from the grave, and set Thee on My right hand, and made Thee a Mediator on behalf of the people I have given Thee." And then the Apostle adds, "Now is the time of the all-prevailing Mediatorship. Now is the time when whosoever shall call on the name of the Lord shall be saved."

This time extends over the whole period between the first and the second Advent. Now is our acceptable time—yours and mine, reader. Now is our day of salvation—now by God's grace we can make our calling and election sure. Now we may lay hold on eternal life. Now we may apprehend that for which we are apprehended by Christ Jesus (Phil. iii. 12).

3. "Giving no offence in anything, that the ministry be not blamed." No offence—*i.e.*, no occasion of stumbling. The preacher of Christ is bound to preach against sin, and false doctrine, and so he is bound to give offence to some. "Woe unto you, woe unto you, when all men speak well unto you, for so did their fathers unto the false prophets." But he must give no offence to the true

4 But in all *things* †approving ourselves ᶠas the ministers of God, in much patience, in afflictions, in necessities, in distresses,

5 ᵍIn stripes, in imprisonments, ‖ in tumults, in labours, in watchings, in fastings;

† Gr. *commending*, ch. iv. 2.
ᶠ 1 Cor. iv. 1.
ᵍ ch. xi. 23, &c.
‖ Or, *in tossings to and fro*.

---

servants of God by a course of living which comes palpably short of his preaching. He is bound, also, to give no needless offence by doctrine or ritual for which men are not prepared. He must be careful to explain what he means, so that men who fear God and trust in Christ should not misunderstand it.

"That the ministry be not blamed." When the minister acts in any way contrary to his profession, he brings not only himself but his office into disrepute. This is the artifice of Satan—to seek some misconduct on the part of ministers that may tend to the dishonour of the Gospel. For when he has succeeded in bringing the ministry into contempt all hope of profit is at an end. (Calvin.)

4, 5. "But in all things approving ourselves as the ministers of God." The whole of the enumeration that follows is written to show that all the tests by which the Lord was accustomed to try His servants were applied to the Apostles.

"In much patience." This may mean "in much patience in bearing with individual souls, and even with Churches;" or it may have reference to what follows, as afflictions. Afflictions are probably the griefs endured from the ingratitude of some, and the falling away of others; the necessities are probably the straits which he endured with regard to his worldly sustenance, which forced him, even for long periods, to work with his own hands.

"In distresses." This may probably mean "straits." "The idea of narrow straits suggests to him the thought of actual persecution of which he gave the three to which he was most frequently exposed—'the stripes,' as in Acts xvi. 23; 'the imprisonments' ('in prisons more frequent,' xi. 23); the tumults and disorders, as in Asia Minor (Acts xiii. 50, xiv. 19)." (Stanley.)

"In labours." Perhaps with his own hands for his maintenance, but rather his laborious journeying, and preaching, and visiting.

"In watchings." These watchings probably mean watchings lest he should fall into some snare of his enemies. Thus, Acts

BY THE WORD OF TRUTH.

6 By pureness, by knowledge, by longsuffering, by kindness, by the Holy Ghost, by love unfeigned,

7 [h] By the word of truth, by [i] the power of God,

[h] ch. iv. 2. & vii. 14.
[i] 1 Cor. ii. 4.

---

xx. 19, "temptations which befell me by the lying in wait of the Jews."

"In fastings." Perhaps voluntary fasts, in the way of disciplining his body (Acts xiii. 2); perhaps long periods of hunger through poverty.

Now he comes to enumerate the virtues and graces of the Spirit by which he had proved himself the minister of God.

6. "By pureness." This, in his case, can scarcely refer to chastity, but probably means purity of intention, and, as the virtue is not mentioned afterwards, sincerity of aim and singleness of purpose.

"By knowledge"—that far extended survey of the whole field of Divine truth of which his Epistles furnish such examples.

"By longsuffering." This, I think, must be ministerial longsuffering—bearing long with the faults, and failings, and dulnesses, and declensions of those whom he has converted to the faith.

"By kindness"—not only by a charitable heart, for without that a man cannot be a Christian, but by a kind, sympathizing demeanour.

"By the Holy Ghost." This probably means by the Spirit's gifts and manifestations, because, all the other graces enumerated, pureness, longsuffering, kindness, are the fruits of the Spirit.

"By love unfeigned." Let love be without dissimulation. It is soon seen whether the appearance of love be assumed, and, if so, all its virtue in attracting others is gone.

7. "By the word of truth." Not necessarily the Scriptures, but the word of the Gospel. Still there must be an intimate knowledge both of the letter and spirit of Scripture, if the workman is not to be ashamed. How can he rightly divide the word of truth unless he knows it? (2 Tim. ii. 15.)

"By the power of God." Dean Stanley explains this "by the power of working miracles." Calvin, "by the power of God showing itself in magnanimity, in efficacy, in the maintenance of the truth, in the propagation of the Gospel, in victory over enemies, and the like."

by ᵏ the armour of righteousness on the right hand and on the left,

8 By honour and dishonour, by evil report and good report: as deceivers, and *yet* true;

9 As unknown, and ¹*yet* well known; ᵐ as dying, and, behold, we live; ⁿ as chastened, and not killed;

10 As sorrowful, yet alway rejoicing; as poor

ᵏ ch. x. 4. Ephes. vi. 11, 13. 2 Tim. iv. 7.
ˡ ch. iv. 2. & v. 11. & xi. 6.
ᵐ 1 Cor. iv. 9. ch. i. 9. & iv. 10, 11.
ⁿ Ps. cxviii. 18.

"By the armour of righteousness on the right hand and on the left." On the right hand and on the left—*i.e.*, thoroughly equipped on all sides. Blunt says: "The sword of the Spirit in the right hand for attack, and the shield of faith on the left arm for defence."

8. "By honour and dishonour." It is no matter whether in some impending struggle the honour of a brilliant victory of the Gospel is to be attained, or some dishonour through apparent want of success.

"By evil report and good report." Sometimes those whom he had won to Christ, spoke evil of him, as being himself insincere; sometimes they turned round, and called themselves by his name as the head of their party.

"As deceivers, and yet true." As accounted even by the members of the Church which he had planted "a deceiver;" and yet true—true to his Master and the souls He had committed to him.

9. "As unknown, and yet well known"—*i.e.*, obscure, so that the world knoweth them not as it knew Him not—well known to God, and to all true believers.

"As dying, and, behold, we live." "In deaths oft." "I protest by your rejoicing which I have in Christ Jesus I die daily." "Always bearing about in the body the dying of the Lord Jesus." "We which live are always delivered unto death for Jesus' sake."

"As chastened, and not killed." The chastisement always coming short of depriving them of life, and yet always increasing their trust in God, and working them more abundant gain.

10. "As sorrowful, yet always rejoicing." Sorrowful, because of the opposition of the world to its own salvation; always rejoicing, because their sorrow, sooner or later, turns to joy when they see the Gospel triumphing through opposition.

CHAP. VI.] OUR HEART IS ENLARGED. 369

yet making many rich; as having nothing, and *yet* possessing all things.

11 O *ye* Corinthians, our mouth is open unto you, °our heart is enlarged.   ° ch. vii. 3.

"As poor, yet making many rich." "As poor," so that he had no property, no home, no income guaranteed to him by any church or society. "Yet making many rich," with contentment, with a citizenship far above the world, with the knowledge of God—in a word, with the unsearchable riches of Christ.

"As having nothing, and yet possessing all things." "Having nothing." This is his description of the Apostolic life: "Even unto this present hour we both hunger, and thirst, and are naked, and are buffeted, and have no certain dwelling place" (1 Cor. iv. 11); and this of the Apostolic riches: "I am persuaded that neither death, nor life, nor angels, nor principalities, nor powers ... shall be able to separate us," &c. (Rom. viii. 38).

Chrysostom has a singular comment: "If thou marvellest, how is it possible for one that hath nothing to have all things, let us bring forth this man himself into the midst, who commanded the world, and was Lord not only of their substance, but of their very eyes even. 'If it had been possible,' he says, 'ye would have plucked out your own eyes, and have given them unto me' (Gal. iv. 15)."

11. "O ye Corinthians, our mouth is open unto you, our heart is enlarged." He now reflects upon what he has said as the utterance of what he feels. Out of the abundance of his heart his mouth had spoken. He had appealed to the life and spirit of his ministry among them, his pureness, his sincerity, his long-suffering, his kindness, his disregard of honour and dishonour, of evil report and good report, his willingness to be poor and unknown, if he could but save them; and so he exclaims, "Our heart is enlarged. It can contain all, and welcomes all. We are not straitened, but ye are. Your divisions, your suspicions, your envyings so narrow your hearts that ye cannot receive me, your father in Christ, and those who in work and love are one with me, into your hearts."

12 Ye are not straitened in us, but ᵖye are straitened in your own bowels.

13 Now for a recompence in the same, (ᑫI speak as unto *my* children,) be ye also enlarged.

14 ʳBe ye not unequally yoked together with unbelievers: for ˢwhat fellowship hath righteousness with unrighteousness? and what communion hath light with darkness?

p ch. xii. 15.
q 1 Cor. iv. 14.
r Deu. vii. 2, 3. 1 Cor. v. 9. & vii. 39.
s 1 Sam. v. 2, 3. 1 Kings xviii. 21. 1 Cor. x. 21. Eph. v. 7, 11.

---

12. "Bowels" here stands for affections. It is usually associated with the idea of yearning affection in the Old Testament.

13. "Now for a recompence in the same, (I speak as unto my children,) be ye," &c. I have abundantly shown my fatherly love in Christ to you. I speak now to you as children. As it is the duty of parents to nourish their children, to instruct them, and to defend them, so it is the dictate of equity that children should requite their parents.

Here, apparently, there is a break, though some suppose that there is an undercurrent of thought between this and the next verse, for the evils which had well nigh shipwrecked their Christianity had been mainly owing to their want of fellowship with their spiritual father, and their too intimate fellowship with idolaters, and with impure persons, who looked back with pleasure to the licentiousness of their former state, and with whom they had contracted alliances in marriage and friendship, and so he writes:

14. "Be ye not unequally yoked together with unbelievers: for what fellowship," &c. The reference is to the Levitical law, forbidding that the ox and the ass should be yoked together at the plough (Deut. xxii. 10).

"Fellowship" means not only fellowship in marriage, but in friendship, in companionship, and perhaps in public office and business.

"For what fellowship hath righteousness with unrighteousness?" How can they converse together, for instance, about the future, when one has no hopes of the life to come, and the other lives his whole life as if an eternal future depended upon it?

"And what communion hath light with darkness?" What intercourse can two persons have on things which most concern immortal

15 And what concord hath Christ with Belial? or what part hath he that believeth with an infidel?

16 And what agreement hath the temple of God with idols? for ᵗ ye are the temple of the living God; ᵗ 1 Cor. iii. 16. & vi. 19. Ephes. ii. 21, 22. Heb. iii. 6.

16. "Ye are the temple." So C., E., F., G., K., most Cursives, f, g, Vulg., Syriac, Arm., Goth.; but ℵ, B., D., L., P., a few Cursives, d, e, Cop., Æth., read, "we" ("we are the temple").

beings when the mind of one is full of light on such subjects as God, and Christ, and His Gospel, and His Church; and the other utterly disbelieves in the existence of these things? Or it may allude to the deeds of light and the deeds of darkness respectively. What fellowship can there be between him who loves chastity, and him who loves adultery; between him who loves truth and uprightness, and him who loves falsehood and fraud?

15. "And what concord hath Christ with Belial?" The word Belial here is a name of the evil one, as being all vileness and worthlessness. It is made up of two Hebrew words, beli, without, and yaal, profit, and implies the emptiness and vanity of the sin to which he tempts men. Thus in Proverbs vi. 12, "the man of Belial (translated, naughty person) walketh with a froward mouth, he winketh with his eyes, he speaketh with his feet, he teacheth with his fingers," &c. Here Christ and Belial are contrasted as infinite worth and truth with utter vanity and falsehood.

"Or what part hath he that believeth with an infidel?" There is nothing really in common between the believer and the unbeliever, because their spirits, and so the whole aim of their existence, are different. The one delights in contemplating God in everything, the other sees Him in nothing—sees nothing but nature—nothing but what is visible and palpable. And so with the Bible. The one sees a revelation of God everywhere; the other sees only what any other man could have written, and perhaps written better.

16. "And what agreement hath the temple of God with idols? for ye are," &c. In the temple of Jerusalem there could be no representation of the one true God. In the temples of the heathen other statues of false gods might be erected besides that to the tutelar deity, but the temple of God was erected to God's honour, not as one amongst many gods, but as the One living and true God:

u Ex. xxix. 45. Lev. xxvi. 12. Jer. xxxi. 33. & xxxii. 38. Ezek. xi. 20. & xxxvi. 28. & xxxvii. 26, &c. Zech. viii. 8. & xiii. 9.	as God hath said, ^u I will dwell in them, and walk in *them;* and I will be their God, and they shall be my people.
x Is. lii. 11. ch. vii. 1. Rev. xviii. 4.	17 ^x Wherefore come out from among them, and be ye separate, saith the Lord, and touch not the unclean *thing;* and I will receive you,

and so it was with the Church. The whole spiritual building, and every stone of it, was erected to the Father of Jesus Christ. It was all builded together in Christ for an habitation of God through the Spirit. Notice how he assumes that the whole Church was the temple of God, just as he assumes everywhere that the whole Church, and every part of it, was the Body of Christ.

"As God hath said, I will dwell in them, and walk in them," &c. This quotation is from Levit. xxvi. 11, 12. In the Septuagint it runs, "I will set my tabernacle among you, and my soul shall not abhor you, and I will walk among you, and be your God, and ye shall be my people."

"I will dwell in them." Both in the whole Church as a body, and in each member.

"And walk in them." This seems to teach that God will not be in His spiritual temple as an immovable statue is in a building, but that He will be active among them, moving from one to the other, as it were, making every spiritual stone conscious of His Presence, inciting all to peace and purity, to love and good works.

"I will be their God, and they shall be my people." For God to be a God to a nation, or a person, implies that He is to it all that God can be, Protector, Deliverer, Redeemer, Saviour, Father, Guide.

17. "Wherefore come out from among them, and be ye separate." This is taken mainly from Isaiah lii. 11. "Depart ye, depart ye, go out from thence, touch no unclean thing; go ye out of the midst of her; be ye clean, that bear the vessels of the Lord." This is applied by the Apostle figuratively to the Corinthian believers. As the Israelites, when they departed from Babylon, were to keep themselves pure from all contact with the pollutions of idolatry, especially because they bore the consecrated vessels of the temple (see Levit. xxii. 2, compared with Ezra viii. 28), so the Corin-

CHAP. VII.]   I WILL BE A FATHER UNTO YOU.   373

18 ʸ And will be a Father unto you, and ye shall be my sons and daughters, saith the Lord Almighty.   ʸ Jer. xxxi. 1, 9. Rev. xxi. 7.

thians were to keep themselves pure from the pollutions of their wicked city, because they bore the name of Christ, and were baptized into His Church, and had His Word, His Sacraments, and His ministry among them.

"Touch not the unclean things." As he writes in Ephes. v. 11, "Have no fellowship with the unfruitful works of darkness." 2 Thes. iii. 6, "Withdraw yourselves from every brother that walketh disorderly," or Rom. xii. 9, "Abhor that which is evil."

"And I will receive you."

18. "And will be a Father unto you, and ye shall be my sons and," &c. But had not God already received them? Had He not given to them—to some, at least—repentance unto life? had He not converted them all from the worship of idols to the worship of Himself? did they not one and all confess that Jesus was the Son of God, and could this have been, unless God had received them and been a Father to them? Yes, this is true; but still the reception by God is a continuous one. As long as men abide in His Son He receives them. If they sunder themselves from the fellowship of Christ they have to be restored. But this place assures them that God is willing to restore them if they return to Him and draw near to Him.

CHAP. VII.

HAVING ᵃ therefore these promises, dearly beloved, let us cleanse ourselves from all filthiness   ᵃ ch. vi. 17, 18. 1 John iii. 3.

1. "Having therefore these promises, dearly beloved, let us cleanse ourselves from all filthiness of the flesh and spirit," &c. "These promises," *i.e.*, those mentioned just before. "Touch not the unclean thing, and I will be a father unto you, and ye shall be," &c.

of the flesh and spirit, perfecting holiness in the fear of God.

2 Receive us; we have wronged no man, we have corrupted no man, ᵇ we have defrauded no man.

3 I speak not *this* to condemn *you*: for ᶜ I have said before, that ye are in our hearts to die and live with *you*.

ᵇ Acts xx. 33. ch. xii. 17.
ᶜ ch. vi. 11, 12.

"Perfecting holiness in the fear of God." It has been supposed, and with much probability, that the idea of a temple, brought forward in verse 16 of last chapter, is here resumed; the holiness referring to the consecration of all our faculties to God, as living stones of His mystical temple, as well as to our purification from defilement.

2. "Receive us; we have wronged no man, we have corrupted no man," &c. "Receive us," literally, make room for us in your hearts. Ye have made room for, at least ye have not cut off from your fellowship, those who as false apostles wronged you by taking maintenance from you, to which they were not entitled, and have corrupted you by their false teaching, both in faith and morals. And ye have yet retained in your fellowship those who do wrong and defraud (1 Cor. vi. 8). We have done none of these things, though accused of them by our slanderers; yet, as we have written to others, "Ye know how holily and justly, and unblameably we have behaved ourselves among you" (1 Thess. ii. 10). The reader will remember how Moses makes a similar appeal to God respecting his integrity (Numb. xvi. 5); and Samuel calls all Israel to witness that in nothing had he wronged them.

3. "I speak not this to condemn you," *i.e.*, I do not desire to blame you and make you ashamed, so much as to urge you to admit me willingly to a place in your hearts, as ye are already in mine.

"Ye are in our hearts to die and live with you." The commentators, following Cornelius à Lapide, illustrate this by the example of those among the heathen who made contracts with one another to live and to die together. Thus the members of the Theban Legion mentioned in Plutarch (ἱερὸς λόχος), and the Soldurii among the Gauls (Cæsar, De Bello Gallico, iii.), Nisus and Euryalus in Virgil's Epic, and Horace offering to kill himself if Mæcenas

OUR FLESH HAD NO REST.

4 ^d Great *is* my boldness of speech toward you, ^e great *is* my glorying of you: ^f I am filled with comfort, I am exceeding joyful in all our tribulation.

5 For, ^g when we were come into Macedonia, our flesh had no rest, but ^h we were troubled on every side; ⁱ without *were* fightings, within *were* fears.

6 Nevertheless ^k God, that comforteth those that are cast down, comforted us by ^l the coming of Titus;

7 And not by his coming only, but by the consolation wherewith he was comforted in you, when he told us your

^d ch. iii. 12.
^e 1 Cor. i. 4. ch. i. 14.
^f ch. i. 4. Phil. ii. 17. Col. i. 24.
^g ch. ii. 13.
^h ch. iv. 8.
ⁱ Deut. xxxii. 25.
^k ch. i. 4.
^l See ch. ii. 13.

---

should be taken away, "Ille dies utramque Ducet ruinam," Od. ii. 17, but it is doubtful whether such illustrations are in place, and do not lower the Apostolic words.

And now he seems to resume the connection which had been broken off at ii. 13, 14, and reverts to the joy which he had received by the news which Titus had brought him.

4. "Great is my boldness of speech toward you, great is my glorying of you." "Boldness of speech," freedom, confidence. Before Titus showed him their real state of feeling towards him, he could not speak to them freely. There was a cloud on both him and them; now this is removed, now he can not only speak to them without reserve, but he can boast or glory of them as in former times.

5. "For when we were come into Macedonia, our flesh had no rest." We were wearied and weighed down by a load of troubles.

"Without were fightings." No doubt persecutions on the part of the heathen.

"Within were fears." Lest the report of Titus should be unfavourable, and he should lose the church in which he had received so many seals to his ministry, so many souls whom he had fondly hoped would have been his crown of rejoicing in the day of the Lord.

6, 7. "Nevertheless God that comforteth those . . . . so that I rejoiced the more." Titus had, as the reader knows, been sent to Corinth, to ascertain the effect which St. Paul's first Epistle had

earnest desire, your mourning, your fervent mind toward me; so that I rejoiced the more.

8 For though I made you sorry with a letter, I do not repent, ^m though I did repent: for I perceive that the same epistle hath made you sorry, though *it were* but for a season.

^m ch. ii. 4.

9 Now I rejoice, not that ye were made sorry, but that

---

produced on the Church. The report which he brought went very far to remove the Apostle's anxieties, and to fill him with comfort. Notice the exceeding naturalness of this account. It would have been a great comfort to the Apostle to receive back again such a son in the faith and earnest fellow-helper as Titus; but the consolation was beyond measure increased when he found that his letter had produced the effect which he had hoped and prayed for. This effect was manifested in their earnest desire both to see him and to please him; their mourning for having caused him distress respecting their spiritual condition, their fervent mind, literally their zeal, not so much towards him as on his behalf against his adversaries and calumniators.

8. "For though I made you sorry with a letter, I do not repent." "With a letter," rather, "with the letter," his first Epistle.

"I do not repent." Rather as the Revisers translate, "I do not regret it," though for a moment I did regret it. It is better to adopt the term regret, as it keeps the word repentance of verse 9 clear for indicating the spiritual state.

"For I perceive that the same epistle hath made you sorry, though it were," &c. The expressions of blame and condemnation in the first Epistle were very strong, but he no longer regrets the temporary pain they gave, because of the blessing with which God accompanied them.

9. "Now I rejoice, not that ye were made sorry, but that ye sorrowed," &c. The least infliction of pain on a fellow-creature is matter of regret to a good man, and his only consolation is that the temporary evil is the occasion of more permanent good. This permanent good was repentance towards God. The translation in our Authorized and in the Revised, "Ye were made sorry after a godly manner," is much too feeble a rendering of κατὰ Θεόν. It is

ye sorrowed to repentance: for ye were made sorry ||after a godly manner, that ye might receive damage by us in nothing.

|| Or, *according to God.*

10 For ⁿgodly sorrow worketh repentance to salvation not to be repented of: ᵒ but the sorrow of the world worketh death.

ⁿ 2 Sam. xii. 13. Matt. xxvi. 75.
ᵒ Prov. xvii. 22.

---

as Wordsworth renders, "With a view to God, and not with an eye towards yourselves or to the world."

"That ye might receive damage by us in nothing." The infliction of pain is, for the time, a damage or loss, unless it be compensated for by subsequent advantage. The probing of an ulcer is attended by acute pain, but that is forgotten in the renewed health. Note the gentle and loving spirit of the Apostle, how he dwells apologetically on the temporary pain, as having no right to occasion the smallest distress unless there was absolute need. How different from the conduct of those who care not how they ruffle and wound by sharp words and ill-natured surmises the souls of those who have done them no wrong whatsoever.

10. "For godly sorrow worketh repentance to salvation not to be repented of," &c. Mark, the Apostle does not call godly sorrow repentance, but says that it *worketh* repentance, for repentance is more than sorrow; it is a change of mind with respect to God, and with respect to sin. There may be much sorrow without any permanent change, and there may be a permanent change without much apparent sorrow in duller or in more equable minds.

"Worketh repentance to salvation." Repentance that leads to Christ and so issues in salvation through Him, through inherence in Him and the reception of His nature through His Sacraments, and His Intercession.

"But the sorrow of the world worketh death." The sorrow of the world seems more especially to be sorrow for the consequences of sin, rather than for sin itself; and yet if we look upon the chastisement as not coming naturally, but as sent by God, this may sanctify the sorrow, and make it the precursor of true repentance.

If the sorrow of the world means sorrow for the loss of wealth or position, or worldly reputation, then, unless raised into something higher by the grace of God, it worketh death, it worketh dis-

11 For behold this selfsame thing, that ye sorrowed after a godly sort, what carefulness it wrought in you, yea, *what* clearing of yourselves, yea, *what* indignation, yea, *what* fear, yea, *what* vehement desire, yea, *what* zeal, yea, *what* revenge!

---

content, moroseness, and despair, and drives men from God rather than attracts them to Him.

11. ." For behold this selfsame thing, that ye sorrowed after a godly sort, . . . yea, what revenge ! " &c. This verse is generally understood as referring to the conduct of the Corinthian Church in the matter of their treatment of the incestuous offender. This godly sorrow, this grief with a view to God, what carefulness it wrought in you, *i.e.*, earnestness; ye were at first indifferent about the evil of complicity with such sin, now ye have become thoroughly alive to the danger of such allowance of wickedness, and have exhibited this "in humble deprecation," ($ἀπολογία$); ye *were* puffed up (I. Cor. v. 2), now ye confess, and make excuse, and urge something in extenuation, as that ye were not aware of the extent of the evil, or did not realize it, and so forth.

" Yea, what indignation." Not merely against the sinner, but against yourselves for having tolerated it for a moment.

" Yea, what fear." Fear lest God should visit it on the Church, or fear perhaps of the Apostle's coming, and his further indignant reproofs.

"Yea, what vehement desire." Perhaps rather longing, *i.e.*, that he should come again, and find them what he would have them to be.

" Yea, what zeal." For the glory of God—for the souls of the sinners among them—for their perfect cleansing from all filthiness of flesh and spirit.

" Yea, what revenge! " This is generally taken to denote the exercise of corrective discipline against the incestuous person, but ought it not rather to be understood in the sense of revenge on themselves, for having connived at the evil—so that they should punish themselves by humiliation and confession, perhaps by fasting and self-denial ? [1]

---

[1] Thus Cornelius à Lapide:—"Vindictam, ut desidiam et peccata vestra vindicaretis, tum dolore et lacrymis vos affligendo, tum aliis modis corpora animasque vestras macerando et puniendo." And he quotes a passage from Calvin. " Postremo est vindicta:

In all *things* ye have approved yourselves to be clear in this matter.

12 Wherefore, though I wrote unto you, *I did it* not for his cause that had done the wrong, nor for his cause that suffered wrong, ᵖ but that our care for you in the sight of God might appear unto you. ᵖ ch. ii. 4.

---

12. "Our care for you." So a few Cursives, Vulg., Goth. ; " your care for yourselves," א, D. ; " Your care for us," B., C., E., K., L., P., seventy Cursives, Syriac, Copt.

"In all things ye have approved yourselves to be clear in this matter." Clear, that is, in respect of present complicity with the offending person in his sin, though at the first they were culpably lax in taking due notice of it.

12. "Wherefore, though I wrote unto you," &c. The wrong which the incestuous person did, and the wrong which his father received, was not in the eyes of the Apostle so grave a matter as the complicity of the Church in the wickedness. This was by far the greatest cause of anxiety to the Apostle, and so he puts it forth here as the one cause of his writing, only he somewhat veils his meaning; instead of saying, "I wrote to warn you against a moment's toleration of so hideous a sin," he says, "I wrote that our care for you in the sight of God might appear." He felt that it was no small thing to recover the confidence and love of his converts. Unless he had this he felt that they were not right. He was God's ambassador and representative. He was their spiritual father in Christ. The power of God, and of Christ, had been manifested in him towards them; so that there was the greatest fear that their hearts were not right with God and Christ unless they were right with him. There is substantially the same meaning if we read "your care for us:" because in that case it would be the "fruit of our care for you." Both imply restored confidence.

13. "Therefore we were comforted in your comfort: yea, and exceedingly the more," &c. Another punctuation and division of

---

quo enim severiores in nos sumus, et acriore censurâ quæstionem habemus de peccatis nostris, eo sperare debemus magis propitium et misericordem Dominum. Et certe fieri non potest, quin anima Divini judicii honore perculsa, partes ultionis in exigendâ de se pænà occupet."

13 Therefore we were comforted in your comfort: yea, and exceedingly the more joyed we for the joy of Titus, because his spirit ᑫ was refreshed by you all.

ᑫ Rom. xv. 32.

14 For if I have boasted any thing to him of you, I am not ashamed; but as we spake all things to you in truth, even so our boasting, which *I made* before Titus, is found a truth.

15 And his † inward affection is more abundant toward you, whilst he remembereth ʳ the obedience of you all, how with fear and trembling ye received him.

† Gr. *bowels.* ch. vi. 12.
ʳ ch. ii. 9. Phil. ii. 12.

---

13. "Therefore we were comforted in your comfort: yea, and exceedingly the more," &c. After "in" insert δε, with ℵ, B., C., D., E., F., G., K., L., P., a few Cursives, Ital., Vulg., Goth., Syriac, and place a stop after "comforted." So Revisers read, "Therefore we have been comforted; and in our comfort we joyed the more exceedingly for the joy of Titus," &c. Most Cursives, but no Uncials, read as in Rec. Text.

14. "Our boasting." B. and F. (Greek) read, "your."

the sentences yields a better, and no doubt the true sense. "Therefore we have been comforted, *i.e.*, with the effects which we heard had been produced on you by my Epistle, such as I have mentioned in verse 11; and over and above this our comfort we rejoiced more exceedingly for the joy of Titus, because his spirit was refreshed by you all. The joy with which your conduct had inspired him communicated itself to us, and was a fresh source of joy."

14. "For if I have boasted anything to him of you, I am not ashamed." St. Paul before sending Titus, spoke much in praise of the members of the Corinthian Church. At one time, perhaps, his heart misgave him, fearing that he had spoken too well, but now he is rejoiced to find that he has not. "As we spake all things, though they were severe reproofs to you, in truth, so now our boasting to Titus of your grace and good qualities turns out to be the word of truth."

15. "And his inward affection is more abundant toward you, whilst," &c. His memory dwells on your obedience, which all seemed to share, and withal how you received him, not in a spirit of self-will and anger at being reproved, but recognizing in him, as my messenger, the messenger of God; so that you received him with reverence and awe.

16 I rejoice therefore that ⁸ I have confidence in you in all *things*.

ˢ 2 Thess. iii. 4. Philem. viii. 21.

16. "I rejoice therefore that I have confidence in you in all things." Confidence seems too strong a word. The Revisers render it, "I am of good courage concerning you."

CHAP. VIII.

MOREOVER, brethren, we do you to wit of the grace of God bestowed on the churches of Macedonia;

2 How that in a great trial of affliction the abundance of their joy and ᵃ their deep poverty abounded unto the riches of their ǁ liberality.

ᵃ Mark xii. 44.
† Gr. *simplicity*, ch. ix. 11.

1. "Moreover, brethren, we do you to wit of the grace of God," &c. There is now, we are thankful to say, a change of subject.

"We do you to wit of." An archaic expression for "we make known to you" the grace of God bestowed on the churches of Macedonia—Philippi, Thessalonica, Beræa, &c.

Notice how the Apostle calls Christian goodwill and liberality a grace of God.

2. "How that in a great trial of affliction," &c. No doubt from the persecution of the heathen, or from the violence of their own unbelieving countrymen. (1 Thess. ii. 14).

"The abundance of their joy and of their deep poverty abounded," &c. What a remarkable conjunction. Their joy in God and in Christ made their open-heartedness to abound to all who belonged to God and Christ, and this was enhanced by their deep poverty. Their poverty prevented them from giving as much as they desired, but it made what they did give far more in the sight of God than the gifts of those who had given much more: just as the Lord says respecting the widow, "Verily, I say unto you, this widow hath cast in more than they all." The deeper their poverty the more rich their liberality.

3 For to *their* power, I bear record, yea, and beyond *their* power *they were* willing of themselves;

4 Praying us with much intreaty that we would receive the gift, and *take upon us* ^b the fellowship of the ministering to the saints.

^b Acts xi. 29. & xxiv. 17. Rom. xv. 25, 26. 1 Cor. xvi. 1, 3, 4. ch. ix. 1.

5 And *this they did*, not as we hoped, but first gave their own selves to the Lord, and unto us by the will of God.

---

4. "That we would receive." Omitted by א, B., C., D., E., F., G., K., L., P., most Cursives, Ital., Vulg., Syriac, Copt., Æth.; retained by many Cursives. Translate with Revisers, "beseeching us with much intreaty in regard of the grace and the fellowship in the ministering to the saints."

This poverty, in all probability, was not confined to the Christians of Macedonia, but affected the whole district. We are told that it never recovered the effects of three desolating wars, the first between Cæsar and Pompey, the second between the Triumvirs and Brutus and Cassius, the third between Augustus and Antonius. "Under Tiberius they petitioned for a diminution of their burdens, and were accordingly for a time transferred from the jurisdiction of the Senate to that of the Emperor as involving a less heavy taxation" (Plumptre).

3, 4. "For to their power I bear record .... fellowship of the ministering to the saints." They were willing of themselves, they did not wait to be asked to give, but, on the other hand, prayed the Apostles with much entreaty to receive what they had contributed apparently of their own accord and unprompted. The words of the original are stronger: "Praying us with much entreaty for the grace and the fellowship of the ministering to the saints. "They implored us (as Wordsworth paraphrazes it) to allow them to be associated with us in the privilege of giving alms to their poorer brethren at Jerusalem."

5. "And this they did, not as we hoped, but first gave their own selves," &c. "Not as we hoped" means "beyond our hopes." They did more than he expected; they not only gave liberally of their substance, but they gave themselves. It is a question as to what this means. Did it mean the ordinary dedication which every Christian performs, first at his Baptism and then all through his life? It could not mean this, for the Apostle evidently alludes

CHAP. VIII.] AS YE ABOUND IN EVERY THING. 383

6 Insomuch that ^c we desired Titus, that as he had begun, so he would also finish in you the same ‖ grace also.

^c ver. 17.
ch. xii. 18.
‖ Or, *gift*.
ver. 4, 19.

7 Therefore, as ^d ye abound in every *thing*, *in* faith, and utterance, and knowledge, and *in* all diligence, and *in* your love to us, *see* ^e that ye abound in this grace also.

^d 1 Cor. i. 5.
& xii. 13.

^e ch. ix. 8.

8 ^f I speak not by commandment, but by occasion of the forwardness of others, and to prove the sincerity of your love.

^f 1 Cor. vii. 6.

---

7. "Your love to us." So אּ, C., D., E., F., G., K., L., P., most Cursives, Ital., Vulg., Goth., Æth.; but B. and some Cursives read, "our love to you."

to something special. Dean Stanley supposes that he alludes to the number of Macedonian Christians compared with those of other Churches who gave themselves to the Apostle as his constant companions. Among these were Sopater of Berœa, Secundus, Aristarchus and Epaphroditus. And he adds, "The number of these Macedonian converts is the more striking, when compared with the few that came from the churches of Southern Greece, none of whom, except Sosthenes, appears as a permanent companion."

6. "Insomuch that we desired Titus, that as he had begun," &c. Titus had begun by initiating the collection amongst the Corinthians, and the Apostle had desired him to complete it when he came to them again as the bearer of this present letter.

7. "Therefore, as ye abound in everything, in faith, and utterance," &c. At the commencement of the first Epistle, he had given thanks to God on their behalf that they were enriched by God in all knowledge and in all utterance; now he adds to this the mention of their faith and diligence, and their love to him. This he could not have done till he had received from Titus the account of their repentance, and their revived reverence and affection for him.

8. "I speak not by commandment, but by occasion of the forwardness of others," &c.—not by Divine commandment.

"By occasion of the forwardness of others." Especially of the Macedonian Christians, but this contribution for the poor Christians of Jerusalem was taken up very cordially by Christians in all parts

9 For ye know the grace of our Lord Jesus Christ, ^g that, though he was rich, yet for your sakes he became poor, that ye through his poverty might be rich.

^g Matt. viii. 20. Luke ix. 58. Phil. ii. 6, 7.

---

of the world, as in Antioch (Acts xi. 28), and other places (Gal. ii. 10).

"To prove the sincerity of your love." Not only to the poor saints, but to God and Christ, as appears from the next verse.

9. "For ye know the grace of our Lord Jesus Christ, that though he was rich," &c. The grace, *i.e.*, the favour, the kindness, the love towards men.

"That, though he was rich,"—in His pre-existent state, when He was "in the beginning with God." St. Augustine says of this, "'*By Him all things were made*' (John i. 3). It is a greater thing to make gold than to have it. You may be rich in gold, and silver, and cattle, but *you* could not *make* them. But see Him who was rich. 'All things were made by him.' Now see Him who made Himself poor. 'The Word was made flesh and dwelt amongst us.' Who can conceive of His riches? And now think on His poverty. He was conceived in the Virgin's womb. O Paupertas! He was born in a poor inn, wrapped in swaddling clothes, laid in a stable. He, the Lord of heaven and earth, the maker of angels, the creator of all things, visible and invisible, fed at the breast of His mother, veils His majesty, is taken and bound, and scourged, and buffeted, and crowned with thorns, nailed to a tree, pierced with a lance. O Paupertas!"

He not only became man, but chose a poor lot. The Son of man came not to be ministered unto, but to minister. We never read of His having a servant. He lived upon what others gave Him, who ministered unto Him of their substance.

"That ye through his poverty might be rich." This is generally understood of spiritual riches. Thus Chrysostom: "By riches here he meaneth the knowledge of godliness, the cleansing away of sins, justification, sanctification, the countless good things which He bestowed upon us and purposeth to bestow."

But are we warranted in limiting these "good things" to what are called "spiritual blessings." Will not the Christian be raised up in a glorified body, which will have an outward state of wealth

CHAP. VIII.]   I GIVE MY ADVICE.   385

10 And herein ʰI give *my* advice: for ⁱthis is expedient for you, who have begun before, not only to do, but also to be †ᵏforward a year ago.

11 Now therefore perform the doing *of it*; that as *there was* a readiness to will, so *there may be* a performance also out of that which ye have.

12 For ˡif there be first a willing mind, *it is* accepted according to that a man hath, *and* not according to that he hath not.

ʰ 1 Cor. vii. 25.
ⁱ Prov. xix. 17. Matt. x. 42. 1 Tim. vi. 18, 19. Heb. xiii. 16.
† Gr. *willing*.
ᵏ ch. ix. 2.
ˡ Mark xii. 43, 44. Luke xxi. 3.

---

and grandeur answering to it. The Lord will reward the man who has improved his one pound so as to make it ten, by making him "ruler over ten cities." The Lord will reward the man who has made his one pound into five pounds by making him ruler over five cities (Luke xix. 16, 19). The description of the eternal good things of the redeemed, in the last chapters of the Revelations, is beyond measure rich and magnificent, and though they are nothing as compared to that fruition which he will have in himself, yet as God mentions them in the Scriptures, we ought to mention them also. Especially ought they to be affirmed in the hearing of the rich, to fill them with fear lest they rise again, not only without the true riches, but utterly destitute of those good things which alone, whilst on earth, they desired and valued.

10. "And herein I give my advice: for this is expedient for you," &c. The advice is that they make no delay in finishing what they had begun, and moreover had resolved upon a year ago. Having resolved upon it so long, as well as having made a beginning, it was proper that they should soon finish. It seems to be implied that there had been some slight slackness between the resolve and the beginning, or rather between the beginning and the present time, and so he reminds them that they had been beforehand with the Macedonians in their resolve, and ought not to be behindhand in the completion of their resolve.

11. "Now therefore perform the doing of it; that as there was a readiness to will," &c. This is a repetition of his advice, which from some cause or other he felt to be needful.

12. "For if there be first a willing mind, it is accepted," &c. He seems here to inculcate that all should give—no matter how poor

C C

13 For *I mean* not that other men be eased, and ye burdened:

14 But by an equality, *that* now at this time your abundance *may be a supply* for their want, that their abundance also may be *a supply* for your want: that there may be equality:

m Ex. xvi. 18. **15** As it is written, ᵐ He that *had gathered* much had nothing over; and he that *had gathered* little had no lack.

—for a little self-denial would enable even the poorest to give something. God looks with acceptance, not at the amount, but at the self-denial which it entails in each separate case.

13, 14. "For I mean not that other men be eased .... that there may be equality." This seems to mean, "I do not wish that the rich people of Judæa should be relieved of their responsibility on behalf of the poor around them, and the burden laid upon you, but the want in Judæa is such that collections are required from all parts to keep men from starving; it may be, however, that matters will be changed, that you will be affected through war or famine, or most probably persecution, and then their abundance may be a supply for your want; they will then, moved by the grace of God, remember your former kindness, and the more willingly assist you in your straits."

15. "As it is written, He that had gathered much had nothing over," &c. The word equality suggests to the Apostle the miraculous law which God ordained in the matter of the distribution of the manna. The manna which each household gathered was put together, and measured out, and it was found that though one may have gathered more, and another less, there was always an omer for each man.

The lesson which the Apostle gathers from the incident is this. It is the intention of the Almighty that each man should have a competent share of the good things of this life for his maintenance. But God has also ordained a great inequality, so that some have, or gather, more and some less, and it is his intention that those who have the more should contribute liberally to supply the needs of those who have less, that there may be the equality typified by the equal distribution of the manna notwithstanding the unequal gathering. It is one of those many places which teach us that the

16 But thanks *be* to God, which put the same earnest care into the heart of Titus for you.

17 For indeed he accepted ⁿ the exhortation;   ⁿ ver. 6. but being more forward, of his own accord he went unto you.

18 And we have sent with him ᵒ the brother,   ᵒ ch. xii. 18. whose praise *is* in the Gospel throughout all the churches;

19 And not *that* only, but who was also ᵖ chosen   ᵖ 1 Cor. xvi. 3, 4.

---

design of God in permitting the unequal distribution of property is not that those who have more should selfishly enjoy their abundance, but that they should share it to the uttermost with those in need. There are a few—very few—who act on this principle, and their reward is set forth in the words of the Lord in Matth. xxv., and in the words of David, "He hath dispersed, he hath given to the poor, his righteousness endureth for ever; his horn shall be exalted with honour," &c. (Psalm cxii. 9, quoted in verse 9 of the next chapter.)

16, 17. "But thanks be to God which put . . . he went unto you." Notice how all earnest desires for the spiritual welfare of others are ascribed to God—the God from Whom "all holy desires, all good counsels, and all just works do proceed."

"He accepted the exhortation." Titus had been sent with the first Epistle, in which the collection holds a very subordinate part, and little or no exhortation to liberality was given—the letter being occupied with graver and more pressing matters—but now he willingly offers to be the bearer of the Second Epistle.

When St. Paul writes, " of his own accord he went unto you," he does not allude to a past journey, but to the one in which Titus was the bearer of this present letter, the tense employed being the Epistolary Aorist; it is the same as if he said, "he now goes to you," because when they received and read the letter, the setting off would be a thing of the past, and according to the rules of Greek epistolary correspondence, would be treated as such.

18, 19. "And we have sent with him the brother . . . declaration of your ready mind." The greatest difference exists amongst commentators as to whom this person thus so honourably

of the churches to travel with us with this ‖ grace, which is administered by us ᑫ to the glory of the same Lord, and *declaration of* your ready mind :

‖ Or, *gift.*
ver. 4, 6, 7.
ch. ix. 8.
ᑫ ch. iv. 15.

20 Avoiding this, that no man should blame us in this abundance which is administered by us:

---

19. "With this grace" (σύν). So ℵ, D., E., F., G., K., L., most Cursives, d, e, g, Goth., Syr. B., C., a few Cursives, and Vulg., read, " in " (ἐν).

"The same Lord." So ℵ, E., K., most Cursives; but B., C., D., F., G., L., a few Cursives, d, e, f, g, Vulg., omit " the same," and read " of the Lord."

"Our ready mind," read by ℵ, B., C., D., E., G., K., L., P., most Cursives, Ital., Vulg.; " your," by a few Cursives.

mentioned was. Chrysostom, and after him Theodoret, suppose it to be Barnabas. Ignatius, in his Epistle to the Ephesians (ch. xv., longer recension) writes : " Our Lord and God Jesus Christ, the Son of the living God, first did and then taught, as Luke testifies, whose praise is in the Gospel through all the churches." Baronius speaks of Silas ; Jerome and Anselm of Luke. Amongst moderns, Alford thinks it may have been Trophimus ; Stanley that it was Trophimus, and the other nameless companion of verse 22, Tychicus. Wordsworth devotes much space to show that it was Luke, and principally relies on this, that St. Luke alone of those who could have been chosen by the Macedonian churches, accompanied St. Paul all through his journey to Jerusalem as his constant companion.

Amongst such diversities of opinion, especially among the ancients, it is impossible to pronounce with certainty. Most moderns seem to think that the words, " whose praise is in the Gospel," cannot refer to the written Gospel of St. Luke, but it is not probable that St. Paul would suffer the churches planted by him to be without a written Gospel, and this Gospel would, in all probability, be that of St. Luke.

" Chosen by the churches "—probably by show of hands ; " with this grace," that is, with this freely-given contribution.

20. " Avoiding this, that no man should blame us," &c. So pursued was he by calumny and misrepresentation that in this matter of bearing their contributions to Jerusalem he insisted on having others with him, chosen, not by himself, but by the churches, that these independent witnesses might bear testimony to the uprightness with which he discharged his trust.

CHAP. VIII.] WE HAVE SENT OUR BROTHER. 389

21 ʳProviding for honest things, not only in the sight of the Lord, but also in the sight of men.   ʳ Rom. xii. 17. Phil. iv. 8.

22 And we have sent with them our brother, 1 Pet. ii. 12. whom we have oftentimes proved diligent in many things, but now much more diligent, upon the great confidence which || *I have* in you. || Or, *he hath*.

23 Whether *any do enquire* of Titus, *he is* my partner and fellowhelper concerning you: or our brethren *be enquired of, they are* ˢ the messengers of ˢ Phil. ii. 25. the churches, *and* the glory of Christ.

---

21. "Providing for." So C., a few Cursives, Copt., Goth.; but ℵ, B., D., E., F., G., P., 6, 11, 67**, 80, 91, d, e, f, g, Vulg., Syriac, read, "for we provide for."

21. "Providing for honest things, not only in the sight of the Lord, but also," &c. This is a quotation from the Septuagint version of the Book of Proverbs which reads, (iii. 3, 4), "Let not mercy and truth forsake thee, but bind them about thy neck: so shalt thou find favour: and do thou provide things honest in the sight of the Lord and of men." It is also repeated in Rom. xii. 17. What mischief in the Church would have been prevented, if good men had always been careful to maintain an honest reputation in the sight of their fellow men, as well as in that of God. The Church has a right to an explanation of every man's conduct, as well as a declaration of the sincerity of his belief.

22. "And we have sent with them our brother, whom we have oftentimes," &c. This person is also utterly unknown. Chrysostom does not hazard a conjecture. Plumptre supposes that it was Tychicus, or perhaps Clement. Wordsworth suggests Silas. The Revisers translate the latter clause "but now much more earnest by reason of the great confidence which he hath in you," which seems to yield a better sense.

23. "Whether any do enquire of Titus, he is my partner . . . . glory of Christ." Titus was one of those constant companions of St. Paul whom he associated with himself in all his work and counsel, that when he was removed they might take up his work of superintending the churches. (See my chapters on Church Government and Apostolic Succession in "Church Doctrine Bible Truth.")

"Or our brethren be enquired of." These men were on this occasion the representatives of the churches, just as Titus was his

24 Wherefore shew ye to them, and before the churches, the proof of your love, and of our ᵗboasting on your behalf.

ᵗ ch. vii. 14. & ix. 2.

---

special representative. It is quite clear that though he highly praises these persons, they were not so near to him, and so not in such authority as Titus was.

24. "Wherefore shew ye to them, and before the churches." This may mean, "Receive ye them well, and so shew your love," or it may mean, "Let them, and the churches which they represent, see in your contributions the proof of your love to the poor saints, and that we have made no vainglorious boast of your obedience to the Gospel."

CHAP. IX.

ᵃ Acts xi. 29.
Rom. xv. 26.
1 Cor. xvi. 1.
ch. viii. 4.
Gal. ii. 10.

FOR as touching ᵃthe ministering to the saints, it is superflous for me to write to you:

---

1. "For as touching the ministering to the saints, it is superfluous, &c." There seems to have been here a break in the composition of the letter. In this chapter we have the Apostle recurring to several points which he had touched upon in the last chapter, as the forwardness of the Corinthians, the sending of Titus and the brethren, and the abounding in the grace of liberality.

"It is superfluous for me to write unto you touching the ministering to the saints." And yet he does write further on this very subject. This is only natural. A man writes a letter to his friend and says "I need not write to you on such a subject," and yet he does write on the subject, not because the person to whom he writes is ignorant, but because the subject is of such importance that it will bear repetition. A man who wrote to exhibit his excellence of style would avoid such a thing, but a man who wrote full of his subject, and with a single aim at doing good, would make many such repetitions.

THAT YE MAY BE READY.

2 For I know ᵇ the forwardness of your mind, ᶜ for which I boast of you to them of Macedonia, that ᵈ Achaia was ready a year ago; and your zeal hath provoked very many.

ᵇ ch. viii. 19.
ᶜ ch. viii. 24.
ᵈ ch. viii. 10.

3 ᵉ Yet have I sent the brethren, lest our boasting of you should be in vain in this behalf; that, as I said, ye may be ready:

ᵉ ch. viii. 6, 17, 18, 22.

4 Lest haply if they of Macedonia come with me, and find you unprepared, we (that we say not, ye) should be ashamed in this same confident boasting.

5 Therefore I thought it necessary to exhort the brethren, that they would go before unto you, and make up beforehand your † bounty, ‖ whereof ye had notice before, that the same might be ready, as *a matter of* bounty, and not as *of* covetousness.

† Gr. *blessing*. Gen. xxxiii. 11. 1 Sam. xxv. 27. 2 Kin. v. 15.
‖ Or, *which hath been so much spoken of before*.

---

2. "Was ready a year ago." "Hath been prepared a year past," Revisers.

5. "Whereof ye had notice before." So I., K., L., and most Cursives; but ℵ, B., C., D., E., F., G., P., about ten Cursives, Arm., read, "that was promised before." Vulg., "repromissam;" d, e, g, "ante promissam."

2, 3, 4. "For I know the forwardness of your mind . . . confident boasting." As if he said, I know your zeal and earnestness, but I am doubtful about your steadiness of purpose: so to make sure of your not putting me who have boasted of you—not to say yourselves—to shame by your remissness, I have sent brethren whose presence will, as it were, keep you up to your good intentions, and compel you to be ready.

5. "Your bounty"—literally, your blessing.

"Your bounty, whereof ye had notice before"—rather, your afore-promised bounty or blessing. According to the Jewish way of speaking, the designation of the gifts of God, such as the fruits of the earth, as blessings, was extended to the free gifts of men to one another. Thus Jacob says to Esau, when he urged him to receive his present, "Take, I pray thee, my blessing, which is brought to thee" (Gen. xxxiii. 11).

"Not as of covetousness"—*i.e.*, not of extortion, as wrung out of those who gave it grudgingly.

6 ᶠBut this *I say*, He which soweth sparingly shall reap also sparingly; and he which soweth bountifully shall reap also bountifully.

7 Every man according as he purposeth in his heart, *so let him give;* ᵍ not grudgingly, or of necessity: for ʰ God loveth a cheerful giver.

8 ⁱ And God *is* able to make all grace abound toward you; that ye, always having all sufficiency in all *things*, may abound to every good work:

ᶠ Pro. xi. 24. & xix. 17. & xxii. 9. Gal. vi. 7, 9.

ᵍ Deu. xv. 7.
ʰ Ex. xxv. 2. & xxxv. 5. Pro. xi. 25. Rom. xii. 8. ch. viii. 12.
ⁱ Pro. xi. 24, 25. & xxviii. 27. Phil. iv. 19.

---

6. "But this I say, He which soweth sparingly shall reap also sparingly," &c. A great principle of God's dealings in the matter of His final retribution is here expressed. As he had written before, "Every man shall receive his own reward according to his own labour" (1 Cor. iii. 8), so here he lays down, "Every man shall reap his reward in eternity in proportion as he has sown here of his worldly substance for the good of his brethren."

Nothing has contributed to make the hopes of the Christians respecting the joys of the world to come so weak and unreal as the idea of an absolute equality of reward: and of course it must be so if the idea of the heavenly state is that of one vast hall in which the only appreciable difference is a seat nearer to, or farther from, the place of honour, thus utterly ignoring such intimations of the future as we have in Luke xix. 16-19.

7. "Every man according as he purposeth in his heart, so let him give," &c. This seems to teach, "Let each man consider his means, and the just claims upon him, and how he would wish others to behave to himself if he was in deep distress, and then let him purpose or determine, and give accordingly."

"Not grudgingly"—*i.e.*, because others give, and so he is ashamed to withhold: " or of necessity," as if because of the importunity of others he is forced to give when he would rather keep what he has to himself.

"For God loveth a cheerful giver." St. Paul must have had in his mind the Septuagint of Prov. xxii. 9: " God loveth (or blesses) a cheerful and liberal man " [ἄνδρα ἱλαρὸν καὶ δότην εὐλογεῖ ὁ Θεὸς].

8. "And God is able to make all grace abound toward you," &c. All grace, that is, all goodness and favour, . . . having all sufficiency

9 (As it is written, ᵏ He hath dispersed abroad; he hath given to the poor: his righteousness remaineth for ever. ᵏ Ps. cxii. 9.

10 Now he that ¹ ministereth seed to the sower both minister bread for *your* food, and multiply your seed sown, and increase the fruits of your ᵐ righteousness;) ¹ Is. lv. 10.
ᵐ Hos. x. 12. Matt. vi. 1.

11 Being enriched in every thing to all ‖ † bountifulness, ⁿ which causeth through us thanksgiving to God.
‖ Or, *liberality*.
† Gr. *simplicity*.

12 For the administration of this service not only º supplieth the want of the saints, but is abundant also by many thanksgivings unto God;
ch. viii. 2.
ⁿ ch. i. 11. & iv. 15.
º ch. viii. 14.

---

10. "Both minister bread for your food, and multiply." So K., L., and most Cursives; but אּ, B., C., D., P., "shall both minister, and multiply, and increase."

12. "Unto God." B. alone reads, "to Christ."

---

in all things, that is, all sufficiency of this world's good things so that ye may have wherewith to do good, and all sufficiency of heavenly grace that ye may have the will to employ them in good works.

9. "As it is written, He hath dispersed abroad: he hath given to the poor," &c. He hath scattered his alms as a sower casteth broadcast his seed in the furrows.

"His righteousness remaineth for ever." Alms are righteousness. The treasure expended in benevolence is laid up in heaven, "where," as the Lord says, "neither rust nor moth doth corrupt, and where thieves do not break through and steal." This is one of those many places in which we are told that God is pleased to account alms as meritorious; such are Matth. v. 7, vi. 3, 4; Luke xiv. 14; Acts x. 4; 1 Tim. vi. 18, 19.

10. "Now he that ministereth seed to the sower both minister bread," &c. This seems to mean that the bountiful Giver of the fruits of the earth shall give you further and more abundant means of sowing for the spiritual harvest, and so increase the fruits of your righteousness. It is an exemplification of the Lord's saying, "To him that hath shall more be given."

11, 12. "Being enriched in every thing to all bountifulness .... abundant also by many thanksgivings unto God." He considers

13 Whiles by the experiment of this ministration they
^p^ glorify God for your professed subjection unto
the gospel of Christ, and for *your* liberal ^q^ distribution unto them, and unto all *men;*

14 And by their prayer for you, which long after you for the exceeding ^r^ grace of God in you.

p Mat. v. 16.
q Heb. xiii. 16.
r ch. viii. 1.

---

that it is a great spiritual gain to men if they can be brought to thank God. This generous contribution on the part of the Gentile Christians will lift up the hearts of the Jewish sufferers in thanksgiving and praise, and so God will be the more glorified, and souls brought nearer to heaven by their thankfulness to the Supreme Giver.

13. "Whiles by the experiment of this ministration they glorify God for your," &c. It was a great proof of the power of the Gospel —how it could subdue all hearts to God, that alien Gentiles, but a very short time before worshippers of idols, should contribute to the relief of Christians in Jerusalem. It glorified God for a fresh proof of His power in that He had knit together His elect, though dwelling in all parts of the world, in one communion and fellowship in the mystical body of His Son. The Apostle sets forth this as what he was sure would be the first and chiefest part of the thanksgiving, in which also would be included thanks for their liberal assistance of themselves, and not only of themselves, but of all men; for the same Holy Spirit which had inclined the Gentile believers to assist them of Judæa would fill their hearts with love to all.

The Greek of this passage is remarkable. It is literally rendered by the Revisers, "They glorify God for the obedience of your confession unto the Gospel of Christ"—that is, they obeyed and carried into act their confession of faith.

14. "And by their prayer for you, which long after you for the exceeding," &c. St. Paul looks forward with certainty not only for the thanksgivings of the Jewish Christians, but for their prayers on behalf of those who had contributed to their needs. He was sure that prayers which sprung from yearning hearts would receive an abundant answer.

15. "Thanks be unto God for his unspeakable gift." His unspeakable—that is, His indescribable gift. This can only be His

15 Thanks *be* unto God ª for his unspeakable gift.

ª Jam. i. 17.

Grace or His Spirit which enables men to obey the Gospel, and so knits men together in one brotherhood that they deny themselves in order to assist one another, and return thanks for, and pray for, and sympathize with one another, wherever they are.

If, however, we take 1 Corinth. xiii. as our guide to the explanation, the gift is charity, the greatest of God's gifts, greater because more abiding than even faith and hope.

CHAP. X.

NOW ª I Paul myself beseech you by the meekness and gentleness of Christ, ᵇ who ‖ in

ª Rom. xii. 1.
ᵇ ver. 10.
ch. xii. 5, 7, 9.
‖ Or, *in outward appearance.*

1. "Now I Paul myself beseech you by the meekness and gentleness of Christ." We have now another change in the tone of the Apostle's remarks. Hitherto he had been speaking in terms of restored confidence and hope; now he speaks again in tones of severity. It is difficult to account for this, except on the hypothesis that when he had concluded the last chapter, the writing of this Epistle was for some unknown reason suspended, and only resumed after he had received some further account of their state, in which he was made acquainted with some further particulars of the efforts of the Judaizing party to regain their ascendancy, and to deprive him of the reverence and affection of the members of the Church.

"I Paul beseech you by the meekness and gentleness of Christ." This observation of the Apostle's is much to be noted. It implies that the human life of Christ on earth, as portrayed in the Gospels, was not unknown to his converts. On the contrary, they must have been well instructed in it, if such an appeal could be made to them on any rational grounds. I have adverted to this place in the preface to my Notes on St. Luke's Gospel (page xvi.) showing by several instances that the meekness and gentleness of the Lord's

presence *am* base among you, but being absent am bold toward you:

c 1 Cor. iv. 21.
ch. xiii. 2, 10.

2 But I beseech *you*, ^c that I may not be bold when I am present with that confidence, wherewith I think to be bold against some, which ‖ think of us as if we walked according to the flesh.

¶ Or, *reckon*.

3 For though we walk in the flesh, we do not war after the flesh:

---

character could be best gathered from St. Luke's account of Him. One of the most mysterious things in the teaching of St. Paul, as contained in his Epistles, is the very scanty reference to the life of Christ as contained in the Gospel narrative. But from this place we learn that the daily or weekly instruction of the Churches planted by him was not wholly after the fashion of that contained in his Epistles. There was an additional instruction in the accounts of the life of Christ as we know that there was in other Churches.

The setting forth of the meekness and gentleness of Christ, if allowed its due effect, must have been a perpetual reproof of that party spirit, and self-assertion, which particularly characterized the leaders of the Judaizing section.

"Who in presence am base among you." Rather, am lowly and forbearing—not answering those who oppose me after their own fashion.

"But being absent am bold towards you," as is seen by his letters. Or more probably it may allude to the accusations of his adversaries. They accused him of being cowardly in facing them when he was present, but imperious and overbearing in the tone of his letters.

2. "But I beseech you, that I may not be bold when I am present," &c. There sounds something ironical in this appeal. Do not compel me to assert myself—you will see what I can do, if I have to confront those who set at naught our Apostolical power, and treat us as if we had no supernatural help from God to overwhelm gainsayers. Let the reader remember how St. Paul treated Elymas, and threatened the incestuous person. (Acts xiii. 10; 1 Cor. v. 5.)

3. "For though we walk in the flesh, we do not war after the

4 (^d For the weapons ^e of our warfare *are* not carnal, but ^f mighty ‖ through God ^g to the pulling down of strong holds ;)

5 ^h Casting down ‖ imaginations, and every high thing that exalteth itself against the knowledge

d Eph. vi. 13.
1 Thes. v. 8.
e 1 Tim. i. 18.
2 Tim. ii. 3.
f Acts vii. 22.
1 Cor. ii. 5.
ch. vi. 7. &
xiii. 3, 4.
‖ Or, *to God.*
g Jer. i. 10.
h 1 Cor. i. 19.
& iii. 19.
‖ Or, *reasonings.*

---

4. "Not carnal," "not of the flesh"—not meaning that they are actually evil.

flesh." "We walk in the flesh," *i.e.*, we are encompassed by its wants, and necessities, and weaknesses.

"We do not war after the flesh." In our campaign against idolatry and all forms of sin, we use no carnal weapons, only the sword of the Spirit, the word of God.

4. "For the weapons of our warfare are not carnal, but mighty through God," &c. "What sort of weapons," asks Chrysostom, "are carnal? Wealth, glory, power, fluency, cleverness, circumventions, flatteries, hypocrisies, and whatsoever else is similar to these." Do we not forget this Apostolic word when we lay such stress upon men of wealth, rank, influence, and commanding ability being on the side of Christ?

"But mighty through God to the pulling down of strong holds." Mighty, not in their own power, but in the power of God. What words could be weaker in the eyes of the world than the account of the Lord's Incarnation and conception by a Virgin, that a crucified Jew was the very and only Son of God, that His Crucifixion was the reconciling of the world to God, and His Resurrection the power of God against sin and the seed of a new and eternal Life : but these truths when proclaimed shook the fastnesses of Satan both in the world and in the soul.

Dean Stanley supposes that the Apostle here covertly alludes to to what took place in St. Paul's own country during the Mithradatic and Piratical wars. Both of these contests partook of the character here indicated; the second especially, which had been raging amongst the hill forts of the Cilician pirates not more than sixty years before the Apostle's birth, in the very scene of his earlier years, and which was ended by the reduction of one hundred and twenty strongholds, and the capture of more than ten thousand prisoners.

5. "Casting down imaginations, and every high thing that

of God, and bringing into captivity every thought to the obedience of Christ;

6 ¹And having in a readiness to revenge all disobedience, when ᵏ your obedience is fulfilled.

7 ¹Do ye look on things after the outward appearance? ᵐ If any man trust to himself that

i ch. xiii. 2, 10.
k ch. ii. 9. & vii. 15.
l John vii. 24. ch. v. 12. & xi. 18.
m 1 Cor. xiv. 37. 1 John iv. 6.

---

exalteth itself," &c. The strongholds are here said to be imaginations, or reasonings, the proud, daring speculations of men exalting themselves against heaven like forts on the tops of high hills. These the word of God "casts down" by such humbling truths as the knowledge of sin, the consciousness of coming judgment, the atoning worth of the Lord's sufferings, the glory of His Cross, and the power of His Resurrection.

"And bringing into captivity every thought to the obedience of Christ." Just as the heart, the will, the imagination is made subject to Christ, so must the intellect be with its reasonings and speculations. The man who truly accepts Christ as the wisdom of God, will humble beneath Him his own intellect and wisdom, and if there be anything in nature or in philosophy which seems contrary to the doctrine of Christ, he will be content to wait till God is pleased to make the matter clear. "He that believeth shall not make haste" (Isaiah xxviii. 16).

6. "And having in a readiness to revenge all disobedience," &c. Being prepared at once to excommunicate those who trouble the Church with their false and factious teaching till they come to a better mind. This discipline was his only weapon, but it was with God's blessing a most effectual one, as was proved by the example of the repentance of the incestuous person.

"When your obedience is fulfilled." He would not take strong measures till the greater part, perhaps nearly all of them, had submitted. From this place we learn that the recalcitrants were probably a small minority, but exercised an influence out of proportion to their numbers.

7. "Do ye look on things after the outward appearance?" Perhaps rather to be taken in the indicative. "Ye look on things after the outward appearance." Ye have regard to a commanding presence, eloquence of speech, skilfulness in human logic, and such

EVEN SO ARE WE CHRIST'S.

he is Christ's, let him of himself think this again, that, as he *is* Christ's, even so *are* [n] we Christ's.

[n] 1 Cor. iii. 23. & ix. 1.

8 For though I should boast somewhat more [o] of our authority, which the Lord hath given us for edification, and not for your destruction, [p] I should not be ashamed:

[o] ch. xi. 23.

[o] ch. xiii. 10.

[p] ch. vii. 14. & xii. 6.

9 That I may not seem as if I would terrify you by letters.

---

8. "For your destruction;" or rather, "casting down," see note below.

things. "Well," he says, "if any man trust to himself that he is Christ's, let him of himself think this again," &c. Most expositors suppose that the Apostle here alludes to that party whom he mentions as saying, "I am of Christ" (1 Cor. i. 12). They were the ultra Judaizers who would bind on the Gentiles the law in its entirety, because Christ observed it religiously: they would point to the original apostles as the first-called of Christ, and so above one who was called "out of due time." Though these Apostles had on the most solemn occasion repudiated their teaching, they would still exalt them to the personal disparagement of St. Paul. Now to this specious arguing the Apostle answers: If any man, Peter James, John even, says that he is Christ's, so are we. We have every mark of the approval of Christ as being His. We have been called personally by Christ as directly as any of the first-called Apostles. We have had the direct witness of Christ in all the gifts of the Spirit, in the performance of miracles, and in the extraordinary success of our ministry in the conversion of souls. If any are Christ's, we are.

8. "For though I should boast somewhat more of our authority, which the Lord," &c. Though I should magnify somewhat more than I have done the Apostolical authority which Christ has given me, for building you up in Him rather than pulling you down by severe discipline, I should be fully warranted in so doing, and so should not be ashamed. Dean Stanley remarks that the building up and casting down is another reference to the fortresses. "My power is given to me to build men up in Christ, not to cast them down, but if there be a necessity I must assuredly use this latter power."

9. "That I may not seem as if I would terrify you by letters." The connection between this and the last clause is difficult to make

10 For *his* letters, † say they, *are* weighty and powerful; but q *his* bodily presence *is* weak, and *his* r speech contemptible.

11 Let such an one think this, that, such as we are in word by letters when we are absent, such *will we be* also in deed when we are present.

† Gr. *saith he.*
q 1 Cor. ii. 3, 4. ver. 1. ch. xii. 5, 7, 9. Gal. iv. 13.
r 1 Cor. i. 17. & ii. 1, 4. ch. xi. 6.

---

out satisfactorily. Perhaps, as Alford says, we should supply some such words as, "I say this that I may not seem to terrify you by mere letters," and so he proceeds with stating the allegation of his opponents against himself.

10. "For his letters, say they [or, says he] are weighty and powerful, but his bodily," &c. His letters threaten terrible punishments, but when you come to see him you behold a miserable creature, whose appearance inspires you with no fear, and whose speech you despise because of its want of all that can command attention.

All the traditions of St. Paul's personal appearance are in accordance with this, that "his bodily presence was weak." Their testimony is summed up thus in the article in Smith's Dictionary. "They all agree in ascribing to the Apostle a short stature, a long face with high forehead, an aquiline nose, close and prominent eyebrows." But the assertion that his speech was contemptible, was evidently a slander. His letters, written from dictation, contain many passages of great eloquence and beauty. When the idolaters of Lystra would do sacrifice to him, it was as to Mercury, the god of eloquence. But there can be no doubt that in preaching the Gospel he shunned all such graces of oratory as the Greeks delighted in. He presented the Gospel in the plainest language possible, feeling how utterly unsuitable it was that a message of life and death—and that from God—should have a single word in it which might detract in the least degree from the infinite importance of the matter. Where is the place for tricks of oratory when "Jesus Christ and Him crucified" is the one thing to be enforced?

11. "Let such an one think this, that, such as we are in word by letters," &c. This is a repetition of what he had written in the first Epistle. "But I will come unto you shortly, if the Lord will, and will know not the speech of them that are puffed up, but the power ... what will ye? shall I come to you with a rod, or in

ACCORDING TO THE MEASURE.

12 ᵃ For we dare not make ourselves of the number, or compare ourselves with some that commend themselves: but they measuring themselves by themselves, and comparing themselves among themselves, ‖ are not wise.

ᵃ ch. iii. 1. & v. 12.

‖ Or, *understand it not*.

13 ᵗ But we will not boast of things without *our* measure, but according to the measure of the ‖ rule which God hath distributed to us, a measure to reach even unto you.

ᵗ ver. 15.

‖ Or, *line*.

---

love and in the spirit of meekness?" There is, however, this difference, that there he is writing to the whole Church, as if all were in fault, now he seems to single out one person as the centre of the mischief—"Let such an one think." There is a similar allusion to one leading opponent in Gal. v. 10, "He that troubleth you shall bear his judgment whosoever he be."

In this verse he must allude to something over and above the excision from the Church of the offending person, but what that "something" is we cannot say with certainty.

12. "For we dare not make ourselves of the number," &c. The meaning of this difficult verse seems to be, "We desire to take a due estimate of ourselves. In order to effect this we must act very differently to members of a clique who hold themselves to be everything, and all the outer world to be nothing, and so judge themselves by themselves, and compare themselves only amongst one another. They who do this act senselessly, and will always overrate themselves, and will sooner or later be robbed of their self-complacency." In this, of course, he alludes to the conduct of the Judaizers, but it is the bane of all cliques and coteries to ignore all excellence out of their own party, and set up amongst themselves a factitious standard, and so live complacently in a sort of fool's paradise till they are rudely awakened out of their dream.

13. "But we will not boast of things without our measure, but according to," &c. The present verse seems suggested by the word "measuring" (μετροῦντες). It instantly suggests itself to him as soon as he has written the word, that God had measured to him his line or limit of work, beyond which line or limit he had never gone. Under the compact made between himself and the

14 For we stretch not ourselves beyond *our measure*, as though we reached not unto you: ^u for we are come as far as to you also in *preaching* the gospel of Christ:

15 Not boasting of things without *our* measure, *that is,* ^x of other men's labours; but having hope, when your faith is increased, that we shall be ‖ enlarged by you according to our rule abundantly,

16 To preach the gospel in the *regions* beyond

^u 1 Cor. iii. 5, 10. & iv. 15. & ix. 1.

^x Ro. xv. 20.

‖ Or, *magnified in you.*

Apostles of the circumcision, Corinth, as a leading Gentile city, came into his province, and in accordance with the expressed will of God (Acts xviii. 8, 9, 10,) he had preached the Gospel there and gathered out the Church.

And his opponents, the Judaizers, had, as plainly, gone beyond their measure, and set at nought the compact of Gal. ii. 9. If they chose to assert that they represented Peter, James, and John, they certainly had no business in Corinth to act contrary to the Apostle of the Gentiles, and undermine his authority; for they should have had regard to what the three aforesaid Apostles had conceded to St. Paul.

14. "For we stretch not ourselves beyond our measure, as though we reached not," &c. There is something to be supplied here to complete the sense—for we do not extend ourselves beyond our measure, as would be the case if our sphere reached not unto you, for we came before others, even unto you, in preaching the Gospel. Wordsworth paraphrases it, "We are not straining our-ourselves by an unnatural effort (as it were) to grasp at you, as if ye were not within our arm's length. For (he adds) we arrived at you—we did attain to you in an appointed range of preaching the Gospel."

Or it may by adopting another reading be taken as a question, "For do we extend ourselves beyond our measure?" &c. But the meaning is the same.

15, 16. "Not boasting of things without our measure, that is, of other," &c. In saying this, he implies that his opponents, the Judaizers, had been guilty of this; they had entered into his field

you, *and* not to boast in another man's ‖ line of things made ready to our hand.

‖ Or, *rule*.

17 ʸ But he that glorieth, let him glory in the Lord.

ʸ Is. lxv. 16.
Jer. ix. 24.
1 Cor. i. 31.

18 For ᶻ not he that commendeth himself is approved, but ᵃ whom the Lord commendeth.

ᶻ Pro. xxvii. 2.
ᵃ Ro. ii. 29.
1 Cor. iv. 5.

---

of work, and, as far as lay in their power, were spoiling it. "Well," he says, "he will not imitate them, but when their (the Corinthians') faith in God, and in himself as God's Apostle, is increased, he hopes to be enlarged in his further operations against heathenism by their liberality, and adhering to the same rule or limit of breaking up new ground, and not trespassing on that which others have enclosed and cultivated, he will preach the Gospel in the regions beyond them, and not glory in another's province of things made ready to his hands."

17. "But he that glorieth, let him glory in the Lord." Let him glory in what the power of Christ had wrought through his instrumentality, and not boast of the fruit of other men's labours, as if they had been his own. The Corinthian Christians had been won to the Gospel by Christ's blessing on St. Paul's labours, and now these interlopers, because they had succeeded in converting some of them to Judaical rites, claimed them, and boasted of them as theirs.

18. "For not he that commendeth himself is approved, but whom the Lord commendeth." The Lord commended the Apostle and those who worked with him by following up their preaching by the repentance, and faith, and love of those converted by them—these signs being the only ones by which the approval of Christ could be certainly known.

CHAP. XI.

WOULD to God ye could bear with me a little in ^a *my* folly: and indeed || bear with me.

2 For I am ^b jealous over you with godly jealousy: for ^c I have espoused you to one husband, ^d that I may present *you* ^e *as* a chaste virgin to Christ.

^a ver. 16. ch. v. 13.
|| Or, *ye do bear with me*.
^b Gal. iv. 17, 18.
^c Hos. ii. 19, 20. 1 Cor. iv. 15.
^d Col. i. 28.
^e Lev. xxi. 13.

1. "Bear with me a little in my folly." So K., L., most Cursives; but ℵ, B., D., F., G., 17, 118, 121, 137, &c., read, "bear a little folly."

1. "Would to God ye could bear with me a little in my folly," &c. What is this "folly" in which he would have them "bear with him a little"? Evidently his self-assertion, in which he indulges as it were in the greater part of this chapter, and in the next; asserting how he was not a whit behind the chiefest Apostles —how he refrained from being chargeable—how in the real glories of Judaism he was equal with the chiefest Apostles, how he was in labour more abundant, and foremost in every privation and form of distress and persecution. And how in visions and revelations of God he was favoured above all.

All this assertion of himself, and of what he had done and suffered, would be folly, because vain-glory, unless he had been compelled to it for Christ's sake, his Master, Who had conferred on him the grace thus to do and suffer; and for their sakes, that they might see how little the false teachers had to boast of compared with himself.

"Bear with me a little in my folly." Some MSS. read "bear from me a little folly."

"And indeed bear with me." "But, indeed, ye do bear with me."

2. "For I am jealous over you with godly jealousy: for I have espoused you," &c. Because they had been converted by his preaching, and joined to the Church of Christ through his ministry, he con-

CHAP. XI.] I FEAR. 405

3 But I fear, lest by any means, as ^f the serpent beguiled Eve through his subtilty, so your minds ^g should be corrupted from the simplicity that is in Christ.

^f Gen. iii. 4. John viii. 44.
^g Eph. vi. 24. Col. ii. 4, 8, 18. 1 Tim. i. 3. & iv. 1. Heb. xiii. 9. 2 Pet. iii. 17.

3. "From the simplicity." So K., L., M., P., most Cursives, f, Vulg., Syriac; but ℵ, B., F., G., 17, 74, Goth., Æth., add " and purity " (" the simplicity and purity ").

siders them to be his daughter, and he their father who, in converting them, had espoused them to Christ; and so he is beyond measure anxious that they should be presented to Christ uncorrupted, faithful in their spiritual allegiance to the One Husband of the Church, which they would not be, if they yielded to the seductions of the false apostles.[1]

3. "But I fear, lest by any means, as the serpent beguiled Eve through," &c. No one could be conceived more pure from sin and evil desire than Eve, and yet she, in her state of innocence, succumbed to the temptation; and so might the Corinthian Church, though, as a body, they were converted and dedicated to God through Christ.

"The simplicity that is in Christ." Rather, "towards Christ." It means single-hearted devotion to Christ. Some MSS. and authorities add "purity;" see critical note.

Dean Stanley remarks that this is the only passage in St. Paul's Epistles in which there is any reference in the New Testament to the story of the serpent in the Fall. This is hardly correct, at least the inference which the Dean would have us draw is not: Rom. v. 12-19, is far more explicit than this place in connecting the Fall with one man, Adam; and that his fall was not from himself, but from an external tempter. Our present passage says nothing respecting the meaning of the narrative of the Fall, except what lies on the surface—that Eve was beguiled, and that the Corinthian Church must see that it be not similarly beguiled.

4. "For if he that cometh preacheth another Jesus, whom we have not preached," &c. "If he that cometh." By the use of the

---

[1] Mr. Blunt has a valuable remark on this. "This allegory runs, indeed, through the whole of Scripture, but it is always the body of the Church which is represented as the bride of our Lord. The application sometimes made of the allegory to individual persons, as in the case of women devoting themselves to the religious life, is little short of profanity, and is entirely unjustified by Scriptural Theology."

4 For if he that cometh preacheth another Jesus, whom we have not preached, or *if* ye receive another spirit, which ye have not received, or ʰ another Gospel, which ye have not accepted, ye might well bear ‖ with *him*.

ʰ Gal. i. 7, 8.
‖ Or, *with me.*

5 For I suppose ⁱ I was not a whit behind the very chiefest apostles.

ⁱ 1 Cor. xv. 10.
ch. xii. 11.
Gal. ii. 6.

6 But though ᵏ *I be* rude in speech, yet not ˡ in knowledge; but ᵐ we have been thoroughly made manifest among you in all things.

ᵏ 1 Cor. i. 17. & ii. 1, 13.
ch. x. 10.
ˡ Eph. iii. 4.
ᵐ ch. iv. 2. & v. 11. & xii. 12.

---

6. "We have been thoroughly made manifest." So E., K., L., P., most Cursives, Syr., Copt.; but ℵ, B., F., G., 17, read, " have thoroughly made it (*i. e.* by knowledge) manifest."

singular number he seems to point to one leading heresiarch, or false teacher.

"Another Jesus." A better Jesus, one more full of grace and truth.

"Or if ye receive another spirit, which ye have not received." A spirit with higher and more abundant gifts than the Spirit which ye received through my ministrations.

"Or another Gospel." The embodiment of still more glad tidings than those which ye have received.

"Ye might well bear with him." But none of these things are so.

5. "For I suppose I was not a whit behind the very chiefest apostles." In preaching to you Jesus the Son of God; in ministering to you the One Spirit, accompanied with all His supernatural gifts; in preaching to you the pure Gospel of the grace of God.

6. "But though I be rude in speech, yet not in knowledge," &c. The word "rude" is used to describe him who is unskilled in any branch of learning, as compared with him who is learned in it. It thus answers pretty nearly to our use of the word "layman," which is applied not only to the laity in comparison with the clergy, but to the person ignorant of law as compared with the lawyers. He certainly was not rude in speech in the sense of not being eloquent, though he was rude in speech as compared with those who used the rhetorical arts of the Greek sophists and orators.

7 Have I committed an offence ⁿ in abasing myself that ye might be exalted, because I have preached to you the Gospel of God freely?

n Acts xviii. 3. 1 Cor. ix. 6, 12. ch. x. 1.

8 I robbed other churches, taking wages *of them*, to do you service.

9 And when I was present with you, and wanted, º I was chargeable to no man: for that which was lacking to me ᵖ the brethren which came from Macedonia supplied: and in all *things* I have kept myself ᑫ from being burdensome unto you, and *so* will I keep *myself*.

o Acts xx. 33. ch. xii. 13.
p 1 Thess. ii. 9. 2 Thess. iii. 8, 9.
p Phil. iv. 10, 15, 16.
q ch. xii. 14, 16.

---

7. "Freely," *i. e.* "gratis."

"Yet not in knowledge; but we have been thoroughly made manifest." However they may despise his oratory, yet they cannot impugn his knowledge, for all their knowledge of Christianity is derived from him.

"We have been thoroughly made manifest," or perhaps (adopting another reading) "we have thoroughly made it manifest to you."

7. "Have I committed an offence in abasing myself that ye might be exalted?" &c. The thought of his having thoroughly manifested his knowledge makes him think of how this was accomplished. He abased himself among them by not requiring from them that sustenance which, as their Apostle, was due to him. He asks them ironically, "Have I committed an offence in having acted thus?"

8, 9. "I robbed other churches, taking wages of them, to do you service. And when I was present with you . . . . so will I keep myself." "I robbed other churches." I acted as if I robbed them for I allowed them to send contributions for my support, which, on any principle of justice, they were not called upon to do; and so it came to pass that when I preached the Gospel to you I was able to preach it gratuitously, because these brethren living at a distance supplied all my wants.[1]

---

[1] "I was chargeable to no man." This, "I was chargeable," is a word having a very singular derivation. It is derived from the word νάρκη, a torpedo; which, pressing itself

10 ᵣAs the truth of Christ is in me, †ˢno man shall stop me of this boasting in the regions of Achaia.

11 Wherefore? ᵗbecause I love you not? God knoweth.

12 But what I do, that I will do, ᵘthat I may cut off occasion from them which desire occasion; that wherein they glory, they may be found even as we.

ᵣ Rom. ix. 1.
† Gr. *this boasting shall not be stopped in me.*
ˢ 1 Cor. ix. 15.
ᵗ ch. vi. 11. & vii. 3. & xii. 15.
ᵘ 1 Cor. ix. 12.

And with respect to themselves he declares that this will ever be his practice.

10. "As the truth of Christ is in me, no man shall stop me of this boasting," &c. So important was the acting on this principle in the eyes of the Apostle, that he confirms it here with something of the nature of an oath.

"As the truth of Christ is in me." This may be "As Christ has given to me His truth that I may preach it to you and to others," or "As Christ in giving me other graces, has given me to partake of His truthfulness."

11. "Wherefore? because I love you not? God knoweth." Whether he received maintenance from the Church of Corinth, or whether he refused it, was equally turned by these implacable adversaries into a matter of accusation against him. If he received it they accused him of working in the cause of Christ for hire; if he refused it it was either because, not being a real prophet, he felt that he had no right to it; or else it was out of a haughty disdain, quite incompatible with real love—he was too proud to receive anything from such as they.

12. "But what I do, that I will do . . . . even as we." It is somewhat doubtful whether these false Apostles received maintenance or not. Wordsworth supposes that they did, and that they accused him of not doing so because he was conscious that he was not a true Apostle. His refusal to receive maintenance would give him the advantage over them as being the more disinterested

---

against other fish, numbs them, and so makes them its prey. There probably is an allusion to the numbing or deadening effect of the preaching of the Judaizers. Jerome (quoted in Stanley) supposed it to be a Cilicianism. "Multa sunt verba quibus juxta morem urbis et provinciæ suæ familiarius Apostolus utitur; e quibus exempli gratiâ, pauca ponenda sunt: οὐ κατενάρκησα ὑμῶν, *i.e.* non gravavi vos. Quibus et aliis multis verbis usque hodie utuntur Cilices."

CHAP. XI.]   SUCH ARE FALSE APOSTLES.   409

13 For such ˣ *are* false apostles, ʸ deceitful workers, transforming themselves into the apostles of Christ.

14 And no marvel; for Satan himself is transformed into ᶻ an angel of light.

ˣ Acts xv. 24.
Rom. xvi. 18.
Gal. i. 7. & vi. 12. Phil. i. 15. 2 Pet. ii. 1. 1 John iv. 1. Rev. ii. 2.
ʸ ch. ii. 17.
Phil. iii. 2.
Tit. i. 10, 11.
ᶻ Gal. i. 8.

14. " Is transformed," " transformeth himself."

in his work. If, however, they preached gratuitously because they had other means of livelihood, or because they were supported by wealthy Judaizers elsewhere, they would be able to taunt him with preaching for hire, if he claimed his Apostolical right; and so he felt that it was better for him to waive that right, even at the expense of being doubly taunted—as one who loved them not, and as one who was conscious that he was not a true Apostle—rather than that he should lay himself open to the charge of preaching for gain: that was, in his eyes, the most deadly charge of all.

13. "For such are false apostles, deceitful workers, transforming," &c. It is not improbable that they professed to have seen Christ, or to have been amongst those who were converted at Pentecost. Let the reader notice that not all who profess to come from Christ are sent by Him. What was in all probability the teaching of these persons? They professed to set forth the example of Christ, in that He was circumcised, and scrupulously observed the law. Though unable, of course, to reckon themselves with the Twelve, they might easily assume to be such Apostles as Barnabas. It is to be noted that the book entitled "The Teaching of the Apostles," assumes that some ministers, who were certainly not the Twelve, bore this name. "And as touching the Apostles and Prophets according to the command of the Gospel, so do ye let every Apostle that cometh to you be received as the Lord" (ch. xi).

14, 15. "And no marvel; for Satan himself... according to their works." Satan desiring to destroy a Christian soul would never present himself, either outwardly or inwardly, to that soul in the shape of an enemy of God. He would assume the garb of virtue, of holiness, of self-denial, and would profess zeal for the glory of God. In the Apostolic age he endeavoured to subvert the Gospel under zeal for the observance of the elder revelation. In this age

15 Therefore *it is* no great thing if his ministers also be transformed as the ^aministers of righteousness; ^bwhose end shall be according to their works.

16 ^cI say again, Let no man think me a fool; if otherwise, yet as a fool ‖ receive me, that I may boast myself a little.

17 That which I speak, ^dI speak *it* not after the Lord, but as it were foolishly, ^ein this confidence of boasting.

^a ch. iii. 9.
^b Phil. iii. 19.
^c ver. 1. ch. xii. 6, 11.
‖ Or, *suffer*.
^d 1 Cor. vii. 6, 12.
^e ch. ix. 4.

---

he seeks to divide Christ's Church under the cloak of devotion to the cause of the pure Gospel, or to ruin individual souls under the idea that, if they accept Christ, they are absolved from any need of imitating His Holiness. "Christ has done all, they say. It is treason to him to work out our own salvation, though an Apostle has told us that we are to do so" (Phil. ii. 12).

15. "Therefore it is no great thing if his ministers also be transformed." What a terrible thing to contemplate, that a professing minister of Christ may be really a minister of Satan! But it has been so, and it now may be so. Under the cloak of righteousness they may encourage party spirit, divide the Church, preach superstition on the one side, or Antinomianism on the other, disparage sacraments, and in other ways hinder or undermine the work of Christ. At the same time we must remember that there is a vast difference between opposing the Apostles then and opposing their successors now: for none now can pretend to the credentials of St. Paul. Such was his holiness, such were his miracles, and such his success in converting souls and founding Churches, that to oppose him was manifestly to oppose Christ. According to Christ's own words, "He that heareth you heareth me, and he that despiseth you despiseth me, and he that despiseth me despiseth him that sent me" (Luke x. 16).

"Whose end shall be according to their works." "If any man defile the temple of God, him shall God destroy." "Woe to that man through whom the offence cometh!"

16, 17, 18. "I say again, Let no man think me a fool . . . confidence of boasting . . . I will glory also." He says this in order to introduce what he is on the point of saying. "I am no senseless

18 ᶠ Seeing that many glory after the flesh, I will glory also.

ᶠ Phil. iii. 3, 4.

19 For ye suffer fools gladly, ᵍ seeing ye *your-selves* are wise.

ᵍ 1 Cor. iv. 10.

20 For ye suffer, ʰ if a man bring you into bondage, if a man devour *you*, if a man take *of*

ʰ Gal. ii. 4. & iv. 9.

---

20. "If a man take of you." "If he taketh you captive," Revisers; but see below.

person, as my detractors say; yet suffer me for a few moments to play the part of one, and, as senseless people are in the habit of doing, let me display myself a little. In what I am now saying, regard me not as an Apostle speaking by the Holy Ghost, but as a man, a mere uninspired man, who has been defamed and slandered, and so bear with me whilst I seem to assert myself, and proclaim my own doings and sufferings in the cause of Christ. Others assert themselves—see whether I have not sufficient cause, if I am driven to it, to assert myself."

19. "For ye suffer fools gladly, seeing ye yourselves are wise." "In asking you to bear with me a little in my folly, I only ask you to do what you do daily, in respect of these persons who exercise this evil influence over you. You deem yourselves wise, and so ye suffer all manner of things at the hands of these self-exalting persons." He speaks, of course, ironically. He can only account for the patience which the Corinthians exercise towards the Judaizers on the assumption that the Corinthians have too exalted an idea of their own wisdom to take notice of such things—just as full-grown persons bear with the pranks of children.

20. "For ye suffer, if a man bring you into bondage, if a man devour you," &c. These Judaizers bring you into bondage; they would impose a yoke upon you which he whom you look upon as the chiefest Apostle declared that neither he nor his fathers were able to bear (Acts xv. 10).

"If a man devour you." If he presses upon you his claims of wages and maintenance above what you can afford to pay him. The Lord speaks of the Pharisees, of whom these persons were the true representatives, as "devouring widows' houses" (Luke xx. 47).

"If a man take of you"—catches you, makes you his prey. "A metaphor taken from fishing or hunting, and in this passage pro-

you, if a man exalt himself, if a man smite you on the face.

21 I speak as concerning reproach, ¹ as though we had been weak. Howbeit ᵏ whereinsoever any is bold, (I speak foolishly,) I am bold also.

22 Are they Hebrews? ¹ so *am* I. Are they Israelites? so *am* I. Are they the seed of Abraham? so *am* I.

¹ ch. x. 10.

ᵏ Phil. iii. 5.

¹ Acts xxii. 3. Rom. xi. 1. Phil. iii. 5.

---

bably applied to the fascination exercised over the Corinthians by their deceitful teachers." (Stanley.)

"If a man exalt himself"—by pride and boastfulness, which for the time depresses you, and makes you feel how contemptible you are in comparison with him.

"If a man smite you on the face." Apparently a form of insult by no means unfrequent. Thus our Lord's words (Matth. v. 39): "Whosoever shall smite thee on thy right cheek, turn to him the other also " (also Luke xxii. 64, and Acts xxiii. 2).

21. "I speak as concerning reproach, as though we had been weak." The Revisers translate this: "I speak by way of disparagement, as though we had been weak." The meaning of this very difficult verse, on which there are very great differences amongst expositors, appears to be somewhat of this sort. "I speak as disparaging myself, as though, when I was among you, I was weak and pusillanimous, not venturing on asserting my authority in any such ways as these."

"Howbeit whereinsoever any is bold, (I speak foolishly,) I am bold also." However, if it comes to this—that I must assert myself—I say emphatically that, in all their strong points on which they rely, I am as strong as they are.

22. "Are they Hebrews? so am I. Are they Israelites? so am I," &c. He asserts the same, and for the same purpose in Phil. iii. 4, 5, 6, though he there characterizes it as "trusting in the flesh."

It has been supposed that one of the slanders uttered against him was that he was not of pure Hebrew blood. Epiphanius (Hær. xxx. 16) asserts that the Judaizers denied that he was a Jew at all by birth, but was a Gentile, and adopted Circumcision that he might marry the high priest's daughter.

23. "Are they ministers of Christ? (I speak as a fool) I am

CHAP. XI.] IN LABOURS MORE ABUNDANT.

23 Are they ministers of Christ? (I speak as a fool) I *am* more; ^m in labours more abundant, ⁿ in stripes above measure, in prisons more frequent, ^o in deaths oft.

24 Of the Jews five times received I ^p forty *stripes* save one.

25 Thrice was I ^q beaten with rods, ^r once was I

m 1 Cor. xv. 10.
n Acts ix. 16. & xx. 23. & xxi. 11. ch. vi. 4, 5.
o 1 Cor. xv. 30, 31, 32. ch. i. 9, 10. & iv. 11. & vi. 9.
p Deut. xxv. 3.
q Acts xvi. 22.
r Acts xiv. 19.

---

23. "I speak as a fool," "as one beside himself." A different word in the Greek from what has been used before.

more." They profess to be servants or ministers of Christ. Well, what said Christ respecting the lot of his servants? "Ye shall be hated of all men for my name's sake." "If they have called the master of the house Beelzebub, how much more shall they call them of his household?" (Matth. x. 22, 25.) "In this mark or badge of Christ's servants, I am more than they; nay, it is given to me to endure more than any of the Apostles with whose lives I am acquainted."

"In labours more abundant," for I have a far larger field.

"In stripes above measure." Probably meaning the scourgings inflicted by the heathen, which were not limited to the forty stripes save one to which the Jews deemed themselves restricted.

"In prisons more frequent." The only one recorded in the Acts, that at Philippi (Acts xvi. 23), being but one amongst a multitude.

"In deaths oft." As when he was stoned at Lystra, and drawn out of the city as one dead (Acts xiv. 19).

24. "Of the Jews five times received I forty stripes save one." The law prescribed (Deut. xxv. 3) that forty stripes should be given, and the number not exceeded; and so the Jews, in order to make certain of not exceeding, inflicted one short of the number. It is said that it was not unusual to inflict only half, in which case the Apostle was treated with exceptional severity. Not one of these cases is mentioned in the Acts.

25. "Thrice was I beaten with rods," &c. The only case mentioned in the history is that at Philippi (Acts xvi. 22).

"Once was I stoned." This must have been the stoning at Lystra before alluded to, in which he was left for dead.

stoned, thrice I ˢ suffered shipwreck, a night and a day I have been in the deep;

26 *In* journeyings often, *in* perils of waters, *in* perils of robbers, ᵗ *in* perils by *mine own* countrymen, ᵘ *in* perils by the heathen, *in* perils in the city, *in* perils in the wilderness, *in* perils in the sea, *in* perils among false brethren;

ˢ Acts xxvii. 41.
ᵗ Acts ix. 23. & xiii. 50. & xiv. 5. & xvii. 5. & xx. 3, & xxi. 31. & xxiii. 10, 11. & xxv. 3.
ᵘ Acts xiv. 5. & xix. 23.

"Thrice I suffered shipwreck." Not one of these is recorded in the history, for his shipwreck on his voyage to Rome took place long after this letter was written.

"A night and a day I have been in the deep." Of this also no mention is made in the history. Some suppose that the Apostle alludes to his having been immured for twenty-four hours in a deep dungeon at Cyzicus in Cilicia, called by the name of Bythos. The Apostle was probably in an open boat, or on some raft. Good Bishop Wordsworth supposes that for a night and a day the Apostle was swimming, but this is impossible, except by a special miracle.

26. "In journeyings often, in perils of waters, in perils of robbers," &c. "In journeyings often." Look at the tracings of his journeyings on the maps, and remember that from each place where he stayed any time he would make short expeditions to neighbouring places to preach the Gospel. Remember, too, that in many cases there were no roads, and consequently that a journey, even in the most favourable weather, was not the pleasant jaunt it is now.

"In perils of waters," *i.e.*, of rivers whose fords, during the time of rain, were impassable.

"In perils of robbers." Every road in Asia Minor then, as now, was infested with robbers.

"In perils by mine own countrymen." As in Cenchrea, when he was about to embark, and was obliged to change his route (Acts xx. 3), though this took place after the writing of this Epistle.

"In perils by the heathen, in perils in the city." As at Lystra, Philippi, their own city Corinth, and Ephesus.

"In perils in the wilderness." Most probably the wild, thinly peopled regions in Galatia and other parts of Asia Minor.

"In perils in the sea." From storms, and rocks, and pirates.

"In perils among false brethren." From this we cannot but

27 In weariness and painfulness, ˣ in watchings often, ʸ in hunger and thirst, in fastings often, in cold and nakedness.

ˣ Acts xx. 31.
ch. vi. 5.
ʸ 1 Cor. iv. 11.

gather that the virulence of Judaizing brethren against him was such as at times to endanger his life.

27. "In weariness and painfulness," &c. The two same words translated in 2 Thess. iii. 8, "with labour and travail."

"In watchings often." In sleepless nights. Compare the midnight Psalms at Philippi (Acts xvi. 25); the discourse all through the night at Troas (xx. 7-11); the ministrations "night and day" at Ephesus (xx. 31); the working to support himself night and day at Thessalonica (2 Thess. iii. 8). (Stanley.)

"In hunger and thirst, in fastings often." Not so much religious fastings which, being voluntary, he would not have mentioned, but fastings through want of necessary food—not hunger only, but hunger unsatisfied for a long time.

"In cold and nakedness." As in his shipwrecks, or in his journeys over the high land and mountain passes of Cilicia, badly shod and badly clothed.

In pausing to review these enumerations of the dangers and distresses of the Apostolic life, we must remember that there were eight or ten years in store for him of similar affliction and distress—in particular there was the tumult in Jerusalem, the long imprisonment in Cæsarea, the peril of the shipwreck on the coast of Malta, and the two imprisonments in Rome, the last ending with his martyrdom. What a life of hardship in the cause of Christ did the grace of God enable him to lead! "I laboured more abundantly than they all, yet not I but the grace of God."

By far the greater part of the Acts is devoted to his life and labours, and yet how fragmentary it is. Not a tenth part handed down to us! We have not a full account of one single day of the life of this man of God. He kept no journal, and the account which has descended to us is but an imperfect outline of a small part, and yet not one hour of it is lost, for it is all in the memory of Him Whose grace made him what he was, and Who forgets not one moment of pain endured on His behalf. "Almighty God, Who hast knit together thine elect in one communion and fellowship in the mystical Body of Thy Son, Christ our Lord; grant us so to follow Thy blessed saints in all virtuous and godly living, that we

28 Beside those things that are without, that which cometh upon me daily, ᶻthe care of all the churches.

29 ᵃ Who is weak, and I am not weak? who is offended, and I burn not?

ᶻ See Acts xx. 18, &c. Rom. i. 14.
ᵃ 1 Cor. viii. 13. & ix. 22.

---

28. "That which cometh upon me daily." The Text Rec. (following K., L., M., P., and most Cursives), has ἐπισύστασις, which signifies a riotous tumult, a hostile rush of adversaries against one. Thus Chrysostom explains it as "The tumults, the disturbances, the assaults of mobs, onsets of cities," and may refer to the way in which the Apostle was daily besieged by crowds of inquirers, of persons requiring interviews, &c.; but ℵ, B., D., E., F., G., 17, 39, 67, read, ἐπίστασις, which signifies a bringing to a stop, then a halt, and finally thought and anxiety.

may come to those unspeakable joys which Thou hast prepared for them that unfeignedly love Thee, through Jesus Christ our Lord."

28. "Beside those things that are without, that which cometh upon me daily," &c. The Apostle never dreamt of making each Church independent and leaving it to itself, to develope itself in freedom according to its own will. On the contrary, he never let the reins out of his own hands. Through his messengers or Apostolic vicars, as we may call them, he kept a strict eye upon each, discerned the first budding of false doctrine or loose practice, and acted with promptness and decision, and yet with the utmost forbearance and consideration.

"Those things which are without" has been explained as "those things which I omit."

"That which cometh upon me daily," or which presseth upon me. "More possibly," says Stanley, "the concourse of people to see me, to ask advice, &c." "The care of all the Churches." Each Epistle which he has written manifests different causes of anxiety, and different admonitions, and different thanksgivings, and particular prayers for each, so that he must have kept himself perfectly alive to the spiritual necessities of each part of the great mystical Body under his care.

29. "Who is weak, and I am not weak?" "Whom do I hear of that is weak in the faith, and I do not throw myself fully into his position, enter into his doubts, sympathize with the infirmities of his flesh?"

"Who is offended, and I burn not?" Burn not with indignation against him who has thrown an occasion of stumbling in his

CHAP. XI.]   ARETAS THE KING.   417

30 If I must needs glory, ^b I will glory of the things which concern mine infirmities.

31 ^c The God and Father of our Lord Jesus Christ, ^d which is blessed for evermore, knoweth that I lie not.

32 ^e In Damascus the governor under Aretas the king kept the city of the Damascenes with a garrison, desirous to apprehend me:

^b ch. xii. 5, 9, 10.
^c Rom. i. 9. & ix. 1. ch. i. 23. Gal. i. 20. 1 Thess. ii. 5.
^d Rom. ix. 5.
^e Acts ix. 24, 25.

---

brother's way, or, as some suggest, burn with zeal to restore him.

30. "If I must needs glory, I will glory of the things which concern mine infirmities." All the things which he had recounted in verses 23-26, had to do with the weak part of his nature—his body, and the weaknesses, infirmities, deprivations, which he suffered through his body. But if he was forced to glory, he would glory in these infirmities and persecutions, and he gives the reason in the next chapter (verse 9), "Most gladly, therefore, will I rather glory in mine infirmities, that the power of Christ may rest upon me.... Therefore I take pleasure in infirmities, in reproaches ... for when I am weak then am I strong."

31. "The God and Father of our Lord Jesus Christ, which is blessed for evermore." "Which is blessed for evermore." This is scarcely an adequate translation. The words "which is" are really ὁ ὤν, "He which is," "He which exists," "the Eternal One," and is the same as in Rev. i. 4, "*which is*, and was, and is to come."

What need of so solemn an affirmation? Because that which the Apostle affirms of himself that he glories in weaknesses, is so strange, so contrary to flesh and blood, so alien from all that is in the natural man, that he might well call the Searcher of hearts to witness to the truth of what he said.

32, 33. "In Damascus the governor under Aretas .... escaped his hands." The very abrupt introduction of the mention of this incident cannot be explained. Out of many conjectures each one is left to choose that which seems to himself most probable. It will suffice to mention two given by Dean Plumptre—one that the Apostle here commences a fresh account of the various circumstances of his life, of which this, which occurred very shortly

33 And through a window in a basket was I let down by the wall, and escaped his hands.

---

after his conversion, was the first, and that the narrative was suddenly broken off at this point, or (2) that this escape being somewhat undignified and partaking of the ludicrous, was another and the last instance of the indignities suffered by one who, it is said, was sensitively alive to ridicule.

CHAP. XII.

IT is not expedient for me doubtless to glory. †I will come to visions and revelations of the Lord.

2 I knew a man ᵃ in Christ above fourteen

† Gr. *For I will come.*
ᵃ Rom. xvi. 7.
ch. v. 17.
Gal. i. 22.

---

1. "It is not expedient for me doubtless to glory." So ℵ, D., K., M., Copt., most Cursives, Æth.; but B., E., F., G., L., P., 17, 31, 37, 39, 108, 137, and about twenty more, d, e, f, g, Vulg., Goth., Syr., read, "δεῖ." See below for translation.

1. "It is not expedient for me doubtless to glory. I will come to visions," &c. It is very difficult to decide upon the reading of the original, and, depending upon it, the rendering of this passage.

If we read according to the Received Text, then, as in our Authorized, δή should be rendered "indeed," or "verily." Thus Alford, "To boast verily is not to my advantage." If we read with B, δεῖ, then we must render it, "I must needs glory, but it is not profitable to me."

"I will come to visions and revelations of the Lord." It is to be remembered, as the latter part of the passage shows, that these visions and revelations are not introduced as a matter for glorying, but as introducing a state of continuous humiliation and distress. So that the whole account corresponds with what he had written in verse 30 of the last chapter, "If I must needs glory, I will glory of the things which concern mine infirmities," and nothing in his view was such a manifestation of his infirmities as this "thorn in the flesh," of which he is about to speak.

2. "I knew a man in Christ above fourteen years ago (whether

CHAP. XII.]   I KNEW SUCH A MAN.   419

years ago, (whether in the body, I cannot tell; or whether out of the body, I cannot tell: God knoweth;) such an one ᵇ caught up to the third heaven.   ᵇ Acts xxii. 17.

3 And I knew such a man, (whether in the body, or out of the body, I cannot tell: God knoweth:)   A.D. 46. at *Lystra*, Acts xiv. 6.

4 How that he was caught up into ᶜ paradise,   ᶜ Luke xxiii. 43.

---

in the body," &c.). "I knew," rather "I know." He does not say outright that he is speaking of himself, but we can infer nothing else. Above fourteen years ago would lead us back to the time covered by the narrative in the Acts between ix. 30, when on account of the persecution of the Jews he was sent by the brethren to Tarsus, and xi. 25, when he was sought out by Barnabas, and brought to Antioch.

("Whether in the body I cannot tell; or whether out of the body I cannot tell: God knoweth;) such an one caught up to the third heaven." Whatever is meant by this it seems to me quite clear that it excludes all idea of a mere trance. St. Paul knew perfectly well what a trance (ἐκστάσις) was, for he fell into one in the temple, and had therein a most important revelation of the will of Christ vouchsafed to him (Acts xxii. 18).

In the present case he was "caught up" out of this world, instead of the Lord coming or appearing to him, as occurred at the time of his conversion. He was taken up to the third heaven—which, whatever it means, cannot possibly designate a state of rapture occurring here below. And if the transitions of verses two and four be the same, or part of the same event, then he was taken up to some sphere where other spiritual beings were present, for he seems to have heard their voices uttering unspeakable things.

3, 4. "And I knew such a man (whether in the body, or out of the body, &c.) . . . . how that he was caught up into Paradise," &c. What is the third heaven? It seems to me useless, and almost irreverent to quote Rabbinical explanations all put forth hundreds of years after the writing of this Epistle. St. Paul must mean by it the highest heaven, where the throne of God is, and where the angels are.

And what, then, is Paradise? Our Lord says to the penitent malefactor, "This day shalt thou be with me in Paradise." This

and heard unspeakable words, which it is not ‖ lawful for a man to utter.

| Or, *possible.*

---

seems to indicate the place of departed saints, where they rest from their labours. But in Rev. ii. 7 compared with Rev. xxii. 2 it evidently designates the highest state of blessedness, though a future one, for in the first of these places Christ promises to him who finally overcomes, that he shall "eat of the tree of life, which is in the midst of the Paradise of God;" and in the latter passage, this tree of life is said to be on either side of the river which flows out of the throne of God and of the Lamb. I have no doubt whatsoever that one and not two places are meant. How much or how little in these two latter visions is real or objective, how much spiritual or how much mystical, I cannot stop to inquire; but I believe that St. Paul simply means to say that either in spirit only, or in spirit and body united, he was caught up to the highest region in the unseen and spiritual world. Less than this cannot be implied in such a term as "the abundance of the revelations vouchsafed" to him, and that it required a thorn in the flesh to keep a spirit so intensely honoured by God in a state of humility.[1]

"And heard unspeakable words which it is not lawful for a man to utter." He heard them; he understood them; but it was not lawful for him when he came to earth again, either to speak them, or put them into writing. There are mysteries of God which are so infinitely above us that in our present state of knowledge and of sin, we could not dwell upon them without profaning them. It is in the highest wisdom of God that so many mysteries of grace are so dimly or inadequately revealed.

---

[1] Three opinions are held by expositors.

1. That there was one vision or revelation—so Alford and others.

2. That there was one vision or revelation which had, as it were, two stages in it. This is Meyer's view. "Paul relates first how he was caught up into the third heaven, and then adds, as a further point in the experience, that he was transported further, higher up into Paradise, so that the ἕως τρίτου οὐρανοῦ was a break, as it were, or resting place of the rapture."

3. That there were two distinct raptures or visions—one to the third heaven, in which he beheld the throne of God and the angels surrounding it: the other, the one in Paradise, where he saw the peace and rest ineffable, even in their intermediate, and therefore imperfect state, of the souls which had fallen asleep in Christ, and were waiting for their resurrection. Both Dean Plumptre and Bishop Wordsworth hold this third view.

OF SUCH AN ONE WILL I GLORY.

5 Of such an one will I glory: ᵈ yet of myself I will not glory, but in mine infirmities. ᵈ ch. xi. 30.

6 For ᵉ though I would desire to glory, I shall not be a fool; for I will say the truth: but *now* I forbear, lest any man should think of me above that which he seeth me *to be,* or *that* he heareth of me. ᵉ ch. x. 8. & xi. 16.

7 And lest I should be exalted above measure through the abundance of the revelations, there was given to me a

---

5, 6. "Of such an one will I glory .... or that he heareth of me." He separates himself, as it were, into two men—the one exalted with a sight and experience of the highest heaven; the other proportionately depressed and humiliated. And he says that if he is compelled to glory he will glory in the one whom he denies to be himself, for in his present true self, his self which is depressed and humbled by what he is now about to relate, he cannot well glory.

"Lest any man should think of me above that which he seeth me to be," &c. He is compelled to speak the truth about himself, which truth is that what he had experienced was not a false or a mere human vision, but a true one, one from God, and the honour of receiving it was of such a sort that the Lord saw it necessary that he should have in himself a permanent source of humiliation, and he desires that men should regard him, not as he once was for a short time, a very exalted creature, but as he is now, humbled and distressed.

7. "And lest I should be exalted above measure .... thorn in the flesh," &c. The explanations of this "thorn in the flesh" are very numerous, but before recounting some of them, let us see whether we have not some clue given to us by the Apostle himself as to what it may most probably have been, or as to the direction in which we are to seek for the explanation. Such a clue seems to be given us in Gal. iv. 13, 14, "Ye know how through infirmity of the flesh I preached the Gospel unto you at the first. And my temptation, which was in my flesh, ye despised not, nor rejected, but received me as an angel of God, even as Christ Jesus." Now this account seems to me incompatible with any secret form of distress, as for instance, one arising from secret temptations to gratify im-

> ᶠ thorn in the flesh, ᵍ the messenger of Satan to buffet me, lest I should be exalted above measure.

ᶠ See Ezek. xxviii. 24. Gal. iv. 13, 14.
ᵍ Job ii. 7. Luke xiii. 16.

pure desires, which is the view of the temptation mostly entertained by Romanists as Cornelius à Lapide, Bernardino A. Piconio, and others. It was evidently something which struck friend and foe alike as soon as he began to preach: for such can only be the meaning of " at the first " in Gal. iv. 13. Also from comparing this notice in the Epistle to the Galatians with many indications of his sensitiveness to ridicule in this Epistle, it seems to have been something which caused contempt rather than some ailment which was attended with pain. Thus in Gal. iv. 14, " My temptations . . . . ye despised not." Now men would not despise a perpetual headache, or earache, or any other painful malady. They would pity it, but not *despise* it. I think that the passage in Gal. iv. would certainly lead us to believe that it was something connected with his speech, his delivery, his utterance, the sound of his voice, or his collectedness in speaking. To me it seems to have been a something which exposed him to ridicule, and tended to make him, as the saying is, unacceptable. Now this must not militate for a moment against his being naturally, and as a rule, eloquent, but it might have been something that at any moment might mar his eloquence, make it fitful and disjointed, and constantly provoke a smile, or even laughter, in those who were not under the spell of his extreme earnestness.[1]

In writing this I am aware that few take this view. From his calling it a thorn in the flesh many will hear of nothing but a bodily pain, as headache—but such a thing would not be so manifest at first sight as this was. Again, by "the flesh," St. Paul seldom means the mere body: he rather means the whole lower man—glorying in the flesh meant with him glorying in any earthly physical advantage. To suppose, with some of the earlier Protestants, that it was some constantly recurring doubt as to his final salvation seems to me the most absurd conjecture of all. How

---

[1] It might have been, for instance, a sudden forgetfulness of what he desired to say. Thus of the most eloquent preacher of his time in France, Bossuet, it is related that having to preach one day before the king, he totally forgot the beginning of his sermon, and had to descend from the pulpit overwhelmed with shame at not being able to utter a word.

8 ʰ For this thing I besought the Lord thrice, that it might depart from me.

9 And he said unto me, My grace is sufficient for thee: for my strength is made perfect in

ʰ See Deut. iii. 23-27. Mat. xxvi. 44.

---

9. "My strength is made perfect." ℵ, A., B., D., F., G., d, e, f, g, Vulg., Goth., Arm., Æth., omit "my;" but E., K., L., P., most Cursives, Syr., Copt., retain it.

could the Apostle commence his message with the declaration of doubts as to its final efficacy in his own case; and yet Gal. iv. 13 teaches us that the humiliating thing was palpable as soon as he opened his mouth. Some other questions arise, as, for instance, who gave this thorn? It was given for the best of purposes, to keep the Apostle nearer to God, and yet it was the "messenger of Satan." Surely there need be no difficulty about this. Satan out of his own malice would, through this humiliating thorn, buffet Paul with the aim of hindering his work by depressing him, but God would bless the very depression to the real exaltation of the Apostle, and so to the success of his work. The patient bearing of "the thorn" would be an acceptable sacrifice which God would reward with the conversion of souls through St. Paul's means.

8. "For this thing I besought the Lord thrice." When did he thus beseech the Lord? It could scarcely have been at the first time of the infliction, for he would not have had such experience of its humiliating and hindering nature, nor are we certain that the "thorn" was inflicted on him immediately upon his receiving the abundance of the revelations.

"I besought the Lord," *i.e.*, the Lord Jesus, addressing Him as God.

"Thrice," perhaps on three occasions of severe assaults or humiliation.

9. "And he said unto me, My grace is sufficient for thee: for my strength," &c. My grace—My strengthening and refreshing grace is sufficient for thee. This seems to look to the fact that the "thorn" was a hindrance to his enunciation of the Gospel. The Lord assures him that it shall not be so. On the contrary, the more weak he seems the more the power of Christ shall accompany his preaching. God constantly thus exalts weakness and humbles strength. Thus it was in Gideon's victory over the Midianites

weakness. Most gladly therefore ⁱwill I rather glory in my infirmities, ᵏthat the power of Christ may rest upon me.

10 Therefore ˡI take pleasure in infirmities, in reproaches, in necessities, in persecutions, in distresses for Christ's sake: ᵐfor when I am weak, then am I strong.

11 I am become ⁿa fool in glorying; ye have compelled me: for I ought to have been com-

ⁱ ch. xi. 30.
ᵏ 1 Pet. iv. 14.
ˡ Rom. v. 3. ch. vii. 4.
ᵐ ch. xiii. 4.
ⁿ ch. xi. 1, 16, 17.

---

11. "In glorying." Omitted by ℵ, A., B., D., E., F., G., K., fifteen Cursives, Ital., Vulg., Sah., Copt., Arm., Æth.: but retained by L., P., most Cursives, Syriac, Goth.

(Judges vii. 7-22). Thus it was in the victory over the world by such weak instruments as the Apostles.

The Lord seemingly refuses to grant the prayer and yet answers it—refuses the creature's will, and yet meets the creature's deepest needs.

We are told by some expositors that grace here means favour only; but is it usual with Christ to regard a man with favour, and bestow nothing upon him?

Commentators draw attention to the perfect, "He hath said," (εἴρηκε), instead of simply "he said." As if Christ's word was abiding, and nothing can reverse it.

"Most gladly therefore will I rather glory in my infirmities, that the power of Christ may rest upon me." "May overshadow me," as a Schechinah. Mr. Blunt refers well to Isaiah xxxii. 2: "A man shall be as an hiding-place from the wind, and a covert from the tempest; as rivers of water in a dry place, and as the shadow of a great rock in a weary land."

10. "Therefore I take pleasure in infirmities, . . . when I am weak, then am I strong." "For Christ's sake," *i.e.*, endured in His cause, in the furtherance of the Gospel. "When I am weak then am I strong," because when I despise myself then only do I most fully rely on the power of Christ. Let us remember the words of his brother Apostle: "My brethren, count it all joy when ye fall into divers temptations" (James i. 2).

11. "I am become a fool in glorying; ye have compelled me." This may be taken as a question—Have I become a fool in

CHAP. XII.] THE SIGNS OF AN APOSTLE. 425

mended of you: for °in nothing am I behind the very
chiefest apostles, though P I be nothing.

12 ᵠ Truly the signs of an apostle were wrought among you in all patience, in signs, and wonders, and mighty deeds.

13 ʳ For what is it wherein ye were inferior to other churches, except *it be* that ˢ I myself was not burdensome to you? forgive me ᵗ this wrong.

14 ᵘ Behold, the third time I am ready to come

o ch. xi. 5.
Gal. ii. 6, 7, 8.
p 1 Cor. iii. 7.
& xv. 8, 9.
Eph. iii. 8.
q Rom. xv. 18, 19. 1 Cor. ix. 2. ch. iv. 2. & vi. 4. & xi. 6.
r 1 Cor. i. 7.
s 1 Cor. ix. 12. ch. xi. 9.
t ch. xi. 7.
u ch. xiii. 1.

---

glorying? if so, ye have compelled me, because instead of my claims having been commended, or enforced by you, my spiritual children, against my adversaries, ye have been silent about them.

12. "Truly the signs of an Apostle were wrought among you in all patience," &c. If Paul had a special mission, not that of an ordinary Christian minister, but to speak authoritatively in the name of Christ, as did Peter and John, he must prove it in the same way, and so he did. Let the reader remember, "Then all the multitude kept silence, and gave audience to Barnabas and Paul, declaring what miracles and wonders God had wrought among the Gentiles by them" (Acts xv. 12).

13. "For what is it wherein ye were inferior to other churches," &c. In what spiritual gifts which I, as an Apostle, communicate to you, are ye wanting? Thus at the outset of the first Epistle he had written to them, "Ye come behind in no gift." Then he suddenly recollects himself, and exclaims, as it were, "Yes, there is one sign of an Apostle which I did not insist upon—my maintenance at your expense—and then in irony he says, "Forgive me this wrong."

14. "Behold, the third time I am ready to come to you, and I will," &c. No second journey—*i.e.*, no journey between the first one mentioned in Acts xviii. 1, and the one that he is now about to make, is alluded to in the Acts, and so this place has been interpreted as meaning that this is the third time he made himself ready to come: He had made himself ready to come, but determined not to come to them in heaviness (2 Cor. ii. 1) and so postponed the journey till he had heard a better account of them. But most probably there had been a short journey, not recorded, during

to you: and I will not be burdensome to you: for ˣI seek not your's, but you: ʸfor the children ought not to lay up for the parents, but the parents for the children.

15 And ᶻI will very gladly spend and be spent ᵃfor † you; though ᵇthe more abundantly I love you, the less I be loved.

16 But be it so, ᶜI did not burden you: nevertheless, being crafty, I caught you with guile.

ˣ Acts xx. 33. 1 Cor. x. 33.
ʸ 1 Cor. iv. 14, 15.
ᶻ Phil. ii. 17. 1 Thes. ii. 8.
ᵃ John x. 11. ch. i. 6. Col. i. 24. 2 Tim. ii. 10.
† Gr. *your souls*.
ᵇ ch. vi. 12, 13.
ᶜ ch. xi. 9.

---

15. Several various readings of latter part of this verse, which it would be impossible to give fairly without copying out a long note of Tischendorf's. Revisers render, "If I love you more abundantly, am I loved the less?" Vulgate and Syriac agree with Authorized.

the time of his prolonged stay at Ephesus, which would make this the actual third time of his coming.

"And I will not be burdensome to you: for I seek not your's, but you." This seems to mean, I will take nothing from you by way of maintenance till I am sure I have your hearts. When I have sought and found *you*, then it will be time to think of claiming my due.

"For the children ought not to lay up for the parents, but the parents for the children." This seems to be said in a sort of playful irony. Parents maintain their children. Suffer me to act as a parent inasmuch as I am one to you, and so give you my services and labours free.

15. "And I will very gladly spend and be spent for you; though the more abundantly," &c. This is an advance in the avowal of affection beyond the last verse. I will not only act as a parent and give to you rather than take from you, but I will impoverish myself, and that to the utmost, rather than be burdensome. And this I will do even though it is with no hope of return of love—indeed, the contrary.

16. "But be it so, I did not burden you: nevertheless, being crafty, I caught," &c. This is to be taken as an accusation or slander of his adversaries. "Be it so," he supposes them to say. "He himself ($ἐγώ$) did not spunge upon them; but, being crafty, he did the same thing in a deceitful way. He did not burden them

DID TITUS MAKE A GAIN OF YOU?

17 ^d Did I make a gain of you by any of them whom I sent unto you?

18 ^e I desired Titus, and with *him* I sent a ^f brother. Did Titus make a gain of you? walked we not in the same spirit? *walked we* not in the same steps?

19 ^g Again, think ye that we excuse ourselves unto you? ^h we speak before God in Christ: ⁱ but *we do* all things, dearly beloved, for your edifying.

20 For I fear, lest, when I come, I shall not

d ch. vii. 2.
e ch. viii. 6, 16, 22.
f ch. viii. 18.
g ch. v. 12.
h Rom. ix. 1. ch. xi. 31.
i 1 Cor. x. 33.

---

19. "Again, think ye" (πάλιν). So D., E., K., L., P., most Cursives, g, Goth., Syr., Copt., Arm.; but א, A., B., F., G., d, e, f, Vulg., read, πάλαι, "long ago," "ye have long thought."

himself, but he saddled Titus upon them; and he inaugurated the collection for the poor saints at Jerusalem, and how do we know but that he will repay himself out of this?"

17, 18. "Did I make a gain of you? . . . I desired Titus, and with him I sent a brother. . . . in the same steps?" Here he indignantly repels the charge, and in so doing his feelings seem to have mastered, for the time, his powers of expression. "I desired Titus to come and make up your contributions; and that there might not be occasion for even a breath of suspicion with him, I sent a brother—rather, the brother, the one I mentioned (viii. 22). Did Titus make a gain of you? So far from this, we walked in the same spirit of ministering the things of the Gospel to you freely; walked we not, too, in the same steps? Did not he, like myself, work in other ways than preaching for his livelihood?"

19. "Again, think ye that we excuse ourselves unto you?" The oldest MSS. read πάλαι, "long ago," instead of πάλιν, "again;" and if so, the sense would be, "Ye have long ago thought that we merely stand on the defensive on our own account, and make humble apologies. It is not so. On the contrary, we speak not before you, but before God in Christ; but still it is for your sake, for your edification, for if ye think of us as crafty, deceitful persons, the word of God spoken by us will not profit you."

20. "For I fear, lest, when I come, I shall not find you such as I would," &c. "I shall not find you such as I would." To whom

find you such as I would, and *that* ᵏI shall be found unto you such as ye would not: lest *there be* debates, envyings, wraths, strifes, backbitings, whisperings, swellings, tumults:

ᵏ 1 Cor. iv. 21. ch. x. 2. & xiii. 2, 10.

---

does he allude? Surely, we hope, not to the greater part of them; but the Apostle invariably treats a Church as an unit, and if some were sinful or impenitent or remiss, he seems to impute it to the whole, as if mutual exhortation, and internal discipline, and kind consideration would have prevented much, if not all, the evil.

"And that I shall be found unto you such as ye would not." He was their father in God, but he was also the special messenger and ambassador of Christ, to retain, if needful, their sin, and to bind it upon them; and whether, as he writes in 1 Cor. iv. 21, he comes to them "with a rod, or with love, and with the spirit of meekness," depends upon themselves. And so he proceeds.

"Lest there be debates, envyings, wraths, strifes, backbitings," &c. "Debates." This is to be taken in the old meaning of the word, which signifies, not controversies, but quarrels even to bloodshed. Thus in Shakespeare ("Henry IV.," part ii. iv. 4):—

> "Now, lords, if heaven doth give successful end
> To this debate that bleedeth at our doors."

"Envyings"—rather anger, used most frequently in a bad sense. In Gal. v. 20 it is put down as a vice which will exclude from the kingdom of God, though most unfortunately there translated by the almost creditable term "emulations."

"Strifes," or, perhaps, parties—always regarded by the Apostle as sinful—"backbitings, whisperings." The first ought not to be rendered "backbitings," but rather open reproach and obloquy, in contrast with the second, which is rightly rendered "whisperings."

"Swellings, tumults." "Swellings," the same word at the root as that in 1 Cor. iv. 18, and v. 2. It cannot be better translated. It reminds all of the old fable of the frogs puffing themselves out to vie with the oxen.

This passage is much to be remembered. In any body of men where there is freedom of speech, and matters are decided by the majority, there is a tendency—and, in fact, more than a tendency—to quarrelling, and factiousness, and sharp, cutting language, just

21 *And* lest, when I come again, my God¹ will humble me among you, and *that* I shall bewail many ᵐ which have sinned already, and have not repented of

¹ ch. ii. 1, 4.
ᵐ ch. xiii. 2.

---

as in an opposite state of things, where no free expression of opinion is allowed, there are engendered apathy, and spiritual slumber, and want of energy. But if we have the very great advantage—in fact, we should say the privilege—necessary to any healthy condition of the Church, of coming together to consider matters pertaining to the well-being of the Church, we must every one of us consider that all which engenders angry passions, and parties, and schisms, and strife, is deadly sin. Ebullitions of it have to be repented of and confessed, just as sins of uncleanness or dishonesty have. At least we cannot but learn this from the sins which are all classed together as deadly in Gal. v.¹

There should always be freedom of speech, and there should be always the abiding consciousness that the abuse of it is not merely wrong, but deadly. In this it is only in the same category with many other good gifts of God, which in their use are most salutary, but in their abuse most destructive.

21. "And lest, when I come again, my God will humble me," &c. The Apostle held that the souls whom he had gathered into the Church were, as he had said before (1 Thess. ii. 19), his crown of rejoicing. Every impenitent sinner then among them was as a jewel loosened, and ready to fall out. He had gloried in this his beloved Church—but in what? not in their numbers, but in their faith, hope, and obedience. Now he was afraid lest his glorying should be turned into shame.

"Many which have sinned already." Revisers translate "which have sinned heretofore." This cannot well mean before their conversion, as some suppose, but must of necessity mean during their

---

¹ I am writing this at the conclusion of the second Manchester Church Congress. The first was held some twenty-five years ago, and I remember well the fiery weapons which different parties hurled at one another, and the confident prediction by worldly wise people of my acquaintance that the ship of the Church was going all to pieces. But these persons did not take account of one thing—of the presence of the Spirit of God within us. He was provoked to depart, but He has not. And the account of the Second Congress is indeed a proof of this. There was the presence of representative Churchmen of all classes—there was the freest expression of opinion, there was no attempt at a hollow and enforced unanimity, but there was charity such as no one who remembered the first Congress in that city could have hoped for.

the uncleanness and ⁿ fornication and lasciviousness which they have committed.

ⁿ 1 Cor. v. 1.

Christian state. It reads us now a lesson, for there are very many who hold and unblushingly declare that sin is not sin in believers, whereas their belief does not protect them from falling into even gross sin, if they are careless and unwatchful, and unquestionably increases the guilt of their fall.

"And have not repented of the uncleanness and fornication and lasciviousness," &c. Each sin committed has to be repented of and confessed, or it may be written against us in God's books.

Notice how those who, as a Church, "came behind in no gift, waiting for the coming of our Lord," might have their consciences yet uncleansed from these deadly sins of impurity. "O cleanse thou me from my secret faults. Keep thy servant also from presumptious sins, lest they get the dominion over me. . . . Let the words of my mouth and the meditation of my heart be alway acceptable in thy sight, O Lord, my strength and my Redeemer."

CHAP. XIII.

ᵃ ch. xii. 14.
ᵇ Numb. xxxv. 30. Deut. xvii. 6. & xix. 15. Matt. xviii. 16. John viii. 17. Hebr. x. 28.

THIS is ᵃ the third *time* I am coming to you. ᵇ In the mouth of two or three witnesses shall every word be established.

---

1. "This is the third time I am coming to you. In the mouth of two or three," &c.

"The third time." See notes on the fourteenth verse of last chapter.

"In the mouth of two or three witnesses shall," &c. This seems to mean that in investigating each case of sin or irregularity urged against any members of the Church, he will proceed judicially, according to the rule laid down in Deut. xix. 15, and not on mere hearsay.

2 ᶜ I told you before, and foretell you, as if I were present, the second time; and being absent now I write to them ᵈ which heretofore have sinned, and to all other, that, if I come again, ᵉ I will not spare:

3 Since ye seek a proof of Christ ᶠ speaking in me, which to you-ward is not weak, but is mighty ᵍ in you.

4 ʰ For though he was crucified through weakness, yet ⁱ he liveth by the power of God. For ᵏ we also are weak ∥ in him, but we shall live with him by the power of God toward you.

ᶜ ch. x. 2.
ᵈ ch. xii. 21.
ᵉ ch. i. 23.
ᶠ Matt. x. 20. 1 Cor. v. 4. ch. ii. 10.
ᵍ 1 Cor. ix. 2.
ʰ Phil. ii. 7, 8. 1 Pet. iii. 18.
ⁱ Rom. vi. 4.
ᵏ See ch. x. 3, 4.
∥ Or, *with him*.

---

2. "And being absent now I write." So ℵ, K., L., P., most Cursives, Syriac, Arm., Goth.; but ℵ, A., B., D., F., G., 17, 23*, 67**, 80, d, e, f, g, Vulg., omit "I write." The sense is carried on from the preceding verb "(I foretell) to them which," &c.

2. "I told you before, and foretell you, as if I were present," &c.

"Foretell you," *i.e.*, tell you now beforehand, as if, &c.

"I will not spare." This seems to mean something of what is implied in 1 Cor. v. 5. It cannot mean, "I will not spare you in the infliction of reproof," for he could not well exceed in severity the words of reproof written in these two epistles.

3. "Since ye seek a proof of Christ speaking in me," &c. Do you wish to neglect my commands in order that ye may experience the power of my excommunication? Remember that in all which I speak as an Apostle, Christ speaks in me. His word in me has been in former times powerful to separate you from your sins. Do not dare its power to separate you, if you fall back into sin, from His Church and grace.

4. "For though he was crucified through weakness, yet he liveth by the power of God. For we also are weak," &c. In this verse the Apostle asserts that he and those like him who abide in Christ, partake both of the death and the life of Christ. Their union with Him does not raise them above that weakness of flesh by which He died, but it makes them partakers of that life-power by which He lives. Now this power is not only a power to convert and build up in the Church, it is also a power of reproof, of discipline, and if need be, a power of penal correction.

5. "Examine yourselves, whether ye be in the faith; prove your

5 ¹ Examine yourselves, whether ye be in the faith; prove your own selves. Know ye not your own selves, ᵐ how that Jesus Christ is in you, except ye be ⁿ reprobates?

6 But I trust that ye shall know that we are not reprobates.

7 Now I pray to God that ye do no evil; not

¹ 1 Cor. xi. 28.
ᵐ Rom. viii. 10. Gal. iv. 19.
ⁿ 1 Cor. ix. 27.

---

7. "Now I pray to God." So E., K., L., most Cursives, Syr., Goth.; but ℵ, A., B., D., F., G., P., 17, 23, 31, 37, 57, 73, 80, Ital., Vulg., Copt., Arm., Æth., read, "we pray God."

own selves." "Yourselves" being the first word in the sentence, is very emphatic, and seems to throw us back to the words in the third verse. There they sought a proof of Christ speaking in him, now he retorts, "Do not examine me, try, examine yourselves. Try whether ye be in the faith, whether ye yet hold the truths of Christ which I have taught you. See whether ye hold firmly the truth of the Lord's Resurrection: for ye have among you those who say that there is no resurrection. See whether ye hold to the truth of the Mystical Body, that Christ is the Head and ye the members. See whether ye hold to the truth assured to you in the Eucharist, that we being many are one bread and one body; for we are all partakers of that one Bread." I fix upon these three things, because respecting each one St. Paul seems to have had misgivings whether they held the truth of it in integrity.

"Prove your own selves." Prove your faith by your love, in which ye seem so deficient.

"Know ye not your own selves, how that Jesus Christ is in you, except," &c. "Reprobates," rather " spurious," when assayed not found to be true metal. "If you are true members of His Body, if ye are not cut off by God, there must be some tokens of His presence within you."

6. "But I trust that ye shall know that we are not reprobates." There seems something of irony in this. "If we were unapproved by Christ, Christ would leave us to ourselves; but you will see, I trust, that He will not do that: whether we preach, or console, or threaten, or exercise merited discipline, He will show, by His accompanying power, that He has not rejected us."

7. "Now I pray to God that ye do no evil; not that we should

CHAP. XIII.] YOUR PERFECTION. 433

that we should appear approved, but that ye should do that which is honest, though °we be as reprobates.   ° ch. vi. 9.

8 For we can do nothing against the truth, but for the truth.

9 For we are glad, ᴾ when we are weak, and ye are strong: and this also we wish, ᑫ *even* your perfection.

ᴾ 1 Cor. iv. 10. ch. xi. 30. & xii. 5, 9, 10.
ᑫ 1 Thess. iii. 10.

appear," &c. The sense seems to be—" Our earnest desire in our prayers for you is not that we should appear approved of God by your being, as it were, a credit to our ministrations, but that ye should do what is good and right, no matter whether to our credit or not." A very subtle temptation of ministers of Christ is here made manifest. They may pray for their flocks, not with absolute singlemindedness, but that their flocks, or those whom they have converted, may be an honour to them. This is not to be. When we pray for others it must be simply and solely for their own sakes, and our own'selves must not come in in any way.

8. " For we can do nothing against the truth, but for the truth." "If we find you," he says, " in good repute, having driven away your sins by repentance, and having boldness towards God: we shall not be able thereafter, were we never so willing, to punish you, but should we attempt it even, God will not work with us. For to this end God gave us our power, that the judgment we should give should be true and righteous, not contrary to the truth." (Chrysostom.)

9. " For we are glad, when we are weak, and ye are strong: and this also," &c. Weak and strong, here, cannot both be applied to the same thing, as, for instance, faith or hope or charity. St. Paul cannot be glad that he is weak and the Corinthians strong in such things as these: but he rejoices in the presence of his peculiar weakness, most probably his "thorn in the flesh," if only the power of Christ rests upon his converts.

"And this also we wish, even your perfection." This verse is the only place where the noun here translated perfection (κατάρτισις) is used in the New Testament: but the verb is frequently used, as particularly in 1 Cor. i. 10. " Now I beseech you, brethren, that ye all speak the same thing, and that there be no divisions among you, but that ye be perfectly joined together (κατηρτισμένοι) in the

F F

10 ʳ Therefore I write these things being absent, lest being present ˢI should use sharpness, ᵗ according to the power which the Lord hath given me to edification, and not to destruction.

11 Finally, brethren, farewell. Be perfect, be of good comfort, ᵘ be of one mind, live in peace; and the God of love ˣ and peace shall be with you.

ʳ 1 Cor. iv. 21. ch. ii. 3. & x. 2. & xii. 20, 21.
ˢ Tit. i. 13.
ᵗ ch. x. 8.
ᵘ Rom. xii. 16, 18. & xv. 5. 1 Cor. i. 10. Phil ii. 2. & iii. 16. 1 Pet. iii. 8.
ˣ Rom. xv. 33.

---

same mind and in the same judgment." All their evils, for which he had so severely blamed them, arose out of their divisions: and here, at the close of the second letter, he desires that these may exist no longer, but that there may be perfect unanimity in faith, and hope, and practice. This would be their perfection as a Church. Stanley translates it, "Your perfect joining together."

10. "Therefore I write these things being absent, lest being present," &c. He dreaded the thought of being among them in a state of righteous indignation against their unrepented sin—what recriminations there might be, perhaps what passion, what opposition! above all, he dreaded having to use such a weapon as excommunication—cutting off the offending members from Christ's Mystical Body by denying to them the participation in that Most Holy Food which sealed to each his connection with that Body. For the power which Christ had given to him was primarily to build them up in His Body; not to cut them off from it. That use of Apostolical power was abnormal, as it were, though at times most needful.

11. "Finally, brethren, farewell." Literally, rejoice, a different word from that used in Acts xv. 29, but with the same meaning.

"Be perfect," i.e., be perfectly joined together.

"Be of good comfort." Literally, be comforted. Some render it, "Be exhorted: receive my exhortation." Stanley joins the two, "Be comforted and exhorted."

"Be of one mind, live in peace." It is to be noted that this final exhortation is all directed against their divisions, the apparent root of all the evil; but these divisions arose from want of uniform firmness in holding the truths of the Gospel—such truths as the mystical Body and its unity, and the holiness of the bodies of Christians as being members of Christ, and the Resurrection in the power of Christ's glorified Body.

12 ʸ Greet one another with an holy kiss.
13 All the saints salute you.

ʸ Rom. xvi. 16. 1 Cor. xvi. 20. 1 Thess. v. 26. 1 Pet. v. 14.

"And the God of love and peace shall be with you." God cannot be with a divided Church in the fulness of His presence and power. The Church must at least endeavour to be of one mind, and God will second the endeavour; or looking at it from another side, when God, Who is the Author of peace and lover of concord, draws them together, they must obey His drawing.

12. "Greet one another with an holy kiss." Probably this letter would be read at the next celebration of the Eucharist. St. Cyril of Jerusalem notices the kiss of peace as given just before the Sursum Corda. His words, as explanatory of its significance, are—
"Then the deacon cries aloud, 'Receive ye one another, and let us kiss one another.' Think not that this kiss ranks with those given in public by common friends. It is not such: this kiss blends souls one with another, and solicits for them entire forgiveness. Therefore this kiss is the sign that our souls are mingled together, and have banished all remembrance of wrongs. For this cause Christ said: 'If thou bring thy gift to the altar, and there rememberest that thy brother hath ought against thee; leave there thy gift upon the altar, and go thy way; first be reconciled to thy brother, and then come and offer thy gift.' The kiss, therefore, is reconciliation, and for this reason holy; as the blessed Paul has in his Epistles urged: 'Greet ye one another with a holy kiss,' and Peter, 'with a kiss of charity.'" After the reading of such a letter as this, so full of merited reproof of divisions, and such humbling of himself, what a significance this kiss of peace would have!

13. "All the saints salute you." The word "saints" here is used in its widest sense. It includes every member of the mystical body who was dedicated to God, and continued in the outward profession of that dedication. It is impossible to suppose that St. Paul had in in his mind a select number of particularly holy and good Christians as distinguished from the whole Church. In the first Epistle the same salutation runs: "All the brethren greet you." In the Epistle to the Romans it is, "The Churches of Christ salute you."

14. "The grace of our Lord Jesus Christ, and the love of God,

14 ˣ The grace of the Lord Jesus Christ, and the love of
God, and ᵃ the communion of the Holy Ghost,
be with you all. Amen.

ˣ Rom. xvi. 24.
ᵃ Phil. ii. 1.

¶ The second *epistle* to the Corinthians was written from Philippi, *a city* of Macedonia, by Titus and Lucas.

---

14. "Amen" omitted by ℵ, A., B., F., G., 14, 17, 67**, f, g; retained by D., E., K., P., most Cursives, d, e, Vulg., Goth., Syriac, Copt.

and the communion of the Holy Ghost, be with you all." This is the "grace" with which the daily offices of the Church ends. It is the strongest assertion possible of the equality in substance, power, and eternity of the ever-blessed Three. For grace or blessing is invoked from Each, as if Each was the co-equal source of blessing. Who is the Lord Jesus Christ, and Who is the Holy Ghost, that They should be thus placed side by side with the Supreme Being? The only possible answer is in the creed of the Catholic Church. "The Godhead of the Father, and of the Son, and of the Holy Ghost, is all one; the glory equal, the majesty co-eternal."

EXCURSUS I.

OF EATING AND DRINKING UNWORTHILY.

Verses 27, 28, and 29 of 1 Cor. xi. raise the question, What do the wicked receive in the Eucharist? Upon the answer to this question it has been supposed that the doctrine of the real objective Presence of the Body and Blood of the Lord depends—if good and bad alike receive the Lord's Body and Blood, then our faith does not bring about the Presence in the Eucharist. It must be there quite independent of our faith; but if only those who have faith receive It, then it is assumed—I think much too hastily—that we are shut up to the conclusion that there is no Objective Presence in the elements; and this in point of fact signifies that there is no Inward Part which the faithful take and receive, and consequently that there is no Sacrament.

OF EATING AND DRINKING UNWORTHILY. 437

Now it seems to me beyond all manner of doubt that the Apostle teaches that the Body of Christ is so present in the elements which have been blessed and given, as to be capable of being profaned. According to him the Body of Christ requires to be discerned. We become guilty of It if we receive It without discerning It. Whatever meaning we give to the word "discern," such as "considering," it amounts to the same thing. We must discern It in what we take and eat.

Now the Lord's Body can be in but one of three places:—

1. It is in heaven locally.

2. It is in the Bread sacramentally, that is, after some mysterious mode of presence, which no one in our present state can understand, and which leads us into endless confusion and contradiction if we try to define or explain it.

3. It is supposed to be in our hearts spiritually, but this last seems to me an incorrect way of speaking: for "body" and "blood" can hardly be said to be in the heart. The memory of one dear to us, or his love, or his saintly character, or some emanation of his wisdom, may be in our hearts: but surely not his body and his blood in any true sense. And the Scriptures never speak of Christ's Body and Blood being in our hearts: but He Himself tells us that the reception of His Flesh and Blood is a means to an end, which is, that He should be in our hearts, and so He says, "He that eateth my Flesh and drinketh my Blood, dwelleth in me and I in him."

Now it is impossible to suppose that our Lord by saying, "This is my Body," and requiring us to say it in remembrance of Him, meant us to believe and profess that His Body is in heaven, and that what He gave or offered was a symbol of His Body now in heaven—in fact, infinitely distant and apart from and absent from that which He gives to us through His ministers.

And it is equally impossible to explain it as if He meant any of those other means by which He comes into our souls, so that we should love Him, such as by the Holy Spirit or the Scriptures or the preaching of the Gospel. For how is it possible that He should offer to us the Spirit or knowledge by a name which is the very opposite of Spirit, for flesh and spirit are the very opposites of one another?

Now the Lord offers to us a Sacrament, a thing which has, to use most ancient words (those of Irenæus, quoted on page 182), an outward and an inward reality—a thing which, to use the words of the Catechism, has two parts, an outward part or sign, and an Inward Part.

This is what the Lord offers. But what do we receive? It is clear that we must receive that which He gives unless something intervenes between His giving and our receiving to prevent it. And here apparently the matter would rest in our acquiescing in the fact that the wicked receive the same thing offered and given as the good do, though of course not the same benefit : but it does not rest here; for in the discourse in which our Lord prepares His Apostles to expect some extraordinary blessing in the reception of His Flesh and Blood, He only contemplates that Flesh and Blood being received beneficially : " He that eateth my Flesh and drinketh my Blood, dwelleth in me and I in Him " (John vi. 56).

Our Lord here, as I said, was leading His Apostles to expect some very great benefit which He would give to them, but when, and in what form, they were to receive it, He did not then tell them. Shortly after this He ordained the Eucharist in terms which would lead them to think of His previous words respecting eating His Flesh and drinking His Blood, but in instituting this Communion He says not a word respecting either benefit or danger. When His Church was founded it was instructed orally in all necessary truth respecting the Eucharist, just as it was instructed orally in all other truth, because every Epistle of the Apostles assumes that the Christians to whom it was written were grounded in all the truths of the Gospel; for there is no single Epistle which assumes to teach Christian doctrine *ab initio*, as we have to do with children when we catechize them in schools, or as we have to do in the case of ignorant heathen just converted.

An occasion, however, arose very early in the history of the Church in which the Christians of Corinth needed to be sharply reminded that there was great danger as well as great blessing attending the reception of the Eucharist. It might be received to salvation, or it might be received to condemnation. The Christians in question had profaned the Lord's Supper by mixing it up with the Agape, and receiving the consecrated Bread as if it was the bread of the Agape : and the Apostle as the organ of the Holy Spirit speaks to them in the strongest terms about the danger of profaning the Most Holy Food, and the terms which he uses are only consistent with the fact that the Body of Christ was there to

OF EATING AND DRINKING UNWORTHILY.

be profaned, and that men might be guilty of It, and eat and drink their own condemnation in consequence.

These are all the places in the Scriptures which bear directly on this matter. The Lord in John vi. only contemplates His people receiving a blessing from eating His Flesh and drinking His Blood. On His offering to them His Body and Blood on the night of His betrayal, He makes no specific mention of benefits to be received or dangers to be avoided. And His servant St. Paul, speaking as His Apostle and special representative, has occasion to mention only the danger: but let us remember that his view of the danger was that of one who believed thoroughly in the words of Institution, "This is my body," and that the Body of the Lord was there to be received to condemnation; and so that men must discern It in the consecrated element, or they would eat and drink their own condemnation, and would be guilty not of mere carelessness or irreligion, but of the Body and Blood of the Lord.

It is clear, then, that there is but one passage of Scripture to which we must look for direct information as to what we are to warn the wicked against; and if we follow the guiding of this passage we must warn them of a danger in some sort proportionate to the blessing which they may receive, and St. Paul describes this danger as being "guilty of the Body and Blood of the Lord."

Now this would be analogous to the danger we incur in receiving other great gifts of God unworthily, particularly the gift of the Third Person in the Godhead. Men may certainly receive the Spirit of God unworthily. They may receive Him so as to grieve Him (Ephes. iv. 30), even after they have been sealed by Him—so as to rebel against Him and vex Him (Isaiah lxiii. 10), even to quench Him (1 Thess. v. 19), and provoke God to take Him away from Him (Ps. li. 11).

All this could not be said if God, foreseeing men's wickedness, should give them some other spirit, not His own Spirit.

And does not the analogy of God's conduct in this respect lead us to consider that What the wicked eat unworthily and to their condemnation is What the faithful receive worthily and to their salvation? The thought is very terrible, but there is this to mitigate its severity, that the Apostle does not contemplate in the case of unworthy eaters their consignment to eternal misery, but to some temporal punishments which he specifies.

This that I have written would suffice so far as the practical

440 OF EATING AND DRINKING UNWORTHILY.

application of 1 Cor. xi. 27-30, is concerned ; but as I write mainly for Churchmen, it will be necessary to say something respecting this matter of the danger, as it appears in the formularies of the Church of England.

In the Eucharistic service itself, the view taken of the danger is undoubtedly the Pauline view. In fact, St. Paul's words respecting it are reproduced and contrasted with the words of the Lord in John vi., which promise unspeakable benefits. "Ye . . . must consider how St. Paul exhorteth all persons diligently to try and examine themselves, before they presume to eat of that Bread, and drink of that Cup. For as the benefit is great if with a true penitent heart and lively faith we receive that Holy Sacrament; (for then we spiritually eat the Flesh of Christ, and drink His Blood; then we dwell in Christ, and Christ with us (John vi. 56), we are one with Christ and Christ with us (1 Cor. x. 16, 17); so is the danger great if we receive the same unworthily. For then we are guilty of the Body and Blood of Christ our Saviour; we eat and drink our own damnation, not considering the Lord's Body; we kindle God's wrath against us." Nothing can set forth more clearly this, that the same Body is a blessing to the one and a curse to the other. By some It is realized, and by others It is profaned.

But there is a passage in a far more sacred part of the Service (in the prayer of humble access, just before the prayer of Consecration,) which is far more important in its teaching—indeed, seems to comprehend in the fewest words the whole matter: " Grant us therefore, gracious Lord, *so* to eat the flesh of Thy dear Son Jesus Christ and to drink His Blood, *that* our sinful bodies may be made clean by His Body, and our souls washed through His most precious Blood, and *that* we may evermore dwell in Him, and He in us." If words have any meaning, these imply that we may so eat the Flesh and drink the Blood, that we may not be made clean—not be washed—not dwell in Him, and He in us. The whole passage is unintelligible except on the hypothesis that there are two eatings of the same most Holy Thing, an outward one, which must take place wherever the Sacrament is received, and a spiritual one, in which the spirit takes its part in the eating—discerns what it eats, and so eats to life eternal.

One of the thirty-nine articles (the twenty-ninth) deals with this question as to what the wicked receive. From the heading of this

OF EATING AND DRINKING UNWORTHILY. 441

article, we should gather that the wicked in no sense eat the Body of Christ, for it runs: "Of the wicked which eat not the Body of Christ in the use of the Lord's Supper;" but when we come to look to the contents of the article, we find that the categorical affirmation of the heading or title is carefully avoided, for we read that the "wicked, although they do carnally and visibly press with their teeth the Sacrament of the Body and Blood of Christ, yet in no wise are they partakers of Christ." This carefully avoids the direct statement which, contrary to the plain words of St. Paul, would make us hold that the wicked eat a mere symbol, and it is also perfectly consonant with the expressions in the prayer of humble access, that we must so eat the Flesh of Christ as to be made clean, which implies that we may so eat as not to be made clean.

And besides this, the Article recognizes that all who eat eat a Sacrament, *i.e*, a thing which has an outward part and an Inward Part. The Lord offers and gives, not the outward part merely, but the whole Sacrament, when He says, "Take eat, this is my Body," and St. Paul follows this up by saying, "He that eateth and drinketh unworthily is guilty of the Body and Blood of the Lord." Now the Article says that the wicked eat to their condemnation, because they do "eat the sign or Sacrament of so great a thing." The sign here, having regard to the nature of a Sacrament, is a sign of the presence of the Inward Part, and so the fact that the wicked receive both parts to their condemnation is not impugned by the article.

I said at the beginning of this note, that it is clear that we receive that which He gives, *unless something intervenes* between His giving, and our receiving, to prevent it.

Now this is not an impossible supposition. One of our greatest authorities on the Eucharist, Dr. Pusey, in speaking of what the Lutherans hold, writes: "The belief that the wicked too receive that which is Sacramentally the Body and Blood of Christ, even while they can in no wise be partakers of Christ, implied a firm belief in the Objective Presence of that Body and Blood. This was explicitly stated in the Smalcald Articles, the larger Catechism of Luther, and the Formula Concordiæ. The belief in the Objective Presence may indeed be maintained without it, if it be held that God withdraws that presence in such cases, as if through carelessness (as has often happened when the Sacrament has been reserved) the consecrated element be devoured by an animal" (Sermons on the Presence of Christ in the Holy Eucharist," vol. i., Note B, page 36 of Notes).

This withdrawal, however, in the case of the wicked, does not seem consonant with the teaching of St. Paul, which we have been considering.

The reader who has paid any attention to the history of the Prayer Book and Articles is, of course, aware that this article was not in the first draught of the Articles. The Articles in their present form were ratified in 1563, but the 29th was not printed as one of them till 1571. It appears that though approved by Archbishop Parker, it was unacceptable to the court, probably more particularly to the Queen. The Article, especially with regard to its reference to a passage in Augustine, formed the subject of some correspondence between Parker and Cecil.[1] Now I do not mean to infer from this that the Article is not now on the same footing as the other Articles as regards its authority, but this difference of opinion respecting its contents and its non-publication for so long a period assures us that the discrepancy between the heading of the Article, which seems levelled against Lutheranism as well as Romanism, and the sentence in it which merely says that "the wicked in eating in no wise partake of Christ," and carefully avoids saying that they in no sense eat His Body, is intentional. It is impossible to give the author of this Article credit for a mistake. The Article is of too much importance controversially for that, and so we must perforce read into the title of the Article some such words as "to their soul's health"—" of the wicked which eat not the Body of Christ *to their salvation* in the use of the Lord's Supper." In this way only can it be reconciled with the words of the Apostle, with the analogy of God's dealings in giving very great gifts which may be received to destruction, and with many words in the Eucharistic service, especially those in "the prayer of humble access."

With respect to the opinion of Augustine, it is to be remembered that in several places that father very plainly expresses himself as if there were two sorts of eating of the Flesh of Christ. "Do so many who either in hypocrisy eat that Flesh and drink that Blood, or who after they have eaten and drunk become apostate—do they

---

[1] See Bishop Forbes on the Articles, p. 590, fourth edition.

APOSTOLICAL TRADITIONS. 443

dwell in Christ, and Christ in them? Yet assuredly there is a certain manner of eating that Flesh and drinking that Blood in which whosoever eateth and drinketh dwelleth in Christ. He then doth not dwell in Christ and Christ in him who eateth the Flesh and drinketh the Blood of Christ in any manner whatever, but only in some certain manner" (Serm. 71).

Again: "Any one who unworthily receives the Sacrament of the Lord does not, because he himself is evil, cause it to be evil, nor because he receives not unto salvation, has he received nothing, for that was no less the Body and Blood of the Lord to those also to whom the Apostle said: 'He that eateth and drinketh unworthily eateth and drinketh damnation to himself'" (De Bapt. cont. Don., v. 8). I owe these quotations to Bishop Forbes on the 29th Article, where the reader will find more to the same purport.

EXCURSUS II.

ON THE TRADITIONS DELIVERED BY ST. PAUL TO THE CHURCHES.

Verse 2 of Chapter xi. of St. Paul's First Epistle to the Corinthians, in connection with several other passages, forces upon us the consideration of the question, "What was the instruction given by St. Paul to the Churches planted by him in such things as the idea and the conduct of public worship?"

I trust I shall be pardoned if I repeat what I have written on this verse in my notes, as it will serve to make my present remarks better understood.

"'I praise you that ye remember me in all things, and keep the ordinances,' &c. No doubt this means that they followed the directions which he had given respecting a large number of what we should deem secondary matters. The ordinances, or traditions, or paradoseis are the laws and rules respecting public worship and private conduct, which he delivered to them to observe. He did not preach the Gospel to them and then say, 'I have done my part; now you are at liberty to follow your own fancy, and to make what ecclesiastical regulations you think will suit you best.' Nothing of the sort. We find that he uses such expressions as, 'as I teach everywhere in every church,' 'so ordain I in all churches,' 'stand fast and hold the traditions which ye have been taught, whether by word or our epistle.' 1 Cor. iv. 17 ; vii. 17 ; 2 Thess. ii. 15. It may be asked, why have these ordinances and traditions not been preserved and come down to us ? To which we answer, we do not know whether these traditions, many of them, at least, have not come down to us. In all human probability they form part of that body of Church observance, which we find everywhere recognised in the very early Fathers, and prevailing in all parts of the Catholic Church (such, for instance, as the reverent use of the sign of the Cross, the remarkable features common to all the typical Liturgies, Infant Baptism, the early rather than the late celebration of the Eucharist). Anyhow, the ship of the Church, from the first, has gone in one direction, in the Catholic direction, in the direction of Catholic dogmas and marked ritual observance, and it is impossible to conceive how it could have done so if these 'traditions' of St. Paul—and, doubtless, those of his brother Apostles—had been conceived in a Puritan rather than in a Catholic spirit. The direction in which the Church was to sail was given from the first."

I will now explain what I mean with respect to one point, and that is, public worship on the Lord's day.

The large Protestant bodies which took their stand outside the pale of the Catholic Church, and severed their connection with the past at the time of the Reformation, insisted on a fact, for the truth of which they had not a particle of evidence to show, viz., that the Apostles ordained—or at least that the Apostolic Churches fell in with—a type of service which, whatever it was in other respects, was non-Eucharistic and non-Sacrificial. It is assumed to have usually consisted of a psalm for the commencement of worship, a long prayer (in the Continental bodies, I believe, mostly a written or printed form), sermon, a psalm, another sermon, and a concluding prayer, also of considerable length. This service was non-Eucharistic, and therefore non-Sacrificial, for the only service in Christian times to which the idea of sacrifice in any sense could be connected, was the Eucharist. The Eucharist, or Holy Communion (for its celebration among these bodies can scarcely be called Eucharist), was quite separate from the usual weekly service on the Lord's day.

APOSTOLICAL TRADITIONS. 445.

It was observed very few times in a year, certainly not so much as monthly. In the form of observance ordered by Calvin, though prayers are permitted, there is not a single Eucharistic prayer, though the minister is directed to expound the words of the Lord in the Institution. Such was, and to a great extent is, the Divine service of all non-Catholic bodies in Western Europe. It will suffice to say that there is no trace of it whatsoever in any ancient writer, and that it was invented for the express purpose of keeping the Eucharistic idea out of the usual Lord's day worship.

But in two writers, each one of whom dates from the first century, there is a notice of Church worship which is totally inconsistent with this, the ultra-Protestant idea.

One is in an Epistle to the Corinthians by Clement, whom all ancient writers who mention his name identify with the Clement, the companion of St. Paul.[1] This Epistle is mentioned by Eusebius as having been read as a Canonical Epistle in some churches. No ecclesiastical historian puts the writing of it later than the year 100. Most assign it to between 80 and 90 after Christ, that is about twenty-five years more or less after the martyrdom of St. Paul. He writes thus respecting the worship of the Church : "These things being manifest to us, and looking deep into the depths of Divine Knowledge, we ought to do all things in order, whatsoever the Lord has commanded us to perform at stated times. The Oblations and Liturgies to be celebrated ($\tau\acute{\alpha}\varsigma$ $\tau\epsilon$ $\pi\rho o\sigma\phi o\rho\grave{\alpha}\varsigma$ $\kappa\alpha\grave{\iota}$ $\lambda\epsilon\iota\tau o\upsilon\rho\gamma\acute{\iota}\alpha\varsigma$ $\grave{\epsilon}\pi\iota\tau\epsilon\lambda\epsilon\tilde{\iota}\sigma\theta\alpha\iota$), and that they should not take place at random, or disorderly, but at definite times and hours. When and by whom they should be celebrated He has fixed by His own supreme will, in order that all things, being holily done according to His good pleasure may be acceptable unto Him " (first Epistle to the Corinthians, ch. 40); and again, "Our sin will not be small if we eject from the Episcopate those who have blamelessly and holily offered the gifts " ($\pi\rho o\sigma\epsilon\nu\epsilon\gamma\kappa\acute{o}\nu\tau\alpha\varsigma$ $\tau\grave{\alpha}$ $\delta\tilde{\omega}\rho\alpha$), ch. 44. Now I

---

[1] Thus Irenæus describes him as "This man as he had seen the blessed Apostles, and had been conversant with them, might be said to have the preaching of the Apostles still echoing in his ears, and their traditions before his eyes." And then he proceeds to state the occasion on which he wrote the Epistle to the Corinthians. Origen speaks of him as referred to by St. Paul in Philippians iv. 3, and as the third Bishop of Rome (Origen on John i. 29); Eusebius as having been proved by St. Paul's Epistle to have been his fellow labourer. Book 3, ch. iv.

do not intend to discuss this passage as to its orthodoxy or the contrary, but simply to draw attention to the fact that it was written by a friend and companion of St. Paul within, at the outside, twenty-five years after his death, to a church planted and watered by the same Apostle. St. Clement then must have known the traditions which St. Paul delivered to the Churches, and so must the Church to which he wrote, for St. Paul commends them for having kept them. Is it then conceivable that if the Apostle had ordained the typical form of worship which has prevailed amongst ultra-Protestants since the time of the Reformation, *i.e.*, two or three metrical psalms or hymns, two long prayers, and one or two sermons,[1] a contemporary of his should have alluded to it in the above terms? Whatever be the exact meaning of the words used by Clement no terms could possibly be conceived more unfit to describe the worship of the Protestant bodies in Scotland, or Holland, or France.

But though totally inconsistent with the idea of ultra-Protestant worship, these terms are quite in harmony with the Sacrificial Eucharistic terms which we find in all the ancient Liturgies. These Liturgies, of which we have specimens yet remaining, were used in all parts of the world, and all contain sacrificial terms answering to those used by Clement. I give those in two or three of the most ancient. The Clementine, "Wherefore having in remembrance His Passion, Death and Resurrection from the dead, His return into heaven, and His future second appearance, when He shall come with glory and power to judge the quick and the dead, and to render to every man according to his works: we offer unto Thee our King and our God according to His Institution, this bread and this cup, giving thanks to Thee through Him, that Thou hast thought us worthy to stand before Thee, and to sacrifice unto Thee; and we beseech Thee that Thou will graciously look on these gifts now lying before Thee, O thou all-sufficient God, and accept them to the honour of Thy Christ, and send Thy Holy Spirit, the witness of the sufferings of the Lord Jesus on this Sacrifice, that he may make this bread the body of Thy Christ," &c.

This passage, taken from what is undoubtedly the most ancient

---

[1] In Holland, where, I believe, the original form of service of the Calvinists is yet more strictly adhered to, there are two sermons following close upon one another. It is not so, however, I believe, in Scotland.

APOSTOLICAL TRADITIONS. 447

type of Liturgies, fairly represents the Sacrificial expressions found in all of them. In order not to break too much the continuity of my argument, I give a few more instances from other typical Liturgies in a note.[1]

Another instance of this Sacrificial language, applied to the worship of Christians, I shall take from a source representing apparently a very different body of tradition from that of St. Paul —a much more legal one—viz., the "Didache of the twelve Apostles." "And on each Lord's day of the Lord be ye gathered together, and break bread, and give thanks, after confessing your transgressions, that our Sacrifice may be pure. And let none that hath a difference with his fellow come together with you until they be reconciled, that our Sacrifice be not defiled. For this is that which was spoken by the Lord. 'In every place and time offer me a pure Sacrifice (literally, mincha or bread-offering). For I am a great king, saith the Lord, and my name wonderful among the Gentiles.'"

Now there can be little doubt but that the treatise from which this is quoted is of the remotest antiquity. I believe that the writer or compiler was unacquainted with any one Epistle of St. Paul, or was opposed to his claims, as might well be the case if he

---

[1] Thus St. James: "Wherefore, having in remembrance His Life-giving Passion, Salutary Cross, Death, Burial, and Resurrection from the dead on the third day; His Ascension into heaven, and sitting at the right hand of Thee His God and Father, and His Second bright and terrible appearance, when He shall come again with glory to judge both the living and the dead, and shall render to every man according to his works, we sinners offer to Thee, O Lord, this tremendous and unbloody Sacrifice," &c.

St. Mark: "Sanctify also, O God, this Sacrifice with Thy heavenly benediction."

The Malabar: "Lord, mighty God, strengthen my weakness by Thy mercy, and make me worthy of the assistance of Thy grace that I may offer to Thee an oblation for the benefit of all men," &c.

The Æthiopic: "And now, O Lord, celebrating the Memorial of Thy Death and Resurrection, we offer to Thee this bread and this cup," &c.

The Ancient Gallican Office used in Gaul, Britain, and Spain before being superseded by the Roman: "Thou art truly holy, truly blessed, O Lord God, the Father Almighty, by the salvation of them that believe, and the Redeemer of all in Christ; through Whom we pray and beseech thee, that thou wouldest vouchsafe to receive, bless, and sanctify this oblation that it may be grateful and acceptable, which we offer unto Thee for the peace of Thy Church," &c.

These are from Liturgies used in the most ancient times in all parts of the world, and many more might be added. They are to be found in "Brett's Collection of the Primitive Liturgies;" in "The Liturgies of St. Mark, St. James, St. Clement," &c., translated by Rev. J. M. Neale, and a "Translation of Four of the most Ancient" in a volume of Clark's Ante-Nicene Library.

was writing for Palestinian Jews. I believe the treatise was published before any of the Apostolical Epistles were in circulation throughout the Church; for if such Epistles had been received by most churches, such a treatise as this, so legal, so unevangelical, so undoctrinal, never could have been put out as the Didache of the Apostles.

But the important point to be observed is, that the writer, by quoting (partially) the famous passage, Malachi i. 11, as referring to the Eucharist, substantiates, so far as his authority goes, the Sacrificial idea in the Eucharist. In this he is followed by two or three very ancient writers. Thus Justin Martyr, "Hence God speaks by the mouth of Malachi, one of the twelve prophets, as I said before, about the Sacrifices at that time presented by you. 'I have no pleasure in you, saith the Lord; and I will not accept your Sacrifices at your hands: for from the rising of the Sun unto the going down of the same, my name has been glorified among the Gentiles, and in every place incense is offered unto my Name and a pure offering (mincha, bread, or flour-offering).' . . . He then speaks of those Gentiles, namely us, who in every place offer Sacrifices to him, the bread of the Eucharist, and also the cup of the Eucharist." Now, supposing that Justin Martyr was of middle age when he wrote this, his own memory of Ecclesiastical matters would reach to the time of Clement's Epistle, or nearly so, *i.e.*, to within twenty or thirty years after the martyrdom of St. Paul, and to the latter years of the life of St. John.

Irenæus writes, "He (Jesus Christ) took that created thing, bread, and gave thanks, and said, 'This is my Body:' and the cup likewise, which is part of that creation to which we belong, He confessed to be His Blood, and taught the New Oblation of the New Covenant: which the Church, receiving from the Apostles, offers to God throughout all the world, to Him Who gives us the means of subsistence, the first-fruits of His own gifts, concerning which Malachi, among the twelve prophets, thus spoke beforehand." And then he quotes Malachi i. 10, 11. "The oblation of the Church, therefore, which the Lord gave instructions to be offered throughout all the world, is accounted with God a pure Sacrifice, and is acceptable to Him." ("Irenæus against Heresies," Book 4, xvii. 5; xviii. 1.)

Irenæus' personal memory of Church matters would have reached to about A.D. 120; that is, to about twenty years after the

APOSTOLICAL TRADITIONS. 449

death of St. John, and fifty years after the death of St. Paul, at which time it is impossible to suppose that the traditions respecting worship which he had delivered to the Churches had become forgotten or extinct, and that other regulations and ideas of worship of a totally opposite character had taken their place.

The state of the case, then, is this. There are two types or modes of solemn Christian worship in question; one which consists of prayers wholly unconnected with the Eucharist, and hymns or metrical Psalms, and a sermon or sermons: and the other, such a service as has been handed down to us from ante-Nicene times in such a Liturgy as that called the Clementine, and in the Liturgies of St. James and St. Mark, and in Liturgies used in parts so remote from one another as Gaul, Spain, Æthiopia, Mesopotamia, and Malabar, all containing Sacrificial terms and expressions used with reference to the consecrated elements as connected most closely with the words and action of our Lord at the Institution of the Eucharist.

Of the first of these, the non-Eucharistic service, not a single tradition or notice has come down to us. Of the second, the Eucharistic or Sacrificial, we have a continuous series of notices, reaching from the time of contemporaries of the Apostles Paul and John, to 348 or 350 A.D., when a celebrated Father of the Church, St. Cyril of Jerusalem, delivered a catechetical lecture upon it, describing it somewhat minutely.

Now of the things to which St. Paul in this Epistle alludes under the name of traditions or paradoseis, only two apparently have come down to us, and their appearance in the Epistle seems owing to the fact that they had been neglected or not realized. One of these is the veiling of women in church, the other the mode in which the Lord instituted the Eucharist, the latter of which the Corinthians had, for profane and unworthy purposes, confounded with the Agape.

It was not, therefore, beneath the Apostle's notice to lay down very strict regulations respecting the conduct of public worship. Now, seeing that in his time the Sacrificial nature of the Eucharist was fast getting hold on the Church, and seeing that prophecies respecting the nature of the pure worship of the Messianic future were appealed to in support of this, it was surely incumbent upon the Apostle to deliver, either in writing or orally, some such tradition as this: "We ordain, as the Apostle of the Lord, that on

G G

no account is there to be anything in your worship which can be called Sacrificial. Your prayers are to be the utterances of the president of your assemblies at the moment. Your praises and thanksgivings are not to be over the cup or the bread which represents the Lord's Body and Blood; rest assured that you wrongly interpret the prophecies of Malachi and other prophets if you imagine that they refer to the Communion of the Lord's Body and Blood."

The Apostle's zeal for the glory of Christ and the purity of Christian worship would have certainly led him to deliver some such tradition as this; but if he had, how was it that the worship he ordained wholly disappeared, and the worship which he must have denounced was prevalent everywhere, even in his own generation, though his memory was everywhere cherished as the most honoured servant of the Lord?

I am well aware in writing all this of the difficulty which very many Christians have in accepting the Sacrificial idea of the Eucharist, but let such remember that by Sacrifice we mean nothing offered in the least degree after the manner of a Jewish Sacrifice, neither do we mean anything approaching to a fresh immolation of the Lord.

Which mode of worship seems most in accordance with the will of the Father? One in which all is left to the will of the presiding minister or elder, whether he should plead the Sacrifice of Christ at all—whether he should even so much as mention the atoning Death;[1] and if he does, it should be apart from, and, as a rule, wholly unconnected with, the one Rite which the Lord ordained for His people, that in it they should show forth His Death till He comes.

Or one in which the Christian worship should be that which the Lord Himself ordained—in which, no matter how it is celebrated, the Death of the Eternal Son must be set forth—in which Christian people are united together as one Body in the Crucified, whilst the idiosyncrasy of the minister is put as much in the background as possible, and in which, in closest union with the Sacrifice

---

[1] Let the reader remember that in this I am not fighting with a shadow. The Reformed bodies of Holland, France, and Switzerland have been so rationalized or Socinianized that the all-atoning Death may for weeks and months together be not pleaded in the prayers.

of the Redeemer, we are privileged to offer up ourselves living Sacrifices, holy, acceptable unto God, our reasonable service.

Note.—I have fully discussed this subject of the Sacrificial nature of the Eucharist in my "One Offering," to which I refer the reader.

THE END.

www.ingramcontent.com/pod-product-compliance
Lightning Source LLC
Chambersburg PA
CBHW071433300426
44114CB00013B/1416